THE ARMIES OF INDIA

HIS MAJESTY
THE KING-EMPEROR

THE
ARMIES OF INDIA

PAINTED BY

MAJOR A. C. LOVETT

THE GLOUCESTERSHIRE REGIMENT

DESCRIBED BY

MAJOR G. F. MacMUNN, D.S.O.

ROYAL FIELD ARTILLERY

WITH FOREWORD BY

FIELD-MARSHAL EARL ROBERTS

V.C., K.G., K.P., O.M., ETC.

The Naval & Military Press Ltd

Published by

The Naval & Military Press Ltd
Unit 5 Riverside, Brambleside
Bellbrook Industrial Estate
Uckfield, East Sussex
TN22 1QQ England

Tel: +44 (0)1825 749494

www.naval-military-press.com
www.nmarchive.com

Gardner's Horse, 1850

FOREWORD

*I*T *will readily be believed that I have read this short history of the Armies of India, written by Major MacMunn and illustrated by Major Lovett, with the greatest interest. Having spent so many eventful years of my life in India, and having been so intimately associated with the Indian Army, in peace and war, I think that no one is better able than myself to esteem that Army at its proper value, as regards what it has—with the help of British training and example—achieved in the past, or to appreciate what it is capable of doing in the future under the same conditions. And this intimate knowledge of its capabilities enables me to realize to the fullest extent the enormous responsibility which rests upon all who are concerned with the administration and handling of such a splendid and potent machine. It is most imperfectly known in England, and often* *insufficiently understood in India, how diverse and divergent in many respects are the numerous races which we enlist into our Indian Army—in creed, in customs, in temperament, and traditions. Yet each and all of these factors must be attentively studied, and the most careful consideration given to the difference of treatment they impose in arranging the conditions of service for such widely different idiosyncrasies, if we would maintain and develop the fighting efficiency of our Indian soldiers, and the strength of the bonds of loyalty and devotion by which they are attached to our service. Major MacMunn's masterly review of the methods by which the existing army has attained its present state of perfection will greatly help to a proper understanding for the necessity of carefully studying the varying characteristics of the several Indian races; while the admirable illustrations by Major Lovett clearly depict the fine physical types we have in our Indian soldiers. For these reasons I cordially recommend this book to all who are interested in the welfare and prosperity of our great Indian Army — more particularly to all officers of the British and Indian Services whose duty must constantly bring them into contact with Indian troops.*

In conclusion, let me say that no account of the Armies of India would be complete which did not include a description of the Imperial Service Troops organized and maintained by the Rulers of the great Feudatory States of Hindustan; and I am pleased, therefore, to see that the origin and development of these fine, serviceable troops are fully set forth in this volume. Encouraged by the British Government, and advised and assisted by British officers, these corps—personally led by their own Princes—have more than justified the high expectations formed of them when their organization was first proposed; and they constitute, at the present time, a moral and material accession of strength to the paramount power which can hardly be overrated.

The joint authors of this interesting volume have done their work well, and I hope that their interesting and instructive narrative will have the wide circulation which it deserves.

ROBERTS, F.M.

CONTENTS

CHAPTER VI

CHAPTER VII

CHAPTER VIII

LIST OF ILLUSTRATIONS

xi

Also nineteen smaller line drawings in the text.

THE ARMIES OF INDIA

CHAPTER I

THE ARMY OF THE HONOURABLE EAST INDIA COMPANY

" By the legion's road to Rimini."

THE English have as yet ruled in India barely one-half the time that the Romans ruled in Britain, though their rule in the East has much in common with that of Rome north of the Channel. For the last century and a half have the English legions, European and Indian, tramped the trunk roads of Hindustan as those of Rome tramped Merry England before it was England at all. Up and down the length and breadth of India, as up and down Watling Street and the Via Fossa, or up and down "the legion's road to Rimini," at the legion's pace, have tramped those English legions since Clive decided that there

1

should be one king and not a dozen in India, and that one, neither French nor Dutch nor Portuguese.

And the marvel of it all is that these tramping disciplined legions are not the beef and porridge and potato-reared lads of the Isles, but for the most part men of the ancient races of Hindustan, ruled and trained and led after the manner of the English.

From the doorkeepers and trained bands that first guarded the factories of the early merchants, the army of John Company *Bahadur* grew and prospered, by the secret of ever-increasing scope and labour, till it became the great shako-clad army of the Line that vanished for the most part in the tragedy of '57.

Of the three great presidential armies, the larger part, that of Bengal, and part of that of Bombay, disappeared, and with it the glorious record of successful war and faithful service, in a storm of unreasoned and uncalled-for mutiny, that buried in a month the tradition of a century.

The army that now upholds the Empire of Hindustan, is based on a systematic grouping of men by race and sept and clan, with a view to the full development of race efficiency.

CORPS PRESENT AT THE SIEGE AND ASSAULT OF DELHI, 1857

10TH DUKE OF CAM-
9TH   BRIDGE'S OWN
HODSON'S HORSE   LANCERS
(Hodson's Horse)

57TH
WILDE'S RIFLES   32ND SIKH PIONEERS
(Frontier Force)   55TH
                      COKE'S RIFLES   QUEEN'S OWN CORPS
1ST   (Frontier Force)   OF GUIDES
KING GEORGE'S   (Lumsden's)
OWN SAPPERS   22ND
AND MINERS   SAM BROWNE'S   54TH SIKHS
                      CAVALRY   (Frontier Force)
21ST PRINCE   (Frontier Force)
ALBERT VICTOR'S   127TH QUEEN
OWN CAVALRY   3RD QUEEN   2ND KING   MARY'S OWN
(Frontier Force)   ALEXANDRA'S   EDWARD'S OWN   56TH PUNJABI   BALUCH LIGHT
(Daly's Horse)   OWN GURKHA   GURKHA RIFLES   RIFLES   INFANTRY
                      RIFLES   (The Sirmoor Rifles) (Frontier Force)

This careful grouping has been the subject of much attention during the last twenty years, and has called for a thorough study of the clans and tribal systems of India, ending in a method of recruiting which is remarkable, and of a rank and file which is numerous and admirable. It is also well calculated to prevent the decline of martial qualities, which follows so quickly in the East on an era of peace. The results of twenty years of this system it is the object of this book to describe and illustrate. To arrive, however, at the present stage, and to understand that vast organization by class and clan which are illustrated herein, it is necessary to trace the rise of the armies of India through their separate presidential exist-ence, to one vast whole.

It is proposed to deal with the subject in the following order :—

> The Army of the Honourable East India Company.
> The Army of the Great Mutiny.
> The Armies as transferred to the Crown.
> The Military clans and tribes.
> The Indian Army of to-day.
> The Armies of the Feudatory States.

The army of great John Company took its origin from three separate nuclei, separated by many

miles of road and sea and hostile territory.
These three centres originated in, first, "an ensign
and thirty men," reinforced by a "gunner and his
crew," stationed in Bengal towards the end of the
seventeenth century ; second, a detachment sent
to garrison Bombay, the dower of Catherine of
Braganza, Charles the Second's bride ; and third,
the forming of companies and soldiers from factory
doorkeepers and watchmen in Madras.   These
curiously haphazard beginnings were the unmedi-
tated foundations of three immense armies of
horse, foot, and artillery.

The raising of actual native regiments was first
undertaken by the French, and it was due to the
coming struggle for mastery in Southern India
that we owe the first conception of a regular native
army.   In 1748 Dupleix raised several battalions
of Musalman soldiery armed in the European
fashion in the Carnatic, and a few years later
Stringer Lawrence followed suit in Madras.   The
distances that separated the three presidencies
resulted in each force growing up on divergent
principles and with different organizations, of which
the ill results survive to some extent even to this
day.   European companies were formed from detachments sent from England, from runaway sailors,

GOVERNOR-GENERAL'S BODYGUARD

Daffadar

Sayyid of Shahpur (Musalman)

men of disbanded French corps, from Swiss and
Hanoverians, from prisoners of war, and any white
material in search of a livelihood.   In 1748 the
regular European corps of the Company's service,
who now form part of the British Line and the
Royal Artillery, were first formed from these
heterogeneous detachments and scattered companies.   In 1754 the first Royal troops came to
take their share in garrisoning the East Indies, the
39th foot being the "first in the Indies."   By 1759,
two years after Plassey, six regular native battalions
existed in Madras, and a few years later similar
corps were formed in Bombay.

During the constant wars with the French,
with Mysore and the Mahrattas, the presidential
armies grew and developed and were brigaded.   In
1793 the fall of Pondicherry for the last time ended
once and for all the power of the French in India,
though their influence lasted for many years after,
and even in the year of grace 1911 there are old
native officers to be found in the Feudatory States
who can drill their men in French.   When this
great struggle came to an end, and Lord Cornwallis
had humbled the Tiger of Mysore, and, after the
manner of the English, given him one more chance,
it became high time to put some organization and

system into the mass of troops that had grown up during the years of war. So in 1795 we come upon the first general reconstruction, on a definite principle, throughout the three armies. At this date there were 13,000 Europeans in the country, King's and Company's, and some 24,000 native troops in Bengal and Madras respectively, with 9000 in Bombay. The reorganization took the accepted form of collecting artillery companies into battalions, cavalry troops into regiments, and forming the infantry into two-battalion regiments. This of course meant renumbering the whole of the battalions in each of the three armies except the first half, and incurring the usual dislike of corps for a change of the number under which they have won fame, however necessary that be. The uniforms of corps were more strictly assimilated to those of the King's troops, and a regular army came into being.

The result was as follows :—

Bengal.—European Artillery.   Three battalions of 5 companies each.
    European Infantry.   Three battalions of 10 companies each.
    Native Cavalry.   Four regiments.
    Native Infantry.   Twelve regiments of 2 battalions.

GOVERNOR'S BODYGUARD, MADRAS
Madrasi Musalman

Madras—European Infantry.   Two battalions of 10 companies.
      Artillery.   Two European battalions of 5 companies each, with 15 companies of lascars.
      Native Cavalry.   Four regiments.
      Native Infantry.   Eleven regiments of 2 battalions.
Bombay.—European Artillery.   Six companies.
      European Infantry.   Two battalions of 10 companies.
      Native Infantry.   Four regiments of 2 battalions and a marine battalion.

In those days the whole of India swarmed with men of military predilections.   The Afghan races, who for the last sixty years have been cribbed and confined to their own hills, wandered at will through the land to sell their sword to the highest bidder. Every native chief had Arab and Afghan soldiery. Afghan soldiers of fortune, on the waning of the Mogul authority, had hacked their way to power and were forming principalities.   The Rohillas, the descendants of Afghan and Turki settlers, still preserved many of their original characteristics, and drew fresh recruits from relatives in the border hills.

The old coast armies were largely filled by these adventurers or their half-bred children, or else by low-caste men, who on European food and with

European leading gladly fought the high - caste races that had oppressed them. The irregular horse, which came into being in Lord Lake's time, was largely recruited from the soldiers of fortune and masterless men that broke away from the falling fortunes of the crumbling States. It should be remembered that in few cases were the rulers then going down before us more than mushroom kings—adventurers who had themselves displaced the old rulers or the old Mogul governors; in hardly any case had they more claim to power than "the good old rule; the simple plan." The slackening of the Mogul authority had been the signal for a vast scramble among the free-lances, in which the cruelty and oppression endured by the long-suffering peasantry was beyond belief. To every district from which British successes had driven the free-lance and the alien *Schwartzreiter*, the British uniform and the white face were a sign of freedom and mercy, when the peasant dare till the field and the woman creep out from her hovel.

Then, too, because in every land, but more especially in the East, it is good to be on the winning side, soldiers of all kinds flocked to the Company's colours, and the leader of free-lances tried to preserve some *izzat*[1] in serving the new master, who at any rate paid regularly.

In 1798 Lord Mornington, later the Marquis Wellesley, "The great Marquis," became Governor-General, and, seeing farther ahead than most, realized that whatever the folk at home would say, the British in the East must either go forward or be overwhelmed, and that forthwith, and so determined that however so much others might care to fritter away an empire, he would have none of it. Already far-seeing men had settled that there was to be one European power in Hindustan, fighting the French wherever they found them, and Lord Mornington had determined that there should not only be one European power, but only one paramount power in the Peninsula. With the fall of the French State, French soldiers of fortune had drifted to most of the native courts of India, ready to minister to the desire for what then seemed the secret of power, troops trained on the European model. Mahratta and Musalman States, alarmed at the might of the English, were preparing to destroy the power of the Company. Buonaparte himself was openly trafficking with Tippoo in Mysore, with Scindia, with Holkar and the Bhonsla, the leading chiefs of the

---

[1] Prestige.

Mahratta confederacy, while the French Isles of France and Bourbon harboured privateers to prey on the Indiamen, and formed a base for designs on India itself.

So the great Marquis started forth himself to strike first, lest worse befall. Tippoo, the Tiger of Mysore, profiting little by the chance given him six years earlier by Lord Cornwallis, again broke a lance, and fell once and for all to General Harris. Arthur Wellesley and Stevenson broke the power of Scindia in two pitched battles and a dozen successful sieges and assaults. General Lake, the Commander-in-Chief, led his troops from Bengal against the chief gatherings of the Mahrattas, defeating Scindia's trained forces, the army that De Boigne and Perron had organized with such care, at Deig and Laswarrie. Delhi fell, the old blind Mogul was rescued from his Mahratta jailers and pensioned, and Holkar was chased by Lake for 350 miles, till he fled to his own country.

Then came the swing back of the pendulum, and the British took reverses that lessened their hold on the imagination of the East for many years to come. General Lake left the final pursuit of Holkar to a force under Colonel Monson of the 76th Foot, and that officer followed far away from

GOVERNOR'S BODYGUARD, BOMBAY
Musalman Rajput

his own base and into the season of the rains, till
Holkar, tampering with his auxiliaries, and even
with his regular troops, turned on him. Monson was
compelled to retire, and the withdrawal gradually
changed to a flight, and the flight to a debacle,
despite the heroism of his Europeans, and some of
his native troops. The second reverse was the
Commander-in-Chief's failure to take Bhurtpore,
the capital of a Hindu State. Time after time were
his columns, usually headed by the 76th Foot, hurled
back from the impracticable breaches with heavy
loss, till at last the old soldier reluctantly determined
to abandon the siege of the great mud fortress ;
and for years after, when our action was thought
high-handed, we were told to "go bully Bhurtpore."
With the exception of these two failures, the three
years' campaign against the Mahrattas was conspicuous by its success, and by the treaties which
brought the States concerned, not within the actual
British Empire, but to a definite state of allied
feudatories, with in many cases their power for
evil at any rate much curtailed.

There is an old medal, so old that its youngest
wearer has long passed to his rest, which commemorates the days when the great sepoy army
was evolving itself in the school of experience as an

army of the Line, in battle and march and siege, earning much fame in the process. It bears the inscription, " To the Army of India," and its tally of clasps includes the history of the wars of the Marquis Wellesley, of Arthur Wellesley, his brother, and General Gerard Lake, the Commander-in-Chief, as well as the later victories of Lord Moira and Malcolm and Hislop. " Assaye," " Argaum," " Ghawilghur,"   " Asseerghur,"   " Laswarrie," " Allighur," " Battle of Deig," " Capture of Deig," " Battle of Delhi," " Defence of Delhi," are among the honours that the medal commemorates, and which were borne on the colours of corps till, for the most part of the Bengal Army, they were wiped off the record in the whirlwind of Mutiny.

During these wars more regiments, both horse and foot, were continually being raised, and after them the army became still more regular and con-trolled by regulation, in close touch with the increasing garrison of King's troops, and more and more European in its dress and equipment. Irregulars too were added to the army at this period, and as the question of regulars versus irregulars has been hotly argued in India in the past, it may be well to understand the difference. To-day, the Silladar Cavalry are the legitimate

1st DUKE OF YORK'S OWN
LANCERS
(SKINNER'S HORSE)

Hindustani Musalman

3rd SKINNER'S HORSE

Musalman Rajput

heirs of the old irregulars, and the whole native army is largely modelled on what fifty years ago was termed the Irregular System. The regular army, both horse and foot, resembled in its organization the British Line. The establishment of officers resembled that of the King's service, and companies and troops were commanded by the British officers, while the native officers were but understudies promoted by seniority, and not for efficiency, and were men of great age. On the cross over the long trench graves on the battlefield of Chillianwalla are inscribed the names of two Brahman subadars, and against their names is recorded their ages, 65 and 70. In war time men no doubt came to commissioned rank earlier, but in peace under the regular system the native officers were aged figure-heads. In the irregular corps the British officers were few, and native officers had definite command of companies and troops, and came to great authority and efficiency thereby. The irregular cavalry were enlisted on the old system of the country—the silladar system—whereby in return for a sum down the soldier came with horse, arms, and accoutrements complete. This is the system which, considerably developed, holds in the Indian cavalry to-day, with the exception of the three light cavalry regular

regiments of the old Madras cavalry, which still
exist as part of the old line, and which still wear
the French grey and silver of the old regular light
cavalry that played so leading a part in the Mutiny.

The irregulars were not esteemed at their worth
by the rest of the army, till the wars in Afghanistan
and the Punjab showed the immense value of the
power of resource and initiative that they possessed.
This was probably accentuated by the fact that
while this spirit was far more present in all ranks
in the earlier wars, the *Pax Britannica* had killed
it among the peasantry and it only remained among
a smaller class.

It should be remembered that during the
earlier years of the nineteenth century the Indian
army fulfilled an essentially imperial rôle.   The
reduction of the oversea colonies and naval stations
of our European enemies during the Napoleonic
wars was entrusted to it.   The oversea expeditions
were numerous, and this power to commence
expeditions from a self-supporting base, was and is
one of the great strategical assets which India adds
to our imperial power.

So early as 1762, an expedition composed of
Madras troops took part in the war with Spain by
capturing Manila.

In 1795, an expedition from India captured Ceylon from the Dutch and French, the native troops being from Madras, with the exception of some artillery companies from Bengal.

In 1795, an expedition from Madras captured Amboyna and the Spice Islands from the Dutch.

In 1801, a force from India under Sir David Baird proceeded to join the British force in Egypt, the 2nd and 13th Bombay Infantry and some native artillery taking part.

In 1808, a force of volunteers from the Bengal army proceeded to occupy Macao with a view to forestalling the French.

Native Officer,
Calcutta Native Militia,
1795.

In 1810, the depredations of the French privateers on British commerce demanded the capture of Mauritius (Île de France), Bourbon and Rodrigues. Expeditions, in which Bombay and Madras corps and volunteer battalions from the Bengal army took part, reduced the islands with little difficulty.

In 1811, a large naval and military force

proceeded to capture the Island of Java from the Dutch and French. The troops included several volunteer battalions from Bengal, and some horse artillery and pioneers from Madras. The expedition met with considerable resistance, and was entirely successful. Sir Samuel Auchmuty was in command, and the famous Gillespie was one of the brigadiers. The accounts of the actions, the capture of Weltevrede and the like, read like actions of the South African War, from the well-known Dutch names which occur.

The end of the Mahratta Wars of 1803-4 meant no prolonged peace for the Indian Army. In 1814 broke out the war with Nepal due to Gurkha inroads, and after preliminary disasters was brought to a successful conclusion when General Ochterlony took the field—the terrible "Lony Ochter" of the lullaby—with fresh troops and selected generals. From this time, after the manner of the English, the conquered race was formed into soldiers, and from it spring the Gurkha battalions that are such a famous part of the Indian Army of to-day.

In 1817 two causes once more involved India in a far-reaching war. The Mahratta States, chafing under treaties, and garrisons that prevented their

BRITISH OFFICERS

5TH CAVALRY

23RD CAVALRY
(Frontier Force)

17TH CAVALRY

26TH KING GEORGE'S
OWN LIGHT
CAVALRY

11TH KING
EDWARD'S OWN
LANCERS
(Probyn's Horse)

4TH CAVALRY
Daffadar
Jāt Sikh

16TH CAVALRY
Jemadar
Jāt

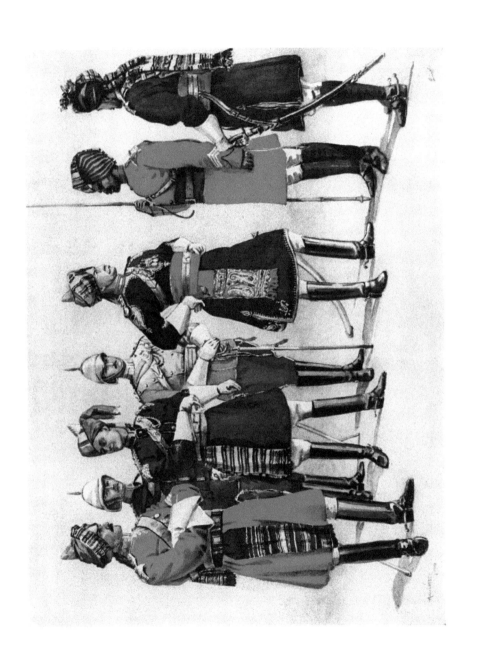

overrunning the territories of their weaker neighbours, were busy planning fresh resistance, while
allied with them and even a worse evil, were the
Pindaris.   This was the name given to the
enormous bands of free-lances, who, seizing strongholds and forming centres wherever they pleased,
scourged the country round, swept and raided
where they listed, and brought half India to the
state of Europe in the days of Wallenstein and
Tilly.   These vast bodies of masterless soldiery,
chiefly horse with many odd guns, had grown from
the gradual break-up of Mogul armies, and had
continually been reinforced from Afghan tribesmen, Arabs, and any adventurous and lawless lad
who liked to hear the lark sing rather than the
mouse squeak, and they lived at their ease on the
peasantry of India.

The horror they inspired in the people has
hardly been forgotten to this day, and still perhaps
keeps the grandchildren of those who suffered,
grateful to the British who saved them.

In 1817, therefore, things had come to such a
pass, that if we were to keep India as a land for
honest men to live in, the Mahratta confederacy
must be reduced to a proper status, and the
Pindaris driven from the land.   If we realize that

the Pindaris were operating over a country about twice the size of France, and provided by nature with every kind of bolthole and fastness, we shall perhaps understand the task that Lord Moira, the Governor-General, had set himself. The combined forces of the Mahratta States and the Pindaris amounted to at least 100,000 horse, 70,000 disciplined foot, and over 500 guns. Against these, the Indian Army took the field in two large forces —the Army of the Deccan, commanded by Sir Thomas Hislop, consisting of seven divisions, and the Grand Army, commanded by the Governor-General himself, consisting of four divisions. Both armies were strong in cavalry, there being several regiments of Rohilla horse, with Gardner's and Skinner's Irregulars, and most of the regular native cavalry, as well as several regiments of British light dragoons, which were reduced in subsequent intervals of peace.

The events of this campaign are too numerous to be described in detail, but among the most famous are the defence of Seetabuldee (the Nagpore Residency), the battles of Kirkee against the Peshwa, the battle of Mahidpore against Holkar, and the famous battle of Corygaum near Poona, where the 2nd/1st Bombay Infantry (now the

102nd Grenadiers), with 250 horse and a detachment of Madras Artillery, resisted the most desperate attacks of the whole of the Peshwa's army. The medal to the Army of India already referred to bears for these campaigns the clasps, "Kirkee," "Poona," "Kirkee and Poona," "Seetabuldee," "Nagpore," "Seetabuldee and Nagpore," "Maheidpoor," "Corygaum." When the main forces opposing us had been crushed as an army in being, many weary months followed in chasing Mahratta and Pindari bands from one stronghold to another, and reducing innumerable hill forts, till the land had peace. Perhaps the feature of this war was the increasing number of irregular horse, who proved far the best suited to the final stage of the work, and the subsequent attempt to improve the organization of the army, that had shown defects in the wide strain put on it.

It must not be supposed that in all these years of an alien army there had not been mutinies; a large army controlled by a trading company, with large ideas on the subject of profits, was bound to have passed through periods of well-founded grievance. In 1806 had been the serious mutiny of Vellore—that should have been as the writing on the wall—and in 1824 the corps ordered to

Naik,   Bombay Grenadier Battalion, 1801.

march to Arracan had refused to go. These will be referred to in the chapter on the Great Mutiny. In 1824 the whole of the armies were reorganized and renumbered, the double-battalion regiments being abolished, and the line in each army was renumbered from 1 upwards by single battalions, receiving their new numbers in accordance with their original date of formation. The Army of 1824, therefore, was composed as follows :—

Bengal.—Three brigades of horse artillery of four troops each, of which one troop was native. Five battalions of artillery of four companies each.

A corps of sappers and miners, with a cadre of 47 engineer officers, and a corps of pioneers.

2 battalions of European infantry.

8 regiments of light cavalry (regulars).

5 regiments of irregular horse.

68 battalions of native infantry.

Several local corps and legions.

Madras.—Two brigades of horse artillery, one European and one native.

3 battalions of foot artillery of 4 companies each, with 4 companies of lascars attached.

3 regiments of light cavalry.

2 corps of pioneers.

2 battalions of European infantry.

6TH KING EDWARD'S OWN CAVALRY

8TH CAVALRY

Jāts

52 battalions of native infantry.

3 local battalions.

Bombay.—4 troops of horse artillery.

8 companies of foot artillery.

A corps of engineers and pioneers.

3 regiments of light cavalry.

2 regiments of irregular horse.

2 battalions of European infantry.

24 battalions of native infantry.

It will be seen, therefore, how fast the great armies were growing, to keep pace with the territories we had acquired, and the responsibilities we had undertaken.

From the close of the Pindari wars, the expedition to Burma in 1824, and the capture of Bhurtpore, were the chief military events till we come to the First Afghan War. It will be remembered how, in 1805, Lord Lake was compelled to abandon the siege of Bhurtpore after losing 446 killed and 2479 wounded, in four separate assaults. In 1825 the insolence of the rulers of this virgin fortress knew no bounds, and circumstances forced the Government to reduce it. The Commander-in-Chief, Lord Combermere (the Stapleton Cotton of Peninsula and Waterloo fame), advanced against the place in December 1825, with a force consisting of a cavalry and two strong infantry divisions, backed up, by what Lord Lake so lacked, half the heavy guns in India. The fortress was eventually stormed, with the loss of close on 1000 killed and wounded, and a loss to the garrison computed at 8000. The prestige thus regained by the British was great, and the last clasp on the old medal was for "Bhurtpore." The Burmese War which was going on during 1825, was also commemorated by a clasp for "Ava," and its history, while devoid of large engagements, is a record of difficult and harassing operations in hill and swamp and jungle, both in Burma itself and in the Assam and Arracan districts.

About this time the whole of the infantry, including the local battalions, were clothed in scarlet with white pants, the only exception being the rifle battalions. The head-dress, though resembling a shako, was still made of black cloth on an iron, and later a wicker frame. The regular cavalry were all in French grey with various facings, the officers being dressed as dragoons, hussars or lancers. The horse artillery officers were in the English dragoon helmets, with varying crests and plumes, and the native horse artillery wore high Persian skin head-dresses. The irregular horse were in varieties of native clothing, the officers the same, though we see portraits of James Skinner, or "Old Sekunder," as he was called, at the head of his regiment dressed as an officer of dragoons.

For twelve years after the fall of Bhurtpore the army had comparative peace. As a result of the Marquis Wellesley's policy, and that followed by the Marquis of Hastings (Lord Moira) after the close of the Pindari war, there grew up many contingents paid for by the native States, but commanded by Company's officers, drilled like our own troops, and enlisting, in the case of the majority, the same races as the Bengal Army. Service in some of them was much sought after, and the Gwalior contingent came to be regarded as a *corps d'élite*, famed for its discipline and appearance.

In 1838 a policy was adopted which was to involve India in four years' war, immense disaster and chagrin, and a loss of prestige to which perhaps the Mutiny is of all causes most directly traceable. This policy consisted of forming a friendly Afghanistan to assist in opposing the advance of the Bear. The rightful ruler of Afghanistan, Shah Soojah ul Mulk, driven forth by his own folk by reason of his incompetence, was a pensioner in our midst. He had apparently sufficient following to justify our restoring him as our ally, should that course seem desirable, which to the brains of the time it did. There was no question of right or wrong. On all and every occasion Afghans had swept into Hindustan to slay, to rape, to loot, and to devastate. If, in the policy of security and good government, it was desirable to turn the tables, it was only a question of expediency and counting the cost, and the pros and cons. At any rate, to those in power the course seemed good, and the famous "Tripartite Treaty" was signed between ourselves, the Shah, and Ranjit Singh, the Maharaja of the Punjab. To place His Highness on the throne of his fathers and maintain him there, a contingent was raised in India, with British officers, of Hindustanis and Gurkhas, and to support it the Army of the Indus was collected. Since, however, the Punjab was foreign, and not too trustworthy, it was decided to advance into Afghanistan by the lengthy if easier route of Sukkur, Quetta, Kandahar, and Ghuznee. The force consisted of a brigade of cavalry, a Bengal division, a Bombay column, and the Shah's contingent, 6000 strong. The campaign that ensued, with all its successes, disappointments, disasters, and controversies cannot be discussed here. The

10th DUKE OF CAMBRIDGE'S OWN LANCERS
(HODSON'S HORSE)
"THE QUARTER GUARD"

| BRITISH OFFICER | Dogra | Punjabi Musalman | Sikh | Punjabi Musalman | Pathan |

force under Sir John Keane reached Kabul in 1839, after the successful storming of Ghuznee, and immense trouble due to want of carriage, cold and sickness, and after abandoning the useless baggage and camp followers responsible for much of the trouble. All was *couleur de rose*. The Shah sat on the throne of his fathers; much of the army was withdrawn; English officers rode freely over the country; the Khyber route was opened; ladies, children, soldiers, families, flocked to the canton-ment at Kabul; the contingent garrisoned the outposts, the brigades of occupation sat in Kabul and Kandahar. All was peace and content on the surface. We read in Sir Neville Chamberlain's life, of officers riding in from Ghuznee to Kabul for the races The Shah was to present a medal to the troops for the storming of Ghuznee; he had already started a magnificent order of Knighthood, the "Order of the Douranee Empire," and had conferred it on the leading lights of the army and political service, to the derision of those who did not receive it. Then came the sinister rumours, the gathering of the storm, the murder of the Envoy Sir William Macnaghten and the Envoy-elect Sir Alexander Burnes, the squabbles of an effete commander and inefficient garrison, the attempt to evacuate Kabul in the snow, the taking of hostages, and lastly, the massacre of half-frozen troops and frost-bitten followers—such a disaster and humiliation as had never before happened to British arms. Bright spots there were. The defence of Kelat-i-Ghilzai by the 3rd Shah's, now the 12th (Kelat-i-Ghilzai) Regiment, under Captain Craigie, with a few European artillerymen, the defence of Jellalabad by Sale and the "Illustrious garrison," the sturdy demeanour of Nott at Kandahar, with his "splendid Sepoy regiments," all were bright spots, to redeem incompetence and pusillanimity. But the world looked at the failure; a British brigade annihilated under most pitiable circumstances was what the Eastern world saw, and rejoiced at. Then came the avenging army under Pollock, with trembling sepoys to be heartened and redisciplined at Peshawar, and a final advance, not so much to rescue the English men and women in captivity as to help the sturdy Nott, who had agreed with Pollock to carry out the orders to evacuate Afghanistan by coming *via* Kabul on their joint responsibility. This method of evacuating Afghanistan enabled vengeance to be taken on the guilty capital, and the British prisoners to be rescued. Besides the medal for the storming of Ghuznee in the first phase, special medals were given for the defence of Kelat-i-Ghilzai and Jellalabad respectively, and another to the avenging armies, bearing the inscription "Victoria Vindex." The armies of Nott and Pollock then marched down from Kabul, and after traversing an almost hostile Punjab, passed the British frontier into Ferozepore, to find an immense reception awaiting them from the Governor-General, Lord Ellenborough, at the head of a reserve army. An interesting incident of the times, was the intense camaraderie between the 13th Foot and the 35th Bengal Native Infantry, parts of the "Illustrious garrison," which ended in the whole of the latter feasting their British comrades before parting at Ferozepore. Even the 35th, however, went under in '57, and with them the battery of artillery on whose guns Lord Ellenborough had engraved a mural crown for its share in the defence. Despite, however, the triumphant finale, the maimed and frost-bitten remnants of the earlier occupation, rescued from begging in the Kabul bazaars, told a tale of lessened prestige that was not forgotten for many years.

During the strain of the Afghan War, however, India was still able to find troops for Imperial oversea purposes.   In 1840, a large amount of British property had been destroyed by the Chinese in an attempt to solve by a short cut the opium problem, and an expedition under Sir Hugh Gough was sent to South China.   The major por-tion of the force were troops of the Madras Line, for, as it had become a habit for the Bengal Army not to cross the seas, the usual volunteer battalions alone represented the Bengal Army.

A Grenadier Sepoy of 30th Regiment of Bengal Native Infantry, 1815.

An aftermath of the Afghan wars was the trouble in Scinde, ending in Sir Charles Napier's short and famous campaign, in which three Bombay Cavalry and two Bombay Infantry regi-ments took part with the 22nd Foot.   The annexation of Scinde that followed, still further extended the responsibilities of the sepoy army, and necessitated more battalions.

This same year, 1843, was to see an important though short campaign in internal India.   A minority in Scindia's domain, the State of Gwalior, had resulted in dissensions between two factions.

11TH KING EDWARD'S OWN LANCERS
(PROBYN'S HORSE)

RISALDAR
Durrani (Afghan)

The army took opposite sides to that supported by Government, and the army was a very considerable force, still retaining the European organization and drill that it had learnt in the days of De Boigne and his successors. Gwalior was a large Hindu State, and there was considerable danger of an attempt to combine with the other great Hindu power, the Sikhs of the Punjab. To obviate any outbreak of the Gwalior troops, an army of exercise was collected as a precautionary measure near Agra, and another force at Jhansi. Eventually the state of affairs at Gwalior necessitated a move of the British troops on the capital, but it was not expected to be more than a promenade, and some ladies even accompanied the force. While Sir Hugh Gough advanced from Muttra, Sir John Grey advanced from Jhansi, and to every one's surprise, the Mahratta army was found in position near Maharajpore, and also at Punniar. The former force opened fire on Sir Hugh Gough, and a severe engagement ensued, in which the Gwalior artillery was especially well served. The battle at Punniar was also a severe one, though on a lesser scale. These two victories, however, completed the overthrow of the Gwalior troops and ended the disturbing conditions in the Durbar. A six-

pointed bronze star was awarded the troops, with
a silver centre, and the words " Maharajpore" and
" Punniar" respectively in the centre.

In the winter of 1845 the most serious trouble
that had threatened India for many years came to
a head.   The Sikhs, who had lost the firm hand of
the sagacious Ranjit Singh, and were burning to
invade British India, finally crossed the Sutlej
in large numbers near Ferozepore.   The Sutlej
campaign with its hard-fought battles, its vicissi-
tudes and successful conclusion, is a story by itself,
and has often been told from many points of view.
The native troops that took part in the campaign
were entirely from Bengal, and acquitted themselves with varying credit.   The Sikhs were far
the severest foe that had been met in India, and
the climate was rigorous to natives of Hindustan,
while there was considerable feeling towards the
last Hindu State.   The bulk of the fighting fell on
the European troops, whose casualties were very
severe.

Large additions were made to the army at the
outbreak of the campaign, including the formation
of eight more regiments of cavalry.   The canton-
ing of a force of occupation at Lahore during the
minority of the young Maharaja, put some strain

on the army, and a special force was raised for the garrisoning of the Jullundur Doab.

The attempt to bolster up the Sikh State, that was adopted as a definite policy after the First Sikh War, was soon doomed to failure. The Sikhs had not yet made up their minds to accept even British domination, and an outburst was precipitated by the murder, at Mooltan, of two British officers lent to the Durbar. This took place in the early summer of 1848, and it was some time before a force for the reduction of Mooltan, into which Mool Raj, the rebellious Sikh governor, had thrown himself, could be assembled. Events, too, soon showed that the outbreak at Mooltan was likely to become general, and a large army was organized at Ferozepore, consisting of four brigades of cavalry and three divisions of infantry.

The reinforcement of the force attacking Mooltan, by a Bombay brigade, the final capture of the fortress, the passing of the Chenab, the hard-fought battle of Chillianwalla, the final crushing of the Sikhs at Gujarat, and the surrender of the Sirdars and their followers at Rawalpindi, with the pursuit of the Afghan horse to the Khyber, are all matters of history and of full record.

Suffice it here to say that the Bengal native army formed the bulk of the force, reinforced for the crowning victory of Gujarat by the Bombay brigade that had taken part in the storm of Mooltan. The brunt of the heavy fighting in this war fell as usual on the European troops, but some of the native infantry corps were especially distinguished and suffered very heavy casualties. The losses sustained by the British troops in these two Sikh wars were very severe, far more so than any portion, especially the native infantry, had been accustomed to experience for many years.

The annexation of the Punjab was followed by more additions to the native army, with very little corresponding increase in the European garrison, while the exigencies of holding the immense area annexed, and of watching the Afghan frontier, demanded a grouping of the European troops in the North of India, and a very large native garrison. The frontier brigade organized in the Jullundur Doab was moved to the Afghan border, and from it, with the addition of several new corps, recruited largely from the Khalsa regiments that had been disbanded, the Punjab Irregular Force was formed, which, known later as the Punjab Frontier Force, has become so famous a portion of the Indian

12TH CAVALRY

JEMADAR

Dogra

Army. Lord Dalhousie's policy of annexing States in hopeless anarchy, or which had no successor in heredity on the demise of the reigning chief, added considerably to the demands on the native force in the country.

In 1854 the annexation of Nagpore necessitated the formation of a local force, and the annexation of Oudh in 1856 was perforce followed by the immediate formation of the Oudh Irregular Force. It should be realized that the state of the country, with its poor communications and immense hilly and jungle tracts, demanded far more effective forces than police, for the ordinary pacification and maintenance of order in the districts. In countries where might had been right for perhaps a couple of hundred years, and the hand alone had kept the head since the memory of man, there were scores of reiving barons and robber chiefs to be dealt with. To make the barons and their retainers pay revenue, obey the law, and cease to spoil the peasant and the trader, was for many years beyond the power of mere police, and it was this need, coupled with the fact that revenue was by no means ample, that demanded troops, and those of the cheaper, or native, kind. The policy, therefore, dangerous though it seemed, was an almost unavoid-

5

able one, given the conditions as they appeared to men at the time.

The war in the Crimea had withdrawn some European troops from India which had not been replaced in 1857. The Second Burmese War, unavoidably thrust on us in 1853, had called for still more troops of occupation, and in 1856, a Persian expedition removed several European corps for the time beyond the seas. Several native corps of the Bombay Army took part in the Persian expedition and gained considerable distinction. Between 1849 and 1857 the new frontier at the foot of the Afghan hills gave much trouble, and numerous small frontier expeditions, to impress the laws of *meum* and *tuum* on the tribes, were necessary.

The foregoing in brief is the outline of the causes which gradually formed the huge Indian Army, and of the magnitude and the vastness of the services it rendered both in India and in the Empire generally. Minor infidelities and mutinies there had been, and many failings of the service as a whole had been often pointed out, with many aberrations of judgment on the part of the administration. The fact remains, however, that come rain come shine, this vast alien force had, for

14TH MURRAY'S JAT LANCERS
RISALDAR-MAJOR

a hundred and fifty years, rendered the most faithful military service to their masters, while an immense feeling of attachment had grown up between officers and men.   So much so that when the storm came, the retired officers from India could not credit the news.   "What! dear old Jack mutiny, kill his sahibs, murder their families— impossible!"   Such were the views of the mass of officers who had spent happy and often glorious careers with the sepoy regiments.   However, blow up that sepoy army did, with all the romance and tragedy and inconsequence imaginable; and to understand in outline how and why it did so, is essential to a right understanding of the conditions of to-day.   The Indian Army, as we now know it, is the result of the evolution of the portion of the army that remained faithful, and the reconstruction of that that fell away.

That great army stood in 1857 at 311,538 (Imperial Gazetteer), with 39,500 Europeans, King's and Company's.   It was, too, dressed and equipped for the most part on a pedantic model of the British Army.   In the great lines of battle drawn up to meet the Sikhs, the European and Native Infantry were dressed in their scarlet coatees and white ducks, with tall black shakos

and white buff cross-belts. The artillery and
cavalry, other than the irregulars, were also dressed
much as their European brethren. For the most
part, too, corps fought in their full dress, after the
manner of the time. The 24th Foot at Chillianwalla, for instance, had their shakos pulled off
forcing their way through the thorn jungle to get
at the Sikh guns. Some corps, like the 61st Foot,
however, went into action in shell-jackets and
forage-caps with white covers. How this enormous
army, in its European costume of coatee and
shako, came to mutiny and rue untold, and how
the modern army grew up in its place, will be
outlined in the following chapters.

CHAPTER II

IN the foregoing chapter, the history of the army from its inception to the Mutiny has been run through in outline. Allusion has been made to the great campaigns, but to describe these in detail and write a history of the wars of the Company's Army would require many volumes. Nor is it possible to dwell on the exploits of the native regiments, and the actions in which they individually came to fame, even if this were confined to those that still figure on the Army List. There are, however, two great campaigns in the early portion of the nineteenth century which are specially remarkable, and which, more than any others, formed the real India of to-day, and resulted in that consolidated Indian Army which lasted till 1857 in Bengal, and practically to this day in the other Presidencies.

37

These campaigns are the two great Mahratta wars, of which the first lasted from 1803 to 1806, and included the famous battles of Sir Arthur Wellesley and Lord Lake ; and the latter, from 1817 to 1819, represented the final conclusions with the Mahrattas, and the ridding of the country from the scourge of the Pindari bands of free-lances and robbers. The Sikh wars and the First Afghan War are well known from the many histories and biographies that bear on them. These two Mahratta campaigns, however, are little known, yet many of the most famous battle honours of the surviving Company's regiments, as well as those of the British Line, are derived from them.

The enemy who fought against us were principally the Mahratta chiefs, who controlled immense bands of mercenary horse and foot, largely trained and officered by Frenchmen, and comprising every lawless man in the country-side, with Persians, Arabs, Afghans, and even negroes. There was no case of the patriot fighting for his country-side, and the campaigns have, to a great extent, but confined the Mahratta chiefs to their rightful provinces, and curbed the immense pretensions and scrambling conquests that had ensued on the collapse of the Mogul Empire. The country-side only longed

15TH LANCERS (CURETON'S MULTANIS)

Honorary Native Commandant
NAWAB SIR HAFIZ MUHAMMAD ABDULLAH KHAN, K.C.I.E.

for deliverance from an era like to the worst days of the Palatinate.

The daring of some of these troops is clearly evinced in the casualties that they inflicted on the victorious British, while the political conceptions of some of the chiefs were magnificent. None of them, however, possessed the power to consolidate a Hindu rule, and their pretensions resulted in constant devastation of their neighbours' or rivals' territories, including our own.

The result of these campaigns brought the British paramount to the borders of the Punjab, bestowed peace on millions of people, and gave our own territories, for the first time, complete immunity from cruel raids. Incidentally, it broke the fortunes of many of the barons who lived by raiding and pillage and adventurer service, and of the thousands of hereditary and mercenary soldiers for whom there was no place in our ranks. Several thousands were absorbed in our irregulars, but the remainder had, perforce, to turn peasant.

The campaigns that brought this about it is now proposed briefly to describe, as a fitting complement to the outline history of the Company's Army, more especially as in these extremely arduous campaigns the backing of British troops was far smaller than in later years. Some of the events, too, such as the defence of Seetabuldee and the fight at Corygaum, both in 1817, against overwhelming odds, with only a small force of European artillery in the way of backing, are among the most famous events in the whole military history of our Empire.

THE FIRST MAHRATTA WAR, 1803-6

The history of the Governor-Generalship of Lord Mornington, afterwards the Marquis Wellesley, is one of struggle against the French influence in India, as revived by the plans and ambitions of the Emperor Napoleon, and against the hostility of the Mahratta princes. When Sivaji, the Mahratta prince and leader known to the Moguls as "the mountain rat," had established his Hindu kingdom among the mountains of Western India, he had formed a barrier to the power of Islam and its proselytizing influence which at first had promised to revive some of the glories of the old Hindu rule in India. On his death, however, the solidarity of the Mahrattas soon passed away. The nominal sovereignty remained in the hands of the Rajas of Satara, but the high officers of state soon raised

18th KING GEORGE'S OWN LANCERS

Honorary Lieutenant
Hon. MALIK UMAR HAYAT KHAN, C.I.E.
Tiwana of Shahpur

(*Punjabi Musalman*)

طال حيات خان سوار

A.C.LOVETT

semi-independent principalities for themselves.   The
Rajas of Satara exercised nominal control through
their Peshwa or hereditary minister of the crown,
who soon also became a territorial ruler.   The
Mahratta princes, of whom the principal were
Scindia, whose capital was Gwalior; Holkar, the
ruler of Indore; the Bhonsla at Nagpore, together
with the Peshwa at Poona, were always at war
with their neighbours in some form of confederacy,
or else individually among themselves.   Combined
against the Mogul power, against the Nizam, or
against the British, fighting the Rajput princes,
and scouring the territories of their neighbours
with hordes of horse, they and their name had been
a horror and offence in the land for generations.

The first steps necessary to counteract the
French influence had been to destroy, once and for
all, the cruel and impossible ruler of Mysore,
Tippoo Sultan, son of the great Hyder Ali.   The
history of his and his father's wars with the
British, and his own implacable and unreasoning
behaviour, had resulted, as has been related in the
previous chapter, in his death at the final storming
and capture of Seringapatam.   In Hyderabad the
Nizam had a force of 15,000 men trained by
M. Raymond, and officered by many of the

French officers left out of employment when the French power had died out, and reinforced by officers from Europe. Some were royalist refugees, others sent by Napoleon to push French influence. The Governor-General insisted, as a price of his protection of the Nizam against the demands and invasions of the Mahrattas, that this force should be disbanded and replaced by a British subsidiary force. To fortify the Nizam in his resolution, four Madras battalions and some guns marched into Hyderabad, and the French-trained force was disbanded, the officers coming to the British for protection, and many of the men re-enlisting in the British service. This took place at the end of 1798.

The ground was now clear for compelling the Mahratta princes to enter into agreement with the British, to cease from attack and raid on British territory and that of its allies, and combine for the defence of Hindustan against the Afghan invader.

For several years after the death of the Peshwa Madho Rao, intrigue and counter-intrigue, killings, poisonings, and inter-Mahratta battlings with European leaders on each side, had torn the States to distraction. At last, in 1802, Jeswant

Rao Holkar defeated the joint forces of the Peshwa and Scindia close to Poona, and Bajee Rao, the former, fled to British territory and signed the Treaty of Bassein, whereby he vowed alliance with the British, in return for a subsidiary force of some European artillery and six battalions of sepoys to protect him in his capital.

The other Mahratta chiefs were much incensed at the Peshwa's defection from the cause of independent and combined hostility to all and every neighbour. For twenty-five years the confederacy had avoided all foreign alliances, and now the head of them had accepted it. Holkar proclaimed Bajee Rao's brother, Amrut Rao, Peshwa in his stead, and it became necessary for us to support Bajee Rao, and generally obtain some settlement.

The foregoing description is necessary to understand the situation that brought General Arthur Wellesley in the Deccan and General Lake, the Commander-in-Chief in Hindustan, into the field for the campaign that practically made the modern India.

The British had been organizing for some time for a war that was obviously inevitable. The theatre of war was enormous, and necessitated the employment of several entirely separate forces.

The Army of the Deccan

General Wellesley advanced on Poona with 8000 foot, 1700 cavalry, and 2000 Mysore horse from Mysore, through the Southern Mahratta States, to reinstate the Peshwa, bringing in his train many Mahratta chieftains to support their head.   Colonel Stevenson came up with the Subsidiary Force, and the Nizam's troops from Hyderabad, the latter numbering 9000 horse and 6000 foot.

The Commander-in-Chief advanced with 10,500 men on Delhi, leaving 3500 in reserve at Allahabad. Eight thousand men under General Stuart moved into the Southern Mahratta States, and 8000 under Colonel Murray entered Gujarat.   Five thousand were also sent towards Cuttack, which province was held by the Bhonsla (the Raja of Berar). The British force totalled 50,000 men, which was far larger than any hitherto put into the field.

Assaye

The first move consisted of a forced march, to save Poona from being burned by Holkar.   General Wellesley then stormed the town and powerful fortress of Ahmednagar, which became an excellent

19TH LANCERS (FANE'S HORSE)
Punjabi Musalman

base to store his reserve supplies. The storming of the town wall was a remarkable feat, and cost 169 men ; while the fort, one of the strongest in India, surrendered after two days' bombardment. It is not possible to follow the details of the campaign, but suffice it to say that General Wellesley shortly after found himself in a position to strike at the combined forces of Scindia and the Bhonsla near Jalna, in the territory of Aurunga-bad, with the troops under his immediate command. Swollen rivers prevented Colonel Stevenson from joining him, though only a few miles off, and Wellesley found himself in front of some 55,000 Mahrattas, posted in the fork of two rivers, the Jua and the Kelna, the swollen Kelna being a mile in front of their position. Scindia and the Bhonsla had with them a magnificent park of artillery, massed in the vicinity of the village of Assaye.

The enemy's position indicated no particular desire to come to action for the time being, but the opportunity was too good to be missed, despite the fact that the British numbered but 4500.

With that audacity which has never failed the combatant in the East who is ready to grasp the nettle danger with the hand of courage, the British

leader decided to attack.   How to get at the
enemy was the difficulty, for at present their line
faced him, with a swollen and unfordable river in
their front.   The quick eye of General Wellesley,
however, showed him two villages opposite each
other on the river, which, he felt, must mean a
practicable ford.   The British were at once moved
in that direction, and succeeded in crossing, to find
that the enemy, pivoted on the village of Assaye,
had changed front half left to meet them.

The total number of the British was but 4500,
of whom some 2200 were cavalry.   This small
force, immediately it could form up, advanced with
enthusiasm on the enormous force of the Mahrattas,
and their immense line of artillery.   The enemy's
infantry included 116 regular battalions, 600 men
of M. Pohlman's brigade, and 2500 of M. Dupont.
Four battalions belonging to the Begum Sumru
were also present.   The impetuosity of the British
attack resulted in a determined counter-attack
by the rallied enemy and the descent of their
cavalry, only driven off by determined charges
of the British dragoons and native cavalry.   After
three hours, however, the enemy were in full
flight, leaving 1200 dead and 98 guns on the field.

The British casualties were over 2000, in which

THE FORMER "HYDERABAD CONTINGENT" CAVALRY

30TH LANCERS (GORDON'S HORSE)
Lance Daffadar
Jāt

20TH DECCAN HORSE
Sikh

29TH LANCERS (DECCAN HORSE)
Risaldar
Dekhani Musalman

all corps shared heavily. The 74th Foot lost the most, with 10 officers killed and 6 wounded, and rank and file in proportion, while the 1/4th and 2/12th battalions of Madras native infantry lost heavily also. The native corps that took part were a party of Madras sappers, the 4th, 5th, and 7th Native Cavalry, and the 1/2nd, 1/4th, 1/8th, 1/10th, 2/12th battalions and the Pioneers. Of these only three are still in the service, besides the sappers, viz. the 1/2nd, now the 62nd Punjabis; the 1/4th, now the 64th Pioneers; and the 2/12th, now the 84th Punjabis. The present 63rd Palamcottah Light Infantry and 73rd Carnatic Infantry were with Wellesley at Ahmednagar, while the present 66th, 79th, 80th, 81st, and 82nd were with Colonel Stevenson's force a few miles from Assaye. It will be seen that it was the old Madras Line, then at the zenith of its fame, which formed the entire native portion of the victorious army in the Deccan. The reductions that the piping times of peace have necessitated have unfortunately removed from the Army List all the corps of Madras cavalry that gained such fame in this campaign, as well as H.M. 19th Light Dragoons.

After Assaye, Colonel Stevenson moved on to capture the immense hill-fortress of Aseergurh,

then belonging to Scindia, which eventually
capitulated.   During these operations several
French officers and non - commissioned officers
surrendered on various occasions.   Some had
already been found dead after different engagements, an officer of high rank being found on the
field of Assaye.

ARGAUM

After reforming his force that had fought at
Assaye, General Wellesley moved on to complete
the overthrow of the Bhonsla's forces, as Scindia
had arranged an armistice pending negotiations.
On the 28th of November Wellesley, having
joined with Stevenson for the purpose of moving
on the strong hill-fort of Gawilgurh, in the north of
Berar, came on a large force of the Bhonsla's and
Scindia's troops drawn up at the village of
Argaum.   The troops of Scindia were there in
contravention of the armistice, and though late
in the day, the General decided to attack.   The
enemy's position was five miles long, and his force
included large numbers of Persian and Arab
mercenaries.   The fighting was desperate, the 1/6th
Madras native infantry, now the 66th Punjabis,
repulsing an overwhelming charge of Scindia's

25TH CAVALRY (FRONTIER FORCE)

BANGASH

(*Pathan*)

horse. The fire from the heavy batteries of the Mahrattas, however, succeeded in disorganizing many of the native troops at the earlier stages, and it was not till late in the evening that the enemy were in full flight, with the loss of much of their camp and treasure and 38 guns. The British loss was 346 all told.

GAWILGURH

From Argaum, Wellesley pushed on at once to the Bhonsla's fort of Gawilgurh. On the 12th of December breaching batteries were opened, and the place was stormed on the 14th, in the face of determined opposition. Our losses amounted to 146.

The storming of Ahmednagar, the battles of Assaye and Argaum, and the capture of the impregnable fortresses of Aseergurh and Gawilgurh, were the main features of General Wellesley's campaign, and were followed by overtures for peace on practically our own terms. They were all operations of more than usual severity. The battle of Assaye was as desperate as any in our history, and full in its promise of the power of leading, possessed by the newly discovered "Sepoy General." The casualties, in their proportion to

7

the size of the force, were as heavy as any on record. When, close on half a century later, the British Government came to make up its jewels and award medals for half-forgotten services, clasps for all these actions, except Ahmednagar, were added to the medal "To the army in India." They have been described in some detail here, because it was in this war and that of 1817 that the real Indian Empire was founded, by the old Indian Army, and the corps that took so continuous a share in the campaign in the Deccan still survive intact.

THE GRAND ARMY

The other campaign of the same war, that conducted by Lord Lake himself, equally famous, was so far as the Indian Army is concerned chiefly the work of corps lost in the cataclysm of '57. There are, however, still four corps on the rolls of the army who marched with the Commander-in-Chief, and a briefer outline of this phase of the war is therefore desirable for the glory of Jack Sepoy and the famous 76th Foot, who formed the kernel of this sledge-hammer army. The Indian corps who remain are the 1st Cavalry (Skinner's Horse), the 1st Brahmans (then the 1/9th of the

Bengal Line), the 2nd Queen's Own Rajput Light Infantry (then the 2/15th), and the 4th Prince Albert Victor's Rajputs (then the 2/16th).

The Grand Army had been assembling at Kanauj, where the large force of cavalry, three regiments of dragoons, and five regiments of native cavalry had been exercised together for some months and trained as a division.   It was here that the first horse artillery was formed, by attaching two six-pounder galloper guns to each cavalry regiment. The infantry of the force consisted of one

17th Regiment Bengal Irregular Cavalry, 1850.

European battalion, the 76th, and eleven native battalions.

The immediate object was the destruction of the large force belonging to Scindia, which was disciplined under M. Perron, the successor of De Boigne. This force numbered nine brigades, with a total of 43,000 men and 464 guns. It was maintained by the revenue of what was known as "The French State," being the Doab between the Ganges and the Jumna. This had been assigned to the administration of De Boigne and Perron, to defray the cost of the force and the pay of the Europeans. In August the Grand Army slowly moved up towards the Mahratta frontier, and on the 28th was at Coel, within a few miles of M. Perron's army at Alligurh. A regular advance of the army on the 29th so impressed the Mahrattas that General Perron moved off after a skirmish to Delhi, leaving a Colonel Pedron in the fort of Alligurh.

ALLIGURH

As Alligurh was General Perron's headquarters, in which he had built his barracks and stores, it was decided to storm it at once, in spite of its twice triple series of gates and bastions. The assault was made early on the 4th of September, and carried with a loss of 260 killed and wounded, in which the 76th Foot, who were always to bear the brunt of all Lake's battles, lost 5 officers and 19 rank and file killed, and 4 officers and 62 rank and file wounded, the 1/4th Native Infantry losing almost as many, including 1 British officer killed and 4 wounded. The enemy's loss was very heavy. M.

27TH LIGHT CAVALRY

BRITISH OFFICER

26TH KING GEORGE'S OWN
LIGHT CAVALRY

DAFFADAR

Madrasi Musalman of the Carnatic

Pedron was captured, with 281 guns of all kinds, and large quantities of sepoys' uniform of French pattern.

BATTLE OF DELHI

No time was lost in following the enemy to Delhi, but General Perron himself rode in with some of his European officers, to surrender, before another battle took place. On the 16th of September, after a march of 18 miles, Lord Lake's force were pitching their camp near the Hindun river, a few miles from Delhi, when they found the Mahrattas, numbering sixteen of M. Louis Bourquien's regular battalions, and several thousand horse with plenty of artillery, were drawn up within a mile or so of them, hidden by long grass. Their guns soon opened on the British outposts. Lord Lake decided to attack at once, and did so, himself leading the attack. The furious and ordered attack of the British into the teeth of the Mahratta artillery fire was irresistible, and the whole of the enemy were routed with severe loss, and all the regulars, except two battalions, cut up. Sixty-three guns were captured, with a considerable amount of treasure. The British loss was 477, of which the 76th, as usual, lost the most (137);

and the 2/4th Native Infantry again suffered nearly as heavily, while the 2/15th, now the 2nd Rajputs, the only corps of the Indian Army taking part in this battle that is still extant, lost an officer and 16 men killed and 9 men wounded.

The next day Lord Lake entered Delhi, and rescued the Mogul Emperor, the blind Shah Alam, from his Mahratta jailors, who, while ruling under his seal, maintained him in poverty and squalor. On the 19th M. Bourquien and four of his officers surrendered, anxious for protection against the people of Delhi. After leaving a garrison at Delhi, and arranging treaties with minor chiefs, the British Army returned south towards Agra, to capture that stronghold, which still maintained many regular troops, and the gun foundry, where a Scotchman turned out many of the numerous guns in the Mahratta hands. *En route*, a treaty of alliance was concluded with the Jat Raja of Bhurtpore. On arrival before Agra, the fort and garrison were summoned to surrender; and on refusing, the force of several battalions camped on the glacis were attacked and dispersed or driven within the huge sandstone bastions. Twenty-six guns were taken, the British loss amounting to 228. The 2/9th, now the 1st Brahmans; the

31st DUKE OF CONNAUGHT'S OWN LANCERS

DAFFADAR

Dekhani Mahratta

2/15th, now the 2nd Rajputs; and the 1/16th, now the 4th Rajputs, took part in these operations, the 2/9th having two British officers killed.

After some negotiations Colonel Sutherland, the commandant of the fortress, completed arrangements for a surrender, which included 164 guns, and all the stores in this immense stronghold and palace. The great gun of Agra, weighing 96,600 pounds, with a calibre of 23 inches, was among the trophies.

Laswarrie

Still a further portion of Scindia's organized forces required to be dealt with. Some battalions which had escaped from Delhi, and the Chevalier Dudrenac's brigades which had come up from the Deccan, had taken post on the flank of our communications with Delhi, and needed attention. The Chevalier himself, with two officers, had surrendered shortly before Lord Lake's arrival at Agra. The Governor-General had issued a proclamation calling on foreign and British (European) subjects now serving with the hostile States to leave their service, promising safe conduct and protection for their property, and many were availing themselves of this offer, hastened by the fact that in several cases the troops had turned on their officers and murdered them.

On the 27th of October 1803 Lake marched from Agra in the direction of Deig. Lake himself, anxious to bring the enemy to battle and end the campaign, pushed on ahead with the cavalry division of three regiments of dragoons and five of native cavalry. On November 1, in the early morning, hearing that the enemy were at Laswarrie, he pushed on, covering the 25 miles in six hours, the infantry following behind. Before the day was far advanced the cavalry came up with the enemy and at once closed, with the object of, at any rate, forcing the Mahrattas to keep their ground. The enemy deployed an enormous line of guns linked with chains, but up and down and through this the eight regiments charged, and charged again. The British dragoons lost 8 officers and 34 men killed, and 19 officers and 89 men wounded, and 310 horses. The native cavalry lost 1 officer killed and 5 wounded, with 17 troopers killed and 69 wounded, and 172 horses. No better instance of the cavalry spirit can be quoted, and it was rewarded with entire success. The enemy changed position slightly, and formed again for battle. By noon up marched the unfailing infantry, done to a

32ND LANCERS

LANCE DAFFADAR

Musalman Rajput

33RD QUEEN'S OWN LIGHT
CAVALRY

DAFFADAR

Kaimkhani

34TH PRINCE ALBERT VICTOR'S
OWN POONA HORSE

Ratore Rajput

turn, but ready for more.   They had marched 65 miles in forty-eight hours, while the cavalry had done 45 miles in twenty-four hours.

After a short halt the whole force went into battle in the full heat of the sun.   The enemy's cannonade was terrific, and by evening the British losses had totalled 834, but the whole of the Mahratta army was destroyed, large numbers killed and many prisoners, and 71 guns were taken.   The 76th lost 2 officers and 41 men killed, and 4 officers and 170 men wounded.   The 2/12th N.I. also lost heavily.   The 1st Brahmans, the 2nd Rajputs, and the 4th Rajputs took part, under their old numbers losing 16, 37, and 87 respectively of all ranks killed and wounded.

The victory of Laswarrie would have closed this phase of the campaign but for the activity of Holkar.   Scindia, the Bhonsla, the Raja of Bhurtpore, and most of the minor Rajas had now entered into offensive and defensive alliances with the British, as a result of this and Wellesley's campaign.   The forces in Cuttack and Bundelkhund had been equally successful.   In the former campaign some Madras native infantry had taken part, of which the present 69th Punjabis are the sole survivors.   Gwalior, Scindia's capital, had been reduced, in which service the present 1st Brahmans also shared, and the troops had some hopes of going into summer quarters to escape the daily growing heat. The attitude of Holkar, however, in threatening the Doab, and endeavouring to stir up the chiefs who had made peace, necessitated one more effort, and Lord Lake in person made an advance in force towards Holkar. This campaign involved many minor actions, and much skirmishing with the Mewatis in the broken country between Agra and Rajputana, but without any opportunity offering of bringing Holkar and his main forces to book.

SUMMER OF 1804

At last the army withdrew towards the Jumna, and moved into cantonments, after enduring heavy losses, especially among the Europeans, from the intense heat. Many corps did not get into quarters till the commencement of the rains. To cover the Doab, Colonel Monson was left on the Chumbal with a considerable detachment.

MONSON'S RETREAT

It was this detachment which was to experience the first real disaster to British arms in India, and which was to prolong the war to 1806. In July the news that Holkar had advanced, induced Colonel Monson to leave his camp and move to meet him. As Holkar withdrew Monson followed for many marches, till, fearful for his supplies and communications, he decided to fall back. This was the signal for the advance of vast hordes of the enemy, and for the general hostility of all those through whose country he passed. Want of supplies and swollen rivers reduced the troops to the greatest straits, and though fighting constantly, demoralization at last set in, and the force, entirely native, at last fell to pieces, the survivors arriving by detachments at the British border. Of the five infantry battalions composing the force, the 2/21st, a newly raised battalion, did well (now the 5th Light Infantry), and is the only survivor on the Army List.

DEFENCE OF DELHI

The news of this disaster to the invincible English spread rapidly. Lord Lake at once took steps to collect the army from its summer quarters, and on the 1st of October advanced towards Muttra from the vicinity of Agra. Holkar had already occupied Muttra. As the British advanced the Mahrattas fell back, always refusing an engagement, and it then became known that his regular infantry were besieging Delhi. The Commander-in-Chief at once pressed on to the relief, regardless of the swarms of horse who harassed flanks and rear. The Mahratta force had appeared before Delhi on the 7th of October, but Colonel Ochterlony, the Resident, had already summoned in Colonel Burns' corps and several detachments of local troops, and managed to hold certain portions of the dilapidated and lengthy bastioned wall. Heavy breaching batteries were brought against the wall, and a hot cannonade kept up. The crumbling walls were, however, repaired at night, and the garrison, always on the alert, made continual sorties. The enemy, however, after being repulsed in an assault on the 14th, disappeared on the 15th as suddenly as they had come, and shortly after Lord Lake marched up.

LAKE'S PURSUIT OF HOLKAR

It was then discovered that Holkar was making for the Doab to ravage our territories, so after him marched Lake himself with the three dragoon regiments (8th, 27th, and 29th) and two regiments of native cavalry. General Fraser followed with

37TH LANCERS
(BALUCH HORSE)
Baluch

35TH SCINDE HORSE

KOT DAFFADAR
Baluch

36TH JACOB'S HORSE
Pathan
(All of the Derajat District)

the main body of the force. Lake's pursuit of
Holkar is one of the great cavalry feats of history,
and it was not till 350 miles had been traversed in
the short space of a fortnight, that, marching all
night, Holkar's cavalry camp was ridden down at
dawn by a charge of the British force, which
destroyed a large number of his horse, took many
prisoners and all his guns and baggage, and almost
got that desperate Mahratta himself.

BATTLE OF DEIG

In the meantime General Fraser, marching
south, came up with Holkar's infantry and
guns underneath the walls of the fort of Deig,
in the territory of the Raja of Bhurtpore. This
force consisted of 24 regular battalions with 160
guns and some irregular horse. The usual
audacious attack on the part of the British
followed, led also, as usual, by the 76th. The
enemy were completely overthrown with the loss
of 87 of their guns. The British loss was 643.
The 2nd Rajputs (2/15th) took part, losing a
British officer killed and another wounded.
General Fraser himself was mortally wounded,
and Colonel Monson brought the battle to its
victorious close.

CAPTURE OF DEIG

The battle of Deig, however, was by no means the last that the British were to see of the place. It belonged to Bhurtpore, and as an aftermath of the Monson disaster, our ally of Bhurtpore had fallen away from his agreement. The fortress of Deig opened its gates to Holkar's troops after the battle, as did also Bhurtpore itself. As the land could have no rest so long as Holkar was burning and slaying all and sundry, with friendly haunts to do it from, it was necessary to reduce Deig. On the 11th of December the British appeared before the walls. On the 24th the breaches were ready, and by dawn on Christmas Day the place was ours, with the loss of 43 killed and 184 wounded. A hundred cannon of sorts were taken.

SIEGE OF BHURTPORE

Next to reckon with was Bhurtpore itself. By this time the army with Lord Lake had been considerably reinforced, and shattered troops relieved by fresh ones, saving always the 76th, whom nothing daunted, and the dragoon regiments. On the 1st of January 1805 the British encamped before the virgin fortress, which was protected by immense commanding bastions of solid mud.   Not all the daring of the 76th, however, nor the devotion of their native comrades, was to put Lord Lake inside Bhurtpore.   Two assaults were repulsed with appalling loss.   Then there arrived a division of Bombay troops under General Jones.   With it were the 2/1st, the 2/2nd, the 1/3rd, and the 1/9th of the Bombay Line, now the 101st Grenadiers, the 104th Rifles, the 105th and 117th Mahrattas.   The new troops were burning for action.   Another determined attempt to storm failed hopelessly, though again and again daring spirits carried the colours up the breach.   Still a fourth and larger attempt was made, and then the force stood back, having lost 103 officers and 3100 men.

Summer of 1805

Immense preparations were made for a blockade and prolonged siege, while various forces moved against bodies of Holkar's horse that threatened communications or ravaged the Doab.   In the meantime the Raja of Bhurtpore sued for peace, which was made on reasonable terms.   The diminished but still jaunty army then moved off to clear Bundelkhund of Mahrattas, and finally went into summer quarters about Agra and Muttra, Holkar

still being at large, though with his forces for the
time being dissipated. The three regiments of
dragoons, it is recorded, spent the rains in the
immense courts of Akbar's tomb at Sekundra,
near Agra, the officers and their families occupying the tombs of the Omras round, as their
dwellings. Many troops were cantoned at Fatteh-
pur Sikri.

The Pursuit of Holkar to the Punjab

As the rains passed the activity of Holkar
became more marked, and was having its influence
on Scindia. Finally, Holkar made his way towards
the Punjab, with a view of inducing the Sikhs
to overrun the Doab with him. The year before,
Lord Lake had had to drive large bodies of Sikhs
from the vicinity of Delhi, and the possibility of a
Hindu combination of this nature was very serious.
So in October 1805 once again the Grand Army
had to take the field, and marched north from
Agra and Cawnpore and Muttra, two brigades of
cavalry and one of infantry leading. This force
marched straight past Delhi, after Holkar, to the
banks of the Beas, where it halted, Holkar being
with the Sikhs at Amritsar. This display of force
resulted in the Sikhs refusing to support Holkar,

38TH KING GEORGE'S OWN CENTRAL INDIA HORSE

LANCE DAFFADAR

Gakkar (Punjabi Musalman)

and, after much negotiation, a treaty with Scindia and Holkar on a reasonably satisfactory basis being concluded.   In January 1806 the war-worn army commenced its march south, and the Great Mahratta war of three years was at an end.   The Marquis Wellesley, who had conducted affairs through so many stirring years, had returned home, and a change of policy had taken place, on account of which possibly another Mahratta war was yet to come.   And in the years to follow, the hordes of the Pindaris were much reinforced by the disbanded soldiery of this war.

The medal to the Army of India, awarded to the survivors half a century later, recognized the campaigns of Lord Lake by clasps for "Capture of Alligurh," "Battle of Delhi," "Defence of Delhi," "Laswarrie," "Battle of Deig," "Capture of Deig." Bhurtpore, the most desperate business of the lot, was not of course rewarded, since the fortress never fell, till Lord Combermere captured it in 1825, for which capture the medal bears the clasp "Bhurtpore."

THE MAHRATTA AND PINDARI WAR, 1817-19

The reversal of policy that had followed the successes of Lake and Wellesley had prevented

9

anything approaching a permanent settlement. The Mahratta chiefs were continually intriguing, while the Pindari bands, bandits of every race and tribe, originally formed on the break-up of the Mogul armies, had grown to enormous size. They were overrunning the whole of Hindustan, far down into the British provinces, with fire and sword and torture. In 1817 things had come to such a pass that it was decided to organize a vast force, and tramp out the immense area involved. The Marquis of Hastings, the Governor-General, called on the Mahratta chiefs to aid him against the common enemy, but received little more than promises. The general plan of operations was to advance from all sides on the fastnesses bordering the banks of the river Narbudda, at the foot of the Vindhya Mountains, along which the Pindaris had long established their centres. The forces of Holkar, Scindia, the Peshwa, and the Bhonsla were to be watched at the same time, lest they, too, should elect to side against the cause of law and order.

Two large armies were formed, the Grand Army of four divisions which assembled at Cawnpore under the Governor-General himself, and the Army of the Deccan, under General Sir Thomas

QUEEN'S OWN CORPS OF GUIDES (LUMSDEN'S)

INFANTRY	CAVALRY
Tanaoli (Pathan)	DAFFADAR
	Adam Khel (Afridi)

Hislop, consisting of seven divisions, acting from different points.

The Peshwa had again been in trouble, and after the entirely purposeless murder of the Gaekwar's envoy, who was at Poona on a mission, had been compelled to agree to an arrangement which gave some promise of curbing his wayward character. Irked, however, by the trouble that he had brought on himself, he was watching for an opportunity to vent his hostility on the British. The Pindari trouble seemed to him an excellent opportunity to arouse the Mahratta chiefs, combined with all the Pindari hordes, against the British.

At this time the forces that a united combination might have brought into the field were extremely numerous, and were approximately as follows :—

Scindia	.	.	1,500 horse,	16,000 foot,	140 guns.
Holkar	.	20,000 „	8,000 „	107 „
Peshwa	.	. 28,000 „	14,000 „	37 „
Bhonsla	.	. 16,000 „	18,000 „	85 „
Amir Khan	. 12,000 „	10,000 „	200 „
Pindaris	.	. 15,000 „	1,500 „	20 „

Such a potential and even probable enemy, with the vast power of the Pindaris to recruit their ranks with every bad character in India, who preferred plundering his neighbours to working for himself, was ample justification for the vast preparations of the Governor-General.

KIRKEE AND POONA

Matters were soon quickened by the action of Bajee Rao. Poona had been filling fast with levies of all descriptions, ostensibly to help us against the Pindaris. Their general behaviour became insolent and threatening, and various detached British officers were murdered. A battalion of the Bombay European regiment had been pushed up to support the subsidiary force cantoned at Dapuri near Kirkee. The Peshwa now demanded the withdrawal of the European battalion, and advanced on the 5th of November 1817 to attack the British force, which had withdrawn from its cantonment and was drawn up on a ridge at Kirkee, close to what is now the grand trunk road running through the present cantonment. The British under Colonel Burr was joined by Mr. Elphinstone, the Resident, who had with difficulty escaped from Poona. The Mahratta force numbered some 18,000 horse, 8000 foot, and 14 guns.

The British numbered some 2000 native troops with 800 Europeans. In addition to the Bombay

European regiment a detachment of the 65th Foot was present, with some native artillery, and five Bombay native infantry regiments, with one auxiliary battalion. This latter eventually formed what is now the 123rd Outram's Rifles, while the other battalions that still survive are the 102nd Grenadiers, and the 112th and 113th Infantry. The glory in this battle of Kirkee lay in the *audace, encore l'audace*; for the small force advanced against the huge hordes that had poured out of Poona over the Mutha river,

On the March.

65th Regiment of Bengal Native Infantry, 1840.

and swarmed round it on the plain between Ganeshkind and Bamburda. As the force advanced, the Mahratta horse swept round it, to the confusion of some of the native corps, who, however, quickly rallied. The good Atkins of the day led the charge, a cannon-ball struck down the Mahratta banner, a grape - shot killed the leader of horse,

one Moro Dixit, and the huge force broke away
from the field, to tell its fears to the Peshwa,
praying to heaven from the gilt-topped temples
of Parbutti Hill.   Since a fine daring often brings
its own reward, the British casualties were not
severe.   The Kirkee force was then left unmolested, and shortly after, on the 13th, the
advanced portion of the 4th division arrived under
General Smith and, forcing the ford near what is
now the Bund at Poona, drove the enemy from
the city to the hills beyond.

SEETABULDEE AND NAGPORE

At Nagpore, the Bhonsla's capital, the Mahratta
chief had been assembling his own forces, ostensibly
to assist against the Pindaris, and the moment
news came of the trouble at Poona and the
Peshwa's outbreak, his troops at once became
threatening.   The British subsidiary force at Nagpore consisted of three troops of the 6th Bengal
Cavalry (not the present 6th), the 1/20th and 1/24th
Madras Infantry, and some details of artillery, with
some local troops.   The Bhonsla, as did most of
the other chiefs, maintained a large force of Arabs,
and these to the number of 3000, with huge bodies
of horse, swarmed round the Residency.   So

No. 31 MOUNTAIN BATTERY

GUNNER

Punjabi Musalman

threatening had been their attitude that the British moved out of their lines on the 15th of November and occupied the two small hills of Seetabuldee which overlooked the Residency, and entrenched themselves. All that night and the next day the Arabs and Mahrattas attacked the position, the Arabs being most daring in their attacks. The unfortunate troops had left their families in the lines, and heard the shrieks of the occupants, who were killed and ill-treated. Captain Fitzgerald made several desperate charges with the 6th Cavalry, in which young Hearsey was wounded and achieved great distinction, being long known as "The Hero of Seetabuldee." This officer, as General Sir John Bennet Hearsey, commanded the Dinapore division when Mangal Pandy, just before the Mutiny, shot his adjutant and thus shed the first blood in the great rising. The Seetabuldee main hill was definitely held, the smaller one was taken and retaken, though the enemy finally broke off the fight, not, however, before the British had lost 121 killed, of whom five were European officers, and 241 wounded, of whom 13 were European officers. In the period of strained relations, word had been sent calling up the 2nd division under General Doveton, and this

force reached Nagpore on the 12th of December,
and on the 16th attacked the enemy who, to the
number of 21,000, were entrenched in villages and
gardens near the city.   After several hours' fighting they were in full flight, leaving 64 guns on
the field.   Five thousand Arabs and Hindustanis,
however, threw themselves into the city, and it took
several days of bombarding and attempted assaults
before the garrison surrendered.   The British
losses at Nagpore were 141, chiefly from artillery
fire.   It is very noticeable in this war that the
casualties were not nearly so heavy as in the earlier
one.   Lord Lake and General Wellesley had
destroyed the trained infantry that each chief
maintained.   With the exception of the Arabs,
who fought most courageously, and who were an
object of immense dread to our native troops, the
forces against us were chiefly masses of elusive
irregular cavalry, who could not be destroyed in
one pitched battle, and it took months of weary
pursuit before they could be accounted for.

Of the troops that shared in the desperate
defence of Seetabuldee, only the 61st Pioneers
remain, then the 1/24th, but who had for a long
time been the 1/1st.   The troops who took part in
the battle of Nagpore that are still on the Army

2ND QUEEN'S OWN SAPPERS AND MINERS

"THE WORKSHOPS"

HAVILDAR

SUBADAR

Christians

List are the 1/22nd Bengal Infantry, now the 6th Jats, and the present 61st, 62nd, 81st, 83rd, 86th, and 97th, and of course the ubiquitous Madras Sappers and Miners.

CORYGAUM

While the Bhonsla was adding his share to the confusion, and losing his throne thereby, General Smith and the troops at Poona were pursuing the Peshwa, who had retired to his chain of forts in the Western Ghats, from which every sort of opportunity existed for successful doubling. At the end of December, evading General Smith, he was again threatening Poona. Colonel Burr commanding there then called to his assistance the garrison of Sirur, which place lies between Poona and Ahmednagar. Captain Staunton in command marched with the 2/1st Grenadiers, now the 102nd Grenadiers, 2 guns of the Madras Artillery under Lieutenant Chisholm, and 250 Reformed Horse under Lieutenant Swanston. These latter were some partly organized horse recently in the Peshwa's service. On marching into the village of Corygaum they found the whole of the Peshwa's force encamped on a stream opposite the village. Twenty thousand horse with 8000 infantry,

10

including 3000 of the dreaded Arabs, immediately advanced on this small force, which threw itself into such of the village enclosures as were not already in the possession of the enemy. By noon the British were closely invested and cut off from the water, and exposed to the most desperate attacks of the Arabs, and a heavy artillery fire. Till 9 P.M. that night the attacks continued, when at last the disappointed Arabs and Mahrattas drew off after suffering severe loss. In the fight almost all the European gunners were killed or wounded, and Lieutenant Chisholm's head was cut off and taken to the Peshwa. One of the guns was carried by the Arabs, and Lieutenant Pattinson, a gigantic subaltern of Grenadiers already mortally wounded, led his men to recapture the gun. This mortally wounded giant of six feet seven, in his dying effort, himself accounted for five Arabs, and exhorted the failing troops to renewed efforts. Assistant - Surgeons Wyngate and Wyllie led the men equally with the combatant officers, the former being killed later in the day by the enemy, who captured the courtyard in which he was lying wounded. Lieutenants Swanston and Conellan, who were lying severely wounded with him, were only rescued at the last moment.   The losses of this determined band were more than heavy.   Out of the 24 Europeans of the Madras Artillery 12 were killed and 8 wounded, while the Grenadiers lost 50 killed and 105 wounded, and the Reformed Horse had 96 casualties.   Only Captain Staunton, who commanded, and two other officers were unhurt.   A tall basalt column to this day stands to commemorate the gallantry of this small band, and the Grenadiers yearly keep festival on the anniversary.

At daylight next morning the Mahrattas, scared by the news of General Smith advancing to the rescue, made off and broke up.

Mahidpore

While the attacks on their subsidiary forces by the Peshwa and the Bhonsla had been taking place, with the troops that they had assembled ostensibly to help us against the Pindaris, the other divisions of the Army of the Deccan and the Grand Army had advanced into the area which contained the various strongholds of the commanders of the different Pindari *darras* or bands.   These various hordes were driven from their fastnesses and gradually broken up.   Sir

Thomas Hislop, commanding the Army of the
Deccan, had crossed the Narbudda and advanced to
Ujein, keeping, however, one eye on Holkar lest his
forces, too, should play us false.   Holkar himself
was a lad, under the guardianship of Tulsi Bai, a
mistress of the famous Jeswant Rao Holkar of the
former wars.   Tulsi Bai was in favour of peace
with the British, whereon the war faction in the
State chopped her head off and set their troops
in motion.   Sir Thomas Hislop then advanced
towards   them,   negotiating   with   the   Durbar
as he went, with a view to the preservation of
peace.   Peace, however, was not to be, and on
the 20th of December 1815, the British found
that   the   Mahratta   force   was   at   Mahidpore,
a few miles ahead, and consisted of some 5000
infantry with 100 guns and 30,000 horse.   There
were, however, many with that small British force
of 5500 men who had fought a larger number of
Mahrattas with even smaller numbers at Assaye,
and knew the value of *l'audace*.   So before day-
break on the 21st Sir Thomas advanced with Sir
John Malcolm, commanding a strong advanced
guard.   The enemy were as usual drawn up with
a river on their front (the Sepra), one flank opposite
the village of Mahidpore, the other on the river.

3RD SAPPERS AND MINERS

LANCE NAIK
Brahman of Oudh

JEMADAR
Dekhani Mahratti

The details of the battle were as many of its forerunners. The infantry crossed the stream and attacked in the face of a long line of guns, followed by the cavalry and artillery, and the Mahratta horse broke away at once, though the infantry stood their ground, and the gunners died at their guns. The whole of the immense camp and treasure was captured, with supplies and munitions of all sorts. The British loss was as heavy as in some of the battles of the earlier war, though nothing like so serious as Assaye. It totalled 174 killed and 604 wounded. The troops engaged consisted of the flank companies of the Royal Scots, and the whole of the Madras European regiment, while the native troops all came from the Madras Army, and the Russell Brigade. The following corps that took part are the Madras Sappers and Miners, the 63rd, the 74th, the 87th, the 88th, the 91st, the 94th, and 95th (both of the Russell Brigade, which was later the Hyderabad contingent), and the 28th Light Cavalry. A pursuit was organized a few days later, and Holkar's Durbar concluded a treaty.

The Capture of the Peshwa and the Break up of the Pindaris

Scindia, it should have been explained, had been overawed by the advance of the Grand Army, and had not joined, or let his troops join, with the Pindaris. Holkar was now settled with, and little remained but the weary task of finishing up the operations, and completing the destruction of the Pindaris. It was to take, however, over a year more of pursuits and sieges. The mountains in the theatre of war were covered with inaccessible forts, while numerous strong walled towns and fortresses in the plains acted as continual havens of rest to the enemy. The pursuit of the Peshwa after the action at Corygaum was taken up on all sides in succession, and he was run up and down the country, as were the remnants of the commanders in South Africa. Bajee Rao himself finally surrendered to Sir John Malcolm in May 1818. The chase of Bajee Rao is still famous in the country-side, while the people say that the beat of the hoofs of his thousands of horse may still be heard o' nights. He was removed to Bithur and pensioned, dying there in 1854.

After this there still remained the Bhonsla and

the Pindari chief Chetu, with dozens of lesser bands. Numerous columns reduced the mountain forts, while the mounted corps pursued the broken horse. Appa Sahib, the Bhonsla, eventually fled to the Punjab. Chetu Pindari, hunted and solitary, was killed by a tiger, and there only remained Aseergurh, which belonged to Scindia, but whose governor refused to obey his order to surrender. It had become the refuge of the desperate, and finally fell, after a siege and a loss of 323, to the British. The garrison surrendered a few days before the storm, and were almost entirely the Arab, Mekrani, and Sindi mercenaries from the State troops and Pindari bands. Among the many more important sieges in which the Arabs were also the principal garrisons, were Malegaon and Garhakotah. In the Southern Mahratta country the sieges of Belgaum and Sholapore were important. With the fall of Aseergurh the land had peace till the Mutiny once again stirred Arab and Pathan and free-lance to run riot over Central India, and a similar campaign to that against the Pindaris was necessary to free the land and hunt down Tantia Topee.

The big Mahratta States, as a result of this war, were once and for all confined to their legitimate territories and such conditions as suited us, and did not again dispute with the British the overlordship that they had tried to wrest from the Mogul. The army of Scindia, it is true, did break out owing to domestic disturbances, and was destroyed in the short Gwalior campaign of 1843, and with it the last trace of the old French military pattern, except so far as a few traces endured in the Punjab.

To that belated medal "To the Army of India," already alluded to, were added the following clasps for this war: "Kirkee," "Poona," "Kirkee and Poona," "Seetabuldee," "Nagpore," "Seetabuldee and Nagpore," and "Maheidpoor." It will have been noticed that the bulk of the heavier fighting fell to the Madras Army, which was still at its prime. The Grand Army, though engaged in plenty of harassing work, was more immediately concerned with watching some of the larger States and preventing the Pindaris from breaking into the Doab and Bundelkhund.

After the war the military organization of the three armies was overhauled, and some uniformity of system introduced, with many improvements in enlistment and equipment, for which the experience of the Peninsula and recent wars in India was utilized. These two prolonged wars are certainly

1ST AND 3RD BRAHMANS

SUBADAR

Brahmans of Oudh and North-West Provinces

noteworthy as the two greatest wars in which the army of John Company had been engaged, and also the hardest.   The employment of eleven divisions at once, besides many detachments, is striking proof of the large force which their responsibilities and dangers had enforced the Company to maintain. How the demands on them still further increased with their responsibilities in Afghanistan, Scinde, and the Punjab, has already been referred to, and the result that followed in its train, as many think inevitably, must now be described before the modern army that rose from the ashes of the old can be treated of.

CHAPTER III

THE ARMY OF THE GREAT MUTINY

THE hard-fought battles of the Sikh wars and the annexation of the Punjab bring us within a few years of the turning-point in the history of the Indian Army. It has been shown how that army grew from a force of doorkeepers and watchmen, to an army of 311,000 native soldiers, regular, irregular, and local. We have seen how at one time the remnants of the fighting forces of the free-lances and warring barons flocked to the British standard, and how the low-caste Hindu became an efficient soldier in the coast armies. Then gradually, if we may believe the diaries and the autobiographies of the old officers, there came what is spoken of as the "brahmanizing" of the native army. That is to say, as war became less constant, the consideration of other matters than securing the best fighting animal, actuated the authorities. The race of adventurers began to die out, and the need for employing disbanded hostile soldiers became less pressing, while our officers came to know more of the better classes of the people. It was perhaps thought desirable to get them into connection with the army. At any rate, the desire became general to confine enlistment to high-class races, to whom certain other classes, that had made such good soldiers, were beneath contempt as fellow-men. To get these men of social prejudice to serve, it was necessary to discontinue enlistments of the lower castes in the same corps. The army came to consist largely of the better castes, men who were chiefly the yeomen peasants of the country. Now there can, of course, in many ways be no better stock than this for a soldiery, but in the East, long years of alien rule and constant invasion had reduced many of the peasantry of the South to a state of spirit that made them unsuited to military service.

In the eyes of many of the old officers the higher castes in Southern India were by no means the best soldiers, and generations of oppression, or years of peace, had deadened the habit of the sword. In Bengal, however, the same tendency had different if not less harmful results. The population of Behar and Oudh consisted of a manly and warlike peasantry of fine physique and martial appearance, and withal orderly and obedient. Gradually, the whole of the army in Bengal, with the various contingents and local corps dependent on it, and corps to which the Bengal officers were appointed, enlisted more and more of this convenient and suitable material.

In 1857, in Bengal alone, irrespective of contingents, locals, and military police, there were 137,000 regular troops, of whom close on 20,000 were cavalry. A very large number of these were Poorbeahs, as they were called, or men of the eastern provinces ; in other words Rajputs and Brahman clans from Oudh. In the ranks of the regular army, men stood mixed up as chance might befall. There was no separating by class and clan into companies. The Bengal regiments were leavened with a considerable number of Muhammadans, and after the Sikh wars with some Sikhs.

These latter, by reason of their wild appearance, were not welcomed, and were only enlisted in deference to stringent orders of Government. In the lines, Hindu and Muhammadan, Sikh and Poorbeah were mixed up, so that each and all lost to some extent their racial prejudices, and became

RAJPUT REGIMENTS

7TH DUKE OF CON-
NAUGHT'S OWN
RAJPUTS
Havildar

16TH RAJPUTS
(The Lucknow Regiment)
Subadar

Bhisti

13TH RAJPUTS
(The Shekhawati
Regiment)

8TH RAJPUTS

11TH RAJPUTS

2ND QUEEN'S OWN RAJPUT
LIGHT INFANTRY

inspired with one common sentiment. When the trouble came, the Sikhs in the Bengal regiments, either infected with sympathy for the men of their corps or too isolated and distributed throughout the companies to dare assert their own feelings, joined in the Mutiny in the first instance, while their compatriots flocked to the British standards. At any rate, by 1857, the mass of the Bengal Army consisted of the same material, the soldierly and obedient Brahmans and Rajputs of Oudh and Behar, chiefly the former. The gradual regularizing of administration, the desire of the Court of Directors for information, the call for statistics and all the bureaucratic tendency of a vast government, militated against the discipline of the army. The power of commandants of corps had been reduced, petitions from sepoys to superior authority received attention, the bonds of discipline slackened. The vast increments to our dominions called for many Europeans to fill the various offices of government. It was economical to draw on regiments for officers for civil and semi-civil appointments. The regimental cadres were large, on the scale of the British service, viz. 1000 privates, 120 N.C.O.'s, 20 Native, and 24 British officers. It is true that some of the best corps were the irregulars, which had but three

British officers, but the irregular system especially developed the initiative and responsibility of the native officer.   In the Line the British officer did most of the work ; and though as many officers were not required in peace as for war, still, the process of selecting officers from corps, without filling up their places, resulted in many of the best men preferring employment in the interesting work of developing new provinces, to the humdrum routine of station life.   The regiments of late years had therefore lost some of their best blood.   The vast increase in the numbers of the native corps, without any counterbalancing increase in the Europeans, due to the vast new tracts to be held, has been already noticed.   This, added to what has already been described, and the loss of prestige due to our disasters in Afghanistan, together with the un-expected severe casualties suffered by the troops in the Sikh wars, had gradually reduced the prestige and content that had appertained to military service.

Added to this was the fact that the permanent occupation of districts that had already been occupied as a temporary measure induced Govern-ment, whose financial position always affected their actions, to abolish the field - allowances usually granted to temporary garrisons in districts outside British India.   This latter step was the signal for considerable show of insubordination. The 66th at Wazirabad showed such ill-feeling that the Commander-in-Chief, Sir Charles Napier, in the absence of the Governor-General on a sea voyage, ordered the immediate disbandment of the corps.

During the hundred years that had elapsed between the battle of Plassey and the Mutiny, many acts of mutiny of varying gravity had occurred, and usually over the question of pay and allowances. On two occasions had these mutinies been on the part of the British officers of the Company's Army. In 1764 the Bengal sepoys had mutinied for higher pay and gratuities, and only two years later the British officers in Bengal conspired, and ceased from duty on a question of *batta* (field-allowance), and this mutiny was only put down by the determination of Lord Clive.   1806 was specially remarkable for the mutiny at Vellore, which was far more serious than any of its predecessors.   In its significance it might well have been regarded as a warning.   At Vellore dwelt the pensioned family of Tippoo Sultan, the ousted ruler of Seringapatam, who had fallen in the final storming of the fortress. His family were removed and pensioned in favour of the Hindu dynasty, that he himself, or rather his father Hyder Ali, had supplanted. It is probable that the discontent of a dispossessed family and their entourage had resulted in an endeavour to tamper with the fidelity of the native troops. An unthinking order regarding the wearing of caste-marks in uniform, and the pattern of turban to be worn, gave light to a conflagration that had been preparing for some time. The native troops of the Madras Army garrisoning Vellore fell on the British troops also in the fort, and killed many before they recovered from the surprise. The remnant were barely able to defend themselves with considerable further loss, till relieved at the last gasp by Colonel Rollo Gillespie of the 19th Light Dragoons at the head of an advanced detachment of his regiment. This mutiny was found to have widespread ramifications.

In 1809 the British officers of the Madras Army rebelled, owing to certain real or imaginary grievances, and had to be suppressed with a heavy hand. Again, in 1824, some Bengal infantry battalions, under orders to march towards Arracan, refused and were severely handled for their pains. After the occupation of Scinde and the annexation of the

5TH LIGHT INFANTRY   6TH JAT LIGHT INFANTRY

HAVILDARS

Musalman Rajput   *Jāt*

Punjab, the troubles and insubordination regarding the *batta* came to be acute, as already described.

For some time occasional warnings had been uttered against the native army, organized, as has already been described, in a vast imitation of a European Line.   To many of the statesmen who had served in India, Sir Henry Lawrence and others, the huge possibilities underlying the preponderance of this vast mercenary force over its European counterweight had the obsession of a nightmare.   The warning utterances, however, had not sufficient weight, or were given under circumstances that deprived them of their value, such as Sir Charles Napier's criticisms, and the letters of Colonel Jacob criticising the discipline, organization, and efficiency of the Bengal Army.   The Bombay Army of those days had a practical efficiency far ahead of the Bengal troops. In Herbert Edwardes' book, *A Year on the Punjab Frontier*, he tells (himself a Bengal officer) of his seeing the Bombay brigade join the Bengal troops under General Whish, before the fortress of Mooltan.   He relates how struck he was with the practical equipment of the troops, which included water-bottles and haversacks, and with their military alertness, so superior to that of the

12

Bengal battalions, but which he attributed to the
—to his ideas—dangerous custom of promoting
non-commissioned officers and native officers for
their military efficiency apart from their length of
service. Safety apparently in the Bengal Army had
been provided for by assuring that no man should
come to any status till he was past the age of
activity. The inscriptions on the cross alongside
the long trench graves at Chillianwalla, as already
related in the preceding chapter, is a witness to the
age of the native officers, and in the Company's
service the same system prevailed for British
officers. In the old graveyard at Saugor, sometime the headquarters of a division, may be seen
the grave of a general officer who died in " command
of the Narbudda division of the army" at over
eighty years of age. It is hard to expect the
characteristics of the soldier at even three-score
years and ten.

It is interesting to note how the army, modelled
on the safe system of incompetence, was the one
to blow up so soon after this comparison had
been drawn.

Lord Dalhousie, as may be seen from his private
letters that have only recently seen the light, was
very fully aware of the volcano on which he sat,

PIONEER REGIMENTS

128TH PIONEERS
Yusufzai (Pathan)

12TH PIONEERS
(The Kelat-i-Ghilzai
Regiment)
Jat

34TH SIKH PIONEERS
Naik
Jat Sikh

81ST PIONEERS   64TH PIONEERS   61ST KING GEORGE'S OWN PIONEERS
Tamils   Madrasi Musalman

48TH PIONEERS
Labana Sikh

23RD SIKH PIONEERS   34TH SIKH PIONEERS
Jemadar   Subadar-Major

Mazbi Sikhs

106TH HAZARA PIONEERS
Subadar-Major

107TH PIONEERS
Kaimkhani (Musalman Rajput)

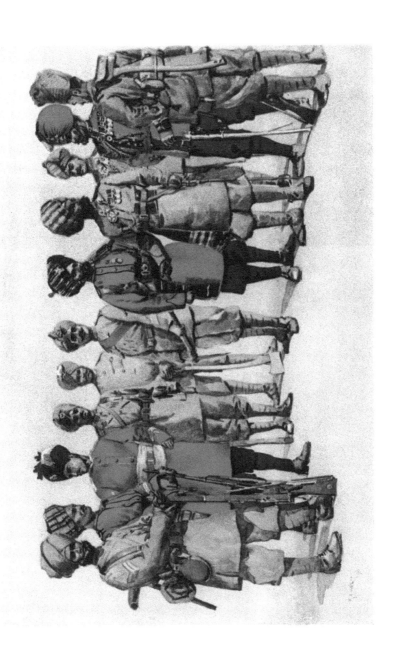

and long proposed to himself to try to reform it ;
but constant pressure and growth of territory were
to prevent him from putting his hand to the
difficult ploughing.

So, despite warning and premonitions and head-
shakings, and a universal feeling that however well
the army was dressed and the belts pipeclayed
there was something rotten, 1857 found us with
the army as described, with peace on the surface
and a canker below.   The literature that has
described the Mutiny and discussed its causes is
perhaps only beaten in its volume by that of the
American War of Secession, and its various phases
need only be lightly passed over here.   Though,
however, Lord Dalhousie had recognized that the
native army was out of all proportion, wrong in
its constitution, and deficient in European counterweight, still he himself confessed in these same
letters of his, written in this case during the Mutiny,
that he had never foreseen anything in the way of
a general mutiny and massacre, and that with a
hundred years of fidelity and more behind it, there
was ample reason for some confidence.   On the
other hand, the private accounts of the Sikh wars
constantly allude to the accepted belief that the
Sikhs had been tampering with the Poorbeahs, and

that the reluctance of some corps to advance was due to this.

Be that as it may, 1857 opened in considerable peace and contentment; the Ganges Canal had not long been open, and its hundreds of miles of ample water had brought much promise to many thousands of peasants. Oudh had been annexed with unexpected simplicity. A new Governor-General found little to harass him. Then came the outbreak at Barrackpore, whence the general name of the mutineer was derived. Early in January of that year came the first news of the greased cartridge incident. It had flown all over India with extraordinary speed. In the end of February, the 19th at Berhampore in Bengal refused to take the ordinary exercising blank cartridge. After threats and persuasions they took them in sullenness and flew to arms that night. The officer commanding the station marched down the native artillery and cavalry to the 19th lines, and the men were finally persuaded to replace their arms, without recourse to force, which probably the other troops would have refused to use.

At Barrackpore, the headquarters of a division, to which the 19th had now been ordered to march, were the 34th Bengal Native Infantry, who had openly avowed their sympathy with the 19th.   In the evening of the 29th of March, the guard of

the 34th were reported in an excited state, and one, Mangal Pandy, shot the adjutant who rode up, and the European sergeant-major who came up also and called on the guard to protect their officer.   The guard then struck them with the butts of their rifles.   The divisional commander, General Hearsey, famous as a leader of sepoys, and known when a lad as the " Hero of Seetabuldee," coming up at this juncture, rode straight at Mangal Pandy, who then tried to shoot himself.

1st Gurkha Regiment, 1861.

A Soldier out of Uniform.

The disturbance was then quelled, and the General at once promoted a naik who had come to the rescue of his adjutant. It is interesting to know that the General received a wigging for doing so from the Military Department.   Some show of promptness in the way of punishment did follow, however, for Mangal Pandy and the native officer in charge of the guard were shot before a month had elapsed.   By this time the state of the army was the absorbing interest.

The classes at the musketry schools had spread the
tale of the greased cartridge all over India.   Officers
were discussing the affair with their native officers,
but no apprehension of a large mutiny was entertained.   All over the country, officers professed the
most profound confidence in their own regiments.
This, curiously enough, continued up to the last
stages of the Mutiny, and however much neighbouring corps might misconduct themselves, officers had
full confidence in theirs.   This attitude, so much
derided by outsiders at the time, was perhaps one
of the most remarkable tributes to the innate
faculties that enable British officers to lead alien
troops.   When you have lived with soldiers for
years, led them to victory, and heard all their
troubles, who will believe that they are about to
rise ?   Who would expect, for instance, the 35th
Native Infantry, the portion of the " Illustrious
Garrison " who, emulating Clive's sepoys at Arcot,
had given up their rations to the Europeans of the
13th Foot in Jellalabad, and feasted these same
comrades at parting, would mutiny ?   This same
spirit of trust between British officers and their
men exists to-day, and only so long as it exists will
the native army be a fighting force.   With the
great shadow behind, however, it cannot be carried

15th LUDHIANA SIKHS

" THE COLOUR PARTY "

Jāt Sikhs

to the blind extreme that so honoured the sepoy officers of 1857.

It is agreed by all who have studied the subject, that the greased cartridges were a fortunate incident, from the plotters' point of view, which merely gave head to a movement that had had many different centres for many years.   The British rule, with its immense weight, its different ethics and standards, and its craving for administration, had become unpopular, for many reasons that need not here be reviewed.   To the dread of many of the princes and the hatred of the priests, was added the long-felt disgust of all those classes, to whom the free-booting services and conditions prior to the Pindari war had brought so congenial a livelihood.   It is always hard for the Baron and his men-at-arms to settle down to a reign of peace and simple agriculture.   The greased cartridges, the admitted thoughtlessness of a military department, were a god-sent incident to act on the arrogance of a spoilt but reasonably contented army of mixed religions, and it was used to its full by the extremely capable heads who were pulling the strings of the move-ment.   After this occurrence rumour followed rumour, and discontent and uncertainty appeared at many stations, with unexplained fires chiefly in

officers' quarters.   Then at Meerut came the well-
known test parade of the 3rd Cavalry to receive
their old ammunition, under the eyes of the large
European garrison.   The refusal of 85 men to
take the cartridges, their trial by a court-martial of
native officers, their heavy sentences, the manacling
parade of the whole garrison to see the fetters
riveted on the mutineers, and the outbreak on the
evening of the next day, Sunday, the 11th of May,
are well - known matters of history.   As the
Europeans were parading for evening service at
Meerut the native troops broke into open revolt,
murdering every Christian man, woman, and child
that they came across.   The stupor of surprise that
allowed the mutineers to escape need not be described
here; the fact was patent that, in the words of the *Red
Pamphlet*, "THE BENGAL ARMY HAD REVOLTED."
How those mutineers made off, unpursued, to the
old Imperial city of Delhi, and were joined by the
troops there, and the rabble that surrounded the
mock court of the pensioned descendant of the
Great Mogul, to likewise slay all the English they
could lay hands on, is equally a twice-told tale.   In
a few weeks, from Patna to the Peshawar valley,
the Army of Bengal was in open mutiny, and half
the Barons in the country-side with it.

19TH PUNJABIS

LANCE NAIK
Jat Sikh

Afridi of Tirah

BANGASH
(*Pathan*)

*Pathan of Upper
Swat Valley
(Out of Uniform)*

JEMADAR
Yusufzai (Pathan)

Punjabi Musalman

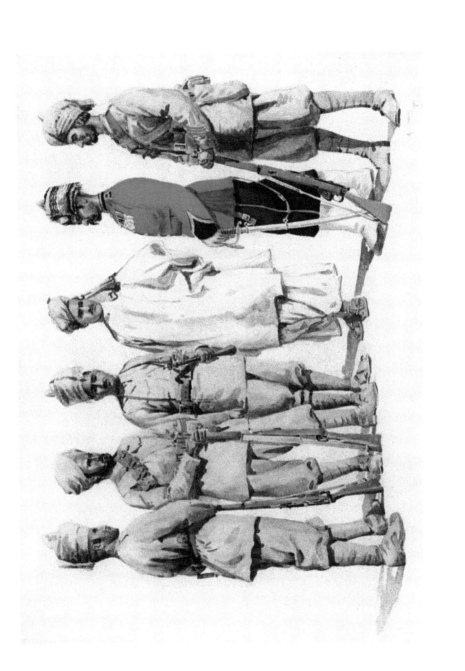

The mutineers, largely Hindu soldiers from Oudh, proclaimed the re-incarnation of the Mogul Empire, compelling the aged pantaloon Bahadur Shah, son of blind Shah Alam, to pose as the Emperor of India. Then as the tally of regiments mutinied in all the main cantonments, they flocked to the great centre at Delhi and the old Imperial name.

Sir Henry Lawrence in Oudh had held havoc in hand for several weeks, till the mutiny of the large garrison at Lucknow and the Oudh Irregular Force, with the attraction of the Europeans at bay, formed a second focus for rebellion.

The mutinous regiments, under command of their native officers, marched to Delhi, to Lucknow, or to Cawnpore, with their British colours flying, wearing their British war medals, with their bands playing British airs. The British on the ridge before Delhi could often hear the mutineer bands playing the airs their officers had taught them, before the Emperor's palace. The anomalies of the Mutiny were many. In some regiments the officers were murdered with every possible atrocity. In others great pains were taken to conduct them within reach of a place of safety. Some officers received offers to assume command and lead them

13

to the service of the Padishah, after the manner of the European free - lances, whose adventures were still a topic in the land. Here we read of the *subadar-major* taking an affectionate leave of his commanding officer, but demanding his epaulettes or his full-dress coatee as the price of safe - conduct. *Psychologie des foules,* in all its forms, was to be experienced. Careful study of the inner history of the many mutinies of 1857 almost unfailingly elicits the conclusion that the great bulk of the army did not mean to mutiny and massacre its officers. The clever cliques in each regiment, to whom the ferment had been entrusted, knew their game thoroughly.

The soldiery, in many ways simple and confiding as children, were fed on every possible rumour. One day the bulk of the regiment or the older native officers, with tears in their eyes, would protest their loyalty to their colonel and comrade of fifty years. The next morning he and his officers would be dead in the rising sun.

It has been urged as an instance of the inconsistency and perfidy of the Asiatic that it always seemed that the best-beloved officers were the first to fall, as a regiment rushed to its bells of arms, and devoted officers hurried into the lines

to calm their men's excitement.   But does not this
rather tend to show how well the men managing
the rising knew their business ?   In every native
regiment there are always two or three officers
whose disposition has gained them the confidence
and affection of the men in an exceptional degree.
These officers hold a regiment, as it were, in the
palms of their hands.   Once they were out of the
way, the ship would be without a rudder.   It was
no hard matter for the desperadoes, usually the
pahlwans or wrestling clique, to shoot these officers
before the rising clamour had got beyond control.

Then, while the well-affected stood aghast, the
leaven would spread, the desire for blood rise . . .
a few more shots, and the regiment would stand so
committed that all must stand or fall together.
Such, no doubt, was the inner history of most of
the mutinies, at times appalling in their atrocities,
at times astonishing in their mildness.   Corps
mutinied unexpectedly, without regard to time and
reason.   A few, like the 50th Infantry at Nagode,
mutinied even after the fall of Delhi must have
proclaimed the hopelessness of their cause.

How, or when, or at what moment the mutinous
desire seized a regiment, no one could tell.   In the
words of an old mutineer, ' *hawa laga* ' . . . a wind

blew . . ., exactly as a crowd knows not who first kicks the man who is down.

At any rate, the fact was soon patent that the whole, with a few exceptions, of the great Bengal Army had disappeared in this whirlwind, taking with it most of its kindred contingents and affiliated irregulars. Those corps that did remain true to their salt, mostly owed their escape to circumstances and a location that removed them from a participation in the feelings of the rest of the army, or debarred them from the opportunity of displaying their disaffection. The irregulars in some cases failed almost as hopelessly, though not so universally as the regulars, and the local corps were little better. There were, however, a few honourable exceptions, notably the 31st N.I. at Saugor, who, when the rest of the garrison mutinied, remained staunch, and operated vigorously against the rebels, while the 65th and 70th N.I., who had volunteered for China and were serving there while their comrades were in mutiny, may fairly be given the benefit of the doubt. At the end of the Mutiny, fifteen battalions of regular infantry out of over seventy regiments of the Bengal Line, and none of the regular cavalry, remained on the Army List. So departed the glory of the Bengal Army.

30TH PUNJABIS
AWAN
(*Punjabi Musalman*)

20TH DUKE OF CAMBRIDGE'S
OWN INFANTRY
(BROWNLOW'S PUNJABIS)

LANCE NAIK
Malikdin Khel (Afridi)

The Madras Army, however, had been little touched by the storm, for reasons many and various. Difference in race, difference in system, and perhaps the embarrassing custom whereby a sepoy was allowed to have all his family with him in cantonments, and on the march, helped to discount all tendency to rebel. In the still smaller Bombay Army sedition was not so universally absent, for it was not to be expected that the Mahratta would miss so golden an opportunity for intrigue. In the Southern Mahratta country, where there had been a war in 1844, with confiscations and annexations, there was plenty of tinder to help kindle a flame, which, however, never really assumed large proportions. The Madras and Bombay Armies, as well as the Hyderabad Contingent, took an active part in suppressing mutiny and rebellion in various parts of India, notably in Central India.

During the progress of the Mutiny in Hindustan proper, the stern and resolute spirit manifest in the Punjab overawed the Bengal regiments. The garrison at the capital, Lahore, of which Mian Meer was the cantonment, was disarmed by a *coup de main*, while the populace marvelled. Rebellion in the Peshawar valley was stamped out ruthlessly, and only in one or two stations did mutiny raise its head with success. This decision appealed to all the hardy men of the north, who were waiting to see how the cat meant to jump. The Punjab Irregular Force eagerly responded to the call to march south. The disarming of the Bengal Line regiments in Peshawar, and the punishment of those who tried to mutiny, captivated the mind of the border tribesmen, who, at first merely watching, now eagerly flocked to serve.

The Irregular Force, led by the Guides, marched south. Every sort of irregular horse and tribal levy was formed, some to keep themselves in order, others for Hindustan.

The motives that brought the Punjab and the Border to our aid, were no doubt mixed ones. Some content with our administration, some liking for English ways seen at their best in the cold of the Northern winters, some memories of the hard hitting of Sobraon, of Chillianwalla, and Gujarat, a dislike of the Poorbeah, our abetting instrument in conquering them . . . all had, no doubt, their place. Probably first, however, among the motives of those who enlisted in the new corps was the thought of the wealth of Hindustan. To this day, if you talk to a veteran of the siege of Delhi, he will tell you perfunctorily of this skirmish and that fight, and show you on the ridge where So-and-so fell, but his eyes will glisten and his old heart warm, when he tells you of the Chandni Chowkh, the jewellers' street of Delhi. The old soldier who went to the Baillie Guard, the relief and capture of Lucknow, that is to say, will talk as much of the loot he brought away as of the fighting. According to him, the return of the Guides to the frontier was a sight to see, and was talked of in the Punjab for many a day after. Beautiful ladies transferred their affections to the men of the north, and rode in carts behind the baggage of the corps, and with them wealth that was the envy of every soldier of fortune in the country-side.

A Khyberi of the Queen's Own Corps of Guides, 1853.

However, whatever the mixture of primary motives actuating the irregular soldiery that helped the British Line to reconquer India, they followed their gallant leaders unflinchingly, and with loyal affection, and were more than true to the salt they ate. The corps which they went to form, now remain as some of the *élite* of the army, and have served since, with as much distinction as that which they won in '57, in many more of the Sirkar's wars.

The fidelity of the Frontier, or as it was then called, Irregular Force of the Punjab, the alacrity of the Punjabi and frontiersman to serve, added to the steady loyalty of most of the Bombay and Madras corps, together enabled us to reconquer Hindustan. It must also be remembered that though chiefs and Barons and their followers turned against us, and villagers hastened to rob and to loot, the great mass of the people had no desire to see the last of us. The army before Delhi lacked neither supplies nor transport, nor the most faithful domestic service, from even the earliest days.

Among the many irregular corps that came to fame in '57, in addition to the existing corps of the army, were Hodson's Horse, Wale's Horse, Lind's Horse, Cureton's Multanis, the Mahratta Horse, the Sikh Irregular Cavalry (three corps), the Delhi Pioneers, the Sikh Volunteer Infantry (raised from the Sikhs of corps that had revolted), with eighteen regiments of Punjab Infantry, and local levies innumerable. When the last embers of the Mutiny had died out, and the last gang of hopeless Poorbeahs and outlaws had surrendered or fallen in action, the task of rebuilding a new army on the

PUNJAB REGIMENTS

67TH PUNJABIS
Sepoy
Khatri Sikh

25TH PUNJABIS
Subadar-Major
Dogra

93RD BURMA INFANTRY
Subadar
Janjua (Punjabi Musalman)

76TH PUNJABIS
Subadar
Chach (Pathan)

69TH PUNJABIS
Jemadar
Jāt Sikh

91ST PUNJABIS (Light Infantry)
Tanaoli (Punjabi Musalman)

21ST PUNJABIS
Subadar-Major
Adam Khel (Afridi)

28TH PUNJABIS
Subadar-Major
Jāt Sikh

74TH PUNJABIS
Sepoy
Dogra

72ND PUNJABIS
Sepoy
Punjabi Musalman

84TH PUNJABIS
Sepoy
Tanaoli (Punjabi Musalman)

87TH PUNJABIS
Havildar
Talap (Punjabi Musalman)

24TH PUNJABIS
Subadar
Jāt Sikh

29TH PUNJABIS
Subadar-Major
Punjabi Musalman

ashes of the famous red-coated line of the Honourable East India Company, was no light task. The Company hardly knew what its stock of irregular troops was, for they had been raised as emergency demanded and opportunity offered, on authority which, even if existing at one time in writing, was often not forthcoming afterwards. Opinions innumerable existed as to what was to be done. The whole subject was much complicated by the transfer of India to the Crown, and the formation of a Royal instead of a Company's Army. How that task was carried out, and what the measures then taken have ultimately developed into, it is the principal object of this book to illustrate and explain.

CHAPTER IV

THE INDIAN ARMIES UNDER THE CROWN

WITH the raising of the irregular regiments in the Punjab, commenced the Indian Army of to-day. When, a year or so after the Mutiny, the proclamation transferring India to the Crown was read before the large force then garrisoning Peshawar, it is on record that on the left of a long line of troops, clad in the loose khaki clothing that is now so familiar, stood a corps that a twelvemonth had made as extinct in Upper India as the dodo. There stood, in its scarlet coatees, its shakos and white cross-belts, a surviving Bengal regular battalion, that had alone, of the original Peshawar garrison, escaped disarmament and avoided mutiny. The influence and character of its officers must have been far beyond the ordinary, to have kept that regiment still standing under arms.

106

From the discussions that ensued on the close of the campaigns that succeeded the revolt, it had been decided to organize the whole of the native force on what has already been described as the irregular system. The existing nucleus and model was the now famous Punjab Irregular Force. In the first hasty numbering of the newly raised infantry in the Punjab, they had been organized on the same status as the Irregular Force, numbered consecutively after the existing corps, and assumed to be, as that force was in peace time, under the control of the Punjab Government and not of the Commander-in-Chief. The eighteen new battalions had been numbered from 7 to 24. It was now decided to renumber the loyal remnant of the old army from 1 onwards, according to seniority, both infantry and cavalry, and to add on to these the new corps, renumbering them also in succession.

The actual numbering between 1860 and 1861 was altered several times in the Bengal Army, owing to change of policy and plans. At first the Gurkha regiments, which had been extra battalions, were numbered with the new Line. Already the original Nasiri battalion had been taken into the Line as the 66th, when the original

66th mutinied in the 'fifties over the *batta* trouble, and it was first decided to include them all. Then came orders to keep the Gurkhas as a separate Line of their own.

The final numbering of the new Bengal Army was as follows (under **G.G.O.**, 990 of **29.10.61**) :—

1st Bengal N. Infantry.		The old 21st.		
2nd	,,	,,	,,	31st (of Saugor staunchness).
3rd	,,	,,	:,	32nd.
4th	,,	,,	,,	33rd.
5th	,,	,,	,,	42nd.
6th	,,	,,	,,	43rd.
7th	,,	,,	,,	47th.
8th	,,	,,	,,	59th.
9th	,,	,,	,,	63rd.
10th	,,	,,	,,	65th.
11th	,,	,,	,,	70th.
12th	,,	,,	,,	Regiment of Khelat-i-Ghilzai.
13th	,,	,,	,,	Shekhawati Battalion.
14th (Sikhs)		,,	,,	Regiment of Ferozepore.
15th (Sikhs)		,,	,,	Regiment of Ludhiana.
16th	,,	,,	,,	Regiment of Lucknow.
17th	,,	,,	,,	Loyal Poorbeah Regiment.
18th	,,	,,	,,	Alipore Regiment (Calcutta Militia).

This closes, with a few exceptions, the list of the Bengal Infantry corps that escaped the cataclysm.

22ND PUNJABIS
Awan of Shahpur

The 12th had been raised as a battalion of Shah Soojah's Contingent at the time of our first Afghan venture, and after its famous defence of Khelat-i-Ghilzai it was brought into the Company's service as an extra battalion. The 13th, 14th, and 15th had been local battalions, the two latter of Sikhs, raised in the Cis Sutlej States, before the Mutiny. The 16th is a famous corps, in that it is composed of the loyal detachments who stuck to their officers when the Lucknow garrison mutinied, and who formed a very much larger portion of the effective fighting strength of the garrison than is usually remembered. It was remembered at the time and after, but at half a century's lapse we are apt to forget some of those who kept the flag flying during those weary, scorching months. The 17th was formed from similar detachments from various regiments, while the 18th were an old local corps who maintained their honour under trying circumstances.

The new 19th to the 32nd Native Infantry were 14 of the 18 regiments of Punjab Infantry raised in '57-'58, and temporarily numbered in succession with the six regiments of Punjab Infantry in the Irregular Force; while the 33rd to the 40th were various local corps raised as

"Levies" during the Mutiny. The 41st, it is interesting to note, were the 1st Infantry of the

British Officer,
Madras Horse Artillery,
1845.

Gwalior Contingent, and the 42nd, 43rd, and 44th were the old Assam and Sylhet Light Infantry battalions. Three Line regiments that had survived the Mutiny, the 4th, 58th, and 73rd, were disbanded, as well as several local battalions. The Gurkhas were renumbered as follows : the 66th or original Nasiri Battalion became the 1st Gurkhas ; the second Nasiri Battalion, which had broken out into semi-mutiny at Jutogh and scared half Simla into the jungles, before it went down to help keep the Delhi-Punjab road open, was subsequently disbanded. They had been raised to take the place of the original battalion taken into the Line as the 66th already referred to. The Sirmoor Battalion became the 2nd Gurkhas, the Kumaon Battalion became the 3rd Gurkhas, the Extra Gurkha Battalion became the 4th Gurkhas, and the Hazara Battalion became the 5th Gurkhas, remaining as before part of the Punjab Irregular

Force.   A few years later Rattray's Sikhs, raised as a military police battalion after the Sonthal rebellion of 1856, was mustered into the Line as the 45th Sikhs.   The highest number of the Bengal Line remained at 45 for many years.   The cavalry in Bengal were similarly renumbered.   All the regular cavalry and several of the irregular corps had mutinied or been disarmed, or otherwise come under suspicion.   In 1861, orders appeared renumbering the whole of the cavalry, some being old irregular corps, others local horse of recent standing.   Before the Mutiny there were eighteen regiments of irregular cavalry.   Of these eight were finally retained and renumbered, according to their own original seniority, under the same G.G.O. of 1861 as the Infantry, viz. :—

1st Bengal Cavalry, formerly the 1st Irregulars.				
2nd	,,	.,	2nd	,,
3rd	,,	,,	4th	,,
5th	,,	,,	7th	,,
6th	,,	,,	8th	,,
7th	,,	,,	17th	,,
8th	,,	,,	18th	,,

Then to these were added the famous regiments of horse raised for the suppression of the Mutiny:—

9th Bengal Cavalry, formerly 1st Hodson's Horse.

10th	,,	,,	2nd ,, ,,
11th	,,	,,	Wale's Horse (later Probyn's Horse).
12th	,,	,,	2nd Sikh Irregular Cavalry.
13th	,,	,.	4th Sikh Irregular Cavalry.
14th	,,	,,	Murray's Jāt Horse.
15th	,,	,,	Cureton's Multanis.
16th	,,	,,	Rohilkand Horse.
17th	,,	,,	Robart's Horse.
18th	,,	,,	2nd Mahratta Horse.
19th	,,	,,	Fane's Horse.

Fane's Horse was originally raised after the Mutiny from volunteers from other corps, for the expedition to China.

The Punjab Irregular Force, which was not under the control of the Commander-in-Chief, was left at its original strength of 5 cavalry regiments, 4 battalions of Sikh infantry (the old Sikh locals of the Jullundur Doab), and 5 battalions of Punjab Infantry. Their light field batteries and mountain trains were finally fixed at four, and converted to mountain batteries, with one garrison battery. The Madras and Bombay Armies were not renumbered, as mutiny had made no gaps in the former and but one or two in the latter. Certain corps raised and especially developed during the long hunt for Tantia Topee, and the

24TH PUNJABIS

MALIKDIN KHEL SUBADAR
(*Afridi*) *Jāt Sikh*

marauding bands into which the embers of mutiny had turned, remained under the orders of the Government of India, and were not brought into the Line at that time, such as the Central India Horse, the Erinpura Irregular Force, the Deoli Irregulars, etc. Some of these irregular corps comprised both horse and foot, and at one time guns.

The whole of the European artillery and the corps of engineers were transferred to the Royal corps under special conditions. The mutiny of all the native Bengal artillery, and other weighty considerations, had decided the Government to have no native field artillery in future. All the native artillery was therefore gradually disbanded. The only exceptions to this rule were the four mountain batteries in the Punjab Irregular Force (which force was called the Punjab Frontier Force in 1865), and two native batteries in Bombay. These Nos. 1 and 2 companies *Golandaz*, originally used to garrison Aden and man the Jacobabad mountain train in turn, eventually became Nos. 1 and 2 Bombay Mountain Batteries, and later 5 and 6 (Bombay) Mountain Batteries. Another exception were the four field batteries of the Hyderabad Contingent. The whole of this contingent had done excellent service in 1857, and was retained intact. In future, with these exceptions, the artillery service in India was to be found by batteries and companies of the Royal Artillery. A sapper and miner corps was retained in each Presidential Army, officered from the Royal Engineers.

The new corps had all been organized on the so-called irregular system, which has already been described, and which in its early days meant that the command of companies and squadrons was in the hands of the native officers, and that only the command, second in command, and regimental staff, were in the hands of British officers. This had the merit of cheapness, and was well suited to the immediate post-Mutiny military conditions. The term irregular was, of course, an ill-chosen one ; it was only irregular in that it differed from the old sealed pattern organization, that had tried to follow the regimental constitution of Europe.

The question was also taken up of applying this system to the Madras and Bombay Armies, after the moot question had been decided as to whether or no there should be one Indian army or three armies. In that day there was no Suez Canal, and Europe, for troop-transport, was far away. The mass of opinion was in favour of water-tight compartments, by which it was meant that three different armies, organized and constituted differently, were a great safeguard against general mutiny ; and the staunchness of the coast armies in the recent trouble did certainly bear out the argument.

Gradually the whole, however, of these two armies was organized on the same system as regards officers. The whole of the cavalry, except four regiments of Madras Light Cavalry, was organized on the silladar system which obtains to this day. Its whole principle is that Government pay so much per head, and the regiment finds everything except firearms. In the original days of silladar cavalry, it meant that the trooper received this amount and found himself in everything. In these days, when a regiment is expected to have itself equipped in a uniform way, it means that the men are required to enlist with a certain amount of money towards the purchase of their horse, and the regimental commander administers their pay so as to make it gradually cover

British Officer, 3rd Madras Light Cavalry, 1845.

all the various articles of equipment they require as well as to feed the horse. For this sum the regiment also provides its baggage animals. The administration, therefore, of a silladar cavalry regiment requires immense business capacity on the part of a commanding officer. The system has produced some splendid light cavalry, and has appealed to the best material in the country. It has also been admirably suited to irregular and frontier war, and the need for a sudden well-equipped move when the tribes are rising. It is not a very easy system to maintain in a war of any size or duration, while the continual rise in price of horses, food, and equipments always tends to make the silladar rates of pay a little behind the times.

The Madras Line practically retained its old numbers, as did the regiments and battalions of Bombay, the other coast army. The Company's European battalions of the three armies were transferred to the Crown, and as regiments of the Line have much added to their already ample laurels. Three regiments of European Light Cavalry, raised for the Company during the Mutiny, and known to fame as the " Dumpies," by reason of the small and gin-fed recruits that were at first forthcoming, were transferred also as the

26TH PUNJABIS
MALIKDIN KHEL
(*Afridi*)

A.C.LOVETT

19th, 20th, and 21st Hussars. At the time of this transfer, occurred that instance of mismanagement, that while once and for all clinching the argument against a local European force, was both sad and dangerous. The "White Mutiny," as it was called, was a widespread and determined opposition on the part of the Company's Europeans, led in some places by the artillery, to the orders transferring them to the Crown. The Crown had been advised that the terms of the men's engagement included service under the Crown, and that an act of transfer was completely legal. The men thought otherwise, and considered that they should be allowed a discharge or a bounty. The crisis that arose was a source of great anxiety just at the close of the Mutiny, and was by no means creditable to the troops. Before it was quelled, one unfortunate had to be publicly executed. The Government then decided to modify their attitude, and thousands of men took their discharge home to re-enlist in the Queen's troops on arrival. It was one of those unfortunate occurrences of which the inner history is hard to know.

Allusion has been made to the vexed discussion as to whether or no the European troops in India should be local. This waged very acutely, and it is interesting to read in the reviews of the time, that it was held by well-informed men that if there were no local European service the native army would deteriorate to the level of a " Black Militia." So unkindly does print and time treat the prophets.

The transfer of the large cadre of officers of the Indian Army, to a force serving under entirely different conditions (for purchase still obtained in the Royal Army), produced many anomalies and much discontent. The mutiny of about half the army with large cadres of officers, and its replacement with fewer corps with small cadres of officers, meant that very many were without employment. As they had definite rights as regards periods of service, they had to remain on if they wished, and throughout India were to be found officers of the old cadres doing general duty in cantonments or commanding isolated forts and sanatoria.

With the reforming of the Army of Bengal, another controversial question came into prominence, viz. that of class regiments versus class companies. That is to say, whether regiments should consist of only one race, or whether different races should be kept in different companies in the same regiments. It will be remembered that, in the old army, men stood by

DOGRAS

31ST PUNJABIS
Havildar

37TH DOGRAS

27TH PUNJABIS
Havildar

41ST DOGRAS

38TH DOGRAS
Subadar-Major

chance in the ranks, Hindu and Musalman, Poorbeah and Punjabi, cheek by jowl. The object aimed at in the new construction was, to some extent, to put the races into water-tight compartments, while at the same time developing their feeling of clan emulation and martial characteristics to the full. There was much to be said for both of the proposed systems. The balance of argument was on the class company. To put the analogy into English terms, it was as though a battalion should have so many English, and so many Scotch or Irish companies, or so many Catholic and so many Protestant companies, or should be entirely of one race.

Accordingly, the majority of the new regiments became class-company ones, and only a few Sikh and Gurkha corps remained entirely homogeneous. In the older armies the old constitution was to a great extent retained, but the number of Poorbeahs (literally men of the Eastern provinces), the race which had mutinied, was strictly limited. This system of class companies gradually led to a very close study of the clans and races of India, which will be discussed and described in the next two chapters.

Before, however, the new Crown Army had

settled down after the struggle and re-organization, it was once more called on to perform its Imperial rôle. The war in China that had been patched up in 1857, once more broke out, and a strong force from India was hurried off from the campaigning ground of the Mutiny to the celestial capital, in co-operation with a French force in the advance on Pekin in 1860. The force was drawn from all the armies, but some six of the newly raised irregular regiments from the Punjab took part. Even during the Mutiny itself the usual frontier operations were taking place in the Peshawar district and on the Assam frontier, while in 1860 an expedition was sent against the Mahsud Waziris. In 1864-65 operations against Bhootan were necessary, and in the autumn of 1864 we were forced into the operations in the Peshawar valley, which brought in their train the rising of the whole of the tribes in Swat, and the desperate fighting in the Ambeyla Pass. The desperate fighting connected with the repeated capture and recapture of the Crag piquet is a famous incident of the campaign. In 1867-68 the expedition to Abyssinia was undertaken, in which the Bombay Army took a considerable part, with a strong Bengal brigade. Lord Napier of Magdala's march from

33RD PUNJABIS

SUBADAR

Punjabi Musalmans

Zula on the Red Sea to Magdala, with its wonderful arrangements for food and transport over
most difficult country, will always be remembered.
1868 also saw an expedition against the raiding
tribes of the Black Mountain and several other
minor operations.

1878 saw us once more involved in Afghan
affairs, owing to the Amir's reception of a Russian
mission and refusal to receive a British one under
Sir Neville Chamberlain. The war that followed
was a long and costly one, and had two distinct
phases; one, the advance towards Kabul on the
north, and to Kandahar in the south, with the
treaty of Gundamuk and the succession of Yakub
Khan to the throne of his father Sher Ali; and the
second, the advance to Kabul after the murder of
the British agent Sir Louis Cavagnari and his escort
there. The war is memorable for the famous
actions at Ali Musjid, the Peiwar Kotal, and
Charasiab, and the heavy fighting round Kabul;
later on came Ahmed Khel, the disastrous defeat
of Maiwand, and Lord Roberts' march from Kabul
to Kandahar, with the successful battle under the
walls of that city. The conclusion of the campaign left us with a more convenient and logical
frontier, and especially with the possession of British

16

Baluchistan.   The Bengal Army and Frontier
Force formed the bulk of the Kabul Army ; and
the Bombay Army, the Kandahar Army, while
several units from the Madras Army
were moved up on to the lines of
communication.

Daffadar.
13th Duke of Con-
naught Lancers.
Watson's Horse,
1885.

Just before this war, an Indian force
had been sent to Malta in readiness
to join a British force to act if need
be in the Russo-Turkish War.   In
1882, a strong Indian contingent joined
Sir Garnet Wolseley in Egypt, and
shared in the decisive fight at Tel-el-
Kebir, eighty years after the original
brigade under Sir David Baird had
sailed to join the British there.   In
1885 Indian troops again went towards Egypt, this time to the Soudan ;
while the same year the situation
brought on the Third Burmese War,
in which representative corps of the
whole three armies took part, and which ended
in the annexation of Upper Burma.

During the Afghan and Burmese wars it had
become evident that several corps in all three
armies were recruited from material that was no

longer suited to the trying climate and arduous conditions of the modern theatres of war. Several regiments of the Bombay and Madras Armies were reconstituted with Baluch, Pathan, and Punjabi soldiers in the ranks. The Madras regiments thus altered were located in Burma, the Baluch and Pathan regiments in Scinde and Baluchistan. In the Bengal Army, more battalions of Gurkhas were raised, and also a corps enlisted from a kindred hill-race in Garhwal. The Madras Army had made immense efforts, too, to improve its quality by tapping certain likely races within its own territorial limits ; and Moplahs, an uncouth race from the western coasts, with hillmen from the uplands of Coorg, were enlisted into class corps. Experience eventually led, however, to the corps being broken up.

The immense expenditure incurred in the prosecution of the war in Afghanistan led to the reduction of several corps of cavalry and infantry in 1882. In 1885, however, the necessity for war preparation that was the sequel to the Penjdeh incident, had seen half the Indian Army mobilized to take the field in Central Asia, and the demand for troops showed the shortsightedness of the '82 reductions. Most of the reduced corps were restored to the establishment, under an improved class constitution. The few blank numbers that a scrutiny of the Indian Army List will reveal as still vacant, are mostly a relic of the '82 reductions.

During the 'eighties, in addition to the overseas expeditions recorded, there were several small frontier operations, including the Sikkim expedition, which brought us regularly into touch with Thibet. 1888 to 1892 brought two expeditions to the Black Mountain, one to the Samana, and one among the mountains of Hunza Nagar on the borders of the Pamirs, as well as several minor expeditions in the Chin and Kachin hills of Upper Burma. So that some portion of the Indian Army was always under arms.

In 1894, the fierce fanatical attack on the escort to the Boundary Commission in Waziristan, forced on us an expedition against the Mahzud Waziris for the third time, and brought us into closer relations with a more than usually faithless and fascinating class of tribesman. In 1895, the British Agent at Gilgit had occasion to visit Chitral, on the occurrence of one of the usual cataclysms in the reigning dynasty, and was attacked and shut up in Chitral fort by Pathans from neighbouring States. This resulted in the Chitral Relief

35TH SIKHS

SUBADAR

Expedition, with its fight at the Malakand Pass, *en route* to Chitral, from the Peshawar Valley, and Kelly's sensational march from Gilgit in the north. In 1897, events of many kinds, the encroachment of civilization, salt dues, the joy of possessing better arms, and the drum ecclesiastic rolled after the triumph of Turk over Greek, combined to produce such a crop of simultaneous frontier risings as we had never before seen. First Waziristan blazed off, in the treacherous attack on a small escort at Maizar. Then in the north, the tribes of Swat threw themselves for days in succession against the British garrisons at the Malakand and Chakdara, for the glory of God and the Prophet. While the force that had relieved these posts was inflicting punishment on the offending tribes, the Mohmands further south threw themselves across our borders, and were defeated at Shubkadr. Before the troops could gather to repel the Mohmands the fiery cross had sped, the tribes of Miranzai and the Samana were in a blaze, and as troops were hastened there, the Afridis of Tirah must needs attack the Khyber posts and close the road. By this time the situation had become most difficult, and the Government all at once had some four different campaigns on hand, of more than usual dimensions. From the north to the south of India, troops of all kinds and classes had to be put in motion, and operations lasted for practically ten months. Some of the events, notably the storming of the Dargai heights on the road to the Afridi Tirah, are well known. The close of the campaigns found us for the time being with considerably increased garrisons, till in Lord Curzon's viceroyalty the policy of local levies, on the old Black Watch principle, was extended, and the troops themselves gradually withdrawn.

During the period covered by these campaigns, many changes had been in progress within the army itself. In 1886, the Punjab Frontier Force was transferred from the direct control of the Government of India, to the ordinary control of the Commander-in-Chief in India; while in 1895 came the great change which had been long foreshadowed, viz. the abolition of the Presidential Armies, as separate armies under separate governments, with separate Commanders - in - Chief. After the Mutiny this question was much discussed, but at that time railways were hardly even in their infancy in India. Central control was almost impossible, while the water-tight compartment seemed the immediate lesson to be derived from

39TH GARHWAL RIFLES

Garhwalis

the Mutiny. As India had modernized, and the railway system had overcome the difficulty of the vast distances, it was evident that three Commanders-in-Chief were an anachronism ; and at last, after much discussion, the Bengal Army was split up into two commands, and these with the Madras and Bombay Armies were constituted into four Lieutenant-Generals' commands, with a Commander-in-Chief over all. The numbering of the various units of the army was, however, for the time, left to stand, with the many anomalies that such an arrangement presented. There were in the army, liable to serve side by side, both in peace and war, and often actually during the latter, the 1st Bengal Infantry, the 1st Bombay Infantry, the 1st Madras Infantry, the 1st Gurkhas, the 1st Infantry Hyderabad Contingent, the 1st Punjab Infantry, the 1st Sikhs, the 1st Burma Infantry, the 1st Baluchis, and almost as many 1st cavalries, etc. It was not till Lord Kitchener's period of command that this big question of renumbering could be successfully tackled. The abolition of the armies in 1895, however, was the forerunner of the general numbering.

Then during this period, the recruitment of class and clan and the recruit-yielding capacity of

the various races began to be most carefully
studied, and as one class after another came to
show the results of years of peace, the search for
a better soldier - bearing stratum became more
stringent.   Orders appeared from time to time,
altering the constitution of regiments as experience and change of times proved the need, till
gradually the present arrangements, which it is
now proposed to describe, were evolved.

CHAPTER V

THE MILITARY RACES OF INDIA

IT is one of the essential differences between the East and the West, that in the East, with certain exceptions, only certain clans and classes can bear arms; the others have not the physical courage necessary for the warrior. In Europe, as we know, every able-bodied man, given food and arms, is a fighting man of some sort, some better, some worse, but still as capable of bearing arms as any other of his nationality. In the East, or certainly in India, this is not so. The people of Bengal, even those with the most-cultivated brain, the trading classes, the artizan classes, and the outcaste tribes, are men to whom the threat of violence is the last word. At the bottom of all power and law, disguise it never so carefully, lies the will of the hand to keep the head. Presumably the great conquest of India away back in the mists of time, by the Aryan race, and the subjection of the original inhabitants, is at the bottom of this. Only certain races were permitted to bear arms, and in course of time only certain races remained fit to bear arms. Conquest, pure and simple, with cruel repression, is responsible for it in some places, such as in Bengal and Kashmir. It is extraordinary that the well-born race of the upper classes in Bengal should be hopeless poltroons, while it is absurd that the great, merry, powerful Kashmiri should have not an ounce of physical courage in his constitution, but it is so. Nor are appearances of any use as a criterion. Some of the most manly-looking people in India are in this respect the most despicable.

The existence of this condition, therefore, much complicates the whole question of enlistment in India. It renders any form of levy *en masse* impossible, or any form of Militia service, while it emphatically forbids the English system, whereby the well-to-do pay for the lower orders to do their fighting for them. In India itself certain classes alone do the soldiering and kindred service. These are, roughly, in central and northern India the yeoman peasant, the grazier, and the land-owner. Very good classes, too, as every one can see, and in India there is no exodus from the land

40TH PATHANS

MALIKDIN KHEL

(*Afridi*)

to the crowded city.   The peasant in India, that is
to say, the yeoman peasant, is a well-born man,
distinct from the mere helot of low birth who in
some parts helps on the land.

Now the people by tribes from whom' we take
soldiers in India itself are as follows :—

(1) The ancient Aryan races, who invaded India in prehistoric times, viz. Rajput (lit. sons of princes)
and Brahman, who for practical purposes may be
divided into two distinct classes, those of Hindustan
and those of the Punjab.

(2) The races of Jāts or Jăts, and Gūjars.

(3) The Pathans and the Moguls of India.

Then from outside the limits of India :—

(4) The Pathan and Afghan of the frontier hills.

(5) The Gurkha.

Then we have a further division which is by
religion, and also another by country.

For instance, we have the Sikhs, who are largely
that portion of the Jăt race which embraced the
calvinistic reformed Hindu teaching of the Sikh
gurus, and who live in that part of Upper India
known as the Punjab, the land of the five rivers.

Then we have the Muhammadans of the
Punjab, who are of many mixed races, but who
largely consist of Rajput tribes converted to

Islam at various times in the past.   They describe themselves as Rajput rather than Muhammadan.

The Muhammadans of India are either the descendants of conquering or serving foreigners of that faith, or of converts.   In whichever category they may claim descent, they will generally be of mixed origin by now, and those who claim Pathan and Mogul descent will have lost the characteristics of their race, and even their features, for it is rare to see a sign in these days of the Tartar origin of the Moguls.

Then, again, in the Southern Plateau we have the Deccan, of which the people are largely Mahrattas or Marathi-speaking, and, mixed with them, Muhammadans of varied origin.

For the purposes of describing the military tribes and castes it will be as well to do so by countries and provinces with certain exceptions. The gradual raising of the military standard by the change of times and terrain, and the enervating effect on Asiatics of a few generations of peace, have already been referred to.   It has resulted in a gradual enlistment of an increasing number of men of the northern races, whom a cold winter, and a lesser period of the enjoyment of peace, have for the present preserved from military deterioration.

42ND DEOLI REGIMENT

Honorary Major
H.H. SIR UMED SINGH BAHADUR, G.C.I.E., K.C.S.I.
Maharao of Kota (Rajputana)

M. Ahmed Singh

It will be reasonable, therefore, to commence with the races of the north, viz. of the Punjab and the North-West Frontier.

The Military Classes of the Punjab

The Sikhs.—It is not correct to speak of the Sikhs as a race ; they are, properly speaking, a numerous religious sect, which, starting as a persecuted set of reformers, became a powerful sect embracing many of all the Hindu tribes and races of the Punjab. The first *guru* or spiritual teacher of the new faith was Baba Nanak, born in 1469, near Lahore. Brought up within the influence of the teaching of a one and only God as conceived in Islam, he taught a reformed or puritan Hinduism, in which simplicity, kindliness, purity, and brotherhood were among the leading principles. Stimulated by repression and persecution, the sect grew and flourished. Nine *gurus* succeeded father Nanak ; the tenth *guru*, the famous Govind, succeeding his father at the age of fifteen, on the former's suffering death and torture at the hands of the Mogul. In the hands of the tenth *guru* the religious and peaceful community was changed into a powerful military sect, that constantly obtained fresh recruits and became the champion of the Hindu inhabitants against the Musalman. The faith spread to most of the Hindu tribes of the Punjab, more especially to the vast cultivating race, the Jăts, which to this day is spread over the whole of Upper India.

H.H. Raja Sir Hira Singh Bahadur of Nahba, Hon. Colonel 14th Sikhs.

Because the Jăts form, perhaps, two-thirds of the Sikhs, the term Sikh (which means disciple) is largely associated with the *Jăts*. These same Jăts, however, number many hundreds of thousands who embraced the hostile creed of Islam, while in Rajputana and about Delhi and south of it are numerous Hindus of the same descent who call themselves *Jāts* (*q.v.*). To the generic title of Sikh or disciple, the warlike Govind added the affix Singh or lion, originally the affix of men of Rajput race.

A Sikh is baptized into his sect and not born into it, so that no man is a Sikh till he has taken the *pāhŭl*, that is to say, till he has been baptized.

Sikhism is an austere faith, demanding some simplicity and rigour of life from its adherents. So much is this so, that for many years there has been a tendency for young men to avoid the *pāhŭl* and grow up as ordinary Hindus, for whom life has few irksome restrictions. But as the value of the Sikh as the simple, faithful soldier, has lain in his adherence to the simple tenets and hardy life of his forebears, no non-baptized Sikh is admitted into a regiment of the Indian Army. So careful are regiments in this matter, and so much are regiments the home of the old martial and simple Sikh principles, that it has been said, not without some shadow of truth, that it is the British officer who has kept Sikhism up to its old standard. The creed of Govind is thus described :—

Emerging from his retirement he preached the *Khalsa*, the faith of the pure, the elect, and the liberated. He openly attacked all distinctions of caste, and insisted on the equality of all who would join him. Resuscitating the old baptismal rite of the Sikhs, he proclaimed it as the *pāhŭl* or gate, by which all might enter the fraternity, while he gave to its members the *pershad* or communion as a sacrament of union in which the four orders of Hindu society should eat from the same dish ; . . . the higher orders murmured . . . but the lower orders rejoiced at the new dispensation and flocked in numbers to his standard. . . . He gave them the outward signs of their faith, in the unshorn hair, the short

drawers, and the blue dress.   He marked the military nature
of their calling, by the title of *Singh* or lion, by the
wearing of steel, and by the initiation by sprinkling water
with a two-edged dagger, and he gave them a feeling of
personal superiority in their abstinence from the unclean
tobacco.[1]

But while Nanak substituted holiness of life for vain
ceremonies, Govind Singh demanded brave deeds and
zealous devotion to the cause as the proof of faith. . . .
Religious fervour was entirely eclipsed by military zeal, and
thus for the second time in history a religion became a
political power, and for the first time in India a nation
arose, embracing all races, all classes, and all grades of
society, and banded them together in face of a foreign foe.[2]

Such in brief is Sikhism and its history.   The
Jăt Sikh forming the bulk of the fraternity are
those who have served us most, and who probably
make the best soldiers.   The *Jăt* is a peasant
farmer before anything else, however.   In spite
of the military tenets of his faith, his sayings are
all of the plough, and a plough is the first toy of
the Sikh's son.   The *Khatris*, who have embraced
Sikhism, form largely the business class, and have
been enlisted in small numbers for their brains
. . . the *Jăt* being proverbially thick in the uptake,
. . . and have served with distinction.   The
Lobana, the hereditary carrying class, have always

[1] *Sikhs.* Bingley.
[2] Sir Denzil Ibbetson, *Ethnography of the Punjab.*

43RD ERINPURA
REGIMENT

COLOUR HAVILDAR
Mina

44TH MERWARA
INFANTRY

HAVILDAR
Mer

108TH INFANTRY

KAIMKHANI
(*Rajputana Musalman*)

done well as soldiers, though not very largely enlisted. The greater demands of the army on the hardier races of the north have, however, caused the recruiter to closely examine the yield in Sikhs of other classes, with the result that certain regiments enlist no *Jăt* Sikhs, but have been successful in some of the smaller and humbler Sikh communities. For instance, *Sanis* or gardeners, *Kumboh* Sikhs, a cultivating race of putative foreign origin, of whom some are Sikhs, the artificer classes, have all been swept into the military net, which only their Sikhism has made possible.

The *Jăt* race, from whom so many Sikhs were made, is described farther on under Jāt and Gūjar, but must be referred to here. There is much discussion as to their origin, but it seems probable that they are in reality of a Scythian race, with whom some identify the Jātii of history and the Magyars and gypsies of Eastern Europe. To what extent, and when, they mingled with the Aryan race, and to what extent the distinction between them and the Aryans is social, it is impossible to tell. The Scythian tribes undoubtedly adopted Buddhism soon after their arrival, and later Hinduism. All *Jăts* are cultivators, and the name

18

has become almost the name of an occupation. The inhabitants of the Indus Valley when that river leaves the mountains are largely Muhammadan Jăts. (See later "Jāts and Gūjars.")

One more Sikh community needs description, since they form so faithful a portion of the Sikh soldiery, and these are the *Mazbi* Sikhs who serve in the Sikh Pioneer regiments. The term *Mazbi* means faithful, and was applied to the sweepers of outcaste tribe who brought back the crucified body of Teg Bahadur, the second successor to Guru Govind. Their descendants of outcaste tribe, and probably those outcastes whom they converted to Sikhism, now have the title. They served under Ranjit Singh, and were formed into a pioneer regiment for service before Delhi, since when their courage and general good qualities have made them famous for the work of the military pioneer.

The military services of the Sikhs in our service are well known. The Sikh regiments, whether those raised just before the Mutiny, such as the 14th or 15th Sikhs, the regiments of Ferozepore and Ludhiana, or the 35th and 45th (originally a military police corps), are equally famous, as are those regiments that enlist class squadrons and companies of Sikhs, and the regiments of Pioneers.

45TH RATTRAY'S SIKHS

"THE DRUMS"

Jăt Sikhs

Their military reputation, so far as our service is concerned, largely dates from the Mutiny, when the Sikhs flocked to our standards. Since those days, the Punjabi generally, but especially the Sikh, has become a world-wide adventurer. In addition to enlisting in every sort of military or police body that will take him, in Africa, China, or the East generally, he is to be found also as watchman in many private firms. High pay is what attracts him, and wealth to spend on his land when he returns home. These attractions, and the devastation of plague in the last few years, have made the Sikh recruiting-market tight, and there is little doubt that we have, if anything, over-recruited from this nationality. The large number of men they furnish, *vide* the next chapter, their importance as a population, and the latent possibilities underlying the tenets of their creed, all make their description at some length desirable. In appearance they are well known: tall, well-knit men, with their long hair pulled up under their headdress, their beards and whiskers neatly curled up close to the face, and their military bearing all stamp the man, even to those with only a bowing acquaintance with Hindustan. As a fighting man, his slow wit and dogged courage give him many of the characteristics of the British soldier at his best.

THE MUHAMMADAN OF THE PUNJAB

The Muhammadans of the Punjab, exclusive of the Pathan, who will be described later, consist for the most part of men of the various Hindu tribes who have at one time or other accepted Islam. The better classes inhabit more or less their own districts and are largely Rajput, and describe themselves as Rajput. They keep themselves separate by clans, and in some cases, such as the Chibs, count kin in some sort with those of the tribe who remained Hindu. There are, of course, tens of thousands of Muhammadans of the lesser castes and classes of no particular descent scattered about in every sort of occupation. It is the zemindar, the land-owning peasant, that the reputable mass of the population consists of, and who claim to be of Rajput stock and clan. Among them are certain clans and tribes who claim a foreign origin, and to have entered with one of the invasions, and, having occupied the lands of others, founded a barony and brought the owners to subjection. Among the latter are a well-known military clan, the Gukkhars, while among the

46TH AND 33RD PUNJABIS

AFRIDIS

HAVILDAR

Zakka Khel   *Malikdin Khel*

Oraksai   *Kuki Khel*   *Kambar Khel*

Rajput clans are the Bhattis, Suttis, Chibs, Janjuas, Tiwanas, etc. The Awans, again, are another large tribe whose origin is uncertain, but from whom we draw many soldiers. The Muhammadan tribes of the Punjab furnish many excellent soldiers, and since all the world over men are prone to exalt their station, so is a man seeking service given to say that he belongs to a better tribe than his own. The greatest care is taken to see that men do not represent themselves to be what they are not. Regiments enlist men of certain tribes and endeavour to keep to men of those tribes, so that in the companies that exist, tribal pride and emulation and even tribal discipline and public opinion may be stimulated. All arms of the service enlist the Rajput Muhammadan, some tribes, such as the Tiwanas, only going to the cavalry. The best of the Musalman tribes come from the Salt Range, that tumbled pile of sand and limestone crag that lies between the Jhelum and the Indus.

Allusion has already been made to the Jăts and the numberless tribes of this race that have embraced Islam. They are so numerous that they have not received any very close study, and it is doubtful if the term *jăt* does more than imply cultivator in many cases, and the ethnography of

the so-called Jăt tribes of the Muhammadan
religion will bear far more study. Jăt Muhammadans, however, are not at present largely enlisted. Each class regiment and class company
regiment has the tribes and clans whom it is to
enlist either laid down by superior authority, or
by regimental rule, and this is strictly observed.
Great precautions are taken to ensure that the men
really are what they profess to be, and their statements as to birth and tribe, etc., are sent to the
civil authorities to be verified and corroborated,
should the guarantee of the Indian officers in the
regiment or other reliable evidence be not forthcoming in the corps. It must always be remembered that in India, military service is a
source of much honour and prestige, so that
pretenders will often try to pass themselves off
as better born than they are. The essential
difference, then, between the voluntarily enlisted
army of the United Kingdom, and the voluntarily
enlisted army of India, is at once evident. The
English soldier does not always come to the ranks
because it is the most honourable career he knows.
The Indian soldier does.

The foregoing describes for the most part the
fighting races of the Punjab other than the Dogras.

"FRONTIER FORCE"

51ST SIKHS
Piper
Punjabi Musalman

59TH SCINDE RIFLES
Gakkhar

56TH PUNJABI RIFLES
Sagri Khattaks

There are members of the great Brahman race scattered all over India, and those in the Punjab have imbibed the hardy habits that the climate has induced. A few are enlisted from the agricultural and land-owning clans, and make good soldiers. The various plates showing Sikhs and Muhammadan groups of the Punjabi regiments, illustrate the different physiognomy of the tribes and races, and also their national fashion of growing hair and beard, as well as the characteristic fashion of tying the pugaree, which in itself serves to distinguish race to the instructed observer.

The Dogra.—The Dogra is among the most valued of all the soldier races of Northern India. The name is really geographical and not racial. Dogras are people who come from the hills between the Punjab and Kashmir, and are the old Aryan Hindu stock and affiliated races who peopled the bulk of India. They are Brahmans, Rajputs, Jăts, and the like, who refused the Koran and the Prophet when many of the other Rajputs succumbed, and who later kept clear of the Sikh movement. Their situation in the foot-hills of the Himalaya, off the trampled path of the legions, may account for their retaining the religion and habits of the Aryan race. Certain of their related tribes, such as the Chibs, have in part, however, accepted Islam, and, when living in the Dogra country, are admittedly entitled to be styled Dogras, though in common parlance that term is applied to the Hindus of the outer hills, and more especially to the Rajput tribes.

Their good behaviour, courtly manners, high courage, and physical endurance, make the Dogra a valued soldier by all who know him.   His enlistment is, however, only come to be widely undertaken during the last twenty-five years, and as a body they have not had the opportunity for acquiring fame that has presented itself to some of the other races.   They have, however, invariably acquitted themselves with distinction.   Three class Dogra regiments exist, the 37th, 38th, and 41st, while numerous regiments take one or more Dogra companies, and the cavalry Dogra squadrons.   The higher class of Rajput is the more favoured, but those who will not themselves set hand to plough are as blue-blooded and as penniless as ever a Laird of Cockpen.   The best clans are perhaps to be found in the cavalry.   The Indian officer of the 12th Cavalry in one of the illustrations is a Dogra of a Rajput tribe.   Another plate shows Dogras of Rajput and other tribes in the class regiments,

"FRONTIER FORCE"

57TH WILDE'S RIFLES	53RD SIKHS
Naik	Subadar
Adam Khel	*Sagri Khattak*
(Afridi)	

37th, 38th, and 41st Dogras, and a Dogra of the
31st Punjabis, which regiment is one of the many
that has a class company of that race. Dogras
come from the Dogra State of Jammu, the
predominant State in the feudatory of Jammu
and Kashmir (whose ruler is a Dogra Rajput of
the Jamwal clan); from the British district of
Kangra in the outer Himalaya, a part of the
Punjab province; and from the foot-hills and
submontane tracts between Jammu and Kangra.
The State of Jammu and Kashmir maintains a
considerable force of Imperial Service troops
(*v.* Chapter VII.), who are chiefly Dogras, and
who came to great distinction in the Defence
of Chitral, Kelly's march to Chitral from
Gilgit, and in actions with the Kohistanis near
Chilas.

Pathans.—We now come to the great Pathan
race, which is so inextricably bound up with the
history of India, of whom many are now settlers in
India, devoid of almost all their racial characteristics. Others live immediately within our North-
West Frontier, while the bulk either occupy the
unadministered hills between our administrative
border and the treaty Afghan frontier, or dwell in
Afghanistan itself.

It has been the fashion for all Afghans and Pathans for the last five hundred years to claim for themselves a common descent, and that descent a Jewish one. The Afghan proper, that is to say, the Durani clans, call themselves the Ben-i-Israel, the Children of Israel, and the legendary ancestor is one Kais, the chief of the descendants of a Jewish settlement in the Mountains of Ghor which lie north-west of Kandahar, and which to this day have never been visited by Europeans. To one of the three sons of Kais, all Afghan and Pathan tribes trace their origin, and cling to the Jewish legend. Kais was said to be 37th in descent from Saul, and lived in the days of the Prophet. There are settlements of professing Jews in Bokhara who preserve what may be an original legend, that they are the descendants of Reubenites, Gadites, and half of Manasseh, carried away to Central Asia by Tiglath-Pileser.[1] Be this as it may, the Afghans hold strongly by their Jewish origin, and their names, Jacob and Joseph and Isaac and Abraham and the like, do not belie the tale.

It is, however, pretty certain that a great many of the Pathan tribes do not belong to the real

[1] *The Kingdom of Afghanistan.* Tate.

Afghan stock, but are some Rajput tribes of the mountains who accepted Islam, and gradually assumed relationship with the Afghan confederacy, or were allowed the privilege of doing so in return for faithful service.   Again, the number-less invasions that swept into India by the Khyber, the Tochi, the Gomal, and the Sangarh passes, have perhaps left in their wake colonies that ejected, or mingled and assumed relationship with older tribes.

Whatever, therefore, may be the pretensions of all the tribes claiming Afghan descent to be of the true blood, the fact remains that the mountain life, cold climate, difficulties of livelihood, and com-munity of religion, have produced peoples that resemble each other in their main attributes, with-out, however, the least homogeneity as a nation. Our venture to Kabul in 1838, to restore the dethroned king, Shah Soojah, to the throne of his fathers, as a British ally, first brought us into touch with the Afghans of Afghanistan and the inde-pendent republican tribes between Afghanistan and the Indus.   Our annexation of the Punjab brought our border and our administration into close relation with them.   Previous to this, however, the Afghan connection with India, dating from the days of

Afghan rulers and adventurers, and always kept up in some form, had brought many Afghans into the ranks of our irregular horse from the time of Lake and Wellesley onward.

Their systematic enlistment dates from the early days of the Punjab Frontier Force, but it was not till the Mutiny that it was at all regularized. The Pathan tribes are organized into many entirely distinct clans, claiming only the common Jewish, or perhaps some more recent ancestor. The clans have many subdivisions, and every clan and every sub-clan, and almost every family, has a feud, smouldering or active, which at times breaks out into raids in force, at times finds vent in the mere moonlighting murder of the Emerald Isle. Hardy, active, alert, and inured to war, are these clansmen of the Afghan hills, endued with considerable courage when well led, and capable of much *élan*. To the best type of Englishman their open, irresponsible manner and delight in all exercise and sport, with their constant high spirits, appeal greatly, and certain types of Englishmen appeal greatly to them also. When in the British ranks all blood feuds are closed, by custom as much as by discipline; and a man may be stalking his right-hand man in the ranks, with knife and martini

CARNATIC INFANTRY

63RD PALAMCOTTAH
LIGHT INFANTRY
Tamil

83RD WALLAJAHBAD
LIGHT INFANTRY
Christian

75TH CARNATIC
INFANTRY
Christian

86TH CARNATIC
INFANTRY
Madrasi Musalman

THE 80TH HONORARY COLOUR WITH
THE INSCRIPTION, "HYDER ALLY,
SHOLINGHUR, HEZIRA, 1195"

80TH CARNATIC
INFANTRY

73RD CARNATIC
INFANTRY

Subadars

Madrasi Musalmans

rifle, the moment furlough is open and they are across the border. Over the border 'tis border law, an eye for an eye and a tooth for a tooth, and the hand must keep the head, so that the young tribesman has his natural combatant faculties sharpened from the day he is weaned.

In addition to the clans beyond the administrative border, there are several wholly and some in part within the British line ; some, those who already dwelt within the Peshawar Valley, when an Afghan province ; others whose hills have for one reason or another gradually come within the administration, or who had come within the Sikh provinces.

All Pathans speak *Pukhtu* or *Pushtu*, as the hard and soft dialects of the language are called. *Pukhtu* is probably derived from the old Zend language written in the Persian character with many Arabic and Persian words. The Pathans or Pakhtŭns are the people who speak *Pukhtu* ; and since Herodotus speaks of the Pactydae who inhabited the Khyber, it is thought that the language and the folk who originally spoke it may have given a name to all who afterwards may have adopted it.

The Pathans who are enlisted in the Indian Army come for the most part either from within the British border, or between the administered border and the Afghan frontier. A few, however, notably in the Guides and the 124th and 126th Baluchistan regiments, come from Afghanistan itself. Great among the Pathan clans are the numerous collection of the Yusufzai, or the sons of Joseph. They live within the Peshawar Valley, or the hills bordering on it, and in the mountains towards Chitral, as well as in Buner, in Swat, and round the Malakand. They also dwell in the hills east of the Indus in the Hazara district, in what was for many years famous as a fighting-ground, viz. the Black Mountain. Their clans are many, and they make excellent soldiers, serving especially in the Guides. Between the Children of Joseph and the Khyber Pass, come the Mohmands and Utman Khel, who serve in our army, and always are prepared to fight us. South of the Mohmands come the Afridis, through whose hills the Khyber itself passes, and who are responsible for its safety and draw blackmail therefor, as many other highland clans before them in other lands. The Afridis are probably a Rajput or at any rate an Aryan tribe, though they have been fitted out with an ancestry of the Jewish community of Ghor. They are intensely republican or, more accurately, democratic, at times even paying no heed to their counsels of elders, every man a law unto himself. They serve in our army more than any other class, and are famous as good soldiers, and, of course, excel as skirmishers. Several thousand are in our ranks, and during the Tirah War (Tirah being the Afridi hills), when they too had been drawn into the wave of fanaticism on the border, the tribal representatives, who came to discuss terms of peace, usually wore British medals earned in our service.

The Afridi has less Jewish features than many of the Pathans, and some of them, with close-cropped fair hair and blue eyes, have a distinctly European appearance. It is curious, too, that on the border, Pathans of beautiful regular features are to be seen, especially among the lads, so that it is not incredible that the traces of the Greek soldier may still be

Subadar-Major, 20th Brownlow's Punjabis. Kambar Khel (Afridi).

visible. Between the Afridi Tirah, in the valley north of the Samana Range, are the Orakzai clans, who also give us soldiers.

South again of the Afridi within our border, are the Khattak Hills, from which comes another widely enlisted tribe, the Khattaks, who also lay claim to the Afghan Jewish descent. They have now been within our borders so long, that they have lost some of the less-desirable characteristics of their wilder neighbours, and make most courageous and reliable soldiers. Closely allied to them are the Bangash in Miranzai. South again of them, beyond the Bangash, up the road from Kohat into Afghanistan, comes the Kurram Valley, partly inhabited by a Shiah tribe known as the Turis. These only enlist into the local militia, but as such have obtained a considerable military reputation. They lay claim to the usual Afghan descent, but are thought to be of different origin.

Farther down the border between the Kurram and Baluchistan comes the tumbled mass of hills known as Waziristan, inhabited by what are now known as the Mahsud clans, the Darwesh Khel, and other Wazir clans. They give us immense trouble, but make remarkably fine soldiers, especially when, as in the case of the Irish, they serve away from their own land. The foregoing are the main clans from whom we take soldiery, who speak the Pushtu, and about whom and whose hills so much is heard

82ND PUNJABIS

Awan
(Punjabi Musalman)

from time to time.   The clans are all, with the exception perhaps of the Afridis, intensely fanatical when stirred by the roll of the drum ecclesiastic. The majority profess a most unenlightened form of Sunni-ism, the orthodox form of Islam, but certain groups of clans, such as the Turis, the Bangash, and others, are Shiahs, and as such, heretics, and, except in war with the unbeliever, obnoxious to the orthodox.

The great race of Afghanistan proper is the Duranis, from Zemindawar and Ghor, and a few of them come to our ranks, especially the cavalry. There are, however, a considerable number of Duranis settled within British India near Multan and in the Derajat on the Indus.   They are ordinary British subjects, but have maintained their ancient valour, and serve in such regiments as the 15th Cavalry (Cureton's Multanis), the 21st Cavalry (Punjab Frontier Force), and in the Baluch Horse.   The Nawab Abdulla, head of the Alizai Section, is honorary native commandant of the 15th, and many of his family are serving or have served in the regiment.   His portrait shows a type of a specially fine class of men, always ready to support us so long as we are true to ourselves.

20

Mention should also be made of the **Hazaras**, who are not Afghans, except in so far as they come from Afghanistan. They are a **Tartar race** and are much the same people as the original **Moguls** and Tartar hordes who overran China and Europe, and who as Moguls conquered India. Their language is the old Persian of Afghanistan and India. They are enlisted in the Baluchistan regiments, and a few years ago, an entire regiment, the 106th Hazara Pioneers, was raised from them, at a time when, owing to trouble with the Amir, many of them had migrated to British territory. They have for many years flocked to India to work as navvies, and make splendid pioneers as well as extremely smart soldiers.

Men of Pathan descent are to be found all over India, among the soldier settlers from old invasions. Until, indeed, the final extension of British rule to the Afghan border, the wild Afghan and Pathan clansmen have habitually sought their fortune in Hindustan, for the hills breed many and feed few.

The Baluchis

The Baluchis or Beloochis are a **Muhammadan** hill-race of probably Arab descent, who entered

THE FORMER "HYDERABAD CONTINGENT" INFANTRY

98TH INFANTRY
Ahir of the Eastern Punjab

97TH DECCAN INFANTRY
Rajput

96TH BERAR INFANTRY
Jat

95TH RUSSELL'S INFANTRY
Hindustani Musalman

94TH RUSSELL'S INFANTRY
Dekhani Musalman

into their present abode from Persia and the Persian Gulf. They occupy a portion of what is now called Baluchistan. In the hills, they have distinct tribal organization like the Pathans, except that they acknowledge implicitly the authority of their tribal chiefs. Many Baluchis of broken tribes are scattered about the Indus Valley as landowners and cultivators. The tribal Baluch of the hills is averse from military service except in local levies, but the broken tribe Baluch of the plains enlists freely. The 127th, 129th, and 130th Infantry are known as Baluchi regiments, but owing to the reluctance of the Baluch of the hills to serve, have but few companies of this race.

RAJPUTS AND BRAHMANS

The history of the Hindu religion and the Aryan race in India is one with which all are familiar. How, back in the mist of ages, the great Aryan race overflowed, or migrated, from the press of others, from the crucible of the human race in Central Asia, down through the passes of Afghanistan to the plains of Hindustan. How, after many generations of war between the original inhabitants, the whole or almost the whole of India owned their sway. How, a few centuries before the Christian era, a prince of the blood, named Gautama or Buddha, founded the reformed religion or rather philosophy known as Buddhism, which spread for some centuries over the land and into Thibet and China, only to lapse back in India, in the course of time, to Hinduism and Brahmanism. The main story, too, of Aryan evolution, so far as it is revealed to us through the many centuries that have elapsed, is common history. The Aryan invaders gradually broke up into three great divisions, the Kshattryas or soldiers, the Brahmans or priestly class, and the Vaisiyas or traders, merchants, cultivators, and the like. The Kshattryas, from being the followers and no doubt the clansmen of the princely leaders, gradually called themselves Rajputs, or the sons of the rulers. The Brahmans soon increased far beyond the power of their priestly craft to bring them bread, and took to cultivation; and all three classes spread over the length and breadth of the land from Swat in the north to the hills on the fringe of the Himalaya, and to the plains of the south and the west.

Rajputs and Brahmans are still to be found all over India. The Rajputs in the Punjab have been

102ND KING EDWARD'S OWN
GRENADIERS
Bagri Jāt

101ST GRENADIERS
. NAIK
Punjabi Musalman

A.C.LOVETT

described already, where, bearing the brunt of the wave of Islamic invasion, after desperate struggles they were compelled to accept the Prophet, but remain Rajput, which is the name of a race and not of a religion.

We have seen that they are to be found as the leading races in the Dogra hills, and also in Nepal, and shall find them far west in the Deccan. In India, however, especially in so far as recruiting is concerned, the term Rajput is usually understood to mean Rajputs of Rajputana and Delhi, usually spoken of as Western Rajputs, and Rajputs of Oudh or Eastern Rajputs. The chief centre of Rajput power finally came to be in the country of the Ganges and its tributaries, with Kanouj and Adjudya as the capitals. The wave of Islamic invasion, however, broke these kingdoms, and drove the Rajput centres to the edge of the Bikanir desert. The Rajput principalities, then formed in what is now Rajputana, held their own to a greater or less extent against the Musalman, and were finally admitted into alliance with the Mogul Empire. The Rajputs of Oudh took to agriculture, and, their tribal power broken, for many generations served as mercenaries in the Muhammadan armies. The Rajputs of Rajputana maintained their feudal system and held aloof from actual agriculture. Both classes have preserved many of their military traits, those of Rajputana being famous as horse soldiers and those of Oudh as footmen. The Rajput and Brahman of Oudh unfortunately formed the bulk of the army that mutinied, and lost their place in the army from henceforth. The few old regiments still enlist them, and of late years the principle of class and clan regiments has been extended to them, and has been carefully followed with far-reaching results.

The Rajputs are traditionally divided into three great branches, the Lunar race, the Solar race, and the Agnicular or fire clans, the latter being supposed to be Scythic clans admitted into the Rajput circle for political reasons. In fact there is no doubt that many of the aboriginal chiefs were endowed with Rajput ancestors exactly on the same principle as the Heralds' College will find ancestors of renown for parvenu families. The three Rajput races are subdivided into thirty-six recognized and so-called royal clans, which are to be found in various parts of the country independent of religion.

The Brahman race is roughly divided into the Gaur and Dravira divisions, with many clans in

MAHRATTA INFANTRY

110TH MAHRATTA
LIGHT INFANTRY

116TH AND 114TH
MAHRATTAS

Konkani Mahrattas

103RD MAHRATTA
LIGHT INFANTRY

Subadar

Dekhani Mahrattas

each.   The former are generally found north and the latter south of the Vindhya Mountains.   The military qualities of the Rajputs of Rajputana are famous in history and saga.   The military services of the Rajputs and Brahmans of Oudh in the service of the Company in the pre-Mutiny days are equally famous.   Since the Mutiny, Rajput and Brahman corps have taken part in minor wars with distinction.

The 2nd, 4th, 7th, 8th, 11th, and 16th regiments of infantry are Rajputs of Oudh and Delhi; the 13th are Rajputs of Rajputana; while several other regiments, infantry and cavalry, enlist Rajput companies and squadrons both Eastern and Western Rajputs.   The 1st and 3rd Infantry enlist Brahmans only.   The pride of race in both Rajput and Brahman is intense; the former, especially the Rajput of Rajputana, being especially proud of the military history of his forebears.

THE JĀTS AND GŪJARS

The Jāt or Jăt race has already been referred to as one of the distinct races which are to be found under different religious banners in different parts of India.   As Jăts, those of them who form the bulk of the Sikh community have been already discussed as well as those who range under the crescent in the Punjab. The Jāts, Getae or Jātii of history, were a Scythian race who from Bactria have entered India by way of Southern Afghanistan and Scinde. Originally, it is believed, embracing Buddhism, they eventually joined the Brahmanical

10th Jāts.
A Jāt from Shekhawati.

revival, and some of their leaders were admitted to the status of Rajputs, and given Rajput genealogy as the Agnicular or "fire-born" race. The term Jāt is now universally accepted as referring to the Hindu Jat of Hindustan, and of Rajputana, Delhi, Rohtak, etc. Their history in the past has been that of a powerful warlike race, and in 1806 and 1826 they tried conclusions with the British, who twice besieged the Jāt fortress of Bhurtpore. The failure of Lord Lake after repeated and costly assaults, and the success of Lord Combermere, with a heavy battering-train, twenty years later, has been already referred to. It is not necessary to further describe them, except to say that they

are a fine sturdy race of cultivators, who till the
land while the Rajput looks on. They have been
long considered excellent horse soldiers, and of
late years class Jāt regiments have been carefully
recruited, while many regiments take Jāt companies
and squadrons. The 14th Cavalry (Murray's Jāt
Lancers) and the 6th and 10th Infantry are Jāt class
regiments, that is to say, Hindu Jats of Rajputana
and Hindustan. A reference to the Indian Army
List will show many other regiments with one or
more Jāt squadrons or companies. As with other
races, class enlistment has much improved their
military value. The Gūjars are also a people found
scattered in tribal communities far and wide over
India, and largely in the Punjab, in Kashmir, and
in Gujarat. They are also believed to be a
Scythian race known to history as the Yūchi, who
came into India slightly earlier than the Jāts.
They colonized both banks of the Indus from
Scinde to the Hazara district and spread to Gujarat,
Rajputana, and Delhi. In the Punjab they eventually adopted Islam, but had originally given up
their serpent worship for Hinduism. They have
of recent years been enlisted in certain class company regiments with success. They are largely
graziers in modern times, and to a great extent the

21

term Gūjar is applied to grazing people irrespective of their real race, just as Jăt is often applied to cultivator. They are a powerful, strong-featured race, best known to the European world from seeing those of them who feed their flocks on the Kashmir hills.

THE GURKHA

The Gurkha differs very considerably in many ways from the ordinary soldier of the Indian Army. He is like the Hazaras, whom he closely resembles but for a difference in height, also the inhabitant of an independent kingdom. The term Gurkha is now applied to the majority of the inhabitants of the kingdom of Nepal, but in strict ethnography belongs to those races which formed part of the old kingdom of Gurkha, a comparatively small part of Nepal. The inhabitants of Nepal consist of varying races. There are the Aryan and Rajput clans who spread to Nepal to fight for kingdom and barony in the days when the Aryan Rajput and Brahman races spread over Hindustan, and also the Mongolian races whom they supplanted or conquered. In the early days of the enlistment of Gurkhas, only the Mongolian tribes were taken, and those chiefly from Central Nepal. Their

RAJPUTANA INFANTRY

104TH WELLESLEY'S
RIFLES
Subadar-Major
Gujar of Gujarat

112TH INFANTRY
Subadar
Sayyid Musalman

109TH INFANTRY
Khanazadah
Rajputana Musalman

119TH INFANTRY
(The Multan Regiment)
Subadar
Gujar of Jaipur

123RD OUTRAM'S
RIFLES
Lance Naik
Ratore Rajput

122ND
RAJPUTANA
INFANTRY
Rawat

113TH
INFANTRY
Subadar-Major
Gujar of the Punjab

Hinduism was of the simplest, and, in fact, they were, and are, more Buddhist than Hindu. The principal tribes thus preferred were Magar and Gurung, of which there are many clans. As the demand for more men of Nepal increased, recruits were taken from the tribes of Eastern Nepal, known as Limbos and Rais, also belonging to tribes of Mongolian origin. Then the Nepalese of Aryan stock claiming Rajput origin have now been enlisted under the general name of "*Khas*" Gurkhas. They include what are known as the Khas tribes and the Thakurs. The principle of class and clan is here also strictly preserved and insisted on by the army authorities. The *Khas* Gurkhas go to one double-battalion regiment, the 9th, and Magars and Gurungs chiefly to the older regiments; Limbos and Rais to the newer corps. There are twenty battalions of Gurkhas in the service, as well as a few in the Guides and in the Kashmir Army. Their language is *Khas-khura*, which is somewhat similar to Hindi and is derived from the Sanskrit. Their enlistment dates from the days of the Nepal War, after which certain regiments took companies of them, and three local battalions were raised, viz. the Nasiri, the Sirmoor, and the Kumaon battalions. The Gurkha soldier is clothed as a rifleman and wears in moderate weather the old Kilmarnock cap, the universal army forage-cap of the Crimean days. The Magar and Gurung are short and powerful with a bullet-shaped Mongolian head. Limbos and Rais are taller, and the *Khas* approaches more to the Aryan height. The services of the Gurkha soldier generally, the intense camaraderie existing between himself and his officer, and between him and British troops who can forget their Saxon awkwardness, are well known. All are dressed in rifle green, while the 2nd, the old Sirmoor battalion, wears the same uniform as the 60th rifles, in memory of the day when they and the 60th held the exposed flank of the Ridge before Delhi, come rain and shine, against all comers from the first to the last of the famous siege. The 1st, 2nd, 3rd, 4th, 6th, and 9th Gurkhas are represented in the plates.

The Garhwali

The term Garhwali is a geographical one, being applied to the inhabitants of the country known as Garhwal, which hangs under the buttress of the Himalaya in the hills west of Nepal. The term in its military sense applies chiefly to the Khasia race, who are probably an aboriginal race absorbed

124TH DUCHESS OF CONNAUGHT'S OWN BALUCHISTAN
INFANTRY

"THE QUARTER GUARD"

LANCE NAIK

Khattak

Punjabi Musalman   *Hazara*

to some extent by custom and intermingling with
the Aryan Rajputs, and also certain purer Rajput
immigrants.   The Khasias demand, and are practically accorded, the status of Rajputs.   Garhwalis,
of the tribes and races referred to, were till comparatively recent years enlisted among the rank
and file of ordinary Gurkha regiments, in
which they gained considerable reputation as
soldiers.   The advance of ethnological knowledge
resulted in their being separated very properly
from Gurkhas, and gradually eliminated from
Gurkha battalions.   The 39th Bengal Infantry
was finally made a class battalion of Garhwalis, and
later a second battalion was added.   The Garhwali battalions are dressed in the well-known
Gurkha style of rifle uniform with Kilmarnock
cap.   Though not such soldiers by instinct as the
Gurkha, they are a courageous hill-race who make
active and obedient soldiers of considerable fighting
value.   They are a small people, but not so thick-
set and muscular as the Gurkha.

MAHRATTAS

The Deccan, or country south of the river
Narbudda, was among the last of the districts to
which the early Aryan conquerors penetrated.

The Vindhya Mountains and the forests of the Deccan long harboured fabulous aboriginal tribes who were overcome only after years of difficult advance and struggle. This country was known as Maharashtra or Mahratta, and its principal population was either the Aryans who had absorbed many of the conquered tribes, or the original tribes only tempered with a leaven of Brahmanism. The Mahrattas of to-day and of modern Indian history claim somewhat vaguely to be Rajputs, and no doubt one of those mysterious absorptions of a newly conquered race did take place, as in the case of Scythian-descended agnicular Rajputs. The Mahrattas, the inhabitants of modern Maharashtra, are the land-owning class of the Deccan proper, viz. the high plateau and the seaboard of western India. They first came into fame in the struggle made by Sivaji, a Mahratta of the Bhonsla family, to overthrow the power of the Muhammadans and restore a Hindu *Raj*. This rôle as the champions of Hinduism, to this day attaches to them to some extent. The history of the successes of Sivaji, the "mountain rat," in his struggles against the power of Islam, the growth of the Mahratta power and confederacy, their seizure of the person of the great Mogul, their defeat and slaughter by the

125TH NAPIER'S RIFLES

SUBADAR-MAJOR
Jāt of Jaipur

HAVILDAR
Punjabi Musalmans

Afghans, near the " Black Mango tree " at Paniput, are all famous in the history of India.   Well known also is the long series of wars which they insisted on waging against the British and their allies, to their undoing.   Several of the famous Mahratta chiefs of the old confederacy, however, still rule over feudatory States.   The Mahrattas are divided, in modern parlance, into Dekhani and Konkhani, the former from the upland plateau east of the great mountains of the Ghats, the latter the inhabitants of the seaboard.   They have long served with credit and distinction in the Bombay Army, and several class regiments exist, while several others have class companies and squadrons.   The Mahrattas have a reputation for great wiriness and endurance. The 103rd, 105th, 110th, 114th, 116th, and 117th Infantry are Mahratta regiments, each enlisting six companies of Mahrattas and only two com- panies of other classes.   Marathi is an offshoot from the Sanskrit, and is spoken by many people of the Deccan who are not Mahrattas.   Mahratta Brahmans are merely Brahmans who have dwelt for many centuries in Maharasthra, and have developed an extreme reputation for ability and intrigue.   In the days of the Mahratta Con- federacy they wielded much of the power in the various offices of state, a lost position to which no doubt they are keenly alive.

THE MUHAMMADANS OF INDIA

Reference has already been made in previous chapters, and in the foregoing notes on various races, to the different classes of Muhammadans within India, both those who have been converted to Islam from among the races of India, such as the Muhammadan Rajputs, and those who have entered India and settled there in the train of the various Muhammadan conquerors. The Musalman races of the Punjab have been described at length. Throughout India are to be found those who claim foreign descent and who are putatively either Pathan, Mogul, Sheikh, or Saiyid. Pathan and Mogul are recognizable as descendants of conquering races; Saiyids or elders are properly the descendants of Fatima, daughter of the Prophet; while Sheikhs are members of the Koreish tribe to which the Prophet belonged. Converts of low caste, however, have constantly claimed to belong to one of these races. Muhammadans who claim to be of these races are therefore enlisted more if they come of land-owning and cultivating stock than for any purely race claim, while, of course, the

127TH QUEEN MARY'S OWN BALUCH
LIGHT INFANTRY

Brahni   *Baluch from*
            Dera Ghazi Khan   *Punjabi Musalman*

SUBADAR-MAJOR
Baluch of Khelat

Muhammadan Rajput tribes, such as the Rangars from the neighbourhood of Delhi, are freely enlisted. They are all taken into class companies and squadrons, more in accordance with the province they reside in than with racial distinction, viz. as "Muhammadans of Rajputana," etc. The descendants of Pathan and Mogul settlers, who are clearly recognizable as such, make splendid cavalry soldiers, and in the past have been most distinguished in the irregular cavalry. The 5th Light Infantry and the 17th and 18th Infantry are class regiments of Musalmans of the Eastern Punjab and Hindustan, and the 1st Skinner's Horse is entirely composed of Muhammadans of the Eastern Punjab, Delhi, and Hindustan, many of Rajput descent, while all the Indian cavalry regiments from 1 to 8 have one or more squadrons of this class.

THE MILITARY RACES OF THE CARNATIC

Constant references have been made in the preceding chapters to the services of the Coast Army—the Army of the Madras Presidency—and the various recruiting experiments that have been resorted to, to obtain satisfactory recruits fit for modern conditions of war. Most of the experi-

22

ments with special races, such as men of the Coorg
hills and that strange Arab-descended race the
Moplahs, have been abandoned.   The recasting
of the three armies into one Line enabled the
authorities to proceed with the question purely on
its merits as part of one general policy.   It was
possible to resist the feelings and sentiment of the
older officers of the Madras Army, who had that
natural attachment of the British officer for the
classes and men they have so long led, and definitely
decide on the number of regiments to be recruited
from the Madras Presidency.   The Madras Army
had for some years been divided into two portions
in the minds of the authorities, viz. in one the
sapper and miner and pioneer corps, and the other
the ordinary Tamil and Madrasi Musalman corps.

The two former classes of corps had long enlisted
men of the artizan classes ready to go anywhere,
eat anything, and turn their hands to anything.
They had been famous for useful semi-military
service in many parts, and were eminently desirable.
The actual number of Line battalions was to be
restricted to eight, and these, with the three pioneer
corps and the corps of sappers and miners, with
about half a squadron in each of the three Light
Cavalry regiments, were alone to enlist men of

2ND KING EDWARD'S OWN GURKHA RIFLES
(THE SIRMOOR RIFLES)

SUBADAR-MAJOR

Gurung Gurkha

King Edward's last Indian Orderly Officer

सु मे सन्तवीर उ.रं श/२ गोर्खा

Madras. The reduction of the demand on recruiting centres has naturally enabled corps to raise their physical and mental standard for recruits.

The military races of Madras consist of the Tamils and the Muhammadans. The Tamils and other Hindus are of the Dravidian races who were only affected by the Aryan invasion many centuries after the rest of India. Brahman and Rajput blood and influence have to some extent affected them as it did all the original races that the Aryans met, but only to a small extent. The Tamils are divided into many classes and castes. One large caste, the Telinga or Telegus, are now no longer enlisted, though at one time serving in considerable numbers. An outcaste race, the Parraiyans or Pariahs, have long been enlisted, especially in the pioneers and sappers, and to a small extent in all corps, and have many useful qualities.

The Muhammadans consist, as in other parts of India, of the converted races and those who claim foreign descent, Pathan, Mogul, Sheikh, or Saiyid. To these, as elsewhere, converts have always tried to claim affinity. The Muhammadans who enlist in the cavalry are probably nearer to the Pathan than anything else, coming as a rule from Vellore, round which most of the descendants of Hyder

Ali's following are to be found. Hyder Ali himself was of the foreign-adventurer breed.

The soldiers of Madras have many inherent
military qualities. They shoot well, drill well, and
stand well under arms, and so far as this part of
their professional requirement goes, foreign critics
have been known to say that it was not till they
got to Madras that they saw regular native soldiers.
The eight Carnatic battalions of the Line enlist
4 companies Muhammadans, 2 companies Tamils,
2 companies Pariahs.

4TH GURKHA RIFLES
Magar and Gurung Gurkhas
'' A REAR-GUARD ACTION ''

CHAPTER VI

THE INDIAN ARMY IN 1911

In Chapter IV. the reconstruction after the great
Mutiny was traced, with the gradual evolution of
the carefully calculated modern system of enlistment, and in Chapter V. the various military castes
and clans as recognized to-day. When Lord
Kitchener came to India, the whole army stood in
four subordinate armies, yclept commands, under
the one Commander-in-Chief. The regiments of
the three presidential armies still retained their old
numbers, with the resulting multiplication of
similarly numbered units already described. The
Empire had just been through a war on a large
scale. Russia and Japan were at war, and war and
the dangers of unpractical or complicated organization, or the lack of it, were uppermost in everyone's minds. Armies must either be organized for
the immediate business of war or must be abolished.

So in the many changes that this spirit was working in the Empire, there was enough driving force to overcome the valuable though at times dangerous attachment to old names and old principles.

The fiat went forth that the old armies were to be renumbered on one roster, and that the Bengal Army, though not the oldest, should stand first on the roster, followed by the Punjab Frontier Force, then the old Coast Army of Madras, then the Hyderabad Contingent, and lastly, the famous faithful old Army of Bombay. To minimize the blow, and to bear testimony to the fact that the authorities were not hopelessly blind to the value of military sentiment, the opportunity was taken to give to corps titles connecting them with the officers who had raised them, or with their early history, or some suitable title of a similar nature.

The regiments of the Bengal Army therefore headed the Line, both Cavalry and Infantry. To enable corps to keep their own digits, that is to say, corps that were originally one to still have the figure one among their number, each army began its numbering as the first of a series. Thus the numbering of the Bengal Army and the Frontier Force stopped at 59. The number 60 was left

6TH GURKHA RIFLES

vacant, and the old 1st Madras Infantry became the 61st, and the old 1st Bombay Grenadiers became the 101st Grenadiers. Those numbers that had been vacant owing to the disbanding of corps after the Afghan wars were left vacant so as not to disturb the digit of those corps following it. Occasion, however, was taken to bring into the vacant numbers one or two corps that had been recently raised. The Frontier Force was partly accounted for in a similar way, the numbers 49 and 50 being left vacant, and the 1st Sikhs became the 51st Sikhs (Frontier Force). The Punjab Infantry of the Frontier Force and the Hyderabad regiments had to lose even this much trace of their older numbers, but the Frontier Force Cavalry were enabled to take up the numbers from 21 onwards.

Shortly after this the 9th Bengal Infantry (Khas Gurkhas) were removed from the general Line, and put into the separate Gurkha Line, as the 9th Gurkhas, while the 42nd, 43rd, and 44th Light Infantry Gurkhas who had been localized in Assam were also brought into the Gurkha numbering, and their place in the Line taken by certain special irregular battalions that had existed as local corps in Central India. The old 10th Madras

Infantry, changed in 1890 to a Gurkha battalion, finally became the 10th Gurkhas.

The result of this renumbering was as follows :—

THE CAVALRY

First the Cavalry of the Line received their present numbering from 1 to 39, without break, except that the number of the old 4th Punjab Cavalry of the Frontier Force, reduced after the Afghan War, has been left vacant and there is no 24. The two regiments of the Central India Horse, famous relic of the numerous irregular horse that the suppression of the Mutiny called forth in Central India, or composed of loyal remnants, received the numbers 38 and 39. These with the Guides Cavalry, an independent squadron in the Deoli and Erinpura Irregular corps, the Aden troop, and the three Bodyguard corps form the regular cavalry of India. The 26th, 27th, and 28th are Light Cavalry, and are non-Silladar. They are, that is to say, troopers, mounted on Government horses as are the British Cavalry. They are the only survivals of the Light Cavalry of the pre-Mutiny days, and still wear the French grey and silver of the older times. Only three of the cavalry regiments are " class " corps, viz. the 1st Skinner's Horse, composed entirely of Muhammadans of Hindustan and the Southern Punjab; the 14th Murray's Jāt Lancers, entirely of Jāts; and the 15th Cureton's Multanis, entirely of Multani Pathans and kindred neighbouring races. The remainder of the regiments consist of class squadrons, of which the principal divisions are Sikhs, Dogras, Pathans, Punjabi, Hindustani, or Dekhani Muhammadans, Jats, and Rajputs. The various plates of the men of these regiments depict one or other of these classes, and clearly show the distinctive features and methods of wearing the lungi (head-dress) of each race. The cavalry soldier generally comes from the more wealthy cultivating and land-owning members of the classes described.

17th Infantry (The Loyal Regiment).
A Rajput from Hissar.

Of the exploits of the various regiments it is impossible to speak here; suffice it to say that they are numerous and varied, but that the fact that many of the corps date from the Mutiny accounts

for the shorter tally of fame of some. The
Indian Army List details the class composition,
the previous history, the uniform, and the battle
honours of each corps. A few may perhaps be
referred to as typical. The 1st of the post-Mutiny
Line, formerly the old 1st Irregulars, was raised by
the famous half-breed James Skinner, long affectionately known to his friends in the army as " Old
Sekunder."   It practically came over to the British
in 1803 from the remnant of the De Boigne-trained
Mahratta Army.   After much service in the pacification of India in the early days, it marched to
Kandahar in the First Afghan War, having previously taken part in the storming and capture
of Bhurtpore.   Its later services have been in the
last Afghan War, and the relief of Pekin in 1900.
The 2nd Gardner's Horse has a history nearly as
old, having been raised in 1809, and later numbered
as the 2nd Irregulars ; while the 3rd are also
Skinner's Horse, having been the second of two
Risalahs raised by Colonel James Skinner.   The
3rd took part also in the First Afghan War, while
the 2nd served in the First Burmese War and both
the Sikh wars.   The 1st is noted for its uniform of
bright canary, the fancy of " Old Sekunder."   In the
Skinner Church at Delhi is a stone on which is

9TH GURKHA RIFLES

A Khas Gurkha

टेकाका ठाकरे ब्रो

recorded the name of all the commandants of the corps. The Mutiny record of most of the corps is more than distinguished. Of late years, the 11th in Swat in 1897, and the 13th led by Atkinson, in a timely charge over extremely bad ground at a critical moment at Shabkadr, have given evidence of the dash that is inherent in this branch of the Service. The Guides perhaps have found opportunity to enhance their own and the Sirkar's fame, more than has been vouchsafed to other corps. No opportunity was ever wasted, from the days of the staunch old native officer who knew no more drill than the principle of the attack contained in " Draaw swaards and Hulla," to the accomplished and equally dashing modern trooper. Their charge at Fattehabad, when another Battye fulfilled his weird, the hopeless, dogged defence of the Residency at Kabul, in the last Afghan War, the repeated charges in Swat in '97, were all opportunities for service rendered and honour gained that were seized to the full. The cavalry of the Frontier Force, since their formation, have spent a life of raid and counter-raid on the border : an eye for an eye and a tooth for a tooth, which is always border law. Among many incidents might be recalled the charge of the 25th Cavalry, Vousden leading, at the King's Garden near Sherpore, in the Afghan War. When we come to the three Light Cavalry regiments, the 26th, 27th, and 28th, we touch the very origin of Indian military history so far as the British are concerned, from Sholinghur and the Carnatic wars to Seringapatam and Mahidpore, and then on through the last century. Two out of the cavalry regiments of the old Hyderabad Contingent served in the burning Central India Campaign. The 31st to the 37th, the cavalry of the Bombay Army, have a long record, of which perhaps the 33rd charging the Persian squares at Kooshab in 1857, and the 34th, when newly raised, sharing in the famous stand against the Peshwa's hordes at Corygaum, are the most notable.

THE INDIAN ARTILLERY

The Indian artillery of to-day consists of twelve mountain batteries numbered from 21 to 32. The lower numbers are borne by the British mountain batteries, of which there are eight, with vacant numbers to spare for any possible increase. The first four Indian batteries are the old light field batteries and mountain trains of the Frontier Force; 25 and 26 are of older origin, being the only relic of the native artillery of the Company's army,

Hon. Major-General
H.H. MAHARAJA SIR PRATAP SINGH BAHADUR
G.C.S.I., K.C.B.

Hon. Aide-de-Camp to His Majesty
Commandant Imperial Cadet Corps

formerly numbers 1 and 2 companies of Bombay
Golandaz.   The remainder are of more recent
origin, 27 and 28 having been raised at the time of
the Third Burmese War, with the original numbering of 1 and 2 Bengal mountain batteries.   All the
Indian mountain batteries consist of Punjabis,
half Muhammadan and half Hindu, the latter
being almost entirely Sikhs.   The gunners are
specially selected for their height and strength,
with a view to the rapid assembling and dis-
mantling of the guns from off and on to the backs
of the powerful mules that carry them.   Mountain
artillery is practically a special arm peculiar to
India so far as our army is concerned, and has long
been famous for its mountaineering capacity.
The services of this branch of the artillery are
more than notable.   The 21st, 22nd, and 24th
batteries in the last Afghan War, the 22nd in the
Kurram and on the Samana, the 25th at Maizar
in Waziristan, and the 28th at the Malakand and
in Bajour in the '97-'98 frontier campaigns, gained
more than average distinction.   On the frontier
one more artillery corps exists, formerly known as
the Punjab Garrison Battery, and familiarly the
" Blokes " (owing to its being formed of veterans
from the mountain batteries past their prime on

the hillside), now the Frontier Garrison Artillery. Their name describes their rôle. A plate shows the mountaineer gunner.

In addition to these mountain batteries, reference must be made to the Indian soldiers serving as a portion of the European batteries of artillery. The horse and field batteries have a few native drivers, while the ammunition columns, which are fully horsed in India, have native drivers and native gunners as waggon-men. The British mountain batteries have British gunners and all native drivers. The heavy batteries similarly have British gunners and native drivers. These men are enlisted from the usual fighting classes of the Punjab. A few come from Hindustan. The drivers of the mountain batteries have long been established, and have acquired a high reputation. Those in the heavy batteries and ammunition columns are a comparatively new experiment. Driving powerful " Waler " horses is quite different work from leading mules, which is what mountain artillery driving consists of, but the men promise to be as good at the one as the other. It is in the artillery alone that British and Indian personnel serve together, and the two races do succeed in striking a happy *modus vivendi*. In the mountain batteries many of the drivers are old soldiers with several campaigns to their credit.   Atkins is wont to borrow their bemedalled tunics to be photographed in, which is a fair token of camaraderie.

THE ENGINEERS

The rank and file of the Royal Engineers do not come to India save for a few non-commissioned officers attached to sapper companies.   The engineer services are, therefore, all Indian, so far as the men are concerned, and consist of several consecutively numbered companies grouped into three corps, which corps are the lawful successors without break of the three famous engineer corps of the three Presidencies.

62nd Punjabis, Subadar.
A Dhund from Rawal Pindi.

The 1st Prince of Wales' Own Sappers and Miners are the old Bengal Sappers and Miners, and consist of six service companies and various attached special sections.   They enlist Sikhs, Pathans, Punjabi Muhammadans, and a few Hindustanis of various classes. Their battle honours include every campaign of any importance since the storming of Bhurtpore. The 2nd Queen's Own Sappers and Miners are the old Madras Sappers and Miners, with headquarters at Bangalore, and consist also of six service companies, with one company localized in Burma and enlisting Burmese. The remainder enlist Madrasis. Several special sections are also attached to this corps. Their war record is even more complete than that of the 1st, and commences from a far earlier date. The 3rd Sappers and Miners are the old Bombay Sappers and Miners, consisting of six service companies and a fortress company with certain special sections. The class composition of the companies is very varied, and Sikhs, Mahrattas, Rajputs, and Muhammadans are all drawn on. Their record also is varied and distinguished, commencing from the fight at Beni-Boo-Ali in 1823 on the shores of the Persian Gulf.

The British officers of the Sapper Corps are, of course, Royal Engineers, with a few N.C.O.'s from the corps for special duties.

Four divisional signal companies have been added recently to the army with the object of

managing all the signal services of a division (one company per division) in the field. These companies have also been formed as engineer units, and their personnel, though drawn from the army at large, are classed and rated for the time being as Sappers.

THE INFANTRY

The infantry, as has been explained, is numbered in two separate lines — the ordinary Line and the Gurkha Line. The Line itself consists of battalions numbered from 1 to 130, of which 14 numbers are vacant, and one, the 39th Garhwal Rifles, is a double-battalion corps. That is to say, that 117 battalions remain, and the infantry of the Guides. In the Gurkha Line there are ten two-battalion regiments, numbered 1 to 10; thus the total number of battalions of Indian Infantry is 138.

The constitution of them under the careful system of class recruiting has now resulted as follows :—

> 41 class-company Punjabi battalions, in which the classes are some variation of Muhammadan, Sikh, Pathan, or Dogra.
> 9 Sikh battalions, of which three enlist Mazbi Sikhs.

24

3 Dogra battalions.

2 Brahman class battalions.

7 battalions of Hindu Rajputs from outside the Punjab.

2 Jat (Hindu) battalions.

28 class-company battalions, of which the classes are not exclusively from the Punjab.

6 purely Muhammadan battalions, of which three are from outside the Punjab, and three exclusively from the Punjab and the transfrontier.

6 Mahratta battalions, exclusively Mahrattas save for two companies of Dekhani Muhammadans each.

1 battalion of Afghan Hazaras.

1 two-battalion regiment of Garhwalis.

11 battalions recruited from the classes of the Carnatic.

20 battalions of Gurkhas.

Of these battalions, 12 are pioneers with special training in road and rail making and rough engineering work, and equipped to that end, but also trained as infantry. India alone of the British Empire has pioneer corps, since India alone expects campaigns by way of goat-tracks and mountain watercourses.

The foregoing describes the fighting troops of the Indian Army, which, with the British troops forming part of the garrison, are combined into formations of the Imperial war organization, being grouped by brigades into divisions. The war organization of the Empire is by strong three-brigade divisions with brigades of mounted troops, and the Empire has practically copied India in discarding thoughts of army corps, and preferring to find the force required by the grouping of strong divisions. This Indian Army of British and Indian regiments and batteries is able to furnish nine war divisions and several cavalry brigades, after furnishing the internal garrisons for the support of peace and order and the civil power. But since an army crawls on its belly, and masses of battalions and regiments and batteries do not make an army, or even divisions of it, administrative troops are an essential component. A quarter column of bakers' carts does not convey the pomp of war, though a file of ambulances may suggest the pity of it, yet these are the services that make men with muskets into an army, and should not be forgotten in the tally for their more outwardly effective comrades.

The administrative troops of India are principally the Indian Subordinate Medical Service, the Army Hospital Corps, the Army Bearer Corps, and the Supply and Transport Corps. None of these are in themselves war formations. That is to say, they do not exist, with certain exceptions as regards Transport Corps, as units that take the field in the same formation as they stand in peace time, as do

the fighting troops of an army. They exist as
corps which form, as it were, a pool from which
war units are mobilized. The Army Bearer Corps,
for instance, supplies the bearers for regimental
ambulance carriage and also for the field ambulances. The Supply and Transport Corps mobilizes
the various supply units that accompany a force in
the field. The men of the bearer corps are enlisted
from that class, or, rather, those classes who are
hereditary bearers by caste and practice. India for
ever has been a land without roads, as we know the
term, and even when trunk roads and railways
traverse it, the majority of the villages are off the
road along tracks. Brides and bridegrooms, who
form the pageant of the East, and purdah ladies,
and corpulent folk in general, have ever been carried.
Therefore has a caste of hereditary carriers existed
from time immemorial. Special thews and sinews
to lift the weight and bear its pressure have
developed, and from these classes alone do good
bearers come. The change of life that is so rapidly
coming over the East, as a result of the energy and
movement of the West, is decreasing the men who
are, by profession, bearers, especially in Oudh,
whence come the Hindu Kahars, who are the best.
There is a question connected with bearers which

ALWAR LANCERS

COMMANDANT
Chohan Rajput

illustrates one of the difficulties of organization in India.   The rules of caste being specially strict where food and drink are concerned, the wounded Hindu will starve or die rather than take food or water from an unfit man.   The Kahar of Oudh, however, is an hereditary servant, and from him almost all Hindu soldiers will take food and water. Efficient bearer corps should, therefore, contain this class, for, if chance bearers are entertained in war-time, apart from their physical incapacity to carry the dandies, fighting men have to be taken from the ranks to tend Hindu soldiers in hospital.   The devotion of good bearers to the wounded they carry has often been borne testimony to.

The Transport Corps are of several kinds, and these do exist to some extent as permanent war formations, but many corps, of course, are mobilized from reserve and registered animals.   The majority of the transport personnel comes from the Punjab, either from smaller-sized men of the classes enlisted in the regiments, or from the lesser clans and castes.   Mules and camels being more bred and used in the Punjab than elsewhere, it is but natural to enlist from the classes used to them. There are two varieties of camel corps which are interesting.   They are the Silladar Corps and the

Grantee Corps.   Silladar Camel Corps are raised somewhat on the same principle as the silladar cavalry.   Camel-owners are paid a sum down to serve with their own camels.   The troops of the camel corps have two rates of pay, an employed and an unemployed rate.   They are called up by troops for work at times during the year, and at other times are doing their own work at their homes on unemployed pay.   Grantee Camel Corps are furnished by men who have received grants of land on the new canal lands in the Punjab on condition of producing certain camels whenever required.   They are embodied for a short period each year.   The Camel Corps men come from the Muhammadan tribes—Baluch, Jat, etc.—of the sand and karoo-like plains between the Ravi, the Jhelum, the Chenab, and the Indus.   The march of irrigation is, however, driving the camel from off the land.   The camel-owners are wild, picturesque, long-haired rogues, almost as weird as their camels.

JODHPUR SARDAR RISALA

Ratore Rajput

CHAPTER VII

THE ARMIES OF THE NATIVE STATES

IT is often forgotten that the portion of British India that is not under direct rule is almost as large as the portion that is. The Indian feudatory chiefs are many, and the extent of their territories is in some cases very considerable. The nature of their tenure varies in almost every case, in accordance with treaties and sanads granted or entered on during the course of the rise of our power; it has ever been our policy to adhere rigidly to our treaty obligations. Circumstances at times have caused us to go back on them, but in every case those circumstances seemed at the time to have been forced on us. Native States that occupied themselves with their own affairs, and did not engage in the numerous intrigues and coalitions to expel the foreigner, are still our trusted allies, as favoured now and unmolested as when we first

entered into relations with them, little dreaming of
the extent to which our rule would extend. The
Nizam of Hyderabad is a case in point. It is more
than a century ago since the Nizam was guaranteed
protection from the Mahrattas and other encroach-
ing neighbours, and compelled to get rid of his French
allies as the price of protection. Since those days
the relations between his State and the sovereign
power have remained practically unchanged.

At the end of the 18th century the independent
States, as well as the Feudatory States, had large
armies organized to some extent on European lines.
French, English, Italian, and American officers—
some adventurers, others deputed officers—were
training and commanding these State armies. They
often led the armies of their respective masters
into action against each other. Scindia's and the
Nizam's services were organized on lines resembling
our own. De Boigne, the Savoyard, in the service
of Scindia, Maharaja of Gwalior State, had a
regular establishment and cadet service like the
Company's; the Nizam's service was similarly
organized. Later Ranjit Singh, the Maharaja
of the Punjab, had a similar service, while Golab
Singh of Jammu and Kashmir organized many
corps on the same lines.

BIKANER GANGA RISALA

Ratore Rajput

The armies of these States were entirely separate from the various contingents which were officered by officers of the Company's Army, and were only a portion of the State forces in so far as the State concerned paid for them, or assigned districts to the British to pay for them. To this day the State armies preserve some trace of the days when their armies were organized on European lines to enable them to oppose, if necessary, the irresistible force of the trained British sepoy. They even preserve the dress of the early Victorian period.

The large armies that some of the States maintained, were at one time a source of anxiety to the supreme government, as much for the unnecessary drain on the resources of the States as for their possible danger in the event of disturbance, for their discipline was never as a rule in a satisfactory state. They, however, represented the outward and visible sign of power and dominion to the rulers, and as such were naturally dear to them. In the Mutiny some of the troops of the native States were able to render excellent service, especially those of the Cis Sutlej States, Jind and Patiala and Nabha, in keeping the road open from the Punjab to Delhi. In Rajputana, too, their services were freely given.

Now and again since the Mutiny, if not before, discussion had taken place as to what was a fair contribution, if any, of native States towards the expense of the protection under which they flourished.   It is not a century and a half since the

Sadul Light Infantry.   Havildar.
A Rahtor Rajput of Bikaner.

great invasions from the north had ceased to flow across the Indus to loot and to slay.   To the smaller States the Mahratta pretensions and power were always a menace and a nightmare, and to the larger the terror of the north was never absent. It had been argued that they owed some assistance to the government that gave them peace, and, in the case of many, a protection from outside that they had never known before. In the slow progress of evolution that was going on, it was well to let things develop by themselves. The dangers of a large war, however, so strongly brought home to all in India after the Penjdeh incident, impressed on the rulers of the States how necessary it was that they should stand in with the supreme government in some of the burden of military preparation. 1885 saw half the army in India on the move to the Bolan, and immense sums were spent in preparing for a war that seemed inevitable. The Nizam of Hyderabad offered a large sum from his revenues to Government in aid of the war chest. His patriotic and spontaneous example was promptly followed by others. Government, however, did not feel that a contribution to the war chest was so desirable as an entry into some share of empire by the maintenance of a portion of the troops required for defence. From, therefore, the Penjdeh incident and the patriotic offers of the Feudatory States, sprang what is now known as the Imperial Service Troops. Government suggested that, in lieu of money offers, some portion of the troops in each State should be trained and improved so as to be fit to take their place in the field alongside the Indian Line. The offer was very eagerly accepted, and there had already from time to time been proposals put forward for organizing some of the State troops.

The result of this movement has been that almost every State of any size has contributed a force. These troops are in the same relation to their rulers as the older and less-organized corps from which they were formed. The Government offered up-to-date arms, and lent officers to train the troops. From the first beginnings has risen a force of many thousand men. The service of training and inspecting has been for many years thoroughly organized. An officer was appointed Inspector-General of Imperial Service Troops, with a staff of inspecting officers and assistant inspecting officers, who are in no way the servants of the States. They are deputed to assist in the training of the troops, to advise the Durbars (the official terms for the State governments) on military matters connected with the troops, and to see that they generally do attain that standard of efficiency that will justify the authorities in accepting them as part of the recognized contingent. The States are grouped into circles for this purpose, and an inspecting officer with assistants presides over each, and visits each State in turn.

MYSORE TRANSPORT CORPS
Musalman

MYSORE LANCERS
Madrasi Musalman

The result of this experiment has been a happy one. In addition to providing a satisfactory career for the feudal gentry of the States, it has brought the best class of sirdar into touch with the best class of British officer. The States are lavish in their offer of troops for service whenever there is a war or threat of war. The Imperial Service Troops have been engaged in many operations since 1895. The Relief of Chitral, Tirah, the campaign across the Swat river, the Mohmand Expedition, Somaliland, China, have all been shared with State troops. In the South African War, since their troops could not share, horses and equipment in charge of State personnel were freely sent.

The State of Kashmir enjoys a peculiar position in that it not only marches with the outer boundary, but with, or practically with, a part of the Russian frontier, which is an entirely different condition from that obtaining in other States. Her troops therefore garrison her own frontier districts, and have constantly been engaged with tribes on her border, and have seen a very considerable amount of frontier service. The defence of Chitral was largely carried out by the Kashmir troops; while in the Hunza Nagar campaign they bore a considerable share in the earliest days of their

organization on modern lines.   Kashmir alone has
Imperial Service Artillery, two mountain batteries
being organized principally for the defence of the
Gilgit frontier.   One, however, took part in the
Tirah Expedition of 1897-98.

The upkeep of highly trained and well-equipped
troops costs more than the older units they replaced,
which for fifty years had purely existed for guard
and ceremonial purposes.   The various States,
therefore, while retaining what are styled their
regular troops, have in most cases considerably
reduced their numbers to meet the extra cost of
the Imperial Service Corps.

It will be remembered how, in the days of the
Mutiny, several rulers, who staunchly maintained
the British authority in every way in their power,
were themselves betrayed by the action either of
their contingents or of their other troops.   The
contingents, it should be remembered, were bodies
of troops maintained by treaty for their own protection, officered by British officers.   In most
parts of India these contingents were not recruited
from the population of the State whose troops they
titularly were.   They were not actuated by
personal loyalty to their chief, but were largely
drawn from what had become so universal a

recruiting - ground, viz. Oudh and Behar. They followed the example of the Bengal Army, and not of their ruler. The leading case is that of the famous Gwalior Contingent as well as the other troops of Scindia. The Gwalior Contingent was one of the *élite* forces in India. The loyalty of Scindia was beyond dispute and his actions were unequivocal, but his mercenary troops and the contingent followed the prevailing wind. It has therefore been decreed that the Imperial Service Troops shall be subjects of the ruler they serve, so that they may be expected to follow his lead and that of no one else. Certain exceptions are allowed to this rule, notably in Kashmir, where it has been the custom, far older than our days, for Gurkhas to serve in considerable numbers in that State. An Imperial Service and also a regular battalion in Kashmir enlist a large number of the men of Nepal.

In many States the rulers themselves command their own corps, or appoint their sons and relatives to do so, so that these troops are Royal Troops in the old - fashioned sense of the word, and the feudal spirit and system does really exist. A plate shows the Maharaja of Bikaner, a Rajput of famous race, as the Colonel-in-Chief of one of his own Imperial Service Corps. It is no uncommon thing to see the chiefs lead their troops in review past some high authority, with a dash that they are equally prepared to maintain in the field.

The corps of a State army bear names reminiscent of the names in the days of the Mogul forces. The regiment of the sun, the battalion of victory, the lightning battery are common terms. The regular forces, as distinct from the Imperial Service, have the arms and equipment and often the clothing of the early Victorian or Georgian period, and at a review in some State capital one is able to step back a couple of generations. Side by side with the troops of an old régime, are the highly trained, modern - armed troops of the Imperial Service, which stand on parade as stand the troops of the Indian Army. The uniforms, especially the full dress, are more elaborate in many cases than our own, and the Imperial Service cavalry are often superbly dressed, especially the officers. For manœuvre and service the dress is of course the regulation khaki and plain accoutrements of India. It has taken years to inculcate the principle in all armies, that however you may dress your troops in glory for gala occasions, the war dress must be as simple and easy as possible ; and yet nothing betrays more clearly the strength of purpose behind

BHARATPUR INFANTRY

The Commandant

Jāt

R. C. LOVETT.

a disciplined army than the mass of loosely clad active men in a drab or khaki dust-proof dress.

It will be convenient to refer to the troops of each State in the circles to which they are arranged for the convenience of inspection and expert advice, at the hands of the Government of India, as these circles are grouped for geographical reasons.

The status of these States, however, should be first explained. Their relations to the Army and to the Government are practically those of the troops of allies. The States offer to maintain troops on our model, we promise to assist, and then in times of stress and strain the States place them at His Majesty's disposal. The troops are subject to the military law of the States both in peace and war, which is assimilated to the Indian Articles of War (recently remodelled into the Indian Army Act). The disciplinary Acts of the States, however, enact in most cases that the commander of the British force in the field, with which they are acting, shall be the higher legal authority referred to for the various purposes of the Acts. The situation is therefore clear and understandable.

The State maintaining the largest contingent is Jammu and Kashmir, which has one squadron, two mountain batteries, and three battalions of infantry.

26

The frontier conditions peculiar to this State demand a considerable force, and in the days when Chitral and Hunza were more prominent factors, the number of battalions was six. Reference has been already made to the peculiarity of this State, for historical reasons, enlisting aliens, viz. Gurkhas. Next to Kashmir, or perhaps equal to it, is Gwalior. It has three regiments of lancers and two battalions of infantry, with a strong transport train of 300 carts. The latter corps has often taken part in frontier expeditions. The Maharaja Scindia being himself an enthusiastic and well-read soldier, this force benefits by a considerable share of his personal attention. Outside these two States it will be simpler to refer to the States according to the circles already referred to. In the Punjab we have Patiala with one

9th Bhopal Infantry. Subadar-Major.
A Suni Musalman.

regiment of cavalry and two of infantry, of whom the first took part in the frontier campaign of

1897 ; Nabha, Kapurthala, and Jind, the other Sikh States, each furnish a battalion of infantry ; while Bahawalpore furnishes a camel transport corps of 966 camels, properly disciplined, with its own mounted escort as a military camel corps. The action of the Sikh States, in keeping open the road to Delhi in 1857, by which the Punjab was able to send down its men and material unmolested, is a matter of history.   In the Multan rising in 1848, it was the Daudputras, the troops of Bahawalpore, who first came up to assist Herbert Edwardes, alone with his levies and doubtful Durbar troops from the Derajat.   Sirmoor, Malerkotla, and Faridkot each maintain a company of sappers and miners, a form of contingent as specially useful as the transport corps.   Tehri, a State in the hills of Garhwal, also maintains a company of sappers.   Alwar maintains a regiment of lancers and a battalion of infantry.   Bharatpur (the Bhurtpore of earlier history) has a battalion and a transport corps.   Rajputana and the Rajput States are naturally the centre of loyal service and soldierly instinct.   Bikaner has a battalion and a camel corps 500 strong, which served both in China and Somaliland.   Jodhpore has two lancer corps, the famous Sardar Rissalah, with the bluest blood in

Rajputana in its ranks. Jaipore has a double-strength transport corps of 550 carts. Rampore maintains two squadrons of lancers; Junagarh and Navanagaar and Udaipore each maintain a squadron of lancers. The Muhammadan State of Bhopal has a lancer regiment, Bhavanagar has two Rajput squadrons, and Indore a transport corps with an escort squadron. Down in the Deccan and farther south, the movement still holds good. The ancient State, and our ancient ally Hyderabad, has two regiments of cavalry, and Mysore a cavalry regiment and a transport corps.

The total then of this force voluntarily organized by the more important States as the best way of contributing their share to the burden of empire is as follows: Cavalry, ten regiments of four squadrons each, and one of three squadrons, with eight squadrons in corps of lesser strength than three squadrons. Infantry, six eight-company battalions and six six-company battalions; then two mountain batteries, four companies of sappers, five mule or pony cart transport corps aggregating 1650 army carts, two camel transport corps aggregating 1200 camels, a fighting camel corps of 500 rifles, and three transport escorts for the protection of transport corps provided by the State. This

IMPERIAL SERVICE TROOPS

PATIALA RAJINDRA LANCERS — *Jāt Sikh*

KASHMIR MOUNTAIN BATTERY — *Dogra (Hindu)*

KAPURTHALA INFANTRY ⎫
JIND INFANTRY ⎬ *Jāt Sikhs*
NABHA INFANTRY ⎭

INDORE TRANSPORT CORPS — Commandant *Dekhani Musalman*

BAHAWALPUR MOUNTED RIFLES AND CAMEL TRANSPORT

1ST KASHMIR INFANTRY — Commandant *Dogra (Hindu)*

SIRMOOR SAPPERS — *Brahman*

RAMPUR LANCERS — *Rohilla*

1ST HYDERABAD LANCERS — *Mogul Musalman*

2ND GWALIOR LANCERS — *Mahratta*

ALWAR INFANTRY — *Shekhawati Musalman*

BHARATPUR INFANTRY — *Jāt*

JAIPUR TRANSPORT CORPS — Commandant *Rajput*

force means a very considerable accession of fighting strength, while the transport corps and sappers are an asset far above their actual numbers in value.

Such in outline are the forces maintained by the feudatories of India, forces which are now enlisted on the same class lines as the Indian Army, and which are composed of the races already referred to in Chapter IV. The uniform has already been referred to as being of the same general style as the Indian Army, and of the same simplicity in its field service order, but more varied, and more elaborate in its full dress. More varied, because a dozen or so different States are concerned ; more elaborate, because they often form troops necessary to the ceremony of the various households. Among the plates will be found the uniforms of the Bikaner Camel Corps, the Jodhpore, Alwar, and Mysore Lancers, and some of the chiefs who lead them. It is in the feudatory courts, especially at the Rajput courts that felt the Mogul influence the least, that the old traditions and customs of the Hindu kingdoms of centuries ago are still to be seen ; while in Rajputana itself, the old Rajput chivalry, with pride of race and pride of weapons, still remains, and hence provides a mounted soldier

second to none. How long in the process and
change that railways are carrying to the uttermost
ends of Hindustan, is a matter for reflection, and
perhaps sad reflection. The lament of the days
that are passing is to be read in Sir Alfred Lyall's
verses, and there are many who mourn the days
that are going—

When I rode a Dekhani charger with the saddle-cloth gold laced,
And a Persian sword and a twelve-foot spear, and a pistol at my
*   waist.*
My son he keeps a pony and I grin to see him astride,
Jogging away to the market and swaying from side to side.

And again, the old Rajput chief:

I cannot learn in an English school,
Yet the hard word softens and change is best.
My sons must leave the ancient ways,
The folk are weary, the land shall rest,
And the gods are kind for I end my days.

It is from the Feudatory States, and above all
from Rajputana, that the born horse-soldier comes ;
for the legend of the hand keeping the head is barely
dead a generation. Hard knocks and border law,
the *Schwartzreiter* and the baron, are the factors
that make the horse-soldier and the men-at-arms
from the cradle. In British India, even the
tradition is almost gone, so quickly does peace
enter into a race's bones, but in the States the

THE KHYBER RIFLES

Malikdin Khel

A.C.Lovett

past is barely yet a legend. In British India, to make the yeoman and the peasant into the necessary number of citizen battalions and preserve as much as necessary of the old spirit, is the aim and object of the class by clan grouping that has been described.

CHAPTER VIII

" If the salt have lost its savour, wherewith shall it be seasoned ? "

THE foregoing completes the description of the regular native troops of India, though it does not comprise the whole tally of armed forces at the disposal of the Governor-General. A detailed description of these other forces is outside of the scope of the present work, but some allusion to them is necessary to complete an account of the Indian Army.

In all districts where the ordinary civil police with their truncheons and lockups do not suffice for the maintenance of law and order, some mailed fist is necessary. In ordinary places this is represented by the military garrison which is brought into play on rare occasions. In frontier districts where an uncivilized neighbour is always tempted by the wealth of others, and where the civil force is always an object of enmity, something between the wielder of the truncheon and the regular soldier is required. The requirements of armed escorts, armed arresting parties, treasure guards, and the like are harassing and undesirable for regular soldiers. In the thousand-mile-long marches of India from the Mekran coast round to the extremity of Burma, there exists, therefore, a semi-military force, entirely under the control of the civil power. This force exists in varying forms. It is most highly developed in the corps of the North-West Frontier militia, which under the command of army officers carries out the functions performed for many years by the Punjab Irregular Force. Its name is a misnomer, as it is a permanent force, on irregular lines, under the civil power. It is raised on the old border plan of "set a thief to catch a thief," on which the original Black Watch was raised. It is recruited, that is to say, from the border tribes. Two other varieties of irregulars exist on this portion of the frontier—they are the border military police, organized by battalions who hold the frontier posts, and the tribal levies. The levies are armed un-uniformed retainers of chiefs and

27

headmen, who, in return for certain allowances, contract to police and protect certain roads and districts. The militia are more highly disciplined and trained than the border military police (known as the *barder*), and the *barder* are better than the *livy*. The levies are more familiarly known as "catchies," or "catch 'em alive ohs," not from their methods of catching raiders so much as for the mysteries of the tribal toilet.

Along the marches of Assam, which deals in large tribal frontiers, military police corps guard the frontier, while after the annexation of Upper Burma the necessary military garrison, if raised as regular troops of the Line, would have been costly in the extreme. A large force of military police, from the fighting races of India, was therefore raised on military lines, and largely assisted in the pacification of the country and the destruction of the bodies of armed dacoits into which the disbanded soldiers of Theebaw had resolved themselves. As the need for these corps diminished with the settling of the country, the best of them were taken into the Line, but a large number still remain for the necessary watching of the unadministered tribal tracts and the actual frontiers. The military police in Assam is largely recruited from Gurkhas or

KURRAM MILITIA

SUBADAR
(Out of Uniform)
Turi

kindred races, and those now in Burma from the Punjab, but some of the local tribes also do excellent service. The total of this military police force, though scattered along many hundred miles of frontier, is very considerable.

After, therefore, due reference to this force that bears much of the burden of ordinary come-and-go on the borders, little remains but to review the Indian Army as it stands . . . one of the marvels of modern times. It is not profitable to consider at any time the question of its faithfulness, since the measure of the fidelity of this great force is the measure of the fidelity of all mercenary armies, that is to say, of all armies that serve voluntarily for a wage. We may rest content with the situation as it is, and the fact that so long as India as a whole acquiesces in our presence, and has faith in our prestige and our equity, and our power to give peace in the land, so long will the Indian Army continue to give us, and incidentally their own land, faithful military service. To expect more is to ask for the impossible. We may more profitably content ourselves with observing the marvellous nature of the glamour which the handful of English officers has from the earliest times been able to throw over these men of an alien race. The men of the Indian Army follow their alien officers with a devotion and a gallantry that has no precedent. We see this handful of white men controlling many many thousands of men of high courage, and occupying the position to some extent of demigod, but at any rate a leader as well as guide, philosopher, and friend. From no one does the sepoy get more disinterested and more freely given help and advice, than from his British officer, that man of alien race and a widely different faith.

Quite how or why we know not, but the fact has remained that for two centuries, with the exception of the madness of 1857, come weal come woe, come rain come shine, the sepoy has followed and trusted that unintelligible entity his sahib. From the plains of Madras to the snows of the Hindu Kush, from the Deccan to Burma, from the Punjab to China, through snow and frost and fiery furnace, the sepoy has followed the sahib, chanting the old chant of the patient East—

> *Kăbhi sŭkh aur kăbhi dŭkh*
> *Angrez ka naukar—*

which may be interpreted, "Sometimes pleasure, sometimes pain, the servant of the English."

Regular pay, due sympathy, and prompt justice may, and do, appeal to the mercenary soldier, and bring men of martial proclivities to a service in which profit and suitable recognition of devotion follow on services.   But the reasonable fulfilment of the written word, the acting up to the provisions of an attestation paper, is not to account for the deeds of the Indian soldier.   It was not the fulfilment of a contract that made Clive's sepoys at Arcot give up their rations to the European soldiers, or the 35th Native Infantry do the same when the earthquake killed the remaining live stock in Jellalabad.   It was not the acting up to the letter of the law that kept some hundreds of Poorbeah sepoys true to their salt within the shattered defences of Lucknow, or took the Gurkha and Punjabi soldiers up and through the Delhi breaches, or made the Guides escort in Kabul sell their lives for the sake of their British officer, to the mob and the dog Heratis.   No contract alone takes the native of the plains to serve the Sirkar in the snows of the Afghan hills, and to tramp the burning desert, or down to the swamps and the fever of the eastern frontier.

Some love of service, some power of the white man for attracting faithful service and admiration, must be the motive power that brings Hindu and Musalman, Afghan and Indian, Sikh and Gurkha, to an alien ruler and an alien race, to serve for small guerdon and smaller pension. For honour, no doubt, and hereditary love of the sword the

man of a martial clan takes to military service ; but there is more than this, and it would seem that so long as the British are worthy of it, so long as courage and justice and the strong arm keep up the confidence of a hundred races in our power to keep the ring, so long will the soldier races of the East serve the Sirkar.

The Poona Horse Standard, surmounted by a silver hand, captured at the battle of Kooshab.

It is the fashion among the unthinking to say that the bayonet of good British Atkins alone keeps us in India, and that we hold and rule India by the sword. Except, however, in a very very limited manner, and strictly subordinate sense, this is the result of a great misconception. Sir John Seeley especially pointed out the limits of this conception. He pointed out that, in the suppression of the Mutiny of the Bengal Army, the small British forces never wanted for ready assistance. Transport supplies, military followers, and domestic servants thronged to our assistance. Never for a day was the force clinging to the Ridge at Delhi in want for anything that the natives round could supply. That is to say, there was no feeling of sympathy with the rebels, or that it was disgraceful to give assistance to those opposed to the brave Indians trying to shake off an alien yoke. There was no feeling that the patriot fought for his country-side. And why? Probably because every one knew that the sepoy could not keep the peasant and the trader in peace and safety; nay, that he was among the first to prey on them.

Here indeed we do strike the point where the 75,000 British bayonets hold India, viz. in the confidence that they give as the strong arm, to maintain that civil power that gives safety to all races and all religions, to live their own lives against all comers. Since no other rule has done the same for over a thousand years, small wonder that the length and breadth of the country, trodden out by the companies of free-lances and the wars of the barons, welcomed those that let the old man and the maiden sleep secure o' nights. The British bayonets and that sign of might, power, and majesty and dominion that bulks so large to the Eastern mind, the "twenty yoke of the forty-pounder train," as the outward and visible sign of a strong will, *do*, in this sense, hold India. But it is not the holding of India by the sword, but rather the possession of a sword to draw against those that disturb the people. The distinction is not even a subtle one.

It was Sir John Seeley who pointed out, and any one who knows India will acknowledge it, that it is only necessary for a feeling to arise, that it is impious and disgraceful to serve the British, for the whole of our fabric to tumble like a house of cards without a shot being fired or a sword unsheathed.

Fortunately it is impossible also to imagine such a situation. For many a year, nay for many a generation, it is only the presence of the strong if alien rule that can keep religion from the throat of religion, race from race, the prince from the peasant, and the thief from the banker. Because the English can do this for a long-distracted country, with their reserve police force of 75,000 hearty English Atkinses, therefore the mass of the people serve for a wage willingly, and while serving give true and faithful service. Because

OFF TO PENSION

(A SIKH OFFICER)

also it is well to be in the train of the strong and successful, so do the martial men of India gladly serve the ruler alongside those same Atkinses.

It is no part of the scope of this book to inquire what the future may bring forth, or to peer into the crystal globe to see how long the anomaly of West nursing East to peace and prosperity and national ideals must continue, nor to discuss the pace at which the East shall share its own government with the West. To the wisest the crystal has little to tell, and we plod on trying to play the game, so that pleasure and profit may ensue to those for whom we do it. It will be enough if in the future we shall have deserved success in a problem as large and as difficult as ever faced the Empire of Rome.

The strategical aspect of the great army in India also is far removed from this, the outline history of how the great army has grown and come to its present stage. But since armies in modern times do not exist for the pleasure and pomp of kings, but to some stern purpose, the extraordinarily favourable position of India and the Indian Army for the purposes of empire may be alluded to. Amphibious war, war by land and by

28

sea, has for many years been a peculiar asset of
the British Empire.   The power of transporting
troops to distant scenes, and to protect them on
the high seas, has belonged to Britain.   Since ships
do not sail over dry land, it is not the omnipotent
navy alone that can clinch a war.   The peculiar
power that we have possessed in the past, to land
our troops at that point where their very presence
must produce an effect far out of proportion to

Havildar,
Marine Battalion, 1885.

their actual numbers, is one of
those that only the mistress of the
seas can hope to wield.   This
power and all it stands for is aptly
described by Captain Mahan, when
talking of the influence of sea-
power, and the small red ulcer
that it enabled us to keep open in
Spain.   He writes of the "Storm-
beaten ships, on which the Grand
Army never looked, that stood
between it and the dominion of
the world."

These same storm-beaten ships
equally protected expeditions overseas from India.
From India as from a fresh base we are able to send
forth expeditions at the bidding of an ocean cable

which other powers can but start from Europe. Time after time has India sent her native army over the sea on Imperial quests in return for the peace we give her. Manila, Macao, Java, Bourbon, Egypt in 1801, Egypt in modern times, China time after time, have seen the native troops from India bearing their share of an Imperial purpose. The army of India exists for its own protection and security, but, in return for the British backing that forms its nucleus, is ready, when its own immediate needs are not pressing, to contribute to the general purpose of empire. The sepoy has carried the Eagles in triumph from the shores of the Mediterranean to the Great Wall of China, and to those who see fit to inquire how long he will continue to do so, the answer is perfectly straightforward. Just so long as our rule in India fulfils the conditions that have hitherto made it acceptable to a people longing for peace and protection.

A Russian officer who has lately given to the world his impressions of a tour in India, in paying tribute to the faithful soldiery and their military bearing and efficiency, has exactly described the situation. He is mindful that the Indian soldier has for centuries served the ruler, and remarks that he, like the cat, is attached to the house rather than to the master.

For at present

Khălk-i-Khuda
Mulk-i-Sirkar
Hukm-i-Sahiban Alishan.[1]

---

[1] Mankind belongs to God,
The land to the Government,
And power to the powerful Sahibs.

INDEX

THE END

Lightning Source UK Ltd.
Milton Keynes UK
UKHW050145190821
389007UK00005B/38

No Author Better Served

———————————————

For Maurice and John Connelly with kindest Good wishes, Maurice Harmon

No Author Better Served

The Correspondence of

Samuel Beckett & Alan Schneider

Maurice Harmon

Edited by **Maurice Harmon**

Harvard University Press

CAMBRIDGE, MASSACHUSETTS
LONDON, ENGLAND / 1998

Publication of this book has been supported through the generous provisions
of the Maurice and Lula Bradley Smith Memorial Fund

Library of Congress Cataloging-in-Publication Data
Beckett, Samuel, 1906—
No author better served : the correspondence of Samuel Beckett
and Alan Schneider / edited by Maurice Harmon.
p.   cm.
Includes bibliographical references and index.
ISBN 0-674-62522-6 (alk. paper)
1. Beckett, Samuel, 1906–   —Correspondence.
2. Theatrical producers and directors—United States—Correspondence.
3. Authors, Irish—20th century—Correspondence.
4. Schneider, Alan—Correspondence.
I. Schneider, Alan. II. Harmon, Maurice. III. Title.
PR6003.E282Z495   1998
848'.91409—dc21
[B]   98-5207

Contents

Introduction

From the beginning Samuel Beckett and Alan Schneider got along well together. Invited to direct *Waiting for Godot* in America (1955), Schneider went to Paris to meet the playwright. What was to have been a brief encounter became an extended exchange of views, and they went to London to see Peter Hall's production of *Waiting for Godot* at the Arts Theatre Club. The nature of their professional relationship appears at once in their correspondence. In the first letter (14 December 1955) Samuel Beckett writes, referring to *Waiting for Godot* which he has given to Schneider to direct, "I feel my monster is in safe keeping." It was, however, the enclosed copy of a letter to Peter Hall about the London production that showed what Beckett expected from directors. The letter focuses on specific points: the degree of emphasis and of hesitancy, the amount of irony, the speed of delivery for particular lines, the length of a silence, the pronunciation of a word, tones, verbal echoes, the importance of the sound of Pozzo's whip, the symmetry of stage positions.

Beckett's next letter (27 December 1955) is even more enlightening. Pozzo, he explains, is a "hypomaniac and the only way to play him is to play him mad." Then he remarks on actors who seek to "clarify" the role and to give it "unity," trying, he writes, "to establish it from without." The sources of Pozzo's behavior, he explains, do not lie in the external world, but "in the dark of his own inner upheavals and confusions." Beckett insists now and later that all he knows is in the text. He distrusts psychological photofits and actors and directors who try to build a character from the outside. The "she" in *Not I*, he writes (16 October 1972) is "purely a stage entity, part of a stage image and purveyor of a stage text. The rest is Ibsen."

The first of Alan Schneider's letters catches the flavor of all his letters to Beckett: news of the various plays he is directing or has seen; reports of conversations with Beckett's American publisher, Barney Rosset of Grove Press; plans for the production of *Endgame* at the Cherry Lane Theatre, his search for a suitable cast, details about the opening, about publicity and photographs, the size of the theater; and, finally, specific questions: did Hamm have a "rag" over his knees; are "ending" and "dying" interchangeable; is there any specific reason why Clov says "*my* light"? He ends with news of his family.

It is the beginning of a pattern that almost never alters. Schneider pioneered five of Beckett's plays in America. Usually, he went to Europe to discuss a forthcoming production. Then, as he worked on the text, came the exchange of letters, postcards, and phone calls, all of which provide a fascinating portrait of their relationship. To the questions given above, Beckett responds (21 November 1957): "rag" is a printer's error for "rug"; "end" is stronger than "die"; "in *his* kitchen it is *his* light, *his* life." Beckett claims that he is unable to talk about his work, but his explanations are clear and helpful, as when he writes of the characters in *Endgame*, "They endure their 'thing' by projection away from it, Clov outwards towards going, Hamm inwards towards abiding. When Clov admits to having his visions less it means that his escape mechanism is breaking down. Dramatically this element allows his perception of life (boy) at the end and of course of the rat to be construed as hallucinations." Beckett speaks of vocal levels in Hamm's story, noting that certain exchanges should be played as "*farcical parody of polite drawing-room conversation.*" Amusingly, when he reveals the play's philosophical theme—"the impossibility of catastrophe. Ended at its inception, and at every subsequent instant, it continues, ergo can never end"—he adds: "Don't mention any of this to your actors!" "Birth," as the Speaker says in the opening line of *A Piece of Monologue*, "was the death of him."

Schneider, wisely, concentrated on what could be shown on stage. He understood what the next letter (29 December 1957) famously declared about the "extreme simplicity of dramatic situation and issue . . . we have no elucidation to offer of mysteries that are all of their own making. . . . Hamm as stated, and Clov as stated, together as stated, *nec tecum nec sine te,* in such a place, and in such a world, that's all I can manage, more than I could." Impatient with elaborate interpretations of his work, and of what he continues to regard, with considerable justice, as misunderstanding, Beckett insists on the simplicity of means by which his work lives. Schneider trusts Beckett, refuses to depart from the text, and thereby ensures, much to Beckett's satisfaction, that the work is performed as the playwright sees it. Of *Endgame* Schneider writes: "no production has given me greater pleasure in the doing" (23 January 1958).

Schneider's virtues included a rigorous attention to technical matters; an affective nature that enabled him to respond openly to each new Beckett play; an appreciation of the finer points in a script; a persistence in getting a deeper and surer understanding of the play in hand; an appreciation that every actor contributes his own visual and vocal individuality; and an ability, and a policy, of getting his cast to work together. Trusting Beckett's directions, he used them to discover levels of meaning through scrupulous adherence to what the playwright wanted, believing that the truth was discoverable in that way and that to do otherwise would be to muffle the play's integrity and purity. He deeply regretted the one time (1964) when, yielding to pressure from his producers and failing to follow Beckett's instructions, he allowed *Play* to be performed without the *da capo*. He would have liked Beckett to have been present for some rehearsals, but Beckett did not like America. Beckett's one visit in 1964 was for the making of *Film* with Buster Keaton; his detailed technical instructions (letter of 29 September 1964) and the subsequent correspondence show how well he understood this medium. Not until the rehearsals for the National Theatre production of *Not I* with Billie Whitelaw (1982) did Schneider have the satisfaction of directing in Beckett's presence. In his letter of 16 December 1982, he declares himself grateful for Beckett's "continual patience and understanding . . . I was especially glad because you have never been around with me when I was working on a stage piece of yours . . . we weren't starting from scratch but at least you had a glimpse."

The production of *Happy Days*, "all poised on a razor-edge and no breather anywhere" (13 July 1961), created a number of technical problems. First of all, Winnie's mound had to have the exact measurements that Beckett had in mind. What color, Schneider asked, should the backcloth be, what texture should the mound have, what kind of bag was Winnie carrying? Beckett sent a drawing of the mound and sketches of Winnie. The mound, he said, should extend across the entire stage, sloping down to a few inches on each side; the texture should suggest scorched grass, but smooth; the whole scene should be characterized by a pathetic unsuccessful realism; Winnie should have a "desirable fleshiness . . . gleaming opulent flesh" in the first Act, to be remembered in the second by their absence. As for her voice, he wanted "vocal monotony and relying on speech rhythms and speech-gesture complexes, eyes, switching on and off of smile, etc., to do the work, all these in their turn requiring, if they are to operate fully, vocal tranquillity & transparency" (17 August 1961). The letters about *Happy Days* go back and forth for weeks and show just how reliable Schneider was in getting as close as he could to Beckett's exact technical requirements as well as to the play's meanings.

This play was crucial in Beckett's development. On the threshold of that great innovative period in which he would expand the drama still further, he was interested in what the "professionals" would say about it (15 September 1961) because they would help him to decide whether the play was "really a dramatic text or a complete aberration and whether there is justification for trying to push further this kind of theatre." Schneider had no doubts (19 September 1961): "By all means, go on, Sam, do what you feel you should, write the way you want to, stretch everything the way you'd like." The reviews, in fact, were disappointing, but Beckett's friends—Harold Pinter, Kay Boyle, George Reavey—reported so favorably on the production that he could write in happy appreciation (23 September 1961), knowing, as the letters show, just how hard Schneider had worked: "I've a feeling no author was ever better served."

From the woman embedded in sand it was a natural progression to heads suspended, a mouth in midair, disembodied voices. *Play*, Schneider told him, was "opening up new pathways," but once again the technical demands were daunting. Beckett wanted the three urns to touch and the light "snapping from face to face," all three and the light belonging to "the same separate world." The faces should be "as little differentiated as possible. Three grey disks. Voices grey and abstract as the faces, grey as cinders." He wrote (26 November 1963) that he wanted "complete expressionlessness." Schneider managed the technical needs: the finger of light stabbed unerringly through the darkness, the urns were exactly as Beckett had drawn them for him. "They touch, they are trapped, and the heads stick out of the lip as you intended." The voice was as "toneless" as humanly possible, expressionless and staring (26 December 1963). Later, Schneider described the successive refinements he had made: "I decided on the curve and shape and size and texture and location of the urns . . . I worked out the aesthetics and mechanics . . . of that omnipresent light beam." During the rehearsals and previews, "I was able to arrange and rearrange and select and sample and change and change again the symphony of tones and volumes and rhythms and sounds and silences which together determined the particular texture and shape of this particular production of Beckett's PLAY" (Alan Schneider, "What Does a Director Do?" *New York Theatre Review*, Spring 1977, 18).

Beckett's comments are often brilliantly succinct. Krapp, he said (4 January 1960), "has nothing to talk to but his dying self and nothing to talk to him but his dead one." His visualization of the voice in *Eh Joe* (7 April 1966) is similarly effective: it should be whispered, it should be a "dead voice in his head. Minimum of colour. Attacking. Each sentence a knife going in, pausing for withdrawal, then in again." It could be dramatized by lengthening certain pauses within paragraphs as, for example, before "Imagine if you couldn't," "Imagine what in her mind," "That's love for you," and even within sentences, as in "Gets out . . . the Gillette," "Gets out . . . the tablets." Of the voice in *Not I*, he said (16 October 1972): "I hear it breathless, urgent, feverish, rhythmic, panting along, without undue concern with intelligibility. Addressed less to the understanding than to the nerves of the audience which should in a sense *share her bewilderment*."

The history of the reception of Beckett's plays is also present in the letters. Despite the initial and indeed recurrent adverse reaction to each new play, his work found an increasingly interested and responsive audience. By the time Schneider directed *Waiting for Godot* at the Sheridan Square Playhouse in New York in February 1971, a greatly acclaimed production, a whole new generation was coming to the theater. Beckett had become part of the university curriculum, his novels and plays studied in literature and drama courses, his work always in print.

Schneider's 1972 Beckett Festival, consisting of *Not I, Happy Days, Krapp's Last Tape*, and *Act Without Words II*, was successful. When he sent the script of *Not I*, Beckett told Schneider (25 July 1972) that it "must go very fast, no pause except for breath and the two big silent holds after the screams." Schneider solved the technical problems by lighting the mouth with a "gallery light," and draping the set and actress in black to exclude everything else on stage. He cleverly lit the mysterious figure of the Auditor so that he was visible without being intrusive, his few helpless gestures suggesting a grieved, ineffectual response to Mouth's obsessive monologue. *Not I* was one of Beckett's most daring innovations. With Jessica Tandy as Mouth, Schneider assures him (24 November 1972), it was one of the most electric evenings he had ever spent in the theater. "Don't let anyone tell you *Not I* doesn't work or cannot work as a theatre piece. . . . The image of that mouth moving in space across from that mysterious shadowy figure will remain with anyone who has seen it forever."

Schneider invariably met the fresh challenges. In a letter of 27 July 1975 he says that *That Time* is "beautiful, fascinating, difficult," and despite the technical task of making clear the modulation in the voices of A, B, and C without breaking the continuous flow, he finds the play "extremely powerful, terribly moving, and terribly delicate" (1 September 1975). In 1981, when directing *Rockaby,* Schneider realized that it was different from the other shorter plays. Again, the technical details—the lighting, the movements of the rocker—occupied his scrupulous attention. Beckett thanked him (22 April 1981) "for the excellent and meticulous job." Schneider also recognised the purity of *Ohio Impromptu,* the impact of its stage images: "Strong image of black and white. The white table strongly lit, the two mirror-images, blackness around" (16 May 1981).

The last years of their relationship produced a series of innovations. Beckett's fame spread. "Everybody all over the place is talking about you and you'll just have to get used to it" (17 February 1974). Seminars, symposia, productions, festivals—the expansion of interest continued unabated. At the end of the correspondence (2 March 1984) Schneider delighted in opening the Samuel Beckett Theatre in New York, 16 February 1984, when seven Beckett plays were "lighting up off-Broadway."

During the thirty years of this correspondence, Beckett created his own kind of theater and his own audience. From the "vaudeville" turns of *Waiting for Godot,* with its symphonic structure and strange ambiguities, he moved to the stark, mathematical shapes of his final plays. From a time in which his audiences were bewildered by the antics of Vladimir and Estragon, when theaters were reluctant to put on his plays, he arrived at a time when his plays were performed throughout continental Europe and across America. It is a remarkable development. Beckett's theater is based on fundamentals. On stage there are ambiguities and uncertainties; what looks and sounds like dying may not be death or may even be a haunted region of afterlife. Sounds come from a vast silence, from blackness; a light strikes the still faces; incidents happen in a repetitive manner; forces press in upon the individual. Winnie sinks into the sands of time, May paces the narrow strip of her life, Krapp holds onto his dead past. The Mouth in *Not I* torments itself, the brain in *Footfalls* flickers "like mad." In *That Time* the head of an old man confronts his life. In *Eh Joe* a voice stabs. The stream of consciousness is a fragmented babble. In the dreaming-back process Beckett lets in the threatening chaos, accommodating it in precise and careful structure. The form is flexible and strong, a vehicle for the haunted figures who linger astride the grave. To cease would be a release, but they do not cease. The head that sinks at the end of *Rockaby* may not have found release; the cry of "More" suggests a necessary hold on life, however dwindled. In *Play, Footfalls,* and *Not I,* death appears to flutter out of range.

The bareness of means limits movement and speech. Over and over Beckett asks Schneider for stillness, for voices in monotone. Over and over he makes minimal use of properties: a rocker, a suspended head, a mouth and an Auditor, three heads in urns. His images are powerful and challenging. From *Happy Days* to *What Where* they become increasingly startling. The settings make no pretense of being representational. In the drama of immobility, Beckett controls space through spare sets, minimal movements, and concentration on dramas of the interior of the mind. He hacks away the trappings of representational drama and modifies the tongue's expressive power. The roots of Beckett's drama go back to Yeats and his ideas for verse plays, the ideal of stillness, the stylized figures of *The Hawk's Well* and other plays, the haunted memory of *Purgatory,* the eerie medium in *Words Upon the Window Pane,* suddenly possessed by Swift's huge presence, J. M. Synge's visionary tramps, O'Casey's clowns. His plays have connections with continental European drama in Maeterlinck and Pirandello. Beckett writes boldly with an extraordinary sureness of touch, as his letters to Schneider show. To be an artist, he said, is to fail, "as no other dare fail." He presses on, struggling to put his theatrical ideas into practice. The strain of these engagements is a recurrent theme in the letters, as are the tension and effort that go into the writing: "To think writing was once pleasure" (4 February 1982).

Alan Schneider was remarkably receptive to Beckett's technical innovations, and thus the correspondence is virtually a history of Beckett's growth as a dramatist as well as a reminder of how he wants his plays to be staged. "Make sense who may," as we are told in *What Where.* The later plays are particularly challenging, the stage images starkly evocative: in *Ohio Impromptu* the old man in black tells his tale

over and over to his alter ego; in *Cascando* the story is "panted." A break
has developed between the teller and the tale. The creator in *Cascando*
cannot create; the creative imagination endures disruption. The fluency
and control of the oral narrator have been lost; he is a bereft and
struggling repository of tales that sometimes are turned outward but at
other times are directed inward, as in *Eh Joe*. In Irish tradition when we
listen to the severed head, we hear what the spirit speaks, the drama in
the deeps of the mind. In Beckett's plays our perceptions of age and
death, of isolation and the void, are given unforgettable shape.

But the creative joy that Yeats celebrated has lost much of its self-de-
lighting ease. Forces beyond human control impinge and disturb. A
goad probes, light stabs, phrases pierce. Despite the harrowing of the
self, the speaker can only appeal for more of the same. One of the most
poignant images in Irish storytelling is of the teller of tales who no
longer has an audience and therefore must tell the stories over and over
to himself. In *Embers* we hear the speaker's pain: "Stories, stories, years
and years of stories"; the speaker wants someone "to be with me,
imagine he hears me, what I am, now." Terrified of silence, Winnie
prattles, knowing Willie is near. "Ah! les beaux jours" (Verlaine, "Collo-
que sentimental"). Outside of these "Profounds of the mind," is the
nothingness of extinction, and even then, it seems, in the dreaming
back, haunted figures cling to remnants of the past, with little sign that
they will one day escape from the cycle. Pathos, repetitiveness, loss,
loneliness, impassive faces, toneless voices, communication more by
chance than by design, consciousness a barely tolerable flow in the
mind: stage space dwindles, movement slows, tawdriness and decay
encroach. Beckett sees man in severe decline, but does so with infinite
compassion and objectivity, through a brilliant mastery of stage techniques and images. He was fortunate that in Alan Schneider he found a
director whose understanding and love of the theater enabled him to
rise to the challenges.

The letters range beyond the issues of particular productions.
Schneider frequently mentions his other productions in New York and
Washington, as well as university and regional theaters. Beckett relates
what is happening in Paris, London, or Berlin, frequently referring to
productions of his own plays, telling Schneider what he thinks of directors, actors, or theaters. As Beckett becomes more involved in production, Schneider is eager to study recordings, to know about sets, costumes, voices, to consult the production notebooks. How did such
and such an actor speak? What did he look like? In turn, while increas-

ingly clear about how he wants a play to be performed, Beckett trusts Schneider to do it his way: "Do it any way you like, Alan."

They became affectionate friends. Although there are some restrictions on what personal material can be published, enough remains to convey the warmth of the friendship and the character of the two men. Beckett tends to focus more on practical matters; he is restrained and economical with words, but from time to time mentions how he feels, and responds to what Schneider tells him about his own state of health, or about his family. Schneider, more outgoing, with a dynamic, restless temperament, tends to pour out his current interests and concerns.

Although Schneider's career was less well known, especially in Europe, he influenced the course of avant-garde theater in America. Not only was he the pioneering director of Beckett's plays, but he also directed plays by Edward Albee, Harold Pinter, and Brecht. He liked what he called "unexplored territory," that is, innovative plays that helped to change the nature of the theater. His respect for Beckett's contribution to the theater never waivered. It was the same quality that he admired in Brecht and Albee: the intense theatricality; they pushed out and enhanced the resources of the stage. He recognized and valued Beckett's extension of the possibilities of stage language, his restoration of metaphor and myth, his creation of stage images of classic proportions. What is most admirable about Schneider's relationship with Beckett is his ability to respond positively to the successive stages of Beckett's evolution as a dramatist. He is as excited and challenged by the possibilities of plays in the early 1980s as he had been in the mid-1950s, and just as prepared to study them, to consult with Beckett, to plan meticulously in advance, to get actors working together and to guide them, knowing when to take hold and when to leave alone. A director, he said, is a necessary evil, a means to an end. He did not intrude upon the work but submitted himself attentively to it, discovering its imaginative inner life, most pleased in the end if his contribution to the play's successful performance could be unnoticed. He put artistic interests first, taking care to do plays at the right time, in the right theater, with the right cast; sometimes, as in the case of the 1971 *Waiting for Godot*, he worked for nothing.

As Beckett and Albee both testified, Schneider strove above all to get the playwright's work on stage the way the playwright intended. A director, he believed, should not be inventive just for the sake of being inventive. "I have always held to the old-fashioned belief that a first production—certainly of a living author, especially of an author as clear

and as explicit in his directions to all concerned as Beckett has always
been (and is increasingly becoming)—should try to bring to stage life
the author's play" ("'Any Way You Like, Alan': Working with Beckett,"
28). He measured his development as a director by his success in working more creatively with actors and stagehands. In his view the group
was more important than the individual. The ideal theater, for him, was
one of people joined together over a period of time with a common
view, dedicated to the work of a particular author. What he had in mind
was Brecht's Berliner Ensemble, or the Group Theatre's championing of
Clifford Odets. There was nothing like that in America in his time. He
chafed against the prevailing conditions—the commercialization of the
theater, the insufficient rehearsal time, the forces that lured actors away
to television and film, Equity's rule about the use of actors from abroad,
the blindness of drama critics; these and other complaints are heard in
the course of his communications with Beckett.

He saw Beckett as a compassionate observer of man's state and
recognized Beckett's central view that we must go on, no matter what
the circumstances—old age, pain, loneliness, or what Schneider termed
the "corruption and despair permeating our pores." He had little time
for those who found Beckett negative. "I don't think man's *striving* for
life," he declared, "man's *zest* for life, man's *capacity* for life has ever
been stated more strongly or specifically than in his plays" (Alan Levy,
"The A* B** B*** of Alan Schneider," *New York Times Magazine,* 20 October 1963, 52).

When he tried to explain how Beckett's plays worked, Schneider
turned to musical analogy. His plays, he said, tend to be musical in both
form and overtones. There is always a strong connection with musical
composition. His remarks on how *Play and Other Plays* should be approached also hold true for the other plays. They represent, Schneider
declared, "a kind of theatrical chamber music. In them, sounds and
silences, cadences and rhythms, are selected, arranged, pointed and
counter-pointed—as would be the scenes and acts, the plots and coun-
terplots, the characters and dialogue of more conventional playwrights" ("I Hope To Be Going On With Sam Beckett—And He With
Me," *New York Times,* 18 December 1977, sec. 2, 5). The actors are asked
to function almost as musical instruments on which Beckett's special
brand of auditory and visual music may be played. The director conducts.

Editor's Note

The Samuel Beckett–Alan Schneider correspondence is held in the John J. Burns Library at Boston College and is made up of letters, postcards, telegrams, and notes to productions. The correspondence runs from 14 December 1955 to 2 March 1984, terminated by the accidental death of Alan Schneider in London where he was directing James Duff's *The War at Home*. Ironically, Schneider had crossed the street to mail a letter to Beckett and was struck by a motorcycle as he returned.

In this edition the term "letters" includes all of this material, which has been transcribed as accurately as possible. Samuel Beckett's handwriting is sometimes difficult to read, and occasionally a word or group of words remains illegible. Such failings are indicated in the text by square brackets; a question mark within square brackets in front of a word indicates uncertainty in deciphering. Schneider's letters are usually typed.

In general, spellings, typographical errors, occasional repetitions, and minor flaws have been corrected. Where a word has been emended, the correction is placed in a square bracket. The position of addresses and dates has been styled uniformly, although Beckett sometimes writes across the page, with the date in the left-hand corner. The dates have been transcribed as they are in the manuscript, although this results in some variation in Beckett's case: he writes both "April 30th 1957" and "16.4.57," but uses the latter form more frequently. In his address Beckett sometimes writes "Paris 15me," or "Paris 14me," but occasionally uses superior letters. These have been regularized. His address at Ussy-sur-Marne is often written as "Ussy"; this practice has been retained.

In addressing Schneider—"Dear Alan"—Beckett uses no punctuation. Similarly in conclusion—"Yours ever/Sam." Both these practices have been retained. His letters, whether typed or handwritten, are signed.

Some of Beckett's drawings—diagrams and pictorial illustrations—have been reproduced from the originals in the John J. Burns library.

Only carbon copies of Alan Schneider's letters, usually typed, have survived, and not all are signed. When missing, the word "Alan" has been inserted in square brackets for ease of identification. In some cases the final line or lines on a page were not reproduced. Sometimes Schneider rectifies the omission by an almost illegible hand, noted in square brackets. Schneider follows his salutation with a comma, punctuates the address consistently, and usually closes with a period, all of which have been reproduced.

Beckett writes the ampersand and the dash somewhat loosely, making it difficult to distinguish one from the other. The choice may not always have been correct. Furthermore, Beckett does not always make a clear distinction between lowercase and capital letters at the beginning of sentences. Again, the choice may not always have been correct.

Beckett is not consistent in underlining titles of plays, books, periodicals, and newspapers, but this has been regularized. Nor does he always use capitals for proper names, but this, too, has been regularized. Both he and Schneider sometimes italicize foreign words, sometimes not. In the text they have been italicized. Play titles, which vary greatly in the course of the letters, have been given a consistent form. Schneider capitalizes but does not italicize the titles of plays, and this has been retained. Abbreviations have also been kept.

The individual idiosyncrasies of both Beckett and Schneider in writing ellipses and use of question marks have been retained. Schneider, for example, uses as many as seven or more question marks as a form of emphasis. Schneider varies the number of periods in an ellipsis, while Beckett's typical practice is to use three. Their use of ellipses does not mean that words or sentences have been omitted.

Both writers use American and British spelling interchangeably, and this too has been respected. Beckett uses double quotation marks, Schneider single.

In the case of productions of Beckett's plays, full annotations are usually provided, but only the names of theaters and dates of opening are provided for plays by other dramatists. Although opening dates are as accurate as possible, there are times when conflicting evidence among playbills, theater reference books, reviews, and letters has made it difficult to decide for one date over another. The actual difference is usually not more than one or two days.

Given the busy nature of Alan Schneider's life, it is remarkable that so much of this correspondence has survived. He kept Samuel Beckett's letters and kept carbon copies of his to Beckett. Inevitably, there were losses. Some of these are noticeable within the correspondence, where one or the other will refer to a letter that is missing. Those absences are noted, but there are undoubtedly many that are not accounted for.

Samuel Beckett's letters have been edited in accordance with the wishes of the Samuel Beckett Estate, which stipulates that only letters, or parts of letters, relevant to Beckett's work may be published. Since most of the material in this correspondence relates to performances or to information about the theater, there has not been significant loss. Letters that refer only to travel arrangements have been taken out, and material within letters of a personal nature has been omitted. In Alan Schneider's letters, some personal material has also been removed.

Omissions within letters by either writer are indicated by four ellipses followed by explanatory footnotes. Handwritten insertions are indicated within the text.

The originals of all letters may be read in the John J. Burns Library, Boston College.

Acknowledgments

I wish to acknowledge the help of many people in the preparation of this book. First, my thanks are due to Robert O'Neill, Librarian, the John J. Burns Library, Boston College, who invited me to edit the Samuel Beckett–Alan Schneider correspondence when I was the John J. Burns Library Scholar in Irish Studies. It was through the generosity of John J. Burns, Jr., that Boston College was able to acquire this valuable collection. I am grateful also to Edward Beckett, Samuel Beckett's nephew, whose help and encouragement I have greatly valued. Jérôme Lindon, literary executor of the Samuel Beckett Estate, was gracious and helpful. Jean Schneider was both helpful and courteous whenever I sought her help.

Barbara Brown, my research assistant, helped at all stages of research and editing. I am grateful for her meticulous attention to detail and fact. Rüdiger Imhof gave me much information about productions of Beckett plays in Germany, and Jacques Chuto answered many queries about productions in France. I received useful information also from Kristina Karatnytsky in the New York Public Library (Theatre Collection).

Many individuals answered specific questions; I wish to thank Jocelyn Herbert, Henrioud Charles (known as Matias), Antoni Libera, Jacek Gasiorowski, Siegfried Unseld, Walter D. Asmus, Herbert Blau, Tadashi Suzuki, James Knowlson, Ruby Cohn, Marek Kedzierski, Francis Warner, Julian A. Garforth, Michael Bott, John Attaberry, Tina Hunt

Mahony, Judith Douw, Barney Rosset, Joy Small, Dina Kosten, Edward de Grazia, Beth Sweeney, Marilyn Norstedt, Ann Saddlemyer, Mary Seitz, Lawrence J. McCaffrey, Thomas E. Hachey, Ronald Hill, Richard Caldicott, James C. C. Mays, Terence Dolan, Brian Lynch, Mary Pountney, Linda Leet Howe, Sheila Harvey Tanzer, Hugh M. Olmstead, Claire Kelm, Guido Davico Bonino, Janet Lynn Krell Becker, Stephen E. Novak, Susan J. Ellis, Vi Marriott, Janet Birkett, Martin Jenkins, Colin Smythe, Poul Nielsen, John Calder, and René Agostini.

Staff in the following institutions kindly answered queries: the John J. Burns Library, Yale University Drama Library, Stanford University (Department of Drama), Princeton University Program in Theater and Dance, Dartmouth College Library, the Juilliard School (New York), Seeley G. Mudd Manuscript Library (Princeton University), T. P. O'Neill Library (Boston College), the James E. Morrow Library (Marshall University), the Stapleton Library, Indiana University of Pennsylvania, CPEDERF (Paris), Japanese Embassy (Dublin), Embassy of the Russian Federation in Ireland, Royal Netherlands Embassy (Dublin), Embassy of the Republic of Estonia (London), Reading University Library (Archives; the Beckett International Foundation), The Playhouse, Oxford, Piccolo Theatre Company, Young Vic, Royal National Theatre, The Theatre Museum (London), BBC (Radio Drama), Independent Television Commission, British Film Institute, Lord Chamberlain's Office (Buckingham Palace), Theater Institut Nederland, La Biennale di Venezia (Archives), Der Kongelige Bibliotek (Dramatisk Bibliotek), Copenhagen, Radio Telefis Eireann Reference Library, RTE Sound Archives, the Mercer Library (College of Surgeons, Dublin), the National Library of Ireland, Trinity College Library, University College Dublin Library, the Computer Centre (University College Dublin), the National Theatre Society (Abbey Theatre), the Gate Theatre (Dublin).

Finally, I wish to thank my neighbor, Michael Hayden, for his assistance with computer matters.

But even after I've got back each time, there have always been after-thoughts, new questions, new explanations. Never has there failed to be a further exchange of ideas and problems between us, a dialogue via air mail. Continued and regular cross-currents of air letters, post cards, or just little pieces of paper, typed or printed, or scrawled so unintelligibly as to challenge the CIA's top cryptographers. Over the years now, seemingly hundreds of them, suddenly part of theatre history, though once read and re-read and studied and cherished for their apt responsiveness to a particularly crucial confusion.

ALAN SCHNEIDER,
"'Any Way You Like, Alan':
Working with Beckett"

✺

6 Rue des Favorites
Paris 15me
December 14th 1955

My dear Alan

Herewith some notes I have sent to Peter Hall,[1] and letter with after-thoughts. I thought you might like to have them.

It was finally decided in London that a new production during performance was not feasible.

I got back here last Sunday. I have decided not to go to the States. Having worked with you so pleasantly and, I hope, profitably, in Paris and London,[2] I feel my monster is in safe keeping. All I ask of you is not to make any changes in the text without letting me know. If their way of speaking is not the American way it simply cannot be helped. Not, as you know, that I am intransigent about changing an odd word here and there or making an odd cut. But do please let me have the opportunity of protesting or approving.

It appears my publisher has been making things difficult. We have done all in our power to cawm him and I do hope peace now reigneth.

I hear there was talk in your papers of Wilder coming to our rescue with an adaptation of my play. This would make me laugh if it was not prohibited.[3]

All the best, Alan. Let me have your news.

Yours
Sam [handwritten]
Sam Beckett

1. Sir Peter Hall (b. 1930), British theater, opera, and film director, theater manager; as Managing Director of the Shakespeare Memorial Theatre, 1960–1968, Hall created the Royal Shakespeare Company and acquired a lease of the Aldwych Theatre in London where he introduced modern plays into the repertoire; director of the National Theatre, Old Vic, 1973–1978; 1980 joint Director of the Olivier and the Cottesloe Theatres. Directed premiere of *Waiting for Godot,* Arts Theatre Club, London, 3 August 1955. Peter Woodthorpe (Estragon), Paul Daneman (Vladimir), Timothy Bateson (Lucky), Peter Bull (Pozzo), Michael Walker (A Boy). The play moved to the Criterion Theatre, 12 September, and ran until 19 May 1956. Hugh Burden played Vladimir and was subsequently replaced by Richard Dare and William Squire. *En attendant Godot,* 1952, English trans. by SB, *Waiting for Godot,* 1954. SB's letter to Hall and the notes follow this letter.

2. Prior to directing Michael Myerberg's American premiere of *Waiting for Godot*, in January 1956, AS visited SB in Paris to discuss it. They saw the London production six times; see Schneider's autobiography, *Entrances: An American Director's Journey*, Preface by Edward Albee, 1986, 225.

3. Thornton Wilder (1897–1975), American novelist and playwright, Pulitzer Prize for *Our Town*, 1938, and *Skin of Our Teeth*, 1942. AS wrote that the daily meetings on board ship between Wilder and himself were so detailed and regular that a rumor circulated that Wilder had rewritten *Waiting for Godot*. "Thornton may have been amused by that thought: Beckett was not" (*Entrances*, 222–223). SB may be remembering that the American director and producer Garson Kanin, probably with Thornton Wilder, had sought the rights of adaptation for England and America. See James Knowlson, *Damned to Fame: The Life of Samuel Beckett*, 1996, 398–399, 781. Hereafter cited as JK.

6 Rue des Favorites
Paris 15me
December 14th 1955

Dear Peter Hall

Herewith a few notes, depressingly inadequate.

When Lucky dances a third time instead of thinking he should begin exactly the same movements as the first two times, and at the same place, and then get to his thinking place under Pozzo's orders.

The correct lighting in both acts is:

1) Unvarying evening light up to boy's exit.

2) Then suddenly darkness.

3) Then suddenly moonrise and moonlight till curtain.

I don't suppose this can be done without serious disturbance. But it seems to me you could have the moon rise, through an arc of 90°, i.e. from horizon to zenith. This should last about 10 seconds. Vladimir watches it in silence. I do feel this is important and need not upset anything.

Important also to get Pozzo to vary his tone.

With best wishes to you all,

Yours sincerely
Samuel Beckett

["notes": three pages of notes follow; the numbers refer to the text of *Waiting for Godot*]

 8 *AP-PALLED.*   More emphatic
 9 *and the other . . . damned.*   He should take longer to find the word.
   or thereabouts.

Give more irony to this parenthesis, suggestion being they were keeping out of trouble.

11 *But what Saturday? etc.* Much slower and more broken. Pause after each question. Each question a *banderilla.*[1] Let each day sink in before passing on to next.

DON'T TELL ME. More anguished.

12 *If it hangs you it'll hang anything* better than ... *it'll hang you.*

13 Long embarrassed silence after *horse*

I'm hungry. More violent.

14 *Ti-ed.* Two syllables.

For the moment. Longer pause before.

17 *Oh I say . . . It's the chafing.* A little too fast. More value to five successive *it's.*

A trifle effeminate etc. A little too fast.

18 *Basket.* Immediately upon *Can't you see he wants to rest?*

Lucky should not grab at bones. Bateson[2] knows about this.

19 One should feel that Estragon's *Ah that's better* is an echo of Pozzo's, p. 18.

21 Not *Well, that's what I think* but *Well, that's that, I think.*

22 *The tears of the world, etc.* Much more lyrical.

Swine. Meaning Lucky.

24 *You missed a treat.* Addressed to Vladimir.

Black night. Better than *Darkest night.*

Ask me again. Much more an aside.

Whip should crack here and elsewhere as indicated. It was mute throughout.

25 *What is your name?—Adam.* Why omitted?

Good? Fair? etc. Cascando of tones from hopefulness to gloom.[3]

26 Lucky dances for Pozzo who should not turn his back, but manifest his disgust.

27 *My left lung etc.* Much hoarser, followed by series of feeble coughs.

But my right lung etc. More ringing.

Wait.

Wait. Longer. Parody of anguished concentration.

Wait.

Nothing happens etc. More anguished and out of longer silence.

28 Lucky's speech. *Wastes and pines* more emphatic.

29 [sic]

31 *Adieu.* Pronounced adioo.

33 Correct boy's *sirs.*

34 *In the loft.*   Simply. No pointing to heaven.
        [handwritten]
    Not really.   Ironic. Grock's *Sans blâââgue.*[4]

37 Song.   Air herewith. Vladimir should advance to extreme front,
        parody attitude of amateur cantatrice and sing with
        exaggerated feeling. What stops him is the word tomb. He
        broods on death.

38 *What a day.*   Out of a silence.

39 Full value to silence between Estragon's *We are happy*
    and
    What do we do now etc.

40 *Say something.*   Anguished. Full value to preceding silence.

41 *Say anything.*   Do.   Do.
    This is awful.   Do.   Do.
    What is terrible is to have thought.   Accent on have.

42 They concentrate bare-headed. Longer. More parodic.
    Same effect as in Act 1 when Vladimir, Estragon and Pozzo
    concentrate.
    We spent blathering about nothing in particular better than *We spent
    talking etc.*

44 *Not sufficiently* better than *Not enough.*

45 Vladimir's walk in his shirt-sleeves should last longer.
    The coat should fall to the ground when Estragon wakes with a
    start.
    Don't tell me.   More vehement.

47 Vladimir should inspect audience at much greater length before
    saying *Well I can understand that.* All this passage played too fast.

48 Strict symmetry of position when watching out. Vladimir was too
    far from wings. Burlesque peering from under eye-screening
    hands.

49 Long silence before *How time flies etc.*
    Let's just do the tree. Sketch herewith.

It is the hands pressed together as though
in prayer that produces

Estragon's *Do you think God sees me?*
["Pozzo" written in margin here]
53 *We are men.* Very solemn.
54 Cloud passage. Between long silences.
Silence before *Perhaps he can see into the future.*
55 *7 o'clock . . . 8 o'clock.* More hesitating and separated by
longer inspection of sky.
Much longer silence before Estragon's *Expand.*
Don't question me. More vehement.
It's indescribable . . . There's a tree. Suggest all three totter round,
where they stand, in a full circle,
to look at the place. Lines to be
spoken as they do so or when
they come back to their original
position. [from "to" to "place"
handwritten]
56 Estragon's *exactly.* Ironical.
Make sure he's alive . . . if he's dead. Not enough made of this.
57 *They give birth etc.* Much more lyrical.
Don't tell me. More vehement.
58 Not *The air is full of cries* but *The air is full of our cries.*
Correct boy's *sirs.*
Full value to silences throughout dialogue between boy and
Vladimir.
59 *Two other . . . men.* Long hesitation before *men.* [penciled slash
after first period]
Christ have mercy on us. Almost unintelligible ejaculation. Keep
hat on.
From now on to curtain *dead numb tone* [underlined by hand] for
Vladimir.
Everything's dead but the tree. Dead numb tone.

1. *"banderilla":* a decorated dart used in bullfighting.
2. Timothy Bateson (b. 1926), English actor, Lucky in the London production, won the Clarence Derwent Award for best actor. The Derwent Award, 1945, was named after Clarence Derwent (1884–1959), President of the Actors Equity Association of America for two terms, for many years President of ANTA (American National Theatre and Academy).
3. *"Cascando":* a music term, indicating a diminishing of sound.
4. Adrian Wettach, called Grock (1880–1959), Swiss circus musician and clown, German speaking. One of his well-known expressions was *"Nicht möglich,"* which in French means *"sans blague!"* and in English "no kidding" or "you don't say so!"

6 Rue des Favorites
Paris 15me
December 27th 1955

Dear Alan

Very glad to have your letter. I much appreciate your having found the time, in the stress of rehearsal, to write to me at such length and I am very interested by all you tell me. There is no point in my commenting from here on your problems, if anyone can solve them you can. Very pleased by your remarks on your Vladimir, he is the spirit of the play and his wrongness in London was little short of disastrous. Not much point either in my adding at this stage to the suggestions I made in London. But one or two things occur to me that may help your actors. If you feel they won't you needn't mention them. One has to do with Pozzo. He is a hypomaniac and the only way to play him is to play him mad. The difficulty always experienced by actors with this role (apart from its mechanics which are merely complicated) results I think from their efforts to clarify it and to give it a unity and a continuity which it simply cannot receive. In other words they try to establish it from without. The result at the best is lifelessness and dulness. Pozzo's sudden changes of tone, mood, behaviour, etc., may I suppose be related to what is going on about him, but their source is in the dark of his own inner upheavals and confusions. The temptation is to minimize an irresponsibility and discontinuity which should on the contrary be stressed. The uniformity of Peter Bull[1] in London was unbearable. Such an understanding of the part is perhaps a lot to ask of an actor, but I am convinced it is the only proper one and, what is more, the only possibly effective one. Played in any other way Pozzo is just dead, artificial and tedious. The other point is simply that Estragon is inert and Vladimir restless. The latter should be always on the fidget, the former tending back to his state of rest. One should hear Vladimir's feet. But I think we talked this over in London.

I am not coming to the States just now because I am tired and cannot face the fuss. If I don't get away by myself now and try to work I'll explode, or implode. So I have retreated to my hole in the Marne mud[2] and am struggling with a play. Later on, if *Godot* makes any dollars, and when the dust settles, if any is raised, I'll come along under my own wheezy steam. In all I have had one brief letter from Myerberg.[3] I have written him that I cannot get away at present. The Wilder story came from my NY publisher.[4] I don't know where he saw it, or how crooked.

Why the platform? Is it just rising ground?

Good of you to send me a list of your changes. If I had not met you I'd be on a hot griddle!

I saw Kenneth Tynan[5] in London before I left. When I told him you had Ewell and Lahr he folded up with speechless joy.

Warm greetings to you all. *Et courage! On les aura!*[6]

Yours

Sam

1. AS letter is missing. Peter Bull (1912–1955), English actor and author, Pozzo in first London production; see "On Playing Pozzo," *I Know the Face, But . . .,* 1959, 166–191; reprinted in *Casebook for "Waiting for Godot,"* ed. Ruby Cohn, 1967, 1987.

2. SB's rural retreat, a two hours' drive, 30 miles from Paris near the village of Ussy-sur-Marne.

3 Michael Myerberg (1916–1974), American theatrical producer; when AS returned from seeing SB in Paris and London, Myerberg had already cast American actors including comedians Tom Ewell (1909–1994) and Bert Lahr (1895–1967), who began his career in vaudeville and burlesque.

4 Barney Rosset (b. 1922), liberal-minded American publisher and editor, Grove Press (1951–1986); became SB's publisher and agent in America, close friend and correspondent. "Sylvia Beach who first seriously talked to me about Samuel Beckett, in New York, in 1953 . . . recommended him to me in the warmest terms as a coming writer of importance. . . . And so we got our most important author, and shortly after that I went to Paris for the first of many meetings with Sam." See Rosset, "Beckett is the Ideal Author," *As No Other Dare Fail: For Samuel Beckett on His 80th Birthday by His Friends and Admirers,* ed. John Calder, 1986, 97. Sylvia Beach (1887–1962), American owner of the Left Bank Paris bookshop Shakespeare and Co. in the rue de l'Odéon, original publisher of James Joyce's *Ulysses.*

5. Kenneth Tynan (1927–1980), English drama critic, *The Observer* (1954–1958, 1960–1963), *The New Yorker* (1958–1960). Review: "New Writing," *The Observer,* 7 August 1955; Sir Harold Hobson's review in *Sunday Times* also was supportive.

6 *"Et courage! On les aura!":* Courage, we'll win, or we'll beat them to it.

                                          to Cocoanut Grove Playhouse
                                          Miami(Flo)
                                          January 3 1956

CROSSING EVERYTHING HEART IN MIAMI SUCCESS TO YOU
ALL[1]

    SAM

Western Union telegram

1. Myerberg's production of *Waiting for Godot*, directed by AS, opened at George
Engel's new Coconut Grove Playhouse, Coral Gables, Florida, near Miami, 3 January
1956. Bert Lahr (Estragon), Tom Ewell (Vladimir), Arthur Malet, Charles Weidman's
understudy (Lucky), Jack Scott Smart (Pozzo), Jimmy Oster (A Boy). First nighters included playwrights Tennessee Williams and William Saroyan, Hollywood stars Joseph
Cotten and Joan Fontaine, columnist Walter Winchell. See "800-Seat Theatre Is Opened in
Miami," *NY Times*, 5 January 1956; Helen Wells, "Grove Playhouse Impressed Audience
Even If Play Didn't," *Miami Herald*, 4 January 1956. Myerberg had advertised the play
with Lahr and Ewell as "the Laugh *Sensation* of two Continents."

                                          6 Rue des Favorites
                                          Paris 15me
                                          January 11th 1956

My dear Alan
    Many thanks for your letter received this morning. What a hell of a
time you have had, with everybody and everything, you must be in
tatters.[1] It is easy for me here. Success and failure on the public level
never mattered much to me, in fact I feel much more at home with the
latter, having breathed deep of its vivifying air all my writing life up to
the last couple of years. And I cannot help feeling that the success of
Godot has been very largely the result of a misunderstanding, or of
various misunderstandings, and that perhaps you have succeeded better than any one else in stating its true nature. Even with Blin[2] I never
talked so unrestrainedly and uncautiously as with you, probably because it was not possible at that stage. When in London the question
arose of a new production, I told Albery[3] and Hall that if they did it my
way they would empty the theatre. I am not suggesting that you were
unduly influenced by all I said or that your production was not primarily your own and nobody else's, but it is probable our conversations

confirmed you in your aversion to half-measures and frills, i.e. to precisely those things that 90% of theatre-goers want. Of course I know the Miami swells and their live models can hardly be described as theatre-goers and that their reactions are no more significant than those of a Jersey herd and I presume their critics are worthy of them. It is of course impossible for me to judge, with so confused a situation and so many factors operating of which I know nothing, but I think if Myerberg had maintained his programme, instead of caving in the way he has, he would perhaps not have had reason to regret it.[4] My New York publisher Rosset is now set on giving the play a Lys Theatre production, Capalbo and Chase[5] being apparently very keen. But from what you tell me Myerberg retains the rights, though his contract with Albery was for a Broadway production, so I suppose the usual disputes will arise. For the moment all I can say and all I want to say is that this Miami fiasco[6] does not distress me in the smallest degree, or only in so far as it distresses you, and that the thought has not crossed my mind that you are in any way to blame. On the contrary I thank you more warmly than ever for your faith in the play and for the way you have laboured, in an impossible set-up, to present it as we agree it should be presented, and I send you my affectionate friendship and esteem.

Sam [handwritten]
Sam Beckett

I am writing an even worse affair and have got down the gist of the first act (of two).

1. The letter from AS is missing, but he gives a detailed account of his difficulties in *Entrances*, 229–236. *Variety* and critics Walter Winchell and Jack Anderson ("Mink-clad Audience Disappointed in *Waiting for Godot*," *Miami Herald*, 4 January 1956) were "savage." The production was badly received, audiences left, and Myerberg closed the show after two weeks.

2. Roger Blin (1907–1984), French film and stage actor, director, designer, made his name with production of *En attendant Godot*, Théâtre de Babylone, 5 January 1953; created the roles of Pozzo and later Hamm in *Fin de partie*; directed *Fin de partie (Endgame)*, 1957, *La Dernière bande (Krapp's Last Tape)*, 1960, and *Oh les beaux jours (Happy Days)*, 1963.

3. Donald Albery (1914–1988), producer, managing director, Wyndham Theatres Ltd., London.

4. Originally Myerberg had booked the play in Washington and Philadelphia prior to the opening at the Music Box Theatre in New York, then canceled the bookings and opened at the Coconut Grove Playhouse where Engels had guaranteed him a two-week run (*Entrances*, 228–229).

5. "Lys Theatre": Theatre de Lys, off-Broadway. Carmen Capalbo (b. 1925), and Stanley Chase (b. 1928), American producer-directors, occasional collaborators.

6. "this Miami fiasco": the Miami production of *Waiting for Godot*. AS later wrote in *Entrances*, 236, that his anguish was "unrecordable": "I not only wanted to shoot myself and blow up the Coconut Grove, I wanted to leave the theater forever." He also noted that later audiences in the two-week run responded better.

6 Rue des Favorites
Paris 15me
April 12th 1956

Dear Alan

Glad to have news of you and to think of you heading for this poor old world. I expect to be in Paris or the very adjacent country for the rest of my life, including this summer, so look forward to seeing you. Tell me more about your Arts Theatre production.[1] I have no news of the John Golden affair[2] and have not been able to work up much interest. Afraid no plays to show you. I did finish another, but don't like it. It has turned out a three-legged giraffe,[3] to mention only the architectonics, and leaves me in doubt whether to take a leg off or add one on. All the best and write me soon from London.

Yours ever
Sam [handwritten]

1. AS would direct the American playwright Horton Foote's (b. 1916) *The Trip to Bountiful* at the Arts Theatre Club, London, 4 July 1956, and at the Olympia Theatre, Dublin, opening 20 August 1956. See *Irish Times*, 21 August 1956.

2. "the John Golden affair": probably refers to the new Myerberg production of *Waiting for Godot*. Presented by Myerberg and directed by Herbert Berghof, the play opened at the John Golden Theatre, New York, 19 April 1956, and ran for 59 performances. Bert Lahr (Estragon), E. G. Marshall (Vladimir), Alvin Epstein (Lucky), Kurt Kasznar (Pozzo), Luchino Solito De Solis (A Boy). Ten years earlier AS had criticized Golden's "too narrow view of the American theatre" in his article "On That Golden Gift," *NY Times* (*Entrances*, 85).

3. SB alludes to *Fin de partie (Endgame)* in this mocking tone; its power to "claw" is mentioned in the following letter.

Paris
June 21st 1956

Dear Alan

Many thanks for your letter. Look forward greatly to seeing you end July. I had a letter from MM[1] announcing reopening in October. I have no clear picture of the production. Much seems to get across, but to the exclusion of too much else, probably. Revival here in second week at the Hébertot,[2] a fine theatre. Slow start, but improving now. Have at last written another, one act, longish, hour and a quarter I fancy. Rather difficult and elliptic, mostly depending on the power of the text to claw, more inhuman than *Godot*. My feeling, strong, at the moment, is to leave it in French for a year at least, so tired by *Godot* and all the misunderstanding. I'm in a ditch somewhere near the last stretch and would like to crawl up on it. They kill me, all the translating and silly fuss. Hope you are pleased with your *Trip to B.* A big success for you would give me more pleasure than I can tell you. All the best, Alan. *Et à bientôt.*[3]

Ever
Sam [handwritten]

1. "MM": Michael Myerberg's "reopening in October" was postponed until January 1957; he had planned a revival of *Waiting for Godot* with an all African-American cast, opening announced in *Newsweek* (24 September 1956) as 11 November. The production finally opened 21 January 1957. SB's reaction to the proposed revival is recorded in a letter to Nancy Cunard, 23 September 1956: "*Godot* reopening Broadway November with an ALL NEGRO CAST! That's my best news." See Deirdre Bair, *Samuel Beckett, A Biography*, 1978, 402, and JK, 424, 432–433.
2. The Paris revival of *Waiting for Godot* opened 13 June 1956 at the Théâtre Hébertot.
3. "*Et à bientôt*": see you soon.

6 Rue des Favorites
Paris 15me
October 15th 1956

Dear Alan

Many thanks for your card from the ruins of the Moira[1] where as a Trinity scholard I ate large steaks copiously hawked upon by the consumptive grillman, and for your letter with photos and cutting. Miami looks good to me, Ewell in particular. Delighted that *Bountiful* went so well at the Olympia. I wonder did you put your nose into the Dolphin²—gone to hell too I'm told.

I don't in my ignorance agree with the round and feel *Godot* needs a very closed box. But I'd give it to you with joy if I were free to do so. So all I want—all!—is the OK from MM and Rosset.

I liked Myerberg. He has great charm. We had a rather dismal evening together in that filthy famous joint La Pérouse.³ I'm very pleased at the thought of the all black production and hope it comes off.⁴ I also met Lieberson⁵ of Columbia Records complete with *Godot* recording. Another very pleasant man.

Have begun work on the new play with Blin and Martin⁶ (Lucky). A very long one act, over an hour and a half I shd. think. We hope to have the Hébertot but it is not yet quite definite. With the desert mime⁷ to follow as last straw. I feel at the moment strongly disinclined to translate the play. I am panting to see the realisation and know if I am on some kind of road, and can stumble on, or in a swamp.

Best of luck with Swollen Feet⁸ and the Arena.⁹ Come back both of you to Paris soon.¹⁰

Yours ever
Sam [handwritten]

1. Hotel close to Trinity College where SB had been a student (1923–1927), subsequently Lecturer in French (1930–1932). "Trinity scholard": SB probably echoing James Joyce's *Finnegans Wake*, 1939, 215: "Latin me that, my trinity scholard, out of eure sanscreed into oure eryan." This may even be a reference to SB, whose knowledge of Greek may have discomfited Joyce, who knew more Latin. But the phrase was current in Dublin.
2. Theater in Dame Street, Dublin; the "Dolphin": a Dublin hotel.
3. Restaurant in Paris.
4. Myerberg's all-black revival of *Waiting for Godot,* directed by Herbert Berghof, opened Ethel Barrymore Theatre, 21 January 1957, closed 26 January. Manton Moreland (Estragon), Earle Hyman (Vladimir), Geoffrey Holder (Lucky), Rex Ingram (Pozzo), Bert Chamberlain (A Boy).
5. Goddard Lieberson (1911–1977), president of Columbia Records (1956–1966). *Waiting for Godot*, Columbia Masterworks No. 02L238.
6. Jean Martin, Lucky in first production of *Waiting for Godot* in Paris, 1953.
7. *Acte sans paroles.*
8. Sophocles, *Oedipus the King,* Omnibus, NBC-TV, New York, 1 December 1956. Donald Davis (Tiresias).
9. Arena Stage (theater-in-the-round), Washington, D.C., founded by Zelda Fichandler and Edward Mangum, first production in 1950; AS began directing there in 1951, and was associated with the theater for seventeen years; acting producer, 1973–1974.
10. "both of you": AS's wife, Eugenia Rosa Muckle (Jean), whom he met in England in 1952.

6 Rue des Favorites
Paris 15me
16.4.57

Dear Alan

Many thanks for your two letters.[1] I can't face my typewriter these days so you'll have to make the best you can of my foul fist.

We "created" *Fin de partie* and mime at Royal Court and played from April 1st to 6th.[2] The press was hostile. A fine article from Hobson.[3] We go on here at the end of the month at the Studio des Champs-Elysées. Much advance hostility in the air, and the papers, here, which I do not understand, but rather welcome. I shall probably take control of U.S.A. performance rights away from Curtis Brown and give it to Rosset. But I have not yet got down to translating the play into English. I have undertaken to have it ready by August and to give U.K. rights to the Royal Court. The text will lose much in translation of whatever quality it may have, and my feeling always was against translation. But if I had not contracted to it for the Royal Court the week in French in London would have been financially impossible.

I left London very tired. *Fin de partie* is very difficult to get right. Perhaps I have the wrong idea as to how it should be done. Blin and Martin have done a very good job—in spite of me! And the work in London improves our chances here.

A group of American students are doing *Godot* in English in a little theatre near the Halle aux Vins (5th *arondissement*), opening I think today. At the moment I am in the country and aspiring to stay there.

Write and tell me of your own doings. Enough about this old bastard, meaning

your friend
Sam

Kindest remembrance to Jean.

1. Missing.

2. *Fin de partie (Endgame)* and the "mime," *Acte sans paroles (Act Without Words)*, were first performed, in French, at the Royal Court Theatre in Sloane Square, London, 3 April 1957, produced by George Devine, directed by Roger Blin, designed by Jacques Noël. *Fin de partie*: Roger Blin (Hamm), Jean Martin (Clov), Georges Adet (Nagg), Christine Tsingos (Nell). *Acte sans paroles* was directed and danced by Deryk Mendel (Man), for whom it was written, with music composed and performed by SB's cousin, John Beckett (piano), with Jeremy Montagu (percussion), T. G. Clubb (xylophone).

3. Sir Harold Hobson (1904–1992), English theater critic, *Sunday Times*, 4 and 15 April.

6 Rue des Favorites
Paris 15me.
April 30th 1957

Dear Alan

Many thanks for your cable and letter. I have not yet disposed of USA rights of *Fin de partie*.[1] I have not even begun the translation. I have until August to finish it and keep putting off the dreaded day. In London the rights, or the option, belong or belongs to the Royal Court Theatre. If I kept to the *Godot* pattern I should let Curtis Brown handle the USA rights as well. But I have a strong wish to deviate from it and to give disposal of USA rights this time to Barney Rosset. I have not yet mentioned this to Curtis Brown (so keep it under your hat for the moment) and nothing has been signed except in the UK with the Royal Court and with Curtis Brown as agents for that contract. But I think it is pretty certain—unless Curtis Brown produces from the depths of the bag some unexpected document binding me to their agency for USA as well as UK rights—that I shall be able to offer to Barney Rosset disposal of former. I suggest therefore that you discuss your plans with him, pending my getting the position clear with Curtis Brown. It goes without saying that I shd be very happy for you to direct the play in the theatre and with the actors of your choice and I shall not fail to confirm this to Rosset when next I write to him. But you will appreciate also that if Rosset has the disposal of the rights the final decision must rest with him. It seems funny to be making plans for a text which does not yet exist and which, when it does, will inevitably be a poor substitute for the original (the loss will be much greater than from the French to the English *Godot*). The London week was useful insofar as it got our steam up for the run here. I thought the critics (those I saw)—with the exception of Hobson whose moving article you may have seen—were stupid and needlessly malevolent. Their ignorance of French explains the former, but hardly, or not entirely, the latter. We opened here last Friday 26th at the Studio des Champs-Elysées. The *générale*,[2] with the CRRRITTICS, this evening. The reactions so far are good and I have not much misgiving as to the outcome. Blin, after a shaky start in London, is now superb as Hamm. I have nothing but wastes and wilds of self-translation before me for many miserable months to come. You certainly have not been misspending your time since *Bountiful*.[3] I am so pleased to hear of your success. *Hommages* to Jean and good growth to the growing.

Yours ever
Sam [handwritten]

I quite agree that my work is for the small theatre. The Royal Court is not big, but *Fin de partie* gains unquestionably in the greater smallness of the Studio.

1. Missing; apparently AS asked about performance rights for *Fin de partie (Endgame)* in America.

2. *"générale"*: dress rehearsal.

3. AS has directed Arthur Miller's *A View from the Bridge*, opened Arena Stage, Washington, D.C., 7 November 1956; Tennessee Williams's *The Glass Menagerie*, opened The New York City Center, 21 November 1956; and Jean Giradoux's *The Opening*, Boston University, 3 May 1957. Arthur Miller (b. 1915) and Sidney Lanier (Tennessee) Williams (1911–1983), both American dramatists; Giradoux (1882–1944), French playwright.

> 6 Rue des Favorites
> Paris 15me
> August 12th 1957

Dear Alan

Forgive my not having replied before now to your letter of June.[1]

I have finished translation of *Fin de partie* and am sending it to Barney to-day. I have told Curtis Brown that I want Grove Press to handle the U.S. rights.[2] Now it's up to Barney and you—if your interest survives a reading of the script. Whatever the two of you decide is, in advance, O.K. with me.

The creation in French at the Royal Court was rather grim, like playing to mahogany, or rather teak. In the little Studio des Champs-Elysées the hooks went in.[3] We closed for the vacation in July and reopen September 12th. It would be fine if you get over to see it. You know by experience what little help I am with my own work and I have little or no advice for you. But simply to see the production here, for which I am very grateful, while not altogether agreeing, might be of some use to you.

I spend most of the time at Ussy, regretting I can't spend all. No work in sight except translation of *L'Innommable*,[4] more misery, and another little act without words.[5]

Kind remembrance to Jean.

Yours ever
Sam [handwritten]

1. Missing.

2. Published *Fin de parti, suivi de Acte sans paroles,* 1957, trans. by SB, *Endgame: A Play in One Act followed by Act Without Words, A Mime for One Player,* 1958. Curtis Brown: SB's dramatic agent in London.

3. *Fin de partie* opened 26 April, same cast as in London, except for Germaine de France (Nell).

4. *L'Innommable,* a novel completed in January 1950 and published in 1953.

5. *Acte sans paroles II.*

6 Rue des Favorites
Paris 15me
September 30th 1957

Dear Alan

After sending you the cable this morning I rang up the theatre.[1] According to them a prolongation is not "most probable," to quote my hasty expression, but—if business improves—just possible. And the closing date is not—to quote my impetuous expression—the 11th, but the 10th. In other words, if you want to be absolutely sure of seeing this production, you will need to arrive on 10th at latest and in time to get to the Avenue Montaigne by 21 hours GMT approx. I have the feeling Barney does not like the production, though he has not said much, and it is possible you may not either. But I think it would help you considerably to see it. No mention being made of the mime *(Act Without Words)* in the contract Barney showed me, I should make it clear that I want *Endgame,* too short (one hour and a half) to provide a full evening's agony, to be followed in NY by the mime (20 minutes), and not by another short play by someone else. If this were specified in the contract I'd sign right away. That's the sad position. Try and get here by the 10th. Or arrive on 14th as you planned and chance it. In any case you'll have the great benefit of seeing me and getting another dose of my stutterings.

Looking forward to you.

Ever
Sam [handwritten]

1. Telegram about closure of *Fin de partie:* "CLOSE OFFICIALLY ELEVENTH PROLONGATION MOST PROBABLY WRITING SAM" (30 September 1957).

26.10.1957

Dear Alan

Thanks for your letter. Hope you had a good and restful crossing and found all well with Jean & Vicky[1] to whom my salutations. It was good seeing you. Sorry I wasn't of more help about the play, but the less I speak about my work the better. The important thing was for you to see the production.[2] Barney left abruptly and must have been back in N.Y. before you. Here I'm trying to learn the quiet life again. It's coming. Perhaps I'll be able to find Clov's song.[3]

Ever
Sam

1. Viveca (Vicki) Schneider (b. 5 April 1955).

2. After a run of almost a hundred performances, the French production of *Fin de partie* was in its last week when AS arrived in Paris. AS does not mention that *Acte sans paroles* was on the same bill. AS thinks he saw the play "three times, twice with Sam" (*Entrances*, 249).

3. In *Endgame* Clov says "I want to sing," but doesn't. SB discusses the song later (see letter of 21 November). He omitted it from the English translation (1958) and from the production text of his Schiller-Theater *Endspiel*, 1967. SB referred to a French proverb: "everything ends with a song." The words of the song are given in Dougald McMillan and Martha (Marty) Fehsenfeld, *Beckett in the Theatre*, 1988, 175.

November 8, 1957

Dear Sam,

Well, back two weeks now, and Paris seems as far away as it normally does though memories of it are very close at hand. All the photographs came out, several of them remarkably well; they are being enlarged, and I'll send you some as soon as they are ready. The copy of MISS LONELYHEARTS[1] is on its way to you, with some trepidation. And those photographs of the FIN DE PARTIE production which you sent Barney are marvelous and have been especially useful all around—with actors, publicity men, and allied interests. For which many thanks.

Have been in constant touch with Barney, in fact have been going through his 'Beckett files' assiduously the past two weeks; don't know how much he has passed on to you. The situation looks very good and about as hoped-for. We shall probably be opening in the middle of

January and at the Cherry Lane theatre as planned.[2] PURPLE DUST[3] will complete its year there on December 28; business has been slackening off, and they will close it shortly afterward. We will rehearse in the theatre, and have an additional week at least after they close for final technical needs and considerations. Practically every designer in NY wants to do the set; we have narrowed the choice down to two of those who are actually available and can meet the budget and the fee, both excellent; one has done LONG DAY'S JOURNEY and ICEMAN COMETH[4] recently; the other did CIRCUS OF DR.LAO[5] and SKIN OF OUR TEETH[6] among others. There is tremendous interest all around, from the actors whom we have contacted, and from theatre people in general; and they are fascinated by both the script and the photographs. (I also have a set from the Royal Court.)[7]

The issue of a companion-piece has been set aside; everyone, including the theatre manager, has agreed that ENDGAME can and should stand by itself. We are planning to make the theatre lobby as interesting as possible with an exhibition of photographs and posters (and may call on your publisher for some of those he has indicated are available), and will probably start around 8:45 or 8:50 p.m. each evening. The actual date of opening cannot yet be set because there are many variables. Apart from not yet knowing the exact closing for PURPLE DUST, we also want to open on a good night as far as critics' availability is concerned, and when Broadway is not especially active, etc. etc. But the middle of January sounds reasonable. Actually, I have turned down BACK TO METHUSALEH for the Theatre Guild,[8] and the possibility of a motion picture in England; so you may be pretty sure.

Now, to the main question: the cast. We have been seeing people for two weeks now, and are beginning to make our final choices. We have no problem with Nagg and Nell. There are several possibilities for Clov, and we are working on that at the moment. Hamm remains our biggest question mark, and, of course, the crucial one. For Nagg, we have P. J. Kelly, originally from the Abbey,[9] as well as two other strong possibilities. For Nell, any one of three or four excellent character women who will be touching and comic at the same time. For Clov, we have narrowed it down to about 8 candidates, one of them the fellow who played Lucky in Miami. For Hamm, we have only glimmers so far, but are now concentrating our efforts in various directions. Paul Muni,[10] who was an excellent idea, is under doctor's orders to rest; his understudy is at present working in COMPULSION[11] and not available. The actor who played Tiresias in the TV OEDIPUS I did last year is a strong possibility. Sam Jaffe[12] (do you know this name?) is possible. . . . We could cast the other three parts in the next few days. For Hamm the search for the best one goes on. I'm afraid Roger Blin has spoiled me for lesser breeds without the law. But . . . . courage . . . .

Barney has been terribly helpful in every way, including a copy of MURPHY[13] through which I am now journeying. He is trying to bring the book out for our opening, and to coordinate the publicity campaigns, advertising, and other necessary evils. He has used that photograph of Hamm with the handkerchief over his face for the book cover, and it is most terrifying and effective.[14] The plan is to see whether that will work as a poster although we are also thinking about something with the garbage cans for the latter.

By the way, the Cherry Lane is suitably trapped so that the garbage cans can be placed wherever we want them downstage. And the size and feeling of that theatre seem to me just right, a bit larger stage than the Studio, and a bit smaller auditorium. Everyone will see and hear perfectly.

Have, naturally, been pursuing the script further in a search which will never end. But have a few questions at the moment which, if you're not too busy, would like to have answered or at least dwelt on. I'll use the pagination of the galley-proofs, because now that we have mimeographed scripts we have various systems of numbering pages. So here goes:

Page 1: In the beginning stage direction, you say Hamm has a rag over his knees. I don't remember this. Did he have a rag (in addition to the handkerchief?) What happened to it?

2: Am I correct in assuming that you use the ideas of 'ending' and 'dying' interchangeably throughout? Or is there some reason why you use one word instead of the other at any given place?

3: We may have to find a more understandable or familiar equivalent for Spratt's Medium.[15] Have discovered no one over here has heard the phrase.

4: Is there any specific reason why Clov says '*my* light'? (Hamm, of course, catches him on this.)

7: So far, we think we can do the tailor story as written; if censor trouble, will let you know. (Kelly is marvelous in this!)

9: Not quite clear to me what Hamm means when he says he *saw* inside his breast.

11: Also not clear why Clov says 'So you *all* want me to leave you'. And Hamm's answer: 'You can't leave *us*'. Is that 'royalty', 'editorial', ?????????? Why particularly in this sequence?

12: What are Clov's visions?

15: ANYTHING YOU WANT TO TELL ME ABOUT HAMM'S STORY WILL BE WELCOME!

17: Not entirely clear to me, or at least I'm not sure, why Hamm says 'Keep going, can't you, keep going' *angrily?*

19: Not entirely clear (though perhaps I'm making too much of it) about the line where Hamm says, *absently, head bowed,* 'That's right'. Why that particular stage direction? At that moment?

20: Have you remembered who 'that old Greek' was?[16] And I don't know if I get why Clov says: 'Is your throat sore?' Does he mean to imply that Hamm should himself answer the call of the earth???????????

P.S. How's Clov's song?

There's a possibility that the NY TIMES wants me to write an article on you and the play before our opening, and I've been doing some preliminary thinking as to what to say and what not to say. If I do one, I want you to read the mss. before it's printed. We shall see.

Glad to be home and with the family. All are well, luckily, and the daughter is growing up. Can even set up a chess-board now, though her endgame is sloppy. Jean asked about you in great detail, and she is only sorry she couldn't come with me to see you. It was good that I could come, and you know how much the experience of seeing the production meant to me. My best to Suzanne,[17] and I shall continue to keep you posted on progress.

[Alan]

1. By American dramatist Howard Teichmann (1916–1987), directed by AS, Music Box Theatre, New York, 3 October 1957.

2. Off-Broadway, 189 seats. AS has taken an option on *Fin de partie* for $500 and is exploring off-Broadway theaters. At the Cherry Lane Theatre, Noel Behn is the manager; AS writes: "Noel and his producing partners, lawyer Jerome Friedman, publicist Barry Hyams, and actor David Brooks—who were establishing themselves as interesting and successful off-Broadway entrepreneurs—would have preferred acquiring the rights directly from Sam, but since I had already optioned the play, they had to deal with me" (*Entrances*, 247).

3. Sean O'Casey (1880–1964).

4. Both by Eugene O'Neill (1888–1953); David Hays designed the set for *Endgame*.

5. Novel by Charles Finney, dramatized by Nathaniel Benchley (1915–1981), directed by AS at Edgewater Beach Playhouse, Chicago, 9 July 1957.

6. Thornton Wilder.

7. *Fin de partie*, Royal Court Theatre production.

8. George Bernard Shaw (1856–1950). The "Theatre Guild": influential New York producing organization, founded 1919, Guild Theatre taken over by ANTA, 1980.

9. P. J. Kelly (1883–1960), played with the Irish National Dramatic Company (not the Abbey Theatre) in 1902; in 1904 accepted an invitation to work in America, where he remained.

10. Paul Muni (1896–1967), Austrian-born American actor.

11. *Compulsion*, based on the novel by Meyer Levin (1905–1981), opened Ambassador Theatre, 24 October 1957.

12. Sam Jaffe (1893–1984), American actor.

13. SB novel, 1938, French trans. by SB, 1947, reprinted 1965.

14. Grove Press *Endgame* had cover photograph of Hamm with the handkerchief over his face.

15. A dog biscuit.

16. In his next letter (21 November) SB thinks the "old Greek" was Protagoras.

17. "Suzanne": Suzanne Deschevaux-Dumesnil, SB's companion whom he married in 1961.

Ussy-sur-Marne
November 21st 1957

Dear Alan

Forgive delay in replying to your letters. I am only just back in the country after another bout in Paris where I could not settle down to dealing with your queries.

I hope the enclosed answers will help you.

Many thanks for good news of prospects and preparations.

With regard to *Godot* complication, I confess I do not see exactly why such a revival should be damaging, but I take your word and Barney's that it would tend to. I wrote forthwith to Curtis Brown (Kitty Black), asking if Myerberg has the right to do productions of *Godot* when, where and with whatever elements he likes without consulting me and whether I have or have not any contractual authority to intervene in such a matter. Also whether his control of *Godot* in US is everlasting or terminates after a specified period. So far no reply. Barney suggested I should write directly to Myerberg asking him to postpone his production till after *Endgame* opening. I think we should wait to have more definite information about his plans before I do this, also that there is little likelihood of his changing them just to please me. As soon as I hear from Kitty Black I shall let you know what she says. It goes without saying that I shall do whatever you and Barney think most advisable.[1]

Blin is off to Vienna in a few days to direct *Endgame* in the German language production to be given there in January. No news from Devine.[2]

Salutations to Jean and daughter.[3]

Yours ever
Sam

1. "Rag" is a printer's error for "rug." Blin didn't use one. Unimportant.
2. I think in this text "end" is stronger than "die." As far as I remember Hamm and Clov never use "die" referring to themselves. Their death is merely incidental to the end of "this. . .this. . .thing." But there is no system on my part here and the terms are used as naturally as possible. I do not say "deathgame" as I do not say that Mother Pegg "ended" of darkness. [in margin in AS hand] "existence the universe. ."
3. The French is *"biscuit classique."* If in US there is no particularly well known brand of dog biscuit you could fall back on "classic biscuit" or "standard biscuit" or "hard tack."
4. In *his* kitchen it is *his* light, *his* life. To replace *his* by *the* normalizes and kills the line.
9. Presumably in a dream—"last night"—he saw the inside of his chest.
11. "All" because Nell has just told Clov to "desert." "Us" means Hamm, Nagg and Nell.
12. I only know the one alluded to—his light dying. This if you like is an ironical allusion to Acts 2.17.[4] They endure their "thing" by projection away from it, Clov outwards towards going, Hamm inwards towards abiding. When Clov admits to having his visions less it means that his escape mechanism is breaking down. Dramatically this element allows his perception of life (boy) at the end and of course of the rat to be construed as hallucinations.
15. What more can I say about Hamm's story? Technically it is the most difficult thing in the play because of the number of vocal levels. Dramatically it may be regarded as evoking events leading up to Clov's arrival, alone presumably, the father having fallen by the

way, and to the beginning of the particular horror to which this play is confined. It also allows Clov's "perception" of boy at end to be interpreted as vision of himself on last lap to "shelter" (which term use instead of "refuge" throughout if you wish).

17. [in margin in AS hand "p. 50"] "Keep going etc" means "keep asking me about my story, don't let the dialogue die." Repeated ironically by Clov a little later with same meaning. Cf. "return the ball" in *Godot*. I think this whole passage—up to the recurrence of "end" motif—should be played as *farcical parody of polite drawing-room* conversation.[underlined by hand]

19. Because Hamm is groggy. Justify it if you like by Clov's refusal to touch him.

20. Hamm's voice spent after scream (second "What'll I do!"). Clov's "pity" means "pity you don't give me the opportunity of saying 'There are no more lozenges.'"

Old Greek: I can't find my notes on the pre-Socratics. The arguments of the Heap and the Bald Head (which hair falling produces baldness) were used by all the Sophists and I think have been variously attributed to one or the other. They disprove the reality of mass in the same way and by means of the same fallacy as the arguments of the Arrow and Achilles and the Tortoise, invented a century earlier by Zeno the Eleatic, disprove the reality of movement. The leading Sophist, against whom Plato wrote his Dialogue, was Protagoras and he is probably the "old Greek" whose name Hamm can't remember. One purpose of the image throughout the play is to suggest the impossibility logically, i.e. eristically, of the "thing" ever coming to an end. "The end is in the beginning and yet we go on." In other words the impossibility of catastrophe. Ended at its inception, and at every subsequent instant, it continues, ergo can never end. Don't mention any of this to your actors!

Clov's song: There is a quatrain by James Thompson might do the trick. I haven't got the text here and can't quite remember it:

> Bid me sigh on from day to day
> And wish and wish the soul away
> Till hope (?) and youthful joys (?) are flown
> And all the life of life is gone.

It figures in the "addenda" to *Watt*,[6] so you can check above version with Barney. The trouble is that the air I used for the French song would be quite unsuitable for this. I don't mind if the song is cut.

But if you like the idea of using the Thompson I'll ask John Beckett to do a setting for us. It's entirely as you wish.

1. At least one letter missing.
2. George Devine (1910–1966), English actor and theater director, founded the English Stage Company at the 400-seat Royal Court Theatre, 1955; supported new-wave dramatists like SB, Harold Pinter, and Edward Albee.
3. Vicki Schneider.
4. "And it shall come to pass in the last days, saith God, I will pour out of my Spirit upon all flesh: and your sons and your daughters shall prophesy, and your young men see visions, and your old men shall dream dreams."
5. English poet (1700–1748).
6. SB novel published 1953, French trans. by Ludovic and Agnès Janvier with SB, 1968. Ludovic Janvier, critic and Professor of Literature at University of Paris, *Pour Samuel Beckett*, 1966, and *Samuel Beckett par lui-même*, 1969. The Thompson quatrain is on p. 248. SB corrects this version later (see letter of 10 January 1958).

Paris
29.12.57

Dear Alan

Thanks for your letter.¹ You know how anxious I am to help you and Barney with that uncrackable nut. But I simply can't write about my work, or occasional stuff of any kind. Please forgive me.

It would be impertinent for me to advise you about the article you are doing and I don't intend to. But when it comes to these bastards of journalists I feel the only line is to refuse to be involved in exegesis of any kind. That's for those bastards of critics. And to insist on the extreme simplicity of dramatic situation and issue. If that's not enough for them, and it obviously isn't, or they don't see it, it's plenty for us, and we have no elucidations to offer of mysteries that are all of their making. My work is a matter of fundamental sounds (no joke intended), made as fully as possible, and I accept responsibility for nothing else. If people want to have headaches among the overtones, let them. And provide their own aspirin. Hamm as stated, and Clov as stated, together as stated, *nec tecum nec sine te*,² in such a place, and in such a world, that's all I can manage, more than I could.

I like the idea of the bare walls and the added space it gives. Paint the windows on them if you like. Glad you are pleased with your cast. In London the Lord Chamberpot³ demands *inter alia* the removal of the entire prayer scene! I've told him to buckingham off.

Congratulations on TV Great Cham.⁴ Yes, I always had a passion for that crazy old ruffian.

Salutations to Jean and Vicky.

Ever
Sam [handwritten]

1. Missing.

2. *"nec tecum nec sine te"*: neither with you nor without you.

3. Lawrence Roger Lumley, Earl of Scarborough (1896–1969), Lord High Chamberlain (1952–1963), was in charge of theater censorship and the granting of licenses for plays. Private or club performances were outside his jurisdiction. Succeeded by Cameron Fromanteel, First Baron Cobbold (1904–1987), who served 1963–1971, although censorship powers were abolished under the 1968 Theatres Act. SB's efforts were unsuccessful.

4. In a letter to John Wilkes, 16 March 1759, James Boswell referred to Samuel Johnson as "that Great Cham of Literature." In 1936 SB planned to write a play entitled *Human Wishes* about Johnson's relationship with Mrs. Hester Thrale Piozzi, but did not. AS directed the *Life of Samuel Johnson* by James Lee (b. 1923) for CBS-TV; Peter Ustinov played Samuel Johnson and received an Emmy; AS and Seymour Robbie took a Sylvania TV Award for "Distinguished Achievement in Creative Television Technique" (*Entrances*, 245).

January 5, 1958

Dear Sam,

Well, we're in rehearsal, in fact have been for several days; I feel very good about the cast—things have been going so well so far that I am almost afraid—Hamm is, I believe, going to be excellent if he keeps going in the direction already evident, Clov is beginning to shape up into something—though the needs of the role seem somehow less definable than Hamm's as yet—and the two old people are terribly touching and very funny—and very true. I have been trying to achieve what you would call 'the right tone', but, of course, this is not always knowable or achievable. But coming. We shall open either the 27th or the 29th depending on what Broadway openings there are that week.¹ . . . .

The main thing is that we are progressing, that the work is good, that everyone is enthusiastic and anxious to do the work, that the actors love the play and respect each other, that we have no axes to grind or egos to coddle—that the play is the thing. The rest is in the laps of fortune. . . . . .

By now, you may have received from Barney that Sunday 'article' for the NY TIMES. For your approval and comments. I tried for weeks to write a conventional-type essay on your work and you; but the results didn't seem to me to be worthwhile or clear enough. Between trying to please the TIMES, you, Barney, Noel Behn,[2] and myself, I was really not pleasing anybody. Then I hit on the idea of showing the progression of events leading up to the play (through our correspondence) and at the same time revealing things about the play and you indirectly and yet most truthfully. This seemed to be an individual and important contribution. I showed the rough draft to Barney first, and he liked it very much. As did everyone. Then we sent it on to you to see what you thought. (I had saved all your letters, and the quotations therefrom are verbatim—though, of course, I had left out whatever was unrelated). There will have to be cuts made, I'm sure, but basically this is the idea. If there is anything that bothers you, please let me know, and it can be eliminated. The article is to appear on the Sunday before we open. Next week the *Herald-Tribune* man is interviewing me about you—and I will try to say all the right things. Will get all the material that gets into print, adverts, announcements, etc. to you. Barney is a bit worried that our publicity man is using the ash cans in the advertising. Actually I cannot control either the theatre or the publicity policy and am somewhat in the middle on the point; but I do agree with the theatre that book-jackets and theatre advertisements may have to be treated somewhat differently. I like the book-jacket very much. And I am beginning to like the ash-can ads also. We are not fooling anyone about the play the way Myerberg did in Miami,[3] but the ashcans are an immediate symbol, very powerful and immediate in impact. We have had a very high response to our first mail-orders; and the ad today in the TIMES will probably bring a great many more requests for tickets. We are all extremely optimistic about prospects. If the critics are anything at all, we should be OK for a good run. Keep your fingers crossed.

Have looked all over NY for a whistle that sounded as good as the one you had in Paris. Is there any chance of your having someone connected with the Paris production locating another one and sending it to us vite? We'll pay the duty, if any. Otherwise, we use an American-type whistle which doesn't have the age and experience of yours. Thanks.

Will try to take a snap of the set to send you. Did you ever receive those snapshots of our Paris adventures? Or is that why you haven't written lately?????

Some questions that have come up during this week of rehearsal, some not really significant, but any help would be appreciated:

Why are the faces of Hamm and Clov 'very red' and Nell and Nagg 'very white'?

(Has this to do with age, energy, 'blood-pressure'?)

We like idea of having rug (blanket) over Hamm's knees at beginning and throughout; could Hamm therefore say later when he asks for a blanket, 'another blanket' (rug)?

That matter of Clov's light: Still not clear to me why Hamm says: "Take a look at me and then come back and tell me what you think of *your* light."

When Hamm says: "I don't like that. I don't like that", I assume he is referring to his own gag to Clov: "Why? Have you shrunk?" Is that correct?

When Nagg says in the middle of his long speech, "One must live with the times", sequence of thought not entirely clear.

Why does Hamm say: "Am I very white?" (This is related to my first question.)

Still wish you could get a stronger word than 'petting parties'. That doesn't mean much over here. 'Orgies' is better; but maybe you can think of another one.

I hear George Devine is having censorship problems.[4] Over here, we think of only two rough spots:

The pee—which we probably will get away with

The bastard! He doesn't exist,—which we probably won't get away with and may have to cut: The bastard.

The real puzzle to me: "A few more gags like that and I'll call". I assume Hamm means the gag: Peace to our . . . . arses . . . . but why does he say . . . "and I'll call."?

Did you or Roger Blin concern yourselves with the problem of not seeing the irises of his eyes—since "they have gone all white"? I don't remember this. I have even thought of contact lenses though the actor may not be able to wear them. Otherwise, though, we *do* see his eyes when he takes the glasses off unless he keeps them closed, which begs the question.

How is the production in Vienna doing?[5]

The Thompson quatrain, we all like very much though Barney has not yet found his WATT to give me any corrections in the text. We are at the moment trying to find an old English or French air which might fit it—though if you want John to write a bit of a tune, fine. Either way, I am delighted to have the four lines in . . . .

In my *Webster Abridged*, wind velocity is measured by an: ANE-

MOMETER. Is that OK with you??????? (Doesn't actually matter very much.)

And so on.

Can't tell you how much I am enjoying working on the play, how strongly I feel about it, how much we're all getting out of it. It's a real privilege. I just wish you were here with us every day. As soon as we're open, will redouble my efforts to lure you over. Should we be in for a good run. . . . .

Have been reading some most interesting and revealing articles on your work by Rexroth and others, and Barney tells me there are more to come.[6] I do hope you are well and working. Jean sends her love, and Vicky is growing up at an astonishing rate.

All the best.

[Alan]

1. First American production of *Endgame,* presented by Noel Behn and the Rooftop Productions, opened at Cherry Lane Theatre, 28 January 1958, designed by David Hays. Lester Rawlins (Hamm), Alvin Epstein (Clov), P. J. Kelly (Nagg), Nydia Westman (Nell).

2. Noel Behn (b. 1928), American producer, manager of Cherry Lane Theatre (1956–1961), received an Obie Award (the *Village Voice* off-Broadway award) for this production of *Endgame,* rated "Best Foreign Play" of the year.

3. Tom Ewell remembered Myerberg's advertisement as "a French farce, the laugh hit of two continents."

4. SB explains "censorship problems" (see letters of 9 January 1958 and 10 January 1958, and JK, 447–451).

5. *Endspiel (Endgame).*

6. Kenneth Rexroth (1906–1982), American poet, translator, and painter, associated at this period with the Beat poets; "The Point is Irrelevant," *The Nation,* 182 (14 April 1956), 325–328 (reprinted as "Samuel Beckett and the Importance of Waiting" in *Bird in the Bush: Obvious Essays,* 1959).

Paris

9.1.58

Dear Alan

Your letter of Jan. 5 today. Shall answer it properly (?) tomorrow or this evening. This in haste to get something off my muckheap of a mind.

I received from Barney yesterday jacket of book and extracts from our letters, with no indication of what the latter was for. This disturbed me as I do not like publication of letters. I wrote to him at once saying I shd prefer the letters not to be used unless it was important for you that they should be. I see from your letter that it is and this is simply to say all right, go ahead. I may want to remove some phrases and shall indicate any corrections in my next letter. Thanks for the photos, they do me full justice. Glad you are pleased with progress. Some of your questions look unanswerable. I have refused to allow the prayer passage to be touched in London and my feeling is it must not be. The bastard he does not exist is most important. More tomorrow and thanks for all your efforts. I like ashcan ad.

Greetings to Jean and Vicky.

Ever
Sam [handwritten]

Paris
10.1.58

Dear Alan

Here goes to elude your teasers:

1. Faces red and white probably like Werther's green coat,[1] because the author saw them that way. Don't seek deep motivation everywhere. If there is one here I'm unaware of it. Actually illogical that H and C, living in confinement, should have red faces. Scenically it serves to stress the couples and keep them apart.

2. Even if H uses rug throughout "give me a rug" is much better than "give me another rug". He is so cold he doesn't realize he has one already.

3. I thought we had had this. Every man has his own light. Hamm, blind, is in the dark, his light has died. What he means is: "Think of me in my black world and don't come whining to me because yours is fading". I hope this accounts for importance of stressed "your".

4. Yes, "that" is the shrinking of Clov.

5. Typical illogism. Life is an asking for and a promising of what both asker and promiser know does not exist.

6. This is also related to 10. H does not know he is red. He thinks

he is (bled) white (immediate cause of line being cold from open window if you like), as he thinks his eyes are white. That in reality his eyes are not white is unimportant. Blin also thought of contact lenses. But this is the Antoine approach and wrong here.[2] H's preoccupation with white appears also in dog scene. The need of white and light of the blind.

7. Perhaps "leching". Good strong old word and follows well on "lick your neighbour". I used "petting parties" for its sneer.

8. To please Lord Scarborough[3] I have consented to change "pee" to "relieve myself" and, when it occurs later as noun, to "relief", "arse" to "rump" and "balls (of the fly)" to "hames". But I have refused to touch the prayer passage the omission of which was demanded. It is indispensable this should be played as written. If you must change "pee" I prefer "leak" or "urinate" to "relief". "He doesn't exist" without "the bastard" is simply inacceptable to me. Devine is coming over to see me. There are limits to the damage one can accept.

9. What H is doing here is putting off, with the help of such "business" as the gaff, toque, glasses, verse and story, the moment when he must whistle for Clov ("call") and call out to his father, i.e. the moment of his definite dereliction. His whistling for Clov throughout play is with growing fear of its remaining unanswered (cf. notably at end of previous monologue beginning "you weep, and weep etc"). This time he feels certain that Clov will not "come running" and that his father will not answer. But he cannot be *absolutely* certain until he has whistled and called in vain. (This also explains why Clov must enter throughout play ["throughout play" is handwritten] immediately when whistled.) It is this absolute and final certainty that H shrinks from with his "business". "Gags" is not good. In the English edition[4] I changed it to "squirms", which is not good either but perhaps better expresses Hamm's situation. Perhaps "business" would be possible. "A little more business like that etc."

10. Cf. 6.

11. Roger left for Vienna yesterday. Opening end of February.

12. Thompson quatrain: Line 1 read "us" instead of "me". Line 3: "Till youth and genial years are flown." Rest correct. Bit late in the day to ask John for music now. Leave it to you. Or no song at all.

13. Anemometer of course correct. My bad proof-correcting. With Blin gone to Vienna, probably with whistle, not much I can do about that. If I find another I'll send it on.

Herewith letters with one or two cuts.

Thanks for all you are doing and the great trouble you are taking. Greetings to the players.

All the best to Jean and Vicky.

Ever
Sam

[signature and following handwritten]

All I received from Barney was correspondence, not your connective stuff. In fact just the pages I am returning herewith.

1. Johann Wolfgang von Goethe (1749–1832), *Die Leiden des jungen Werthers* (*The Sorrows of Young Werther*, 1774).

2. André Antoine (1858–1943), French actor, director, theater manager, founded the Théâtre Libre (1897) to promote naturalistic drama; for SB "Antoine approach": "wrong."

3. Lord Scarborough, then Lord High Chamberlain (see letter of 29 December 1957, n. 2).

4. *Endgame*, 1958.

January 23, 1958

Dear Sam,

Want this to get to you by the time of our opening, which is now definite for next Tuesday, January 28. We had to do some last-minute shifting around because some Broadway-bound shows changed their schedules, and in order to get the Criticks on our opening, we must pick a clear night . . . But Jan. 28 it is.

Tonight, we had our first preview, the first time in English before an audience. All I can say is that despite the nervous tenseness of the actors, especially Hamm, the audience response was tremendous—both in the serious sections and in the lighter moments of Hamm-Clov playfulness. We had their rapt attention at all times, the silence in the theatre—except when they laughed—was thick enough to be cut with a knife; the applause at the end was tumultuous. And we had applause along the way several times, for Nagg and Nell, for Nagg's story, for some of Hamm's sallies, etc. etc. We had a full house, some of it 'paper'—but at the last minute had to turn some 30 or 40 away from the door. They'll come another night. There's always lots of off the street last-minute buying for off-Broadway.

Anyhow, I am very happy at the moment with the show—though

we are still working and still far from satisfied. Visually, it looks great, the bare walls, the windows painted on the walls but seemingly lit from outside; the chair on which Hamm sits, Hamm's costume, the general 'ambiance' of a grey interior. Our Hamm is really quite remarkable. I didn't want to tell you but couple of weeks ago, we replaced the first actor we had hired; his general heaviness and European accent were just too much tho he was a good actor. The fellow we have now, Lester Rawlins,[1] has a face of granite, a wonderful deep and resonant voice, and in addition, real comic expressiveness. You would love him. And if we run, I do hope we can lure you over on the q.t.

For the rest, my cable told you.[2] Talked with Barney this evening—he isn't coming again till Saturday—and he is pleased too. . . . The publicity and advertising is beginning to pick up as we get closer, and the sale of tickets is brisk if not an avalanche. The notices are terribly important with us. I honestly don't know what they will say, they are unpredictable. I can say that I am grateful to you and to the cast for a really unparalleled experience in the theatre. I think it's getting close to what you would want, and to what I want. No production has given me greater pleasure in the doing.

Your last set of answers much appreciated. Forgive my curiosity and persistence. Hamm *is* saying 'Give me a blanket' (rug), and not using one throughout. We are sticking to 'petting parties'—sounds great. We are not cutting a word—including 'pee', 'the bastard', whatever. Stick to your double-barrels. (The audience tonight loved every word, loved everybody—and especially the author.) "A little more business like that" doesn't quite work yet. The Thompson quatrain sounds fine the way Clov does it.

About the chronicle of letters: sorry about all the confusion. I checked with Barney before I started, and he thought you wouldn't mind. And I had already cut the two sentences you had 'edited' in the copy you returned. But, as it turns out, the TIMES has decided not to use the material for the time being. We are hoping they'll run at least a decent production photograph. We had some excellent ones taken (not as good as the French though) last week, and will get you copies as soon as we can browbeat the photographer.

All in all, we're getting on. By the time you read this we'll be even closer, and we hope wiser. The text continually fascinates and amazes me as it opens up in theatrical seams. We wish we had more time, but we always would. We have had problems, but our joys have been boundless. Nothing has been less trouble and more delight. My Jean thinks we are doing well, which gives me great comfort as she knows and does not hide the truth.

Thanks again for all your faith.

[Alan]

1. Lester Rawlins (b. 1924), actor, charter founder of Arena Stage, Washington, D.C., where he worked with AS, replaced Boris Tumarin (see *Entrances*, 251–253).

2. Missing.

Ussy sur Marne
29.1.58

Dear Alan

My old Japy is bust,[1] hence the foul fist.

Your good letter this morning, shortly after your call. It was good to hear your voice, and Barney's, and to feel you were pleased. Forgive my being so stupid on the phone. I had just dragged myself out of bed and was still three quarters asleep, i.e. about a quarter more than usual.

Your letter is very encouraging, if the critics don't slug us now. I imagine they'll find it hard not to. What you say about the actors and the set and the integrality of text pleases me greatly. I had an enthusiastic cable from George Reavey[2] who is not so easy to please. And that this production has meant so much to you gives me more pleasure than I can tell you and will make up for any disappointment that may be in store. If we don't get them this time we'll get them the next!

The tapes of the BBC readings (2) are on their way to Barney, if they have not already reached him. The shorter (20 minutes) is of the text published in the last issue of the *Evergreen Review*.[3] The possibility occurred to me of its being used to lengthen the programme. In any case I'd like you to hear them. I think Magee's performance is very remarkable.[4]

I am sorry I could not find anything to say to the two producers who spoke to me on the phone.[5] Will you excuse my somnolence and assure them of my gratitude for their faith in the play and their support.

I am slogging away at the *Unnamable*.[6] When it's out of the way I'll take what's left of my head in my shaky hands and have another go.

All my thanks again, dear Alan, for your enthusiasm and devotion. All the best to Jean and Vicky.

Ever

Sam

1. SB's French typewriter.
2. George Reavey (1907–1976), Irish-born publisher, Russian translator and poet, SB's friend for many years, helped to arrange the publication of *Murphy*, 1938, and promoted the work of Irish "international" writers.
3. *Evergreen Review,* an avant-garde journal launched (1957) by Barney Rosset of Grove Press; published "From an Abandoned Work," 1.3 (1957), 83–91.
4. Patrick Magee (1924–1982); SB was impressed by this Irish actor when he heard him reading extracts from *Molloy* and "From an Abandoned Work," BBC Third Programme, 10 December 1957, directed by Donald McWhinnie. Began to write the "Magee Monologue" in February 1958.
5. There were three producers: Jerome Friedman, Barry Hyams, and David Brooks (see letter of 8 November 1967, n. 2).
6. Translation of *L'Innommable.*

Thursday,
January 30, [1958]

Dear Sam,

Great to talk to you though we're sorry we woke you up. But when Atkinson's review came in (he's our closest equivalent to Harold Hobson), both Barney and I felt we had to talk with you. We had also seen Kerr's notice (he's our Tynan (?)) but not yet the others.[1] They came in yesterday morning and were somewhat disappointing no matter how prepared one tries to get for them. Actually, we all felt that our opening night performance was probably our best one—but that audience, made up of half a house-ful (80 out of 179 seats) of newspaper critics and reporters seemed not only like teak but petrified teak.[2] Every other night of our five previews and last night (when we had the second night press and magazine people in) we have had wonderful response throughout the show, the proper proportion of laughs and serious feeling. On Tuesday, they sat in silence, though it was an attentive silence. And, of all nights, the steam pipes in the theatre made a helluva racket for a while, much more than they had ever done in a month of rehearsals and all the previews.

In spite of all this, the actors were excellent and gave their finest performances. We were just terribly upset that we hadn't gotten the normal quota of laughs—legitimate ones—we had gotten every other night. Atkinson's review at least seemed an attempt to understand, and we had hoped for a bit more from Watts.[3] The other three are sub-literates, and don't matter anyhow. As a matter of fact, Atkinson is the one who counts as far as business is concerned; and we seem to be doing well at the box-office. Not that it's an avalanche, but doing well. And we find that if we had more lower-priced seats, we'd do even better.

Evidently, the critic for TIME[4] liked the play very much and will say so next week, and the other magazine people last night seemed to enjoy it too. But I don't believe anything till we see it. In the meantime, we are giving it all the publicity possible, contacting various student groups, etc. etc. And keeping our fingers crossed. Everyone at the theatre seems to think that the play will do well, and the general impression on Broadway is that we have a big 'hit'. So keep your fingers crossed.

My own feeling is that I am generally pleased with the actors and the production, and think you would like it too if you could see it. Certain things we achieved later than we should have, and I'm sure certain things we didn't get at all. But Barney, for example, feels that Rawlins was as good as Blin (I think he was *almost* as good), that Epstein was much better than Jean M, and that Nell was infinitely superior in our version; he doesn't think P. J. Kelly was as good as Adet—but I must say it's darn close; Adet had elements P. J. couldn't have, and vice versa.[5] . . . The tone of the play doesn't strike either of us as gloomy or depressing; and I felt a real element of dignity and beauty present. From the time Clov does his last speech to the end, you can hear that clock ticking all the way back in the theatre—and that means they're keeping pretty quiet in the auditorium.

We are gradually getting into the consciousness of NY, though people like Walter Winchell,[6] who still can't admit even to GODOT, are enjoying saying that the whole idea of ashcans is sordid and etc. There are plenty of Americans who consider anything other than a 'petting party' as something depressing. But there are plenty who love it nightly and tell us so after the show. And the general word-of-mouth seems to be very good; many people are buying tickets because their friends have urged them to.

There will be a flock of other notices, and either I or Barney will keep you up to date. There are also photographs, but getting them from the photographer will, as I said before, take a little time. So far, he has printed copies only for publicity purposes.

The night before opening, we changed one word: NIGHTMAN (which no one understood) to DUSTMAN, which was clearer and had a similar beat. I resisted this for some time from the producers; but finally, after checking with Barney, agreed. We didn't think you'd mind. The rest remains as you wrote it. And great it is.

I can't think of another play I enjoyed doing more; and I feel reasonably happy about what I was able to do with it. Seeing the Paris production helped no end, and the choice of the cast proved a good one. No one in the audience walks out (since one of the previews when a couple of girls took offense at the PEE line) and they LISTEN! And your sense of humor really comes thru, though those CRRITTICKS sure didn't concentrate on telling anybody. . . . .

All kidding aside, in a couple of months when the weather gets better and we hope to be running smoothly, maybe you would consider coming over for a week or two. You could come completely incognito, stay quietly with Barney, see the show and New York, and get a change of milieu for a while. Then back to Paris.

Barney and I are already talking about getting you to write the next one in English. After all, if the BBC can commission you, so can we.

Will keep in touch about any developments and progress.

Vicky and Jean send their love.

And our best to Suzanne.

How are the moles?[7]

[Alan]

1. Brooks Atkinson (1894–1984), *NY Times* theater critic, journalist, editor, Brooks Atkinson Theatre; review, *NY Times,* 29 January 1958; Walter Kerr (b. 1913), drama critic for *NY Herald-Tribune* and *Sunday NY Times,* author, director, Walter Kerr Theatre; review, *NY Herald-Tribune,* 29 January 1958.

2. SB had referred to the audience for *Fin de partie* at the Royal Court Theatre as "rather grim, like playing to mahogany, or rather teak" (see letter of 12 August 1957).

3. Richard Watts, Jr. (1898–1981), drama critic for the *NY Herald* (1936–1942), the *NY Post* (1946–1974).

4. Louis Kronenberger (1904–1980), drama critic for *Time* magazine.

5. See letter of 5 January 1958, n. 1.

6. Walter Winchell (1897–1972), newspaper journalist and drama critic, radio and television personality on ABC, associated with the *NY Daily Mirror.*

7. SB tried to control the moles in his garden at Ussy.

6 Rue des Favorites
Paris 15me
6.2.58

Dear Alan

This in haste to thank you for your letter with programme and the reviews which I here do solemnly declare well up to standard. I do hope they will not have too averse an effect on the booking and that you and your actors—to whom my warm greetings—will be repaid for all your work and enthusiasm by a reasonable canter.

By all means "dustman". I am so glad you have been able to preserve the text in all its impurity.

I can't write to commission and I declined to be commissioned by the BBC in the ordinary sense. I just promised I'd do my best and that's what I promise to you and Barney as soon as I get the *Innommable* finished. I must confess I feel the old tug to write in French again, where control is easier for me, and probably excessive. If my present presentiments are worth anything I probably won't succeed in writing in either. But I'll do my best.

I liked the photo of Hamm and Clov and they sound fine. Thank you again, dear Alan, for all you have done and are doing and will do.

Salutations to Jean and Vicky.

Ever
Sam [handwritten]

[?Feb 20 1958]

[Dear Sam,]
[first page missing with probable reference to a "blizzard" that affected the box office]

Business, however, has been helped by the Atkinson article.¹ Off-Broadway there is usually very little advance sale, mostly comes a day or so ahead or even at the door; and we are doing well by those standards. We got another bad break when the TIME review by Louis Kronenberger, evidently a 'rave' for the play and production, was not printed through some space limitations. We are trying to get a copy of the article anyway but TIME is reluctant to let us have it. I believe Barney sent you the VILLAGE VOICE review, which was our most intelligent and literate notice, by Jerry Tallmer.[2] But that paper has, unfortunately, little influence. We are in the process of working out some 'symposiums' during the next couple of weeks. And so on. Nagg and Nell were on NIGHTBEAT, a very provocative TV program last week, complete with ashcans; and they were just fine. One real break would help us a great deal; in the meantime, we are doing reasonably well. The show seems in pretty good condition to me—I'm there two or three times a week—and audiences have responded well. How I wish you could see it! If we could only persuade you to fly over incognito and stay with Barney for a week or two. I'm even sure that I could get the management to foot the transportation. We've had some disagreements on our advertising and publicity program, but none about the show itself. Suppose we sent you an airline ticket?????????????????

Gather you have been having your problems with both London and Dublin. Sorry about the Royal Court. Is it possible that they could do the play as written at the Arts Theatre (a club) but under Royal Court sponsorship?????? How inconsistent that whole censorship policy is! And ridiculous! . . . And I certainly think you did the right thing about the Dublin Festival.[3] . . . .

Barney presented me with hardback edition of the play with your signature. Many thanks. We are all proud and delighted with the gift. . . . As well as to be part of the production here. . . .

Hope your translating coming along, and that you will have a breather soon. Think of you often. Even Vicky talks about her 'Uncle' Samuel Beckett in Paris.

All the best from all of us.

[Alan]

1. Brooks Atkinson championed off-Broadway theater.

2. Jerry Tallmer (b. 1920), associate editor, drama critic; "Beckett's *Endgame*," *Village Voice*, 5 February 1958.

3. When the Archbishop of Dublin, John Charles McQuaid, refused to celebrate a Votive Mass to mark the opening of the International Theatre Festival, Sean O'Casey's *The Drums of Father Ned* and Alan McClelland's *Bloomsday*, a dramatization of a portion of James Joyce's *Ulysses,* were dropped from the program. O'Casey then refused to allow any of his plays to be put on in Dublin, and SB imposed a similar ban.

6 Rue des Favorites
Paris 15me
4.2.58 [4.3.58]

Dear Alan

Thanks for your letter. You are very generous to offer to pay my fare to NY and I thank you very warmly. But as I said before I simply can't make it now. Forgive me.

I'm sorry box office is not better and that a blizzard scattered BA's charitable words[1] and that *Time* stood still with the rave. That the play went on at all and then had the nerve to run a few weeks is for me a thing to be deeply thankful for. But I can understand the disappointment of those who were hoping for a better return.

I'm working on a short stage monologue (in English) for Pat Magee, whose voice you may have heard on the tapes I sent Barney. It looks as if it might come off.

Endspiel in Roger Blin's *mise en scène*[2] opens in Vienna day after tomorrow, in a small new theatre (Theater am Fleishmarkt). Alternance with Ionesco, Genet and Ghelderode, so I'm in good company.[3] Genet's new play, *Les Nègres*, is very fine.

I had a note from Barney's secretary Judith Schmidt[4] saying she had seen the play again and been very impressed by acting and production.

Hope the flu is gone. Write when you have a moment. Salutations to Jean and to my niece.

Ever
Sam [handwritten]

1. The missing first page of AS's letter (20 February 1958) probably referred to this blizzard, a record snowfall of more than 36 inches; "BA": Brooks Atkinson.

2. *Endspiel (Endgame)*, directed by Roger Blin, opened 8 March. George Bucher (Hamm), Karl Schellenberg (Clov), Franz Ibaschitz (Nagg), Mela Wigandt (Nell). *mise en scène*: staging (the total visual impact of a theatrical production, including settings, costumes, lighting, and the positions and movements of the actors).

3. Eugène Ionesco (1912–1994), Rumanian-born French playwright; Jean Genet (1910–1986), French playwright and novelist; Michel de Ghelderode (1898–1962), Belgian playwright.

4. Judith Schmidt [Douw] (b. 1926), Barney Rosset's secretary and general factotum at Grove Press, became one of SB's regular correspondents.

[March 12] 1958

Dear Sam,

Good to hear from you again. The flu is gone, spring stirs, and there's even the possibility of coming to London this summer for a play.

ENDGAME over 50 performances and coming along. In spite of whatever difficulties, climatic and otherwise, we are doing well. If the management could afford lower prices oftener, we'd be getting even more people in. As it is, we're getting on.

A new Clov went in last week, Alvin Epstein going off to another venture. The new actor is Gerry Hiken,[1] who won the Derwent Award for the best supporting actor (in THE SEAGULL) a couple of seasons ago; he's an old acquaintance having worked for several years with me at Arena Stage in Washington. Gerry is smaller, lighter, simpler and very effective—even more so as he plays it a while. He was not available at the time we originally cast the play. So we feel fortunate to have him.

The performance generally seems quite effective to me, the once or twice a week I'm there, although I'm sure it varies in quality. The older people are very good, much more relaxed than they were, they are straining less and achieving more. Alvin was excellent, I thought, although that last speech of his was always a problem. And I like Rawlins as Hamm, though I wish he were ten years older, what he lacks especially is Blin's sense of maturity; but his voice is very good, and he is remarkable in the long story. Still not satisfied with the way we've carried out the ending, but don't yet know what to do. . . .

And I've been meaning to ask you: Why you cut out that much of the scene relating to the small boy coming. In the French version, it's quite a scene, in the English just a few lines. (I meant to ask you while we were first rehearsing, but hesitated. . . . .)

Understand completely about your not coming over. So please forgive my asking.

What happened to the production in Vienna? Searching the papers here, but no word . . . Gather that George Devine is trying to get the Arts Theatre for it in London, a logical and good idea and a further showing up of the ridiculousness of that kind of censorship.[2]

Barney finally got the tapes on to me. Enjoyed listening to them no end, and that voice of Pat Magee's is fantastically interesting. We have talked about using them prior to ENDGAME; but the management seems to think we're going along very well as we are; and that the additional problems of equipment, wiring, and perhaps stagehands are too much to overcome. Barney and I were kind of hoping something could be done, especially with the MOLLOY.[3] We shall see.

Took some production photographs last week, and will try to send you some as soon as they are ready. The original set was shot by Gjon Mili[4] mostly for display; he hates to make copies; but the girl who took the new ones will make all the copies needed.

We've been having some Sunday evening 'symposiums' after the show; apart from some of the far-fetched nonsense that gets spouted, we find most enthusiastic responses for the play and your work in general. And some violent disagreements; which is all to the good.

Am serious about the London possibility mentioned above.[5] If it works out, I may be in London all summer, and will do all possible to get over to Paris at least once.

Hope you are well, finishing the translation, and getting to work on something new.

Jean and Vicky send their love.

[Alan]

1. Gerry Hiken (b. 1927), American actor, had played in Anton Chekhov's *The Seagull*, October 1956.
2. The Arts, a small theater club associated with the Royal Court Theatre, London, was not under the jurisdiction of the Lord Chamberlain.
3. SB's novel *Molloy*, 1951, English trans. by Patrick Bowles and SB, 1955.
4. Gjon Mili (1904–1984), American, born in Albania, innovative photographer, film-maker, lecturer, and writer. See *Gjon Mili: Photographs and Recollections*, 1980.
5. *The Deserters* by Thaddeus Vane, directed by AS, toured in England in August.

Paris
March 17th 1958

Dear Alan

Thanks for your letter of March 12th and news of *Endgame*. Delighted to hear it is still moving in spite of difficulties, and that you are pleased with the new Clov. We cut most of the boy scene during rehearsals here because we found it dragged and also because Blin couldn't bring it into line with his interpretation of the role. It's not important and I think the play is better without it. It seemed to break the tension.

The Vienna production opened with fair success ten days ago.

Suzanne and John Martin went. It shares the week (3 performances) with Genet's *Maids* and a Ghelderode-Ionesco bill (2 performances each). They hope for a two or three months run.

I'm glad you liked the tapes. I was very impressed by Magee, now playing in *The Iceman* at the Arts.[1] I have just written a short stage monologue[2] for him and shall be sending it to Barney this week. The idea on which it is based has endless possibilities and I hope to use it again for a French text. The realisation is another matter. I shall be very interested to hear what you think of it.

The news from Devine is that he is trying to create a club at the Royal Court. It depends on his being able to convince his committee. It is up for discussion this month. If it comes off he hopes to present *Endgame* in May. If he took the Arts he would not be able to produce himself.

I look forward to your production photographs. It is good news that you may be over again in the summer. It would be fine to talk with you again.

I have finished first draft of *Innommable* translation and it only (!) remains to revise and type it out clean. It should be out of my way by the end of April and then down to serious matters.

Love to Jean and Vicky.

Ever
Sam [handwritten]

1. Eugene O'Neill's *The Iceman Cometh* opened 29 January 1958.
2. "a short stage monologue": *Krapp's Last Tape*.

March 24 195[8]

Dear Sam,

I love *Krapp's Last Tape*; it's absolutely marvelous. And both Barney & I feel it would have been a great curtain-raiser—or curtain-follower —for ENDGAME. [handwritten at beginning of letter]

In fact, I'm trying to convince producers to let me try it with the show for the next few weeks—subject to your approval. Though this has various practical problems, paying another actor since it does not seem right to use actor from ENDGAME, working out some way not to reveal the ENDGAME set. Etc. All of which may make it impractical at Cherry Lane. But somewhere. Eventually.

Another problem came up last night. We're losing our Clov again, this time to Giradoux's THE ENCHANTED,[1] which is opening off-Broadway in a few weeks. They offered the part of the Supervisor to Hiken, who has evidently accepted. Which would have been all right for at least two or three weeks because he could have rehearsed during the day and played at night with us. But suddenly he also got a TV show, which meant that he has to rehearse ENCHANTED at night. So he's leaving after Sunday's performance, although I'm trying to work out an arrangement whereby the understudy—who is not too bad—could play one week (until the TV show is over), then Hiken would come back and play until he had to leave for the other show. This may nor may not work out. If it doesn't, we must either try to get Epstein back or find another Clov. And Hiken was excellent! *Is* excellent. But the off-Broadway problem is always and constantly losing actors to other and better paid jobs. We do what we can.

The management of the theatre has announced our closing date as of April 20—though they tell me we might run a bit longer if business warrants. We have held fairly steady for several weeks now. But, ironically enough since it was also the case with the Studio des C.E., they have evidently made a deal with another production (THE BOY FRIEND)[2] to come in the end of April or beginning of May for the summer months, since it's a light musical. Anyhow, we've had more than a little canter. Though, of course, it's always sad to think of a closing night.

We are going on a small tour, which might be not so small if dates and actors could be intertwined. We shall see. There have been about a dozen requests for the play's availability from groups throughout the country who want to do it themselves. And I'm sure it will have continued interest.

I'm so glad you are writing, and that the translation has gotten past the first draft. Looking forward always to everything you do.

We are making up a set of photos for you and for Barney, but these photographers take forever. Eventually, you'll receive them. . . . Glad about Vienna, wish I could see it. Though I'm hoping to catch it at Royal Court. I'm supposed to sail May 21st and go into rehearsal in London on June 20th. We shall see.

Jean sends love. And Vicki talks of you constantly.

[Alan]

1. *The Enchanted (Intemezzo)* opened at Renata Theatre, New York, 22 April 1958.
2. *The Boy Friend* by Sandy Wilson (b. 1924), English dramatist, ran for over four years in England and for fifteen months on Broadway; *Endgame* closed on 27 April after 104 performances.

Paris
March 30th 1958

Dear Alan

I'm glad you like the monologue. I think it would be a pity to rush it into production. It requires a pretty hefty actor and the magneto-phonics very careful rehearsal. It could eventually raise the curtain for *Endgame* without any set complications, as the whole thing is played, apart from the two or three retreats backstage, in a small pool of light front centre, the rest of the stage being in darkness (I presume this is technically feasible). I have had no reaction from Devine so far, but if he wants to take it on and if he succeeds in organising club conditions at the Court for production of *Endgame* in May, I should be inclined to go to London and make a nuisance of myself at *Krapp* rehearsals and we could talk about it then.

I'm told Clov carries skis at the end of *Endgame*. I think I understand your idea, but I feel this is wrong, stylistically and because "no more snow". Load him down as much as you like with shabby banal things, coats, bags and a pair of spare boots hanging from his neck if you like, but not skis. He once asked Hamm for a pair and was told to get out to hell. I know it's only a wretched detail.

I'm sorry you are losing Hiken and having such tiresome juggling to attend to. I consider we shall have had a very good run—for such a beast!

Love to Jean and Vicki.

Ever
Sam [handwritten]

Paris
27.4.58

Dear Alan

Many thanks for your letter and photographs. I like the look of the set very much and certain photos of Hamm are very impressive. It is good of you to keep me so fully informed of your changes and chances. I am very pleased with the way things have gone after such an obtuse press and I thank you all again, you and your actors, for all you have done to [?]defend this difficult play.

I have corrected proofs of *Krapp* for Barney and made a few minor changes which please note. I have no further news from George Devine who is on the continent at the moment. I hope to see him here next week. It seems to me very unlikely that his production will be next month, particularly as the *Iceman* has become a commercial success and that Magee will not be free for the monologue.

There is talk of a short revival of *Fin de partie* here, previous to their tour in Holland. They are also to give two performances at the Venice Biennale in July.[1] Talk also of a film (Alain Resnais)[2] of the French *All That Fall*.[3] I have not yet given the green light for this, but so admire Resnais that I probably shall.

I saw Tallmer's 'Endgame Revisited' in the *Village Voice* and was pleased by his tribute to your [?]care & [?]exacting control of production.[4]

It will be good to see you soon again.
Greetings to Jean and Vicky.

Ever
Sam

1. Roger Blin's "Le Théâtre D'Aujourd'hui" took part in the "Holland Festival 1958": *Fin de partie* opened on 21 June at the Rotterdamse Schouwburg, Rotterdam, 22 June at the Schevingen Kurhauscabaret, and 24 June at the Nieuwe de la Martheater, Amsterdam, directed by Roger Blin, designed by Jacques Noël. Roger Blin (Hamm), Jean Martin (Clov), Georges Adet (Nagg), Alice Reichen (Nell). *Acte sans paroles I* also opened, directed by Deryk Mendel, designed by Jacques Noël, music by John Beckett. Deryk Mendel (Man). They opened at the Teatro del Ridotto, 3 July 1958, as part of the XVII International Theatre Festival, La Biennale di Venezia.
2. Alain Resnais (b. 1922), French film director.
3. *All That Fall*, 1957.
4. "'Endgame' Revisited," *The Village Voice*, 2 April 1958. Returned after two months, Tallmer found "a much better production and, consequently, a better play, more lucid, funnier, much more moving . . . an over-all tightening, sharpening, and recovery from opening-night chillblains." Schneider, he said, had "stayed closely on top of the production."

Ussy-sur-Marne
15.5.58

Dear Alan

This hurried line to thank you for *Endgame* photos which I received only today because of forwarding confusions here. They are very fine and give me some idea of production. Thank you also for announcement of Chicago production.

I dropped everything and went to Berne for a few days and am now faced with mountains of work and the problem of preventing Spring growing into the house. It's all getting a bit too much for me.

You will soon be, if you are not already, on your way to England. I have no news of Devine, but hope to meet him soon.

Forgive more now. Greetings to Jean and Vicky.

Yours ever
Sam

Ussy
26.5.58

Dear Alan

This just to bid you welcome to our [?]mess and to thank you for your letter and for all the trouble you have gone to over the *Endgame* recording.[1]

I have promised Barney *The Unnamable* for next week and am up to my eyes in it, so won't attempt a proper letter now.

I have had neither sight nor news of Devine and have no idea what his plans are for *Endgame* and *Krapp*. Blin and his merry men are rehearsing for their tour in Holland next month. They will also be at the Venice Biennale.

Things very bad here, *mais ils ne passeront pas!*[2]

Greetings to Jean and Vicky. I hope I'll see you all in London.

Yours ever
Sam

1. Letter missing; *Endgame* recording with Lester Rawlins, Gerald Hiken, and others, reissued by Evergreen Records EUR 003 Ster 1968.
2. *"mais ils ne passeront pas"*: but they will not pass.

Ussy
10.6.58

Dear Alan

Your letter here this morning.[1] I'm sorry you are having such botherations and hope you are now comfortably settled in somewhere and
down to work. I do not expect to be in Paris this week. Perhaps next,
but not sure either. I'm disgustingly tired & stupified since finishing
L'Innommable[2] and writing seems more than ever before a quite impossible enterprise.

Not a word from Devine, nor from Barney since he telephoned to
chivvy me on with the translation. A cable from Tallmer announcing
Endgame has been given the *Village Voice* off-Broadway Award.[3] I don't
know what that is. And a letter from a Washington group who seem
pleased with their *Godot* production and said they had seen you.

We shall certainly meet before you go back. About when will that
be? When you have a moment let me know your plans and dates more
fully. If you can't come to Paris I'll skip over to London before you
leave.

Things here are dark, to put it brightly. Something like the end of the
last resort, for many.

Ever thine & [?]thine's
Sam

1. Missing.
2. "*L'Innommable*": trans. *The Unnamable*, 1958, 1959.
3. The Obie Award.

6 Rue des Favorites
Paris
7th July 1958

Dear Alan

Thanks for your letter.[1] I'm off for a jaunt to Belgrade and environs
tomorrow, to get rid of my *Godot* and *Molloy* dinars, and won't be back
in Paris much before the end of the month. I still don't know if I shall
go to London in September or not, it mostly depends on Devine. In any
case if you could skip over for a few days in August after your opening,

if would be fine. My only news of the Royal Court is that last Friday they were to give a private reading of *Endgame* (perhaps you were there) in the presence of the LC and the hope of getting him to change his "mind".[2] Which means I presume that the project of a Royal Court Club has been abandoned.

Blin's group toured the play briefly in Holland (Rotterdam, Amsterdam, The Hague (Scheveningen)). In this last place fire destroyed set and props, including the tape for the mime, and all had to be replaced for Venice where they played last Thursday and Friday.

My movements in Jugoslavia are too uncertain for me to leave instructions about forwarding of mail, so I'll be without letters till the end of the month. I hope then there will be one from you announcing your visit in the second half of August.

Things are very quiet here now and seem likely to continue so.

Greetings to Jean and Vicky.

Yours ever
Sam [handwritten]

1. Missing.

2. He did not, but the ban was eventually removed on 6 August 1958. It had become a matter of public controversy: *The Observer*, 9 February 1958; *The Times*, 10 February; *News Chronicle*, 10 February; *Daily Telegraph*, 10 February; *Daily Mail*, 10 February; *Evening Standard*, 11 February.

6 Rue des Favorites
Sept. 17 1958

Schneider
CHERRY LANE THEATRE (38 COMMERCE ST) NYK
PENSEES AFFECTUEUSES A TOUS[1]

SAM

1. Affectionate regards to all.

Ussy
18.10.58

Dear Alan

Thanks for your letter. Not sure where you are, so writing this to NY. I'm going to London on Tuesday for the last rehearsals of *Krapp* and shall probably stay on to eve of opening Oct 28th.[1] Wish you could be there. Devine came over and we had lunch and went over *Endgame*. He had compared the French and English very carefully and pointed out omissions (involuntary) in my translation. If you ever revive it I'll let you have them. I've been sweating on the French text of *Krapp* and have now a more or less tolerable version at last—and agreeable to the translator! I've gone wrong on the other act[2] I was telling you about and shall have to try it again, if after London there is anything left of me. I hear Barney is safe home, after having got lost in the fog somewhere. I would have caught up on the ravelled skein but for invincible insomnia and concomitant wanderings. However, all in the day's colossal joke. It was indeed good seeing you and Jean and meeting Vicky and her divine ignorance of her whereabouts. Thank you again for all the Endgames, I know what trouble it cost you and what affection is behind it, I'll be at them this winter in the long country evenings.[3] Working on *Krapp* it occurred to me that "Wonderful old woman though" is perhaps better than "Wonderful woman though". If you agree will you make the change in your script? As I said to Barney I leave it now to you and him to do it when and where you like. I think there may be two more short 'uns before the merry new year, but I can't guarantee, and if you feel like going ahead with *Krapp* go ahead.

Affectionately, dear Alan, to you all.
Sam [handwritten]

1. Letter missing; *Krapp's Last Tape* opened at Royal Court Theatre, 28 October 1958, directed by Donald McWhinnie. Pat Magee (Krapp). With *Endgame*, directed by George Devine. George Devine (Hamm), Jack MacGowran (Clov), Richard Goolden (Nagg), Frances Cuka (Nell). Both designed by Jocelyn Herbert. SB attended rehearsals and advised.

2. "the other act": unidentified, but see JK, 456, suggesting it may have been reworked as *Theatre II* or *Rough for Theatre II*.

3. During his visit to Paris in October 1957, AS found a bookshop along the quays that specialized in books on chess; he presented SB with Henri Rinck's *150 Endspielstudien*, 1909.

6 Rue des Favorites
Paris 15me
21.11.58

Dear Alan

I have just read your article in the *Chelsea Review* and am deeply touched by its great warmth of attachment for my dismal person and devotion to my grisly work. Thanks from my heart.[1]

I want to tell you about *Krapp* in London. I worked on it for about 5 days with McWhinnie and Magee before we opened. I am extremely pleased with the result and find it hard to imagine a better performance than that given by Magee both in his recording and his stage performance. McWhinnie, who has not worked in the theatre for years, proved an admirable director and controlled Magee as I think no one else could have.[2] In the course of rehearsals we established a certain amount of business which is not indicated in the script and which now seems to me indispensable. If Barney ever brings out the work in book form I shall enlarge the stage directions accordingly. The stage management of the technical difficulties was also extremely good. How I wish you could have seen it! It ran over 35 minutes, to my astonishment. Before leaving London I arranged for a studio recording to be made and the tape sent to Barney, but have not yet heard if this has been done. If I could only see you and go into it again in detail. All the things we talked about together here were used and worked (with the exception of the banana peel into the pit which had to be cut because of proximity of front stall seats!). He simply boots it out of his way towards the wings. The most interesting discovery was the kind of personal relationship that developed between Krapp and the machine. This arose quite naturally and was extraordinarily effective and of great help in the early stages whenever the immobility of the listening attitude tended to be tedious. If you have not already begun to work on it I think it might be a good idea for me to send you an annotated script. Things cannot be made quite clear in this way and I shall not remember the precise incidence of certain effects, but it would be perhaps better than nothing. Let me know what you think. At the very end, when "I lay down across her etc." comes for the third time, the head goes down on the table and remains down until "Here I end etc", on which it comes up and the eyes staring front till the end. At this point too he has his arm round the machine. Because of the apron at the Royal Court the table with recorder and boxes is visible before the curtain from the outset. Lights out, Krapp slips into place from behind the curtain, then the sudden full blaze on him. At the end on the contrary we had a fade-out and the quite unexpected and marvellous effect of recorder's red light burning up as the dark gathered, this unfortunately visible only to half the house because of the position of the machine at the edge of the table to Krapp's left. Krapp's route from table to shadows was the roundabout one I foresaw. With the script before me I'd find more to tell you, but I'm in the country and haven't got it with me. Don't feel I want to interfere with your interpretation or that I think there is no other way of doing it but ours. All I suggest—if you agree, and when you do—is that I send you a detailed account of all this material and that then you use it or not as you please.

I returned to Paris very tired and jumpy with the text non-stop in my head in the usual way. . .

Blin is doing a reading of the French *Krapp* on December 12th in a new series of *"lectures à une voix"* at the Vieux Colombier organised by Duvignaud and Claude Sarraute.[3] No plans for a stage performance that I know of, though vague talk of a revival of *Fin de partie* for a month's run before they go on tour with it in January to Switzerland and Rome.

Hope all is well with you, and with Jean and Vicky, and that you are engaged on something worth while. Drop me a line and let me have your news and your views.

Affectionately to you all
Sam [handwritten]

1. "Waiting for Beckett: A Personal Chronicle," *Chelsea Review*, 2, Autumn 1958, 3–20.

2. Donald McWhinnie (1920–1987), Assistant Head of Sound Drama at the BBC, where he had directed *All That Fall* and the Magee readings. He directed a number of SB plays beginning with *Krapp's Last Tape* at the Royal Court Theatre production, Jack MacGowran's "End of Day: Entertainments from Works of Samuel Beckett," Dublin Theatre Festival, 1962, and *Endgame* at the Nottingham Playhouse, 1964.

3. *Krapp's Last Tape*, French trans. by Pierre Leyris and SB, *La Dernière bande* in *Les Lettres nouvelles*, 1958; *"lectures à une voix"*: one-man readings; the Vieux Colombier: a theater in Paris. Jean Duvignaud (b. 1921), French critic and scholar; Claude Sarraute (b. 1927), French journalist.

Paris
27.11.58

Dear Alan

This line in haste to thank you for your letter[1] and answer your *Krapp* and letters queries.

There is no point in your holding up *Krapp* on the chance of a new play from me to go with it, there will be none now for a long time as far as I can foresee. So do it as soon as you like, when and wherever.

I prefer those letters not to be republished and quite frankly, dear Alan, I do not want any of my letters to anyone to be published anywhere, either in the *petit pendant* or the long *après*.[2]

. . . .[3]

Love to Jean and Vicky.

Ever
Sam [handwritten]

1. Missing.
2. *"petit pendant . . . après":* neither in the brief now nor during the long thereafter.
3. SB comments on "murk and gloom" in Paris.

Ussy-sur-Marne
27.1.59

Dear Alan

Many thanks for your letter. I am sorry to hear of the worry you are having with your father. I hope he is by now well over the attack and that you can return to NY with a fairly easy mind.[1]

. . . .[2]

Have been mostly here in the country ever since trying with scant success to work. But nothing to do with theatre or radio, from which I need a long rest. Having no tape-recorder and been so little in Paris I have not yet been able to hear the *Endgame* recording. I'll ask them to play it for me at the BBC Paris studio one of these days. I felt very strongly in London how completely wrong and damaging to the play the Noël set is.[3] Not his fault, mine. The hearts of oak were very sour and disapproving of such indecent preoccupation with sorrow and the show just hobbled on a month. However Magee's performance made up for everything.

Nothing of interest in Paris except possibly the new Anouilh *("L'Hurluberlu")* opening shortly at the Champs-Elysées and the Camus adaptation of Dostoevsky's "Possessed" which plays 4 hours! *Couturière* tomorrow at the Antoine. Blin and Martin are both in it. What little theatres are left are having the hell of a time, flop after flop. Ionesco's *"Tueur sans gages"* is having stormy rehearsals at the onetime cinema Récamier.[4]

I have given an old half-baked radio script to the 3rd, perhaps just worth doing. I'll be sending it along to Barney soon.[5]

Affectionate greetings to Jean and Vicky.

Yours ever
Sam [handwritten]

1. Letter missing; his father: Leopol [Leo] Victorovitch (Lyova) Schneider.

2. SB has been to Dublin.

3. SB thought Noël's set for the Royal Court Theatre's production of *Fin de partie*, 1957, was too elaborate, preferring Jocelyn Herbert's for the 1958 production at the RCT.

4. Jean Anouilh (1907–1987), *L'Hurluberlu (The Fighting Cock)*; "the Camus Dostoevsky": Camus's adaptation of Dostoevsky's *Les Possédés* at the Théâtre Antoine, 25 February 1959; *couturière*: the rehearsal preceding the full dress rehearsal when alterations are made to the costumes; Ionesco's *Tueur sans gages: The Killer*.

5. *Embers*: written in English, sent to BBC February 1959, published in *Evergreen Review*, 1959, French trans. by Robert Pinget and SB, *Cendres*, in *Les Lettres nouvelles*, 1959.

February 22 (1959)

Dear Sam,

Just a quick one this time. About KRAPP.

Barney and I have been investigating various possibilities since the fall, and for one reason or another they have fallen through. One fellow had a theatre which didn't open. Another wanted to do it but had a fight with his partner (on another issue) and quit. Another theatre became unavailable. Etc. Standard NY confusion. On the other hand, there was Lortel and that matinee at the De Lys Theatre, a one-shot with Eli Wallach which we didn't want to commit ourselves to.[1]

A while ago, we got a couple of new ideas. The problem of getting a theatre is tied up to the fact that KRAPP is too short to do by itself, it is too difficult evidently to find something suitable to go with it which will please a theatre owner, etc. So we thought of two other kinds of possibilities; doing it not in a theatre at all but in a kind of 'night-club', jazz-spot; or doing it in a small theatre on Monday nights when the theatre was dark—and doing it two or three times in one night.

Now, as it turns out, both alternatives are possible. THE FIVE SPOT, a rather well-known bohemian cabaret which has been flourishing a year or so and which in addition to its diet of jazz combos has had poetry readings by Rexroth and others with some success, is interested in the idea. We would have to work out financial and physical arrangements, but the former could be settled—it's only the latter which worry me. That is, the amount of space, distance from the audience, lack of proper stage, proscenium, lighting, etc. There are, however, things which could be done; if you indicated your willingness, we could investigate them seriously. We have already discovered that by stopping the sale of liquor before and during the performance, we could fit into the legal requirements.

The other possibility is to make a deal with the owners of the Cherry Lane, Circle in the Square, or other small (preferably Greenwich Village) theatre to rent their house on its dark night, Monday, and see if we couldn't get a run out of it that way. I believe it would also be possible to get Equity to agree to more than one performance a night. Thus by charging a small price, say one dollar, two or three times a night, we might have something financially viable in terms of an actor's salary, lighting and publicity. If success is overwhelming, then we might take it from there. But we would start out with the Monday night idea. And two or three managements are interested.

Barney leans to the first idea more than I do, but likes the 2nd as well. I'm genuinely worried about the possibility of getting a proper performance in a night-club atmosphere, smoke-filled and talk-filled as it tends to be. I might be wrong, and it might be just the right off-beat situation. Anyhow, let us know your sentiments, and we shall be guided by them.

By the way, Barney said something about another radio play you had completed. If so, or if you've made progress on another one [ending missing]

[Alan]

1. Lucille Lortel (b. 1912), American actress, producer, and theater proprietor, owned the Theatre de Lys, in Greenwich Village, later renamed the Lucille Lortel Theatre, 1981, where she started the ANTA Matinee Series of innovative plays. She presented SB's *Embers* (1960), but her major involvement with his work came when she coproduced the

world premiere of *Ohio Impromptu, Catastrophe,* and *What Where* (1983) and *Enough, Footfalls,* and *Rockaby* (1984) at the Samuel Beckett Theatre. AS directed these later productions. Eli Wallach (b. 1915), American actor who might have played Krapp.

Ussy
3.3.59

Dear Alan

Glad to have news of you. All wishes for a happy new pa and ma ternity.[1] You don't say how your father is. Much better I hope.

With regard to *Krapp* I don't much like the night club idea, I think it could only be bungled in such an atmosphere. The Monday performance, though not exhilarating, would I think be preferable. It is a delicate and technically rather ticklish production and needs at least quiet. Another possibility is just to leave it for the moment, until there is or I have something to go with it. It is not because it is there written that you must feel it must be done at once, I was never in a hurry about such things. There will be no more theatre or radio from me now until I have done something that goes on from *The Unnamable* and *Texts for Nothing*[2] or decided there is no going on from there for me, either of which operations will take a long time probably. I have sent the other radio text (two years ago) to Grove, but apart from the air it can only be done as a reading, no question of a stage performance. It is not of any great interest in any case. It will be broadcast by the 3rd I think in June.[3] As typing shows tired tonight after slogging all day for nothing, it seems to produce metatheses, I've often noticed it. Have been in Paris lately and saw the Camus Dostoevsky and the new Ionesco both depressing to me and a reading of Arrabal[4] at the Montparnasse Poche, a good evening that. Back here now until some convivial pal pops up in Montparnasse, always irresistible. Have to be in Dublin early July,[5] otherwise no plans. Hope you'll have a production in Europe this summer. In the meantime good luck to all your projects Broadway, off and road and affectionately to you all.

Sam [handwritten]

1. Alan and Jean Schneider's son, David Alan, was born 9 April.
2. *Nouvelles et textes pour rien,* 1955, English trans. by Richard Seaver, Anthony Bonner, and SB, *Stories and Texts for Nothing* in *No's Knife: Collected Shorter Prose 1945–1966,* 1957.

3. *Embers* broadcast on BBC Third Programme, 24 June 1959, directed by Donald McWhinnie. Jack MacGowran (Henry), Kathleen Michael (Ada), Kathleen Helme (Addie), Patrick Magee (Music master/Riding master).

4. Fernando Arrabal (b. 1932), Spanish dramatist and novelist, associated with the "theater of the absurd" and "theater of cruelty."

5. SB received an honorary D. Litt. from Trinity College Dublin, 2 July 1959.

Paris
6.9.59

Dear Alan

Good to hear from you after so long.[1] I was hoping you might be over this summer. Next without fail please. I was in Dublin for a week in July, then briefly in London on the way back, where I heard the tape of EMBERS. Good performance and production but doesn't come off. My fault, text too difficult. Good luck with GODOT in Texas, I am so glad you are directing it again.[2] Struggling with new work in French,[3] nothing to do with theatre or radio, hope to get back to that society game in about a year. KRAPP with SQUARE would please me much or with Pinget's DEAD LETTER (2 acts) also done lately on the 3rd.[4] They would let you have the script. Congratulations on such activity and second paternity. Greetings to all involved in GODOT at the Alley. Love to Jean and Vicky. Let me know how it goes.

Yours ever
Sam [handwritten]

1. Letter missing.

2. *Waiting for Godot* opened at the Alley Theatre, Houston, 9 September 1958. Sidney Kay (Estragon), John Astin (Vladimir), John Wylie (Lucky), Carl Bensen (Pozzo), Neil Tucker (A Boy). SB did not believe it could be done successfully in the round. AS discussed theater-in-the-round in "Four in the Round," *Theatre Arts*, April 1957, 72–73, 91–93.

3. *Comment c'est*, 1961, English trans. by SB, *How It Is*, 1964.

4. Earlier at the Théâtre de Poche Montparnasse, SB had seen *Le Square (The Square)* by dramatist Marguerite Duras (1914–1995), born in French Indo-China; Robert Pinget (b. 1919), Swiss-born novelist and playwright.

Ussy
21.9.59

Dear Alan

Many thanks for your interesting letter.[1] So glad you are pleased with production and reception. Can't see it in the round but my fault.

Back in the country working after a quick trip to Italy. Have an idea for 2 variants on the *Krapp* theme but can't do anything about it till I finish what I'm doing. [?] . . . would be situation if instead of sacrificing the girl in the boat for the *opus . . . magnum* he had done the reverse. You see the idea, triptych, three doors closed instead of one, the one with [?]girl alone dates no. 3.

> 1. Krapp, Mrs Krapp, child.
> 2.   "   "   childless
> 3.   "   alone.[2]

Nice thing to offer the public. Looking forward to Barney next week. And to you and I hope Jean next spring. Good luck with *Summer.*[3] What a worker you are!

Affectionately to you all
Sam

1. Missing.
2. SB also considered Krapp with his wife; Krapp with his wife and child; Krapp alone. "I thought of writing a play on the opposite situation with Mrs. Krapp, the girl in the punt, nagging away behind him, in which case his failure and his solitude would be exactly the same." Quoted in Dougald McMillan and Martha Fehsenfeld, *Beckett in the Theatre*, 288–289.
3. Ray Lawler (b. 1922), *The Summer of the Seventeenth Doll.*

Paris
20.11.59

Dear Alan

To introduce my friend Robert Pinget, French novelist & playwright. I have great esteem for his work. He is in the States on a theatre research scholarship. I'd be very grateful if you'd show him round a bit and introduce him to some of the theatre crowd.

Write me some time.

Affectionately to you all.
Sam

6 Rue des Favorites
Paris 15me
7.12.59

Dear Alan

Many thanks for your letter.

I am very fond of Robert Pinget.[1] He is a remarkable writer. He has written a short play *(Lettre Morte)* which you shd have a look at. It was produced by the BBC 3rd programme. He has also written a radio play which I have translated for the BBC. He could show you the text. It is not definitive. If you could show him something of the theatre ropes I'd be most grateful. He sounds very homesick for Europe from his letters.

By all means an off-Broadway revival of *Godot* on one condition— that *you* direct.

I met Albee here at a rehearsal of Genet's *NÈGRES*. As you may have heard his *Zoo Story* was billed with *Krapp* in Berlin and elsewhere in Germany.[2] I read the play and liked it. He mentioned in a letter that there was talk in N.Y. of the same double bill. What wd you think of this? It'd be all right with me. Pretty gruesome evening though.

Sometimes of an evening play Endgames with myself from your book. I'm struggling with very difficult new work, but nothing to do with the theatre.[3]

Glad you are pleased with your new home.[4] Must be much better for both children & parents. I'm afraid I don't know when life begins. I'm still waiting personally.

Affectionately to you all. Let me know how things go, and come over soon.

Ever
Sam

1. Letter missing; Robert Pinget was the leading exponent of the *nouveau roman*. Pinget's *La Lettre morte* was performed by the BBC Third Programme, 27 July 1959; his *La Manivelle*, trans. by SB, *The Old Tune*, produced by Barbara Bray, was broadcast on 23 August 1960, with Patrick Magee and Jack MacGowran. Published in *Evergreen Review*, 1961.

2. Edward Albee (b. 1928), American dramatist, director, producer. *Das Letzte Band* opened at Schiller-Theater Werkstatt, 28 September 1959, directed by Walter Henn, designed by H. W. Lenneweit. Walter Franck (Krapp). *Die Zoo-Geschichte* opened on the same night, with the same director and designer.

3. *Comment c'est.*

4. Hastings-on-Hudson.

Ussy
4.1.60

Dear Alan

Thanks for your two letters, second today. I hasten to reply. First your specific points:

1. *Spool* instead of *reel* if you wish.

2. *Post Mortems* by all means.

3. Instead of *weir* suggest *sluice* or *lock*.

4. Should prefer you to keep *stem*.

5, If *dell* is clearer than *dingle* by all means. Same thing.

Now the rest.

Know nothing whatever about "extra speaker to tape recorder" in Berlin and am not sure what this means.[1] If it does what I fear it is plain murder and unpardonable. I dream sometimes of all German directors of plays with perhaps one exception united in one with his back to the wall and me shooting a bullet into his balls every five minutes till he loses his taste for improving authors. Krapp has nothing to talk to but his dying self and nothing to talk to him but his dead one. I think we discussed the technical problems raised by the machine. The text re-corded should be spoken obviously in a much younger and stronger voice than Krapp's for his last tape (though as McWhinnie remarked voices don't always age abreast of the rest), but unmistakably his. The visible machine on the table should obviously be a dummy (too risky otherwise with all the violent manipulations), by which I mean of course a real machine visibly working and stopping when switched on and off but the tape silent. The machine heard has to be worked off stage which involves very delicate cue work from the wings but there seems no other way of doing it. By the way for God's sake make sure in your script that there are no omissions or variations in the repeated passages. What helps for the cue is for Krapp to have a very special gesture for switching on and off which though it has to be abrupt may be prepared by a change of posture (straightening a little out of his crouch for example), the same each time. Hard to explain these things in writing. When writing the piece if I had been more familiar with tape recorders I might have had Krapp wind back and forward *without* switching off for the sake of the extraordinary sound that can be had apparently in this way (Blin did it), but it would certainly complicate things technically and better not try it. I told you about the beautiful and quite accidental effect in London of the luminous eye burning up as the machine runs on in silence and the light goes down. It is not visible from all parts of the house unless you can manage two eyes, one on each side, or the eye in front in the middle! This requires of course a slow fade out at the end which I think is good in any case, but not a fade on at the beginning. It is better the curtain should go up on a dark stage and then suddenly full blaze on Krapp seated at his table. He should be in a pool of light and of course near the front (just enough room between table and edge of stage for banana gag and walk back-stage). All backstage as black as possible, he can disappear through black drapes for his drinks and dictionary. Nothing whatever on stage but table. We also I think discussed his itinerary from table backstage. The one I recommend and which we used in London is quite unnatural but correct dramatically, it is

and has the great advantage of lengthening the walk (to compensate immobility) and of allowing Krapp to be inspected in motion as he would not be if he took the normal route in a straight line from behind table backstage. I think this is important. With regard to costume it should be sufficiently clear from text (don't be afraid of exaggerating with boots). Black and white (both dirty), the whole piece being built up in one sense on this simple antithesis of which you will find echoes throughout the text (black ball, white nurse, black pram, Bianca, Kedar—anagram of "dark"—Street, black storm, light of understand-ing, etc.) Black dictionary if you can and ledger. Similarly black and white set. Table should be small (plain kitchen table) cluttered up with tapes and boxes until he sweeps them to the ground (maximum of violence). In the light everything as visible as possible, hence unnatural opening of drawers towards audience, i.e. when he extracts spool from left drawer he holds it up so that it can be seen before he puts it back, similarly with bananas as soon as taken from drawer, similarly with envelope and keys and whenever else possible, almost (only almost!) like a conjuror exhibiting his innocent material. Another good effect is for the transition from repose to motion to be made as abrupt as possi-ble. He is motionless at table then suddenly (shock) in laborious mo-tion, not fast because he can't go fast, but looking fast because of sud-den start and effort entailed. Similarly when having eaten first banana he broods. What next? Suddenly back to table. Similarly when after second banana he "has an idea." Sudden turn and as fast as he can backstage. At the end, towards close of third repeat of boat passage, he can steal his arm round machine and sink his head on table. Then slowly up and staring front on "past midnight etc" to end. Throughout when listening to tape even if crouched down over machine he should have his face up and full front maximally visible, staring eyes etc. Lot to be done with eyes. They can close for example for boat passage. Pity Davis is tall.[2] I saw Krapp small and wizened. What else? Can't think. Bit late in day anyhow. Hope you have the right old tune for "Now the day etc." Herewith in case not.[3]

Hope these hurried notes may be of some service. Let me know how it goes.

Affectionately to you all.
Sam [handwritten]

1. Both letters missing. One mentioned "extra speaker to tape recorder" to which SB responds.
2. Donald Davis (b. 1928), Canadian actor.
3. "right old tune": the Irish chorale for "Now the Day is Over" (see McMillan and Fehsenfeld, *Beckett in the Theatre*, 286).

Saturday Jan. 16 [1960]

Dear Sam,

Well, by now you have read the notices and I have slept 48 hours straight—so we can talk. It went well Thursday night, very well, and I think you would have been pleased.[1] The critics, of course, showed their usual lack of perception; but the response was generally favorable even if they didn't know what or why. Davis was superb, both on the tape and live. In spite of his height I think you would have liked him, and there are times when he looks a bit like Pat Magee even . . . And one thing is certain: you could have heard half a pin drop except in all those places where they were laughing.

Your letter came a week ago in last stages of rehearsal, and followed as scrupulously as circumstances permitted. I was delighted by your comments regarding that extra speaker because I had had a big argument with Ed Albee about it. He said it had worked well in the Berlin production and gave me the impression you had approved, which is why I asked. We used one standard RCS tape recorder, with an EYE which we added since it didn't have one of its own. Visible from all parts of the house and very effective . . . You may be surprised, however, that we actually have Davis manipulate the tape, finding the cueing from offstage (there is no offstage at the Provincetown—where O'Neill got started, by the way) practically impossible. Have settled the winding and re-winding problem very simply although explaining it is complicated, using a new kind of unbreakable tape, and Davis has never missed a cue! And we even get some of Blin's extraordinary sounds on the recorder when Krapp goes forward or backward. . . . Our lighting is also very good, I think, albeit simple. Krapp in a pool of light except when he literally disappears upstage center for his stuff there. The only liberty we have taken and I trust it is not enough to justify any type of firing squad is to have a plain black funnel of an overhead lamp with an actual light bulb in it, which helps to create the pool, light Krapp's face, make him stoop more, and in general give the feeling of a work table. We didn't start out with it, but soon found that in order to see his eyes we needed a light source closer and more directly overhead than was possible in this particular theatre . . . Don't be misled by the publicity photos which appear with some of the notices; they were taken weeks ago before rehearsals started and in no way resemble our present Krapp. He has no mustache, no scarf of that kind, etc. We'll send you some actual photos as soon as there are any. . . . Davis does wonderful things with his eyes, hands, entire body; subtle yet always meaningful.

I love the play, it moves me every time, and I can hardly stand the ending. Really beautiful and true, and I could kill a critic who says 'no enduring value'[2] when every moment will be equally true one hundred years from now . . . Judith Schmidt equally moved, sorry Barney away, he'll come. . . . . . In the meantime, business is good, management pleased, the other play strange but interesting. . . . You know, this is first time I have directed one of your plays without seeing a previous production; maybe this turned out well in the case.

Kept 'Stem', naturally. Also dingle. LOCK for weir.

The weeklies should be even better because more intelligent. And I saw Jerry Tallmer tonight, who said he liked it very much.[3] Looking [ending missing]

[Alan]

1. Produced by Theatre 1960 (Richard Barr, H. B. Lutz, and Harry Joe Brown, Jr.), *Krapp's Last Tape* opened at the Provincetown Playhouse, New York, 14 January 1960. Donald Davis (Krapp). Performed in conjunction with Albee's *Zoo Story*, directed by Milton Katselas, who was Albee's original choice, then "let go"; Barr and Albee directed, although Katselas's name was on the program (*Entrances*, 275). Settings and lighting, William Ritman. Moved to Players Theatre 19 April, then Cricket Theatre, closed 21 May after 582 performances. Davis succeeded by Henderson Forsythe, then by Mark Rickman. Reviews: Walter Kerr, *NY Herald-Tribune*, 15 January 1960; Richard Watts, Jr., *NY Post*, 15 January; Brooks Atkinson, *NY Times*, 15 and 31 January; Frank Aston, *NY Telegram*, 15 January; *New Yorker*, 23 January; *Saturday Review*, 30 January; *Time*, 8 February. Each play received Obie Awards for "Distinguished Plays," Davis for "Distinguished Performance."

2. "no enduring value": Brooks Atkinson, *NY Times*, 15 January 1960.

3. *Village Voice*, 15 January.

Paris
23.1.60

Dear Alan

Many thanks for your letter. Judith sent all the morning paper notices. Surprisingly indulgent I thought. All my thanks for all the trouble you have taken and regard for my suggestions. Your lamp over the table sounds excellent, wish we had thought of it in London. Will you please, if you write again, explain to me exactly what they did in Berlin and what "extra speaker" means. Davis sounds fine. Please thank and congratulate him for me and all concerned. No sign at the moment of anything new for the theatre, few surviving energies hopelessly tied up in quite different work and no end in sight. Only solution to have two things going at once. Shall try soon.

Had a very pleasant session with Blau.[1]

Judith said how much she was moved. Hope it has similar effect on Barney.

No idea what rights Myerberg has.[2] I shouldn't think many now. We shd try to get a copy of his agreement with Donald Albery. I don't think it's too soon for a revival of that old cracked chestnut, in a nice small theatre far from Broadway. I'm for it. For you and Barney to decide.

Thanks again—dear Alan, for all your devotion to my work, and care of it.

Affectionately to you all
Sam

1. Herbert Blau (b. 1926), director, playwright, and postmodern critic, cofounder with Jules Irving (1925–1979) of the San Francisco Actor's Workshop (1952–1966), where they pioneered the work of SB and Brecht; became Artistic Director, Lincoln Center, New York (1965–1967). Wrote *The Impossible Theatre: A Manifesto*, 1964; *Blooded Thought*, 1982.

2. Michael Myerberg held the American production rights for *Waiting for Godot*, that "old cracked chestnut."

Boston
February 12, 1960

Dear Sam,

Sorry so long answering your last letter, which was much awaited and much appreciated by KRAPP cast and staff. Assume through Judith you have been kept informed and supplied with stream of notices, comment and general 'indulgence' to quote you. I do hope you are pleased. We did the show I think you wanted, and the fact that it came off as it did has been most welcome. We all, and I especially, wish you could come over and catch a glimpse before it gets run down or has to change performers, but I understand and appreciate your reluctance. Still you can't blame us for trying. . . .Some of the weeklies seemed much more discerning and, of course, Tallmer more than most. We seem to be selling out nightly—the theatre is just the right size: 192— and audiences most enthusiastic. Did you read the letter in the TIMES comparing it to a Rembrandt?????[1]

Production seems to be holding up, and Davis is excellent. What pleased us also was fact that when we lost Davis for a weekend to a TV show (this is standard practice off-Bway because of starvation wages paid to actors) our understudy did well and most people didn't realise it wasn't Davis though we told them. We have now lost understudy to another show and are breaking in a third Krapp. And so it goes.

Glad you liked lamp idea. Seemed simple and organic enough and was a great visual help, focus, source of actual illumination of Krapp's eyes. About that 'extra speaker' business from Berlin which I did not use, I'm not really sure just what they did do there because I was only told of this by Albee who gave me impression you knew and approved. I gather idea was that there was the tape machine on the table and next to it an extra attached and portable speaker (like a lid or box) which Krapp moved around, carried, held in his lap, etc. Frankly, it seemed tricky and contrived to me—especially as all our tape recorders in USA have their own built-in speakers so there was no logical reason for extra speaker. Also it seemed much more right and moving to me for Krapp to handle actual machine, lean, touch, handle, etc. As it turned out, you agreed. And one of the most effective moments is when he moves machine closer to him at the end and actually embraces it. Really lovely. And comes from actor and director carrying out author's stage directions, which we have tried to do throughout (although, I must confess, you are practically the only author whose stage directions seem so right and so much a part of what you are writing.)

Anyhow.

Loved figuring out handwriting on your last note. Kept me occupied for hours. In addition, was involved with replacements for CHERRY ORCHARD in Washington and SUMMER OF 17TH DOLL off-Broadway, both of which have recently ended their runs. Now in Boston doing University production of Kingsley's DETECTIVE STORY for financial gain. Seems as though KRAPP will be up here for one week in March when we lose Provincetown to previous booking. Catholic Church very strong in Boston and very rough on theatre, we shall see what happens . . . hah! Luckily several other commitments for the spring, one an interesting new play for Blau's group in San Francisco. And then MEASURE FOR MEASURE for NY Shakespeare Festival in July.[2] Trouble is won't be coming to Europe in summer as had hoped if time and finances permit. But latter especially rough, what with two kids, new house, medical bills, and general confusion. Luckily family is well apart from [part of line missing] of my involvement with [end of line missing]. No developments I know of on GODOT, either TV or Off-Bway, but presumably may be at any moment. Will keep you posted. And you know how much I am grateful for your feelings about my directing. Thanks, Sam.

Do hope you are well, not too depressed with French politics,[3] writing, and taking care of self.

Best to Suzanne. Jean joins me in sending affectionate regards.

[Alan]

1. AS gave an interview about *Krapp's Last Tape:* Louis Calta, "Director Defines Play by Beckett," *NY Times,* 6 February 1960.

2. Anton Chekhov's *Cherry Orchard* opened at the Arena Stage, 5 January 1960; Lawler's *Summer of the Seventeenth Doll,* Player's Theatre, New York, 13 October 1959; Sidney Kingsley's *Detective Story,* Boston University, 24 February 1960; *Measure for Measure,* New York Shakespeare Festival, Central Park, 25 July 1960.

3. France's Algerian problem and the sometimes violent repercussions in Paris form a background to the correspondence in these years. In December President Charles de Gaulle went to Algeria and was met with hostile demonstrations by settlers. On 10 and 11 December Muslims in Oran and Algiers demonstrated in favor of the Algerian republic, the National Liberation Front, and de Gaulle. This was seen as a turning point in the war, but the unrest continued until April 1962.

Ussy
25.2.60

Dear Alan

Many thanks for your good letter. The news of KRAPP is fine. Thanks again, dear Alan, for all you have done for this play and for me, and thanks again to Donald Davis.

It is going on in French (LA DERNIÈRE BANDE) at Vilar's second theatre (Récamier, near the old Babylone) next month, Blin directing himself, with Pinget's LETTRE MORTE directed by Jean Martin who plays the barman. Vilar guarantees us a minimum of 60 performances. The theatre, all done up by the TNP when they took it over 6 months ago, is very pleasant, one balcony, 580 seats. Whole setup most satisfactory, technically and financially, paradise after the Babylone and Studio. *Générale* I think March 27.[1] I wired the good news to Robert over a week ago and have had no answer. He was in Hollywood then or said to be. God knows where he is. Mexico probably. Great pity he's not here to help with the rehearsals. It's not an easy play to put over, but I think it will work very well. Levert is a fine role. It is sure to be running anyway when he gets back. The Berlin production of KRAPP and Z.S. is coming to the Théâtre des Nations in June, so then I shall see their bright idea[2] if I can face it.

Nothing much to relate. Slogging away intermittently at the French work. Moving in April to a new apartment other side of Montparnasse (Bd. St.-Jacques), after over 20 years Rue des F. More space and I love the quarter. Shall let you have full address later on.

Judith sent me your article on me.[3] I liked it very much. In the next you may add a 2 HP Citroen to the telephone. I've had it since April and probably told you already. Great help.

BBC GODOT next month, McWhinnie directing. I think Pat Magee will do Lucky. Other players not yet decided.[4] MacGowran unfortunately not available, booked at Stratford for whole season. There's grandeur for you. I am trying to translate opening of new work[5] for Magee to read at some literary-musical do in the Festival Hall Recital Room in April I think? Poor man!

Voilà. Affectionately to you all.

Sam [handwritten]

1. Jean Vilar (1912–1971), French actor, director, founder of the Avignon Festival, 1947, was in charge of the Théâtre National Populaire (TNP), Théâtre Récamier, 1951–1963. *La Dernière bande* opened 22 March, directed by Roger Blin. R. J. Chauffard (Krapp). Robert Pinget's *La Lettre morte*, directed by Jean Martin, was on the same program. SB, who attended a few rehearsals, offered the part of Krapp to Roger Blin, who preferred to direct, to SB's disappointment.

2. Albee's *Zoo Story*, 1959; "their bright idea": the "extra speaker" for Krapp's tape recorder (see letter of 12 February 1960).

3. See letter of 21 November 1958, n. 1.

4. The BBC Third Programme broadcast *Waiting for Godot*, 25 April 1960, produced and directed by Donald McWhinnie. Wilfrid Brambell (Estragon), Patrick Magee (Vladimir), Donal Donnelly (Lucky), Felix Fenton (Pozzo), Jeremy Ward (A Boy), Denys Hawthorne (Narrator). Repeated 17 May 1960.

5. Patrick Magee read from *How It Is*, described on the program as a new, unfinished novel, at a *Music Today* concert in the Royal Festival Hall Recital Room, 5 April 1960 (see Deirdre Bair, *Samuel Beckett*, 436).

April 9, 1960

Dear Sam,

Just back from Florida (and TWO FOR THE SEESAW)[1] in time for my son's first birthday—and Vicky's fifth—and to hear about the success of KRAPP in Paris. Congratulations. I am most pleased, and hope someday to be there when it is played.

Here, we are going strong, the show holding up and business good in spite of our shifts from theatre to theatre, made necessary by previous bookings at the Provincetown. On May 15th we are getting a new Krapp as Donald Davis goes off to Stratford, and I am keeping fingers crossed. He is Henderson Forsythe,[2] also an Irishman, one with whom I've worked, but quite different from Donald. Will keep you posted.

Am hoping before Donald goes to get the whole show recorded as we all think it will make an excellent record—or tape! Also I have great regrets personally that it won't be recorded on film because I think it

would be as beautiful in that medium. Every time I watch it, I think of
what a well-handled camera would do to get the subtleties and nuances which the last rows are bound to miss. I know how you feel
about film, but I wish you'd think about this—not on a commercial
basis but something experimental, or at least a record of what the show
looked like.

By the way, have I ever mentioned to you an idea I once had of a
film of ENDGAME—with Chaplin playing all four roles? What do you
think![3]

The TV people have begun to talk about GODOT but not clear
when, as there is some sort of strike on which gets in the way. But
they'll do it if we can cast it, etc. Again, thanks for your support. . . . . .

Life goes on. I'm casting MEASURE FOR MEASURE for the summer, also preparing first American stage version of TWELVE ANGRY
MEN,[4] which has had much success abroad. And so on. . . . Don't know
where Robert Pinget is; he disappeared after a couple of meetings here,
perhaps on the West coast. . . . . Barney was out to see the new house in
the country and approved. . . . Doesn't look as though I'll be getting to
Paris this summer, but one never knows. . . . Do hope you like your
new place, that you are writing, and that you are taking care of yourself. Best to Suzanne, and love from my two girls.

[Alan]

1. William Gibson's play, *Two for the Seesaw,* opened at the Royal Poinciana Playhouse,
Palm Beach, Florida, 28 March 1960.
2. Henderson Forsythe (b. 1917), American actor.
3. Charlie Chaplin (1889–1977).
4. Reginald Rose's play opened at the Bucks County Playhouse, New Hope, Pennsylvania, 23 May 1960.

Saturday, May 14, [1960]
Dear Sam,

Saw Barney on his return from your neighborhood, and meant to
write earlier in the week; but Jean has been in the hospital all week
having her thyroid operated on—luckily all is well!—we have been
rehearsing a new Krapp, and I've been getting ready to go off to do
TWELVE ANGRY MEN.

Got most of the news from Barney, and wish I could get to Paris to talk over with you personally. There is a minuscule chance that I may drift in for a week in June when the Berliner Ensemble are there,[1] but finances are getting in the way. Heard about all your troubles with the Paris KRAPP; the Irish version-to-be and its visit-to-come. Cusack[2] is, in my opinion, an excellent choice—we had even thought of him for here when we were going to do the play a couple of seasons ago, but he was not available and no off-Broadway management could afford his fare and fee. On the other hand, I gather he says he can do the play without a director, with which point of view I do not agree. He needs a strong one. Nor am I sure that Howard Sackler is what's needed. Sackler is a kind of semi-hemi-demi hanger-on in the theatre who went to Dublin several years ago and got to direct Cusack in a disastrous Hamlet.[3] Beyond that I gather he has done nothing but some recordings of verse-readings and the like. What disturbed me a bit was Barney's saying that Cusack was going around telling everyone (including you?) that we had done the play all badly in NY, that Davis' performance was terrible, and that he was the only one who knew how to do it right. He has a perfect right to his opinion, and of course every actor thinks he alone is the source of all knowledge and talent. But Davis was marvelous in KRAPP, and we both tried to do it the way you would want it. Not that we succeeded in all respects, but we tried. Now with the new Krapp, one Henderson Forsythe, we have a somewhat different character—as is inevitable with another actor—but an equivalent. Details are different but essences remain, we hope. He is in some respects more interesting than Davis, in some less so. We are fortunate to have him. Every actor contributes his own visual and vocal individuality, and so will Cusack. I just hope he won't disturb you too much by giving you the impression that we were all wet here. Wish you could see it yourself. . . . . . .

Anyhow, we may be doing a recording of Davis for Spoken Arts Records. And Canadian Broadcasting is evidently doing a TV version, though not yet for certain.[4]

Everything otherwise about the same. Hope you are well, writing, and enjoying the countryside. How about another play in English? With four characters? Or two? Loved your second Mime w.o. words.[5] Jean sends her love, also Vicky.

Also our four goldfish named Hamm, Clov, Nell and Nagg. Poor P. J. Kelly died last week and we were all much distressed.

All the best. And do take care of yourself. If I find I am going to be in Paris will get in touch beforehand and let you know. Hello to Suzanne.

[Alan]

1. The Berliner Ensemble was founded in East Berlin, January 1949, by Bertolt Brecht (1898–1956), radical playwright, and his wife, Helen Weigel (1900–1971), together with Erich Engel (1891–1966).

2. The Irish actor Cyril Cusack (1910–1993) played in *Krapp's Last Tape* at the Queens Theatre, 20 June 1960, prior to a European Festival tour that took in Rotterdam, Amsterdam, The Hague, Utrecht, then the Théâtre des Nations Festival.

3. Howard Sackler (1929–1982), American dramatist, screenwriter. Cusack's *Hamlet* opened at the Gaiety Theatre, 28 October 1957. SB saw Cusack as Christy Mahon in J. M. Synge's (1871–1909) *Playboy of the Western World* in Paris, 1954 (see letters of 23 May and 4 August 1960).

4. Davis (Krapp), Spoken Arts Records 788 1961; CBC broadcast of *Krapps's Last Tape*, 24 October 1965.

5. "second Mime w. o. words": *Acte sans paroles II*, 1963, 1966, trans. by SB, *Act Without Words II*, 1967.

Paris
May 23rd 1960

Dear Alan

Many thanks for your letter. I am very sorry to hear of Jean's operation and relieved that all is well.

I do indeed hope you will be able to get over. KRAPP folded up at the Récamier a few days ago after a last week of packed houses. The whole thing was very distressing and as Barney has told you about it I won't go into it further.[1] I think Barney must have exaggerated Cusack's reaction to the NY production. He simply said in a letter which I showed Barney that he didn't like it and I know nothing of his abusing it to all and sundry. I replied I was sorry to hear so as I had every reason to think it was excellent. I think he was here very briefly, but we didn't contact, unfortunately, as there was a lot I wanted to say to him—for him to take or leave. He wrote that he planned to play KRAPP a couple of times at the Abbey in June, then bring it here to the Théâtre des Nations for four performances with ARMS & THE MAN. I liked his PLAYBOY and he should give an interesting performance, but with which I don't expect to agree! Vocally he should be all right. I've raised my interdict on my work in Dublin and the Pike will now do ENDGAME and probably revive GODOT.[2]

No new play in sight I'm sorry to say. I'm still floundering in the French prose work I begun over a year ago. It will be out of my way by the end of the year—I mean either published or abandoned. Working in Paris has become impossible and I am obliged to be here more and more frequently, especially at this time of year. The next effort in any case will be a full length theatre play, whether in French or English I don't know. The disappointment with Blin doesn't encourage the former. But the writing of the kind of thing I have very vaguely in mind will have better chances in French. Apart altogether from interruptions I work with increasing difficulty—like writing on a pinhead with fading sight and trembling hand. . . .[3]

Thank Davis again for his performance and greetings and good wishes to Forsythe. Congratulations on V. V. award.[4]

Affectionately to you all
Sam [handwritten]

1. SB wanted Blin to play Krapp and was annoyed when Blin cast R. J. Chauffard instead. He did not like Chauffard's performance (see JK, 468–469).

2. The Pike Theatre Club, Dublin, closed in 1961; plays not produced (see JK, 466).

3. SB comments on move to new address, 38 Boulevard Saint-Jacques.

4. See letter 16 January 1960, n. 1.

Ussy
4.8.60

Dear Alan

The Bartók record is superb and we are delighted to have it.[1] All our thanks. As you will see from enclosed Suzanne wrote at once, but I held it up hoping to hear from you. I suppose you have been up to your eyes with M FOR M. I hope all went well. Cusack's KRAPP was very disappointing, no feeling for the thing or the wrong feeling, under-acted out of existence, recording inaudible, synchronisation unspeakable, direction execrable when there was any. All the more disappointing as he is a remarkable actor with great presence and properly handled could have been excellent. The Mihalovici opera is finished and as far as I can judge a very fine job.[2] Barr very kindly sent me a tape (entire play recorded live).[3] I have not yet had a chance of hearing it. I had lunch with Driver, very pleasant and understanding.[4] Fed up as you can imagine with all this NTA botheration. Won't sign anything till things are clarified and notably Myerberg's obstructions. Unless you can do it exactly as you wish with the actors of your choice and the play as it stands we'll drop it altogether.[5] The Big Banana film was obviously out of the question, even with controls and guarantees it would have been a disaster.[6] I have told Curtis Brown, who urged me to accept, that I shall never allow such a film to be made and asked him to send me a copy of Myerberg's GODOT contract which I have never seen and which takes on a more and more mythical air. I finished my still titleless book last night (revision and typing) at last and think now I can send it forth.[7] I have not been able to give much thought or none to give to the play we talked about. I shall start stalking it soon. I should like to know what exactly he has in those pockets—what he had.[8]

It was good seeing so much of you when you were here and may it not be too long before you are over again.

Bd. St-Jacques not yet ready to enshrine us. Defaulting carpenters painters plumbers and like moguls.

Love to Jean and the children.

Yours ever
Sam [handwritten]

1. Béla Bartók (1881–1945), *Music for Strings, Percussion, and Celesta* (1937).

2. Marcel Mihalovici (b. 1898) used *Krapp's Last Tape* as a libretto for an opera called *Krapp, ou la Dernière bande.* Elmar Tophoven translated it into German, *Das Letzte Band.*

3. Richard Barr (1917–1989), American director, producer (see letter of 16 January 1960, n. 1); "tape": New York *Krapp.*

4. Tom F. Driver (b. 1925), educator, writer, drama critic for the *Christian Century* (1956–1962), *Reporter* (1963–1964); "Out in Left Field," *CC,* 5 March 1958, 282–283; *Romantic Quest and Modern Query: A History of the Modern Theatre,* 1980.

5. NTA: WNTA-TV, Newark-NY, a commercial station, operated by National Telefilm Associates (NTA), sought release of film rights for *Waiting for Godot.*

6. "The Big Banana film": proposed film of *Waiting for Godot* with Bert Lahr, who had referred to himself when playing in the Miami production as "Top Banana," i.e., the comic lead.

7. SB's "still titleless book": *Comment c'est.*

8. "he": at this stage SB saw the protagonist in *Happy Days* as a man.

August 17, 1960

Dear Sam,

Finally.

After a month of shilly-shallying back-and-forth, changes and confusion, calling it off and putting it back on, our friends of NTA are finally going ahead with GODOT.

Won't bore you with grotesque details, casting ideas, and general lack of thought which characterised entire sequence of days. I tried to get them to understand what kind of a play they were doing, if at all; fought the more ludicrous casting ideas by not agreeing to fading Hollywoodens as Vladimir, and generally convinced them I meant what I said. What control I will have from this point and once we get into the camera work, technical morass, and Madison Avenue psychology is not entirely clear but will do my best.

Have kept in close touch with Barney on all the Myerberg details. We were all rooting for you to make some money but quite understand your attitude. Will do all we can to protect the situation vis-a-vis NTA. They are not Myerberg but suffer all the other sins of commercial and even non-commercial TV.

The cast is not bad, and I am especially pleased to have gotten Burgess Meredith for Vladimir and Zero Mostel for Estragon. Meredith was our 'Hamlet of 1940' though he never played it, very good imaginative sensitive thoughtful, was an excellent George in OF MICE AND MEN. Mostel is the guy who played Bloom in ULYSSES IN NIGHT-TOWN, also in London and Paris, where he received best actor award. A real eccentric comedian, marvelous pantomimist. By the way, he made a short film in London last year of ACT WITHOUT WORDS— did you know that? To be shown at Venice Festival, I think. Didn't know you had given permission. I think John Beckett wrote the score.

Lucky is Arthur Malet, who did it in Florida and has improved since; Pozzo is Kurt Kasznar of Broadway cast. Honestly, I wasn't sure of him; but Barney said you liked his voice on the record, he looks good; and we had a terrible time getting someone. All the good ones not available; and the ones they wanted terrible. So settled on Kasznar, trust OK with you. . . . The boy is lovely, small, sandy-haired. . . .[1]

And so on. Has been a rough month, not knowing from day to day what was going to happen. I'm sure all this fuss hasn't helped you either. But am delighted you have finished novel and at work on the play. Let me know how it goes. . . . Glad you liked the Bartók. Thanks, Suzanne, for the note. . . . Take care. And I will write along the way to let you know about our progress or lack of it. Rehearsals start Saturday and we're reading it a bit beforehand privately. . . . . All the best.

[Alan]

1. In December 1960, AS directed *Waiting for Godot* for WNTA's series, "Play-of-the-Week," presented during the week of April 3–8, 1961. Zero Mostel (Estragon), Burgess Meredith (Vladimir), Alvin Epstein (Lucky), Kurt Kasznar (Pozzo). Epstein, not Arthur Malet, played Lucky (see *Variety*, 5 April 1961). The play was not a success on television: see Jerry Tallmer, "The Magic Box," *Evergreen Review*, 5 (July-August 1961), 17–22. Mostel (1915–1977), actor, comedian, and clown, did not make a film of *Act Without Words* in London. SB regarded *Act Without Words* not as film, but, as he told Barney Rosset, "primitive theatre," a codicil to *Endgame*, requiring "that this last extremity of human meat—or bones—be there, thinking and stumbling and sweating, under our noses, like Clov about Hamm, but gone from refuge" (27 August 1957). Meredith (1908–1997), American actor, director; Kasznar (1913–1979), Austrian actor.

Paris
23.9.60

Dear Alan

Thanks for your letters. When I heard from Barney you were in London I was hoping you might make the hop. He was saying you might bring the *Connection* to London. I do hope that comes off soon and that we shall meet again then. Who knows—I might have something to show you.

You must have had a hard time with NTA *GODOT* and I am sure you are relieved it is over. Thank you again, dear Alan, for all you do for my work. I listened to the KRAPP tape and liked it very much. Please tell Davis. I received 2 copies of HORIZON and liked the article.[1] The French work is now at last off my hands and will be out in December. I don't see the play at all clearly, but a little more so. The figure is a woman as far as I can see. Bright light, flowers and a large handbag containing all vital necessities from revolver to lipstick. Would like to try it in English but fear it will have to be in French again. Don't expect to get down to it seriously for a month or so, with the flit to Bd. St. Jacques and other botherations. Shall let you know how it goes.

Copious photographs from Blau of his *Endgame*.[2] Looks pretty good. . . . .[3] So glad to hear of success of your Park Shakespeare.[4]

Affectionately to you all
Sam

1. Robert Hatch's "Theater: Laughter At Your Own Risk," *Horizon*, 3.1 (September 1960), 112–116, about Donald Davis's performance in *Krapp's Last Tape* at the Provincetown Playhouse.

2. With this production of *Endgame* the San Francisco Actor's Workshop opened the Encore, a second theater in the basement of the Marines Memorial Theater, where they began in 1955. They took their production of *Waiting for Godot* to the San Quentin State Prison, 19 November 1957, because it was the only play in their repertory without women; directed by Herbert Blau, the cast included Jules Irving (Lucky). The result was the formation of the San Quentin Drama Workshop and Douglas ("Rick") Cluchey's involvement in the work of SB.

3. SB has seen Barney Rosset.

4. *Measure for Measure*, New York Shakespeare Festival, Central Park.

November 26, [1960]

Dear Sam,

Was going to write to you last Sunday when KRAPP was to close, full of sentimental thoughts on almost a year's run—but then we got extended, and the sentiments will have to wait.

Too long anyhow since I've written. The days and weeks seem to go by much too rapidly, crammed with nothingness, the confusion of detail and the details of confusion. The summer went by and I have absolutely no awareness of summer, only MEASURE FOR MEASURE, and a collection of more abortive efforts. For the past month I have been waiting to go into rehearsal on a new Albee one-act, AMERICAN DREAM, quite different from ZOO STORY; but no proper theatre available. As of yesterday it seems as though we're getting one finally. Then around middle of December off to San Francisco for a place called the Actors Workshop of which you've heard (Herbert Blau's) where I'm doing a 'new' play written in 1947 and never done.[1] Then, I hope, to London for THE CONNECTION—if we get work permits. And if I do get to London, I'll get to Paris.

And so on.

Actually, as you can tell by my mood, am in period of depression and general uncertainty. Decisions piling in, continued and worsening ill health of my parents, the whole New York situation theatrically and the world situation morally and politically. Compensated for somewhat by growth of the two small ones, the efforts of my Jean, and the shelter of Hastings-on-Hudson. Have been offered permanent artistic directorship of Washington's Arena Theatre, which opens a new build-

ing next year. Am tempted but unsure about leaving New York, free-
lancing, off-Broadway potentialities. Washington would offer a place
and continuity of effort instead of this jiggling around; but not sure
how much could be accomplished in situation there, how much freedom, etc. We shall see. . . . . . .

In meantime, have caught glimpses of Barney at work and play,
liked THE END² exceedingly and am looking forward to the next novel
when in English. Barney tells me you are pleased. And how is the play
coming? I gather we'll have to find an actress this time! A handbag
offers more opportunities than pockets??????????????? By the way, I
told Judith I was making an offer for the rights myself this time, sight
unseen. Much easier to keep it from getting mucked about.

The TV GODOT now scheduled in December. Barney liked it and so
did Jean; I thought its better moments good and wished we had provided you with more of them . . . The KRAPP record also on its way,
and Arthur Klein enthusiastic.³ And so it goes. The Beckett influence in
my life considerable and growing. Now Harold Pinter wants me to
direct BIRTHDAY PARTY here. I gather [part of line missing] CARE-
TAKER in London in June and pleased [ending missing]⁴

Trust you are well and not too harassed by visiting Americans. Although I'd like to be one of them. Don't know when that's going to
happen at the current rate of exchange. Our new home in the country is
slowly dropping the bank balance down, but we love it, and Vicky
deliriously happy. Just half an hour away from the Provincetown, so
not bad. This summer not yet clear although I may be doing a Shakespeare for one of the Festivals here, and numerous prospects are looming. So long as I am healthy and can do a Beckett play once in a while, I
won't ask more of [ending missing]

   [Alan]

1. *The American Dream* opened at the York Playhouse, New York, 24 January 1961;
Twinkling of an Eye by H. W. Wright and Guy Andros opened at San Francisco Actor's
Workshop, 11 January 1961.
2. Written in 1946 after the war, "La Fin" ("The End") is about SB's leaving Ireland to
live in Paris, published in *Nouvelles et textes pour rien,* 1955; English trans. by Richard
Seaver and SB, *Stories and Texts for Nothing,* 1967, and *No's Knife: Collected Shorter Prose,
1945–1966,* 1967.
3. Arthur J. Klein (1932–1993), entertainment attorney.
4. AS did not direct *The Birthday Party* in New York until 1967; *The Caretaker* opened at
the Arts Theatre Club, London, 27 April 1960, directed by Donald McWhinnie.

Paris
9.12.60

Dear Alan

Thanks for your letter. You sound rather low and I hope things are better. Washington would probably be depressing at the beginning, but it might work out all right if you could make provision for a certain period of absence. Pleased to hear that *Krapp* has been extended in extremis, looks as if the old ruffian might pant on to 1961. I hear there were four of them at the party and wish I had been with you.¹ I am badly stuck in the new play after about half an hour and haven't yet found out whether the thing is possible or not. An hour and a half necessary, exclusive of interval. Two acts, the second considerably shorter than the first. Same set for both. The first problem was how to have her speak alone on the stage all that time without speaking to herself or to the audience. Solved that after a fashion. No movement possible in first act except of *Oberleib*, no movement of any kind possible in the second. No help from anywhere once the situation has been established except from bag (pockets if it had been a man as was originally the case). Bag obviously better dramatically and of more helpful content. In first act she is imbedded up to waist in a mound, in second up to neck. Empty plain, burning sun (she wonders mildly if the earth has lost its atmosphere). Scene extended to maximum by painted backcloth in *trompe-l'oeil* as *pompier* as possible. This to give you some idea. Too difficult and depressing to write about. Bag of no help except visually in 2 as she has no longer access to it, but the memory of the help it was a great help I hope, in fact I am counting a lot on memory of 1 for 2, which is stupidly said, I mean a kind of physical post image of 1 all through 2. Opulent blonde, fiftyish, all glowing shoulders and *décolleté*. Enough, *Gott hilfe mir, amen.*²

. . . .³ Finishing correcting proofs of new book for Editions de Minuit, title COMMENT C'EST, due out early January. Glad you liked THE END, apart from a few poems it was my very first work in French. THE CARETAKER *(LE GARDIEN)* in rehearsal at the Lutèce with Pinget's MANIVELLE, both directed by Martin, Blin playing the tramp in the Pinter, Adet (Nagg) the organ-grinder in the MANIVELLE. Things are going well and Pinget and Martin very pleased, have not yet seen a rehearsal. Opening Jan. 17th. Pinter due over beginning of Jan. I look forward to meeting him. Have seen nothing but Rogosin's marvellous ON THE BOWERY, went two nights running and want to go again.⁴ Have promised to go to Germany (Bielefeld) late Feb. for opening of

Mihalovici's KRAPP opera, hope you will see it in NY some day. All I know of the music is what he could show me on his piano, I was impressed. We had to go over the script together (English) and modify a few things, as he composed his music on the French text.

Voilà. Affectionately to you all and premature wishes for a happy Xmas and New Year.

Sam

Read an article by Blau in recent theatre magazine—a letter to his company. Very intelligent, rather superior about European theatre.[5] [handwritten from signature]

1. "four of them": the four actors who had played Krapp were probably Donald Davis, Henderson Forsythe, Cyril Cusack, and Herbert Bergdorf.
2. *"Oberleib"*: the upper part of the body; *"trompe-l'oeil"*: designed to give an illusion of reality; *"pompier"*: overplayed, described in the text as "Very pompier trompe-l'oeil backcloth" and described by SB as "laughably earnest bad imitation" (18 August 1961); *"Gott hilfe mir"*: God help me.
3. SB comments on the new apartment.
4. Lionel Rogosin (b. 1924), American documentary film producer-director; *On the Bowery*, 1954, was his first film.
5. Herbert Blau, "Meanwhile, Follow the Bright Angels," *Tulane Drama Review*, 5 (September 1960), 89–101.

38 Boulevard St. Jacques
Paris 14me
Port-Royal 96.60
13.1.61

Dear Alan

Glad to have your letter from San F. Great news that I'll be seeing you in Feb. Might have something to show you then. Have had very little time or quiet for work recently. New book in French just out,[1] very difficult proof-correcting, and all the complication of the move now completed. Please note address. I'm approaching nevertheless end of 1st act—very rough version—and shall certainly go on.[2] But still don't know if the thing is possible theatre or not. Had a heavy evening with Pinter whom I liked. He tells me Donald McWhinnie is bringing his *Caretaker* to NY (Broadway) in the Fall and that his *Birthday Party* is also scheduled for NY production.[3] I liked the *Krapp* record very much.

Again congratulations and thanks. Extraordinary that it shd be still running. Hope the news of your parents is not too bad and that you're feeling a bit more cheerful.

Affectionately to you all
Sam

1. *Comment c'est.*
2. *Happy Days,* earlier called by SB *Many Mercies* or *Tender Mercies.*
3. Harold Pinter (b. 1930), English actor, playwright, director, CBE in 1966; *The Caretaker* opened at the Lyceum Theatre, New York, 4 October 1961. *The Birthday Party,* first American Pinter production by the San Francisco Actor's Workshop, 1960.

38 Boulevard Saint-Jacques
Paris 14me
Port-Royal 96.60
1.2.61

Dear Alan

Good to have your letter,[1] know you so near and that you will be coming over. My only commitment is last week of February in Germany. Otherwise yours to command. Note new address and telephone. Definitely installed here and all Favorites dust shaken off. Much better here from at least 15 points of view. I'll be able to show you first act of play which I'm revising (first act). I'll be very glad of the chance to talk to you about it and hear what you think. Beyond a few notes have done nothing on the impossible second act. You'll see in any case the kind of actress we need. In England Plowright[2] would be the ticket if she'd take it on. Terrible rôle, all evening alone on stage and for last 20 minutes without a gesture to help voice. Perhaps its just madness. You'll tell me. Good luck with CONNECTION[3] and all news when we meet.

Affectionately
Sam [handwritten]

1. Missing.
2. Joan Plowright (b. 1929), member of the English Stage Company and Royal Court Theatre, m. Sir Laurence Olivier (1907–1989).
3. AS, in London for rehearsals of Jack Gelber's (b. 1932) *The Connection,* did not go to Paris. Similar in structure to *Waiting for Godot, The Connection* opened at the Living

Theatre, New York, 15 July 1959, surprising people by its amoral presentation of drug addicts. Opened at the Duke of York Theatre, London, 22 February 1961; "'Connection' Booed at London Opening," *NY Times*, 23 February 1961; AS did not direct it (*Entrances*, 290–292).

Folkestone
9.3.61

Bien cher Alan

....¹ The trip to Germany was a success but very tiring. Bielefeld performance of *Krapp* opera very fine—superbly sung by a young American by name of Dooley. There is talk of its coming to Théâtre de Nations.² In Frankfurt too all went well, great friendship and warmth from everyone. Drove back with friends via Amsterdam. Saw Barney on Tuesday in great form. A hurried evening as I had to be up at crack of dawn next day, but I gathered there is talk of a *H.D.* company. I have come here with the car for a few weeks for a bit of a rest and to deal with that little matter I mentioned to you.³ I haven't looked at *H.D.* since I saw you—but have it with me here. Your comments were a great help. I'll try and improve it now and provide you with final script some time in April.⁴ *Godot* revival I told you about seems almost certain, rehearsing already with Raimbourg & Martin—other roles more or less open, talk of Vitold for Pozzo. Serreau very keen and Bruzzichelli also. May-June in alternance with *Maids/Amédée*.⁵ Then perhaps Royal Court and tour from September on. Glad to have good news of *American Dream* and less good of *Connection*. Had lunch with Hobson & wife, Blin & Martin, at the Closerie. Pinter in Paris down the drain, coming off I think day after tomorrow, replaced by adaptation of Dostoevsky's *Nuits blanches* with Martin and Blin's Nicole II.⁶ Nice to be sitting unknown and undisturbable with nothing in the window but sea, sky and Jules Vernes mist,⁷ and little car before the door to take me to Dover or Canterbury. The hop from Le Touquet to Ferryfield was marvellous and I'll never come to England any other way henceforward.

Much love to you all
Sam

1. SB refers to gifts he and Suzanne had sent to the Schneider children.
2. William Dooley (b. 1932), American bass-baritone, sang Krapp in premiere of Marcel Mihalovici's *Krapp, ou la Dernière bande*, Städtische Bühnen, Bielefeld 1961, performed

"en concert" at TNP (Palais de Chaillot) 13 February 1961. The French version was broadcast on 16 May 1961 by RTF/ORTF (Office de Radiodiffusion Television Française, RTF until 1964). The German version, with libretto by Elmar Tophoven, was sung by William Dooley at the Théâtre des Nations, 3 July 1961. SB went from Bielefeld to Frankfurt where Dr. Siegfried Unseld had arranged an evening in his honor: the "Seventh Suhrkamp Publishing House's Evening" ("Hommage à Samuel Beckett in Anwesenheit des Autor"). It was held at the Cantate-Saal on 27 February. SB drove from Cologne to Paris via Amsterdam with Elmar and Erika Tophoven, his German translators. (See JK, 478–479, 795.) Unseld (b. 1924), SB's German publisher, Suhrkamp Verlag, Frankfurt.

3. SB was arranging his marriage to Suzanne; under British law he had to live in England for two weeks before the wedding, 25 March 1961.

4. Richard Barr and Clinton Wilder (b. 1920), American producers, Theatre 61, agreed to produce SB's new play "sight unseen." AS flew to Paris to discuss it with SB.

5. *En attendant Godot* opened at the Odéon-Théâtre de France, 8 May 1961, directed by Roger Blin, SB supervised. Etienne Berry (Estragon), Lucien Raimbourg (Vladimir), Jean Martin (Lucky), Jean-Jacques Bourgeois (Pozzo), Jean Levy (A Boy). Tree designed by Alberto Giacometti (1901–1966), Swiss-born sculptor and surrealist painter, friend of SB, living in Paris. Michel Vitold (b. 1914), Kharkov, Russsia, did not play Pozzo. Jean-Marie Serreau (1915–1981), avant-garde director at the Théâtre de Babylone, pioneered work by SB, Brecht, Genet, Ionesco, and Max Frisch (b. 1911), Swiss dramatist, novelist, essayist. *"Maids/Amédée"*: Genet's *Les Bonnes (The Maids)*; Ionesco's *Amédée ou Comment s'en débarrasser (Amédée or How to Get Rid of It)*, 1953. Aldo Bruzzichelli, a Florentine-born industrialist, associated with Serreau and the "Theatre nouveau" company.

6. Pinter's *Le Gardien (The Caretaker)* opened at the Théâtre de Lutèce, Paris, 27 January 1961, but was badly received by the critics; Sir Harold and Elizabeth Hobson; *Nuits blanches (White Nights)*, adapted from Dostoevsky's novel of the same title, opened on 24 March 1961. "Nicole": Nicole Kessel (the young girl), Jean Martin (Dostoevski).

7. Jules Verne (1828–1905), French novelist (*Around the World in Eighty Days*, 1873).

38 Bd. St. Jacques
Paris 14me
20.5.61

Dear Alan

Thanks for your letter. I hope the children are quite well again now and all apple-pie order in H.o.H.[1]

Had a hard time here with *Godot* rehearsals in absence of Blin and Serreau rehearsing Raimbourg's part till a week before opening. But we made out and it is now doing very well at Odéon.[2] I could do nothing else while it lasted but since beginning of May have been working on the new play, and hope to start typing definitive text next week and to send it out towards end of month. You could go on labouring for ever on these things, but the time comes, and I think it has come here, when you have to let them go. You won't find much difference from the script you read—got in the bubbly in both acts and think the song will be the Valse Duet *(I love you so)* from the *Merry Widow*[3]

> "Though I say not what I may not
> Let you hear,
> Yet the swaying dance is saying
> Love me dear . . ."
>   etc

Perhaps a bit late (1908) for a musical [?]for popularisation, but there is a Regina recording (same quality of sound)—I'll let you have details and reference in due course. Willie's costume is changed for appearance at end and Winnie has on her hat through 2nd act. Other odds and ends—but essentially unchanged. I saw Bessler *(Schlosspark)* and he wants it for Berlin Festival Sept.-October.[4] I have written to Grove about this. I don't know if you attach importance to a N.Y. world premiere or if you would authorize eventually prior productions in London (McWhinnie Royal Court) & Berlin. Though if Cherry Lane is available in Fall you will almost certainly be the first. I'll be going to England late June and look forward to talking to McWhinnie who will have read the script by then. There's a bad jinks on revival of *Godot* at Stratford E. which was sprung on me & which I tried to stop, but couldn't. All Irish and uproarious. Very upsetting, the more so as McW. now rehearsing TV *Godot* for release June 26th.[5]

New flat is working out all right. Have decided to sell Ussy. Don't seem to be able to get there any more to look after it, or to want to. Better get rid of it.

Affectionately to you all
Sam

1. Letter missing; "H.o.H": Hastings-on-Hudson.
2. "in absence of Blin": Roger Blin was in London directing Genet's *Les Nègres* (see letter of 9 March 1961, n. 4).
3. By Franz Lehár (1870–1948), Hungarian-born Austrian composer. Available on Westminster XWN 18964 (1961). When asked by SB whether he preferred "The Merry Widow Waltz" or "When Irish Eyes Are Smiling," AS said the Waltz, and when asked which he thought the better title, *Many Mercies, Tender Mercies,* or *Happy Days,* chose the last (*Entrances,* 293–295).
4. Albert Bessler (b. 1905), dramaturge, actor, associated with both the Schiller-Theater Werkstatt and the Schlosspark Theater, Berlin. *Glückliche Tage* opened at the Schiller-Theater Werkstatt, 30 September 1961.
5. Billed as the "laugh riot of two continents," *Waiting for Godot* opened at the Thea-

tre Royal Stratford E., 15 May 1961, directed by Alan Simpson, designed by John Ryan. Brian Phelan (Estragon), David Kelly (Vladimir), Derek Young (Lucky), Nigel Fitzgerald (Pozzo), Patrick Byrne (A Boy). BBC 1, 22 June 1961, directed by Donald McWhinnie. Peter Woodthorpe (Estragon), Jack MacGowran (Vladimir), Timothy Bateson (Lucky), Felix Felton (Pozzo), Mark Mileham (A Boy). Dublin-born MacGowran (1918–1973) was named Television Actor of the Year for his performance. See Louis MacNeice, "'Godot' on TV," *New Statesman*, 62 (7 July 1961), 27–28.

College of Letters and Science
Department of Speech
The University of Wisconsin–Milwaukee
3203 Downer Avenue
Milwaukee 11
Wisconsin
Thursday, July 6, 1961

Dear Sam,

Finally, the pictures! And what combinations and permutations of time and space, sunlight and daughter, to get them. The daughter looks a bit peaked but that's not organic, she's actually blooming. Do hope you and Suzanne like them. And we are forever grateful for the little yellow flowers in our garden. . . . .

As you see by the over-done letterhead above I'm back in the academic life, four weeks of summer session here, 'teaching' a class in stage direction, giving a lecture or two, and directing a program of one-acts: THE CHAIRS, DOCK BRIEF, and Shirley Jackson's THE LOTTERY.[1]

Delighted to have HAPPY DAYS at hand, although I haven't really gotten hard to work on it yet, was busy with a Voice of America project,[2] a small operation on my bottom, and then getting ready for Wisconsin. But have read it a half-dozen times, soaking it in a bit more each time. I love the music box tune, and have already investigated the possibilities of getting a music box to play it. To tell you the truth, I didn't find very many changes from the script as I read it that day in Paris. And am still a bit confused about the exact geography of Willie's position in and out of his hole. That is, I think it is clear to me how and when you want him to be seen, but how to do this exactly and in the particular theatre????????? We shall investigate with the scene designer—the same one who did KRAPP.

Now as to administrative matters: I had thought you *wanted* us to do the premiere, somehow had gotten that impression. We are not actually rushing on that account. It just happens that the Theatre 61 management[3] has the Cherry Lane on lease, which is good for us, that it would be better and easier to go after the actors we want earlier in the season, I am tied up the last three weeks in October, etc. The management's present plans—if all else works out and if we have your approval—are to open late in September. There is also an interesting idea in the talking stage, depending on how the Albee plays,[4] which are now in the Cherry Lane, are making out by then. That is, the idea of introducing HAPPY DAYS in repertory with Albee, starting it at four times a week, and perhaps going into 5 or even 6 eventually. (If Albee peters out by then, of course, we won't be able to do it.) But both Barney and I like the idea, partly because of its unusual quality and partly because we would much rather get the Cherry Lane than any other theatre. Provincetown might be available but again we'd have to move out almost immediately as in the case of KRAPP. What do you think? Would love to get your ideas on time, theatre, repertory, etc. Neither Barney nor I want to do anything contrary to your real wishes, so do please tell us. As you know, he and I are taking the option, and then assigning it to Theatre 61, but keeping artistic control, control of future productions, etc. We are working out that arrangement now, and there are as yet some unsettled problems.

As far as casting is concerned, I have been thinking about that ever since I returned from Paris and seeing you. I had hoped at one time that we might lure Zero Mostel to play Willie—but that would depend on who played Winnie, a star, a big name, both of which I'm against. As it turns out, Zero is not available and not interested enough in Willie. We are after a fellow named John Becher, a little rather lively type, Irish, very good comedian, now playing 'Daddy' in Albee's DREAM. We have all sorts of ideas for Winnie—but it's not easy. What we need is someone like Tallulah Bankhead was before she became Tallulah Bankhead.[5] There's a girl named Ruth White whom you wouldn't know but whom we all like.[6] (Are you really getting Joannie Plowright for London????)

Really wish you were coming over to work on the show with me, but I guess that's too much to hope for. You know, NY is only about 6 hours away from Paris.

Will be spending some time on the script during the month here, then going off to a lake for a week to sit and think. Will keep you posted and interrogated as per usual.

Hope you are well, getting away from the Americans in Paris now and then, and relaxing a bit. Have you seen Tom Driver's article?[7] I haven't read it, but gather it's coming out or is out already. . . . . .

Wish I could take a hop over again this summer really to talk things over with you in detail. But doubt if that'll be possible. We'll keep wooing you to come in this direction.

Love to Suzanne from us all. And let me hear from you when you have a chance.

[Alan]

1. *The Chairs* (Ionesco), *The Dock Brief* (John Mortimer, b. 1923, English dramatist), *The Lottery* (Shirley Jackson, 1916–1965, American fiction writer) opened at the University of Wisconsin, 25 July 1961.

2. Voice of America: U.S. Government foreign-language radio, broadcasts worldwide in English and many other languages; began in 1942 "to inform the world of America's role in World War II."

3. Barr and Wilder.

4. Edward Albee's *The American Dream*, opened at the York Playhouse, New York, 24 January 1961, directed by AS, together with William Flanagan's *Bartleby*, directed by Bill Penn. *Bartleby* closed 5 February, replaced by Albee's *The Death of Bessie Smith*, directed by Lawrence Arrick. *The American Dream* reopened 28 February, moved to Cherry Lane Theatre, New York, 23 May.

5. John C. Becher (b. 1915), Tallulah Bankhead (1903–1968).

6. Ruth White (1914–1969).

7. "Beckett by the Madeleine," *Columbia University Forum*, Summer 1961, 21–25.

Ussy
13.7.61

Dear Alan

Thanks for your letter with photos of children. They're a bonny pair and the boy a great chip of old you.

It's the first time I won't have been able to collaborate in the first production of a stage-play of mine, and naturally I'm sorry. No question I'm afraid of my getting to N.Y. It looks as though you will be the first to do it. At Berlin Festival it is scheduled to open September 30th— though German text not yet available! In London (now definitely Royal Court, direction McWhinnie) rehearsals as far as I can see can hardly begin before mid-October at earliest. We should try to get Plowright (in spite of imminent baby). Don't rush it in any case, without adequate actress it hasn't a hope in hell. I'm not keen on repertory set-up, wd.

Willie's route end of Act I

rather have the issue clearer, but if it helps you won't hold out against it. Enclosed a few sketches [preceding pages] which may help you, though of course the proportions are all wrong. I think in Act I she should be sitting on a high stool (standing, unless a very small woman, will make it too high), and in Act II on a low one. I can't see why, if the mound properly constructed, there should be any difficulty with Willie's concealment. He should never have to move except (1) when he is required to sit up with head and hands visible and (2) when he appears at end of play. The "abrupter fall"[1] can actually if necessary overhang as (seen from side)

If he is invisible no problem obviously with hole, his "movement" towards it being simply expressed by Winnie's text and play. And if he cannot be completely hidden, then no problem either, he has merely to crawl *off-stage* to hole.

Wish we could meet and go over it all in detail. Since we can't we must just do the best we can by letter. It's a much more difficult job I've given you here than any so far—all poised on a razor-edge and no breather anywhere.

Affectionately from us both to you all
Sam

1. The stage direction reads "Back an abrupter fall to stage level."

Ussy
as from 38 Bd. St. Jacques
Paris 14me
25.7.61

Dear Alan

Thanks for your letter.[1] It is very good of you and Barney to be so concerned with my wishes and I appreciate it very much. If I had a definite and not too distant opening date from the Royal Court, say sometime in October, I would be tempted to accept your offer to hold up N.Y. and come to London. But they have told me nothing, except that Plowright is away and has not yet read script, which doesn't help things forward. So I think you should go ahead and do it in Sept. at Cherry Lane, rep or no rep. The Berlin opening is confirmed for Sept. 30 and Tophoven has finished his translation (excellent on the whole in spite of unavoidable losses). But I'm not trying to do anything about that, it's the production in English that's on my mind. We can't do much by letter, but we can do a certain amount, so don't scruple to let me know your problems, major and minor. A few photos of your set might be worth sending too. I don't want to go to N.Y., really don't want to, and have not an exaggerated opinion of my usefulness. But if as production develops you feel you really need me and if some way cd. be devised of protecting me from the jackals, I might screw myself up to it. It's things like tone and timing that can't be dealt with outside the theatre, but perhaps I am wrong in thinking they are of peculiar difficulty and importance here. Anyway don't let my nervousness make you nervous, if it doesn't work I know it won't be your fault, but the play's. So go ahead with Sept. production plans and let me give you by letter whatever help you think I can. You have all my confidence, dear Alan.

Affectionately to you all
Sam

McWhinnie will be in N.Y. in August and it might be useful to meet him and hear his reactions to the play and the problems it suggests to him.

———

Had a note from Harry Joe Brown Jr., whom I saw briefly in Paris, saying he would be happy to produce *H.D.*[2]

1. Missing.
2. Barney Rosset had sold the option on *Krapp's Last Tape* to Harry Joe Brown, Jr. (see letter of 16 January 1960, n. 1).

Sunday, August 13 [1961]

Dear Sam,

Back home again—after a week's vacation on a lake that had never heard of a theatre—and feeling fit and ready. Wisconsin turned out fine, though hard work, and I was glad to get a bit of rest. Your letter with the drawings most helpful, and I especially appreciate your taking time and energy to be so specific. You are also very good to let us go ahead, and we are going ahead with plans and procedures to open late in September, depending on available dates. Main reason I'm glad is that we have Ruth White, the girl I wanted—who is up for two other shows and whom we might have lost if we were opening later in the season. Ruth is actually fortyish but has exactly the right quality, tone variety, humor, pathos for Winnie; she is much like Shirley Booth—whom you may know.[1] She was and is our first choice and I feel fortunate that she was available. We shall probably start rehearsals the beginning of the week after next as we want to have four weeks plus previews. The theatre is ideal in size, shape, the rake of the auditorium floor, etc. And I am also pleased with Willie, a tiny Irish actor named John Becher, who currently plays the father in AMERICAN DREAM. As I mentioned before, the current idea is to start in repertory (alternating) with the Albee play; but I'm not so sure how much longer the latter will be holding on, so we may find ourselves playing anywhere from 4 to 8 times a week. Naturally, all depends on our reception. The interest is enormous, as is the curiosity. . . . .

Have been discussing the setting with our scene designer (same guy who did the set for KRAPP). The mound is going to be exactly as you pictured it, the exact scale and height depending on dimensions of stage and rake of auditorium floor. Proscenium opening at Cherry Lane is 18 feet; the mound will be about 12 feet wide from end to end and about 3 to 5 feet in depth, with the overhang behind for Willie, as you indicated. . . . . The backdrop poses more problems. If it is flat, then the stage must be masked on both sides with 'wings', black or painted, neither of which is satisfactory. Would you object to a curved drop, painted as you indicate, but which went off on each side into infinity? Have you any preferences for color of the backcloth? Of the mound? How about the texture of the mound? (I am asking mainly because you are so far away and this will be the premiere and we all want to do what you want.) As soon as the designer has a model, we shall take a photograph and send it on to you to see what you think. In the meantime, here's a rough diagram of what I mean: [diagram missing on carbon]

We are also beginning to think of properties and effects, etc. Are trying to make that umbrella (parasol) really go up in flames, if possible, for a moment. Have you any preference as to color? Also, you indicate that you wanted Winnie's bag to be of the shopping variety rather than an actual handbag. Would not the latter be logical in view of what it contains? Or do you want a shopping bag???? The music box tune we are getting, also the right bell. . . . . .

As you say, the problems and questions will develope mostly as we get into rehearsal. I am so excited and so eager that I can hardly think of anything else. I've been moved and fascinated each time I started to work on one of yours; all I can say is that this one touches me as deeply as any, perhaps more. From the first reading in your flat that day in February till each rereading daily now as I think in practical terms of the problems involved. Am hoping to talk with McWhinnie while he is here—don't think he's come yet. And if Barney and I can persuade you to come over during rehearsals, so much the better. You know how much I'd love to be working with you in the same theatre at the same time. But I also know how much it goes against your grain to come; even to broach the possibility is something. . . . . .

1. Gather you don't want us to see Willie in entirety at all until the end of the play; until then, we see only an arm, a hand, the paper, the back of his head, etc. Therefore we shall take the first of your alternative suggestions: he shall crawl from his normal sitting position to the hole without being exposed to audience at all, only indicating the movement through Winnie's head movement—rather than having him crawl offstage in which case he would have to be seen. (Actually, the actor will move very little if at all, until he comes round at the end of second act.)

2. That means, by the way, does it not that audience in entire beginning will simply *sense* that Winnie is talking to someone or at someone who is around somewhere, presumably behind her, whom they do not see or hear—until his head appears, bleeding, on page 4 ???????????? (This must be carefully built up in suggestion through first 3 pages, that is that someone else is THERE but not seen.)

3. Page 3. Is there anything special you could or would say about sequence of lines from 'holy light' through 'blaze of hellish light'? In terms of tone you want, contrast implied, attitude, anything. . . . .

4. Page 4. I assume that 'Now the other' at bottom of page refers to what I think it does.

5. Page 5. Not sure what you mean by 'Pale flag' in relation to 'Ensign crimson'. Is this meant ironically???????

6. Page 6. Is there anything you would say about . . . 'the happy day to come when flesh melts at so many degrees and the night of the moon

has so many hundred hours'. Or should I not try to interpret that? (The actor will ask.)

7. Page 10. Is there, by any chance, a word left out about two thirds of the way down this page???? "... when I must learn to talk to myself a thing I could never bear to do (in) such wilderness." I was just not sure.

8. Page 13. Does Brownie refer to Browning? Or to the gun? Or to both? (Are you making a pun here?)

9. What is Willie's attitude to his 'Sucked up?' Is he intrigued, surprised, fascinated at the idea? I ask because of your underlining.

10. Page 14. Two thirds of way down. Why cannot Winnie put down the parasol and get on to something else? (The actor will ask me.)

11. Page 16. How do you want us to pronounce Shower? Sho*w*-er, or Sho-er?

12. Page 17. Am I correct in assuming what Willie is eating, at top of page?

13. Page 17. Last line. Should word be "Strange thing*s*" or "Strange thing"?

14. Page 22. Near top of page. Does "... beechen green" refer simply to what was????

15. Page 23. Near top of page. Does "them" refer to "mercies"? Things? Something else?

16. Page 26. Middle of page. What does "bumper" mean?

17. Page 5. "Bast" is not clear in American English. Is there another word perhaps?

Please forgive pettiness and stupidity of these questions? I'm just trying to make sure your intention and specific meaning is clear in each case ... And there'll be others as we go along ... Trust you won't mind.

[Alan]

1. Shirley Booth (b. 1907).

Ussy
17.8.61

Dear Alan

Thanks for yours of Aug. 13 here today.

Mound: I see it extending across entire opening, sloping down to a few inches above stage level at either side

i.e. less hump than undulation. Texture: perhaps a kind of brown canvas with something to suggest scorched grass—but smooth, i.e. no stones sticking up or such like, nothing to break monotony of symmetry. What should characterise whole scene, sky and earth, is a pathetic unsuccessful realism, the kind of tawdriness you get in 3rd rate musical or pantomime, *that* quality of *pompier,* laughably earnest bad imitation. A curved drop is all right with me. Colour: that which best conveys heat and dessication. But this will be more a question of lighting than of painting. Hot blue sky (if blue can be hot, which I doubt) and yellow-brown scorched earth. Suggest striped parasol, echoing striped ribbon of Willie's boater, say blue and yellow again. The bag *must* be a marketing bag (bottom of p. 21). I see it like the big black capacious French *"cabas."* The bell as shrill and wounding as possible. In case I didn't give you musical-box reference, there is an American recording of a Regina (big box) playing this tune: Old Music Box Melodies, RCD4, information from Bornard Music Box Co., 139 Fourth Avenue, Pelham, N.Y. If this box too big for bag or not a "winder," it can be played off and Winnie have small dummy of kind we need.

1. Willie invisible need not move at all, except to sit up etc., till end of play. It's only if he cannot be hidden completely that he wd. need to crawl offstage.

2. I think it must be obvious from outset (p. 2, "Hoo-oo" . . . "poor Willie") that someone is there behind mound. She leans well back & down to her right and apostrophizes him, then when she comes back front comments on his capacity for sleep. May mention here that all this leaning and turning and motion of arms and bust in Act I should be as ample and graceful *(memorable)* as possible, in order that its absence Act II may have maximum effect. Hope your girl has desirable fleshiness. Audience throughout Act II should miss this gleaming opulent flesh—gone.

3. No, just say lines, same tone throughout, polishing mechanically, no emotion on "blaze of hellish . . .". What tone? This of course is *the* problem. I can find no better word for it than "mild." That is the basic tone throughout and should only be deviated from as indicated (voice breaks, murmur, scream). In a word I am asking here for vocal monotony and relying on speech rhythms and speech-gesture complexes, eyes, switching on and off of smile, etc., to do the work, all these in their turn requiring, if they are to operate fully, vocal tranquillity & transparency.

4. Yes, what you think.

5. "Ensign crimson . . . pale flag," Juliet's lips, Act III I think, I'll let you have exact reference when I get back to Paris and other quotation references. No irony. Mild blank tone.

6. If you have to explain this passage you may describe Winnie's "reasoning" as follows: when no further pains are possible (in pursuit of information) one has only to sit tight and lost knowledge will come back into the mind, the examples given (duration of lunar night & degree of heat at which flesh melts) being obviously prompted by her situation.

7. Above all no "in." "Never bear to do such wilderness" straight through, imperturbable, ex. of vocal normality—speech abormality mentioned in 3.

8. No one will get this reference, *tant pis*.[1] It is to a line of Browning "I'll say confusedly what comes uppermost."[2]

9. Willie feels "*fucked up*," not "*sucked up*." His surprise is at the s.

10. She simply can't move, that's all. Times when she can't speak, times when she can't move. Her problem is how to eke out, each "day," and organise economy of these two orders of resources, body and speech (the 2 lamps). Act of God required when both burn down together.

11. Sho*w*er (rain). Shower & looker are derived from German "schauen" & "kuchen" (to look).[3] They represent the onlooker (audience) wanting to know meaning of things. That's why (p. 17) she stops filing, raises head & lets 'em have it ("And you, she says. . .").

12. Snot from his nose.

13. "Thing" is right, meaning this Shower-Looker episode.

14. "Beechen green": Keats's "beechen green and shadows numberless," and of course referring back to "horse-beech" (p. 5) under which she sat on Charlie Hunter's knees.

15. "Them": all these objects she can see.

16. "Bumper": brimming glass. Drink a bumper, toss off a brimming glass. It's the "happy days" toast.

17. "Bast." Fibrous twine used by gardeners, also called "bass." Always gets into a tangle. Same thing as "raphia" which more familiarly replaces it.

P. 17 line 17 between . . "put on my glasses" and "(Finishes left hand, etc. . .)," insert "(Pause.) Too late now."

Frustrating to have to deal with all this by letter, everything cries out for nuance & enlargement. Better than nothing I suppose, hope you agree.

Berlin is confirmed for Sept. 30th in the very small "Werkstatt" theatre, with Berta Drews (good it appears, & well-known, but rings no bell in me). No news from Devine or Plowright, I think Donald McWhinnie leaves in about a week, Pinter also going over. It's as well you should know my plans: back to Paris day after tomorrow Aug. 19th. Aug. 20th–23rd Etretat. Paris then till Sept. 1st. England then till Sept. 11th. Then Paris and Ussy.

At your entire disposal for any help I can give.

Affectionately to you all
Sam

1. *"tant pis!"*: never mind!

2. Robert Browning (1812–1889): "Paracelsus," *The Poetical Works of Robert Browning,* 1983.

3. *schauen*: to look; *kuchen*: to peer. The name Shower is derived from *shauen* and Cooker from *kuchen*. Winnie puns on these names.

Paris
25.8.61

Dear Alan

Herewith promised references. Hope they're worth having.

Best

Sam [handwritten from "Dear Alan"]

P.3 11. 3–4.   "Woe woe etc." *Hamlet*, Act III Sc. 1:

". . . O woe is me
To have seen what I have seen, see what I see."

P.4 11. 27–28.   "Oh fleeting joys etc." *Paradise Lost.* Loc?
          [Book X, 741–742]
                                  "... O fleeting joys
               Of Paradise, dear bought with lasting woe."

P.4 1.47   "Ensign crimson ... Pale Flag." *Romeo and Juliet,* Act V Sc. 3.
        "... Beauty's ensign yet
        Is crimson in thy lips and in thy cheeks
        And death's pale flag is not advanced there."

P.10 1.8   "Fear no more the heat o' the sun."
        Cymbeline, Act IV, Sc. 2.
        "Fear no more the heat o' the sun
        Nor the furious winter's rages;
        Thou thy worldly task hast done,
        Home art gone, and ta'en thy wages.
        Golden lads and girls all must,
        As chimney-sweepers, come to dust."

P.12 11. 19–20   "Laughing wild ..."
        Thomas Gray: On a Distant Prospect of Eton College.
        "And moody madness laughing wild
        Amid severest woe ..."

P.12. 1.30   For "happiness" read "paradise." Omar Khayyam.
        "A book of verses underneath the bough,
        A loaf of bread, a jug of wine, and thou (?)
        Beside me singing in the wilderness,
        Ah wilderness were Paradise enow."

P.13. 1.7   "uppermost. ."
        Robert Browning: "I say confusedly what comes uppermost."

P.16. I.23   "bird of dawning ..." *Hamlet,* Act I, Sc. I.
        "Some say that ever 'gainst that season comes
        Wherein our Saviour's birth is celebrated,
        The bird of dawning singeth all night long."

P.21. 1.11   "Hail, holy light!" *Paradise Lost,* Book III, Line 1.
        "Hail, holy light! Offspring of heaven first-born."

P.22. 1.14   "beechen green ..." Keats. *Ode to a Nightingale.*
        "In some melodious plot
        Of beechen green and shadows numberless ..."

P.22. 1.46   "damask" *Twelfth Night* Act II, Sc. 4.
                     ". . . She never told her love,
             But let concealment, like a worm i' the bud,
             Feed on her damask cheek."

P.25. 11. 7–11.   "Go forget me etc." Charles Wolfe (1791–1823).
                  "Go, forget me—why should sorrow
                     O'er that brow a shadow fling?
                  Go, forget me—and tomorrow
                     Brightly smile and sweetly sing.
                  Smile—though I shall not be near thee;
                  Sing—though I shall never hear thee."

P.26. 11. 42–43.   "Flowers . . . That smile today."
                   Herrick. *To the Virgins to make much of Time.*
                   "Gather ye rosebuds while ye may,
                      Old Time is still a-flying,
                   And this same flower that smiles today
                   Tomorrow may be dying."

                                         Monday, Aug. 28, [1961]
Dear Sam,

   Thanks for your good letters, the second of which came today. They
are invaluable, revealing, helpful, wonderful for us all. We went into
preliminary rehearsals last week, mostly with Winnie (Ruth White),
reading, trying to catch some of the tones and overtones, digging into
the golden lode of the script. It is beautiful, Sam, and I can't tell you
how privileged I feel to be working on it. Ruth is marvelous, just
the right physical image, I think, and we are trying to make her hair a
bit blonder; but face and shoulders, bust, etc. are just right—something of a younger and not so attractive Tallulah Bankhead. She works
very well, some trouble learning the lines—which is normal as they
are tricky—but great love and devotion. . . . Willie is also fine, a small
partly dapper and partly sad-eyed Irishman; good comedian, cooperative in all his logistical problems of sitting and disappearing, etc. . . . .
The mound has been made exactly as you described and wanted, the
width of the stage, 3 feet high, simple and symmetrical, places for all
the small props to be placed, etc. We have found a *cabas*; we have sent
to Switzerland! for a music box which will play the proper tune—that

place in Pelham is not listed by phone but we have written and are hoping for an answer. (How did you ever locate it??????) Our real problem is the parasol which bursts into flame or at least smoke, but we are working, trying, consulting various magicians, etc. . . . . . The backcloth is being painted, haven't seen it yet. . . . . We may have to open on Sept. 17th instead of the 19th because of a conflict with another show—not sure yet. Also possibility of the 21st. In any case, we shall have had 4 weeks rehearsal, maximum allowed by Equity . . . And Ruth White is working all the time, turned down two big TV shows to play the part—and just last Friday turned down a little one which would have paid her well and only required 4 days rehearsal—I told her OK to do it and we would rehearse at night (customary to do this in case of $45 weekly off-Bway salaries); but she herself decided NO, in order to devote all energies. . . . . .

Now to some more questions, which have come up during the rehearsals. Again, forgive obvious stupidity but often it helps me to know that I'm actually right—or wrong:

I'm assuming Willie is supposed to be completely nude in Act I. (Only hat)

Do you want steel-rimmed spectacles? Like yours? You don't want horn rims?

Our idea of a collapsible parasol is one whose handle folds about half way? Is that OK?????

Would you like to draw an outline of Winnie's hat? We're getting one to your description and one that looks good on Ruth—but another of your original drawings might be even more exact.

Presumably you wanted Willie entirely or almost entirely bald since you do not mention white hair although you do mention white mustache. The problem of a bald wig in a small theatre is a tough one. Do you mind a fringe of white hair (same color as mustache) on Willie? (Will help to hide jointure of wig.)

(They're interviewing me for Sunday TIMES next week since they can't get you. Now I know why you don't want to come . . . . What do I say???????????)

Some some [*sic*] harder ones:

1. P 3. Top. Still not entirely sure of Winnie's attitude on "-holy light-" etc. sequence. I get what you say about tone, but what is she thinking? Why does she say it? Key to this would help me and actress. Please forgive my pursuing. We're OK up to there. Anything you might think of to say?????

2. P 3. Near bottom.[1] Is 'butt' of parasol, the middle ?????

3. P 5. Near middle. Raffia clearer than bast. If you like one syllable word, how about rope?

4. I assume smile on 'old style' each time is fond memory of the past.

5. Has Winnie ever before noticed inscription on toothbrush? Always before? Why is she so interested? (I have ideas about this but would appreciate yours especially.)

6. P 6. Top line 14. Does Willie go after postcard because he hears word "setae"?????????

7. P 8. Line 4. We all assume 'old joke' is Winnie herself . . . . .?

8. P 9. Middle. We just want to make sure that you actually mean: ". . . don't like sprawling there in this. . . . ." Somebody thought it was misprint for ". . don't lie. . ."

9. Great problem in supposed actual location of Willie's hole. If he crawls 'left' as indicated, impossible not to see him—i.e. we should be able to see him since mound is not high enough at edges to hide him. Solution we have at moment—subject to your assistance—is to assume hole is directly upstage center. Then he disappears (right stage—left audience) and she cranes right round following his supposed course although we do not see him at all. The actual actor playing Willie then can pitch his voice to sound a bit far away—and we have the hole . . . Is this OK with you? Is it clear???????

(This typing on both sides is awful.)

10. P 12. L 5. Is she saying: "God must have been involved" or "There goes God with one of his jokes again." or "Could it be God?" or "What a joke on God" or ????????????????????

11. P 12. L 16.   The two different things; She's laughing at the 'little joke', Willie is laughing at his pun or the idea of formication . . .?

12. P 11. Bottom.   By the way, what is [Willie] really trying to tell her—in relation to the eggs and formication?

13. p. 13. 1.7–8.   We're still not entirely clear about Browning the poet and Browning the revolver? You do intend the pun, *n'est-ce pas?* Is Brownie only the gun in her reference, or does she start by using Brownie to refer first to Browning and then to the revolver?

14. P 17–32.   Does 'Ditty' refer to the bag or to his body??????

15. P 18–20.   Anything you would want to say to describe the 'gesture' specifically?

16. P 18. Bottom.   Is he crawling for a moment on his belly? Which
                    is why she stresses knees?????
17. P 19–7.   The unrecognizable is related to the Recognizable on
              p. [*sic*]. Although I'm not entirely sure of her meaning
              in the second case.
18. P 19—Middle.   Presumably Winnie has not heard exactly what
                   Willie is saying, but is responding to the fact
                   that he is responding?????
19.   That's enough for now. And anyway we haven't really done
      much to the second act, so I'll leave that for now.

Anything and everything you have to say on these or other matters
will be most appreciated.

Don McWhinnie and Harold Pinter are in town but I'm having difficulty locating them. Pinter is being wined and dined, but he has my
number and may call me. In any case, I shall get in touch.

Hear good things about the GODOT at the Récamier (?) Were you
pleased? And how about the BBC?[2] They're doing ACT WITHOUT
WORDS off-off-Broadway, and some day I'm going to get away from
HAPPY DAYS to see it.

Enclosing some items of interest.

Trust all is well. Best to Suzanne. And thanks.

20. P 11–29.   Asking for moon etc. Presume you don't mean
               American slang term, but rather reference is to night
               of the moon, previously mentioned.

First act about an hour, second about 35 minutes. And the bill holds.

Ever,
Alan

1. The pagination and directions about locations are written in by hand. No. 20 and
following entirely handwritten.
2. *En attendant Godot* opened at the Odéon-Théâtre de France, not the Théâtre Récamier (see letter of 9 March 1961, n. 4). "BBC": see letter of 20 May 1961, n. 4.

Surrey
3.9.61

Dear Alan

This all looks silly written out but hope it will help.[1] Your letter came
last Friday just as I was setting out from Paris. Wrote part of above at Le

Touquet Airfield waiting for mist to rise. Couldn't do anything yesterday. So glad you are pleased with progress. Tell Ruth White how much
I appreciate her devotion. Very interested by your timing. I thought
about 50 & 25 and am pleased it works out longer. I hear KRAPP
is coming on again with Davis. Fine. BBC TV GODOT not good I
thought.[2] GODOT revival at Odéon (Théâtre de France—Théâtre nouveau) good. Nothing at Récamier. Here for another week, then back to
Paris.

Best
Sam

Willie naked in Act I.
Steel or gold-rimmed preferable to horn.
Parasol: telescopic system. The *whole* handle pushes in when not in
use, so that it can be carried in a handbag. Only beak of handle emerges
when closed. Saw a Swiss one.

———

Don't see hat clearly enough to draw. Kind of fussy toque with long
feather (what French call a *"couteau"*). Close-fitting, brimless, casting no
shadow on face. Sorry to be so vague.

———

OK for fringe of white hair. Becher looks almost thin enough on top
to dispense with *"faun crâne."*

———

No ideas for the *Sunday Times.* Sorry.

———

1. If she were blind there would be no more light, hellish or holy,
   no more objects ("What wd. I do without them?"). She comes
   therefore to these lines from the last lines of p. 2. Light holy &
   to be missed in so far as a condition of seeing (which helps her
   through the day), hellish and not to be missed because
   emanation of the "hellish sun" which is burning her. "Bob up
   out of dark"—dark of sleep shattered by bell.
2. By "butt" I mean ferrule, lower extremity.
3. Prefer *raphia* to *rope.*
4. "Old style" and smile always provoked by word "day" and
   derivatives or similar. There is no more day in the old sense
   because there is no more night, i.e. nothing but day. It is in a
   way an apologetic smile for speaking in a style no longer valid.
   "Old style" suggests also of course old calendar before revision.

"Sweet old style" joke with reference to Dante's *"dolce stile nuovo."* [SB underlines *"nuovo"*][3]

5. No deep intention behind deciphering of toothbrush handle. An occupation to help her through the "day"—"to speak in the old style." She has no doubt done this many times before—and forgotten—or always in vain till now. Wonder what your idea is.

6. Dirty postcard nothing to do with *Setae*.

7. "Old joke" not Winnie, rather the joke of being that is said to have caused Democritus to die of laughter.[4] To be related also if you like to Nell's "nothing is funnier than unhappiness etc." Same idea in *Watt* (the 3 smiles).[5]

8. It should of course be "don't *lie* [double underlining] sprawling." For God's sake tell Dick Seaver,[6] in case I didn't correct it in proof.

9. Very pertinent question. Your solution very good, i.e. that he shd. crawl straight up stage, Winnie craning to her right and back as far as she can.

10. "God." *(mild)* [AS underlines] is simply "good God!" as the implications of swarming ants dawn on her. It is also in the event another of God's "little jokes" and

11. they are both duly diverted by it. By "two different things" I am not quite sure what she means, possibly that Willie is not seeing the joke from the same angle as she, i.e. he laughing at the image of the ants devouring her and she at the image of the ants devouring herself. Nuance?

12. "To Formicate" means to swarm, speaking of ants, or to have the sensation on one's skin of ants swarming. The eggs contain the promise of swarming (devouring) ants to come. This shd. be remembered in Act II when she has no longer arms to defend herself with.

13. The revolver is called "Browning—Brownie"—not because there is a weapon of that name—but because it is always uppermost. If the line was by another poet the revolver wd. be called by the name of that other poet.

14. "Ditty" means a sailor's bag, a kind of "hold-all."

15. A gesture of hand or hands towards objects she is putting away, or towards them and bag. Perhaps a simple opening of arms with palms uppermost with rueful implication "this unspeakable way." Same quality of gesture p. 15, 1.27.

16. Yes, presumably dragging himself along on his belly, hence her insistence on knees.

————————

17. Yes, echo here, but no need to stress. If he is still recognizable, it is perhaps because she sees him daily, whereas he seems never to look at her (p.11). So at end of play he may be looking at her for the first time after numberless days—*(smile)*—"to speak in the old style."

————————

18. Winnie happy because Willie has answered. Doesn't matter to her what he says, as long as he speaks to her.

20. *Moon.* Don't know American slang phrase. "To ask for the moon" means to her to demand the impossible. And of course echo of "night of the moon." In the hellish sun *moon* means coolness & freshness.

1. Letter and date come after the notes.

2. See letter of 20 May 1961, n. 4.

3. Dante Alighieri (1265–1321).

4. Democritus (c. 470–400 B.C.), pre-Socratic philosopher known as the "laughing philosopher"; SB impressed by his remark "nothing is more real than nothing."

5. "Watt smiled.

No offence meant, said Mr. Spiro.

Watt's smile was further peculiar in this, that it seldom came singly, but was followed after a short time by another, less pronounced it is true. In this it resembled the fart. And it even sometimes happened that a third, very weak and fleeting, was found necessary, before the face could be at rest again. But this was rare. And it will be a long time now before Watt smiles again, unless something very unexpected turns up, to upset him." (*Watt*, 27).

6. Richard (Dick) Seaver, managing editor, Grove Press at this time, member of the Merlin group in Paris; "Collection Merlin" published *Watt*, Olympia Press, 1953; "Samuel Beckett: an Introduction," *Merlin*, 1(Autumn 1952), 73–79; ed. and introduction, *I Can't Go On, I'll Go On: A Selection from Samuel Beckett's Work*, 1976.

Wednesday, Sept. 6, 1961

Dear Sam,

Thanks for your letter and comments. Sorry about having to write it on the fly. . . . Things are getting clearer—then dim again—then clearer. And we seem to be making progress slowly. Judith came in today and watched a bit and seemed pleased with Ruth White's work—as we all are. Biggest problem is learning the lines, which are tricky, deceptive in their variation within similarity, rhythms, etc. But I think you would generally be pleased with her character, voice, tones, etc. . .

The mound is fine, and we have finally licked the problem of keeping her absolutely still for the second act without developing cramps and aches. A real neck-piece. . . . The music box arrived from Switzerland and is lovely, clear as a bell; the bell is definitely wounding; the parasol is still a problem—the flame part of it. We thought we had it, then yesterday it just wouldn't work. Still trying and will, will succeed. The problem is that it is on stage so long before the flames that whatever inflammable material we use gets dry under the lights. But we are trying various things. And indeed even toying with idea of an exact rigged duplicate which Willie would hand back to her after she lets it slip. This would help the 'time of drying' problem. . . . . We also have smoke, and if the worst comes to the worst, we shall settle for smoke only—but I am holding out for the flames, which is very effective.

Running time remains about an hour for I, and 30–35 for II. And holds like a rock.

Saw Pinter for a bit on Sunday. McWhinnie deep in his rehearsals;[1] am trying to get him for a drink. Harold loved the play.

We checked the printed script and all is corrected with exception of substituting PARADISE for HAPPINESS (enow).

Working on her dress (blouse) and hat. After much fruitless search, we are making both. Will be exactly as you indicate.

Trouble with using Becher's own hair is need for whitening it; and small size of theatre makes it look too much like makeup. But we are trying. And he DOES have a lovely bald patch in a perfect place. We shall try all ways.

The KRAPP-ZOO re-do was a sudden idea of the producers, and everyone thinks its good public relations all around. We're opening Tuesday for a month's run.[2] I'm working with Donald, same set, costumes, etc. . . . By the way, the response at the box-office to the adverts on HAPPY DAYS has been excellent. Previews start next week, and we are still opening Sept. 17 or 19, probably the latter. . . .

Thanks for answers and thoughts on all questions. They may sound silly or obvious or puzzling, but basically they give me a chance to talk with you from afar in place of the talking we would be doing if you were here. I appreciate your tolerance.

Just a few on the second act:

1. p. Why don't you start Narrative tone at start of her story? Do
        you want this actually to be a sort of prologue????? Any
        other reason?

2. p.   Is her 'But no./No, no.' in relation to 'Drop dead!' The whole
        event? Not entirely clear.

3. p.   Why does Willie wait until this point to come out? Has he
        been waiting for proper opportunity? Is he just ready now?
        Is it coincidence? (I know you need it for the end of the act,
        but I mean from an acting point of view.)

I thought second act would be tougher, but it's actually first; second
is taut, direct, terribly moving. First still comes and goes. We're working. Audiences will help us next week. Will write again after first audience, and will keep at it. The play is throbbing away at us all each
minute, and we are all grateful . . . Miss you . . . Trust you are not too
nervous. . . . And will keep you posted. . . . All the best.

[Alan]

1. *The Caretaker* (see letter of 13 January 1961, n. 3).

2. *Krapp's Last Tape* and *Zoo Story* opened at the East End Theatre, New York, 12
September 1961, for 32 performances. Donald Davis (Krapp). AS wrote: "The success of
Krapp and *Zoo* gave me a new lift and a new image; I was 'an off-Broadway direc-
tor'. Suddenly I realized that I liked the shape and scale that this description represented.
I liked working in the less frenzied, more intellectually and emotionally stimulating,
and at the same time more intimate theater. I had not been at home on Broadway, even
though I knew that the large rewards still rested there. . . . After my three efforts off-
Broadway, *Endgame, Doll,* and *Krapp,* I regretted not having come upon the scene earlier"
(*Entrances,* 278).

Sunday, [Sept. 10, 1961]

Dear Sam,

Have had one and a half audiences, and I hasten to send progress
report. Yesterday, just a brief scattering (15), though it turns out a friend
of yours—unidentified—who is evidently writing to you. Today, 50,
mostly writers, actors, friends, etc. Also Donald McWhinnie—whom I
met last night.

Response has been overwhelming, especially this afternoon. Complete attention—even in intense heat—absolute silence, and the laughs
coming. In spite of extreme nerves on part of actress, loss of lines,
incompleteness of set, lites, etc. General reaction is one of being intensely moved, shattered. They say they have rarely if ever felt this way
in a theatre. . . .

Donald seemed to like it—at its present stage—in fact rhapsodic. Judith Schmidt also. Barney coming tomorrow. I called George Reavey and he is coming tomorrow. The week of paid previews starts Tuesday, and will also be helpful.

I feel we are a quarter of the way there. Ruth played the first half of the first act really remarkably today, perfect control and ease, graceful and ample—as you said. She hasn't found it after the Parasol sequence—which we have now licked though not perfectly (both flames and smoke afterward). Recovered towards end of act. She's very uneven in II, largely because of uncertainty with lines, which are most difficult as you understand. She works on them all the time and was four times better today than yesterday; I have no doubts of her ability to get them perfectly this week. Just takes time. . . . The set, the mound, I think is fine; the lighting still being worked on; the props just right, bell fine.

Running time: Act I almost exactly and consistently an hour; Act II just over half an hour.

The opening of each act, I'm very happy with; the end of II also; we are off on timing somewhat for end of I. Am working.

I'm reporting all I know. The reaction pleases though frightens me. I do think the play is remarkable but I don't yet trust the 'professionals' reaction; will feel better after a few laymen have seen it. But there's no question that the experience affects people directly and strongly. We shall see.

We miss you.

And thanks.

[Alan]

Paris
12.9.61

Dear Alan

Back from England last night. Your letter today.[1] I feel the great effort you are all making and am very grateful. No, I am not nervous, just curious about the work's viability. On re-reading I realise Act I more vulnerable than II. I too thought reverse when writing. Better so I suppose. Congratulations on musical-box, neck-piece, parasol flames, set, etc. Try and accentuate eyes in II. It's a tremendous job for an actress. Please tell R. W. how much I am with her in thought and admire her courage. Had a letter from Herbert Myron[2] who crashed a rehearsal and was much moved.

1. Narrative tone only for this particular day's instalment. "She is now 4 or 5 etc" to be regarded as synopsis of previous instalments. All this has already been told in narrative tone on countless preceding days.

2. "But no etc" refers only to "Let go of me . . . Drop dead." On the contrary they continue hand in hand.

3. Willie's behaviour never tied up with Winnie's. He is not reacting to her. It is not even certain that he hears her. Coincidence therefore. German translator asked today if his "collapse" (P. 9) depended on his hearing word "blessing." No. Coincidence. Sorry.

Affectionately to you all.
Sam [handwritten]

1. This letter replies to AS letter of 6 September 1961.
2. Herbert Myron (b. 1906), American academic, Theatre Collection of Harvard College Library.

Thursday, [Sept. 14, 1961]

Dear Sam,

Just a quick note before hastening to rehearsal. Both to let you know things are progressing, and to tell you not to worry about the letter just previous—asking a couple of silly questions about the second act—which will arrive too late for you to answer anyhow. (The bloody postoffice department returned it to me a week after I had mailed it because it had one penny too little on it; no wonder we're losing to the Russians!)

Anyhow.

We have had three more audiences since I last wrote, and the show and reception are both getting stronger and stronger. The last two nights have been paid previews, which means no friends and relatives, few theatre people, just people who come as laymen. Their response is as strong as the others; while the laughs sometimes come differently, the attention is as definite, and the applause at the end tears the roof off. We have been taking 6 curtain calls and they keep applauding through the house lights coming up; we could take a dozen or more. Including Bravos.

Curtain calls are a bit of a problem. Actually I'd prefer not to have any, but it's very customary here and the audience feels cheated. We can't get Winnie out of the mound in a hurry, and besides I hate to see the hole in the mound in the call; so we keep her right there, and Willie as he is on hands and knees. I don't know a suitable and artistic alternative.

The parasol burning works marvelously, flames and smoke. Just hope the fire dept won't come in the middle one day, as it's strictly illegal. . . . . . Have taken some pictures for publicity purposes—but long before set, costumes, props, etc. ready; are taking production shots next week which will be more accurate. Hope you like them. . . . . The hat is lovely, feather and all; Winnie looks marvelously Irish, we think, blonde, ample, and gleaming.

Ruth is just marvelous, we think. I know I do and am grateful for having her, really don't know another actress in USA who could have done the job as well and been so cooperative. Last night her first act was 95 per cent there, the second act is about 75 per cent and climbing. The night before the second act was best ever. Am trying to get both to peak for Sunday.

And John Becher is just right for Willie. Their scene from the hole ('Yes!' and 'Eggs. .' etc. . .) is just great. The newspaper business, the head and hankerchief. . . . . my only regret is that you won't see. We'll keep trying to lure you if the notices are good. Hah! Who knows what those guys will say. And, honestly, it has been such a pleasure and joy to be working on this one, and we have all been so involved and moved by the whole thing that we feel optimistic. Win, lose, or draw I am [words missing] grateful for your confidence and trust. Keep [ending missing]

[Alan]

Paris
Friday 15th [Sept. 1961]

Dear Alan

This scribble in haste to thank you for your letter of last Sunday arrived only today. Naturally very pleased by all you tell me and appreciate very much your finding time to write at such a busy & anxious time for you. I think myself that a commercial success is very unlikely and don't anticipate much mercy from the critics. So I am interested in the "professional" reaction in the sense that it will help me to decide whether this is really a dramatic text or a complete aberration and whether there is justification for trying to push further this kind of theatre. I am surprised by length of running time. Probably I have made [Act] I a bit too long. My heart goes out to Ruth White, it must be a big ordeal for her. Thank you all again for your devotion. I'm not sure when you open so can't send you a cable. Think of me as right with you whenever it is—and no matter how it goes.

Ever [handwritten]
Sam [handwritten]

Tuesday, [Sept 19, 1961]

Dear Sam,

The past 48 hours has flown like mad, a vast jumble of hope and confusion; the frantic hours of waiting for the notices, watching the faces of the audience, hoping that Ruthie would move them as much as she has before, etc. And waking you up in the early hours again. . . . .

The opening went very well,[1] Ruthie terribly shaky and nervous and a shade out of kilter here and there in the first act, but really soaring in the second. House packed with press—almost a hundred out of 180—impossible to keep those vultures out; and their response not as overt as the previews (same as at ENDGAME) but rapt with attention throughout, sometimes the silence as intense as a surgical operation. The heat wave broke Friday, which was a real break for us. No steam pipes this time either.[2] Applause tumultuous. Bravos, I think one or two from Harold Pinter.

Then those ghastly hours of waiting for the notices, though we all kept trying to tell selves we didn't care. Because we were pleased with the show, with Ruth and John, the set, the general tone, the feeling that you too would have been pleased. . . . Nevertheless, the longest three hours in history. Then a quick glance at the NEWS, favorable though illiterate (as is the paper); then the marvelous one in the TIMES—we all said Taubman sounded like Atkinson used to sound before he retired last year—and then our friend Walter Kerr and his constipated evasion in the TRIB. Two out of 3, and the other one saying at the end that it was worth thinking about! So to bed and then the afternoons: a good one from the *World-Telegram,* a disappointment in Watts—whom we'd been hoping for though he's not considered any great shakes as a critic—and the stupid one from the Hearst rag. Oh, and a tidbit from the other Hearst rag out later in the morning. . . . Of course, the TIMES is the one which gets on everyone's breakfast table, so general impression is that all the notices are good and that we have a hit![3] In fact, lots of people are calling in to see if it's possible to get seats. In fact, we had a sellout (with second night press) the second night, and almost full tonight. The show Monday was best ever, full and relaxed, and every laugh. Roar of applause at the end, including the press. We shall see what we shall see in regard to the weeklies. In the meantime, response has been more than good. Not that I think we'll have a sellout for a year; but am quite sure unless the hurricane hits that we'll have a respectable run and attention. So I slept a few hours today.

Your letter arrived today, thanks.[4] All our thanks to you; we have all had a wonderful and rewarding experience, I can never tell you how much it has meant to me to be working on this play. In a certain way, it has moved me more than any other one—though each one seems to do that when one is working on it. In a way, I think, we came closer to what you [?]were [?]aiming at—from casting to tone—than any of the others. I know Ruth is great in it, & I think you would agree. And every little prop worked out also—eventually. You can't [?]always tell from the pix because we didn't yet have everything when they were taken. Kay Boyle[5] was there on Friday & sends her regards—she seemed to be most responsive. Pinter loved it, wishes Ruth could play it in London. Some of our leading [?]stars [?]actresses have been coming & will continue. We'll know more in a week as to how play is really [?]doing [handwritten and almost illegible from "that when one is"]

The critics show their usual—or unusual—range of opinions; I am pleased with the way Taubman expressed his liking.[6] Maybe some of the weeklies will be intelligent, favorably or otherwise. . . . All I can say is that no one emerges unmoved—I don't see how Kerr could have unless he wanted to. By all means, go on, Sam, do what you feel you should, write the way you want to, stretch everything the way you'd like. I do hope the response to this one has given you a little encouragement. Certainly, there is no question of HAPPY DAYS [not] being viable in the theatre or possible or effective. Its effect on most people is absolutely shattering. And I think it gains through repetition, reading, and re-reading.

Delighted to hear your voice, apologies for waking you, all my thanks and good wishes. Will keep in touch as things develope.

[Alan]

1. *Happy Days* opened at the Cherry Lane Theatre, New York, Sunday, 17 September 1961, produced by Barr and Wilder, directed by AS, designed by William Ritman, played in repertory with Albee's *The American Dream* and *The Death of Bessie Smith* for 28 performances, closed 3 November 1961. Ruth White (Winnie), John C. Becher (Willie). Ruth White won an Obie for her playing. *Happy Days*, 1961, French trans. by SB, *Oh les beaux jours*, 1963.

2. During the American premiere of *Endgame* the radiators at the Cherry Lane Theatre clanked well into the second act.

3. Reviews: Herbert Mitgang, "Waiting for Beckett—and His Happy Days Premiere," *NY Times*, 17 September 1961; Howard Taubman, "Beckett's 'Happy Days,'" *NY Times*, 18 September; Walter Kerr, "Happy Days," *NY Herald-Tribune*, 18 September; Norman Nadel, "Beckett's 'Happy Days' Opens at Cherry Lane," *NY World Telegram*, 18 September; Richard Watts, Jr., "The Wasteland of Samuel Beckett," 18 September, also "Two on the Aisle," *NY Post*, 1 October; Jerry Tallmer, *Village Voice*, 21 September; Taubman, "Reason to Live," *NY Times*, 1 October 1961; Robert Brustein, *New Republic*, 2 October; Tom Driver, *Christian Century*, 11 October, 208–209, wrote: "Alan Schneider has done an unusually skilled job of directing. He understands Beckett better than any other director in America."

4. SB, Friday, 15 September.

5. Kay Boyle (1903–1992), American novelist, short story writer, and critic, friend of SB since 1929.

6. Howard Taubman (b. 1907), American journalist, author, music editor, and critic for the *NY Times*, succeeded Brooks Atkinson as drama critic. His review began: "with 'Happy Days' Samuel Beckett has composed a song of rue that will haunt the inner ear long after you have heard it," and "Mr. Beckett's threnody is grim, but in its muted, tremulous way it shimmers with beauty." Of Schneider, Taubman writes: "Alan Schneider has directed the play with a memorable combination of delicacy and strength."

Paris

23.9.61

Dear Alan

Glad to have your Tuesday letter. It's been an exhausting and nerve-racking time for you and I hope you're having a good rest before the next. It was good to hear your voice Monday morning. Judith sent me a packet of notices. I suppose one should be thankful for them but good bad or indifferent they get me down—and wondering what possesses these people to be writing about the theatre. I like the look of Winnie exceedingly—and of the set. Becher too looks fine. A cable from Harold Pinter congratulating on play and "superb production & performance," *et Dieu sait que c'est difficile!*[1] Also a very moved note from Kay Boyle— & warm reactions from George Reavey. Barney will be over soon and tell me all in detail. I look forward to your photos and wish I could look forward to you in person in the near future. No inkling of future work, buried upside down in translation, one foot emerging with what might be a wasp on it. All I know is that if there's ever another it will be a very different kettle of fish. That's what you say. Thanks and affection again to you all for all you've done. I've the feeling no author was ever better served.

Best to Jean & children.

Ever
Sam

1. *"et Dieu sait que c'est difficile!"*: and God knows it is difficult!

November 8, 1961

Mr. Samuel Beckett
38 Boulevard St. Jacques
Paris X1Ve, France

Dear Sam,

Only a combination of physical and mental exhaustion has kept me from writing sooner and please forgive the haste of this note. I have just finished a production of Brecht's CHALK CIRCLE at Arena in Washington and am now on a work of Albee's there.[1]

Last week I saw the next to the final performance of HAPPY DAYS. Ruth was wonderful, the house was full and warmly responsive and I cannot tell you how sad I was at the idea of its closing. Why we were doing no business I just don't know but evidently we weren't. The reviews seemed favorable enough but we didn't get either Kerr or Watts and for a play of this kind that is fatal. Dick Barr wants to do a limited run of four weeks or so in the Spring and I hope that will be possible especially if Ruth is available. We would have lost her in a month anyhow and God knows how we would have replaced her.

This doesn't begin to tell you how I feel about the show, our doing it, and the fact that it didn't run. All I can say is thanks again for your trust and confidence and I hope you don't feel too upset.

Best regards to Suzanne. Will write again at greater length.

Ever,

[Alan]

1. *The Caucasian Chalk Circle* opened at the Arena Stage, Washington, D.C., 30 October 1961; *The American Dream* with John Mortimer's *What Shall We Tell Caroline?* opened at the Arena Stage, 28 November 1961.

Paris
11.11.61

Dear Alan

Thanks for your letter. You sound in need of a good holiday and I hope you'll be able to have one after the Albee.

I'm sorry the play did not do better, but am not at all upset. When one makes these efforts in the theatre one knows what to expect from the Kerrs & Wattses. Perhaps some day it will be possible to survive without their [?]praise.

I see no point in a revival in the Spring and would be opposed to it.

A thousand thanks again to you and Ruth White for what you did.

Best to Jean and the children.

Affectionately
Sam

December 17, 1961

Dear Sam,

At long last. Much too long last, but you'll understand. After the Brecht I was on the point of actual exhaustion, physical and mental. And I still had to do a double bill of AMERICAN DREAM and WHAT SHALL WE TELL CAROLINE (John Mortimer) at the Arena. Somehow it got on . . . and then off I want just to do nothing for two weeks:

reading (biography of Joyce), writing letters, and cleaning up the basement. Or just walking up and down the streets. Assiduously turning
down off-Broadway offers, which are coming faster and more furiously
than ever . . . Trying to recharge the battery.

The Brecht really turned out well, in every respect, and I am hoping to persuade that theatre to let me do GALILEO[1] next year. Or
THREEPENNY OPERA.[2] I am now Associate Director there, committed to 3–4 shows a year, which gives me a bit of financial stability,
something of a base, and a reason for turning down the ordinary stuff
here. . . . I know how you feel about theatre-in-the-round, but wish you
could see a first-rate production there.[3] . . .

The only play I know of that just can't work in Arena is HAPPY
DAYS. Because of Willie. (Although it works wonderfully in proscenium; and don't let its relatively short run discourage you.). . . By the
way, we've been getting some additional notices which are interesting,
one from COMMONWEAL (liberal Catholic) and one in PLAYS AND
PLAYERS (English trade journal); will get Judith to send on copies if
she has not already done so. Also there was an excellent response in
THEATRE ARTS.[4] . . . .

Hear Plowright to do HAPPY DAYS in London. She's just the one
you wanted, so congratulations. She's a remarkable actress; and while
her physical qualities are not exactly as described by you, I'm sure she
will be brilliant. I understand George Devine is very ill, a nervous
breakdown from which he is slowly recovering. Would Tony Richardson[5] direct, or someone else? Or will you wait until Don McW. gets
back from USA? (I hope the latter.)

Judith was out to the house today. She's a bit low, I feel, about her
personal situation and we tried to cheer her up. Barney seems fine,
dashing about as usual and having all sorts of law suits. He is amazing
in his resilience . . . I gather you are busy working on the translation of
COMME C'EST, and I know how difficult that must be for you. Do
hope you are well, taking care of yourself, not getting distracted by too
many visiting Americans and/or the vagaries of the current political
situation. . . .

Almost forgot: found a lovely quote about critics which I wanted to
pass on to you. 'I compare critics to bats, owls and fleas. They are
always upside down, hoot too much, and are always nipping you.'
N'est-ce pas?

Jean and the kids bear up well under all this. Vicky playing piano
and taking ballet. David playing baseball and listening with relish to

Beethoven's EROICA. So there's hope . . . Best to Suzanne. And the most happy hopes for the New Year.

[Alan]

1. Brecht.

2. Kurt Weill (1900–1950).

3. Arena Stage, Washington, D.C.

4. *Commonweal*, 75.3 (13 October), 69–70; *Plays and Players* had no review; *Theatre Arts,* 8 November 1961.

5. Tony Richardson (1928–1991), English director and producer, associated with English Stage Company at Royal Court Theatre, American films include *Tom Jones*.

Paris
21.12.61

Dear Alan

Thanks for your letter. Your last created great fatigue and I'm so glad to hear you're having a rest and feeling better.

Suzanne is just back from a few days in Germany where she saw the premiere of *H.D.* at Düsseldorf and then the Cologne production. Neither of them right, but good acting (Wimmer and Mosheim) and great conscientiousness and care.[1]

Situation at Court very confused. Had vague notes from Richardson & Devine in reply to my query on reading announcement in *Times* that George was to direct. There is no question of this and it is McWhinnie who will direct—unless he has changed his mind.

I'm doing two little radio scripts, one in English for BBC and John Beckett, the other in French for the RTF & Mihalovici. Then back to 3/4 completed *How It Is*.[2]

Things more and more sinister here politically, manifestations, counter [?], *plastiquages*[3] day & night and town crawling with bestial cops. Long to get to Ussy for a long spell but impossible before next month.

Affectionate wishes to you all for Xmas & the N.Y.

Ever
Sam

1. The German premiere, directed by Walter Henn, designed by H. W. Lenneweit, had opened 30 September at the Schiller-Theater Werkstatt during the Berliner Festwochen.

Berta Drews (Winnie), Rudolf Fernau (Willie). *Glückliche Tage* opened in Cologne, 5 November 1961, directed by Hanskarl Zeiser, designed by Joachim Streubel. Grete Mosheim (Winnie). Opened at the Schausspielhaus "Tribune," Düsseldorf, 17 December 1961, directed by Karl Heinz Stroux, designed by Pit Fischer. Maria Wimmer (Winnie).

    2. The "radio scripts": *Words and Music* in English for the BBC and *Cascando*, 1963, 1964, 1966. *Comment c'est*, 1961, trans. by SB, *How It Is*, 1964.

    3. *"plastiquages": plasticages;* terrorist bombings.

January 15, 1962

Dear Sam,

    Just a few words, and a belated greeting for the new year, which will no doubt contain the same confusions and uncertainties of the old ones. Nevertheless, all the best in the best of all possible years.

    Time rushes on, somehow, in spite of daily lassitude. Since returning from Washington, I have been trying to catch up on reading, writing, and the arithmetic of my income tax return. Still reading Ellmann's biography of Joyce, and then recently discovered Malraux's TEMPTATION OF THE WEST.[1] Do you know that?. . . . Also studying Russian on my own, a useful tongue and an impossible one. You know the definition of an opportunist here is the fellow who's learning to eat caviar with chopsticks.

    Dick Barr planning to do a spring 'Festival of the Absurd'—as I assume you know via Judith—and hoping to include ENDGAME and GODOT, if rights on latter are cleaned up.[2] Barr is enterprising and honest, but he pinches pennies and tries to get by with things a bit more than he used to; I still think that with different public relations and scheduling we would have run longer on HAPPY DAYS. But this is hard to control unless one actually does the management oneself—money, theatre and all—and this may be what should be done. . . . Assume Judith has told you of two one-night stands of HAPPY DAYS, one at Princeton last week—which was very well received—and one at YMHA tonight. Ruthie is in good shape; one of my friends who is book editor on *Newsweek* told me she was giving best female performance he had seen since late Laurette Taylor.[3] And Brooks Atkinson, who retired too soon, told me he thought play was your best, and he loved the performance. Wish he had written about it, but he felt he couldn't after Taubman.

    And so it goes. Am off to Washington in March to do a new play called BURNING OF THE LEPERS, set in France of 14th century; then UNCLE VANYA. In the fall, a Pinter double-bill off-Broadway.[4] Meanwhile, teaching, reading scripts, and hoping. Have been asked to be critic for THE NEW LEADER, a small liberal weekly, and may do so if doesn't get in way of my directing.[5]

[Alan]

1. André Malraux (1901–1976), French novelist, art historian, and government official, Minister of Cultural Affairs in the Charles de Gaulle government (1960–1969); *Temptation of the West* (*La Tentation de l'Occident*, 1926; trans. 1961).

2. Myerberg still retained American production rights to *Waiting for Godot.*

3. The Barr-Wilder production of *Happy Days* played at the McCarter Theatre of Princeton, 12 January 1962, directed by AS, designed by William Ritman. Ruth White (Winnie), John C. Becher (Willie). Opened at The Little Theatre in the YW-YMCA building, New York, 19 January. Laurette Taylor (1884–1946).

4. *Burning of the Lepers* by Wallace Hamilton (1919–1983) opened at the Arena Stage, Washington, D.C., 20 March 1962; *Uncle Vanya* by Anton Chekhov opened at the Arena Stage, 17 April 1962; Pinter's *The Dumbwaiter* and *The Collection* opened at the Cherry Lane Theatre, New York, 26 November 1962.

5. AS resigned in 1965.

Ussy
19.1.62

Dear Alan

Thanks for your letter.

I said OK to Judith for Barr's ENDGAME & GODOT directed by you and promised her six bottles of Pernod if she breaks Myerberg's stranglehold on latter. Barr's handling of *H.D.*, to judge from friends' accounts, sticks in my gullet, but no doubt I do him an injustice.

Suzanne had a brief jaunt in the Rhineland and saw Düsseldorf opening of *H.D.* and next day the Cologne production. Not right, but loving performances by Maria Wimmer & Grete Mosheim respect.[1]

I had lunch with George Devine last week. He is much better and back in the theatre. He confirms—subject to Donald being available, as seems likely—*H.D.* with Plowright directed by Donald beginning of September, rehearsals August. It can't be earlier, Joan having promised Larry to do something at Chichester. George was troubled by erroneous report in London papers and said there had never been any question of his directing and that Joan would be pleased to work with Donald. *Nous verrons.*[2]

Translation of *Comment c'est* advances slowly. It's the most distasteful job I ever took on and I'm often on the point of giving up.

I have done two short radio scripts, one in English for BBC and my cousin John, the other in French for RTF & Mihalovici.[3]

No importance.

Yes, I have Esslin's book & Kenner's, and like them, though don't always see the connection.[4]

. . . .[5]

Not an idea in my head for new work of any kind—but then there never was.

Affectionately to you all.

Sam

1. See letter of 21 December 1961, n. 1.

2. *Happy Days* opened at the Royal Court Theatre, London, 1 November 1962, directed by George Devine, designed by Jocelyn Herbert. Brenda Bruce (Winnie), Peter Duguid (Willie). Chichester Festival Theatre, Sussex, England, opened 1962; Sir Laurence Olivier was Artistic Director until 1966. *"Nous verrons"*: we shall see.

3. "radio scripts": see letter of 21 December 1961, n. 2.

4. Martin Esslin, *Theatre of the Absurd,* 1962, 1968; Esslin's title came to denote the anti-literary movement in drama, of which *Waiting for Godot* was the pre-eminent example. Esslin (b. 1918), Hungarian-born critic and radio producer, joined the BBC in 1940, Head of BBC Radio Drama Department 1963–1976, where he produced many Beckett radio plays and readings; editor of *Samuel Beckett: A Collection of Critical Essays,* 1965. Hugh Kenner, *Samuel Beckett: A Critical Study,* 1961, 1968.

5. SB mentions his dislike of Paris.

January 22, 1962

Dear Sam,

Have just made a serious decision which I want to communicate to you, and I'm sure you will understand. Have discussed the matter fully with Barney and he concurs.

As you know, Dick Barr is planning a "Festival of the Absurd" for the spring, some ten plays: DEATHWATCH, THE KILLER, AMERICAN DREAM, ZOO STORY, GALLOWS HUMOR, and some others.[1] He also wanted to do ENDGAME and GODOT—for which he had permission from you. And, surprisingly enough—I didn't expect it—he got permission just a day ago from Myerberg on GODOT.

He's put all this together very fast, just since Thursday, altho he has been talking generally about the idea for a while. He had to wait until a show opened (and closed) at the Cherry Lane, on Wednesday evening. The actors are to be basically those who have worked for Barr before, or who have been in some of the shows originally.

Now, with ENDGAME, we have not had a serious problem. It is about time for a revival; many people who have come to know it in the past couple of years did not originally see it. And we have been able to line up a fairly good cast—although none of the original people turned out to be available. Hamm is in a Broadway show, Clov in a new play by Arthur Kopit,[2] Nell on tour, and Nagg died last year. But we have the actor who played Willie for Nagg, a very good Nell (Grandma in *American Dream*), someone who read for and almost played Hamm originally for us, and a very talented young actor named Ben Piazza for Clov. So I agreed and went along.

With GODOT, it has been entirely different—and the only reason I didn't make an issue with Barr earlier was that I didn't think Myerberg would release the rights at this time. I feel that the actors Barr has available are just not strong enough, and that the play could not get an adequate production under the circumstances. The Pozzo would be the boy playing Hamm, but the only idea for Lucky was the gal playing Grandma (which would be possible but not ideal). We have neither an Estragon nor a Vladimir; and the ones suggested by Barr are in my opinion completely incapable of doing those parts on a level necessary. I was quite content with Meredith and Mostel—regardless of the critics—but with none of the actors available here. And to do this difficult play, with two weeks rehearsal, with an inadequate cast, seemed to me entirely wrong. I think we should do it sometime for a regular run with a first-rate balanced cast and let NY see it in a version other than Bert Lahr's (which was fine except that the balance was thrown off.) Anyhow, I have said No to Barr on it, with great regret because I'd love to do GODOT—but this is not the way. ENDGAME, I think we'll do all right with.

That's about it. Tentative opening date on ENDGAME is Feb. 16.[3] On March 1, I go to Washington to do a new play, THE BURNING OF THE LEPERS, set in 14th century France, but immensely contemporary. Then VANYA.[4] Then the summer. In the fall, Pinter. [lines missing]

[Alan]

1. Barr and Wilder, "Theatre of the Absurd," included *Deathwatch (Haute surveillance)* by Genet; *The Killer (Tueur sans gages)* by Ionesco; *Gallows Humor* by Jack Richardson. The others were *Bertha* by Kenneth Koch; *American Dream, Zoo Story,* and *The Sandbox* by Albee; *Picnic on the Battlefield (Pique-nique en Campagne)* by Arrabal; and *Endgame*.

2. Arthur Kopit (b. 1937); his play *Oh Dad, Poor Dad, Mamma's Hung You in the Closet and I'm Feeling So Sad* opened at the Phoenix Theatre, New York, 26 February 1962.

3. *Endgame* opened at the Cherry Lane Theatre, New York, 11 February 1962, directed by AS, designed by William Ritman. Vincent Gardenia (Hamm), Ben Piazza (Clov), John C. Becher (Nagg), Sudie Bond (Nell).

4. *The Burning of the Lepers* opened at the Arena Stage, Washington, D.C., 20 March 1962; *Uncle Vanya* opened 17 April 1962.

Ussy
29.1.62

Dear Alan

Thanks for your letter.

Approve unreservedly your decision not to undertake *Godot* under such conditions. Hope you'll be able to do a proper revival some day.

Good luck with *Endgame.*

Thanks for news of *Happy Days* one night. Kay Boyle wrote me about it too.

Hope to finish first draft of *How It Is* this week.

Best to you all.

Ever
Sam

Ussy
20.2.62

Dear Alan

. . . .[1]

So glad you are pleased with *Endgame.* Jean Reavey wrote saying they liked Clov, whom Judith didn't like! I agree that *Theatre of the Absurd* is about as vague as Cubism & Fauvism. Kay Boyle wrote that you had invited her.

I've been here some weeks now and hope to hang on into next week. Finished 1st draft of *H.I.I.,* but very rough.[2] Tried to get going on something new, but in vain. Frankly don't see much hope of going on.

John Beckett has done his music for *Words & Music* (BBC).³ No idea yet what he has done, but have full confidence.

. . . .⁴

Love to Jean when you write and to the children when you tuck them up for the night.

Best always
Sam

1. SB is sorry to hear that Jean's mother is ill.
2. "H.I.I.": *How It Is*, English trans. of *Comment c'est*.
3. *Words and Music*: first production commissioned by BBC Third Programme to mark the BBC's Fortieth Anniversary; broadcast 13 November 1962, directed by Michael Bakewell. Felix Fenton (Croak), Patrick Magee (Words), music by John Beckett. Published in *Evergreen Review*, 1962, French trans. by SB, *Paroles et musique* in *Comédie et actes divers*, 1966. See "Beckett's Play for B.B.C.," *Times*, 1 November 1962.
4. SB comments on the bombing of a friend's apartment in Paris.

Ussy-sur-Marne
12.5.62

Dear Alan

Many thanks for card. Very touched that you shd remember the day.¹

Saw Barney with Ann on way to Formentor & without Ann on way back. I thought he seemed harrassed and worried. Big party after Joan Mitchell's *vernissage*.² I told him a little about an idea for a short play (1 act, 1 hour). The idea excites me immoderately and the difficulties appal ditto. Have not yet begun writing. Shall tell you more about it if it comes to anything.³

A letter from Devine saying that McWhinnie cannot direct Plowright in *H.D.* at the Court this Fall and asking me to let him do so. That shook me all right. Not a word from McW. Don't quite know what to do. Let Devine go ahead I suppose (I know Plowright wants him) and try and keep him on the tracks. His *Endgame* was disastrous. He'll be coming to Paris to talk it over.

Wish I could look forward to seeing you this year. . . .⁴ *How It Is* still in the inchoate stage and all efforts to get going again abort.

Blin in Geneva directing Swiss in *Fin de Partie* and playing Hamm.⁵ Opening in a few days. Not going.

Affectionately to you all.
Sam

1. AS invariably sends birthday greetings to SB for the 13th of April.

2. Joan Mitchell (b. 1928), American abstract expressionist, married Barney Rosset 1950, divorced 1952, friend of SB in Paris; *vernissage:* varnishing day.

3. *Play,* written in English, 1962. First published in German, *Spiel, Theater Heute,* 1963; as *Play,* 1964; in French trans. by SB, *Comédie,* 1967.

4. SB says he is "in poor form."

5. *Fin de partie* opened at the Théâtre de Carouge, Geneva, Switzerland, 15 May 1962, directed by Roger Blin. Roger Blin (Hamm), Maurice Aufair (Clov), Marc Fayolle (Nagg), Valerie Quincy (Nell).

Paris
16.6.62

Dear Alan

Thanks for your letter. Very disappointed. Do hope you'll make it in August.[1]

Saw Devine. Donald can't direct *H.D.* Some other engagement. Hard to understand, but there it is. Position now is that George will direct—with whatever help I can give him. Plowright as Winnie. Willie not yet cast. Set by Jocelyn Herbert. Opening 1st week October. I'll be in London for last 10 days of rehearsals. Great if you could be there then.
. . . .[2]

Thanks for receiving Obie. I read *V.V.* account and some description from Judith, including your "I shall abstain etc. . . . Walter Kerr."[3] Good for you.

New play festers away on the way to, back from & during *rendez-vous.* Have got 3 pages down—more or less acceptable. No [?] pillars—*pace* Esslin. Difficult to write about. Keep it till we meet. Know what's going with me, but not where I'm going. Endless possibilities in *ideas.* In great fear of spoiling them.

Affectionately to you all
Sam

1. In an omitted letter, 6 June 1962, SB is anticipating seeing AS in Paris and is very disappointed when AS is unable to come. The AS letter to which SB refers is missing.

2. SB has too many visitors.

3. *Happy Days* received an Obie Award as "Best Foreign Play" of the 1961–62 season. *Endgame* had won the same award for the 1957–58 season, and *Krapp's Last Tape* was a "Distinguished Play" in 1959–60. According to the *Village Voice,* Lotte Lenya announced the award and added "with judge Walter Kerr wishing to be announced as abstaining." After a brief hush, there was "a scattering of hisses, boos, and some small applause." Co-judge Edward Albee "indulged in a brief, dry smile."

University Theatre of Wisconsin
Milwaukee
Wisconsin
June 21, 1962

Dear Sam,

My first week done at the University, and just wanted to say Hello. Because I was going to see you and then didn't see you, feel especially that we haven't seen each other too long. Wondering how you were, and whether you were feeling any better. Got the impression from your last letter that you were down a bit.

Am hoping now that it will still be possible for me to have my quick visit (to see Harold Pinter and his play at the Aldwych) in late August before embarking on rehearsals. Depends on many factors, most important whether play is still running. It opened Monday and I have gotten no news as yet.[1]

What is happening on HAPPY DAYS? I know how upset you were in the last letter about George Devine's doing it. Have you talked with him? Is Plowright set? A date? I just do not understand how McWhinnie would not have talked this over with you before withdrawing. And if it were not too presumptuous of me, I would say that I would move heaven and earth (and commitments) for the opportunity of directing HAPPY DAYS in London—or anywhere. But I would expect both Plowright and the Court would want an English director, no matter what.

Anyhow. We're having our own problems here with the mime. Trying to cast it even reasonably adequately. I told them that unless it could be done properly there was no point, and that I was sure you would agree with that point of view. But I am hoping we can come up with something. I think I may have John C. Becher (who played Willie) for B; my problem is A—and how to get the goad in properly in an arena theatre. Hah! Have become enamored of this one, and hoping to do it somewhere if not at Wisconsin. Meanwhile starting work on Wilder's PULLMAN CAR HIAWATHA (30 characters) and DUMB-WAITER, if we can cast it. Then on to Brecht's MANN IST MANN in California. A busy summer.[2]

Sam, we're all a bit worried about you, not sure of your physical and psychic state of the moment, and hoping to find out from you. That's another, and the main, reason why I'm upset I didn't get over last week. I do hope you're OK, relaxing a bit, and taking care of yourself. And am keeping fingers crossed that I'll see you at the end of the summer.

In the meantime, Jean sends her love, the kids say Hello, and I wish you all the best.

[Alan]

1. Pinter's play *The Collection* opened at the Aldwych Theatre, London, 18 June 1962.
2. The "mime" *Act Without Words II* opened at the University of Wisconsin, 10 July 1962, with Harold Pinter's *The Dumbwaiter* and Thornton Wilder's *Pullman Car Hiawatha. Mann ist Mann* opened at Stanford University, 9 August 1962. The "goad" appears in the mime: "Enter goad right, strictly horizontal . . ."

Paris
28.6.62

Dear Alan

Just a scribble to let you have latest opening date of *Happy Days,* in London: October 11th.[1]

George writes wondering if you could help him with musical box. Any chance of sending it over, or another, or of bringing it if you come in August? I'd be very grateful if you would get in touch with him about this.

Best ever
Sam

1. *Happy Days* opened 1 November.

Ussy
11.7.62

Dear Alan

Thanks for your letter.

I'm all right. Just tired . . . .[1] Perhaps I won't do much more work. I can't work mechanico-professionally, have to get excited about something, and it doesn't come. And all the arrears of self-translation have me paralysed. I've been struggling with the new play. Nothing but false starts till now, but this past week have perhaps got hold of it at last. The shape at [?] least—and a few pages of "exposition" good enough at least to go on from. Re London *Happy Days* nothing would have rejoiced (and relieved) me more than to have you do it. But when Donald defaulted I hadn't the heart not to let George have it. I rather dread the whole thing. I do hope you'll get over before. A talk with you wd. do me a power of good.

Affectionately to you all
Sam

1. SB insists that whatever ills he has are minor.

                                                                    Paris
                                                                    4.8.62
Dear Alan

I want you to see enclosed letter from Lawrence Harvey of Dartmouth University. He is *engagement* on a monumental thesis on your undeserving servant.[1]

My answer that the play is yours in U.S.A. and that I will fall in with whatever you & Barney decide and with nothing that you don't approve.[2]

It seems a little absurd to me, all these plans for one unknown work. I personally presuppose nothing, not even that you will wish to direct it.

I'll give the script to Barney when he comes through mid-September. There is still some [?]poking to be done. It's for the faces and voices of two women and one man, provoked to speech (or silenced) by spots.

Very short—about 35 mins.

No title yet.

If there's no chance of seeing you this summer I'll write you about it. If you're coming over I'll leave it till we meet.

More bad news from London: Plowright pregnant again (baby in Jan.) and availability doubtful. I have suggested Ruth White to George.

Leaving on 7th for a fortnight in Austria. Back Paris end of month.

Best
Sam

Perhaps you would write to Harvey, and let me have letter back at your leisure. [written above address and date]

1. Lawrence E. Harvey (1925–1988), later Professor of Romance Languages and Literatures at Dartmouth College, *Samuel Beckett: Poet and Critic*, 1970.
2. The letter being answered is missing; "the play": *Play.*

August 27, 1962

Dear Sam,

Arrived home late last night from California via the Rocky Mts. and the Shakespeare Festival in Canada—to find your latest letter. Sorry that I was so involved with Brecht at Stanford that I couldn't write earlier. (MANN IST MANN) And I am much relieved that you are feeling a bit better; you know how worried Barney and I were about you. . . . Wish I could get over anyhow, even for a short time, but seems impossible—as I am plunging into production on Albee's first full-length and then the Pinter one-acts. So that I won't be seeing you this summer after all my hopes, please forgive.[1] . . .

Thanks much for your letter and all the news. Am really pleased that you have almost completed the new play. If I had the guts and a few more dollars, I would hop on a plane for a weekend and have you read it to me. In any case, I expect Barney to bring it back with him when he returns from his Frankfurt-Paris commuting. And I would like, with your agreement, to purchase the American option, with or without Barney as he and you prefer. Once that is done, then we can consider the Dartmouth possibility within the framework of how and when we would get the play on in NY. Obviously, it would need another play to go with it on a double-bill; and Barney and I would do all we could either to get another one from you (we'd wait!) or to do it with one you liked. Barney has also spoken of a television play you have in mind.[2] The Dartmouth University has only one real advantage, it seems to me: the possibility of that being a way of getting you to come over. If you agreed to that, then I would certainly encourage it; if you did not feel able to come, then I feel less enthusiastic. I know Clancy and the setup there (in fact, I was offered the job a year ago and did not accept). And I'm certain they could do a good student production; but what the values of such a production would be prior to NY, I'm not sure. I'll write directly to Larry Harvey and pursue some of the alternatives he mentions;[3] but fundamentally both Barney and I feel (I just talked with him) that we want to do it at the right time in the right NY theatre with the right companion piece. And, of course, we are looking forward like mad to just reading it.

Really disturbed to hear of increasing problems at the Royal Court. McWhinnie and now Plowright. Is she definitely out? Heard from George a while back about our music box—which I believe he now has —but he said nothing else. Between us, although I admire Plowright as an actress, I don't think she is the only one in England who could play the part. They have a marvelous group of actresses in that range. What about Brenda de Banzie? Do you know her? And there is an excellent Canadian actress, Kate Reid,[4] who has played in London and whom George might know. We almost used her here until Ruth came along. About Ruth, I'm sure she'd be wonderful there as here—but they may think she's too American for an English production. In any case, she'll be most pleased that you thought of her. (Did you ever read the article Peter Brook wrote on HAPPY DAYS and MARIENBAD in a recent issue of ENCORE? If not, I'll get an extra copy and send it on.)[5]

Judith heard from Curtis Brown about an offer for the movie rights of GODOT. Do you know whom they want to play in it? Peter Sellers? Guinness???????[6] (I still want Charlie Chaplin to do all four parts in ENDGAME.) By the way, Play-of-the-Week showed TV version a few weeks ago while I was away, and I gather that this time the critics didn't fly through the windows.[7] I saw the Actor's Workshop production in San Francisco;[8] a great deal of it was excellent, fluent, funny and moving; and the Pozzo was the best one I have ever seen. But I found the pace [line missing]

He said he would speak to the actors, who were doing it on their own. I must say that I think it the height of amateurishness for actors to ad lib in this play—*à la* Bert Lahr. But, on the other hand, they were very good, very intelligent; and the audience was responding all the way along.

Had a pleasant and rewarding summer. First, the triple bill at the Univ. of Wisconsin, a program of which I'm sending you under separate cover.[9] For a student attempt, I thought it came off well; and the University paid Pinter's way over, so that we had a few days together. (THAT'S the value of Dartmouth!) Then my second Brecht attempt at Stanford. And so on. The family all together for two months, plus a trip across the continent together. Never again though, over all those deserts. The old station wagon I had broke down in Medecine Bow, Wyoming; and I had to junk it and buy another one. . . . Next summer, if all goes reasonably well this year, I hope all of us will come to Europe for an extended stay. In meantime, all the best. Jean sends her love. The kids are great. Be well.

[Alan]

1. Albee's *Who's Afraid of Virginia Woolf* opened at the Billy Rose Theatre, New York, 13 October 1962; Pinter's *The Dumbwaiter* and *The Collection* opened at the Cherry Lane Theatre, New York, 26 November 1962.

2. *Eh Joe.*

3. Dartmouth "alternatives": a student production probably of *Waiting for Godot*, with SB present for some of the rehearsals. James Clancy (b. 1912), Director of Theatre and Professor of Drama (1962–1967).

4. Brenda de Banzie, also known as Brenda Bruce (1920–1996); Kate Reid (b. 1930), both English actresses.

5. "Happy Days and Marienbad," *Encore*, 9 (January-February 1962), 34–38.

6. Peter Sellers (1925–1980), Sir Alec Guinness (b. 1914).

7. A repeat of *Waiting for Godot* (PBS, WNDT-TV, 1961), available in the Theatre on Film and Tape Collection, New York Public Library.

8. The San Francisco Actor's Workshop production of *Waiting for Godot* opened at the Encore Theater, 21 June 1962, directed by Herbert Blau, designed by Robert LaVigne. Robert Symonds (Estragon), Eugene Roche (Vladimir), Alan Mandell (Lucky), Edward Winter (Pozzo), Christopher Bergman (A Boy).

9. "the triple bill": see letter of 21 June 1962, n. 2.

November 4, 1962

Dear Sam,

Much too long since I've written, do forgive. Feel as though I've been in a long dark tunnel marked VIRGINIA WOOLF for as long as I can remember—ever since returning from California in August—and since then in another one marked THE PINTER PLAYS. Since you are responsible for both tunnels, even though you don't know it, feel I owe you an explanation—though have had to wait for my first evening off in 8 weeks to do so.

You probably knew I was directing the Albee play on Broadway, a remarkable work, especially for one so young, and one which none of us expected to have a chance in the commercial theatre—but we were determined to do it anyhow. Well, it opened Oct. 13 and has had fantastic notices—even the unfavorable ones bring us audiences—and a strong response. From all indications should run a year. Since it is over 3 hours long, we have had to put in an alternate cast for matinees—which I have just finished rehearsing, starting the day of our 'evening' opening. So, no rest for the weary; but the satisfaction with the work keeps me going.

It was because Edward Albee saw my work close hand during the KRAPP–ZOO STORY days that he trusted me with AMERICAN DREAM two years ago, and now with VIRGINIA WOOLF. So you see how much a part of my life you always are even when I'm not directing one of your plays. Albee is very fond of your plays, feels and admits being strongly influenced by them, constantly acknowledges his debt to you. I have shown him PLAY, which he loves as much as I do. Barney gave me a copy several weeks ago but I was unable to read it until just recently—and as usual blown overboard by it. Fascinating, terribly theatrical, and certainly opening up new pathways for you. What voices those three must have! And what endurance! Am longing to get to it, though of course we need a companion piece. And actors. And some thoughts. Will get together with Barney soon as I'm through my Pinter production (Nov. 20) off-Broadway. I'd like to get a year's option and then find the right thing to go with it. Perhaps at the Cherry Lane when that is free.

The Pinter duo is lovely, especially DUMBWAITER. Harold is coming over soon for final rehearsals, and I welcome him. He also came to me through seeing my work with you, most especially HAPPY DAYS. (What is happening in London? I can't find anyone who knows the actress' name or when the opening date is? Are you there? Is all well? Wish I could see it.)

There are various chances of my coming over to Europe during this next year though I didn't manage it in the past twelvemonth. Everybody in the world wants to do VIRGINIA WOOLF: London, Paris, Berlin, et al—and various offers for me to direct it in whatever language. If you liked it enough (will send you a copy) and would sit with me in the theatre, I'd love to direct it in Paris with Jeanne Moreau (who may be a bit too young) or Simone Signoret(?).[1] We shall see. In any case, I'm sure something will make my coming over possible in time to talk over PLAY with you—and other things. I just want to see you.

Am dead tired but grateful for the good fortune. My dad and mother both ailing seriously, which is hard to take. Jean and kids fine. Wish we could have you visit us. Have heard nothing more from Dartmouth after first talk. Will write again after Nov. 20. All the best.

[Alan]

1. Jeanne Moreau (b. 1928), Simone Signoret (1921–1985), French actresses; Signoret won an Academy Award for her performance in *Room at the Top* (U.K., 1958).

Paris
7.11.62

Dear Alan

Good to hear from you after so long.

Congratulations and to Albee on hit with *Who's Afraid*. I am pleased. Devine said he was inviting you to direct it at the Court. Great news too.

So glad you like PLAY. It seems to me only difficult technically (how to work spots). Have thought how it might be done and will discuss it when the time comes. In fact I think by far the easiest play of mine you have had. What I should like to know from you and Barney is whether or not I am free to make arrangements in London & Europe. I mean, do you want the world premiere or merely the new world? I have given the script to Devine. I have decided to give Royal Court first option on all my work in the future, this applying both to revivals & to new work. Devine is the nicest and most decent man one could meet and this is very important to me. He is not a great director, but most conscientious and painstaking and will always let me be in on production. *Happy Days* opened Nov. 1 with Brenda Bruce & Peter Duguid. I don't think she carries the guns for the part, but she has done well and got—I am told—great praise. Excellent set by Jocelyn Herbert. I haven't read the notices and don't intend to read any more notices of my work. Friendly or not it's all misunderstanding. Hobson for as usual, Tynan as usual against,[1] my friends tell me. Suzanne came over with a party and was very pleased with the production—said it was infinitely superior to the 2 German productions she had seen at Cologne & Düsseldorf. I worked very hard on it on and off, with George, and got back to Paris last week more tired and shaky than I ever remember having been. Bit better now. I saw neither dress-rehearsal nor premiere—simply can't take it any more.

Faced now with even more than the usual wilderness of self-translation—*Comment c'est* into English, *H.D.*, *Play* into French, i.e. all real work blocked for at least 6 months. *A chacun son petit enfer*.[2] I'll go to Ussy in a few days and start getting down to it—and drinking a little more water!

I do hope you'll be able to ease off a bit after the Pinter opening. Why don't you come over here for a week or so. Perhaps you will have seen Devine in N.Y. on his way to Brazil where he is to lecture. I didn't see Harold Pinter in London I'm sorry to say.

Affectionately to you all
Sam

1. *Happy Days* opened at the Royal Court Theatre, London, 1 November 1962, directed by George Devine. Brenda Bruce (Winnie), Peter Duguid (Willie). Kenneth Tynan, "Intimations of Mortality," *The Observer*, 28 October 1962; Sir Harold Hobson, "The Really Happy Woman," *Sunday Times*, 4 November.

2. *"A chacun son petit enfer":* to each his own little Hell.

December 17, 1962

Dear Sam,

Haven't heard from you for some time, wondering whether all is well, you are well. Assume you're at Ussy busy writing. No need to take time to answer as long as you are OK.

Time bleeds on here. Both VIRGINIA WOOLF and the Pinter plays running on happily, the former paying the bills, the latter just for the heck of it, in spite of our complete lack of newspapers—which has its temporary advantages.[1] I can catch up on the stack sitting on the floor in the study.

Did you ever get the copy of VIRGINIA WOOLF? Or was it so huge it frightened you off? I do hope you might have a chance to read it—as I have a secret vision of you translating it into French and you and I working on it in Paris. Hah! Am trying like mad to find some way of coming over this winter before I have to go off to direct HAMLET in Washington late in February.[2] May wind up with one of my flying visits, and will try to give you all the advance notice possible. Depends on time, money, and the possibility of someone sending me.

Barney and I working out details of buying PLAY together. We both agree that problem is to find proper companion piece, and then a theatre. The Cherry Lane is not at the moment available—the Pinter plays are there—though Barr (and Albee) loves the play. We might look somewhere else. The real-estate situation off-Broadway is getting as bad as on. But if we could get another one to go with it, we'll have something. That's another reason I want to come over during January, to talk with you about the script.

Read THE TIN SOLDIER,[3] and appreciate your suggesting the author send it to me. I liked it, but found it so close to GODOT, without being in same class, that it's going to be very difficult to get producer to put it on. But I'll show it around, and we shall see.

Been reading JOYCE's Letters,[4] and find them remarkable portrait of a writer I wish I had known more about earlier. Also trying to get

farther into ULYSSES than ever have before. I am making myself read
as I have also gotten out of the habit what with nothing but newspapers and magazines to bide me through rehearsals for more than a year.
And to some museums, and listening to Beethoven, and just plain
walking. Yesterday, went ice-skating with both my kids and found it a
rare adventure. We are having winter here, snow and brisk dry cold,
and the countryside is lovely, the city slushy and grey.

Jean has been ailing a bit but not serious, luckily. Both my parents
and her Mum are not well, so we are constantly in one hospital or
another. What can be done? Another happy day! (Saw some pictures of
the London Winnie; wish I could have seen the show, though I would
have been prejudiced in favor of Ruth White.)

Trust you are well, working, not being deluged by too many Americans, taking care of self. Miss you, think of you constantly, have that
snap-shot of you I once took hanging over my desk. Best wishes for
1963. Jean's love goes along also, together with a smile from Vicky and
a puzzled nod [from David].

[Alan]

1. The New York newspapers were on strike from 8 December 1962 to 31 March 1963.
2. *Othello*, not *Hamlet*, opened at the Arena Stage, Washington, D.C., 12 March 1963.
3. Author unknown.
4. Edited by Stuart Gilbert, 1957.

Paris
20.12.62

Dear Alan

Glad to have your letter.

Things much the same here. Got back from London rather groggy.
Better now. Brenda Bruce did her best. Didn't carry the guns. Very
pleasant working with George and team. Excellent set by Jocelyn Herbert. Have finished French translation and given it to Lindon[1] & Blin.
Not in any hurry to see it here. Now have to revise translation of
Comment c'est. Then translate WORDS & MUSIC & PLAY. No chance of
any new work for many a long day.

I did not receive *Who's Afraid*. Having read above you won't be cross
with me if I decline to translate it too.

Re PLAY, not having had any word from Barney, I'm assuming my

hands are free in the Old World to make arrangements for its performance and that you are only concerned with New World premiere.
There's a possibility at next Edinburgh Festival, and the German premiere will probably be in the Spring. With what I don't know in either
case.

. . . .[2] You sound fine. Great if can get over. Congrats. on all your successes.

Affectionately to you all
Sam

1. Jérôme Lindon, SB's French publisher, Les Éditions de Minuit; "First Meeting with
Samuel Beckett," *Beckett at Sixty: A Festschrift*, 1967; "French translation": *Oh les beaux
jours*.
2. SB is sorry to hear of the illnesses in the Schneider family.

Ussy-sur-Marne
6.2.63

Dear Alan

It was good to hear you again and to know I shall be seeing you
again soon.

Many thanks for *Who's Afraid*—safely arrived.

Jean-Marie Serreau was on the phone about it a few days ago, wondering if I wd. translate or supervise translation and wanting my opinion on the play. As I told you I am too submerged with my own work to
be able to take on anything else—and as I have not yet read the play I
had no reaction for Serreau. But from the glance I took and from what I
know of it, adaptation is going to be a big problem here. I shall be
meeting Serreau in a week or so to have a talk about it. But as translator
I'm definitely out. Please tell Albee I'm sorry. I know he'll understand.

Finished French translation of *Happy Days* & gave it to Blin. Madeleine Renaud wants to do it—it appears. Blin is [?]never communica-
tive—and very busy at the moment with his Valle-Inclán production
for Barrault.[1]

The German first of *Play* will probably be in April at Ulm (small
theatre)—in conjunction with the two mimes and perhaps stage presentation of my radio play *WORDS & MUSIC*.[2] No plans so far for English
production as far as I know. Vague possibility at Edinburgh Festival.

All That Fall was done on French TV. Badly I thought—but well received.[3]

Hope to finish this week revision of *Comment c'est* translation and get it off to Barney before end of month. Then take a bit of a rest from translation and try and do a spoken mime for Jackie MacGowran. Had to promise this for reasons too complicated to explain here. Shall tell you all about it when we meet and report progress—if any!

More or less marooned out here with bitter cold and state of roads. Couldn't be better pleased! Absolute silence and peace 24 hours out of 24. Supposed to be going to Ionesco opening on Friday *(Le Piéton de l'air)* but probably won't make it. Saw *Le Roi se meurt* and liked it—though a poor production. Dubillard's *Maison d'os* is most remarkable—best evening in the theatre for years. It was to have come off last week—but the last night the house was packed and it's continuing. Beautifully written, produced, acted and set.[4]

Love to Jean and the children.

Yours ever
Sam

1. Madeleine Renaud (1903–1994), French actress, with her husband, Jean-Louis Barrault (1910–1994), French mime, actor, founded the Companie Renaud-Barrault at the Théâtre Marigny (1947) where they introduced works by Anouilh, Genet, Giraudoux, Ionesco, and SB to Parisian audiences. Barrault headed the state-financed Odéon Théâtre de France from 1959 to the student riots of 1968, also the Théâtre des Nations (1965–1967, 1972–1974). *Divinas Palabras (Divine Words)* by Ramon de Valle-Inclán (1866–1936), Spanish novelist and dramatist. Roger Blin directed and played the sexton; designed by Acquart.

2. *Spiel* opened at the Ulmer Theater, Ulm-Donau, 14 June 1963, directed by Deryk Mendel, who also played the two mimes. *Act Without Words I and II*, designed by Michel Raffaelli. Nancy Illig (f.1 First Woman), Sigrid Pfeiffer (f.2 Second Woman), Gerhard Winter (m. Man). *Words & Music* not included.

3. *Tous ceux qui tombent (All That Fall)* on RTF/ORTF, Paris, 25 February 1963, directed by Michel Mitrani, with Alice Sapricht and Guy Tréjean as Mr. and Mrs. Rooney, Christian Marin, Pierre Palau, Hubert Deschamps. *All That Fall* was written in the summer of 1956 at the invitation of the BBC, broadcast BBC Third Programme, 13 January 1957, directed by Donald McWhinnie, with Jack MacGowran, Patrick Magee, Mary Farell, James Gerard Devlin, Allan McClelland, Harry Hutchinson. Published 1957, French trans. by Robert Pinget and SB, *Tous ceux qui tombent*, 1957 (see letter of 27 April 1958, n. 3).

4. *Le Piéton de l'air (A Stroll in the Air), Le Roi se meurt (Exit the King)*. Roland Dubillard (b. 1923), French playwright and actor. *La Maison d'os (The House of Bones)*.

Ussy
15.3.63

Dear Alan

Many thanks for your note,[1] cheques & *PLAY* contract which I have signed (2 copies) & returned to Judith.

PLAY will have its first performance (in German) at Ulm on June 14th—with the two mimes. My friend Deryk Mendel will play in these and direct *PLAY.* No plans in England so far that I know of. George Devine has the rights.

Translated *Happy Days* at last and gave it to Blin. There is talk of Madeleine Renaud!

Got here a few days ago for a bit of a breather and I hope some work. Struggling with a short piece for Jackie MacGowran.[2]

The film thing has me petrified with fright. To talk with you about it will be a great help.[3] About that and all the rest. It will be great to see you. Please let me have exact date as soon as you can, as we are thinking of going to Austria sometime in June, but it can be late in the month.

Saw Harold with Barney in Paris, in good form, & pleased with off-Bwy. success.

Best of success to yr. Arena productions. Affection to Jean & children.

Yrs. ever
Sam

1. Missing.
2. "short piece": a pantomime not completed.
3. *Film,* written in English, spring 1963.

Paris
23.3.63

Dear Alan

Don't bother replying to this. It is just to thank you for yours of March 19[1] and to tell you that first week in June or earlier will suit me fine. Looking forward extremely to seeing you then. Yes, plenty to talk about, and particularly *Play,* which I have slightly modified (sending changes to Dick Seaver).

Saw Blin's production of Inclán's *Divinas Palabras* last night. Good—but the Odéon is a terrible text-quencher.

Film in abeyance. Struggling feebly with Jacky's pantomime. But hope to have a few images for you in June.

Best ever
Sam

1. Missing.

Paris
2.5.63

Dear Alan

Just heard from Judith of your award.[1] *Bravo bravo bravissimo.* Joy for you in this old ticker.

Sam

1. AS received an Obie Award for his direction of the Pinter plays and a Tony for Albee's *Who's Afraid of Virginia Woolf?* AS told Alan Levy, "Since Virginia Woolf opened a year ago, I've been offered more Broadway plays to direct than in my previous 10 years in New York" (see "The A* B** B*** of Alan Schneider," *NY Times Magazine,* 20 October 1963). The play also won a Tony, as did each of the two stars, Arthur Hill and Uta Hagen, and was named "Best Play" by the New York Drama Critics Circle Awards, established in 1935. Antoinette Perry (Tony) Awards were established in 1947 as a memorial to Antoinette Perry, wartime chair of the Theater Wing.

Paris
11.5.63

Dear Alan

Thanks for your letter.[1] I'll be free Monday evening May 27th, so give me a call when you get in (KELLERMANN 83.11).

I was in the country these last 10 days and did more work on film. I hope to have a fairly detailed (but quite untechnical) script to show you when we meet.[2] Unless I throw my hat at it between now & then!

I sent a slightly revised version of *PLAY* to Judith and asked her to let you have a copy. Hope you won't be too appalled by the *da capo*.[3]

Think vaguely of going to Ulm, not for opening, but towards middle of rehearsals, to stick my nose into things. Any chance of your joining me? About May 30th—June 1st. It's not so far from Switzerland.

Serreau will do *Play* here (at least I've offered it to him), but no idea when. Not yet translated. Renaud still very keen on Winnie (and Barrault too), not at Odéon of course. Roger in one of his deep stupors.

Love to you all
Sam

1. Missing.
2. *Film.*
3. *"da capo": Play* has to be repeated before it ends.

Paris
20.7.63

Dear Alan

Your letter of 12th only yesterday.[1] Don't know why it took [?]so long.
. . . .[2]

The recording did not go at all well. Usual RTF confusion and incompetence and system [?]O and wasted time. The result very unsatisfactory. M's music is fine in itself, but doesn't work with the text.[3]

Do not feel there is any hurry with *PLAY.* It seems to have gone quite well at Ulm—I saw a few unusually intelligent notices—and Deryk has an offer from Schiller Werkstatt to direct it again there with a play by Peter Weiss.[4] It is clear that mistakes were made at Ulm—notably tempo, spots and excessive characterisation of faces—but they can be put right. There seems to have been general doubt as to justification of *da capo.* I am not at all sure of it myself and can't be till I work on a production. Obviously it can be irksome if the pace is not rapid enough but it certainly is a dangerous general indication. I am inclined to think that I'll [?]suppress. But want to see Deryk first, who is away till next month. Serreau—at Barrault's request—is delaying his production till January, so that it won't be on at same time as *Happy Days.* Madeleine still very keen and according to Blin knows the text already! All set for rehearsals to begin middle of August.

They open with I think 3 performances in Venice (Ridotto) and perhaps two in Belgrade before opening at the Odéon, about Oct. 10 I suppose.[5]

From Austria I sent Barney a further note on the film which he'll show you. I find it hard to make it any clearer than in the outline.

Jack MacGowran wrote how pleased he was with his talk with you. He has some offer from the States to tour the first mimes and readings from my work and I expect him over soon to discuss the matter. He is also to do some spoken records for the Columbia collection (directed by Meredith I think) with Pat Magee in some things.[6]

Affectionately to you all
Sam [handwritten]

1. Missing.

2. SB is sorry AS "called in vain" from London.

3. *Cascando*, RTF/ORTF; "M": Mihalovici.

4. Peter Weiss (1916–1982), German dramatist, novelist, and graphic artist. His *Nacht Mit Gästen* was produced with *Spiel*, directed by Deryk Mendel, 16 November 1963.

5. *Oh les beaux jours (Happy Days)* opened at the Teatro del Ridotto during the Venice Theatre Festival at the International Festival of Prose Drama, 28 September 1963; performances almost continuously thereafter in Paris and on tour, including an opening in Belgrade.

6. In 1962 Jack MacGowran had performed his one-man show, *End of Day*, at the Gaiety Theatre, Dublin, and the New Arts Theatre Club, London. The program included *Act Without Words I*, a monologue from *Waiting for Godot*, a speech from *Endgame*, an excerpt from *Molloy*, a passage from *All That Fall*, Krapp's erotic memory of the girl in the boat, and all of *From an Abandoned Work*. Subsequently entitled *Beginning to End*, the new show, 1965, was quite different: the pantomime from *Act Without Words I* was omitted; some poems and excerpts from *Embers* and *Malone Dies* were added. The recording for Columbia did not take place.

Paris
25.8.63

Dear Alan

Thanks for your cable and letter.[1] I'm glad Mostel likes the film and might be interested in doing it. But if he's really too difficult and elusive perhaps better without. I'd hate to have to go to Ireland, but whatever you all decide. About PLAY, you know there is no hurry at all as far as I'm concerned. George is doing it in London next March, for the National Theatre, the companion piece being Sophocles' PHILOC-TETES, all wound and moan. Serreau will do it here about the same time, with I know not what. I have started these last few days scratching round like an old hen in the desert for the structures and text of that face play I told you about.[2] Nothing so far but dubious notes and false starts. Impossible to get down to it properly till rehearsals are out of the way and I can get to Ussy. I have never undertaken anything so tenuous and at the same time so complex. It may take years. So no point in suggesting you wait for it to do with PLAY. It will probably be so short in any case that you would still need something to send them full empty away.

Rehearsals here should begin tomorrow. She[3] says she knows the text. Opening Venice September 27th. Three performances there, then perhaps Belgrade October 5th. Don't know date of Paris premiere.

Do hope you'll get over next month. I'll have nothing to show, but perhaps a little more to tell. Of the ending tale.

Affectionately to you all
Sam

1. Missing.
2. *Not I.*
3. "She": Madeleine Renaud (Winnie) in *Oh les beaux jours.*

Paris
18.9.63

Dear Alan

Thanks for your letter. It was good to hear your voice from London and a disappointment not to see you.[1]

Barr sent me *Funnyhouse.*[2] It beats me, which is neither here nor there, and I have written to him saying I am quite content for it to be presented with *PLAY* if that is your wish & his.

Many thanks for dealing with music box.

Rehearsals are going quite well. It won't be ready for Venice next week, but should be ripe for Oct. 21st when it opens here. It has been very pleasant and interesting working with M.R.[3]

The Edinburgh jinks sound pretty low. I heard of your good story about the man who found truth and was looking for something better. *Bravo.*

Hope Vicki quite over her accident and no scars.[4]

Know you are up to your eyes, so no more hieroglyphics.

Affectionately to you all
Sam

1. Letter missing. AS in London to make arrangements with English coproducer Donald Albery for opening of Albee's *Who's Afraid of Virginia Woolf.*

2. *Funnyhouse of a Negro* by the African-American dramatist Adrienne Kennedy (b. 1931).

3. "M.R.": Madeleine Renaud; *Oh les beaux jours* opened at the Odéon-Théâtre de France, 21 October 1963. SB worked intensively with Roger Blin, who directed; designed by Matias. Madeleine Renaud (Winnie), Jean-Louis Barrault (Willie). SB found MR's performance memorable.

4. The Schneider family had been in a car accident (*Entrances*, 348–349).

October 28, 1963

Dear Sam,

Many apologies for not realizing that HAPPY DAYS was opening already. I have been so involved with BALLAD OF THE SAD CAFÉ that I don't even know what month it is.[1] I do hope you were pleased with the production and that it went well. Maybe I'll get to see it on one side of the Atlantic or the other.

I did hear, however, something about your trials and tribulations with the music box once it had arrived on your side of the port authorities. Presumably you are now well supplied with proper music boxes. Sorry ours took so long to reach you—and then didn't—but we had some difficulty tracing it on its various travels here.

Barney must have told you that it now looks definite for PLAY to be done with Harold Pinter's THE LOVER at the Cherry Lane.[2] We all think the two make a marvelous combination and are only hoping to get the right actors for both. It seems worth waiting for the ones we want. Even if that means a delay in opening. There was some talk of the possibility of going in late November or early December. But two people whom we want are not available until the spring, if then, which means we are now planning on the spring or next fall. There is no question in Barney's mind or mine that THE LOVER is eminently superior to the Adrian Kennedy play or any other possibility as a companion piece. As soon as we have copies I'll send one along to you.

Everything else is about the same only more so. BALLAD opens this Wednesday after which I retire to a monastery for a month. We have just been inundated with various family matters and presences, resulting in our purchasing a larger house[3] to which we expect to transfer sometime after the first of the year. The house in question is a very special contemporary which recently burned down and which we are in the process of rebuilding. It is also in Hastings so that the move is less spatial than spiritual. In the middle of January I shall be coming to

London to do VIRGINIA WOOLF so you may expect me to drop in on you in Paris.

Trust you are feeling well and taking care of yourself.

Ever,
[Alan]

1. Edward Albee's adaptation of Carson McCullers's novella, *The Ballad of the Sad Café*, opened at the Martin Beck Theatre, New York, 30 October 1963; Carson McCullers (1917–1967), American novelist and playwright.

2. *Play* and *The Lover* opened at the Cherry Lane Theatre, New York, 4 January 1964, directed by AS, designed by William Ritman.

3. "a larger house": the Schneiders move from 1 Floral Avenue to 30 Scenic Drive.

Paris
November 19th 1963

My very dear Alan

I know your sorrow and I know that for the likes of us there is no ease for the heart to be had from words or reason and that in the very assurance of sorrow's fading there is more sorrow. So I offer you only my deeply affectionate and compassionate thoughts and wish for you only that the strange thing may never fail you, whatever it is, that gives us the strength to live on and on with our wounds.[1]

Ever
Sam [handwritten]

1. AS's father died 12 November 1963.

1 Floral Avenue
Hastings-on-Hudson
New York
November 21, 1963

Mr. Samuel Beckett
38 Boulevard St. Jacques
Paris, FRANCE

Dear Sam,

Sorry that I haven't written for so long, but as Judith told you, I have been ill since the opening of BALLAD, and then my Father died, which made everything seem even blacker than before.

However, I am gradually pulling myself together, and I shall soon be embarking upon the double bill of PLAY and THE LOVER. It looks as though we shall go into rehearsal early in December for an opening after the first of the year. We are already casting—have got a marvelous gal, Frances Sternhagen, for the wife, and are pushing the other two. Will keep you posted.

I gathered from Richard Barr that you want the urns so designed that it would not look as though the actors were seated comfortably within them. I understand. I have also gotten some information from Deryk about how the Light was handled in Ulm. However, I understand you were not satisfied with the way it was handled there. If you have any ideas or suggestions about the Light, the urns, or anything else, please let me have them when you can. I wish I were coming over for more personal talk, but it is impossible prior to rehearsals. (I do expect to be in London during February, at which time I am hoping to pop over to see you).

The background, for example, confuses me. If it is light, the shadows of the heads cannot help but be visible—as at Ulm. So that presumably, the background should be black drapes so as to isolate the heads in the urns. Also, my designer feels that the Light should hit at a 45° angle from above rather than from below so as to minimize the shadow problem and also to obtain maximum illumination.

Any other ideas on the technical aspects of the show will be appreciated by us all. Our other conversations dealing with the text I have thought and studied.

Barney reports some progress on the general film front, although I must say that Mostel remains elusive. What do you think of Jack MacGowran if we can't pin down Mr. M?

I do hope you are well and getting out to Ussy once in awhile. All the best. Regards from Jean.

Ever,
Alan Schneider

as/lf

Paris
26.11.63

Dear Alan

Thanks for your letter. I did not know that you yourself had been ill and am greatly relieved to know you are better. You drive yourself too hard.

I am perplexed about PLAY and so find this letter very difficult to write. I realize that no final script is possible till I have had work on rehearsals. And as those with Serreau will not begin till after yours, all I can do is try and tell you my doubts and leave final decisions to you.

Suzanne went to Berlin for Deryk's second production[1] and did not like it. But when I saw Deryk himself on his return he was very pleased. It seems in any case to have been well received. They arrived at the incredible speed of 25 minutes, with repeat.

The problems still are:

1. Urns.
2. Lighting.
3. Faces.
4. Voices.
5. *Da capo.*

1. Deryk's urns have their unpleasant bulging shape because the actors are sitting. The ideal is urns trapped and actors standing. If this not possible I am coming round to the idea of actors standing and full length urns as closely fitting as possible and mounted or not on hollow plinth about knee height.

Possibly by means of painting (darkened contours) reduce apparent volume of urns.

Disadvantage: they will no longer appear to be touching. Urns open of course behind. If full length bring them back from front toward mid-stage. Obviously the smaller the actors the better.

2. Deryk said he had got his spot pivoting and moving fast. Suzanne did not feel much speed and said there was little visible beam. There should be a pencil (finger) of light snapping from face to face. But we have been through all this. Deryk worked out some system which I don't understand and can't explain. The man on the light should be regarded as a fourth player and must know the text inside and out. I don't mind if the spot hits from above, provided it does not involve auditorium space. Light, W1, W2 and M belong to the same separate world.

When the play begins, and before spots provoke opening "chorus", there is faint general light in which the urns are just discernible as vague shapes. Enough of this behind them would help kill the shadows. The best background is that which best suggests empty unlit space.

3. Suzanne found the faces excessively made up and characterized: aging missus and exciting mistress, etc. This would be completely wrong. They are all in the same dinghy at last and should be as little differentiated as possible. Three grey disks.

4. I don't see much to add to what I tried to explain when we talked about it. I ask for complete expressionless[ness] except for W2's two laughs and W1's single vehemence. This may be excessive. I simply can't know till I work on it in the theatre. You must feel yourself free to mitigate it if it seems to you desirable. Voices grey and abstract as the faces, grey as cinders—that is what seems to me right. I may be wrong.

5. I still am not absolutely sure that this is right. I think it is, if the movement is fast enough. I asked Deryk to cut all the pauses. Speech reaction to light stimulus now instantaneous, i.e. all those three second pauses cancelled with sacrifice of effect of *effort to speak* and all the five seconds reduced to two or three. Everything for the sake of speed if you adopt the *da capo*. If you decide against it then obviously you should play it slower.

I find it practically impossible to write such a letter. What matters is that you feel the spirit of the thing and the intention as you do. Give them that as best you can, even if it involves certain deviations from what I have written and said.

The actual lines to be spoken are practically without change. I shall send you this week the latest "final" text.

London rehearsals begin May 9th. George has not been well, but is better.

Enthusiastically in favour of MacGowran if Mostel falls through.
Bon courage.

Yours ever
Sam [handwritten]

1. *Spiel* opened at the Schiller-Theater Werkstatt, 16 November 1963, directed by Deryk Mendel, designed by Hans-Martin Erhardt. Nancy Illig (1. Frau), Sigrid Pfeiffer (2. Frau), Gerhard Winter (Mann).

1 Flower Avenue
Hastings-on-Hudson,
New York
November 27, 1963

Dear Sam,

I shall never be able to tell you what your letter meant to me—especially as it happened to come the day President Kennedy was killed.[1] All I can say is thank you for understanding so well.

We have been reading a lot of people and are now fairly certain of our cast. W1 will be Frances Sternhagen. W2 will be Hilda Brawner (who is now playing in THE COLLECTION and who will be the wife in THE LOVER). I have worked with both of them before many times and know them quite well. The Man will be either James Patterson (at present, also in THE COLLECTION) or Michael Lipton. I am quite pleased with the cast; indeed, it is much better than I had ever reason to hope when we first started looking.[2]

We are at present coming to grips with the technical details of Urns and Lights and will keep you posted as to our progress. The designer is Bill Ritman, who did KRAPP'S LAST TAPE, HAPPY DAYS, and the revival of ENDGAME. He is, of course, our first line of regard as far as designers are concerned.

I really wish that we could see each other prior to rehearsals. If you have anything at all to say based on either Ulm or your thoughts since then, please don't hesitate.

Is there *any* chance of your coming over this time?

The events of the past weekend have really shaken us all here—I must say, myself especially. I have a terrible feeling of desolation and uncertainty. But, as always we go on.

All my love.

Ever,
Alan Schneider

as/lf
Dictated by AS; signed by LF

1. Friday, 22 November 1963; AS is responding to SB's letter of 19 November.
2. *Play* opened at the Cherry Lane Theatre, New York, 4 January 1964. Francis Sternhagen (W1), Marian Reardon (W2), Michael Lipton (M). Marian Reardon had replaced Hilda Brawner as W2.

December 13, 1963

Mr. Samuel Beckett
38 Boulevard St. Jacques
Paris, FRANCE

Dear Mr. Beckett,

Alan Schneider is in the midst of rehearsals down at the Cherry Lane Theatre, and so he asked me to send you the following information:

1. The cast for PLAY is as follows:

W1 Frances Sternhagen
W2 Marian Reardon
Man Michael Lipton

Mr. Schneider wants you to know that he has worked with all of these actors before, and he feels that they will all be very good.

2. We are cutting traps in the stage for the Urns.

3. A method is being worked out to make the Light a single moving source.

Mr. Schneider also wants to know if the name "Arsene" can be changed to something less specifically French, such as "Arthur" or whatever you might suggest.

Sincerely,
Linda Feinfeld
Production Secretary

December 23, 1963

Mr. Samuel Beckett
38 Boulevard St. Jacques
Paris, FRANCE

Dear Sam,

Rehearsals are going very well. Haven't heard from you about the change in "Arsene" so we are keeping the name until and unless you approve Anglicized version.[1]

One thing: in order for it to be crystal clear that the Light draws the responses from the people, what would you think of having the 3 people close their eyes each time the Light goes out and open them the moment the Light hits them? This seems to make clearer the cause-and-effect relationship between the Light and their speaking. This is the only deviation from the text that I have used in rehearsal, and of course we will not do it if you object. Aside from that, things are going well. The urns are exactly right, the Light works just the way you wanted it, and all is well.

Ever,
Alan

dict. by AS
typed and signed by lf

1. AS has not received SB's letter of 21 December 1963 suggesting "Erskine" to replace "Arsene."

December 26, 1963

Mr. Samuel Beckett
38 Boulevard St. Jacques
Paris, France

Dear Sam,[1]

Have just finished first run through of PLAY with Light and Urns, and results—excellent. The finger of light (which we call "Sam") stabs unerringly through the darkness at the faces. It moves silently and with precision as well as varying rates of speed depending on its reaction. The Urns, while the actors are still getting adjusted to them, look exactly like the little drawing you drew for me originally. They touch, they are trapped, and the heads stick out of the lip as you intended. In other words, the technical side of the show seems to be under control.

The actors—and I shouldn't forget them—are also fine. I think you will find them about as "toneless" as humanly possible; expressionless and staring; and yet, communicating the three persons involved simply and effectively. The contrast between what they have to say and the tonelessness carries, of course, the humor and pathos of the text. I am most pleased with everything so far and have high hopes that if you were to come, so would you be.

Thanks for the change to "Erskine." It works very well and is much clearer to an American audience.

Our first preview is this weekend, and I will write you immediately about the audience reaction. We are opening on January 4.

Love, in haste, ever,
Alan

P.S. Barney saw a very rudimentary run through a week ago before he left for Mexico and seemed to like it even then.

dict. by AS
typed & signed by LF

1. AS replies to SB's letter of 21 December 1963.

Ussy-sur-Marne
29.12.63

Dear Alan

Thanks for your letter.

Try the eye effect by all means if you find it helps and does not slow down reaction to light.

I replied to your secretary suggesting Erskine instead of Arsene—or anything else you like.

May be going to London next month to rehearse Jack MacGowran & Pat Magee in Michael Blake's production of ENDGAME opening in Paris (Studio des C.E.) Feb. 15 for a short run.[1]

Escaped here before Xmas and hope to stay another week. Struggling feebly and so far in vain to go on.

Madeleine continues to triumph.

Hope to begin work with Serreau soon. Had a very illuminating session with some spot experts.

Bless you again for all you do for my work.

Love to you and *endurable* (better than *bearable*) moments in 1964.

Sam

1. Opened at the Studio des Champs-Elysées, 17 February 1964.

January 2, 1964

Mr. Samuel Beckett
38 Blvd. St. Jacques
Paris, France

Dear Sam,

Four previews under our belt and four to go. General response favorable although I feel we can do better. We have tried it all ways—twice fast, once slowly—in order to judge various reactions. My feeling at the moment is that the *da capo* does not work as well as I thought it would. The audience gets too much the first time, so they resent the second time. On the other hand, if we play it at really lightningspeed, then they resent the first time. However, we are still working.

The tonelessness works fine. And all the technical elements including the Light ("Sam"). And the urns look marvellous; the proportion and distance exactly as planned; the space absolutely limitless and unlit. We will send you some photographs as soon as possible.

Keep your fingers crossed for Saturday night.

Much love,
Alan Schneider

P.S. I almost forgot. We get all the laughs that are there in the first half, and then they are quiet as mice in the second half. Some of the people seem to like it better than any other play of yours. We shall see.

AS/lda

1 Flower Avenue
Hastings-on-Hudson,
New York
January 10, 1964

Mr. Samuel Beckett
38 Boulevard St. Jacques
Paris, France

Dear Sam,

Please excuse my not writing sooner since the opening and for not calling you the night we opened. Actually, since it was a Saturday, the reviews did not come out until Monday, so I had nothing to report. Also, I went to bed fairly early that night, so that it would have been too early Sunday morning to call you just on general principles.

By now you have probably seen the daily notices, which are about as illiterate and stupid as they generally tend to be. Some of the weeklies of which we know already are more intelligent, particularly THE VIL-LAGE VOICE, which I asked Judith to send on to you. Also, interest-ingly enough, THE WALL STREET JOURNAL. There will probably be some others trickling in.[1] The response over-all seems quite good to us, and if all goes well, we should get a good run. I am especially pleased that the technical elements worked out as well as they did. The finger of light and the urns are, I believe, exactly as you envisioned, and the tonelessness, as I said before, is about as well carried out as 3 human voices could make it.

I still expect to be in London on February 6 for the opening of

VIRGINIA WOOLF, and I am planning to come to Paris to see you after that. Would you mind if I showed up around the time of the ENDGAME opening because I would love to see it, also perhaps some of the rehearsals for PLAY? In any case, I will telephone you from London.

Hurriedly, and gratefully,
Alan Schneider

P.S. Have been flat on my back since the opening with an old back injury, but nothing serious, and I am recovering daily. The sea voyage will make all well again, I'm sure, God bless.

dict. by phone by AS
typed and signed by LF

1. *Play* opened with Pinter's *The Lover* at the Cherry Lane Theatre, New York, 4 January 1964. Reviews: Michael Smith, "Play," *Village Voice,* 9 January; Richard P. Cooke, "Beckett and Pinter," *Wall Street Journal,* 7 January; "others": Walter Kerr, "Play," *NY Herald-Tribune,* 6 January; Howard Taubman, *NY Times,* 6 January; Richard Watts, Jr., "The News of Beckett and Pinter," *NY Post,* 6 January.

Paris
18.1.64

Dear Alan

Thanks for your letter of Jan. 10th. Very sorry to hear you have been flattened & hope now fully vertical & mobile again.

Yes, the notices are pretty grim. I gather from them that you are not using the *da capo*.[1] Perhaps I misunderstand them. I look forward to a few photos. I am beginning work on text with Serreau, but won't get down to it properly till I'm back from London early next month. *Endgame* opens at Studio Feb. 17.[2] Madeleine's last Winnies will probably be Feb. 10 & 11.

I leave for London Jan. 16th to begin rehearsals following day.[3] I'm not in good form and am rather dreading it.

Three weeks quiet at Ussy produced nothing, not a line.

Affectionately to you all.
Sam

1. Faced with an ultimatum by his producers (Theatre 1964, Richard Barr, Clinton Wilder, Edward Albee), who strongly objected to *Play*'s *da capo*, AS had it performed only once. For the first and last time in his long association with SB he did something he despised himself for doing. SB was not pleased (*Entrances*, 341–342).

2. Studio des Champs-Elysées.

3. *Play.*

1 Floral Avenue
Hastings-on-Hudson,
New York
March 10, 1964

Mr. Samuel Beckett
38 Boulevard St. Jacques
Paris, France

Dear Sam,

Home again and the usual complications. You know by now about our problems at the Cherry Lane. Business evidently has dropped off the edge of the cliff all over the city, and so much to everyone's surprise, we have been having a difficult time keeping above water. After much deliberation, Messrs. Barr and Wilder decided that the best thing to do would be to drop THE LOVER (it may go on as one of the currently running PINTER PLAYS) but to continue with PLAY supplemented by Arrabal's THE TWO EXECUTIONERS and a new American play.[1] Barney and I have agreed because we want very much to keep PLAY running as long as possible. I saw it again last night and found it in excellent shape and the audience response most enthusiastic.

Anyhow, I hope this meets with your approval.

The real news is that we are now definitely planning the Beckett cycle sometime next season, the plays to include GODOT, ENDGAME, KRAPP, HAPPY DAYS, ACTS WITHOUT WORDS—and with Magee and MacGowran. Barr, Wilder and Albee—not to mention myself—are wild about the idea and are now checking with Actors' Equity Association to make sure about that Irish actor business, but we think it will be possible.[2] The idea is to have a season of say 6–8 weeks at a time when Pat and Jackie and the theatre are all available. Shall keep you completely aware of all developments in this direction.

Wonderful to have seen you, even for that short time in Paris, and so pleased that I managed to see ENDGAME.[3] The boat trip was fine, family even more so, the house remains in the future like Godot, but it will certainly be ready by the time you come over to house you in complete anonymity.

Finger improving slowly but surely. Hope you are well and having a chance to get off by yourself. All the best.

Alan

dict. by AS
signed by LF

1. New play: LeRoi Jones's *Dutchman*, 1964, directed by Edward Parone; Jones (Imamu Amiri Baraka, b. 1934), African-American poet, dramatist.

2. Since Actors' Equity, founded in 1912 to secure equitable contracts between actors and managers, insisted that actors and actresses from abroad be paid star salaries, off-Broadway theaters could not afford them.

3. Presented by a new company known as the English Theatre, originally called the Anglo-American Theatre-Paris, *Endgame* opened at the Studio des Champs-Elysées, 20 February 1964, directed by Michael Blake, assisted by SB. Patrick Magee (Hamm), Jack MacGowran (Clov), Sydney Bromley (Nagg), Elvi Hale (Nell). SB assisted Blake for six weeks in London prior to the Paris opening.

Paris
14.3.64

Dear Alan

In haste to thank you for your letter and to OK modified bill, though very sorry to lose THE LOVER which I shd have thought was the drawing element.

Delighted at prospect of getting Jack & Pat to N.Y. Confirm what I wrote to Barr that in that case I wd. certainly be over making of myself the well known nuisance.

Work with Serreau has produced interesting things which will be useful in London whither this evening. New light especially on repeat.

ENDGAME with Pat & Jack & perhaps the stumps going into Aldwych rep. in June.[1]

Love to you all
Sam

1. When the stumps are put in place in cricket, play (i.e., the game) begins.

Ussy
11.4.64

Dear Alan

Thanks for your letter. Heard from Barr to same effect. Disappointing—but not unexpected.[1] Don't think I'll get over after all. Have been rehearsing practically continuously since Jan. and shall be on again in London in June-July for Aldwych *Endgame* with Jack & Pat. After that simply must go into retirement for a long spell.

Got back from London a few days ago & straight here for a breather. Very tired. Very pleased with production. Three actors & George were marvellous. We got an interesting variation into repeat. Shall tell you about it when we meet. Too difficult to explain on paper. It opened Tuesday. Haven't read notices but understand unfriendly. Perhaps Sunday's better, what the hell in any case.[2]

Resume now, when I get back to Paris next week, rehearsals with Serreau.[3] And a lot of tricky work to be done for second vol. of German trilingual edition. All getting far too much for me.

Hope the new home is coming along as you wish and that you will soon be happily settled in.

Love to you all
Sam

1. *Play* and *The Lover* were taken off 22 March; *Play* reopened 24 March accompanied by Fernando Arrabal's *The Two Executioners* and *Dutchman* by LeRoi Jones; was withdrawn on 19 April after thirty-two performances and replaced by Albee's *The American Dream*.

2. SB went to London for the first production of *Play* at the Old Vic Theatre for the National Theatre Company, 7 April 1964, directed by George Devine, designed by Jocelyn Herbert, light by Anthony Ferris. Rosemary Harris (w.1 First Woman), Billie Whitelaw (w.2 Second Woman), Robert Stephens (m. Man). It was followed by Sophocles' *Philoctetes*. While rehearsing *Play* SB found a solution to the problem of the *da capo*: the reprise worked better when the lighting was dimmed and the volume of the three voices reduced. Reviews: Bamber Gascoigne, "How Far Can Beckett Go?" *The Observer*, 2 April 1964; Herbert Kretzmer, "The Three Faces of Beckett's Contempt," *Daily Express*, 8 April; "Waiting for the Dark," unsigned, *Times Literary Supplement*, 9 April; Sir Harold Hobson, "The Second Time Round," *Sunday Times*, 12 April.

3. Assisted by SB, Serreau directed *Comédie (Play)* at the Pavillon de Marsan, Paris, 11 June 1964, light by Danielle van Bercheycke. Eléonore Hirt (f.1 First Woman), Delphine Seyrig (f.2 Second Woman), Michael Lonsdale (m. Man).

May 26, 1964

Samuel Beckett, Esq.
38 Boulevard St. Jacques
Paris 14me, France

Dear Sam,

Congratulations! I am so pleased about PLAY'S winning an Obie award. Wish I had been there to pick it up for you, but Richard Barr has it. We'll send it on.[1]

Have been meaning to write to you pending some rather fast breaking developments in the film situation. I know how disappointed you must be about the postponement, but I felt it was absolutely necessary to avoid a real shambles. Knowing my own limitations, I couldn't be optimistic about going into a picture without adequate preparation and there simply has been no time here for me to do anything except read the script once or twice, which made me even more aware of the difficulties and pit-falls looming ahead.

The second main problem was that we lost the camera man whom I had met and had great confidence in; the other camera man I would not have met until practically the day before shooting. Since my relationship with him would be of critical value and since it was impossible to find out anything specific about his past work, I am afraid that I was reluctant to trust anyone else's word about his abilities in general.

Originally, as you know, we were going to shoot in July and all my thinking and planning had been on this basis. When ENDGAME came up for Jackie, I was very pleased for him, but terribly upset in terms of our shooting schedule. That is why I wrote to Barney and you in Paris last month. Stilled as my fears were, for the moment, by the news of your coming, they reappeared full-force once I got going on the script and culminated in my making one more approach to Barney.

Since the postponement we have discovered that both Sir Alec Guinness and Buster Keaton are available and we hope that when they read the script one or the other will be interested. Much as I hate losing Jackie, I feel that shooting the film in July with one or the other of these two gentlemen would be much better than going into production the moment I leave here. I do hope that your intention of coming over for the shooting will not change under the present circumstances. Barney tells me that you have elaborated on the first scene and I am anxiously awaiting the revisions.[2]

Do hope you are well and not being bombarded by too much of the same stuff. With all best wishes and regards from Jean.

Ever,
Alan Schneider

1. *Play* was awarded an Obie for "Best New Play" and for "Best Production."
2. AS was very interested in *Film,* his first non-TV film, which had many technical problems. Barney Rosset had the idea of getting three avant-garde playwrights, SB, Ionesco, and Albee, to write three short films. (Only SB actually wrote a script, although Ionesco turned his piece into a TV script.) Since SB felt that the film should have a stylized comic reality similar to that of a silent film, AS thought of casting Chaplin or Mostel but finally chose Jack MacGowran, who became unavailable (*Entrances,* 354–355). Buster Keaton (1895–1966).

Paris
31.5.64

Dear Alan

Thanks for your letter.

I am going to London June 29 to rehearse ENDGAME. We open July 9.¹ From then on I am at your disposal. I could not spend more than a fortnight or 3 weeks at the outside in NY. I should prefer to go straight into it from London. But if you prefer to have me in August, I can manage that too.

Hope you are pleased with the work at Minneapolis and that the opening is a success.²

All news when we meet.

Affectionately to you all
Sam [handwritten]

1. Performed by the Royal Shakespeare Company, *Endgame* opened at the Aldwych Theatre, 9 July 1964, directed by Donald McWhinnie, assisted by SB, designed by Ralph Koltai. With Magee and MacGowran as in Paris and also Brian Pringle (Nagg), Patsy Byrne (Nell).
2. Tennessee Williams's *The Glass Menagerie* opened at Tyrone Guthrie Theatre, Minneapolis, 1 June 1964.

                                                                 Paris
                                                                 13.6.64
Dear Alan

Thanks for your letter of June 9.[1]

Every problem of image in the film is to be solved by reference to the one or other vision. The street is as E sees it. He is looking for O and if there were other *people* in the street besides the 6 couples he would be bound to fix his gaze on them as he does on the couples. So one must assume that these couples are the only people in the opening scene. There may of course be registered very briefly, as he switches from one couple to another, the normal street objects (whatever they are), one or more of which (tree, lamppost) could help to indicate, when the pursuit begins, the direction it is taking, i.e. against the stream.

The same principle obtains during pursuit sequence, with this difference, that E having fastened on O may now legitimately record, blurredly, other human elements, without the question arising as to why he does not scrutinize them as well. The only [ones] to be seen clearly are O and the 7th couple, the latter first by O, then by E, but if you wish there may be a confused presence of other couples all of course moving with the stream, i.e. in direction opposed to that of E and O.

The question of transfers should be clear from the further notes. The point I tried to make was that the two visions are to be distinguished, not only on the plane of absolute quality, but also dynamically, i.e. in their manner of transferring from one object to the next. It is therefore necessary that the samples of O's vision given before the room sequences should involve such transfers, and I specify them, both in the case of the 7th couple and in that of the flower-woman, in the latter case O's eye moving from her face to the tray, from the tray to her hand, from the hand back to the tray, from the tray back to face, more slowly than E's eye a moment later effecting same transfers.[2]

In the midst of apprehension at thought of N.Y. joy at prospect of seeing you all so soon.

Best always.
Sam [handwritten]

1. Missing.
2. AS writes "OK" in the left margin beside "in the latter case O's eye . . ."

Paris
June 29 1964

Dear Alan

It is necessary that the photos

1) Represent O at different ages from his infancy to his present age or thereabouts (the last photo permitting identification) and as far as possible in situations normally associated with these ages.

2) Represent O (with possible exception of last) in *percipi*. This is of course indicated by the fact of his being photographed, but the point is reinforced if, as in the first six I describe, we actually see him being observed (1 by mother, 2 by mother-God, 3 by dog, 4 by public, 5 by young man, 6 by infant daughter). Important in photo 6 to have infant daughter touch his face with finger because of his touching with his photo of hers.[1] Thus the photos and their destruction parallel triple perception (human, animal, divine) from which he seeks to escape and his efforts to obliterate it.

Apart from these two exigencies you are free to deviate as far as you like from photos described in scenario.

I have no photo of a male infant that I wish to use.

The only photo in Judith's series which meets requirements of 2) is that numbered 2.

I suggest we reduce the number of photos to 6, to tally with couples and room elements, by dropping either 1 or 2. The loss of indirect divine in 2 would not much matter, since we have Abu.

In the street scene E first inspects successively all 6 couples as they appear in series 1, then as they appear in series 2, finally as they appear in series 3.

Concerned at the moment with another problem: how to avoid, in room sequences, gratuity of transfer from O vision to E vision and back. I feel that to rely on purely formal considerations is not enough and that we need a principle of necessity justifying these switches. The solution has somehow to do with the angle of immunity, but I haven't yet been able to work it out satisfactorily. I'll have another go on the plane to London this afternoon and let you know results if any.

Yours ever
Sam [handwritten]

1. This sentence: handwritten insertion.

Friday night, Aug. 27 [1964]

Dear Sam,

Just came home from seeing FILM completed (?) and shown on a screen for the first time: black at front and back, all the opticals done, the eye dissolve to the wall, the dolly to the god properly ending square on the eyes, the eye opening on the credits at the end and then shutting for the last time.[1]

I was as nervous as at any opening. Although we haven't even 'opened' in Venice yet!

Gather from Judith that you're not accepting invitation to Venice. But that you might be able to see FILM in Paris. So that if you have strong feelings we can still do something for New York. But it is far from 'unfinished' for Venice.[2]

My feeling was very good. The film has an aura and a sustained cumulative power through the constant repetition of the eyes that I had never felt before in the viewer. I was quite pleased with the Shhhhhh itself—and I don't mind the couple as much as I once did, although they are far from good. The flower woman is fine; I feel real excitement in the hallway scene. And the room.

My only question—and I'd love your response—is whether in the final shot of E at the wall with the nail beside him, we haven't cut the shot too much. We used to have a dolly going in at some length; but I didn't like the dolly with the eye flickering throughout—and you agreed—so we cut it down to the closest possible shot but stationary. How do you like it? What do you think? It's no problem restoring it, the question is do we want to? Sometimes the entire ending seems very powerful to me, sometimes it just misses. Yesterday, as I said, I felt it wasn't entirely there.

The god square in the eyes is very powerful.

I think the animals have been lengthened as much as possible.

Jerry Michaels who took over the last part of the editing when Sidney was unwell did a fine job.[3] He was very conscientious on all fronts. Sidney by the way is much better, just talked with him.

The titles have been designed to fit within the pupil of the eye. We did freeze eye a bit in order to prevent jiggle of titles. Only thing I regret is that titles—designed by Roy Kahlman—are not entirely consistent in style. But they are simple and effective.

I feel the film is more Beckett than Buster, but both work. Wish I could have seen it with you. I hope you're not too disappointed.

How are you?

[Alan]

1. *Film* was produced by Evergreen Theatre, Inc., a subsidiary of Grove Press. Produced by Barney Rosset, directed by AS, cinematographer Boris Kaufman, camera Joe Coffey, editor Sidney Meyers, designed by Burr Smidt. Buster Keaton (The Man), James Karen and Susan Reed (The Couple), Nell Harrison (The Flower-seller).

2. *Film* was awarded the *Prie Filmcritice* at the Venice Film Festival in October 1965 and a Special Jury Prize at the International Film Festival of Short Subjects at Tours in January 1966, among other awards at film festivals. SB, *Film: Complete Scenario/Illustrations/Production shots, with an essay "On Directing 'Film'" by Alan Schneider,* 1969; *Film* in *Eh Joe and Other Writings,* 1967.

3. Sidney Meyers (1906–1969), film editor, friend and correspondent of SB after New York production of *Film.*

Sept. 5, [1964]

Dear Sam,

Well, back once more from various journeys and settling down to work on FILM once more. Sidney just returned from a rather unrestful vacation, I gather, family problems, a bit shaken but anxious to work.

Yesterday, we shot the inserts and should know by Tuesday (because of long Labor Day holiday) how they came out. We got everything except the O pov of covered cage and fishbowl etc.—which we'll have to blow up and treat optically from some of shots we had. It was impossible to get the black overcoats, bowl, lighting, etc. But we shot a batch of pictures of a marvelous fish's eye and eyes and head; the rocker headrest, the eyes of the folder, and the briefcase. Keep your fingers crossed. Did the whole thing in about 3 hours with Joe Coffey. Only thing wrong was that I didn't get a ride back into the city with his Morgan since he was continuing at the studio.[1]

Have started work on next stage of editing with Sidney, and have gone over all your notes—and mine—for entire film. We started putting in changes as we went along but then Sidney got worried that it would take too much time, so we watched and made notes for him to work on. One thing we did do, you will be pleased to note, is eliminate the mail box sequence entirely—and this gave us an opportunity to use the O pov pulse-taking at the mailbox in another place: that is, when O feels his pulse at end of hallway, we cut to it in O pov, and it looks fine. Then we have another one after he closes and locks the door when he gets into room. So three pulses altogether through film. In fact, we have found—I believe—that all the inserts happen in groups of threes, each one getting closer, throughout the picture. That includes: the animals, the parrot, the goldfish, the headrest, the folder, the empty wall. (Not sure whether it's possible with print.) Anyhow, will keep you posted.

Sidney's only worry is that we won't be able to finish before Barney leaves on the 15th. He is certain we cannot get the optical work done: credits, dissolve, blow-ups, whatever.[2] He is going to try to get everything else finished in time but with his family problem, he cannot work as long or as intensively as he would like. As it turns out, I won't be able to work each day and evening either. What I've asked Sidney to do is try, but if he cannot complete the job as satisfactorily as he wants to, then we shall just have to mail the film after the 15th, or send it along with someone who is coming to Paris later.

I meant to say our one disappointment has been that last request of yours about E's eye closing. We have seen all the footage and for various reasons Sidney and I feel that none of the shots work: either they are not with the gauze, or they are clearly Buster blinking to avoid the light. So far we have not been able to improve on the shot we have—although we shall keep on trying.

How are you? I guess you have seen Judith and sent her on to Greece. Are you getting a bit of a rest? Away from all the American invaders? Including those from the *Saturday Evening Post*. Do hope so. And take care of yourself. Jean and I both miss you like mad, and I think fondly of our adventures together wending our way through the maze of film-making. And of your grace under fire.

All the best.

[Alan]

1. Joe Coffey drove an English sportscar known as a Morgan.
2. Technical terms used in this and the following letters: POV = point of view, a shot filmed at such a camera angle that an object or an action appears to be seen from a particular actor's point of view; dissolve = change gradually from one picture to another; blow-ups = enlargements; track = to move a camera to follow an actor, or from one part of a scene to another; cut = to edit a film; pan = to move camera in a horizontal plane; dolly = a vehicle on wheels; rake = the slope of a stage; movieola = an editing machine first made for viewing silent films and later elaborated to accommodate sound.

Sunday,
Sept. 13, [1964]

Dear Sam,

Just spent afternoon with Sidney Meyers (after a week in which he asked me to let him work on the notes previously discussed with him—and about which I wrote you). Saw film several times, and it looks pretty good to my jaundiced eye—though not yet finished. The idea is to get an exact copy made so we could give one to Barney Tuesday morning, and keep one here for protection. So amount of time for work not that much.

Sidney, over this past week, took some liberties with the film, especially the first part, which he wanted me to prepare you for. I cannot say I agree with them all completely, but they are easily enough removed, changed, amended or whatever at your discretion. And besides there was simply not enough time between now and Tuesday to do that much work in two exact copies. So please bear with his whimsy, and let me have your reactions.

1. Main thing he did was play around with that opening examination of wall so that swish to Buster included a fast glance at a couple (I can just see your face!) He thought the swish was bad from the wall to Buster; and he's always had a hankering for those couples. Look at it. (Easy to cut out.)

2. He was not satisfied with our patching together of the wall—nor was I—so we have temporarily put in shot of O-POV wall *before* he bumps into couple. It may be too long. If you are dead against it, we can go back to another try at putting together the two wall shots.

3. The cuts in E's vision of the couple are a bit extreme, but more of the way you wanted it, I believe. Ditto getting O getting around wall. The second swish around corner looks as though it's going in wrong direction, and we shall try to fix it.

4. Entrance into hall works better without mail-boxes. How do you like that insert of pulse-taking? Flower woman in E's vision? Etc.

5. We have amended the entire sequence at the door, outside and inside.

6. The 'three series' and preliminary pan now more or less the way you and I talked about it. Any reactions?

7. The removal of animals now seems about right length.

8. Wasn't time to get dolly to god's eyes printed backwards to eliminate lack of centrality. We will if you want—though I must say I rather like it.

9. We have the new shots of rocker back in. They seem a bit dark to me, can be printed a bit lighter. I like the folder.

10. We are still not completely set on inserts of animals, parrot, fish eye, etc. so let us have reactions pro and con.

11. The photo sequence seems very exciting to me. In fact, from then on to end of picture. I have some small feeling that last view of E by O is somehow too long. (That's related to uncertainty of blinking eye, and impossibility of making real virtue of the . . . Would you mind my trying couple of [line difficult in carbon and ending missing]

There are lots of bits along the way; and my intention once we have heard from you is to sit down with Sidney, and get into third stage of editing, the details, shortening, lengthening, rhythm, exact sizes of inserts, etc. There's really not that much. Besides the 'optical' work, that is the dissolve from eye to first shot, the backwards dolly if we use it, and anything else. (Is the O-POV at covered fishbowl possible for you as it is?). . . . Excuse this lousy typing, my machine on the blink. . . . The house progresses, work continues on various fronts, I have been bitten by the film bug—but not the desire for Hollywood—and I miss you and those morning breakfasts on Sixth Avenue, not to mention all the other times.

How are you? Looking forward to hearing from you and getting all sorts of notes. I hope you can find a good place to look at the film a few times.

We must go into question of credits—and sound for O and E, IF ANY! I'm not certain at this stage that we need ANY.

All the best.

[Alan]

Paris
15.9.64

Dear Alan

Thanks for your two letters. The first, written at Idlewild airport and dated August 19, only arrived today!

Glad to have news of re-shooting and editing. Take your time, I'm in no hurry. Sorry to hear Sidney not so grand. My best to him & Nina.

Happy Days reopened yesterday at Théâtre de France to a good house.[1] Suzanne went & [?]said Madeleine was in good form. I joined up with them afterwards at the *Bist'anana*. Barrault is to direct a *Faust* in N.Y. at the *Metropolitan* September of next year and Madeleine wonders if Barr could arrange some performances of *Oh les B. J.* at that time. Billetdoux's new play, opening in a month, has their hands full at the moment.[2]

A letter from Judith from Dubrovnik. She seems to be enjoying herself and beginning to feel rested. She was very tired when she was in Paris.

Struggling to get the work off the ground again, but no success so far.

Glad you are not going to California and can take things a bit easy till the new Albee.

Love to Jean & the kids.

Yrs. ever
Sam

1. *Oh les beaux jours (Happy Days)* opened 14 September 1964.
2. François Billetdoux (b. 1927), French playwright; *Il faut passer par les nuages* (1964), the "new play," opened at Odéon-Théâtre de France, 21 October 1964.

Mr. Alan Schneider
30 Scenic Drive
Hastings on Hudson
New York U.S.A.

Paris
24.9.64

Dear Alan

Have seen *Film* but don't want to say anything today. Movieoling day after tomorrow and shall write you & Sidney in detail next week. Just lunched with Barney, Chr. [Cristina] & Judith. The former suddenly off to Casablanca! Judith due home next Tuesday, whenever that is.

Love to you all
Sam

Ussy
29.9.64

Dear Alan

Forgive delay in sending these notes.[1] They are no more than suggestions. Don't act on them if you don't agree. The movieola here was
bad and I in poor form. I'm getting the use of a better one in a few
weeks and shall write again then. But don't hold up final cut on that
account if you are in a hurry to get it done or for any other reason. I
don't expect to have much better to offer.

I have had two screenings here, the first with Barney, Cristina and
Hodeir, the second with Suzanne, the movieola girl and again Hodeir
(most helpful).[2] After the first I was not too happy, after the second I felt
it really was something. Not quite in the way intended, but as sheer
beauty, power and strangeness of image. The problem of the double
vision for example is not really solved, but the attempt to solve it has
given the film a plastic value which it would not have otherwise. In
other words and generally speaking, from having been troubled by a
certain failure to communicate fully by purely visual means the basic
intention, I now begin to feel that this is unimportant and that the
images obtained probably gain in force what they lose as ideograms
and that the whole idea behind the film, while sufficiently expressed
for those so minded, has been chiefly of value on the formal and structural level. After the first screening I thought again a lot, and spoke
with Hodeir, about the possibility of reinforcing the E-O distinction
by means of sound. Now I am definitely and finally opposed to any
sound whatever apart from the "hssh" which I think should be as
brief and uninsistent as possible. Suzanne, Hodeir and Miss Movieola
were all I think genuinely impressed. When I get back to Paris I'll show
it, with Barney's permission, to a few close (but outspeaking) friends
and let you have reactions. I described it to Barney after the first screening as an "interesting failure". This I now see is much too severe. It
does I suppose in a sense fail with reference to a purely intellectual
schema, that is in a sense which only you and I and a few others can
discern, but in so doing has acquired a dimension and a validity of its
own that are worth far more than any merely efficient translation of
intention.

Thank you again for all you have done. Love to Jean and the kids.

Ever
Sam [handwritten]

1. The notes that follow have been published in SB, *Film* (see letter of 27 August 1964, n. 2), without the scribbled and often illegible comments made by AS.
2. André Hodeir (b. 1921), French musician, writer, and editor.

GENERAL

[These are the "notes" mentioned in the first sentence of letter of 29 September 1964]

Esse est percipi.

All extraneous perception suppressed, animal, human, divine, self-perception maintains in being.

The search for non-being in flight from extraneous perception breaking down in inescapability of self-perception.

No truth value attaches to above, regarded as of merely structural and dramatic convenience.

In order to be figured in this situation the protagonist is sundered into object (O) and eye (E), the former in flight, the latter in pursuit.

It will not be clear until end of film that pursuing perceiver is not extraneous, but self.

Until end of film O is perceived by E from behind and at an angle not exceeding 45. Convention: O enters *percipi* = experiences anguish of perceivedness, only when this angle is exceeded.

O not in perceivedness:

O in perceivedness:

E is therefore at pains, throughout pursuit, to keep within this "angle of immunity" and only exceeds it 1) inadvertently at beginning of part one when he first sights O 2) inadvertently at beginning of part two when he follows O into vestibule and 3) deliberately at end of part three when O is cornered. In first two cases he hastily reduces angle.

Throughout first two parts all perception is E's. E is the camera. But in third part there is O's perception of room and contents and at the same time E's continued perception of O. This poses a problem of images which I cannot solve without technical help. See below, note 8.

The film is divided into three parts. 1. The street (about eight minutes). 2. The stairs (about five minutes). 3. The room (about 17 minutes).

The film is entirely silent except for the "sssh!" in part one.

Climate of film comic and unreal. O should invite laughter throughout by his way of moving. Unreality of street scene (see notes to this section).

OUTLINE

1. The street.
Dead straight. No sidestreets or intersections. Period: about 1929. Early summer morning. Small factory district. Moderate animation of workers going unhurriedly to work. All going in same direction and all in couples. No automobiles. Two bicycles ridden by men with girl passengers (on crossbar). One cab, cantering nag, driver standing brandishing whip. All persons in opening scene to be shown in some way perceiving—one another, an object, a shop window, a poster, etc., i.e. all contentedly in *percipere* and *percipi*. First view of above is by E motionless and searching with his eyes for O. He may be supposed at street edge of wide (4 yards) sidewalk. O finally comes into view hastening blindly along sidewalk, hugging the wall on his left, in opposite direction to all the others. Long dark overcoat (whereas all others in light summer dress) with collar up, hat pulled down over eyes, briefcase in left hand, right hand shielding exposed side of face. He *storms* along in *comic foundered precipitancy*. E's searching eye, turning left from street to sidewalk, picks him up at an angle exceeding that of immunity (O's unperceivedness according to convention) (1). O, entering perceivedness, reacts (after just sufficient onward movement for his gait to be established) by halting and cringing aside towards wall. E immediately draws back to close the angle (2) and O, released from perceivedness, hurries on. E lets him get about 10 yards ahead and then starts after him (3). Street elements from now on incidental (except for episode of couple) in the sense that only registered in so far as they happen to enter field of pursuing eye fixed on O.

  Episode of couple (4). In his blind haste O jostles an elderly couple of shabby genteel aspect, standing on side-walk, peering together at a newspaper. They should be discovered by E a few yards before collision. The woman is holding a pet monkey under her left arm. E follows O an instant as he hastens blindly on, then registers couple recovering

from shock, comes up with them, passes them slightly and halts to ob-
serve them (5). Having recovered they turn to look after O, the woman
raising a lorgnon to her eyes, the man taking off his pince-nez fastened
to his coat by a ribbon. They then look at each other, she lowering her
lorgnon, he resuming his pince-nez. He opens his mouth to vituperate.
She checks him with a gesture and soft "sssh!". He turns again, taking
off his pince-nez, to look after O. She feels the gaze of E upon them and
turns, raising her lorgnon, to look at him. She nudges her companion
who turns back towards her, resuming his pince-nez, follows direction
of her gaze and, taking off his pince-nez, looks at E. As they both stare
at E the expression gradually comes over their faces which will be that
of the flower-woman in the stairs scene and that of O at the end of film,
an expression only to be described as corresponding to an *agony of
perceivedness*. Indifference of monkey, looking up into the face of its
mistress. They close their eyes, she lowering her lorgnon, and hasten
away in direction of all the others, i.e. that opposed to O and E (6).

E turns back towards O by now far ahead and out of sight. Immediate *acceleration* of E in pursuit (blurred transit of encountered elements). O comes into view, grows rapidly larger until E settles down
behind him at same angle and remove as before. O disappears suddenly through open housedoor on his left. Immediate acceleration of E
who comes up with O in vestibule at foot of stairs.

2. Stairs.
Vestibule about 4 yards square with stairs at inner righthand angle.
Relation of streetdoor to stairs such that E's first perception of O (E near
door, O motionless at foot of stairs, right hand on banister, body shaken
by panting) is from an angle a little exceeding that of immunity. O,
entering perceivedness (according to convention), transfers right hand
from banister to exposed side of face and cringes aside towards wall on
his left. E immediately draws back to close the angle and O, released,
resumes his pose at foot of stairs, hand on banister. O mounts a few
steps (E remaining near door), raises head, listens, redescends hastily
backwards and crouches down in angle of stairs and wall on his right,
invisible to one descending (7). E registers him there, then transfers to
stairs. A frail old woman appears on bottom landing. She carries a tray
of flowers slung from her neck by a strap. She descends slowly, with
fumbling feet, one hand steadying the tray, the other holding the banister. Absorbed by difficulty of descent she does not become aware of E
until she is quite down and making for the door. She halts and looks

full at E. Gradually same expression as that of couple in street. She closes her eyes, then sinks to the ground and lies with face in scattered flowers. E lingers on this a moment, then tranfers to where O last registered. He is no longer there, but hastening up the stairs. E transfers to stairs and picks up O as he reaches first landing. Bound forwards and up of E who overtakes O on second flight and is literally at his heels when he reaches second landing and opens with key door of room. They enter room together, E turning with O as he turns to lock the door behind him.

3. The room.

Here we assume problem of dual perception solved and enter O's perception (8). E must so manoeuvre throughout what follows, until investment proper, that O is always seen from behind, at most convenient remove, and from an angle never exceeding that of immunity, i.e. preserved from perceivedness.

Small barely furnished room (9). Side by side on floor a large cat and small dog. Unreal quality. Motionless till ejected. Cat bigger than dog. On a table against wall a parrot in a cage and a goldfish in a bowl. This room sequence falls into three parts.

1. Preparation of room (occlusion of window and mirror, ejection of dog and cat, destruction of God's image, occlusion of parrot and goldfish).

2. Period in rocking-chair. Inspection and destruction of photographs.

3. Final investment of O by E and dénouement.

1. O stands near door with case in hand and takes in room. Succession of images: dog and cat, side by side, staring at him; mirror; window; couch with rug; dog and cat staring at him; parrot and goldfish, parrot staring at him; rocking-chair; dog and cat staring at him. He sets down bag, approaches window from side and draws curtain. He turns towards dog and cat, still staring at him, then goes to couch and takes up rug. He turns towards dog and cat, still staring at him. Holding rug before him he approaches mirror from side and covers it with rug. He turns towards parrot and goldfish, parrot still staring at him. He goes to rocking-chair, inspects it from front. Insistent image of curiously carved headrest (10). He turns towards dog and cat still staring at him. He puts them out of room (11). He takes up bag and is moving towards chair when rug falls from mirror. He drops briefcase, hastens to wall

between couch and mirror, follows wall past window, approaches mirror from side, picks up rug and, holding it before him, covers mirror with it again. He returns to briefcase, picks it up, goes to chair, sits down and is opening it when disturbed by a print, pinned to wall before him, of the face of God the Father, the eyes staring at him severely. He sets down case on floor to his left, gets up and inspects print. Insistent image of wall, paper hanging off in strips (10). He tears print from wall, tears it in four, throws down the pieces and grinds them underfoot. He turns back to chair, image again of its curious headrest, sits down, image again of tattered wall-paper, takes case on his knees, takes out a folder, sets down case on floor to his left and is opening folder when disturbed by parrot's eye. He lays folder on case, gets up, takes off overcoat, goes to parrot, close up of parrot's eye, covers cage with coat, goes back to chair, image again of headrest; sits down, image again of tattered wall-paper, takes up folder and is opening it when disturbed by fish's eye. He lays folder on case, gets up, goes to fish, close-up of fish's eye, extends coat to cover bowl as well as cage, goes back to chair, image again of headrest, sits down, image again of wall, takes up folder, takes off hat and lays it on case to his left. Scant hair or bald, to facilitate identification of narrow black elastic encircling head.

When O sits up and back his head is framed in headrest which is a narrower extension of backrest. Throughout scene of inspection and destruction of photographs E may be supposed immediately behind chair looking down over O's left shoulder (12).

2. O opens folder, takes from it a packet of photographs (13), lays folder on case and begins to inspect photographs. He inspects them in order 1 to 7. When he has finished with 1 he lays it on his knees, inspects 2, lays it on top of 1, and so on, so that when he has finished inspecting them all 1 will be at the bottom of the pile and 7—or rather 6, for he does not lay down 7—at the top. He gives about six seconds each to 1–4, about twice as long to 5 and 6 (trembling hands). Looking at 6 he touches with forefinger little girl's face. After six seconds of 7 he tears it in four and drops pieces on floor on his left. He takes up 6 from top of pile on his knees, looks at it again for about three seconds, tears it in four and drops pieces on floor to his left. So on for the others, looking at each again for about three seconds before tearing it up. 1 must be on tougher mount, for he has difficulty in tearing it across. Straining hands. He finally succeeds, drops pieces on floor and sits, rocking slightly, hands holding armrests (14).

3. Investment proper. Perception from now on, if dual perception feasible, E's alone, except perception of E by O at end. E moves a little back (image of headrest from back), then starts circling to his left, approaches maximum angle and halts. From this open angle, beyond which he will enter *percipi*, O can be seen beginning to doze off. His visible hand relaxes on armrest, his head nods and falls forward, the rock approaches stillness. E advances, opening angle beyond limit of immunity, his gaze pierces the light sleep and O starts awake. The start revives the rock, immediately arrested by foot to floor. Tension of hand on armrest. Turning his head to right, O cringes away from perceivedness. E draws back to reduce the angle and after a moment, reassured, O turns back front and resumes his pose. The rock resumes, dies down slowly as O dozes off again. E now begins a much wider encirclement. Images of curtained window, walls and shrouded mirror to indicate his path and that he is not yet looking at O. Then image of O seen by E from well beyond the angle of immunity, i.e. from near the table with shrouded bowl and cage. O is now seen to be fast asleep, his head sunk on his chest and his hands, fallen from the armrests, limply dangling. E resumes his cautious approach. Images of shrouded bowl and cage and tattered wall adjoining, with same indication as before. Halt and brief image, not far short of full-face, of O still fast asleep. E advances last few yards along tattered wall and halts directly in front of O. Long image of O, full-face, against ground of headrest, sleeping. E's gaze pierces the sleep, O starts awake, stares up at E. Patch over O's left eye now seen for first time. Rock revived by start, stilled at once by foot to ground. Hands clutch armrests. O half starts from chair, then stiffens, staring up at E. Gradually that look. Cut to E, of whom this very first image (face only, against ground of tattered wall). It is O's face (with patch), but with very different expression, impossible to describe, neither severity nor benignity, but rather acute *intentness*. A big nail is visible near left temple (patch side). Long image of the unblinking gaze. Cut back to O, still half risen, staring up, with that look. O closes his eyes and falls back in chair, starting off rock. He covers his face with his hands. Image of O rocking, his head in his hands but not yet bowed. Cut back to E. As before. Cut back to O. He sits, bowed forward, his head in his hands, gently rocking. Hold it as the rocking dies down.

END

NOTES

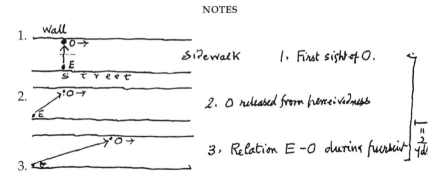

1. *Wall*

Sidewalk   1. First sight of O.

2. O released from perceivedness

3. Relation E–O during pursuit ⊢⊣ $\frac{1}{4}$d.

4. The purpose of this episode, undefendable except as a dramatic convenience, is to suggest as soon as possible unbearable quality of E's scrutiny. Reinforced by episode of flower-woman in stairs sequence.

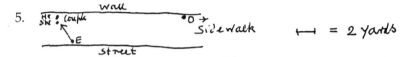

5. *wall* *Sidewalk*   ⊢⊣ = 2 yards

6. Expression of this episode, like that of animals' ejection in part three, should be as precisely stylised as possible. The purpose of the monkey, either unaware of E or indifferent to him, is to anticipate behaviour of animals in part three, attentive to O exclusively.

7. Suggestion for vestibule with 1) O in *percipi,* 2) released 3) hiding from flower-woman. Note that even when E exceeds angle of immunity O's face never really seen because of immediate turn aside and (here) hand to shield face.

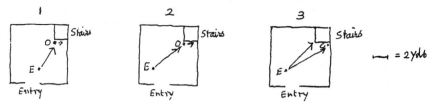

⊢⊣ = 2 yds

8. Up till now the perceptions of O, hastening *blindly* to illusory sanctuary, have been neglected and must in fact have been negligible. But in the room, until he falls asleep and the investment begins, they must be recorded. And at the same time E's perceiving of O, must continue to be given. E is concerned only with O, not with the room, or only incidentally with the room in so far as its elements happen to enter the field of

his gaze fastened on O. We see O in the room thanks to E's perceiving and the room itself thanks to O's perceiving. In other words this room sequence, up to the moment of O's falling asleep, is composed of two independent sets of images. I feel that any attempt to express them in simultaneity (composite images, double frame, superimposition, etc.) must prove unsatisfactory. The presentation in a single image of O's perception of the print, for example, and E's perception of O perceiving it—

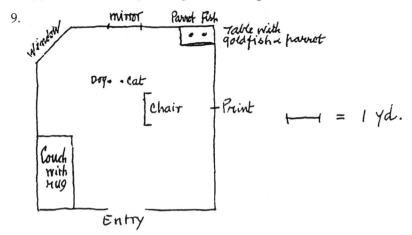

no doubt possible technically, would probably make impossible, for the spectator, a clear apprehension of either. The solution might be in a succession of images of different *quality*, corresponding on the one hand to E's perception of O and on the other to O's perception of the room. This difference of quality might perhaps be sought in different degrees of development, the passage from the one to the other being from greater to lesser and lesser to greater definition or luminosity. The dissimilarity, however obtained, would have to be flagrant. Having been up till now exclusively in the E quality, we would suddenly pass, with O's first survey of the room, into this quite different O quality. Then back to the E quality when O is shown moving to the window. And so on throughout the sequence, switching from the one to the other as required. Were this the solution adopted it might be desirable to establish, by means of brief sequences, the O quality in parts one and two.

This seems to me the chief problem of the film, though I perhaps exaggerate its difficulty through technical ignorance.

Suggestion for room.

This obviously cannot be O's room. It may be supposed it is his mother's room, which he has not visited for many years and is now to occupy momentarily, to look after the pets, until she comes out of hospital. This has no bearing on the film and need not be elucidated.

10. At close of film face E and face O can only be distinguished 1) By different expressions 2) by fact that O looking up and E down and 3) by difference of ground (for O headrest of chair, for E wall). Hence insistence on headrest and tattered wall.

11. Foolish suggestion for eviction of cat and dog. Also see Note 6.

12. Chair from front during photo sequence.

13. Description of photographs.

1. Male infant. 6 months. His mother holds him in her arms. Infant smiles front. Mother's big hands. Her severe eyes devouring him. Her big old-fashioned beflowered hat.

2. The same. 4 years. On a veranda, dressed in loose nightshirt, kneeling on a cushion, attitude of prayer, hands clasped, head bowed, eyes closed. Half profile. Mother on chair beside him, big hands on knees, head bowed towards him, severe eyes, similar hat to 1.

3. The same. 15 years. Bareheaded. School blazer. Smiling. Teaching a dog to beg. Dog on its hind legs looking up at him.

4. The same. 20 years. Graduation day. Academic gown. Mortarboard under arm. On a platform, receiving scroll from Rector. Smiling. Section of public watching.

5. The same. 21 years. Bareheaded. Smiling. Small moustache. Arm round fiancée. A young man takes a snap of them.

6. The same. 25 years. Newly enlisted. Bareheaded. Uniform. Bigger moustache. Smiling. Holding a little girl in his arms. She looks into his face, exploring it with finger.

7. The same. 30 years. Looking over 40. Wearing hat and overcoat. Patch over left eye. Cleanshaven. Grim expression.

14. Profit by rocking-chair to emotionalize inspection, e.g. gentle steady rock for 1 to 4, rock stilled (foot to ground) after two seconds of 5, rock resumed between 5 and 6, rock stilled after two seconds of 6, rock resumed after 6 and for 7 as for 1–4.

Paris

28.10.64

Dear Alan

Saw it again last night with good Italian movieola—hence above.[1]
Shall not bother you with any more notes now—you must be up to
your eyes with *Tiny A*.[2] Shall just show it to a few friends and let you
have any reactions worth having.

Love to Jean & the kids

Yrs. ever

Sam

1. Cut lovers and prolong pan back down wall as long as possible
before appearance of O.

2. Cut O shots of wall and jostled couple.

3. O shot of pulse in lobby. Not only do the hands not match those of
preceding E shot, but letter boxes clearly visible behind.

4. O vision of flower-woman from crouching position under stairs
too long. Start it with hand on flowers or a second before and cut all
preceding frames.

5. Fall of flower-woman. Suggested in previous notes cutting this
shot on look of horror before fall or just as she sways to fall, but feel
now better leave it as it is so as not to break continuity of shot and so as
to show stairs freed for O to get up.

6. Couple of blurred frames as O goes with cat from basket second
time. Reflection in camera lens?

7. Shorten 2nd and 3rd O shots of headrest if they cannot be improved, and 3rd even if they can.

8. Prolong close ups of cat and of fish's eye.

9. First full face of O in E vision closes on open mouth, second opens
with mouth opening. Cut opening frames of latter so that shot opens on
open mouth.

10. Cut opening frames of second and final shot of E in O vision so
that opening of shot not static but already moving in.

1. Notes 1–10 precede SB's brief letter.
2. Edward Albee's play *Tiny Alice* opened at the Cherry Lane Theatre, New York, 29
December 1964.

November 4, 1964

Dear Sam,

Thanks for your note and list of suggestions. You are right about my being up to my eyes or whatever in TINY ALICE but did manage to get together with Sidney last week to make a preliminary stab at your first letter. Can't say that we accomplished all that you wanted yet but it is a beginning but I will keep at him until we do—insofar as it is possible. Please forgive haste and brevity of my reply. We go into rehearsal next week. Jean and kids send their love.

Ever,
[Alan]

P.S. Will try to get a copy of ALICE to you. You might find it more to your taste than VIRGINIA WOOLF. Completely different both physically and metaphysically.

Paris
20.11.64

Dear Alan

Thanks for your letter.

I have thought a lot about that distressing couple. Of course the "sssh" without the look has no meaning. And I don't see how we can eliminate them completely. Again my feeling is to reduce them to their essential functions, the "sssh" & the look, cutting out O's inspection of them and their actual exit from frame.

Harold rang from London very warm about the film & with some good points. He finds Buster's look of horror at the best unconvincing and thinks it might be shortened. I'm inclined to agree. With his suggestions for a sound track ("selective natural sounds") I disagree entirely, as with Fred Jordan's[1] arguments in favour of some kind of sound. I am quite decided now that I want it silent.

I look forward to TINY ALICE. There is talk of a revival of *Godot* very soon at the Royal Court, directed by Anthony Page. He is coming to see me this weekend. I am very sceptical, but George sounds keen and so it will probably come off.[2]

It's great news I'll be seeing you next Spring. I've been having bad trouble with my mouth, but the worst is over and I'll be all right.

Happy & successful rehearsals. Greetings to all.

Yours ever
Sam

1. Fred Jordan and Richard (Dick) Seaver, both associated with Barney Rosset at Grove Press, edited *Evergreen Review*.

2. Opened 30 December 1964; directed by Anthony Page, assisted by SB, designed by Timothy O'Brien. Alfred Lynch (Estragon), Nicol Williamson (Vladimir), Jack MacGowran (Lucky), Paul Curran (Pozzo), Kirk Martin (A Boy). This revival presented the first unexpurgated text. Anthony Page (b. India, 1935), British stage, film, and television director; appointed assistant director, Royal Court Theatre, 1958, Artistic Director, 1970; directed *Krapp's Last Tape* and *Not I*, 1970, assisted by SB.

December 9, 1964

Dear Sam,

Just heard from Judith about your operation and I am glad you are well.[1] We were all terribly worried and concerned with your condition. I only hope that you will have a chance to take things a little easier for a while or even to get away for a vacation. I know you are going to London for the GODOT production but perhaps after that.

Dick Barr is coming to Paris next week and I believe wants to talk to you about the "Beckett canon", which is currently planned to open the Cherry Lane in the fall. The idea is to start with Renaud playing HAPPY DAYS for two or three weeks, then to follow with Ruth White in the English version of the same; and then limited runs of ENDGAME, a double bill of KRAPP and PLAY; and then GODOT for as long as it can run. The idea would be that I would direct most or all of these. What are the chances of you coming for any part of the time? That is late August and September?

I have not seen film lately. I understand there have been some changes made in accordance with your last letter but I simply haven't been able to get away from TINY ALICE. Have you read the script?

Jean and the kids join in wishing you well.

Alan

1. SB had a cyst removed from his palate.

Jan. 4, 1965

Dear Sam,

How good of you to write about Vickie! She was very pleased when I showed her Uncle Sam's letter. Actually, as I believe Judith wrote to you, she is much much better; and we are all breathing a bit more easily after a siege of a couple of weeks which was the darkest we have ever experienced. Without going into too much detail about the accident, what happened was that Vickie's head hit both windshield and dashboard, causing various injuries to the skull and face. For a while we thought the brain was damaged or the ear, and then the eyes. But, luckily, all seems to be clearing up—including the eyes—and we are now hopeful of complete recovery. It's amazing how quickly kids get over their bangs and blue marks. She has been home the past couple of days and in exceedingly good spirits. Soon, she will be able to read again and get back in school. Although we are wrapping her in cautious cotton to keep her from the possibility of any bump at all.

Jeannie is fine too, and in good morale, though her wrist will be in a cast another month or so. David was unhurt, and my few slight bruises went totally unnoticed. We were damn lucky to be alive at all, as it turned out. The car is fairly badly smashed. But the main thing is that we are all together and well. So the long nightmare rapidly recedes into memory.[1]

Had to go on rehearsing with TINY ALICE, and perhaps a good thing I had something to do. The show opened a week ago, and the notices mixed but provocative enough for business to be good, and we are hopeful of a run. A strange play—we did a lot of work on it in rehearsal—but marvelously well written, I think, and with an ambiance of its own. We have an in-joke that says that Tiny Alice is really GODOT, but I'm not sure you would approve.

Am taking things a bit easy until starting on Tennessee Williams duo in a couple of weeks, opening in March.[2] After that, I hope, nothing. And we're probably not going anywhere this spring, just staying put in the new house. Yugoslavia, I've put off for a year if they'll have me then. Vickie really needs rest for a year, and I don't want to go off on my own. There is now a chance that TINY ALICE may go to London in the summer, and I may have to come over for a couple of weeks; but we don't know about that. Will keep you posted in advance if I am coming.

Plans proceed apace for Beckett Festival in the fall. Renaud Sept. 13–26, Ruth White Sept. 28 for 2 or 3 weeks,[3] then *Endgame et al*, culminating in GODOT. . . . Haven't seen FILM since Nov. but Milton[4] is setting up screening for me next week. . . . Heard from Judith that you might have to have another operation; hope all is well and that you are taking care of yourself. Please . . . . House looks great, especially with Giacometti properly framed and hung.[5] We miss you. Jean and both kids join me in all good wishes for New Year and always, and thanks again for thinking of us.

[Alan]

1. "long nightmare": see letter of 18 September 1963, n. 4.
2. *Slapstick Tragedy* (*The Mutilated* and *The Gnädiges Fraulein*).
3. In *Happy Days*.
4. Milton Perlman, a film producer, friend and associate of Barney Rosset's, produced *Film*.
5. By Alberto Giacometti (1901–1966), a full-length drawing of SB, untitled.

Ussy
13.1.65

Dear Alan

Many thanks for your letter of Jan. 4. Delighted to have such better news of Vickie and you all.

Back here at last after 3 months without seeing place—and the worse for wear. London was very hard work. We could have done with another week. It was well received on the whole and seems to be doing well. Williamson (Vladimir) the most interesting of the cast. Jacky not really a Lucky, but it was good having him in the show.[1]

Glad there's a chance of a good run for *T. A.* I didn't much like it when I read it. But too tired and stupid perhaps to get it, shall have another go.

It's good news that the Festival plans hold. I won't come over, dear Alan. I have an idea for a new short play (20 minutes). Terribly complex. It might be ready for the Fall.[2]

. . . .[3]

Do hope you come over in the summer with *T. A.* The new cut of FILM has arrived, but was still in Customs when I left Paris. Robbe-Grillet[4] saw it in Paris and liked it.

Hope to stay here till end of month. Wish it could be for ever. Forgive cheerless letter. Much love to you all.

Sam

1. Nicol Williamson (b. 1938), Scottish actor, director, in Anthony Page's *Waiting for Godot* at Royal Court Theatre, opened 30 December 1964; Jack MacGowran.
   2. "new short play": *Come and Go.*
   3. SB says that his palate has not healed.
   4. Alain Robbe-Grillet (b. 1927), French novelist, literary adviser for Les Éditions de Minuit, leader of the avant-garde New Novelists.

30 Scenic Drive
Hastings-on-Hudson
New York
January 21, 1965

Dear Sam,

Glad to hear from you and delighted to know you are working on a new play. Will be waiting with baited breath.

Had heard GODOT went very well. Hope we do as well for you in the fall. Can imagine how glad you are to be back at Ussy. I do hope that your mouth feels better and that any further work on it won't be too bad.

Saw FILM Tuesday after quite an interval and have some definite reactions which I would like to list for you separately for your approval or disapproval and then we can make the final changes based on your reactions.

Would appreciate your comments as soon as you have seen your copy of the film. I expect to go into rehearsal with the Tennessee Williams on February 8th so there will be a little time between now and then.[1]

The general reaction of people who see FILM is consistently favorable, and I am delighted to hear that Robbe-Grillet also liked it. I am looking forward to the completion of the Pinter and Ionesco sections. Barney thinks the whole thing might be completed by this summer.[2] Because of our accident, I won't be going to Yugoslavia to direct but there is a possibility of my coming over to London for a brief period in which case I will come to see you if only for a day or so.

TINY ALICE continues. Lots of people, of course, don't like it so don't worry about your own reaction. I think the fellow in *The Village Voice* was right when he called it a brilliant first draft.[3]

Take care of yourself Sam and get some rest. Jean and the rest of the family are all doing very well and join me in sending their love.

Best,

[Alan]

1. AS explained that this production of two one-act plays that kept appearing and disappearing was something called either *Slapstick Tragedy* or *Slapstick Tragedies*, depending on how their author, Tennesee Williams, felt (*Entrances*, 365).

2. See letter of 26 May 1964, n. 2.

3. "the fellow": Michael Smith, "Tiny Alice," *Village Voice*, 14 January 1965.

January 21, 1965

From: Alan Schneider re FILM—January 21, 1965[1]

1. The basic problem of the film is to strengthen and clarify the POV business, that is O and E. And to make sure that we know that the camera is *subjective* [handwritten] in both instances. Anything that strengthens this should be done wherever possible. The first place which would help, I am still convinced, is to dissolve from the eye to the wall shot. A dissolve is immediately understood as a connective device. The cut we have now is not (a dissolve is technically and economically possible).

2. I still feel that the closed eye (reptilian texture) should last a few seconds longer before it opens. This is terribly effective but now happens much too fast.

3. I would like to synchronize the eye and the wall. If the eye is moving then we should have the next shot on a moving wall. If the eye is not, the wall should be stationary. At the moment the connection between the two is not clear though a dissolve would help.

4. Are you not bothered by that first cut in O's movement along the wall? I am and do not understand why Sidney replaced a previous shot we had for this sequence.

5. I don't mind at all not having O's POV of wall but I do miss not having the slightest O-POV of Jostled Couple, just as a frame of reference for all subsequent O shots.

6. Agree that Jostled Couple much less offensive but I think to match

Flower Woman and O at end we should hold look of horror shot longer and let Couple start out of frame before swishing back to O.

7. For same reason (strengthening of O contrasting POV's) I still miss the shot of pulse in lobby. I understand that hands don't exactly match previous E shot, although no one knows that; but mail-boxes being visible doesn't clash since in E shot they are masked.

8. At the moment, therefore, the first O-POV shot is Flower Woman. I feel we don't realize as strongly that it is O's POV unless we have the one or two previous O-POV shots before now of Couple and of pulse.

9. This is a new idea. Would like added O-POV of window in second series (I believe). This would be part of build up to his covering window eventually.

10. Animal scene doesn't seem as funny to me when there are bits and pieces taken out of it as there are now. The more constantly E observes O's action the better. We should cut only for O's POV animal in basket each time, and then back immediately to O's movement at the same place where we cut. I found the sequence much more confusing and less funny with bits and pieces taken out.

11. The dolly shot of the God still ends up off center. We have always been told that they would print one of centered dolly shots in reverse; if you still prefer, we should do that.

12. New idea. What would you think if on the last O shot of E we started with the eye open rather than dollying in and then arbitrarily having it opening? I feel that would be strong.

13. I think if I could see the film in a more leisurely manner on a movieola I might want to change timing of some of the cuts, such as O-POV of God the second time, etc. Just a question of relating the cut more specifically of O's action of looking.

1. SB wrote comments in the margin in response to some of the following questions: "1. OK. If first time—each time dissolve & wall moving; 3. OK; 4. ?; 6. Yes; 7. Put back pulse; 11. Prefer centre; 12. Yes?"

Ussy
27.1.65

Dear Alan

Thanks for your letter and list of suggestions.

When I came here a fortnight ago the film had got as far as the

Customs at Orly. I gave what information I could to Barney's agent in Paris and asked for the film to be delivered, in my absence, to the Éditions de Minuit. I have no news of it. As soon as I get hold of it I'll go over it with movieola—and your list—and write you again then.

The little play is written. A page & a half, 4 minutes playing time. It was written for the opening of John Calder's new Soho theatre and I have promised him first performance.[1] God knows when that will be. Here it is [in] any case. Without *colères simples*.[2] You could always use it in any case, if you think it worth it, in your Fall Festival.

Godot is said to be doing well. *Oh les B. J.* is finished for the moment. But she'll play it from time to time.[3]

. . . .[4]

So happy to have good news of V.

Love to you all
Sam

1. *Come and Go*, a "dramaticule," written in English and dedicated to Calder, SB's English publisher of all the work except the plays; Managing Director of Calder and Boyars, founded 1949, and later John Calder publications; editor of *Beckett at Sixty: A Festschrift*, 1967, and two SB *Readers*. French trans. by SB, *Va et vient* in *Comédie et actes divers*, 1966, *Come and Go*, 1967.
2. "*colères simples*": downright fits of wrath.
3. "*Oh les B. J*": *Oh les beaux jours*; "she": Madeleine Renaud.
4. SB says he is "so-so."

30 Scenic Drive
Hastings-on-Hudson
New York
February 4, 1965

Dear Sam,

Thanks for sending me the new play. It is simply lovely and I will certainly plan to include it in the Fall "Beckett Festival". At the moment we are trying to line up casts for the entire series.

Sorry to hear about the problems of your film in customs. Barney mentioned something about it but I had no idea it was still going on. I suggested that he contacted Malraux[1] immediately (Ha!).

I do hope you are feeling better and that the sore is improving. We are all quite concerned here.

Into rehearsal Monday with the new Williams if the money is all raised by then.

Vicki continues to improve. Jean sends her love. Still hoping to see you somehow in late spring or summer.

All the best.

Ever,

[Alan]

1. André Malraux, Minister for Culture at this period.

Paris
3.3.65

Dear Alan

Thanks for your letter.

Thought Buster might like to have enclosed, if you'd be good enough to forward it to him.

Berlin was grim and *Godot* at the Schiller mediocre. The famous Minetti as Pozzo was quite unbelievable & gave the worst performance as Pozzo I have ever seen. It was a relief to get away.[1]

I went again to London for a few days to help Jack with his record for one-man.[2] That was worth while.

Glad you liked *Come & Go*. Have not yet heard from John whether he wants world-first or merely first in England.

Recovered *Film* at last and will be movieoling it—for the last time—next week, in the light of your notes. Shall write you then and leave the final cut to you & Sidney. Pleased to hear that Robbe-Grillet liked it.[3]

Bit of quiet from now on I hope and plenty of Ussy.

Love to you all.

Ever

Sam

1. *Waiting for Godot* opened at the Schiller-Theater, 25 February 1965, directed by Deryk Mendel, assisted by SB, designed by H. W. Lenneweit. Stefan Wigger (Estragon), Horst Bollmann (Vladimir), Klaus Herm (Lucky), Bernhard Minetti (Pozzo), Gerhard Sprunkel (The Boy).

2. *Beginning to End,* assembled and adapted by Jack MacGowran from SB's works, directed by Patrick Garland, broadcast by BBC 1, Monitor, 23 February 1965.

3. SB has forgotten that it was he who told AS that Robbe-Grillet liked the play.

12.3.65

Dear Alan

Herewith notes on your notes. Worked on film last night. Won't do any more on it now. I didn't feel we had gained much with latest cut, in some places perhaps even lost. After opening eye and pan of wall till we get into that room the fact is there is so much wrong with the material that no ingenuity of cutting can redeem it. All we can aim at is to get through it with as little scathe as possible. It is impossible in any case to arrive at anything this way, exchanging notes. It's all such a hairbreadth affair at this stage that the only method would be to get together with Sidney again in the cutting room. So no more about it beyond this one point raised yesterday by Hodeir (who by the way now agrees there should be no sound): the sound made by the silent sound track which he describes as a kind of faint crackling getting more audible and disturbing as the copy gets more worn. If this is so I think we should consider sacrifying [*for* sacrificing?] the "hsst!" and having no sound track at all.

Do you want the film back? I should like to keep it another week or so and show it to a few friends.

Shall write you a better letter soon, from Ussy I hope. I had a hard time in Berlin with *Godot* rehearsals for the Schiller and am pretty well bet.[1] Must have a long time away from it all now.

Love to Jean and the children and to Sidney and Nina.

Ever
Sam [handwritten]

1. Worth trying.
2. OK.
3. Feel wall should be moving when first seen.
4. Agree something very wrong here. The second part of run, after cut, is quite out of keeping with first. The light changes completely. The difference is startling.
5. Quick O shot of couple if you like. I feel E shot of the three after collision is too long. And suggest when E comes back to them after leaving O on his way to the corner that scene should begin with close-up of man. Looked carefully at this several times and feel sure it would be an improvement and that existing opening shots of this scene are superfluous.
7. Put back O pulse if you like.
9. OK.

10. Do whatever you like with this. For me it will never work.

11. Should prefer centre if not too much trouble.

12. The eye widening in midshot always disturbed me. You're probably right—though it's a pity to lose dolly.

Something wrong with timing of O mirror shot before he covers, a kind of hesitation before it comes which seems wrong and then I think the shot held too long.

I am on the whole pleased with the film, having accepted its imperfections, for the most part perceptible only to insiders, and discern how in some strange way it gains by its deviations from the strict intention and developes something better. The last time I found myself submitting, far from the big crazy idea, to a strangeness and beauty of pure image. The few reactions I have had from others are strongly positive. All sound is definitely out as far as I am concerned, except for the hssh.

1. "bet": an Irish way of saying "beaten," done for. The notes at the end of this letter answer AS letter of 21 January 1965.

30 Scenic Drive
Hastings-on-Hudson
New York
March 24, 1965

Dear Sam,

Have your letter and the notes, and have transmitted them to Barney. I am in rehearsal at the moment but as soon as possible we'll all get down to having a look at the film once more. Won't bother you again for a while. Although it would be marvelous if, as you say, Sidney, you and I could have one more bash at it together. On either side of the ocean.

Hope to be in London for a week or so in May and will try to catch a glimpse of you.

How's Jack MacGowran's TV taping? (Would love to see a script of that sometime.)

Do take care, forget about us for awhile, and get back to the moles. All the best from all of us including Vicki—who is much better.

P.S. I hope you won't mind if we include COME AND GO in the

Beckett Canon when we do it. It is absolutely lovely. Plans for the Canon remain fluid depending on availability of actors and scheduling at Cherry Lane. We are definitely doing the Renaud HAPPY DAYS for two weeks in September, followed by Ruth White for two weeks.

[Alan]

Paris
10.4.65

Dear Alan

Thanks for yrs. of March 24.

Showed film to two 2 small groups of friends. Very good reaction—even allowing for partiality. Lindon in particular enthusiastic all for the silence. The tension and beauty of image held them and technical imperfections became minor. Someone suggested doing sound track in silent chamber to eliminate crackle. Anything in this?

What wd. you think of final credits against opening eye shot?

Shall ask Jack to send you script of his TV programme.

Have asked Calder does he want world first or only London. Shall let you know as soon as he replies. Have made a few slight additions. Shall let you have them in due course.

Giorni Felici went well in Turin. Laura Adani—directed by Blin.[1]

. . . .[2]

Rejoice at thought of seeing you [in] May.

Love to all
Sam

1. Produced by the Teatro Stabile, *Giorni felici (Happy Days)* opened at the Teatro Gobetti, 2 April 1965, directed by Roger Blin, designed by Matias. Laura Adani (Winnie), Franco Passatore (Willie).

2. SB has more "mouth trouble."

Ussy
27.4.65

Dear Alan

Shall be sending you soon slightly altered version of *Come & Go*. I have now got things clear with John Calder. He does not hold out for world first so you are free to include it in the series at the Cherry Lane. Is there any chance of your coming to Europe? I had an evening with the Seavers and they were not sure.[1] Next week I'll be seeing Barney on his way back from Formentor Prize.[2] Perhaps he'll have news of other films. I'm working on a short piece for TV at the moment.[3] Delighted to have such good news of Vicky. Love to you all.

Sam

1. "Seavers": Dick and Jeannette.
2. In May 1961 an international group of publishers awarded SB, jointly with Jorge Luis Borges, the *Prix International des Editeurs* or *Prix Formentor*, worth $10,000. Apparently Rosset attended their 1965 meeting.
3. *Eh Joe*, SB's first play written for television and for Jack MacGowran.

30 Scenic Drive
Hastings-on-Hudson
New York
May 9, 1965

Dear Sam,

Just emerged from the TV control room where we have been "redoing" ACT WITHOUT WORDS II.[1]

I must say that even under the difficulties and confusions that existed—the lack of time to rehearse on and off camera, the necessity of using the same props and costumes (although we changed these quite a bit), the necessity of using the same actors—I enjoyed it and felt that it came off reasonably well. As I just said to Judith, at least it was clear, sincere, and Beckett—in contrast to the jumble and glop of the first version, which had no relation to what you had written. We are editing on Wednesday, but there seem to be no great problems in that area. We have two complete taped versions plus some bits and pieces that we had to do over when one of the actors reversed a sequence. It runs between 12 and 13 minutes.

I am grateful to you for straightening me out on that opening stuff. I think you will find the production carries out your wishes. Perhaps it will be possible some day for you to see it. It is on TV tape rather than film which makes it more difficult to carry around and show. This is the version that will be used in all subsequent showings.

I am still not clear when I am coming to Europe. If I do the Tennessee Williams plays I should be departing in the next few days. If I don't I will be coming in June in any case and will spend some time in London and will certainly get to Paris, giving you plenty of advance warning. Thousands of things I would like to talk to you about but will save them for when I get to Paris or Ussy, whichever is more convenient for you.

Vicki continues to improve, and Jean also. The family joins me in sending you their love. There is a strong possibility that they may be coming with me to London.

With all best wishes and regards,

[Alan]

1. First shown with George Bernard Shaw's *How He Lied to Her Husband* and W. B. Yeats's *Calvary* in *Irish Triple Bill,* on Esso Theater U.S.A., sponsored by Standard Oil Co., produced by David Susskind and Daniel Melnick, Channel 5, New York, 17 February 1965; introduced by Walter Kerr with Raymond Biere, Donald Moffat, and Roscoe Lee Browne.

May 30, 1965

Dear Sam,

Forgive this hasty note. Still trying to work out when I'm coming to Europe and Paris.

Trouble is there are so many ifs-ands-and-buts in the situation here that plans keep changing from day to day. Only constant is that I must be in Israel evening of June 18th (flying in from Athens), and that somewhere before that I want to be in London, and perhaps a little town in Germany where Lotte Lenya will be doing MOTHER COURAGE on June 12 and 13th.[1]

Judith tells me you are going to hospital on June 15th, which is just about the time I figured I'd be in Paris. Is this a bad time to come? Would you not want to see anyone? Or could I visit you after the operation? Have we got the date right?

And, most important, how are *you?*

Plans proceeding here for Beckett season in the fall, although lots of problems mostly casting. We are definitely doing two weeks of Renaud-Barrault, followed by two of Ruth White. Then, trying to cast GODOT and, perhaps, ENDGAME. (At the moment, there are plans afoot for immediate production of KRAPP[2] and ZOO at Cherry Lane, to follow current production which is not doing well.) I hope to know more by the time I get to Paris.

TINY ALICE closed. V WOOLF still running in London. And so it goes.

Do take care of yourself, and I hope to be seeing you very soon.

All the best,
[Alan]

1. Lotte Lenya (1900?–1981), Austrian actress and singer, married Kurt Weill, played Jenny in his *Threepenny Opera*, played Mother Courage at the Ruhr Festspiele Reckling-hausen (the Ruhrfestspielhaus).

2. Opened 8 June 1965, directed by AS, designed by William Ritman. George Bartenief (Krapp).

Paris
2.6.65

Dear Alan

Thanks for yours of May 30.

My plans uncertain too. . . .[1] Have written a short (18 minutes approx.) TV piece which I want to show you and talk to you about.[2] Not worth while sending if we are to meet so soon. Suzanne is in Prague and no definite plans until she returns. . . .

Love to you all
Sam

I'm all right whatever that is.

———

Greatly moved by what you said of my unworthy person in the *Tulane Drama Review*.[3]

1. "plans uncertain": the operation on SB's mouth has been postponed; he and Suzanne may go to the mountains.

2. *Eh Joe*, "A Piece for Television," 1967, French trans. by SB, *Dis Joe*, 1966.

3. "Reality Is Not Enough," *Tulane Drama Review*, 9 (Spring 1965), 118–152; an interview with the editor, Richard Schechner.

July 9th, 1965

Dear Sam,

Back home after Israel and off in wilds of Ithaca, sunning and raising three million dollars.

Certainly enjoyed seeing you and spending all that time with you in Paris, not to mention finally seeing Ussy. The latter stays with me more than I can tell you, have described it in detail to Jean. And the trip up and back.

Israel was remarkable, a land of violent contrasts and even more violent emotions. Can't say much about the conference, they're never much, but the people one meets in between, this time a Finn and a Rumanian, make the whole thing worth while. This time there was also the country, and we did manage to get to Jerusalem, Haifa, Sea of Galilee, etc. My biggest disappointment was the shrill tourism of Nazareth; but the fantastic building and planting in the midst of what is a desert impressed me most everywhere else.

Talked a great deal about your work there, and there was even some talk about my doing GODOT in Tel Aviv next summer. All the theatres there invited me, and I may come back and do one show there next June, bringing Jean and kids, and going to Greece or somewhere for a month afterward. To get final rest for the big plunge into Ithaca.

Anyhow.

Wanted to say God Bless on the operation, hoping you had a pleasant and restful month away from us all in Austria, and that you feel a bit refreshed. We are all anxiously awaiting results of July 15th. Judith pleased that you liked the clock, and hoping all will be well with you. All of us.

Jean and kids send their love.

[Alan]

September 2, 1965

Dear Sam,

Just heard indirectly via Barney and Judith that all was proceeding apace in Venice but that you were not coming there—I *had* a sneaking suspicion you might not—so that Judith would be holding the fort, or even defending it against the forces of 'General' Keaton.[1]

Would have loved to have been there myself (Is that grammar?) but still in rehearsal with MacLeish.[2] By the way, did you ever meet him in Paris in the Twenties? He was there and knew Joyce somewhat.

Did you get to see the film?

Are you all right? You know, we all worry about you especially when we don't hear any hard news, only rumors. Did the operation help? Do you have a good doctor? Can we be of any help? Are you all right? (Repeat, as in PLAY)

Have been talking about EH JOE to various people. Summer is a bad time for anything to happen, but after Labor Day, I'll send out a couple of copies to reliable sources. I'm assuming Jackie will be available sometime if and when we do it. Also, what do you think of Rosemary Harris doing the girl's voice? Too young? She's absolutely marvelous in the MacLeish; and she and I have talked at great length about PLAY in NY and London. She worships you, but don't let that stand in your way.[3]

HAPPY DAYS, French and English, being much looked forward to here. But we have had a bit of a blow regarding the Cherry Lane's subsequent use for Beckett Canon and all other matters. Messrs. Barr and Wilder are evidently so broke at the moment, they have had to give up the lease at the conclusion of HAPPY DAYS. Everyone is miserable, but nothing to be done short of taking over the theatre myself—which I've thought about but too expensive. So, unless we find some other absolutely suitable place, we shall have to delay once more. Sorry. Am hoping they'll make some money this year so they can have it again—but am doubly worried about Albee's MALCOLM earning any or even being done.[4]

Did you ever read Harold's HOMECOMING?

But, mainly, just wanted to be assured you were not too bad, were off at USSY away from too many visiting Americans, and were embarked on another project. Will keep you posted on EH JOE and all other matters.

Best from us all,
[Alan]

1. Venice Biennale; a reference to Buster Keaton's film *The General*, 1927.

2. Archibald MacLeish (1892–1982), American poet and dramatist. *Herakles* opened at the University of Michigan, 24 October 1965.

3. Rosemary Harris (b. 1930), English actress (see letter of 11 April 1964, n. 2).

4. Albee's *Malcolm*, an adaptation of James Purdy's satiric novel of the same title, opened at the Schubert Theatre, New York, 11 January 1966.

8.9.65

Dear Alan

Thanks for your two letters. I didn't see your latest cut—it sounds fine—and didn't go to Venice. Judith has held the fort marvellously. I'm afraid it's been a strain for her. She has sent me a lot of cuttings. Quite foolish, not a gleam, but friendly mostly. It shared some kind of mention with other films. I am glad it is to be shown at the Cinematheque. Buster was there parading his incomprehension.[1] Ah well! But you will have had all this news and more from Barney. I do hope you are both pleased. I am.

So sorry to hear that Barr & Wilder are losing the Cherry Lane. I thought they were prospering. I'm not sure about Jack's plans. I know he wants to do *Eh Joe* in London as soon as it can be arranged. I'm waiting impatiently for a date. . . .[2] Serreau is bringing *Play* to Venice next month, but minus both Seyrig & Lonsdale, which means serious rerehearsal. Of course I'd be delighted to have Rosemary do the voice. She was excellent in *Play*, nearly as good as Billie Whitelaw, who may do the voice in London.

Last days of peace here now. Back to Paris on the 13th. I dread the prospect.

Much love to you all
Sam

[in left margin] I never met MacLeish.

I liked Harold's *Homecoming*. His best I think since *The Caretaker.* He has just been in Paris looking at his rehearsals.

1. See letter of 11 April 1964, n. 3.
2. SB has to fit in the operation on his mouth.

Paris
22.9.65

Dear Alan

Sorry to hear N.Y. critics so disapproving.[1] Venice was favourable on the whole. But entirely foolish. Have these people no eyes?

Judith has just gone through to London. Depressed. But perked up a bit while here.

So glad you liked Madeleine.[2]

. . . .[3]

May go to London next month for *Come & Go* and for *Eh Joe*. But nothing definite yet. Jack is free to do the latter now. But hard to get a date from BBC.

Suzanne just back from Milan where Laura Adani is having a hit in *Happy Days*. She had done it already in Turin.[4]

Best of luck with *Sloane*.[5] Regards to Rosemary. So glad to have her for that voice.

Love to you all
Sam

Latest news of George not good. Still in hospital & very critical.[6]

1. In a letter of 15 September 1965, AS told SB of some unfavorable reviews.
2. Madeleine Renaud played Winnie in *Happy Days*, presented by Theatre 66 (Richard Barr, Clinton Wilder, Edward Albee) at the Cherry Lane Theatre, opened 14 September 1965, for 32 performances. Directed by Roger Blin, designed by Matias, with Jean-Louis Barrault (Willie). Ruth White and Wyman Pendleton opened two weeks later, on 28 September, for 16 performances.
3. SB comments on the operation on his mouth.
4. *Giorni felici* opened at the Teatro Gerolamo, Milan, 18 September 1965 (see letter of 10 April 1965, n. 1).
5. Joe Orton's *Entertaining Mr. Sloane* opened at the Lyceum Theatre, New York, 12 October 1965, designed by William Ritman.
6. George Devine had had a heart attack.

January 18, 1966

Dear Sam,

Happy New 1966! Meant to write earlier but seem to be constantly in rehearsal with something or other, usually other. MALCOLM finally opened and clobbered; critics really pounce on Edward when he's vulnerable.[1] It was not good—for him—but if anyone else had written it, would have been respectfully received. But one good thing, maybe he'll stop doing adaptations.

Now, deep in T. Williams, lovely one-acts, and fine cast. Open Feb. 22, and then I hope nothing for a time. Israel this summer, with the family, to do new Weiss play about Auschwitz[2]—then two weeks in Greece before heading for home. Maybe, maybe, through Paris on way there or back.

Big news here is that we have someone who wants to do EH JOE. The only decent cultural and educational station, the logical place, and they responded very favorably.[3] Definitely want to do it if you agree this spring. Several problems: Casting: Rosemary Harris wants to do it, and they and I want her—we must only wait for her Broadway show to open in March. They cannot bring over Jackie for one simple reason. TV actors' union prevents anyone being imported unless of technical star calibre, which means paying $1500 per week, way beyond budget. (In fact, budget and payments are nominal, only $150 for first rights; will go up if redone or sold later.) I told them it was all conditional on getting Jackie—although actually I didn't know what exact situation was. Assume he's doing BBC version. When? With whom?. . . . Alternatives: Cyril Cusack, who will be here for something else and therefore has some sort of 'resident alien' status; I think he's difficult and not that good. Pat Magee, who is here in *Marat/Sade,* but who does not have any resident status and may be going back just as Rosemary is free. Third and most possible, an ex-English actor whom you may or may not know, George Rose,[4] marvelous face and comedian, the 'common man' in MAN FOR ALL SEASONS, Dogberry in MUCH ADO at Stratford, etc. etc. We think he's available and good. The only question is whether you know him or are agreeable to anyone besides Jackie.

Just tell me the truth. Would you rather it were done only on BBC, and then marketed here? Would you want to wait until some other more affluent sponsorship appears—one which could afford Jackie? Would you be willing to accept Rose? (He's well known in London.) Mind you, we're not even sure we have Rose although we're pretty certain about Rosemary.

More important, how are *you*? Have heard only via Judith, Barney et al for much too long now. The operation? The writing? Can't believe it's been ten years since GODOT. Are you going to be in London for a while?

All reasonably the same here, though haven't seen too much of the family since Aug. 1. Kids thriving, Jean surviving. All send their love, would love to see you. How can we lure you over? Can we get you to write a play for the Ithaca Festival?????

All the best.

[Alan]

1. *Malcolm* ran for a week. On 12 January 1966 there were unfavorable reviews: Norman Nadel, *NY World-Telegram;* Stanley Kauffman, *NY Times;* Walter Kerr, *NY Herald-Tribune;* Richard Watts, Jr., *NY Post;* John Chapman, *Daily News;* John McClain, *NY Journal American.*

2. *Slapstick Tragedy* by Tennessee Williams finally opened at the Longacre Theatre, New York, 22 February 1966. The Peter Weiss (1916–1982) play was *Die Ermittlung (The Investigation)*.

3. PBS, WNDT-TV, New York.

4. George Rose (b. 1926), associated with Old Vic, later with Royal Court Theatre.

Paris
11.2.66

Dear Alan

Forgive delay in answering yours of Jan. 18. Have been up to my eyes since Xmas. Preparing & shooting here film of *PLAY*.[1] Then London for *Eh Joe* with Jack[2] and a record and poetry recording with same.[3] Back now finishing film and rehearsing new show at Odéon. *Play, Come & Go,* Pinget's *Hypothèse* and two Ionesco shorts—*Délire à Deux* & *La Lacune*.[4]

Eh Joe went well in London. Jack marvellous. Siân Phillips (voice) adequate and a very good team. Really pleased with result. It will go out in the next few months, but no definite date so far. Please not Cusack. Pat of course if he can. If not by all means Rose. And love to have Rosemary. Voice very low throughout—plenty of venom. Face just listening hard and brain agonizing. Smile at very end when voice stops (having done it again). Of course I'd prefer Jacky to anyone. It was written for him.

Congratulations on Tours award.[5] Those of the *Play* crew who saw it were impressed—and they are hardboiled. I'm glad it's free to be shown with *Play*. Making this was exciting and I'm pleased with result. 10 more days of [?]finicking and lab and there'll be a screening with *Film* for friends.

Going to Stuttgart next month to give a hand with *Eh Joe* there. Deryk Mendel playing Joe. Not looking forward to it.[6]

No more writing needless to say all these past months. Hope to get back to it in April. . . .[7]

Do try and stop off here on your way to or from Israel. Won't have any new work for you. But lots to tell you and ask you and talk about.

Much love to Jean & the children.

Ever
Sam

1. *Play (Comédie)* directed by Marin Karmitz, Jean Ravel, and SB, a filmed version of the Jean-Marie Serreau production of 11 June 1964, was shown at the Venice Biennale in September 1966.

2. *Eh Joe,* broadcast by BBC 2, 4 July 1966, produced by Michael Bakewell, directed by Alan Gibson and SB (uncredited). Jack MacGowran (Joe), Siân Phillips (Voice). Siân Phillips (b. 1934), Welsh actress, then married to Peter O'Toole.

3. "record": *MacGowran Speaking Beckett,* Claddagh Records, CCT-3. Supervised by SB with musical accompaniment by Edward Beckett on flute, John Beckett on harmonium, and SB striking the gong. "poetry recording": *MacGowran Reading Beckett's Poetry,* supervised by SB. Claddagh Records, an Irish firm founded by Garech Browne. SB also supervised a BBC recording of a selection of his poems read by MacGowran and Denys Hawthorne, *Poems by Samuel Beckett I and II,* produced by Martin Esslin, broadcast by BBC Third Programme, 8 March and 24 November 1966.

4. The "new show," *Va et vient (Come and Go),* opened at the Odéon-Théâtre de France, Petite salle, 28 February 1966, directed Jean-Marie Serreau, assisted by SB. Annie Bertin (Flo), Madeleine Renaud (Vi), Simone Valère (Ru). With *Comédie,* directed by Jean-Marie Serreau, designed by Matias. Eléonore Hirt (W1), Danielle van Bercheycke (W2), Michael Lonsdale (M). SB not only assisted Serreau with both productions, particularly *Va et vient,* but is credited as the "director" of the latter. On 18 October 1965 SB had directed Pierre Chabert in Robert Pinget's *L'Hypothèse* at the Musée d'Art Moderne (Biennale de Paris). *The Hypothesis* resembles *Krapp's Last Tape* in that a writer-protagonist reacts to another aspect of himself, in this case through films of his face. Its revival with both *Va et vient* and *Comédie* was part of the Beckett-Pinget-Ionesco *Spectacle,* 14 March 1966.

5. Tours Film Prize for *Film.*

6. *Eh Joe (He Joe)* first broadcast in German at Süddeutscher Rundfunk, Stuttgart, 13 April 1966, directed by SB, designed by Matias, camera Horst Schella, Jim Lewis. Deryk Mendel (Joe), Nancy Illig (Voice).

7. SB comments on the results of his mouth operation.

March 29, 1966

Dear Sam,

Don't know whether you're in Paris or off elsewhere but hoping this gets to you.

Actually, hesitated to write before things here on EH JOE got more definite—we have had so many ups and downs—but as of today got the final call from WNDT, our 'educational' TV station, that all was set: Rosemary Harris, George Rose, an air date on April 18. Am having meetings the rest of this week to arrange rehearsals, setting, etc. Wish you were here, although you must be tired of traveling hither and yonder setting up productions. Also wish I could see the one you made for BBC with Jackie.

Have a few questions, for your reaction. The sooner the better.

1. Evidently, the whole play could be shot with one camera except for Joe's first moves, and even then I'm not sure what you mean by 'Cut to'. Is it because as he turns each time, you want the camera to stay behind him? (But *does* he turn each time?) Is it because you want simply a slightly different angle each time? Sorry to say, it's not clear. Because the action is continuous, and the only cut actually required is from behind Joe to in front of Joe. But obviously, you mean something there and although we may have talked about it last year, I'm not too sure now.

2. How slowly do you think Joe should move in that first series of moves? Seems to me he should have a definite rhythm, fairly slow one.

3. Assume her voice should be as close in perspective as possible, even those you say 'remote' in feeling. An inner voice from the past. *How* remote? (Did you find you had to vary rhythm at all?)

4. Anything based on London version (or others) that you would add or subtract from either script or directions?

George has marvelous mobile face, different from Jackie's, of course, but quite expressive in his own way. He was the finest Dogberry I ever saw. And Rosemary has her own special voice.

Apart from *Eh Joe*, wanted to surprise you with a birthday present of a tenth-anniversary off-Broadway GODOT, and proceeded in that direction past two weeks. But we have had great difficulty getting proper actors—all off in Hollywood or TV—and Cherry Lane got rented out from under us. But we did get some good casting ideas and leads, and the moment we can intend to do it even if not smack ten years after. I still say that if we can cast it right with an ensemble of actors, we should get a really good off-Broadway run.

See Judith fairly often and we drink to your health. Things are at sixes and sevens, much running about, little productivity. Hoping to hang on till summer when off to Israel and, I hope, at least a fleeting visit. Family and all. Will keep you posted.

Also how *Eh Joe* comes out. How are *you????* Can't believe it's been ten years.

Jean sends her love.

[Alan]

Paris
7.4.66

Dear Alan

Thanks for your letter.

"Cut" is a false direction. It is a single unbroken shot. The camera follows Joe from behind round the room and when he gets to the bed and sits down again he has his face turned towards camera now in position for the nine moves in. The opening shot is a long one (hold about 10 seconds) showing Joe hunched on bed and most of room (essential to see window, door and cupboard in this shot). Then camera moves in on Joe, losing cupboard. Joe's first move—takes off one slipper & starts taking off sock [handwritten at top]—sitting on bed, indicating he is going to bed, stops this advance of camera. When Joe moves to window camera follows and stops when Joe stops at window and during play there. Ditto from window to door, door to cupboard, cupboard to bed, camera always moving with Joe and stopping when he stops. Camera has to cheat a bit on cupboard to bed move so as not to get too close to Joe on bed and allow enough space for the nine moves in. It is a help if Joe sits on foot of bed for opening shot and at head when he comes back to it.

Joe must move fairly slowly to let camera catch up and then keep up as camera has more ground to cover (except on cupboard to bed move). The feeling is of camera sneaking behind him hugging walls. From move 5 onward camera's cue to move in is when Joe starts to relax and cue to stop when voice resumes.

Voice should be whispered. A dead voice in his head. Minimum of colour. Attacking. Each sentence a knife going in, pause for withdrawal, then in again. Dramatize by lengthening certain pauses within paragraphs as e.g. before "Imagine if you couldn't," "Imagine what in her mind," "That's love for you," and even within sentences as e.g. "Gets out . . . the Gillette," "Gets out . . . the tablets." Voice starts fading on "All right . . . You've had the best," but may be spoken at same level as rest and lessened technically. I decided that the underlining of certain words at the end was very difficult for the speaker and not good. So I simplified second last paragraph as follows:

"All right . . . You've had the best . . . Now imagine . . . Before she goes . . . Imagine . . . Face in the cup . . . Lips on a stone . . . Taking Joe with her . . . Light gone . . . 'Joe Joe' . . . No sound . . . To the stones . . . Say it you now, Joe . . . No one'll hear you . . . Say 'Joe', it parts the lips . . . Imagine the hands . . . Imagine . . . The solitaire . . . Against a stone

. . . Imagine the eyes . . . Spiritlight . . . Month of June . . . What year of your Lord? . . . The breasts . . . Imagine the breasts . . . In the stones . . . The hands . . . Before they go . . . Imagine the hands . . . Imagine . . . What are they at? . . . In the stones . . ."

I asked in London and Stuttgart for a smile at the end (oh not a real smile). He "wins" again. So ignore direction "Image fades, voice as before." Face still fully present till last "Eh Joe." Then smile and slow fade.

In London the only sound apart from the voice was that of curtains and opening and closing at window, door and cupboard. But in Stuttgart we added sound of steps as he moves round and made it interesting by his having one sock half off and one sock and slipper. Sock half off because at opening he was taking it off to go to bed when interrupted by sudden idea or sudden feeling that he hears a sound and had better make a last round to make sure all is well.

Dead black screens behind window, door and cupboard. All black outside. Black under bed.

Curtains drawn (closed) at opening. Drawing back of curtains, opening window, leaning out, banging window shut, drawing curtains to, all sudden and violent, especially at window.

Hope this some help.

. . . .[1]

Starting on *Eh Joe* again with Madeleine and Jean-Louis. Very tired. Nonstop theatre, film *(Play)*, TV and Radio since before Xmas. Forget what Ussy looks like. Forget what writing is about.

Hope you manage *Godot.*

I'll be around July, August and first half September and looking forward.

Love to you all & to Judith
Sam [handwritten]

["& to Judith" handwritten]

1. SB met his nephew Edward Beckett.

Paris
8.4.66

Dear Alan

1. He does not look directly at camera and is not aware of it. He is aware only of the voice. The eyes are turned inward, a listening look. It is however effective dramatically if at the very end, with the smile, he looks full at the objective for the first time.

2. Whisper *throughout*.

3. From parable of the rich man Luke 12.20. "Thou fool! This night thy soul shall be required of thee."

4. *Thout* misprint for *thou*.

Best
Sam

AVOCA(accent on O):   stress on *o* long as in po
A as in ma

Saturday, April 23, 1966

Dear Sam,

Apologies for the week's delay in writing after *Eh Joe* went on.[1] I had to practically dash out of the studio to catch a plane for Memphis and a speaking date at a University there; and all of this week I have been in Ithaca trying to raise all those millions we need for that classical repertory theatre we are hoping to open there—before 1984.

Well, it went on, twice in fact, and I haven't actually seen it yet except in the studio. There I was quite pleased, I think the best and most faithful of the three Beckett's I have had the good fortune to put on TV. GODOT had excellent sections, and Mostel and Meredith were fine; but everything was put together in too short a space of camera rehearsal, Meredith couldn't remember his lines, Kasznar was weak as Pozzo, etc.; ACT WITHOUT WORDS was more of a piece, but again not nearly enough camera time. An improvement on what had been done the first time, but I would have wanted one more take. For *Eh Joe,* somehow, there's little to complain of. Rosemary was just marvelous; I doubt if George Rose would please you (or me) as much as Jackie; but on camera he turned in an excellent sustained and developed performance. The total impact was considerable, in fact I think that the people involved had little idea how powerful it might be. The play ran somewhat longer than we had thought—mostly because I encouraged Rosemary to take her time. But I don't think you would have minded. Evidently Barney and Judith—and I know, Jean—were very happy. Just sorry you weren't able to be there. Maybe some day you'll be able to see a tape or kinescope.

Just for your curiosity, let me tell you a few of our adventures. We rehearsed about two weeks, sometimes both actors sometimes one, usually in Rosemary's apartment replete with tea and stories of PLAY in London. Lots of questions up and down, and your letters and telegram arrived all in good time, for which copious thanks. Then came camera day (the actors, of course, were playing in various plays at night), and both actors were late, Rosemary oversleeping or setting her clock wrong. Our set had been built the night before, studio not free until then (very much like set in FILM, bare, functional), and was still getting set up. Eventually both actors, and George to be made up, Rosemary to tape her voice. Because of low voice level, we picked up every bit of sound in the world, from air conditioners to ticking of distant clocks. Much scurrying to remedy this. Finally, hours later, Rosemary on tape. Then work with George for some hours to block action on set for first time. Eventually the taping. As it's all one shot, we could not go wrong in any particular without starting from the beginning. Well, after a false start or two with the camera, we got going and into it, absolutely beautifully, and George doing well. Got more than half way through when sound man in studio goofed with one of Rosemary's tapes, and we had to stop and START ALL OVER AGAIN! Everyone horrified because it had been so good. So we had coffee and small talk and gathered our forces and started again, all the way through, the tension building till we got through. Everyone felt it had gone well, some parts better some not so good as in first take; but we did not do another. Much release of tension when all over.

And so you have two English-language *Eh Joe*'s. Would love to see the other one and will perhaps this summer. We're off to Israel on May 15, not clear what happens on way back in July but we'll be [?coming] by.

[Alan]

1. *Eh Joe* broadcast by PBS, WNDT-TV, New York, 18 April 1966, produced by Glenn Jordan, directed by AS. It was the last offering of the first season of The New York Television Theatre. George Rose (Joe), Rosemary Harris (Voice). *Waiting for Godot*, PBS 1961; *Act Without Words II*, PBS 1966.

May 8, 1966

Dear Sam,

Don't know whether you're in Paris or elsewhere but dropping you a note there in any case.

We're heading off for Israel as of next Sunday, May 15, and as of this moment plans have been changed so that it looks as though we shall all be stopping off for a few days in London and then on to Paris for a day or so—I have a package I must deliver to you—and then on to Israel. Not sure that there'll be time on the way back in late July—I'll probably be dashing back home fast to get to work on the new Albee[1]—so we're making sure we'll see you on the way over. Hope you're still there.

Almost a month since EH JOE and people still talking about it. Evidently all our Grove Press friends liked it especially. Barney is having a print made so maybe sometime you'll see it.

Is it true that Jackie made a record of readings from your work? Some Irish company.[2] I just heard vague rumors here. Will try to find it in London.

Should you want to reach me between May 15 and May 18, you could drop me a line c/o Margaret Ramsey,[3] 14 Goodwin's Court, St. Martin's Lane, London W.C. 2. In any case, I'll telephone you from London to see where and how you are. We'd all love to see you.

Jean joins me in fond regards.

All the best.

[Alan]

1. *A Delicate Balance* opened at the Martin Beck Theater, 22 September 1966, produced by Theater 1967 (Barr and Wilder), designed by William Ritman, cast included Jessica Tandy, Hume Cronyn, and Henderson Forsythe. Won a Pulitzer Prize.

2. *MacGowran Reading Beckett's Poetry*, Claddagh Records (see letter of 11 February 1966, n. 3). Second record not released.

3. Literary agent.

January 27, 1967

Dear Sam,

Feel awful about not writing or hearing from you for so long. The time since coming back from Israel this summer has just galloped by, first Edward's play, then Ithaca, a host of lecturing and general confusion, and then the New Year and Judith in the hospital—from which I have just come. She's fine, in good spirits and should be home soon. And very grateful to hear from you.

Personally feel surrounded by a vast theatrical swamp, in which it is getting more and more difficult to move or know where one is going. The Albee play (DELICATE BALANCE) didn't do too badly—critical reception mixed and Kerr hated it[1]—we ran over three months and are now on a national tour which will be as long or longer. I've gotten very good response to my work in diverse quarters and am being offered more new scripts than ever. But somehow or other I don't feel the production came off or was exciting enough in terms of what it might have been. And the scripts I read are uniformly dull or inept or just plain copies of last year's. The only good play I've seen is Pinter's HOMECOMING which is beautiful and superbly done. Naturally, Kerr gave it a contemptuous dismissal in the TIMES (He's now all-powerful) and it is just limping along.[2] Have been seeing a bit of Harold here; I'm hoping to do his BIRTHDAY PARTY next year. Has never been done in New York.

Our Lincoln Center non-commercial theatre attempts have gotten more and more awful, thereby making matters more difficult for anybody else who wants to buck Broadway. Now, having discovered they cannot lick Broadway, the Lincoln Center seems to be joining it. Barr and Wilder have embarked on a series of new and old American plays at the Cherry Lane (backed by a Rockefeller Grant). Interest in off-Broadway GODOT in various quarters, but as always dependent on right actors and a theatre.

Ithaca continues, but with glacier-like rapidity. They are now trying to postpone another year; and I have serious doubts as to whether community support and my own enthusiasm will survive further delay.

More importantly, the war in Vietnam continues, madness escalated. And none of us knows what to do except occasionally to lend our voices and dollars to some kind of protest, which seems to have no effect. This week, we are having a series of events in which the 'angry arts' take a hand in protesting. The real decisions will continue to be made in Washington and Saigon. In the meantime, more killing and suffering and bitterness and hate. And so on.

We go on.

Jean and kids, luckily, all well. Vickie completely recovered, David growing up and surprising me daily with one skill or another. The house remains a refuge from New York's increasing ugliness. Have seen Barney several times recently; they are awaiting Christine's child. Grove Press doing well, expanding into films, posters, and who knows what.

We miss you. Wish you well, hope you are all right. Oh, yes, talked with a Miss Hungerford who is doing a thesis on you. Also Ruby Cohn.[3] Wish I were coming to Paris soon, no such luck. Take care. Write.

[Alan]

1. Walter Kerr, *NY Times*, 23 September 1966.

2. Pinter's *Homecoming* opened at the Music Box Theatre, New York, 5 January 1967. Review: Walter Kerr, *NY Times*, 1 January. Named 'Best Play' in the New York Drama Critics Circle Awards.

3. Ruby Cohn (b. 1922), Beckett scholar and friend; ed. *Casebook on "Waiting for Godot,"* 1967, 1987; *Samuel Beckett: The Comic Gamut*, 1962; ed. *Samuel Beckett: A Collection of Criticism*, 1962; *Back to Beckett*, 1973; *Just Play Beckett's Theatre*, 1980.

Ussy-sur-Marne
8.2.67

Dear Alan

Good to have news of you after so long.

Nothing much to tell. . . .[1] No work recently apart from self-translation both ways—mostly alone, a little in collaboration. Had an idea for a 40 min. play for the *Petit Odéon* (105 seats) and I suppose I could find it again if I looked, but haven't been able to write it. Only the wish to oblige Madeleine in any case, no heart in theatre now.

Saw Edward Albee briefly before leaving Paris. Looking very well and pleased with life and work.

Jack MacGowran has not been too grand . . . He's better now and was over for a few days. He has a production of the *Shadow* coming up at the Mermaid, directing himself & he hopes Pat and Shivaun.[2]

Film was to be shown with other shorts at the Pagoda this month, but Karmitz tells me it's delayed. Saw a very poor film of *2nd Act Without Words* by an Italian. They gave it a prize at Tours Festival.[3] Erwin Leiser whom you may know *(Mein Kampf,)* is filming both for Berlin TV with a Tchech mime (forget name).[4]

. . . .[5]

Forgive feeble letter.

Affectionately to you all
Sam

1. SB and Suzanne have been away.
2. Sean O'Casey's *The Shadow of a Gunman* with Shivaun O'Casey, daughter of the playwright (Minnie Powell), and Jack MacGowran (Seamus Shields). Pat Magee was unavailable.
3. *Act Without Words II,* directed by the "Italian" Carlo Di Carlo, was awarded a Special Jury Prize at the 1967 Tours Film Festival. *Film* had received an award at the same festival in 1966.
4. Erwin Leiser (b. 1923), German filmmaker of the Deutsche Film-und-Fernse-hakademie (the German Film and Television Academy) in Berlin, *Mein Kampf,* 1959. SB gave him permission to present the two mimes with the Prague mime artist Ladislav Fialka.
5. Avigdor Arikha has an exhibition in Paris.

Ussy
24.4.67

Dear Alan

Please forgive my not having written for so long and for not having answered before now your March letters.[1]

. . . .[2]

Had an idea for a short act for the Petit Odéon & Madeleine but it came to nothing. No new work of any kind in sight. Desultorily translating *Watt* into French with Ludovic Janvier & his wife. He has published a work with Minuit on the Nouveau Roman *(sic)* and another on "me" *(resic).* Nice bright young couple (I mean the Janviers).[3]

Booting myself off to Berlin W. May 9 for 48 hours to see the Schiller people. Question of setting up *Endgame* production probably in Schlosspark for September. Perhaps with Ernst Schröder as Hamm. Minetti clamouring for the role, but I worked with him (Pozzo) in *Godot* & never again.[4]

Turned down offer from "Keep Films" to do a film of *Godot* starring (!) Peter O'Toole.[5]

Looking forward to seeing Grovites on their way through this week. Wish I could look forward to seeing you. Any chance?

Haven't seen the Barraults for donkeys. She's still doing her Winnie here and there and will be in Montreal. Nothing new of interest there lately.

Film ran about a fortnight at the Pagoda and seems to have made a bit of a stir. There was a long article by Raymond Federman in some American Film magazine ("Films"?).[6] He had seen the original project and got something of what we intended.

Bought a little German piano for the country. . . .[7]

Jacky had a great personal success at the Mermaid in *The Shadow* & *A £ On Demand*. Shivaun O'C. played the girl in the former. But you've probably read about it. . . .[8] No news of Pat. I think he has signed on again with the Royal Sh. Jocelyn writes a little more cheerful. She did an opera for Sadler Wells.
. . . .[9]

So it goes.

Much love to you all, dear Alan. Keep well. Work well. Write soon.

Sam

1. Missing.

2. SB broke some ribs in a fall.

3. Ludovic and Agnès Janvier, SB's French translators.

4. Ernst Schröder (1915–1994), German actor and director with three major German theater companies, including the Schiller-Theater, Schlossparktheater in Berlin. Bernhard Minetti, Pozzo in Schiller-Theater production of 25 February 1965.

5. Peter O'Toole (b. 1932), Irish-born actor, starred in *Lawrence of Arabia* (UK, 1962); joined National Theatre, 1963, played Hamlet in its first production at the Old Vic; formed Keep Films Ltd., 1962. See "Film of Waiting for 'Godot,'" *Times*, 4 September 1962.

6. *Film Quarterly*, 20 (Winter 1966–67), 46–51.

7. SB describes how he plays, despite poor vision.

8. See letter of 8 February 1967, n. 2. Jack MacGowran has not been well. *A £ on Demand* by Sean O'Casey.

9. SB and Suzanne may go to Courmayeur; her mother is ill.

May 15, 1967

Dear Sam,

Thanks for your good letter. Really delighted to hear from you as it had been so long.

To dinner with Barney and Christine tonight, plus a whole batch of Russians. Assume he will bring me up to date on all your news.

Things here seem in constant flux even though I haven't directed a play since March 13th. That one is doing excellently and should run. No great shakes but gentle and warm humor. Next is THE BIRTHDAY PARTY for the fall.[1]

As a matter of fact I'm off in a few days to see Harold in London to talk about the production. I am coming right back so probably won't get to Paris but I will try to call you one night if that is o.k. Do hope you are well and taking care of yourself. Sorry that you dropped writing the new play but am hopeful. Will talk to Barney tonight about commissioning you to do something, although we could never be as imposing as the B.B.C.

Jean sends her love, kids too.

All the best,
[Alan]

1. Harold Pinter's play opened at the Booth Theatre, New York, 3 October 1967, directed by AS, designed by William Ritman.

July 7, 1967

Dear Sam,

Nothing special. Just that you've been on my mind more than the usual amount lately—two nights ago, I had a long dream about you being in some sort of hospital (along with Richard Schechner of the TULANE DRAMA REVIEW, and with me trying to keep the two of you apart) and not well.[1] And every time I see Barney or Judith, they tell me about you. Sorry that I didn't see for myself when I was in for the quick visit to London a month ago. Did you ever get that letter from the airport—when I couldn't get a telephone line?

Heard about your eyes. Sorry to hear, but glad that you are finally doing something about them. That operation, unpleasant as it is, has been brought under excellent control, and the results are very favorable.[2]

Know how you must be feeling, though, and sympathize greatly. On much smaller scale, have just gone through an operation on my gums—which I dreaded for weeks. Now that it's come—and gone—I feel much better, though the jaw is swollen and I'm on antibiotics.

The month since my return has passed like a swirl. Don't know what I've done except go to various conferences, give various speeches, and cast various plays. Soon at work on BIRTHDAY PARTY, and looking forward to it all.

Jean and Kids OK. We're off to a lake for a couple of weeks very soon. My mum in Switzerland, only happy when she's wandering. But relatively well. The Arab-Israeli thing practically an obsession with me.[3] And Viet Nam remains an open sore. Just don't know if we're ever going to get out of there or recover from what we're doing.

Take care of your eyes. You need them for that next play, Sam. Jean joins me in sending her love.

[Alan]

1. Richard Schechner, editor of *Tulane Drama Review,* associated with Free Southern Theatre (FST), New Orleans; founding director of the Performance Group, New York, and Professor of Performance Studies, New York University; wrote or edited several books on theater (see letter of 2 June 1965, n. 2).
2. SB had cataracts removed.
3. The Arab-Israeli conflict broke out again in June: the Six Day War, 5–11 June.

Paris
15.7.67

Dear Alan

. . . .[1] Very disappointed not to have seen you.

Work in a jam this long time now. Like squeezing an empty tube. I tried hard for the Petit Odéon play but gave it up. It's still there in the wings somewhere. But at the best just another gasp of the old wheeze, of which I'm very tired.

Have undertaken like an imbecile to direct *Endgame* for the Schiller (Werkstatt). Five weeks beginning Aug. 16. Schröder (whom I don't know) and Bollmann (whom I do & like) Hamm & Clov. Latter apparently miscast. But a tubby Clov will be a change. Set by Matias. That shd about finish me if all goes well. Stuttering egos and stammering German. Ah well.[2]

I'm sure you'll have a great time with *The Birthday Party*. I've only seen it in my skull. Full of the crash of *frères*.

. . . .³

Sorry you've been having trouble with your mouth. Hope all well now and no more beastly antibiotics. Have a happy time on your lake, and above all let me see you soon.

Much love to you all
Sam

1. SB has been away.
2. Marks an important development. Prior to this SB had assisted or advised directors like Roger Blin and Jean-Marie Serreau, or George Devine, Donald McWhinnie, and Anthony Page. Now he directed some of his own productions: in Germany, *Endspiel* (1967), *Das Letzte Band* (1969), *Glückliche Tage* (1971), *Warten auf Godot* (1975), *Damals* and *Tritte* (1976), *Krapp's Last Tape* (1977), *Spiel* (1978) at the Schiller-Theater Werkstatt; in France, *Va et vient* (1966) at Odéon-Théâtre de France, *La Dernière bande* (1970) at Théâtre Récamier, *Pas moi* and *La Dernière bande* (1975), *Pas* and *Pas moi* (1978) at Théâtre d'Orsay; in England, *Footfalls* (1976), *Happy Days* (1979) at Royal Court Theatre. In 1980 he directed the San Quentin Drama Workshop's *Krapp* and *Endgame* in London for the Goodman Theatre, Chicago, and "advised" Cluchey in 1984 in a production of *Waiting for Godot*.
3. SB is still getting treatment for his eyes.
4. See letter of 7 July 1967.

Academie der Kunste
Berlin 20
11.9.67

Dear Alan

. . . .¹ Hope all clear now and that you're enjoying *The Birthday Party*. Exciting play.

Here things going not too badly with Schröder (Hamm) & Bollmann (Clov) with whom I've worked before. Very physical expansive actors and Bollmann notably not ideal casting. But they seem to be getting the idea and are working hard. Been at it now 3 weeks and 3 more to go before opening 26th.² We should be ready in plenty of time but I don't think it can be more than just satisfactory, which the previous Berlin production at the Schlosspark with Minetti certainly wasn't, to judge by the photos I've seen.³

Pleasantly lodged here in the Bellevue Park which is beautiful and has me walking in it hours on end.

. . . .[4] No new work on the way. Very busy with French translation of *Watt*.

Much love to you all
Sam

1. SB sympathizes with AS's urological problems.
2. *Endspiel (Endgame)* opened at the Schiller-Theater Werkstatt, 25 September 1967, directed by SB, designed by Matias. Ernst Schröder (Hamm), Horst Bollman (Clov), Werner Stock (Nagg), Gudrun Genest (Nell). Bollmann was associated with National Theatre Mannheim, then Schiller-Theater.
3. *Endspiel* and *Akt Ohne Worte*, 30 September 1957, directed by Hans Bauer. *Endspiel:* Bernhard Minetti (Hamm), Rudi Schmitt (Clov), Werner Stock (Nagg), Else Ehser (Nell).
4. SB mentions holiday plans.

30 Scenic Drive
Hastings-on-Hudson
New York 10706
November 30, 1967

Dear Sam,

Just a few words before heading into rehearsals (Bob Anderson's I NEVER SANG FOR MY FATHER).[1]

Should have written long before this but have kept in touch with your news through Judith and Barney. I'm delighted your eyes are being looked at and soon to be cared for. Also that you had a rest after the Berlin job.

Here all sorts of things in the works: a TV KRAPP, The Open Theatre touring ENDGAME,[2] some further plans for GODOT (we'd hoped to do it in repertory with THE BIRTHDAY PARTY but the theatre's management unwilling), among other things.

Have just heard about your theatre at Oxford and am delighted.[3] Am looking forward to knowing more. Take care of yourself, and with any luck I may be seeing you this spring or summer.

All the best.

Ever,
[Alan]

1. Opened at Longacre Theater, New York, 25 January 1968.
2. The Open Theatre, established 1963–64 as an experimental company to perform new scripts, president, Joseph Chaikin (b. 1935), American actor, director and producer, *The Presence of the Actor*, 1972.
3. Francis Warner and others at Oxford University were raising money to build a theater to be called after SB, but it was never built.

Ussy
6.3.68

Dear Alan

Thanks for your note of Feb. 8 and forgive belated reply.[1]

Have been working hard all these past months on French translation of *Watt* and finished at last today.

Great to learn you will be over in May. Very vague talk of a triple bill at Royal Court that month *(Play, Krapp, Come & Go)* with me directing. Have said neither yes nor no. Probably won't happen.[2]

Olivier & Plowright came up with a hot offer for *All That Fall* at National. I said no but they came over and insisted. Larry kept saying: "It'd make a GREAT SHOW"! [handwritten in margin] However said no again. Impossible in the light. They had worked out some idea with players moving from stage onto screen. They were a bit fed up with me, but very nice.

Same day BBC wanting to do *Happy Days* on sound radio with Dame Edith Evans! *oh là là*. How crossed can garters get?[3]

. . . .[4]

Saw Harold when he was over to see French *Birthday Party*. He let himself in for an excruciating symposium on the stage with actors & public. Never again. He was in good form. He gave me his latest play to read (title escapes me).[5] I liked it very much. It shd work fine.

Edward also sent me *Mao & the Box* which I think is one of his best.[6] I said so to Madeleine who had been listening to nonsense about it.

Suzanne's mother died . . .

Polansky wanted to do a film of *Godot* with Jacky. Sorry.

Gene Searchinger ditto.[7] Ditto.

Jacky has just gone to Australia for three months to film with James Mason.[8] . . .[9]

A card from Pat from Spain where he says it's raining worse than in Connemara.

. . . .[10]

Much love to you all
Sam

1. In his "note" of February 8, AS mentioned that he hoped to be in London in May and that Sir Laurence Olivier and Kenneth Tynan had asked to see FILM.
2. Did not happen.
3. Dame Edith Evans (1888–1976); "how crossed": a joking reference to Malvolio's description of aristocratic dress in *Twelfth Night*.
4. SB comments on his eyes.
5. Probably Pinter's *Silence*, which resembles some of SB's work in that three characters speak, but not consecutively.
6. Albee's *Box* and *Quotations from Chairman Mao Tse-Tung: Two Inter-Related Plays*.
7. Roman Polanski (b. 1933), French director, writer, actor; Gene Searchinger, film producer, director.
8. James Mason (1909–1984), English actor; film: *Age of Consent*, with Jack MacGowran as "Nat Kelly," produced by Columbia/Nautilus, filmed in Queensland, Australia.
9. SB is concerned about MacGowran.
10. SB comments on political situation in America.

Paris
26.8.68

Dear Alan

Many thanks for your June letters from Cal. & forgive failure to reply before now. . . .[1]

Hope you enjoyed Spoleto. No doubt you met Eléonore Hirt. She writes she had a success with her reading.[2]

Fin de partie with Blin as Hamm & directing. Did well up to closing for vacation and is opening again [?]next week. I had little or nothing to do with this production, just a few sessions with new Clov (Martin not being available).[3]

My old friend Georges Belmont[4] seems pleased with his translation of *Box Mao Box* and likes the work greatly. Barrault's plans vague. Have not seen them since I think April. They've had a bad deal from Malraux and Ministry of "Culture".[5]

Much love to you all.
Sam

1. Letters missing. SB says his lung trouble has eased.

2. "Spoleto": Annual Festival of Two Worlds, founded 1958; divides its program between Spoleto, Italy, and Charleston, South Carolina; encourages young artists in several of the arts. AS directed Edward Albee's *American Dream*.

3. *Fin de partie* at the Théâtre 347, Paris, directed by Roger Blin, designed by Matias. Roger Blin (Hamm), Jean Martin (Clov) replaced by André Julien, Georges Adet (Nagg), Christine Tsingos (Nell).

4. Georges Belmont (Georges Pelorson, b. 1909), French translator, journalist, friend of SB since years at Trinity College Dublin.

5. Because Jean-Louis Barrault allowed the state-financed Odéon-Théâtre de France to be used by antigovernment student protesters, Malraux had it closed in May 1968.

September 29, 1968

Dear Sam,

Much too long after I should have, writing to tell you all the things would much prefer to share with you in person at La Coupole. Have been continuously in rehearsal (the Albee-Beckett Repertory)[1] since getting back to New York almost a month ago. Thank you for your good letter, which I managed to decipher, albeit in installments.

Still don't quite know what to believe about your state of health, eyes; but trust you are indeed seeing daylight. All my thanks for that kind note to my Mum, who was most touched. Sorry to inflict her on you at all.

All sorts of things: Have been working both on KRAPP (Donald Davis) and HAPPY DAYS (Sada Thompson, Ruth White being unavailable). This, in conjunction with Edward's BOX-MAO; plus numerous others (not directed by me; AMERICAN DREAM, BESSIE SMITH, ZOO STORY). We rehearsed in New York, then embarked for Buffalo (!) where we had two weeks of break-in time, now back in New York, opening BOX etc. tomorrow evening. Not totally satisfied with this one, as it requires four absolutely virtuoso actors and voices, and ones we have are too ordinary. Also, technical problems galore plaguing us. We shall see. Edward reasonably pleased, I'm not.

As for KRAPP, Donald is fine, even better I think because I've made him simpler. We made a new tape, changed a bit of business here and there in terms of what he had been doing by the end of the long run previously, and I am very happy. If I can get a wig that makes Donald look less like an Italian maestro, all will be well. His performance opening night in Buffalo a week ago was superb.

HAPPY DAYS more of a problem. Really sad about not having Ruth but seemed impossible. Sada is a bit younger, different quality, started off much too dry, I thought. Resisted pauses. I despaired, and we also had some difficulty with her learning the lines. But I can only say that by the time we opened, she surprised us all, was delightful and full and lovely. Lots of laughs (in right places), and quite moving. Since we have now two more weeks rehearsal before opening on Oct. 12, I think she will be even better.

Will send you reviews, Buffalo and New York soon as I can get organised and uninvolved; also pictures, etc., all I can. Can only say that KRAPP and HD have warmed me again, and I see once more after all these years how true and beautiful they are. (Willie, by the way, is fellow who was understudy when Barrault did it here, and actually played it several times. Not great but OK. We have licked umbrella business this time, and mound is fine. We are in largish theatre, 1100 seats, with balcony; so mound is slightly larger than before but well proportioned.)

All sorts of interest in GODOT, from various quarters, and will pursue after we open repertory. Want to make sure of good theatre, cast, and all control. Off-Broadway. The time is ripe, and if production OK, there is excellent possibility of good run. Saw GODOT in Stratford, Canada last month, and although production and acting only fair, audience response very favorable.[2]

Assume you have also heard about Ken Tynan's wanting to include COME AND GO in new revue for New York and London. (Jacques Levy directing.)[3] I told them, and Judith, certainly OK with me if you have approved. She is in hospital, by the way, but better.

And so it goes. Delighted to be home again. Jean suffering some, but improving. Don't know who to vote for—or even what to think.[4] [handwritten paragraph across top of page]

Shocked by dismissal of Barrault, in fact by entire tenor of political situation practically everywhere, from Chicago to Prague. Where does one turn?

Please forgive my not writing you earlier, but I have been working day and night since we started the repertory. Will try to keep you posted on all fronts.

Take care of yourself.

All the best from all of us.

Ever,
[Alan]

P.S. *K.* and *H.D.* got best notices in Buffalo.

1. Albee-Beckett in the Playwrights Repertory, produced by Richard Barr–Edward Albee, opened Buffalo, New York, at the Studio Arena Theatre, 10 September. *Box* and *Quotations from Chairman Mao Tse-Tung,* directed by AS, opened at the Billy Rose Theatre, New York, 30 September 1968, with the voice of Ruth White (recorded); Albee's *The Death of Bessie Smith* and *The American Dream* opened 2 October; *Krapp's Last Tape,* directed by AS, with Donald Davis (Krapp); and *The Zoo Story,* directed by Richard Barr, opened 9 October; *Happy Days,* directed by AS, opened 12 October. *Happy Days:* Sada Thompson (Winnie), Wyman Pendleton (Willie). All designed by William Ritman.

2. *Waiting for Godot* opened at the Avon Theatre during the Stratford Festival, Ontario, 22 August 1968, directed by William Hutt, designed by Brian Jackson. Eric Donkin (Estragon), Powys Thomas (Vladimir), Adrian Pecknold (Lucky), James Blendick (Pozzo), Douglas Birkenshaw (A Boy).

3. SB gave the mime *Breath,* a one-minute sketch, to Kenneth Tynan, who used it for the Prologue to his revue, *Oh! Calcutta! Breath* was first published in *Gambit* 4.16 (1970), *Breath and Other Short Plays,* 1972.

4. AS had considerable choice. On the Republican side were Richard M. Nixon, George Romney, Nelson Rockefeller, Ronald Reagan, and Charles Percy; on the Democratic side were Eugene McCarthy, Robert Kennedy, and George McGovern. Although not in the primaries, Hubert H. Humphrey won his party's nomination and ran against Richard Nixon.

Paris
3.10.68

Dear Alan

Many thanks for writing so fully at such a busy time.

This in haste to say that I have had no request from Tynan for permission to use *Come & Go* in his N.Y. show. What he did ask for was the "breath play". I gave him permission for this on condition that both you and Grove were consulted and had no objection. As a garbled account of this had been circulated I wrote it down for the first time. I am sure I must have told you about it. Here it is in any case.

Shall write a proper letter soon. Eyes no worse. Lung trouble practically cured.

Love
Sam

Breath Play

Curtain.

1. Faint light on stage littered with miscellaneous rubbish. Hold about 5 seconds.

2. Faint brief cry and immediately inspiration and slow increase of light together reaching maximum together in about 10 seconds. Silence and hold about 5 seconds.

3. Expiration and slow decrease of light together reaching minimum together (light as in 1) in about 10 seconds and immediately cry as before. Silence and hold about 6 seconds.

Curtain.

Rubbish: no verticals, all scattered, leaning and lying.

Cry: Instant of recorded vagitus. Important that two cries be identical, switching on and off strictly synchronized light and breath.

Breath: amplified recording.

Maximum light: not bright. If 0 = dark and 10 = bright light should move from about 3 to 6 and back.

November 29, 1968

Dear Sam,

Back home, finally, after a week in London and the shape of the immediate future a bit clearer.

Was delighted to see you and Suzanne, and to be able to spend some time with you. Really must say that you looked reasonably well, in fact better than you had for some time, and both Jean and I are hoping that all will go well and that you will have a relaxed couple of months in Madeira. With the weather we've been having here the past couple of days, I wouldn't mind being there either.

Concluded the film business—except for the gruesome financial details—and it looks as though we are definitely going to shoot in New York starting August 1, with preparation two months before that. With shooting scheduled for 11 weeks plus the editing after that, we get into November or December.[1] So it does not seem possible for me to get to Paris in the fall to do BOX-MAO with Madeleine, much as the prospect pleases and intrigues me. (That is, even if she does not do the play with a French director next spring.) Thank you very much for thinking of this and broaching the idea to her. I am writing Madeleine directly and explaining that it just is not possible to plan this at this time. Although I do hope some day to be able to direct her in if not Edward's play, perhaps something else. She was most charming to us, would hear of nothing but driving us directly to the Madeleine that day; and we even managed to understand each other here and there.

Edward is away in Hollywood somewhere, and then off to London to see rehearsals of DELICATE BALANCE, but I hope to catch him before he goes.

Barney also fairly elusive at the moment, but I have talked with Judith. And about your doing a screenplay of KRAPP. Will be looking forward to hearing from you.

Take care of yourself, enjoy the sunlight, and those writing juices will be flowing, I'm certain.

Best regards from Jean and all of us.

All the best.

[Alan]

1. AS is preparing to direct a film for Paramount, *Piano Sport.*

January 22, 1969

Dear Sam,

Had hoped to hear from you but only slivers via Judith. But glad to hear you're feeling better and hope this continues. Also the sunlight.

Things here highly in flux. Not doing the Schisgal play after all as one of the "stars" objected to my ideas. Starting on another—with no stars—in March.[1] Various flurries on GODOT but hesitate to tell you in detail because all so evanescent. If and when something concrete, will confide in you. In the meantime, closely in touch with Barney on all developments.

We are both most anxious to hear from you regarding screen adaptation of KRAPP, how and when it's coming, as we have serious plans to do this when you're finished.[2] I tried to reach Pat and Jackie in London in November, but they must have already been gone. In any case we are awaiting your script with bated breath.

Edward Albee returned from London, where DELICATE BALANCE seems to be going well, to tell me that Madeleine's BOX and MAO now looks likely for December rather than September. Trouble is my film—ha!—goes from August through end of the year at least, damn it.

Jean and the kids are OK. We've taken up skiing and although no bones broken every sinew is sore.

Love to hear from you. All the best.

Ever,

[Alan]

1. Murray Schisgal (b. 1926), American playwright; the play was probably *Jimmy Shine;* "another": Lyle Kessler's *The Watering Place.*

2. Approached by West-Deutscher Rundfunk, Cologne, for a television version of the Schiller-Theater Werkstatt production of *Das Letze Band,* SB gave them "Suggestions for T.V. *Krapp.*" First shown by Cologne Television, 28 October 1969. In the previous year he told Grove Press he was working on a television script of the play. For details see Clas Zilliacus, *Beckett and Broadcasting,* 1976. *Krapp's Last Tape* was first shown on BBC 2 television, 13 November 1963, with Cyril Cusack as Krapp. AS refers to his plans throughout 1969 but they only came to fruition in 1971 when he directed Jack MacGowran for PBS, WNET-TV, New York, but no commercial network bought it. Another version with Pat Magee was shown on BBC 2, 29 November 1972, directed by Donald McWhinnie.

Cascais
15.2.69

Dear Alan

Yours of Jan. 22 here yesterday on way back from islands.

Forgive my not having written before.

You will have seen by now *Krapp* notes. I realize their inadequacy but I can do no better now. If you can go on from there I'd be happy. If not let's forget it. The principle seems OK to me. Not pleased with treatment of end (when Krapp records etc.) but it could serve. I am the world's worse adaptator—heart not being in it, and of course lack completely technical equipment for TV work. Add to all that (if any room left) the kind of mental stare in which I seem to have frozen and forgive.

No news of Belmont or Madeleine except that she had success in Duras's rewrite of *Les Viaducs* . . . at little TNP.[1]

Endgame over after quite a long run and *Play* on at Montparnasse *Poche* with Lonsdale & 2 darkies, direction Serreau.[2]

10 days here then back to the fumes. Hope to see Dick & Jeannette[3] on arrival.

Much love to you all.
Sam

1. Marguerite Duras, Nathalie Sarraute, Michel Butor, and Alain Robbe-Grillet revolutionized the French novel. *Les Viaducs: Les Viaducs de la Seine-et-Oise.*

2. *Comédie (Play)* opened 21 March 1969 at the Théâtre Poche-Montparnasse, directed by Jean-Marie Serreau. Toto Bissanthe (W1), Danielle van Bercheyke (W2), Michael Lonsdale (The Man).

3. The Seavers.

March 23, 1969

Dear Sam,

Just heard from Judith that your x-rays are okay and that all is well.[1] At least reasonably. Delighted to get the news, and hope you are refreshed from your holiday and feeling generally better.

Please forgive the delay in writing you about your "Krapp" notes. Actually, all I ever received (via Grove) was a badly photostated copy of your letter, although Paul Heller[2] (the producer) has promised me a typed copy. Also, I was in rehearsal at the time, the play opened (and closed), and I went immediately into another one, which opens the end of April.[3] So I have had very little time, unfortunately, to think. I did meet with Heller and with Barney to work out some of the administrative details, schedule, etc.

We all agreed that we want Pat Magee above all, if he were available. I got in touch with Pat, and he is definitely interested, and will let us know about his availability (May or June) within a week. Heller's other idea was Burgess Meredith, whom I respect but distrust; no one seems willing to go with Donald Davis because of his age. There is also another possibility, Henderson Forsythe, who succeeded Davis, and was very good, but Heller wants a bigger "name." So, we are crossing our fingers about Pat.

My own schedule is also a little confused at the moment. I finish THE GINGHAM DOG around the end of April, then have to go to Hollywood to discuss the Paramount film (heaven knows what goes on with that!). We are hoping to shoot KRAPP around the middle or end of May, but I am in desperate need of some kind of rest, and also some thought before embarking on the project. Pat's news will tell us more, and I will keep you posted.

About your "suggestions," I feel that they are basically fine. What you are asking for, in effect, is an objective and a subjective camera; or, a basic long shot, moving back and forth (or from left to right), and a basic close-up, varying in angle, depending on what is to be seen. So long as we are in agreement on these two fundamentals, I am sure that there can be some flexibility within. In any case, we would tend to shoot material from different angles and distances, and judge later what is most effective.

Please forgive me, Sam, for not going into greater detail, but I simply have not yet had the opportunity of studying the script in relation to your notes. I will, and will come back to you with some of my usual stupid questions. I was also hoping that I could get over to Paris between now and the time we shoot, but this seems highly unlikely, though not yet completely out of the question.

If you have any further thoughts, please do let me have them. I am assuming from everything Barney tells me that you will not be able to come over this time for the actual shooting.

Sorry as hell about not being able to do BOX and MAO with Madeleine. I wish that my crazy mixed-up theatrical existence were not so, but in order to survive, one goes on doing what one can. The last one (THE WATERING PLACE), was one of the most interesting plays I have ever worked on, written by a young man of considerable talent. I was called in to replace another director, and had just a couple of weeks of rehearsal, but I enjoyed the work, and liked the play. The critics blasted it, and it ran one night—although, in the long run, I have a feeling it will survive. (I am not sure I will.)

Jean and the kids join me in sending all our love and good wishes.

Ever,
[Alan]

P.S. Heard from Judith that you liked "the article" on FILM. When Grove asked me to do it I was a bit nervous, but then decided to tell the story as directly as I could. Glad you liked it.[4]

1. Refers to chest x-rays.

2. Paul Heller (b. 1927), American producer, director mainly in film and television.

3. Kessler's *The Watering Place* opened, and closed, at the Music Box Theatre, New York, 12 March 1969. "another one": Lanford Wilson's *The Gingham Dog* opened at the John Golden Theatre, New York, 23 April 1969.

4. AS, "On Directing *Film*," in SB, *Film: Complete scenario/Illustrations/Production shots*, 1969, 63–94.

Ussy
27.3.69

Dear Alan

Glad to have your letter today about TV *Krapp.* I do hope Pat can do it, though it seems a bit hard on Davis. I couldn't get to NY for the shooting, but feel very strongly that we should meet before you get going. I'd be at your disposal any time in the coming months and perhaps Pat could join us. Paris or London. My notes are very inadequate. I have been working on the German text and thinking a lot about the play, not televisually, but in view of the Berlin production in September.[1] This has suggested to me certain deviations from the published stage directions which you should know about. I could of course give you some idea of them by letter, but they really need to be *shown.* Two sessions together would do the trick, with a night between for you [to] think it over and come back with queries. A nice Atlantic crossing is just what you need.

Love to you all.
Sam [handwritten]

1. *Das Letzte Band* opened at the Schiller-Theater Werkstatt, Berlin, 5 October 1969, directed by SB, with Martin Held (Krapp) and with Ionesco's *Le Nouveau locataire (The New Tenant).*

May 24, 1969

Dear Sam,

Have just returned from that whore house run by Civil Service, called Hollywood—after sitting around there off and on for almost three weeks. At the end of that time the picture is off-on, maybe, what have you. I still have an agreed-upon contract, so I can't just walk out; but at this point I can only say that I have never been so uncertain, confused and frustrated about a project of this kind in my life.

Had to send you that telegram from out there about not being able to come because the one clear thing was that I could not be definite about being free in July (after July 16, when Pat said he would be free). Really sad about that as, among other things, I had been looking forward to coming to Paris to see you and spend some time talking over KRAPP. This was the day I was coming. (Wrote to the hotel and apologised and thanked them.)[1]

Had Pat only stayed free in June or late May as previously planned, all would have been well, as my services are not legally bound to them until July 15th, six weeks before shooting date (?) of the projected picture. This way, I have told Paul Heller and Barney that I feel we should not go after another actor but wait for Pat to be free for a couple of weeks sometime when I am. Maybe we could even shoot in London. And, somehow I'll get over to talk with you beforehand. Lots of ideas and questions.

Plans here remain uncertain from day to day or even hour to hour. Still under pressure from official auspices to go as one of American delegates to Theatre Conference in Eastern Europe; but if I go (which is far from settled even at this late moment) I'll have to go directly and head back directly as dates and times are fixed. Also I may have to head back to Los Angeles at any time. So I'm gritting my teeth and waiting for each day to develope. May surprise you yet.

Have you heard about Tynan's OH! CALCUTTA! revue with your short piece?[2] Still in preview and selling out; said to be very erotic. Hope to see it soon. Another source of interest in off-Broadway GO-DOT for next season, but don't want to hope too much until more definite.

Jean and the kids reasonable but very pale year; and country degenerating daily. Despair. Thinking about moving to London but impossible to make a living there. We'll see.

Would like to commission you to write a play for four women all of whom can hear but not see each other; or two of whom can see but not hear and two who can hear but not see. How [ending missing]

[Alan]

1. In a letter dated 12 May 1968, SB refers to a missing letter of May 7 and anticipates seeing AS on May 25/26. An AS telegram sent May 20 says AS is unable to come and that "July availability unlikely." The May 24 letter follows.

2. Opened at the Eden Theatre, New York, 17 June 1969, directed by Jacques Levy, with SB's *Breath* as the opening sketch. Levy (b. 1935) was a member of Joseph Chaikin's Open Theatre, New York, at this time.

Paris
30.5.69

Dear Alan

Very disappointed and sad to think of you in such uncertainties. Glad you agree the best thing is to wait till both you and Pat are free.

4 women interesting idea. But fear no more theatre in me. Struggling with a short prose piece with ridiculous difficulty.[1] It was always [?]resisting or writing. But why not writing now? Too dignified I suppose.

Met Mrozek *(Tango).* Tired young Pole.[2]

. . . .[3]

Love to you all.

Bon courage
Sam

1. *Mercier et Camier,* 1970 (see letter of 28 May 1972, n. 2).
2. Sławomir Mrozek (b. 1930), avant-garde Polish dramatist; *Tango* (1965), an explosive and complex play about the destruction of values.
3. SB says his lung is "holding its own."

Academie der Kunste
Berlin
7.9.69

Dear Alan

Forgive my not having thanked you for your letter long ago.[1] So sorry you've had such an exasperating time with those film bastards. We'll do *Krapp* with Pat before they land on Mars. I'll be more of a help after all the work for and with Held. He's good and willing and it should be all right. Opening Oct. 5 in double bill with *Le Nouveau Locataire.* . . .[2]

Much love to you all.
Sam

1. Missing.

2. See letter of 27 March 1969, n. 1. After the plays open SB will go to Tunisia, as he says in the next letter.

Academie der Kunste
1 Berlin 21
Hanseateweg 10
14.9.69

Dear Alan

I'd be grateful if you wd. send to me here a copy of the *Krapp* TV notes. Cologne needs them. I have no copy nor the courage to work them out again.

Enjoying rehearsals with Martin Held. He should be very good. We open Oct. 5. Next morning I take plane to Tunisia and shall be there a month at least.

Love to you all.
Sam

September 18, 1969

Dear Sam,

Delighted to hear from you, and to know that you are well, even if working a little too hard. Sure wish I could be with you.

Attached are the T.V. notes on *Krapp*. I trust they get to you in time. I am still hoping that we can do it with Pat sometime not too far away.

Deep at work on musical version of *La Strada*.[1] In a long dark tunnel until December.

Do say hello to Martin Held.

Best wishes for your work, health and good cheer.

Ever,
[Alan]

Changes
· Table off centre audience right
· In drawer on side   "   "

- Den upstage audience left
- In drawer bananas and virgin reel
- Mike in den brought p. 17 after drink 2
- No keys
- K does not resit between bananas
- Table empty to start with. After banana 2 K fetches 1. Ledger 2. *Tin boxes* 3. Machine
- He plugs in machine to loose lead on floor audience right
- Light on in den to start with, curtain drawn. After first trip to den (to fetch ledger) curtain left half open and remains so throughout. At end light in den dimmed with rest.
- Looks behind in shadow. 1. P. 11 interrupting loading of spool 1. 2. P. 14 on return from drink 1 interrupting movement to switch on. 3. P. 19 interrupting loading of spool 1
- Relationship with machine. Maximum intimacy p. 17 with punt repeat at end of which head on table

1. Opened at Lunt-Fontanne Theatre, New York, 14 December 1969. Book by Charles Peck, Jr., based on the film by Federico Fellini, music and lyrics by Lionel Bart; it was AS's first Broadway musical.

December 31, 1969

Dear Sam,

Figured out that you are probably in Paris or about to get there, and wanted to wish you good things for the new year, say hello, and bring you up to date on variety of confusions. LA STRADA opened and closed the same night, mixed reviews but management had no money left even to try for a run. Wouldn't have traded the experience though a little less agony along the way would have been appreciated. Now embarking on off-Broadway musical supposedly about Crimean War but actually Viet Nam.[1] Have totally lost faith in my judgment on theatrical matters, so expect nothing from enterprise except the work. We shall see.

Judith just lent me book of your ENDGAME production in Berlin, and pictures are fascinating.[2] She'll never get it back from me. Wish I could have seen it. She's coming over to spend the Eve of New Year with us, quietly, sitting around the fire and your Giacometti drawing and just talking (also with her new boy friend, looks serious, I'm glad to say).

Spent an evening with John Kobler and his first editions of your books, rather like him.[3] I gather he will be seeing you this spring. Hoping to do the same this summer, all of us. Am scheduled to teach in some sort of American Seminar at Salzburg[4] middle of June and plan to bring over the whole family and try to drive around Europe for a few weeks afterward, stopping off in Paris to descend in hordes around you. Vicky is 15 and quite mature, and David is constantly astonishing us at almost 11. Jean, as always, indomitable—in the face of all my foibles and a very bad theatre year: four failures.

Plans for off-Broadway GODOT continuing to percolate. We have an interested management if they can raise the dough and get a theatre. (We are getting double-talk and a bit of run-around from the Cherry Lane owners but we're trying.) Approaching some actors. Hoping for the middle of spring. Off-Broadway is as big a jungle as on Broadway now, so can't be sure of anything. Have talked with Barr and Albee about possibility of Beckett Festival, but they are wrapped up in films for the moment. (Albee without a play for over a year.) Everyone going into films and theatre more and more sprawling and self-indulgent. Haven't seen OH! CALCUTTA! yet but they are running on and on.

Lots of interest in the book of FILM; spoke to Marilynn M.,[5] who tells me it's going well. Do you have enough copies? (More interest in the film itself also.) I'm trying to reach Paul Heller, who's off somewhere, to renew interest in KRAPP TV-film. Maybe can see Pat Magee in London this summer.

World continues worrying everybody, and am not too optimistic about 1970. Jean and I continually talk about moving to London to live but problem is how to afford that and how to make a living there? The USA grows increasingly maddening, especially in NY area, but that's where the work is.

Think of you always and hope you are well, have had some sort of rest, and are not too besieged by outsiders all the time. Long to see you and find out how you are.

All the best, ever,
[Alan]

[handwritten]

You know about Sidney Meyers.⁶ Did you know Ruth White had died the same month? A lovely gal & I'm absolutely devastated.⁷ Did you ever meet her? [ending illegible]

1. *Blood Red Roses,* book and lyrics by John Lewin, music by Michael Valenti, opened at the John Golden Theatre, 22 March 1970, closed 22 March after one performance and nine previews. AS does not mention the play again.

2. *Endgame: Notebook for Endspiel (Endgame) at the Schiller-Theater Werkstatt, Facsimile of Samuel Beckett's Production, with Transcription and Translation,* ed. James Knowlson, 1967.

3. John Kobler (b. 1910), American novelist, journalist, wrote *The Life and World of Al Capone,* 1971.

4. Salzburg Seminar in American Studies.

5. Marilynn Meeker, editor at Grove Press.

6. Meyers died on 3 December 1969.

7. AS had written a memoir for the *NY Times,* 14 December 1969.

                                                    hotel cidadela
                                                    CASCAIS
                                                    11.1.70

Dear Alan

Many thanks for your letter rich in news.

Heard of Sidney's death in Nabeul. Very grieved. Had a great fondness for him. . . .¹

Very sorry to hear of Ruth White's death. No, I never met her. . . .²

Jean-Louis and Madeleine are putting on a cycle at the Récamier— *Happy Days, Godot* with Raimbourg (original Didi) directed by Blin and—if I am well enough to direct it—*Krapp* with Jean Martin.³ Will depend mainly on what the occulists tell me. I haven't yet seen that *Endgame* book you speak of.

Dreadful production of *Godot* at the Abbey with O'Toole, licensed by my agent without my authority, on pretext of my inaccessibility in Tunisia.⁴ I could have prevented it at last moment, but hadn't the heart to. All I could do was limit the run to one month and refuse rep. and all subsidiary rights including American TV for which O'Toole's agent offered large sums. Curtis Brown seem to have gone to the dogs since Spencer left, changing personnel every few months.⁵

Sorry to hear of failure of *Strada* musical on top of previous flops. I'm definitely out of *Oh! Calcutta!* for all future productions & notably

London & Paris and in book & disk only on condition that my piece be attributed to me. I was properly let in there.

. . . .[6]

Much love to you all
Sam

1. SB had been on vacation in Tunisia before going on to Nabeul and Cascais; he comments on Sidney Meyers.

2. SB and Suzanne expect to return to Paris in about ten days' time.

3. The three-month Beckett cycle opened 16 March 1970 with *En attendant Godot*, directed by Roger Blin, designed by Hubert Monloup. Marc Eyraud (Estragon), Lucien Raimbourg (Vladimir), Michel Robin (Lucky), Armand Meffre (Pozzo), Philipe Deutch or Denis Alland (A Boy). *La Dernière bande*, directed by SB, opened at the Théâtre Récamier, 29 April 1970. This production closely resembled the Berlin production. Jean Martin (Krapp). *Acte sans paroles* opened 29 April 1970, directed by Deryk Mendel, designed by Matias. Mendel (A), Pierre Byland (B). *Oh les beaux jours* opened 9 February at the Théâtre Récamier. Madeleine Renaud (Winnie), Jean-Louis Barrault (Willie).

4. *Waiting for Godot* had opened at the Abbey Theatre, 1 December 1969, directed by Sean Cotter, designed by Norah McGuinness. Donal McCann (Estragon), Peter O'Toole (Vladimir), Des Cave (Lucky), Eamon Kelly (Pozzo), Dan Figgis (A Boy).

5. Spencer Curtis Brown, director, Curtis Brown literary agency.

6. SB looks forward to seeing AS in the summer.

January 27, 1970

Dear Sam,

Taking time off from deciphering your letter from Portugal just for a brief note.

Told Judith she had better get you a copy of that book on the German production of ENDGAME; hate to part with my copy. Figured the Germans ought to send you one. It's lovely.

I suppose I should have learned by this time never to tell you anything about plans for doing one of your plays before we get really set. Because this damn New York theatre gets harder and harder. All this means is that I am despairing about the off-Broadway GODOT production plan I wrote to you about. The producers are two young guys who are nice and sweet and talked well and I liked them. But when things come round to their delivering what they should, it's another story. Tried for weeks to get hold of them and couldn't. When I did, we sat and talked and they said they were starting to raise money. As of now, they haven't. They said they were going after a theatre—and I pursued the matter on my own because the off-Broadway real-estate situation is just murderous with everyone lying and cheating and stealing (literally)—but every time they told me they were on the track of a theatre, they actually were not. We exchanged lists of possible cast ideas—and when I finally got theirs (delayed) it was incredibly inept and ridiculous. (Apart from anything else, we're still forced to deal with the ghost of Bert Lahr, and anyone who plays in this GODOT has got to be first-rate, not eighth rate. Not talking about stars, just actors.) Anyhow, we were going to get together, and they haven't called me and I cannot reach them. So finally as of yesterday I told Judith I was about to give up. (Apart from all this, they haven't even signed my contract, which was supposed to have been done by Dec. 31.)

Have talked with a couple of producers about the possibility of doing a Beckett Festival (which has so long been the real goal) but they point out the various practical obstacles: casting, theatre, etc. I'm just going to go on in various directions, but NOT going to tell you until things are definite! Please forgive our foibles over here; we just seem incapable of rational organized effort in the theatre.

Delighted you are home by this time, and hope you are getting a reasonable rest. Still plan to come over in July or thereabouts. Best from the family.

Ever,
Alan & Jean
[handwritten "Ever," signed by Alan (and Jean)]

P.S. How about writing
    a play in English for
    two women (who see but
    cannot hear each other)?   excuse the
                                                       presumption

[handwritten]

May 13, 1970

Dear Sam,

Hope this catches you. Judith said you were in Sardinia, so I'm hastening to write there. Forgive my silence for so long. After a spring spent endlessly in rehearsal, the Rosenberg play opened—to good critical response but doing only fair—and I collapsed.[1] Had just been going too long and too hard. And a bad chest cold which I could not shake and still haven't. So I retired into myself, stayed in bed mostly and read a lot, early to sleep and lots of radio music. Am just about pulling out. Don't remember when I have been so exhausted, physically and emotionally.

Couple things that helped: Judith's getting married. Went to the reception afterward and she looked radiant. Sorry you weren't able to see her. Never happier or more youthful.[2] . . . Went to see Madeleine do *Oh les Beaux Jours* again. Too large a theatre but a lovely performance. Spoke to her afterwards, and we made a date for 'tea', which turned out to be orange juice for her and whiskey for me. She's really incredible, so beautiful and so alive. Am seeing Barrault's opening next Tuesday of *Rabelais* and hoping to see her again[3] . . . Met your Parkinson fellow about Jackie's one-man Beckett show, liked him very much, although I strongly advised him to do it off-Broadway rather than on.[4] Not sure he agrees. Anyhow, have heard through various sources that the show went well in Paris and should repeat in London. Wish I could see it, wherever. Am so pleased it's on. Wish I could have helped. And if I can do anything when it's over here? Are you coming?. . . . Heard about the Oxford Beckett Theatre ceremonies from Wolf Mankowitz (who wants me to do a movie for him, which I don't like).[5] Have not heard from Francis Warner for some time, but gather things are moving along there.[6] I'm going to London for a week prior to lecturing for a month at an American Seminar at Salzburg (June 20–July 10)[7] and will ring him up. Not sure whether I can get to Paris before Salzburg but definitely afterward—and will write to you. Must see you. How are your eyes? The rest of you?

Am thinking more seriously than ever of staying in Europe to live and work. USA getting absolutely madly impossible. Just must find a way of surviving economically over there. Would love to work in England, teach, direct, something. The New York theatre completely corrupt, not a chance for serious work on Broadway and off-B succumbing fast. Desperate. Jean & family reasonably well & join me in wishing you good holiday & all well. Let me know how you are. [handwritten after "not"]

[Alan]

1. Donald Fried's *Inquest*, based on the book *Invitation to an Inquest* by Walter and Miriam Schneir, reconstructed the trial of Julius and Ethel Rosenberg, who were found

guilty of espionage in 1951 and electrocuted in 1953. Billed as "a tale of political terror," the controversial play suggests that the Rosenbergs were innocent; reviews were mixed. Opened at the Music Box Theatre, New York, 23 April 1970, closed 16 May.

2. Married John Douw.

3. Presented by Le Treteau de Paris, *Oh les beaux jours* opened at the Barbizon-Plaza, New York, 24 April 1970, directed by Roger Blin. Madeleine Renaud (Winnie), Olivier Hussenot (Willie). Barrault's *Rabelais* opened at the New York City Center, 19 May 1970, designed by Matias.

4. Tom Parkinson produced Jack MacGowran's very successful one-man show, *Beginning to End*, opened at the Théâtre Edouard VII, Paris, 22 April 1970, as part of the SB cycle. SB directed but took no credit. Gloria MacGowran was stage-manager. Reviews: Thomas Quinn Curtiss, "Beckett Is Focus of Show in Paris," *NY Times*, 25 April 1970; "When Friends Collaborate," *Time*, 11 May 1970; Jean Genet, "Letter from Paris: *Beginning to End*, selections from works performed by J. MacGowran," *The New Yorker*, 16 May 1970.

5. Wolf Mankowitz (b. 1924), American dramatist, took part in the "Samuel Beckett Theatre Appeal," 8 March 1970, produced by Francis Warner, at The Playhouse, Oxford. This was a fund-raising event toward building a Samuel Beckett Theatre at Oxford.

6. "Things moving along" may refer to the "Appeal" or to Warner's play, *Maquettes*, or the proposed collaboration between AS and Warner in Toronto (see letter of 16 August 1970).

7. The Salzburg Seminar, founded in 1947 by students at Harvard University, met in the Schloss Leopoldskron and the adjoining Meierhof. The faculty gave their services free of charge.

August 9,
"1970" [handwritten]

Dear Sam,

The week flown by, and I do apologise for not writing earlier. But I did want to wait until I had reached Jackie, which I've just done . . .

He seems to be involved in a New York production of a play on Gandhi, which goes into rehearsal, he tells me, middle of September.[1] If it succeeds, and if I can persuade Barney to provide some funds, I shall try to have Jackie do the Beckett evening on his dark night. If it doesn't succeed, maybe we can make a stand of it somewhere off-Broadway. I still say a large 'maybe' because there are so many indefinite factors here, including Barney, Jackie and myself. But am at least pursuing the matter.

My own situation here highly uncertain. Have received another offer of a West End production, the third, and will be hoping to settle the matter this week. But, of course, not only financing but the question of getting the proper actors is involved. And it's quite conceivable that the management may abandon the entire scheme. Jean is also much disturbed about my whole idea of working in London for a while, as she feels that I am exchanging one rat race for another; and that even should I find work on a regular basis, it will be impossible to make a living there. She may be right. Certainly the prices here are not much lower than in NY while the fees paid out to theatre directors are nowhere near as high. On the other hand, I find the life and atmosphere most congenial, and hope that we can somehow manage the finances to make it possible to stay a while. We go up and down on the toboggan slide daily, if not hourly. . . .

Really glad to see you, even though I'm sorry to have added to the pressures upon you. And apologies for the small accident at the cafe, about which David was inconsolable for a while—but from which he has now recovered. I do hope you can say the same about your trousers. And thanks for coming to see us off. We managed to arrive at Boulogne just as a Hovercraft was taking off that evening—and got on it! Spent the night in Folkstone, which was a great let-down from Montparnasse. Although the English weather has been marvelously welcome in the past week.

Got down to Oxford to see MAQUETTTES.² Production very rudimentary though acting not bad. Critics very bad, and poor Francis was desolate until Hobson's notice appeared last Sunday and saved the day. Spent some time with him talking over what might be done and am going to try to help. [ending missing]

[Alan]

1. Gurney Campbell's epic play, *Gandhi*.
2. Opened at The Playhouse, Oxford, 27 July 1970; "Skin Games," Sir Harold Hobson's review of *Maquettes* ("Emblems," "Troat," "Lumen") appeared in *The Sunday Times*, 2 August 1970. "Emblems" was dedicated to SB.

Ussy
16.8.70

Dear Alan

Many thanks for your letter.

I got the impression from Jack that *Gandhi* was off and *Beginning to End* perhaps on again in N.Y. Must have got it wrong. The cameraman in Stuttgart seems very keen on getting him. He badly needs a break.

Here over a week working away, but nothing for the theatre. An old television idea came back, but can't go after it now.

Warner wrote heartened by Hobson's article. I hope you'll be able to help in Edinburgh & Toronto. He has it in him I feel.

. . . .[1]

It was good seeing you all in such form. May things work out for you for the best, whatever you decide. Let me know how it goes.

Love to you all
Sam

1. SB will see Judith and John Douw in early September.

September 18, 1970

Dear Sam,

Back in New York, finally, after a longish sojourn in London mostly spent in looking for a job, a flat, and some sense of direction. The English being notoriously slow in all matters, I left still in a state of indecision on all points. Though I did meet a lot of theatre people whom I didn't know, including Jocelyn Herbert[1]—who sends regards— who were friendly and helpful. And about half a dozen offers to direct something, although most of these dependent on money being raised, time and circumstance being propitious, and other matters in the laps of non-existent gods. Suddenly, a telegram asking me to direct Edward Bond's SAVED off-Broadway, and I took the next plane home (exactly on the day of all those hi-jackings).[2]

Do hope you are OK. Took all my will-power not to telephone you from London at Ussy, but I knew you were pressured from all sources, so I didn't. I did finally speak with Jackie M. in Dublin who assured me he was coming to NY to do GANDHI. (Your letter to him via me just arrived, and I shall try to get it to him immediately.) I also wrote to him to find out more about his plans, asking him to write back, but he hasn't yet. I'm sure I shall be seeing him in NY. We talked about possibility, if GANDHI goes, of doing the Beckett on a Monday night here somewhere. If *Gandhi* doesn't go, maybe we can keep Jackie and do the 'evening' on some other basis.[3] Also talked about him and Pat doing

GODOT off-Broadway—although that alien business is still a formidable obstacle. Still they have obviously coped with it on GANDHI. (Obviously, a matter of economics more than any other factor, as one, I believe, can hire aliens off-Broadway if one pays them and everyone in the cast a Broadway salary.) I also had tremendous difficulty reaching Pat in London; finally, one morning, I woke him up and he asked me to call him back an hour later, which I did but he had already disappeared. I rather think he is dodging me because he thought I might be calling about F. Warner's MAQUETTES, which he is leery about. (I went up to Edinburgh a few days to help Francis with it, mostly with technical aspects as it was impossible to do much with the cast. It went reasonably well, though audience totally baffled. I have promised to work on it in Toronto—along with BREATH and COME AND GO, so please tell me anything beyond what you've already written about how you want these two done.[4] This to be done to raise money in Toronto (and elsewhere, we hope) for Beckett Theatre. We go into rehearsal November 9 for November 16th opening at Hart House, Univ. of Toronto.) Never reached Pat, sorry to say, he never called back, and I went back to NY. He's had great success with O'Neill's TOUCH OF THE POET, and may be doing it in West End, I gather.[5]

Saw Bettina[6] several times in London, also Harold Pinter. And have talked with Barney here since I returned. We're talking about our doing GODOT ourselves off-Broadway, in the Village, hopefully at the Cherry Lane if we can get it, directly after MAQUETTES. Will keep you posted on this. The Lincoln Center has been so vague about everything including possibility of casting outside of their (inadequate) Company that we're much more happy about other prospect. What we're all concerned about is How Are Your Eyes? And whether the operation is already done. I suppose you've seen Judith, so she'll be telling us the news.

Anyhow this started out just as a short note to tell you the basic news, and look where it's gotten to.

David is still terribly apologetic about the beer-spilling episode; he has started a number of letters to you to tell you how badly he feels, but has torn them up. Everyone back in school and remembering the summer with great nostalgia. I still want to live in London and may yet, but the problem of earning a living there is horrendous.

Jean sends her love, we all wish you well and long for news of you.

[Alan]

[bottom of page]:

P.S. Has Barney told you that he wants to release the TV- tape GODOT (Mostel and Meredith) to schools? There seems to be a great deal of interest.

1. Jocelyn Herbert (b. 1917), English theater designer, mainly with the Royal Court Theatre; designed *Krapp's Last Tape, Happy Days, Not I, Footfalls, That Time;* wrote *A Theatre Workbook*, 1993.

2. *Saved* opened at the Chelsea Theatre Center, Brooklyn Academy of Music, Brooklyn, 20 October 1970. There were four hijackings on 6 September 1980.

3. Gurney Campbell's *Gandhi*, directed by Jose Quintero, opened at the Playhouse, New York, 20 October 1970, but played only one night. Jack MacGowran (Gandhi).

4. Opened at the Jordanburn Theatre, Edinburgh Festival, 31 August as part of the Festival Fringe; Edinburgh Festival: an annual international celebration of music, dance, and theater, instituted 1947; the Fringe, 1949.

5. Pat Magee (Major Cornelius Melody) opened in Eugene O'Neill's *A Touch of the Poet* at the Gordon Arts Centre, London. The Round House, a different theatre, had the same address.

6. Bettina Calder.

[Fall, 1970]

Dear Sam,

Have just come from seeing Jackie M. magically transmitting the essence of you last night, and must share my feelings with you.[1] A grand evening with your words in the air; Judith and her husband and my Jean with me; and all of us thinking of you and wishing you well. Jackie was fine, a great success, and lots of young people in the audience enjoying Beckett. I had been a bit upset with our Jackie because after our conversations on the subject in London and Dublin, and then here while he was in *Gandhi,* I had gone on to make arrangements to present him in the Beckett evening; then, without a word to me, he had gone off to do it at the Public Theatre. Well, the main thing is that the program is on, most warmly received, and he is happy and has made up for the other unhappy theatre experience in New York. Saw him after the show, and he is in great form and spirits. Sorry you couldn't be here to share the evening's triumph. . . . Other things: have just returned from Toronto and Milwaukee[2] where the BECKETT-WARNER evening was also most successful. Assume the management or Francis has sent you reviews. Toronto was splendid to us. I thought COME

AND GO went very beautifully, and although I had to use the Oxford tape (which I was not entirely satisfied with), BREATH glowed. We did it only twice, before and after COME AND GO, so that the two made a unit. Also had a very good actor read ABANDONED WORK, and it went very well. The MAQUETTES, I tried to make as simple and clear as possible, and the audience was most attentive. Mrs. Zacks most pleased, and our friend Al Latner radiant in his first venture as producer. My main concern is how much we managed to raise for the Beckett Theatre, and Bob O'Driscoll assures me we did very well. I hope to be hearing from Francis at Oxford. Anyway, it was a great evening, and the occasion served its purpose. Sorel Etrog there and we talked about you.[3] . . . SAVED now running at the Cherry Lane, though business suffering because of the off-Broadway strike. Who knows how long. Had hoped to be in rehearsal with *Godot* at the nearby Sheridan Square—just to surprise and cheer you—but the strike has stopped everything. For how long? Want Jackie to play Vladimir, and he says he wants to—but his producer has him tied up with Beckett Evening and then a tour for the year. We shall see. At this point, I am keeping all fingers and toes and other parts of anatomy crossed. . . . Jackie says he's heard from you since operation, and that you are reasonably mending. Do take care of yourself, and let us hear from you when you can. In the meantime, Jean joins me in love and good wishes.

Ever,

[Alan]

1. Presented by the New York Shakespeare Festival at the Public/Newman Theatre, New York, *Jack MacGowran in the Works of Samuel Beckett*, staged by Joseph Papp, based on SB's Paris production of *Beginning to End*, opened 19 November 1970. Designed by Ming Cho Lee. In his review (*Women's Wear Daily*, 20 November) Martin Gottfried complained that New Yorkers had not seen a Beckett work for five years, because AS had a "strange hold" on the New York rights to Beckett's work and refused to allow anyone else to stage it in New York. Reviews: Mel Gussow, "The Quintessence of Beckett," *NY Times*, 20 November 1970; Richard Watts, "A Pair of Notable Irishmen," *NY Post*, 20 November; Edith Oliver, "Beckett at Astor Place," *The New Yorker*, 28 November; Walter Kerr, *Sunday Times*, 29 November.

2. *Breath, Come and Go*, directed by AS, and Francis Warner's *Maquettes* opened at the Hart House Theatre, Toronto, 16 November 1970. *Come and Go:* Jenny Earl (Flo), Adriana Lawrence (Vi), Treasa O'Driscoll (Ru). Chris Wiggins read from SB's *From an Abandoned Work*. Also opened 23 November at the Performing Arts Center (Vogel Hall), University of Wisconsin–Milwaukee. "From an Abandoned Work," *Trinity News* 3.4 (1956); reprinted in *No's Knife: Collected Shorter Pieces 1945–1966*, 1967, 139–149, French trans. by Ludovic and Agnès Janvier with SB, 1967, "D'un ouvrage abandonné."

3. Samuel and Ayala Zacks, wealthy Canadians, had contributed toward the SB Thea-

tre at Oxford. Sorel Etrog (b. 1933), sculptor, donated one of his works and designed lithographs for a limited edition of *Imagination Dead Imagine*. The Israeli artist Arikha Avigdor (b. 1929) presented two portraits of SB. The Beckett-Warner Evening, produced by A. J. Latner, was a tribute to the memory of Samuel J. Zacks by the University of Toronto, St. Peter's College, Oxford, and the Irish Theatre Society. Robert O'Driscoll taught at St. Michael's College, University of Toronto, and wrote the program note.

January 1, 1971

Dear Sam,

The first letter of the New Year, and—I hope—a harbinger of a better year to come. Barney just told me that he had seen you since the operation and that your sight and your morale much better. Great news. Judith here last night for some small grog round the fire with us, and we drank a special toast to you.

Real news is that as of tomorrow we are starting on that GODOT off-Broadway. Long-rumored, long-awaited, long hoped-for, and now finally here, I think. I'll believe it when it opens. The off-Broadway strike finally ended about a week or so ago, and we plunged in full steam ahead on casting and production details. Naturally, it would have been great if Jackie could have done it (and Pat, although Pat is doing another show in New York according to the grapevine). But when I approached Jackie after his performance, he was all booked up for the school tour and then London, so not available for a year if then. Would have been difficult if not impossible anyhow because of that alien business. OK in the one-man show because that means they have to pay him a Broadway salary; but when it comes to all the actors having to be paid on that scale, plus understudies, and crew, etc., it's impossible to do the show. So, sad . . .

But we did get what I think is a pretty special cast. Henderson Forsythe, who took over from D. Davis as Krapp, is doing Didi; and a youngish but very talented comedian, Paul Price, is Gogo. (How to banish the shades of Bert Lahr!) Price has played the part before somewhere, though I didn't see him, to great success. The Pozzo is Ed Winter, who left a successful Broadway musical, PROMISES PROM-ISES,[1] to come with us; he was McCann when I did BIRTHDAY PARTY. Lucky is a very interesting actor and pantomimist, Tony Holland. We are in the Sheridan Square Playhouse right in the heart of Greenwich

Village, absolutely splendid theatre and location, even better in some respects than Cherry Lane. Management is really a combination of owners of Sheridan Square plus Mark Wright (who co-produced BIRTHDAY PARTY) and myself. With money situation being very difficult in US at the moment, and with no subsidiary rights available on GODOT for potential investors, we are doing it on minimum cash outlay. Everyone except the actors working for nothing but with potential of something coming in should show run. I'm quite happy with that, just determined to keep artistic elements in proper shape. Designer is fellow who's done all the previous Beckett (and Albee and Pinter), Bill Ritman. We shall see. But here it is finally after all these years, and I know you're pleased about that. If we have reasonable success, we might even branch out a bit with KRAPP and pantomimes, etc. One step at a time. There seems to be good interest from the young people in the play, and we hope to bring them in. Trying to keep ticket prices down. It's awful what's happened to our theatre prices in last few years. . . .

And so it goes. Jackie huge success,[2] and deservedly so. Grove in various troubles, but Barney struggling on. Saw John Calder, who seems embarked on all sorts of ventures and trying to get me to London. Wouldn't mind but don't know how to swing it financially. SAVED had to close in spite of notices and acclaim because of the strike but will live in memory. Can't say my [words missing] truly about [words missing] theatre [word illegible] in NY has changed, but at least am working with marvelous material and with high hopes. Think of you & hope eyes & all else improving. Jean sends love & good thoughts for better New Year. Take care of yourself, will keep in touch. [handwritten from "strike"]

[Alan]

PS Edward A has given his new play to Sir John Gielgud to direct. Haven't read it.[3] [handwritten in left margin]

1. Adapted by Neil Simon (b. 1927); opened 1 December 1968.
2. *Jack MacGowran in the Works of Samuel Beckett* opened at the Kreeger Theater, Arena Stage, Washington, D.C., 16 March 1971.
3. Edward Albee's *All Over*, directed by John Gielgud, opened at the Martin Beck Theatre, New York, 27 March 1971.

Paris
9.1.71
Dear Alan

Many thanks for yours of New Year's Day.

Good news that you are reviving *Godot* off-B. Thanks for all the details. Very touched by your & actors' honorary [?]services and hope a success will [?]reward you. Snatch a moment here & there to let me know how it goes.

. . . .[1]

So sorry Barney in difficulty. I have no clear picture of what it is about. Very sad to think of them without Judith.[2]

Nothing of interest to tell. Self-translating a little, but heart not in it.[3] If possible shall go to Schiller Aug./Sept. to do *Happy Days*. Barlog's last Festival I understand.[4]

With new Minister of Culture here (Jacques Duhamel) faint hopes that things may improve.[5]

Love to you all.
Sam

1. SB cannot understand Jack MacGowran's plans.
2. Having borrowed heavily to expand in 1969, Grove Press was caught by the economic recession of 1971 when sales fell. They accepted an offer from Random House to handle their marketing. Judith Schmidt, who had worked at Grove Press from early 1956 to the end of 1970, was an active supporter of Eugene McCarthy in his election campaigns.
3. SB cannot go to Ussy.
4. Boleslaw Barlog (b. 1906), General-Intendant (director, theater manager) at Staatliche Schauspielbühnen (which included the Schiller-Theater, the Schiller-Theater Werkstatt, and the Schlosspark Theater), Berlin (1915–1972). Seating capacity: the Schiller: 1,100; the Werkstatt: 200; the Schlosspark: 470.
5. Jacques Duhamel (1924–1977), Minister for Culture, 1971–1973.

January 11, 1971
Dear Sam,

Slightly over a week's rehearsal, and I feel pretty good about the cast and the work done so far. Wish you were here to advise and pitch in personally, but I understand why you can't be. (That article on the Berlin production in THEATRE HEUTE has some lovely pictures, including one of you twisting around to show an actor the position you want him to assume.)[1] Anyhow, we are trying to do the play; and I feel of my four attempts so far, this is the one that gives promise of coming closest . . .

Have a few textual matters to ask you about. Some of them I may have asked you about in years past, in which case forgive me. Also, wherever your answer is NO, just say No. Pages are from the Grove edition. I hope you have one.

p. 8 Could we say 'Then I go all strange' instead of 'all queer'? Queer has a special connotation, especially in Greenwich Village.

p. 13A The chap playing Vladimir has been reading the French text. He asked me why you cut that little exchange about Godot after 'At his horse'. I said you probably didn't want that specific a reference. Would you object to our including that section between silences? Could you translate it for us? Or should we just forget about it?

p. 23A 'Pantomime' is not a familiar word for us in this context. Could you suggest another? Or do you prefer that we stick to it?

25 Does Pozzo say 'Even since' or 'ever since'? There are a couple of other typos in this script, and we just want to make sure whether this is or isn't one.

26 etc. Would you object to our finding American monetary equivalents for francs whenever they come up?

35 'Rhone' is not a familiar place name for us. Would you object to our saying 'river'?

39A We'd love something stronger than 'muckheap', if you wouldn't mind. 'Pile of crap'? Something else?

That's about all for now, and it all does seem rather insignificant, to bother you with it. But my asking you some of these small matters makes you come that much closer. If you don't want to bother, I'll understand. Do hope you are getting better with the eyes each day.

Jackie's reading session is ending as of Jan. 24. It could probably go on forever, but he feels it is too great a strain.[2] There is tremendous interest in GODOT. Already, just after the preliminary announcements, the management got a number of phone calls. The advertisement will be in next Sunday's paper; I am trying to make the public relations people pay some attention to previous material, but they usually go off on their own . . . I am most pleased with the physical setting for the play, and happy about the actors. Will continue to keep you posted.

All the best from all of us.

[Alan]

1. *Theatre Heute,* 4 (April 1965), 17, photograph of SB with Horst Bollmann.
2. *Jack MacGowran in the Works of Samuel Beckett* opened at the Public/Newman Theatre, 19 November 1970, closed after 61 performances.

                                                    Paris
                                                    14.1.71

Dear Alan

Thanks for yours of Jan. 11.

First your queries.

1. All *queer.* OK.
2. After *at his horse.* OK.
    Estragon: Let's go.
    Vladimir: Where? *(Pause)* Perhaps to-night we'll sleep under his roof, warm and dry, in the straw, with our bellies full. That's worth waiting for. No?
    [in margin SB writes "'in the straw' archaic 'in childhood'"]
    Estragon: Not all night.
    Vladimir: It's still day.
3. *Vaudeville* instead of *pantomime* if you prefer.
4. EVER since.
5. Prefer you keep *francs.* But as you wish.
6. Prefer you keep *Rhone.* But as you wish. Perhaps *River Rhone.*
7. *Pile of crap.* OK with reluctance. Prefer *pile of shit.*

Glad you are pleased with progress. Wish I could be with you getting in your way. Please let me know date of opening and address of theatre. Starting to translate *Film* into French & reading again your so generous account of proceedings.[1] My warm salutations to actors and all concerned.

Yours ever
Sam

1. AS, "On Directing *Film,*" in SB, *Film.*

Monday, Feb. 8, 1971

Dear Sam,

Writing to you from bed where I've been (with bad throat, intestinal flu, general nervous exhaustion) since the Wednesday opening. Apart from the physical state, however, I feel fine, and delighted with the reception given GODOT.[1] Pleased that it's come off so well after all these years, and only sorry I wasn't able to reach you by phone. Have tried every night, and have just been told by the MacGowrans that you may not be answering the phone. I thought you might have gone away somewhere to rest.

Anyhow . . .

The show went really well. We had a week of previews during which the response got better and better and the actors got used to things. Barney came and liked it very much. Jackie was invited to the first preview but was too tired from his own chores; he and his wife did come the night before the official opening, and I sat next to them. Jackie laughed a lot & seemed most responsive and pleased with basic production. Various other people: Judith, John Kobler, Dick Seaver and Jeannette. George Reavey was supposed to be coming, but I haven't seen him.

The reviews were 90% per cent excellent, which is almost unheard of in New York. And they all recognised the play's greatness and strength. The only bad ones that I know of at the moment are in CUE, a sort of guide to entertainment weekly which I haven't seen but evidently didn't like the production; TIME, which liked the production but doesn't understand the play; WOMEN'S WEAR, whose critic has been waging a personal vendetta against me; and one of the radio critics. I just heard that the VILLAGE VOICE is very good indeed. After the opening, I asked the producers to send you copies of all the reviews; as usual, there's some confusion as to whether they did so, so I am sending you those I have. They're still coming in, and I'll eventually get them all to you. The main thing is that we have been steadily building an audience even before the reviews came out. We were sold out for every single preview, with people—mostly young people—coming and standing in line to buy tickets. There is tremendous interest in the play and in your work, and a whole new generation is availing itself of the chance to see GODOT professionally done. The word-of-mouth must be good because our advance sale has been building by the hour. I am enclosing today's advertisement just to give you an idea.

The theatre is in a perfect location, in the heart of Greenwich Village.

We have a large banner up saying WAITING FOR GODOT, which can be seen from all over (we are two blocks from the Cherry Lane), a photo of you which we got from Grove, and some photos of the actors; plus blow-ups of the TIMES and the POST reviews. It seats only just under 200, but has marvelous intimacy and warmth. The setting, done by the same fellow who did *Krapp* and *Happy Days*, is simple and quite lovely, we think.[2] We were unable to have a cyclorama because of technical reasons, but we project the moon on a textured dark brick wall, and it is most effective. The cast is a balanced one, and there is great sympathy for all of them. Vladimir reminds me much of Raimbourg;[3] he is tall, slender, looks very professorial, and has a great voice (he played Krapp after Donald Davis). Estragon is small, pert, overt, somewhat mousy and terribly appealing. The two of them make a fine combination. (I was very worried that the ghost of Bert Lahr would hover over the proceedings because the myth of his performance is very widespread, but the actor and the combination was so different that the memory did not hurt us.) Lucky is an extraordinarily sensitive young actor who does all the pantomime very well and on opening night was electrifying with the speech—although he varies a bit. Pozzo is the best Pozzo I have seen in English; he is huge with a big voice and a most believable hollow quality when he needs it. The accent (Italian-Continental) is his idea and crutch; I tried at one time to get him not to use it, but it helps him in some way and we kept it. The boy is simple and sincere and lovely. I'm quite pleased with the production—not that it doesn't have many faults or cannot be improved—and Barney told me it is the best GODOT he has seen. What's so marvelous is that the play is so clear and immediate, without any gimmicks or nudity or rock and roll music—which lots of people wanted me to use or thought I was going to use. They're crazy. We get lots of high school and college kids, and they sit there and really eat it up. It's wonderful watching their faces . . . We are selling tickets, the ad says, until the end of 1971, hah! Don't know how long we can keep the actors, but I'm trying. Everyone is quite happy being connected with the show, and morale is excellent on all fronts . . . As for me, I cannot tell you how grateful I am to you for your patience with me and your trust. It's been 15 years that we've been waiting for GODOT to come back. But it turned out to be the right time and the right place and the right combination of chemicals . . . I do hope you are OK and I really missed not being able to talk with you right after the opening. Jackie tells me your second operation will be soon. We are all looking forward to your being over that hump, and to your recovery. Don't worry about answering this letter or anything. And I'll just keep sending things on to you. We also have some photos of the production which will be forthcoming although, as usual, they were shot before we had all the proper costumes and makeup. But they'll give you an idea of what it looks like.

Do take care of yourself. We think of you all the time and feel your presence. Thanks for the opening-night telegram, which the actors and everyone much appreciated.

Excuse the lousy typing and confusion of stationery.

Ever,

[Alan]

1. *Waiting for Godot* opened at the Sheridan Square Playhouse, New York, 3 February 1971, produced by AS and Mark Wright, directed by AS, designed by William Ritman. Paul B. Price (Estragon), Henderson Forsythe (Vladimir), Anthony Holland (Lucky), Edward Winter (Pozzo), David Jay (A Boy). Reviews: Clive Barnes, *NY Times*, 4 February 1971; Martin Gottfried, *Women's Wear Daily*, 4 February; Richard Watts, Jr., *NY Post*, 4 February; *Village Voice*, 11 February; Edith Oliver, *The New Yorker*, 13 February; Marilyn Stasio, *Cue*, 13 February; Walter Kerr, *NY Times*, 14 February; T. E. Kalem, *Time*, 15 February; Harold Clurman, *The Nation*, 22 February; Jack Richardson, *Commentary* 51.4 (April); John H. Reilly, *Christian Century*, 10 May. Martin Gottfried renewed his attack on AS: "he seems to have convinced Beckett that only he can stage this or any of the author's others."

2. William Ritman.

3. In Roger Blin's production, Théâtre de Babylone, Paris, 5 January 1953, Pierre Latour (Estragon) and Lucien Raimbourg (Vladimir) were cast for contrast; since then the casting of the two characters tends to duplicate that contrast. See Ruby Cohn, "Growing (up?) with Beckett," *Beckett at 80/Beckett in Context*, ed. Enoch Brater, 1986.

Paris

12.2.71

Dear Alan

Many thanks for your cable, letters and cuttings. Delighted to have such good news of the production. Warm congratulations to you all.

I'm sorry you've been laid up and hope the worst is over. Also that you've been phoning me in vain. In self-defence I acquired a phone that can be switched off as required and I only answer between 11 and noon.

I have been pottering along with odds & ends of self-translation pending second operation fixed for next week.[1] Finished French *Film* notably which carried me back to those exciting weeks in N.Y. nearly 7 years ago.

. . . .[2]

Love to you all and again *bravissimo.*

Sam

1. *Le Dépeupleur* and *Mercier et Camier.*
2. SB mentions a Synge-Yeats Conference in Toronto.

Sunday, February 28, [1971]

Dear Sam,

Just heard from Barney that your second operation is over, and that all is well, or will be as soon as you've had a few weeks of rest.

You must be glad that's over.

We're all so pleased that it's finally done and you can get some rest and look forward to seeing a lot better.

Got your letter, and the solution to the mystery of your telephone not answering. Thank you. I thought at first of calling you during the witching hour, but then decided to leave you alone for the time being.

GODOT has been on five weeks and nary an empty seat, with the demand for tickets growing steadily, and the responses basically excellent. I see it once or twice per week and give a few notes, but on the whole the show remains consistent. The last time I saw it, the best and most balanced performance. They laugh a lot and they are moved at the end.

We think there is no doubt that it will just go on running, through the year and with a bit of luck, longer. Perhaps a tour to schools and colleges in the fall. There is tremendous interest on the part of the young people; we have them as at least half of our audience every night, and on three or four nights per week usually a school group comes together. They tend to sit there in hushed awe a bit, but then warm up in Act II.

The real problem—typical of off-Broadway—is that our actors get and take other jobs, even though we offer them the maximum salary of which the gross is capable. We've already lost Lucky to a film (he may come back, he says, but I have my doubts), but were very lucky to get another actor who is equally effective though quite different. I have been working with him and in a couple of weeks, he should be as good as the original. Hopefully. There is also a strong possibility of our losing our Estragon (Paul Price) who is off to act in and direct his own film. We are trying to hold on to him as long as possible, but in the meantime, I am rehearsing another fellow, who is quite different physically and rhythmically but very suitable in his own way. Larger, rounder, and very physical. We shall see. The process is endless, and we'll probably have a half-dozen actors in each role before it's over. I know every role and every line, and in a pinch could go on myself—though I cannot imagine doing nearly so well as the actors we have. (We also have understudies.)[1]

I hear there are some other reviews but at the moment, you have received or at least been sent all I have. The main thing is that we are doing well, the word-of-mouth is good, and there is lots of talk.

Miss you and hope you are soon on the mend. Hope I'll get over to see you this summer but present plans not clear. If and when I can, I'd love you to autograph some *Godot* copies for the cast and staff; I'll bring them over. Take care. We will think of you every day. Will return Sat. when [handwritten after earlier "when"; ending missing]

Alan

1. Replacements: for Paul B. Price: Oliver Clark, Warren Pincus; for Henderson Forsythe: Warren Pincus, Jordan Charney, David Byrd, Tom Ewell; for Anthony Holland: Tom Rosqui, Dan Stone; for Edward Winter: Larry Bryggman, Ed Bordo.

Paris
5.3.71

Dear Alan

I feel Mr. Breuer should be allowed to present *PLAY* in the way he describes & wd. be grateful for any help you can give him to that end.[1]

Best always
Sam

1. Lee Breuer (b. 1937), director, playwright, actor, founding member of Mabou Mines, 1963, avant-garde theater company associated until 1973 with La Mama Experimental Theatre Club (E.T.C.); produced SB's *Play, Come and Go, The Lost Ones, Cascando,* 1974–1975.

Paris
14.3.71

Dear Alan

Thanks for yours of Feb. 28.

Very glad to have such good news of *Godot* & sorry for all the trouble you are having with cast. Saw Barney & Christine last night, full of praise for the production. Shall be delighted to autograph books for staff and cast.

. . . .[1] Have accepted Schiller Theater's invitation to do *Happy Days* in the Werkstatt Aug. Sept. Winnie: Eva-Katharina Schultz. Don't know her but she looks good. They are inviting Jackie to give his show at the same time, also in the Werkstatt.[2]

Sorry you have been phoning in vain. . . .[3]

Do hope you get over in the summer. Thanks again for *Godot.*

Love to you all
Sam

1. SB's vision is improving.
2. "show": *Beginning to End.*
3. SB only answers the telephone between eleven o'clock and noon.

March 20, 1971

Dear Sam,

Got your last letter, and glad to hear eyes are progressing. Marvelous news!

Nothing to thank me for on GODOT; I'm the one who should thank you.

Have just arranged to have sent to you a package of photos of the production, as well as a few from previous pieces, taken by Alix Jeffrey,[1] whom you met during shooting of FILM. They are quite good, and should give you some idea of how show looked.

Into our eighth week, and hardly an empty seat. Was there again last night, and about 12 people waiting at the box office for possible returns. The only sad fact is that we now have three new actors, our Pozzo off to do the lead in a Broadway musical. Only original Vladimir remains. But we have been fortunate in replacement actors, and show continues in reasonable shape. We seem constantly to be rehearsing, and I am constantly giving notes; but that's the nature of the beast. New Estragon large and round but similar combination of physical and child-like, the new Lucky is, in some respects, even more terrifying, the new Pozzo quite interesting, but not yet powerful enough to 'shatter the space of the play', as you once told me. We're still working.

Also on the possibility of a college tour in the fall. We have offered Jackie MacGowran Vladimir (or whichever part he wants) but I gather from his agent—Jackie is now away from New York with BEGINNING TO END—that he's probably not going to be available. Although I thought I'd try. Would love to get him into GODOT somehow somewhere.

There's also a future prospect of a 'Beckett Evening' of some of the shorter pieces which haven't been done here yet: the pantomimes, COME AND GO, perhaps PLAY (performed twice with or without the National Theatre variations, as you prefer). I think this should wait a while until we have the right actors and occasion, and until GODOT has run longer. We shall see.

Delighted to hear you are doing HAPPY DAYS in Berlin. I have heard of the actress. Wish I could be there to see you. Don't you need an assistant? If it were the Soviet Union, I could translate for you. Not sure of my summer plans, or whether will get to Europe. Awaiting Francis Warner's new play,[2] which he has asked me to do at Oxford. Also have a possible film, as well as some teaching. General theatre situation just as bad as ever, but lots of activity.

Always lovely to hear from you, but don't feel pressed to answer my letters. I just want to keep you posted. All the best from Jean. [ending missing]

[Alan]

1. Alix Jeffrey, New York photographer.
2. *Lying Figures* opened at the Oxford Playhouse, 21 June 1971; AS did not direct.

Paris
18.4.71

Dear Alan

Many thanks for pneu[1] sent day of departure. Very touched by your kind thought.

I greatly enjoyed our evening together[2] and hope it won't be long before another such.

I had a letter from Jack pleased with his new flat and things generally and looking forward to *Krapp.*

Contrary to what Barlog said his Berlin is by no means off though not yet definitely clinched apparently.

Let me know how it goes when you have time and not before, by it meaning the lot.

Love to you all
Sam

1. "pneu": form of letter service in which the messenger waited until the return form had been completed.

2. AS has seen SB in Paris to discuss the television production of *Krapp's Last Tape* with Jack MacGowran.

Monday, May 3, 1971

Dear Sam,

Finally!

Please forgive my not writing as soon as I got back—and thanks for your kind note—but I took off at once for Sioux Falls, North or South Dakota, was traveling all over the West for a week, came back to a bum tooth and equally bum typewriter and all sorts of matters left undone.

Mainly, I came back to Grove Press' partner, whoever, pulling out of the KRAPP deal, and all gloom with Barney and Joe Liss. Immediately got cracking in various quarters, including the fellow who's making the film in the desert with Jackie. Finally, Mark Wright, one of the coproducers of GODOT managed to get the money, and we are once more back in business.[1] This time, for real. Because I started with Jackie and the text today, and your changes, about which we are both enthusiastic. Rehearse daily, and plan to put on tape (TV) on Monday, May 17. Assuming all goes well. Then Jackie departs for California and the other venture. So, he's busy.[2]

Will keep you posted as much as possible about our progress here, although it's all happening pretty fast. Will do as stated by your notes and adapted by our immediate situation. Am sure all will be reasonably well but you know those technical necessities that are always creeping up, whatever they are and wherever they come from. Would be much simpler, for example, if we didn't have that doorway into the den, and he faded into dark as before. But den is lovely and we're going to do it.

Really enjoyed visit with you, brief as it was, and delighted to find you in good shape and spirits. The evening we were together, you must have thought I looked like a balloon because I was suffering from something swelling up my face. Thought it was sinus or gangrene, but turned out to be infected tooth, which practically killed me in plane, but taken care of the moment I hit the ground. I'm back to normal, which is no great shakes either.

Spoke to Barney about Jeannette's letter, and I gather he has written to you. As I suspected, there's nothing in the rumor that Grove is in any way changing anything in regard to treatment and disposition of your plays. Judith's absence, I'm sure, makes it harder for whoever is dealing with matter to know every detail of the past. But they call Judith and they even call me, so all continues as before, as far as I can tell. André Gregory group, which has had great acclaim for workshop of ALICE IN WONDERLAND is, I've been told, working on ENDGAME for the fall. They're interesting and very Grotowski group, but inclined to use text for own purposes.[3] But with their standing in theatrical community, hard to refuse them permission though not sure you'd be happy with results. PLAY done at Yale, I didn't get back in time to see it, mixed response.[4]

GODOT continues, houses slightly falling but we feel good about getting through summer. Forsythe has had to leave but we hope just for a while until he recovers strength (has been doing TV series all the time also). And so it goes. Everyone most grateful for signed copies. Please forgive scattered missive, am finding some kind of solution . . .[?] & desk . . . play Krapp. [handwritten from "copies"]

A

1. Barney Rosset and Joe Liss wanted to film *Krapp* in New York for PBS, WNET-TV, New York, produced by Mark Wright, directed by AS with Jack MacGowran.

2. Jack MacGowran played The Fool, Paul Scofield played Lear in Peter Brook's film of *King Lear*. Athena-Laterna. The location in the Mojave Desert, California, was chosen to make a film of MacGowran's one-man SB show, entitled *Beginning to End*; there were two versions, one for TV, shown by KCET-TV, Los Angeles, 4 November 1971, and one for cinema. The Pinnacles in the Mojave Desert, prehistoric columns near Death Valley, were regarded as a suitable landscape.

3. André Gregory (b. 1934), director, actor, producer, identified with 1960s avant-garde; founded the Manhattan Project environmental theater group, which adapted per-

formances to suit each group, affiliated with New York University, produced *Alice in Wonderland*, 1970, and achieved immediate fame. Jerzy Grotowski (b. 1933), Polish director, in his experimental theater in Wroclaw wanted actors to achieve a state of trance in order to give a more open performance; influenced Peter Brook's Living Theatre, New York, Joseph Chaikin, and Chaikin's Open Theatre's production of *Endgame*, Washington Square Methodist Church, 30 May 1970, directed by Roberta Sklar. Joseph Chaikin (Hamm), Peter Maloney (Clov), James Barbosa (Nagg), Jayne Haynes (Nell); closed 14 June 1970.

4. The Yale Repertory Theatre presented Georg Büchner's *Woyzeck* and SB's *Play*, 1–14 April, directed by Tom Haas. Sarah Albertson (w1: First Woman), Elizabeth Parrish (w2: Second Woman), David Ackroyd (Man).

May 12, 1971

Dear Sam,

Off we go again!

Have been in rehearsal with Jackie one week, and he is doing marvelously well, slowly but beautifully. We are working very well together, a real collaboration; and each day I feel closer and happier about the work and about him. He's most cooperative, inventive, and hardworking. He's also very glad to be doing KRAPP finally, and we have even talked about possibility of his doing it on stage some time now that he's tackled it. We talk about you constantly, and almost feel sometimes as though you were here. Certainly, there are vibrations all around.

Now, having told you what's good, I've also got to share the other side of the experience with you so you'll understand. We went into rehearsal, with the understanding that Jackie had to leave for California to do the desert film on May 18; so we hired a studio and scheduled the taping for May 17, organising our crew schedule, etc. for that date. There was some preference voiced by Jackie's agent (and by Jackie) for an earlier taping date, say on May 14, if possible (Sat. and Sunday, May 15 and 16 are impossible because the weekend costs are double); but it was obvious that we would be taping on May 17 and Jackie would depart for California on May 18 to start his film on May 20, as scheduled. Then, yesterday morning, his agent informed us for the first time that Jackie *had* to tape on May 14 because he *had* to leave for California on May 15. Jackie concurred, saying he was ready to tape on Friday, although he has admitted since that he is indeed not ready in terms of the lines and business. We cannot tape on Friday, May 14, because the staff and crew and studio are not sufficiently available, I am scheduled in my planning to tape May 17, and Jackie is not ready either.

To make a long story short, my producer here had to give in: which means, letting Jackie go to Calif. Saturday (we tried to get them to postpone there but it is impossible), cancelling all our scheduling here, and postponing everything until Jackie is finished there. So we are now planning to resume rehearsals on May 24, and then tape on June 2 because the previous weekend is a Memorial Day Holiday and nothing is available. Sorry about the delay, but there was no alternative. What most troubles me is that the agent (and, presumably, Jackie) knew all along that we would have to be finished here by May 14 but didn't make that clear to us because they were afraid we would not be able to schedule KRAPP at all in that case. Then they hoped to pressure us during rehearsals to tape in time. This doesn't affect my working relationship with Jackie as an actor, but I must confess it does make me question the goodness of mankind, or at least the theatre. Anyhow, I am happy about the work, and that is the important thing. Also, I want Jackie to be in good shape for the film out there. So, perhaps, all will be well.

In the meantime, let me take advantage of the delay to ask one question. Camera A is OK, fine, throughout as you have indicated. The problem of having Camera B moving around for so long and then stopping as indicated is a serious one. (We tried it in the Studio one day.) The movement is most distracting. Would you object to our getting the equivalent effect by less movement, and then by coming in for very tight close-ups on details: machine, hands, face, etc. as indicated? That would give us opportunity to watch and listen to Jackie & still focus on details. But to move the camera around as planned would not only take weeks of rehearsal with camera (which is impossible) but I'm afraid would not accomplish what you really want; which is to serve as Krapp's listening ear. The best way to suggest that would be in some carefully selected use of closeups. (I mean even closer than Camera B.) We'd still be using two cameras, and one would indeed be objective covering basic action of the scene, and the other more subjective as inner listening perceiving self. Would appreciate your reaction to this alternative, or some other thoughts. Everything else seems OK, and I am looking forward to moving forward as soon as Jackie gets back.

Your Berlin book has been most helpful in all respects, and I am most grateful for having it from you.[1] Wish I had seen Held. Gather the double bill was a great success in London.[2]

Trust your eyes are improving, and that you will soon be able to go to Ussy. Jackie assures me he will be in Berlin. Jean sends her love. Best.

[Alan]

1. SB's "Berlin book": *Samuel Beckett, Das Letzte Band: Regiebuch der Berliner Inszenierung*, 1970, ed. James Knowlson; *Samuel Beckett, Krapp's Last Tape, Theatre Workbook I*, 1980, and *The Theatrical Notebooks of Samuel Beckett, III, Krapp's Last Tape*, 1994.
2. "double bill": *Krapp's Last Tape* and *Endgame* performed by the Schiller-Theater of West Berlin opened at the Aldwych Theatre, London, 29 April 1971, directed by SB, designed by Matias. Martin Held (Krapp). *Endgame:* Ernst Schröder (Hamm), Horst Bollman (Clov), Werner Stock (Nagg), Gudrun Genest (Nell).

Paris
17.5.71

Dear Alan

Thank you for your letters with news of *Krapp*.

Very sorry to hear of Jacky contretemps and hope the interruption won't set you back too far.

Re Camera B use it as you deem best. My notes are no more than suggestions & and have no pretensions to finality.

. . . .[1]

Forgive this poor note and thanks again for your patience & persistence in spite of upsets.

Love to you all
Sam

1. SB has had the flu.

Sunday, June 6, 1971

Dear Sam,

Well, it's all down on tape now, and tomorrow we'll be editing it, and hopefully by the end of the day something. Not too bad.

Actually, when we finished shooting on Wednesday, we were all happy and pleased, and I felt you would have been too. A long and rough day, as expected, with the usual problems and pressures from the technical side. Time and space. We had only one day for the shooting because of costs; and it's a relatively small studio though well equipped. The cameramen were the best two I've ever worked with, quick, cooperative and good; the crew was excellent all around, and we wasted very little time. Just that there was only one day. Space in the control room at a minimum, and various problems throughout the day with sound coming in from outside, etc. In spite of all, we managed to get through the show twice, with two cameras shooting all the time, so that we can edit back and forth. Jackie looked marvelous. He did his own makeup, and I think fine. We had some chance the day before to look at him through the camera. We shot in color video-tape, which looks marvelous, though I must say I also liked it on the black-and-white monitor where we could see it from time to time as we were shooting.

For some reason not clear to anybody, in the first section of the show, Jackie started to stretch the time, and we suddenly found ourselves more than 7 minutes over what we had been running in rehearsals. We picked up time as we went along, but the first taping, roughly, ran over an hour. So that we decided to shoot the whole show over again, this time it was 53 minutes. Now we can use this version as a master, and edit from the other run here and there if we want to. We took from 9 in the morning to block out and shoot in sections through the whole show, finishing at half-past four. Then we shot some inserts, then at 5 started a complete re-run. This time we went through without any technical stops because the crew knew the show, stopping only for Jackie three times when he forgot a piece of business or reversed a line. Every time we stopped, it would take 15–20 minutes to get all the elements together to start again, but we still finished up at 6:30. Really a good show, and the crew most enthusiastic. I must tell you that Jackie was magnificent from an acting point of view. He played beautifully, every moment, and some of his closeups are really alive. His broods, his memories of the eyes, etc. etc.

Wish I could describe the whole thing to you. Basically we started back as far back as we could with Camera A, then moved in to frame the action, which was held throughout, including the door when we needed it. The other camera was moving over the field with very large closeups on face, hands, whatever. We shall make decisions on where Camera B shots will be used when we edit. Then we also shot some additional 'insert' shots, from other angles, above, and so on. Doing TV is considerably different from making a film, in that you see exactly what you are shooting, you do it faster, with less changes of lighting, etc. On the other hand, certain details and subtleties tend to get lost since you do not change the lights for each shot. It's fascinating and terrifying. But all in all, at least as far as we can tell, we have excellent footage, and the only concern now is to put it all together in the best possible way. I cannot believe that when it gets on TV Jackie will not win some sort of award for his performance. (By the way, I was with him when he got the 'Obie', and all of us most pleased.)[1] He seems to be enjoying his NY stay. I just hope that the good luck and work will continue. And I feel very good that we finally got together and got to know each other. Would love for Jackie to do KRAPP (and the panto-mimes) on the stage sometime, and he also wants to. We seemed to hit it off together, and I look forward to further association. . . . Will write again after we have edited. In the meantime, thanks.

   [Alan]

   1. Won Obie Award for Best Actor in an off-Broadway performance, *Jack MacGowran in the Works of Samuel Beckett,* and the New York Drama Critics Circle "Actor of the Year" Award, the first non-American actor to do so (see letter of "Fall 1970," n. 1).

                                                           Paris
                                                           9.6.71

Dear Alan

   Thanks for yours of June 6. It is very good of you to write me such a full account of *Krapp* shooting. Sounds fine. Thank you again for going to such pains. Do hope you will do it with Jack on stage some day. . . . .[1]

   No news from Jack. Hope his desert film went well & Berlin engagement confirmed. Good news he got the Obie. Had not heard. Not much zest for *H.D.* in Berlin.[2] Often wonder who wrote that play and why. Answer to second question coming slowly back.

   Hope interesting work on your horizon and all well with Jean & kids.

   Love to you all
   Sam

1. SB has had a virus, now intends to go to Italy.

2. SB had committed himself to directing *Happy Days* in German for the Schiller-Theater, Berlin Festival, rehearsals at the end of August. Jack MacGowran would also perform his *Beginning to End*.

July 18, 1971

Dear Sam,

Don't know whether you're back from Portugal yet, but hastening to write to tell you the sad news that GODOT is finally having to close the end of this week. Actually, I didn't know until I found out by accident in the papers a few days ago—because the management probably didn't have the heart to let me know. They may have written or be writing to you directly.

Actually, business has, as you can probably tell from the royalty statements recently, not been good for some time now. The general economic recession, the high prices, the heat, and the dangers of New York streets are all tending to keep people out of the theatres. I heard before I left NY early in July that every single show on Broadway was on 'twofers', which means surviving by selling two tickets for the price of one. Off-Broadway cannot do that because of its smaller-size theatres; but we have been selling student tickets and also tickets to special groups at lower prices. As we got into the summer season, this audience lessened, and we got into trouble.

We had hoped to have a new lease on life when we put in Tom Ewell (the original Vladimir in Miami) and Joey Faye just before I left; but as it turned out even that didn't work. Joey couldn't learn the lines and we had to postpone his going in;[1] Tommy was really very good (better than he had been in Miami, and almost up to Forsythe, who had had to leave earlier for personal reasons, sad to say), but business did not pick up enough to justify going on beyond the end of July.[2] At various times, we have had 4 different Vladimirs, 4 Estragons, 4 Pozzos, and 3 Luckys. The boy was indestructible, and so was the spirit of our stage staff.

Naturally, I am sorry to see it end; but happy that it ran so long (six months and almost 200 performances) and to such a receptive response, both critical and audience. I was pleased, relatively, with the production, and happy about the performers who were with us the longest. Off-Broadway, it's becoming increasingly impossible to hang on to good actors for more than a brief time, and the succession is often exasperating. Our stage management performed wonders to keep the show operating on as high a level as possible each night, and I am most grateful to them all. And, most of all, I am thankful to you for the play, and for your patience and trust which made this production possible again after all these years.

The currently-edited version of KRAPP had a small 'preview' last week for Grove Press and a few friends, and the report I received was that the reactions were basically good. I think it could stand a bit more editing, but liked Jackie very much (even though we had great trouble matching various takes of his because he was different each time) and thought the overall impression fascinating, though very special. We are now trying to sell it. Hope either I or Mark Wright (the producer) can bring you a copy of the TV-tape this fall sometime.[3]

Am nearing the end of my month here, directing a show and lecturing. A very alive University and enterprising in the Arts. Lovely theatre and congenial surroundings. Pleasant old-world German town, and beautiful lake-front. Jean and family enjoying it, and a great break from NY. Trust you are well and back in Paris—or Ussy.

[Alan]

1. Joey Faye (Joseph Antony Palladino, b. 1910), American actor, comedian.
2. Review: Mel Gussow, *NY Times,* 29 July, featuring Tom Ewell (Vladimir), who joined the cast on 28 July.
3. A copy of this *Krapp* is kept at the Performing Arts Research Center, New York Public Library; it was never released for public television.

                                                        Paris
                                                        [?]21.7.71
Dear Alan

Many thanks for your letter of July 18. *Godot* has had a great run & I'm not [at] all disappointed or surprised that it has to close. Thank you again for all you have done to keep it going in the teeth of such difficulties.

Distressed to hear from George Reavey that you had run foul of the cops.[1] Hope you are none the worse and that they make you amends.

. . . .[2] Getting ready none the less to take off next month for Berlin and

Happy Days. Talk of Deryk Mendel making a film of the two *Acts Without Words* playing all three parts. Perhaps shoot here in October. . . . .[3]

So you still have thoughts of living in London . . .?
Love to you all.

Ever
Sam

1. AS was assaulted by a policeman in New York on 25 May 1971. Three witnesses filed complaints on his behalf (see Linda Charlton, "Broadway Director Says Policeman Assaulted Him," *NY Times*, 8 June 1971).
2. SB still feels effects of the virus.
3. SB saw Helen Bleu, the sculptor, "yesterday."

August 29, 1971

Dear Sam,

Writing this much too belated a note directly to you in Berlin, hoping to catch you with the latest news.

A harrowing month since I last wrote, but the one ray is that GODOT is not only still running but picking up. We may get killed by Labor Day Weekend, but at the moment things look reasonable on the box-office front, and picking up artistically. More below.

Since I last wrote, I returned to NY from Wisconsin. My mother came back from Israel and Switzerland in very bad shape, having suffered a slight stroke (without telling us), and the night we brought her home from the airport she was hardly there, and we were not sure she would survive the night. . . .[1]

At the same time, I had my trial. Finally. After many evasions and hypocrisies. I was completely acquitted, but the whole affair, not only with the actual cop beating me up but with the process of chasing through the courts just to get some kind of justice was a very emotional harangue on all sides. Thanks for your good thoughts. I didn't really want to burden you with the news, but it seems to have been all over the papers, so you found out anyhow. Basically, it has to do with the police being up-tight at the moment, and the general atmosphere in NY being rather terrifying on all counts. There is not one time that I go in that I am not worried of something happening. Though I would never have imagined that I might get physically assaulted by a policeman in broad daylight for not getting out of his way fast enough. Well, it is all over, and all is well; I am now suing the city (hah!), and of course, I have a complaint against the cop with a special Board for that purpose—though whether anything will happen is not clear. The good thing was that two guys who did not know me came as witnesses on my behalf, and in effect saved me from a possible conviction. Restores my faith in New York people.

About GODOT: I thought it was closing in July when I wrote you. But was surprised to find it still running when I got back. Everyone except actors off salary, of course, but audiences picking up. And Tom Ewell very good. He got several notices, which I am sending to you separately. Big article in today's TIMES,[2] and general interest. We shall see. We have recently gone over 250 performances. Saw the show last week, and it is not bad. Another Estragon goes on this week, and I am now in rehearsal with him. Irish chap, Geoff Garland, you wouldn't know him.[3]

Jackie, I gather is off to Berlin. Best wishes both for HAPPY DAYS and the Beckett program. Wish I were there with the two of you, I'd be much happier. Great interest in the KRAPP tape, but no sale yet. General economic situation here very uncertain. I'd love to live in England but haven't the economic wherewithal. Even wrote to Ireland to see if I'd qualify under non-tax status. Would I like living outside the USA? [last line missing]

All the best.
[Alan]

1. Rebecka Samdilovna (Revecka) Schneider: AS describes his mother's illness and the difficulty of taking care of her.
2. Ira Peck wrote "At Last He's Shaken 'The Seven Year Itch,'" *NY Times,* 29 August 1971, mainly about Tom Ewell and his memories of the Miami production of *Waiting for Godot.* AS had given his memories in the *NY Times* on 31 January: "No More Waiting."
3. Geoff Garland (b. 1926), English-born actor, director, writer.

Selmun
Malta
18.10.71

Dear Alan

Thanks for letter of Aug. 29 and *Godot* notices received a few days ago. Please forgive long delay in writing. Berlin though pleasant as always was difficult and results inferior to those with *Endgame–Krapp*.[1] Schultz a bit young for the part & not quite up to it technically, not to mention being scandalously under strain throughout rehearsals (5 weeks) from having to perform on an average 3–4 evenings a week in 3 different plays! Not to mention your servant's shortcomings. Another 10 days and I think we would have made it more or less. As it was . . . on the right lines (for me). . . .[2]

Jacky gave his show twice in the Werkstatt and they loved him. He left Berlin the same day as me for Dublin invited by the Gaiety for its centenary celebration.[3] Then back to USA for a big tour beginning Princeton I think . . . .[4]

Congratulations & gratitude to you all for continuance of *Godot*.

With me no work except a little dreary belated self-translation.[5]

. . . .[6]

Love to you all.
Sam

1. *Glückliche Tage* opened at the Schiller-Theater Werkstatt, 17 September 1971, directed by SB, designed by Matias, translated by Erika and Elmar Tophoven. Eva-Katharina Schultz (Winnie), Rudi Schmitt (Willie). SB prepared two detailed notebooks on the production of *Glückliche Tage* and made many changes in the text: *Glückliche Tage/Oh les beaux jours/Happy Days*, Suhrkamp, 1975; *Happy Days/Oh les beaux jours*, ed. James Knowlson, 1978.

2. SB was handicapped during rehearsals by arthritis in his shoulders.

3. *Jack MacGowran in the Works of Samuel Beckett* opened at the Gaiety Theatre, Dublin, 26 October 1971.

4. SB comments on MacGowran's health and sympathizes with AS on his mother's condition.

5. See letter of 12 February 1971, n. 1.

6. SB says it will be hard to return to the Paris "cauldron."

October 17, 1971

Dear Sam,

In New York for my day off from the show in Washington, where I've been for three weeks. Just a note to tell you that GODOT finally closed—because Tom Ewell had to go off to deal with his mother who is seriously ill in Kentucky somewhere. We tried to get Henderson Forsythe back, but he was available only for a week or so, so we finally decided we had no equal alternative. Better to close with dignity, or whatever. So . . . . 280 performances or thereabouts. Not bad, considering. And generally good response even near the end. Just sad to see it happen.

Have been calling Jackie M. to see if he's back from Berlin, and to get news of you. No response. Will try again when I'm back in NY once more. Judith told Jean that she had missed you last time she was over, so presumably you may not be in Paris at the moment. How did HAPPY DAYS go in Berlin? And you? And Jackie?

I long for news.

Saw the TV KRAPP again a few weeks ago, and reasonably pleased except for some technical sound problems which they have not yet quite solved but are working on. Did Jackie tell you about the process? Not yet sold but will be.

My police affair is over. I was acquitted, the cop is now facing departmental charges, and I'm suing the city. Nothing will happen but at least there's been a flurry about policemen beating up civilians, which happens every day every hour on the hour in NY.

Enjoying the experience in Washington (Arena Stage) where I am doing a new play, CANCER, which was done last year at the Royal Court in London to favorable attention.[1] Written by a young American writer resident in England, talented and with an individual voice. About a graduating class of American students and how they face themselves. Really lovely Chekhovian play.

Still not sure of future plans. Have a Broadway show in November which I'm not really keen on doing. Thinking seriously of trying to get some sort of teaching base which would support me and still let me go on directing here and there. Really impossible to make a living rattling around. Next summer I'll be conducting a seminar at the University of East Anglia in Norwich, England; hope to get over to Paris in late July, we shall see. And so on.

Trust your eyes are well, and you are having or will have a good rest after the Berlin adventure. Would love to know how it went.

Take care of yourself. Best from all of us.

Ever,

[Alan]

1. Michael Weller's play, *Cancer,* had opened at the Royal Court Theatre, 14 September 1970; as *Moonchildren* opened at the Arena Stage, Washington, D.C., 29 October 1971.

> Paris
> 30.1.72

Dear Alan

Many thanks for yrs. of Dec. 30.[1] Late in day for wishes but best wishes to you all for 72.

Not much to tell. Finished some more of the mindless self-translation & since trying in vain to get on.

. . . .[2]

London perhaps early May for a BBC TV *Krapp* with Pat Magee & perhaps a 2nd Claddagh record with same & Harold. Haven't been over for years.[3]

Ionesco's *Macbett* coming up with Mauclair at Alliance Francaise & Blin working on genuine article for Strasbourg opening April.[4]

. . . .[5]

French *Old Times* coming to a close after a long run. Harold [?]steeping in Proust.[6]

Do hope we'll meet again this summer.

Love to you all

Sam

1. AS letter of 30 December missing; last letter dated 17 October 1971, to which SB replied on 4 November 1971.

2. SB will be in Morocco until early March.

3. *Krapp's Last Tape* shown on BBC 2, 29 November 1972, directed by Donald McWhinney. Pat Magee (Krapp). SB sent an amended script. The "2nd Claddagh record" with Pat Magee was not issued.

4. Ionesco's *Macbett* opened at the Théâtre Rive Gauche, in the Alliance Francaise, 24 January 1972; Jacques Mauclair (b. 1919), French actor, director. Shakespeare's *Macbeth,*

directed by Roger Blin, designed by Matias, adapted by Pierrette Tison, opened at the Théâtre de Strasbourg, 27 April 1972.

   5. SB met Israel Horowitz.

   6. In Harold Pinter's *Old Times* (1971), as in Proust, time shifts forwards and backwards.

April 17, 1972

Dear Sam,

   A thousand apologies for not writing all these weeks. Seems I have been constantly in rehearsal for months, exhausted, tired and depressed, and have only just emerged—to grab a plane and fly out here as Visiting Lecturer and Guest Director for a few weeks.[1] Directing Behan's THE HOSTAGE,[2] and a lovely play it is too. And supposedly conducting a Seminar in Contemporary Theatre, but actually just talking with a flock of young people, the best part of the job. Apart from being lonesome—Jean joins me next week for a while with the kids—am sort of enjoying the change away from NY and the commercial theatre, that mesozoic beast.

   Have had more work and less satisfaction in the theatre this past season than in years. Started the year at Arena in Washington with a new play by a young American living in London; called MOON-CHILDREN, done at the Royal Court as CANCER, a much better title but everyone thought it frightened the audience away. Chekhovian study of American student life and attitudes, sensitive, true, funny, the best American play I've done since VIRGINIA WOOLF. Huge success in Washington, hailed as the best writing in years, all sorts of Broadway characters vying for the rights, and one of them, the worst, got them. Mixed but good notices on Broadway (with more or less the same cast)—and no one came. No one. Had to close in a couple of weeks. Sadness all around, and we were all torn apart. Item one. Then another piece on Broadway, revival of Lorraine Hansberry's SIDNEY BRUSTEIN'S WINDOW, minor piece but a special voice; the critics lambasted us, another closing . . . Item two . . . . Then back to Arena for first English language production of Günter Grass' DAVOR, done in Berlin a few years back. Interesting intellectual exercise about student protest, theatrically interesting. Turned out very well, and now everyone wants it to go to off-Broadway. I don't want to have another fiasco in NY, and am holding back. We'll see.[3]

In between, as you must have heard, the management of GODOT at Sheridan Square, took it out for a short tour, to Philadelphia and Princeton, where it got very good responses all around. With Tom Ewell, irony of ironies, because Philadelphia is where we were originally supposed to go back in 1956 with Tommy and Bert, and instead wound up in Miami. Tommy, of course, played Vladimir the last few months in New York last year, and was excellent. And I did get a chance to rehearse the company before they went out; all had been in the show at one time or another with us, except the Boy. Now there is talk of a longer tour next year, probably concentrating on the colleges; we shall see what we shall see. Would be fine, but I want to make sure that we get decent actors and decent bookings, not something just slapped together. Thought of producing it myself if I could raise the money, but economic situation at the moment, including my own, not the best. Our audiences were full of young kids who knew the play and had read it and studied it and loved it—having never seen it done professionally or clearly before . . . .

Jackie is, as you know, doing sensationally well with the one-man show, his TV will probably win some prizes; he is now establishing himself nationwide.[4] Tried to reach him before heading West (University of California is where I am), but he is normally impossible to get hold of, and never tells me where he is or what doing. I like him immensely, but never know where I am with him. We talked while doing the TV KRAPP of his doing an off-Broadway evening of KRAPP and the pantomimes; but the last time we met he wasn't sure of future plans. Saw the TV tape once more and liked it. Lots of interest but no firm sale yet, mostly because they've 'had' their Beckett for the year. I'm sure it will be sold and shown. In meantime, much interest in releasing it for schools.

What I'm really writing about: How are YOU? The eyes? The rest of you? Thanks for your good cards, but you don't say very much about yourself. Anxious to know how you are keeping. Not sure, after all, that [I] will be coming to Europe. Had been depending on some income from MOONCHILDREN, now not forthcoming. May just have to stay at home and enjoy the family. Sorry. Will let you know in advance if plans change.

Did you ever hear from that Professor from the Univ. of Wisconsin who wants to have a Beckett Festival next year? And to have you come over to lecture. I told him you probably wouldn't come . . . . Also, a nice young free-lance writer, Alan Levy, writing an article on you.[5] Am sure you're besieged . . . .

Grove Press considerably different these days, though I gather going ahead. Dick Seaver elsewhere, sad to say. Barney in bad shape. Hard to know what's going on.[6] The whole country in grip of *malaise extraordinaire*, akin to your Algeria times. See Judith, who is blooming and trying to elect McGovern.[7]

Trust you are reasonably well, and taking care, maybe even vacationing somewhere. And the eyes.

Jean joins me in sending love. We think of you constantly. Next time we meet I'll tell you about getting beat up by NY police. Grotesque.

Best to Suzanne. And yourself.

[Alan]

1. At the University of California.

2. Brendan Behan (1923–1964), Irish dramatist.

3. *Moonchildren,* the Arena Stage production, opened at the Royale Theatre, New York, 21 February 1972. *The Sign in Sidney Brustein's Window,* a musical adaptation of the play by the African-American dramatist Lorraine C. Hansberry (1930–1965), opened at the Longacre Theatre, New York, 26 January 1972. Günter Grass (b. 1927), German dramatist; *Davor (Uptight)* opened 17 March 1972. AS's agitation may be detected in the somewhat confused chronology here.

4. *Jack MacGowran in the Works of Samuel Beckett/Beginning to End,* U.S.–European tour; the TV "Beginning to End," directed by Lewis Freedman, PBS, KCET-TV, Los Angeles, filmed in Trona, California, 4 November 1971.

5. Alan Levy (b. 1935), American journalist, contributed "The Long Wait for Godot" to *Casebook on Waiting for Godot,* ed. Ruby Cohn, 1967, 1987.

6. Seaver had left Grove Press in 1971 to found his own imprint, Richard Seaver Books, at Viking Press.

7. *malaise extraordinaire:* deep unease; Judith Schmidt actually worked in Eugene McCarthy's campaign.

Paris
28.5.72

Dear Alan

Many thanks for yours of April.

So sorry about Broadway flops. I had heard about *Moon-Children.* Hope you do it again with success in a less pernicious area.

Jack did his old chestnut again at even more than usually dim Dublin Theatre Festival and is now—or was a week ago—playing The Tramp in *The Caretaker* at the Gaiety.[1] Poor production by all accounts. He was resting up in a London clinic after the Festival but now seems OK again.

I keep well and have been busy translating—hateful old hat from the late Forties![2] Writing a bit too on the now familiar basis of thousands of words for a viable (?) dozen . . . .[3]

Sitting tight apart from Ussy (too seldom) since return from Morocco. NO plans for more before Fall. Should have gone to London to assist Pat & Donald with TV *Krapp* but couldn't face it in the end. They write very pleased with production.[4] Donald has also just done a new production of *All That Fall* with some of original cast—but Maddy gone the way of all Rooneys.[5] Talk of Peggy Ashcroft in *Happy Days* at Aldwych directed by P. Hall.[6] Still vague. Roger directed *Macbeth* at Strasbourg. Haven't seen him but heard depressing accounts. Tried to do *Breath* with a yogi for opening of Barrault's Théâtre du Nations. But rehearsal facilities nonexistent up to very last moment so withdrew. . . . .[7]

Love to you all.
Sam

Do hope you make Europe in spite of all.

1. Opened on 16 May 1972.
2. SB was translating *Mercier et Camier,* published in English as *Mercier and Camier,* 1974, 1975 (see letter of 30 May 1969, n. 1).
3. SB met Dick and Jeannette Seaver, notes changes at Grove Press where he now knows "nobody."
4. Broadcast by BBC 2, 29 November 1972, on Thirty Minute Theatre.
5. McWhinnie also produced a "modernized" version of *All That Fall,* 4 June 1972. Marie Kean (Mrs. Rooney), J. G. Devlin (Rooney), Alan McClelland (Mr. Slocum).
6. Dame Peggy Ashcroft (1907–1991), regarded as first lady of the English stage.
7. SB can see well now except peripherally.

June 4, 1972

Dear Sam,

Back home from the wilderness of California once more, and greeted almost as I arrived by your most recent note. Many thanks for writing and letting me know all the news. Glad the eyes are better and you're writing a bit again. Dee Bair, who had seen you a few weeks ago, told me you seemed to be feeling reasonably well. She also told me you had written a short play.¹ Delighted that you are at it again, and would love to read if you're willing to let me see a copy. I've gotten to read all the prose pieces as soon as they get into English over here, but had been hoping you'd do another one for the theatre.

Sorry to hear about Jackie being in hospital, among other troubles, and glad he's out and working again. As I told you, I'd tried to reach him lots of times here but he'd disappeared. We had some rumors that you were coming over in the fall to direct him in ENDGAME; and I was looking forward to having you with us for a while—though I was a bit skeptical that Jackie had been able to persuade you to come. Is there a chance you will be coming? Would be lovely.

My own plans for the summer remain uncertain. The Summer School in Norwich, where Martin Esslin and I, among others, were to be lecturing, has been called off for lack of enough students (no wonder, with the tuition they were charging). Can't afford to bring entire family over, but still hankering after coming over myself, even for a brief time, if I can somehow manage it. Will you be in Paris first two weeks of July? Just in case.

Everything over here continues iffy. Have been trying to get to see Barney and find out what's going on over at Grove, but he seems always to be in a crisis or away. Haven't talked with Dick Seaver since he's on the new job. Judith we do get to see once in a while and talk to often—she's heavily involved with the election campaign and seems in good shape. Which is more than I can say for the rest of the country.

Dee Bair, whom I've met only recently and rather like, is giving me copy of her book about you, and I am looking forward to reading it. She has been talking with George Reavey and John Kobler, among others, who have shown her some of your letters to them, which contain biographical information she is looking for. I haven't shown her any of your letters as I consider them private—unless you want me to. I have them all but will keep them private until or unless you would like her to have access.²

Glad Don McWhinnie and Pat working again; would love to see it. There's all sorts of interest in Jackie's KRAPP, which I'd love you to see, but general feeling is it's too special for our TV. We're still trying and hoping. I'm also interested in hearing from Jackie because Hume Cronyn is after me again to do KRAPP and the pantomimes for limited run in the fall. He's very good, but naturally I'd prefer (as I'm sure you would too) Jackie—if he is available and would do it.

Generally a bit depressed about life, theatrical and otherwise, but pulling out of it. New York increasingly impossible, the theatre worse and worse. Arena in Washington a good place to work but we don't want to move there. Would love to be living in London but can't make a living there. So it goes. Meanwhile, we go on.

[Alan]

1. Deirdre Bair; the "short play" was *Not I*.
2. AS may be referring to the ms. copy of Bair's *Samuel Beckett: A Biography*, 1978.

July 2, 1972

Dear Sam

Life pulling a few surprises, nice ones for a change. Looks as though I might be coming over, after all, to see you. Very soon. Had lunch with Barney a while back, and both of us saying we hadn't seen you in too long an age. So I suggested he go, and he suggested I go with him. Yesterday, he told me he had cabled you and had gotten an answer; and now it looks very much as though we'll both be arriving on your doorstep on July 13. Just in time for Bastille doings. Do hope we won't be too much for you.

Another surprise. You may recall the names of Hume Cronyn and Jessica Tandy, two of our finest actors (who have taken over the mantle of the Lunts) and good friends of mine. Jessie is our Peggy Ashcroft; she originated the main role in STREETCAR NAMED DESIRE, and more recently appeared in Albee's DELICATE BALANCE and in ALL OVER. Hume was also in BALANCE and in dozens of others.[1] As I understand it, they were going to do HAPPY DAYS in English in Rome some years ago, but something interfered. We had talked many times about their doing your work because they've both been extremely interested—but they always seemed busy or away. They called me this week, and we've had several talks and come up with something which I believe could be marvelous, a kind of Beckett repertory season. Which you know I've tried to get on before. The idea would be for Hume and Jessie to do an evening of HAPPY DAYS plus ACT WITHOUT WORDS I, and then another evening alternating of KRAPP and something else, preferably giving Jessie something to do. We talked of COME AND GO, but it's really too short, we need something at least 15–20 minutes. They would alternate the two evenings off-Broadway at a very good eastside (accessible) theatre, where the last bill of Pinter one-acts ran.² We have the theatre, the producer standing by, everything but your approval and go-ahead. The idea would be to rehearse in September, play some weeks of previews and then open late October or in November. Keeping prices low enough for general audience, students, etc. I think it's a good idea and time.

I did talk with Jackie while we were doing the TV KRAPP about his doing a program of KRAPP and the two ACTS WITHOUT WORDS some time; but his agent tells me that he is booked up with the tour and with other things and not available. I couldn't reach him directly. Hume is different but an excellent character actor with great flavor and quality, also a mime. He'd make a lovely Willie, akin to Barrault's. As for Jessie, if I hadn't gotten Ruth White that time, I would have tried to get Jessie. And I'd love to get something of yours for her to do on the bill with KRAPP; perhaps you have a small piece or could write one.

Anyhow. The main thing is that I'm pleased to be coming over, albeit not expecting to until this past couple of days. A real lift to this sad year. I wanted to send you a Happy Birthday when I wrote back in April from Calif. but wasn't sure whether you liked to be reminded. Judith read me your last letter, so I decided if she can remember your birthday, I can too. Happy Post Birthday. I'm sure everyone and his brother will be descending upon you this summer, so save an evening for Barney and meself. We've got lots to fill you in on. And you've got to tell me how you made the parasol burn up in Berlin. I saw some photos, and they were super. Is the *Modellbuch* out by now?³

Gather your eyes reasonably responsive, except on the sides. I hope you're driving carefully out at Ussy. How are the moles? Jean and kids join me in wishing you well. Vicki in Spoleto as theatre apprentice, heaven help us.⁴ Hope to see you soon and learn all.

My mouth fine. I'm up, down & sideways. [handwritten]

[Alan]

1. Hume Cronyn (b. 1911), and his wife, Jessica Tandy (1909–1994); Tandy played Blanche Dubois in *Streetcar Named Desire* by Tennessee Williams, 1948, Agnes in Albee's *A Delicate Balance*, 1966, and The Wife in *All Over*, 1971; Cronyn played Tobias in *A Delicate Balance*.
2. The "accessible" theater: the Sheridan Square Playhouse, New York.
3. *"Modellbuch"*: Brechtian term for the "book" that contains suggestions for direc-

tions, including dramatic analysis and notes on characterization, with accompanying sketches.

4. Spoleto Festival, Italy (see letter of 26 August 1968, n. 2).

Paris
25.7.72

Dear Alan

Many thanks for your card from London.

Herewith *Not I* & *H.D.* notes.[1] I'm sending former, by same mail to Royal Court. I am too wearied of it to be of any help. All I feel sure of is the text must go very fast, no pause except for breath & the two big silent holes after the screams. On top of *H.D* a superhuman job for J. T.[2] If she finds it too much just forget about the 2nd evening. Don't hesitate to ask for cuts or consult about difficulties . . . .[3]

It was good being with you both again after so long. Come again very soon.

Love to you all
Sam

1. SB sent a copy of the text of *Not I* and a xeroxed copy of his notes for the Schiller-Theater Werkstatt production of *Glückliche Tage (Happy Days)*, 1971. In a letter dated 7 July 1972 SB arranges their meeting and adds: "Think I may have what you need to go with *Krapp*."
2. "J.T.": Jessica Tandy.
3. SB gives Matias's address.

August 12, 1972

Dear Sam,

Back, finally, from Montreal, Quebec, Maine, Martha's Vineyard, and a couple of other places, various wanderings, some restful, some not so—in the midst of which and directly after my postcard from Canada, our producer lost his nerve or his pocketbook or whatever, and vanished. To this date, I have not heard one word from him, news of his withdrawal coming to me long distance via Hume. So, over the wires, we came up with various other possibilities, the chief of which being the small theatre of the Lincoln Center, the Forum, 299 seats, and the loveliest in New York. Saved from an untimely transformation into a film house last year by the concerted outraged efforts of the theatrical community.

Both Lincoln Center and the erstwhile producers of the off-Broadway GODOT immediately said Yes, without having to read the new script. But both Hume and myself felt the Sheridan Square too small, and really impossible for ACT WITHOUT WORDS; unfortunately, the Cherry Lane, which could have worked, falling apart and unusable. So, it is the Forum,[1] with complete autonomy and artistic control retained by us. A Beckett Festival, two evenings, as planned, opening previews (to students mostly, at student prices) in the middle of October, and officially opening around Thanksgiving, endish of November. All agreed to and though no contracts signed, all elements committed. I'm getting used to a history of hopes thwarted at the last minute, especially with the Beckett canon; but I feel reasonably sure we are on our way this time.

Investigated the question of Matias immediately, but it is not possible.[2] Unions much too strong, especially in an institutional theatre (non-profit) such as Lincoln Center. Using the designer who does most of work there, Douglas Schmidt, excellent painter, and has done great deal of opera, as well as theatre work. Also, lighting man there, John Gleason, is someone I've wanted to get many times before, and never available. Already working on a lamp for NOT I. We shall see. (Actress may have to wear dark makeup around mouth, or mask or something to prevent seeing rest of face; we'll experiment and I'll keep you posted.)

Thanks much for the new text, which I'm now studying, and the HAPPY DAYS notebook. Most helpful, and I'm most grateful. You really did fantastic work on that.[3] I'm trying to get German text here, and shall probably succeed. In meantime, am just starting my own preparation on all four plays. Jessica looking forward to her herculean job; I'm actually starting to rehearse informally last week in August, and then two weeks with them both at home before official rehearsals start on Sept. 18. Thus we have six weeks of rehearsals before technicals, which should reassure the actors—and yourself. I think they'll both be fine, Jessie more like Madeleine than Ruth, Hume perfect for his two. As it turns out, I've just discovered that Jackie will be playing Fluther in PLOUGH AND STARS[4] in larger Lincoln Center theatre at almost same time, so may be seeing something of him. . . . There's been a nibble on the TV KRAPP, but everyone still worried it's too special for a mass audience. We're working on it.

Delighted to see you in such good form, and hope you'll be even better after your holiday. Take care of self, & thank you for all your kindness & help. Love from us all. Jean much pleased with *Not I.* David, with letter. [handwritten after "better"]

Ever,
Alan

1. The Repertory Theatre of Lincoln Center, New York, established 1960; Jules Irving then director.
2. Henrioud Charles (b. 1926), known as Matias, Swiss-born designer for SB's productions in France and Germany; apparently SB had suggested that AS use Matias in the new production.
3. See *Happy Days: Samuel Beckett's Production Notebook,* ed. James Knowlson, 1985, and S. E. Gontarski, *Beckett's "Happy Days": An Analysis of the Manuscript,* 1977.
4. By Sean O'Casey.

Paris
16.8.72

Dear Alan

Thanks for yours of 12.

Yes, had a note from Cronyn about changed places. OK with me if with you. Israel Horowitz,[1] whom I saw on his return from O'Neill jinks, has been invited to work next season at Forum. With Jack fluthering in big theatre that will be a party.

Have written to German publisher to send you a copy of *Glückliche Tage* in appropriate edition in case you can't get one in N.Y. I'm out of mine.

. . . .[2]

Love to you all
Sam

1. Israel Horowitz (b. 1939), American playwright and academic, Professor of English, City College, New York, 1968–1973; Professor of Theater, Brandeis University, 1973–1975.
2. SB has seen John Calder and Martin Esslin; is going to Malta.

August 25, 1972

Dear Sam,

Some day, will write you a plain old letter, with only non-vital matters dealt with, like our upcoming election (which sickens me more and more daily), the new troubles in Ireland, Behan's HOSTAGE—which I worked on in the spring and loved for the fun of it—my mother's aches and pains, my latest reading of THE LOST ONES[1] (which really rocked me), and such.

Today, I'm just writing to tell you that we have tested a possible lamp for NOT I, something called a 'gallery light', which lights paintings in galleries, and it works just marvelously. All you can see is the mouth (we sat a girl down in total darkness in the theatre and tried it out all afternoon; just wish you had been there to see); and the effect is super, just what I think you imagined it to be, alive, organic, a being all of its own. I think it's going to work fine. May have to put dark makeup or a mask of some kind, soft fabric, on Jessie just to make sure there is nothing seen of her face. But we have worked out a way to mask the light, to mount the light, etc. And, mainly, we have a light that's going to do exactly what you wanted it to do.

There's bound to be other problems, so don't get too cheered up.

Also, have neglected to find out from you what it cost to have that Notebook of HAPPY DAYS xeroxed. The production should pay for it, so please just send me the amount, exact or approximate. No reason in the world why you should expend your francs there.

Lincoln Center has lots of things wrong with it, but they have good technical help, and a few bucks in their budget.

Nice note from Alec Reid with a signed copy of his book.[2]

Have been calling George Reavey since I got back to tell him I had seen you, but no answer. Must be away.

Judith off somewhere working for McGovern.

Lunch with Barney and he seems in good shape, especially since we came to see you.

Jessie and Hume off on their tour, but we talk all the time; and I'm starting with them, informally at their home, next week. Two weeks of this, then official rehearsals start Sept. 19 for four weeks, then a week of technicals, then 5 weeks of previews before we officially open in November. Should be enough time.

Thanks for asking Suhrkamp for German text. If they send it, fine. Otherwise, I'm on track of one here. Also have heard of Renaud record of HD, which I'm getting someone to send from Paris.[3] Do you have any special way you want that Revolver to look? Everybody here has different idea of what a Browning is, also about its not being too realistic; should be constructed possibly. We're working on a parasol like one in Berlin.

You see, I have nothing to tell you. Best from us all.

[Alan]

1. *Le Dépeupleur*, 1969, trans. by SB, *The Lost Ones*, 1972.

2. Frederick Alexander (Alec) Reid (1921–1986), Irish drama critic, wrote *All I Can Manage, More Than I Could: An Approach to the Plays of Samuel Beckett*, 1968.

3. Recorded by Madeleine Renaud and Jean-Louis Barrault, Collection l'Avant-Scène ADES TS30 LA 568, Disque 33t, 1964.

Paris
31.8.72

Dear Alan

Thanks for yours of Aug. 25 with good news of lamp.

Cost of xeroxing not worth a claim.

Revolver should be as *conspicuous* as possible throughout from its first appearance. Black probably best. Something strange, length of barrel perhaps. When she decides at end of I to leave it on mound she should put it down in front of her or a little to her left in such a way that it won't be hidden from audience, or from as few as possible, by Willie coming from her right at end of II and so that his right hand reaching up may at the end of its stretch be about half way between it and her face.

Have seen Ruby Cohn & shown her *Not I* which she likes.

. . . .[1]

Love to you all
Sam

1. SB refers to George and Jean Reavey, sends regards to Hume Cronyn and Jessica Tandy.

Sept. [?]3, 1972

Dear Sam,

Not sure whether you're home yet, but trust holiday went well, you're relaxed and tanned from Malta's sunlight. We've actually been in rehearsal with Beckett Festival for more than four weeks, two of them 'official', three more weeks till first preview, and then another four till opening, November 20 and 22. Feel very good so far, though it hasn't been easy. Luckily, two of four very familiar (though still discovering things), a third reasonably so, and fourth (NOT I) fascinating in possibilities and effect. Have millions of things to tell you and ask you and just share with you, and will try, in some sort of order, as far as I can. What's left out will come later.

As always, administrative problems galore. Contract problems, mercifully all settled now, between Grove, Cronyn, Lincoln Center. Publicity problems, name of the enterprise, size of type, dates, prices, etc. etc. As usual, press has been on us, like vultures, and as usual getting things wrong. You saw the *New York* TIMES story,[1] 'quoting' me completely not accurately. When I wouldn't tell him what NOT I was 'about', he took what I said out of context and twisted it to fit his own theories. I said that it was your latest play and, as you had been doing from GODOT through all your plays up to PLAY, was using a theatrical metaphor in a very special way. Never mentioned urns at all, and certainly did not compare NOT I to PLAY. He did, although he's obviously never read PLAY because he mentioned *two* urns. Anyhow. Usual tosh. Sorry, but can't be helped, cannot be helped.

Actors working very hard. Hume very nervous and concerned, Jessie concentrating on HAPPY DAYS, though the past week we've been more on NOT I. At the moment: this afternoon's run-through of HAPPY DAYS was superb (Jessie more like Madeleine than like Ruth, warm with a gentle sadness but also vitality and humor, Hume beginning to get some of Willie's comedy; he was very worried about additional strain of doing Willie, but we've kept after him; he'll be fine); Hume's ACT excellent, including the technical problems of all the props, except that we're not yet satisfied with his entrances, working on them. That's the first bill. Hume is a fine KRAPP, different from all the others, quieter in a way, but very real and very much of a character. He has only one eye, so has been having some problems threading the recorder etc., but working on them. NOT I, we're just beginning to get into. Technical difficulties galore, but gradually solving. The light works, Jessie in dark dress and full mask. We tried the hidden mike and speaker yesterday and marvelous effect. We're building an entire unit to roll on in dark. She's standing, propped up against back-support, mike around her neck, lamp unit fastened on with her so making sure she'll be lit exactly. (We actually have two lamps in case something happens to one.) Because Jessie having great psychological problem with learning lines in HAPPY DAYS and NOT I at same time, we have been working with small 'teleprompter', which has her NOT I lines printed on roller controlled by stage mgr. She'll be using this until quite sure of lines; this mechanism, of course, unseen by audience. Entire effect of mouth floating in space and amplified, however, very very effective and works exactly the way you thought it would, mouth a live organism, not immediately clear what it is. Question of location of Auditor yet to be settled.[2]

I have enclosed floor plan of FORUM theatre, probably best small theatre in New York. Although you may be disturbed because it is not proscenium.[3] Hope you can relate my tracings to the actual floor plan, in each case. Question of Auditor's position will be decided when we get to lighting. I have shown two possible positions, one more or less as it would be in proscenium (but this may look a bit flat since he would be more or less on plane with her), other on a diagonal across the thrust stage. Each of these two possibilities only approximate, and we will work on them to get maximum relationship, tension, dynamic. Thrust, of course, has certain disadvantages but also certain advantages, which you would see if you were here. Works excellently, especially so for ACT and KRAPP, also HAPPY DAYS, though we had problem making sure mound hid Willie and still enabled us to see him when sitting up. It's about four feet high and about size you seemed to have had in Berlin. Don't take my sketch too exactly. For H. DAYS and ACT we use same or similar backcloth; black all around, of course, for KRAPP and NOT I.

The FORUM is where Pinter's LANDSCAPE and SILENCE were done several seasons ago to great response.[4] Nice, intimate feeling. Seats 299 but only a few rows, so sightlines and connection especially fine. Also acoustics. [last 2 words handwritten]

Now for some thoughts and questions. If you could write back, without trouble, would much appreciate:

NOT I

1. We're assuming she's in some sort of limbo. Death? After-life? Whatever you want to call it. OK?

2. Your note about pronunciation of 'any' has steered us a bit into Irish. Also because Jessie wants to have a different voice here from in H. DAYS. OK?

3. In our Paris talks, you kept distinguishing between the VOICE and the MOUTH. Jessie and I trying to make this clear, to ourselves, and to audience; but anything you can add will be helpful. Tension comes from opposition of these two *and* of juxtaposition of MOUTH (emission) and AUDITOR?

4. We're working on proper tone, and also proper tempo. Again, anything you can add to what you said to us in July would be helpful.

5. How does anyone know AUDITOR is a man? Costume? Does djellaba have hood over head (which may make him look like a Monk) or more Arabic something? We have made both.

6. If she never stops talking, how can she stop to listen to the screams twice? (this from Jessie)

7. Auditor's repeated (slightly diminished) gesture works well. Could he start his gesture a bit sooner, or should he wait, each time, until the 'She!'? (this from Jessie, who has difficulty sometimes waiting)

8. I believe there's typographical error on page 4 near the bottom, three lines from the bottom: after 'so far', shouldn't it be 'then thinking . . .'? We've assumed so.

9. As you must surmise, there's no actual 'curtain' at Forum. We start in absolute blackness, with murmur growing with light, and so on. Effect should be what you want. We can also, if you prefer, start murmur as house lights going down, but with mutter of audience, which usually doesn't even stop until house has been black a while, we won't hear anything. To start in blackness after house is quiet seems more effective, I believe.

10. The play has a mesmerizing effect, even without the lighting yet done; though of course interpretations bound to vary, and some are going to wonder what the hell it's all about. I find it chilling. Runs exactly 20 minutes, we find. I'll think of something else to ask. Hate to be too specific because I know how you are about defining meanings. I think she's dead, can't believe it, refuses to believe it, accept it, pushes thought away, can only deal with it in terms of someone else, cannot imagine it for herself. If only she would . . . .

And so on.

KRAPP

1. Know this one pretty well, and have used all your changes, except keys (which Hume wanted to hold on to, and I felt game not worth the

candle to get him to drop.) We are using the same furniture and props Jackie used in TV show (which by the way is going to be put on after we open!) Have only one question: How many girls are involved? Is Bianca girl in raincoat at railway station? Is 'face' nurse's or Bianca's? One girl? Two? Or four? (We *waver!*) (Please forgive my asking.) [handwritten after "Bianca's"]

HAPPY DAYS

1. Know this one too, but of course it's always different. Have studied your Berlin notebook carefully, and followed it as much as humanly possible. American actors don't like to be hemmed in this much, but Jessie has been miraculously marvelously cooperative, she's a rare person and a lovely actress. Got her Madeleine's record, and she's even listened to that for a sense of your intentions.

2. Since FORUM auditorium steeply raked, we had to make mound high enough to hide Willie, but turned out not to be too bad, about four feet.

3. More importantly, in order to make passage possible from offstage to behind mound (for Hume and perhaps for one of stage crew who may have to be behind there for various reasons) we have had to back up outside end of mound up to or very near to cyc. When Willie comes round the mound at the end of II, he will have to climb over this slight elevation, instead of completely around mound. I know this was not your intention; but since stage floor is concrete thus not allowing a trap, and since Hume can't or won't sit there behind mound all the time—he feels he needs to be able to get offstage part of the time when he's not seen—it was either something like that, or another Willie. Actually, the crawling at the end is not that different, I just wanted you to know.

4. Could you explain, once again, why and how Winnie repeats various phrases when she says 'I say I used to think', for example, after 'I used to think'. Does she not stress the *'say'* as though she were not certain?

5. First act ran exactly an hour this afternoon. Second act half an hour.

6. Umbrella as always a problem. We're trying to benefit from all previous experiences on all continents, but umbrella makers and all technical men are very stubborn fellows. Will report more in detail when we are further advanced. Rest of props are very much as you specify.

7. There are various typos in script (Grove Press) which we have discovered via other scripts—Suhrkamp sent me German text and I

thanked them—and rectified, i.e. 'It is because you're still on your two flat feet. . .'.

8. Jessie is getting the lines, but more than that: the life, the variety, and the colors magnificently. She will be superb. I know you're worried about doing anything after it, even if the something is ACT. It's like doing THE CRITIC⁵ after OEDIPUS, a bit of something after a great block of marble. Let's see what happens with the audience, don't pre-judge it.

ACT WITHOUT WORDS

I. We're solving all technical demands, rope breaking is toughest. Hume working like mad, and amazingly athletic, I have to keep him from wearing himself out. We're trying to keep it simple, economical, direct. It's very funny and very touching. No music. (Would you object strongly if we had a short musical intro as house lites down, the moment lights out and music over, up with blaze of light? Would just like to try it one day. No music during piece itself. Contrast is what may be effective. Depends on music, of course.)

Will think of something else. Talked with George Reavey and sent him NOT I. Judith sends regards. Hope I haven't overwhelmed you. Basically pleased. Love from Jean. Look forward to your responses.

Ever,
Alan

Can you come over for opening?

1. *"New York TIMES* story": George Gent, "New Beckett Play, 'Not I', to Bow Here," 29 August 1972.
2. The silent Auditor, standing stage right in a djellaba, raises and lowers his arms in a "gesture of helpless compassion." According to SB, the image of the Auditor in *Not I* was suggested in part by Caravaggio's *Decollation of St. John the Baptist*.
3. SB preferred a regular, picture-frame stage; Forum Theatre, Lincoln Center, has a thrust "apron" stage.
4. Opened 2 April 1970.
5. Famous farce (1779) by Richard Brinsley Sheridan (1751–1816).

Paris
16.10.72

Dear Alan

Forgive delay in answering yours of Sept. 30[1] found awaiting me here on return yesterday.

Not I

1. This is the old business of author's supposed privileged information as when Richardson wanted the lowdown on Pozzo's background before he could consider the part.[2] I no more know where she is or why thus than she does. All I know is in the text. "She" is purely a stage entity, part of a stage image and purveyor of a stage text. The rest is Ibsen.
2. *Anny.* Simply an example of the "certain vowel sounds." No Irishness intended.
3. If I made a distinction it can only have been between mind & voice, not between mouth & voice. Her speech a purely buccal phenomenon without mental control or understanding, only half heard. Function running away with organ. The only stage apprehension of text is Auditor's.
4. I hear it breathless, urgent, feverish, rhythmic, panting along, without undue concern with intelligibility. Addressed less to the understanding than to the nerves of the audience which should in a sense *share her bewilderment.*
5. It is not stated, though suggested by masculine "auditor," that it is a man. The costume, as I neglected to specify, is djellaba with hood. The figure is completely shrouded from head to foot.
6. This is complete misunderstanding. She does not *listen to screams,* she screams herself in illustration of what she might have done if able, if not "numbed." Read: "no screaming for help . . . . should she feel so inclined . . . scream . . ." (*She screams*) ["she" underlined twice] . . . then listen . . . (*Silence*) . . . scream again . . . (*She screams again*) . . . ["she" underlined twice] listen again . . . (*Silence*) etc. Cf. Winnie's screams in Willy story.
7. Auditor cannot react till refusal clear, i.e. after "She!"
8. "*Then* thinking" is correct.
9. Voice should begin before house quite quiet & contribute to its quieting.

Krapp

    1. Four different girls mentioned.
       1. Bianca.
       2. Girl in green coat.
       3. Nursemaid (face).
       4. Girl in boat.
    Not to mention Miss McGlome, Effie, Fanny and the bitch.

Happy Days

    4. Relates to "May one still speak of time?" "I used to think" too
       affirmative, hence "I *say* I used to think." Similarly later "I *say* I
       used to say." Nothing sure but immediate utterance.
    8. Surely *Act W. W. before H. D.* unless technically quite unfeasible.
       After seems to me impossible.

I'm afraid it's all a bit too much.

Thanks for all the trouble you're taking as always. I'm sorry to be of so little help. The remains of some convention seems to lie between us.

I won't be able to be with you at the opening. I'm not even sure I'll make London . . . .[3]

Warm greetings to the Cronyns.

Love to Jean & you all.

Sam

    1. The carbon copy of the letter from AS reads "Sept. 1972"; SB's original copy apparently includes the day: the 30th. He and Suzanne have been on holiday in Malta.

    2. SB's impatience was not entirely justified. Sir Ralph Richardson's commitments at the Old Vic prevented him from taking the part of Pozzo.

    3. SB has "dental trouble" (see JK, 596).

October 22 [1972]

Dear Sam,

Your letter came the day of our first (invited) audience, thank you. Contents read carefully by all concerned and noted, also your evident disturbance at my questions. Do understand. Maybe American actors, or some American actors, most notably 'stars', tied to certain psychological configurations, no matter how much they might wish it otherwise. Half of my questions came from Jessica, and getting your answers firsthand from you has made her believe or trust me bit more.

Anyhow. Have had audiences and first trial of both bills as of today, and want to bring you up to date. Plenty of problems between previous letter and this, and more to come—but we're well on way to something, something taking its course. George Reavey there yesterday, though I told him we weren't ready. He will, I'm sure, report his reactions directly—although he may not repeat what he said to me about Mouth in NOT I 'should be large blow up', *à la* TV screen. Nothing doing. The Mouth perfectly visible, marvelous image, and (when Jessie perfectly still) more than fascinating, mesmerizing. We're still working on lighting Figure of Auditor, which is even trickier business. Last night, we couldn't see his arms well enough, better tomorrow, and so on. Problem is to suspend him in space and yet see him.

For those who are willing to go with it, NOT I works wonders. People stunned, crying, left in seats at end, and so on. For majority of ordinary onlookers, there is confusion and disappointment galore, mutterings, and one or two or more walking out. Expected. Jessica very nervous and not yet settled down, but has moments of real effectiveness, especially today after she had read your letter and realised I had not been leading her astray, although I had said O'Neill rather than Ibsen to her over and over again. She will be terrific in a couple of weeks. Business of starting and ending voice muttering with house lights worked perfectly today, some of them even Shhhhing the others to listen to her. Figure confuses almost everyone, not location but presence. I find the juxtaposition of two arresting but not really explainable. How to explain? To explain? Just to be there? Space between them and relationship maximally effective? We're still trying out his exact position. And lighting him! It's a very special piece, and not everyone's taste, as usual. But today I began to be caught up in Jessie's performance, and began to worry less about technical problems, which have been immense. Time before, lamp slipped as they were bringing her on, and stage manager had to hold it bare-handed (switching hands whenever burn unbearable) on her mouth entire show. Hands burned, but he did it! Lamp anchored more securely. . . . Running time, just under 20 minutes. Wish you could see it.

Hume lovely in KRAPP, though still fussing in various directions, including wig, timing, and costume. Very human, comedic but basically very moving. We have shown him the *REGIEBUCH*[1] and he's very impressed with photos. Very stark and simple lighting, den as in Berlin, shadows, very effective. His vocal quality not as cracked-voiced as I want, but he's still working. Audience visibly and audibly affected; Joe Liss of Grove says best Krapp ever; each one has something others lack, no one best.

Hume also triumphant in ACT, which is really fun; they absolutely loved it. Props and timing really fine, and all pleased by tone and looks. Jean almost fell out of her seat laughing. We saw the French cartoon last week, and I think we have done you better. Getting very fond of this; and when timing is right—a la small board folding—most effective. Very tricky business. HD started out OK today, & then slowed down, Jessie very nervous. Actually, her performance was rich & quite beautiful but she extended all too much. Too serious in Act II. We're still working on mound, including time taken to get her in and out. This is toughest one of all, and will take time. Her quality close to Madeleine's, though she has special humor and verve of her own. Only technical problems have made us end with ACT so far; impossible to assemble mound between without taking half hour or more. When this routined, we will start with ACT, maybe end of this week. Of course HD should be last . . . In case of KRAPP and NOT I, may experiment with KRAPP last, though now it's N.I.
[handwritten from "timing" to "time," then typed]

Our first actual (subscription) audience on Wednesday, and we shall see. Opening on Nov. 20 with HD–ACT and Nov. 22 with KRAPP–NOT I, so there's time. At the run-throughs so far, we have had critical technical problems on all four, irony of ironies, Hume making trouble for self in threading recorder (he has only one eye) in KRAPP, lamp getting jiggled in NOT I, umbrella (which we have rigged to burn for some 7–8 seconds) only sparking for Jessie, and rope in ACT sticking a bit. They coped, and I had conniptions; but each time we learn and deal with. Staff is good, but union stage hands are union stage hands. Main thing is that the performances are there, actors have been encouraged by response—even though a few irate bourgeois have stalked out from NOT I—and improvements will continue. Will keep you posted. Wish you were here. The plays are on their way to where you might be able to stand them. Thanks for trust and all the help. Love from all.

[Alan]

1. *"REGIEBUCH"*: production notebook from Schiller-Theater Werkstatt *Krapp's Last Tape*, 1969, also *Modellbuch* (see letter of 2 July 1972, n. 2).

Paris
5.11.72

Dear Alan

Many thanks for yours of Oct. 22.

Have not heard from George Reavey.

Parasol shd. not burn too long. As soon as she realizes (i.e. almost immediately) she gets rid of it hastily.

The auditor? only answer worth giving: try it without him. The more he disturbs the better.

Seeing Jocelyn, Oscar & Tony Page this evening.[1] Still don't know who chosen for *Not I*. Talks over weekend . . . .[2]

Warmly & gratefully to all.

yrs. always
S

1. Jocelyn Herbert, Oscar Lewenstein, and Anthony Page met to discuss forthcoming Royal Court Theatre production of *Not I*; SB requested Billie Whitelaw, whose voice SB had in mind. Lewenstein (b. 1917), English manager, Artistic Director, English Stage Company, Royal Court Theatre, 1972–1977.

2. SB to go to the dentist.

Paris
9.11.72

Dear Alan

I heard from Harold Pinter who had seen the *Krapp–Not I* evening at the Forum. He was impressed by the latter but had disturbing things to say about Cronyn's reactions while listening to the tape and his "additional dialogue" ("balls," "rubbish") when winding forward the tape (p. 21 of Grove edition). Please have him sit quite still when listening to the recording and refrain from any words that are not in the text. Sorry to have to trouble you with this.

Affectionately
Sam

November 13, 1972

Dear Sam,

Your card re matter reported by Harold P. received this morning, but situation described already previously taken care of. I didn't happen to be at the theatre the night Harold was, which was also—I gather—the night of Martin Esslin's visit. (Have you heard from him? Gather he was favorably impressed, especially with NOT I.) Anyhow. Whatever Harold may have thought of Hume's performance, he seems to me excellent as Krapp, a sad, bedraggled wraith. His 'ad-libbing' that night must have been a shade excessive. Usually he curses, as per text, very much under his breath so that no one knows what he is saying. I have also asked him, again, to be very careful about this . . . Saw both shows twice this week, and he is getting standing ovation, very favorable. Sorry that Harold's report disturbed you, as indeed it well might, but I am trying to make sure it won't go on. As you know, 'stars' don't always listen to directors, but in this case, Hume has been most co-operative.

NOT I continues to improve and hold the audience. Got your previous card, and thought about cutting Auditor. I don't want to do that. You wrote the Auditor and his presence contributes an ambient tension which is marvelous. Jessica is now really holding them; and response at the end is very good. I think the critics are going to be baffled, but then they always are. People are very moved even when they differ in interpretation. The visual metaphor quite striking. And, thank heaven, all our technical problems out of the way now. Mouth very clear. Process of voice starting as house lights dim effective. And so on. Wish you could see it.

Jessie erratic in HAPPY DAYS. Sometimes lovely and bright in Act I, and then falters in II. Or vice versa. Once or twice, she has hit both. And I am still keeping after her. She is similar in quality to Madeleine, I think, though not as subtle.[1] Audiences vary in reactions from much laughter to little. All moved and responsive at end, however. She loses her faith in herself often, and I must constantly encourage her. Has mastered text, and totally faithful to text and physical demands. Didn't mean to make you think umbrella was burning too long. Actually 5–7 seconds just enough time for her to respond and get it put out behind mound. Yesterday, it was perfect.

ACT also going well, though we have had to abandon attempt to play it prior to HAPPY DAYS on bill. Impossible technically. Took crew of four stagehands 45 minutes to assemble mound, and that would make intermission interminable. This way, they set up night before, and strike it for ACT in about 15 minutes. Sorry. But sure you understand that stagehands often control our destinies. Hume is lovely in ACT, and technical things again working well—after all sorts of agonies. I think the show (20 minutes long) is a delight, and wish I could put it on film for you to see.

Haven't been at theatre each night because getting involved in Washington show, and impossible to be at weeks of previews. But word-of-mouth is very very fine, and business improving steadily. We have been selling out for a couple of weeks. Mixture of young and middle-aged, and reactions vary. The KRAPP–NOT I opening is Wednesday, Nov. 22, with other bill on previous Mon. Will send you news of our formal reception. Have high hopes.[2] Lincoln Center having financial troubles, and likely Forum season will begin and end with us regardless of reception on critical front. Deficit too huge. But season likely to be artistic success, with Gorki[3] already opening, and Beckett on the way. Hope you are OK dentally; and please trust me on getting Hume to stick to Beckett. He's not Bert Lahr. Love from us all.

[Alan]

1. Madeleine Renaud had not yet performed in *Not I*. AS remembers her Winnie in *Oh les beaux jours*.

2. "Samuel Beckett Festival," presented by The Repertory Theater of Lincoln Center, New York, opened at The Forum, 20 November 1972, *Happy Days, Act Without Words I; Krapp's Last Tape, Not I*, a world premiere, 22 November 1972, directed by AS, designed by Douglas W. Schmidt. *Happy Days:* Jessica Tandy (Winnie), Hume Cronyn (Willie). *Act Without Words I:* Hume Cronyn (The Player). *Krapp's Last Tape:* Hume Cronyn (Krapp). *Not I:* Jessica Tandy (Mouth), Henderson Forsythe (Auditor). Reviews: A. Alvarez, *NY Times*, 19 November 1972; Douglas Watt, *Daily News*, 21 and 23 November; Richard Watts, *NY Post*, 21 and 24 November; Martin Gottfried, *Women's Wear Daily*, 22 and 24 November, critical of AS; Edwin Wilson, *Wall Street Journal*, 22 and 28 November; *NY Times*, 3 December; Jack Kroll, *Newsweek*, 4 December; T. E. Kalem, *Time*, 11 December.

3. Maxim Gorki (1868–1936), Russian novelist, dramatist; *Enemies* opened at the Vivian Beaumont Theater, 9 November 1972, directed by Jules Irving.

Nov. 24 [1972]
[handwritten]

Dear Sam,

Rang you twixt 11–12 your time this morning at both Paris and Ussy to tell you that we had opened both evenings and response has been enthusiastic—especially to (believe it or not!) NOT I. Naturally, since it was only one of the four not yet seen ever by anyone, interest was greatest. Beyond this, the performance Jessie gave opening night was simply marvelous, chilling indeed, and completely sustained. You may have heard something about her and it from Martin Esslin or Harold or whoever else saw it in previews; but I can only tell you that she kept getting more and more secure and better during previews, up until and through the opening, when she simply held that audience in a dramatic vise with your words and the entire image. Don't let anyone tell you NOT I doesn't work or cannot work as a theatre piece. It worked—beyond everyone's expectations. And exactly as, I believe, you had seen it in your own eye-of-the-mind. And the Auditor was completely part of the tension built, as even some of the critics noted. (Our Auditor was the guy who played Vladimir in last year's GODOT, excellent actor, and completely devoted to you and to the material. He was fine.)[1] Just wish you had been there.

Sorel came from Toronto and from seeing you, also Mrs. Al Latner. And, of course, Barney and Cristina and Judith and George and John K. and my Jean. It was one of the most electric evenings I have ever spent in the theatre; and none of the critics' descriptions or explanations—even though favorable—match the actual experience. The image of that mouth moving in space across from that mysterious shadowy figure will remain with anyone who has seen it forever. Thanks for trusting us with it. And adding it to the canon.

KRAPP went very well also, though here they were expecting it. Hume never more touching. And as controlled as he can be. He's 62, has one eye, and is inclined to get very very nervous at times. We did the play simply, using the changes from Berlin (Hume very much studied the *Regiebuch* of Held[2]—and, in fact, I gave it to him as opening night present.) The two works make an excellent pair. Could not have been a more exciting evening—even if the critics *did* like us! Which they certainly did. Not clear how long the whole affair can stay at the Forum, partly because of Cronyn-Tandy's other commitments and partly because of question of Forum's availability. Will see.

First evening (Monday) also got excellent response for most part, though it started rockily (Jessie in first act of HAPPY DAYS very nervous and not in control.) Then recovered and played second act best ever. And Hume fine in ACT, which has severe technical problems as you well know. He was also very good as Willie (which he had during rehearsals wanted to let Forsythe play, because he felt he had enough of an acting load with Krapp and ACT; I had to really lay into him.) He should have done Auditor too really but afraid of additional burden—not only of playing but of watching his wife struggle. Jessie as nervous as he throughout and sometimes more so. At some point, she lost confidence to deal with NOT I, and I had the toughest job of all weaning her back. That was just before first previews, and your letter most helpful when it arrived. I'm sure they'd appreciate a note from you if you can spare the time. When I see you next, will tell you more about rehearsals. [last sentence handwritten]

Varying interpretations, naturally, of NOT I. But amazing they responded to it as they did and tribute to your vision. We did it exactly the way you envisioned—after series of technical problems galore, including lighting the Mouth, lighting the Auditor, isolating him in space (which gave impression of his being so tall) keeping spill of teleprompter (which Jessie had to use to help her with the words) off of everything, etc. etc. But well worth it. 'Strange, chilling and masterly', one of crix said, and it was. I'm pleased and wish you could see it.

Sorel tells me you're in midst of London preparations. If I or we can be of any help, offer any suggestions, let me know. I'll try telephoning again, but not sure how to reach you if you are indeed in London. Hope your teeth are coming together. We missed you. And I long to see you and share more with you. Reviews will be sent *en masse.*[3] *Bon chance.* Once again, many mercies. [handwritten after "with"]

Love,
Alan

1. Henderson Forsythe.
2. Martin Held (b. 1908), Krapp at the Schiller-Theater Werkstatt production, 1969, directed by SB.
3. See letter of 13 November 1972, n. 2.

November 30, 1972

Dear Sam,

Been ringing you every morning (your time 11–12) in Paris, but no answer. Finally decided you must be away. Taking chance that the rumors of your presence in London accurate. Anxious to hear your voice and share good news personally.

The Beckett Festival is exceeding all expectations: audience response, the critics even, and general enthusiasm. Especially to NOT I. I have asked the Lincoln Center people since we opened to make sure that they immediately send you the reviews, so assume you have some of them by now. Actually, I have not seen all of the second set because I went right back to Washington to work on Thornton Wilder.[1] But have heard them read to me, or have heard about them. Am back in NYC tomorrow to see all four plays, and will check again to make sure notices have been sent, and more to be sent. I did ask Hume to see to it that you got some of our production photos (actually rehearsal photos because they were taken weeks ago before costumes or props or set entirely ready; but they should give you a rough idea.) Gather that he did and that you have them.

Now that shows are on and greeted well, Cronyns are suffering some kind of post-coital let-down. Doesn't mean anything, the nature of the beast, I think, but has to be dealt with. They have both worked very hard, and at their age the experience—physically and pychologically—has not been an easy one. We had all hoped that if business warranted we might extend the runs past December 17. Business is terrific, and tickets are almost unobtainable, especially to KRAPP–NOT I; but the Cronyns are reluctant to go on, both because they have another assignment soon after, and because they are tired, exhausted emotionally. Nor is the Lincoln Center in great economic state; they operate at a deficit, and the longer we run even at capacity the more they lose. So they say. . . .

NOT I would, I believe, please you. Whatever the interpretations and attitudes, it is taut, theatrical and strongly arresting. I do hope that you are managing with it in London. And, I repeat, if our experience with it can be of any help to you or Tony Page, I'd be glad to talk or write or whatever. (I envy them for having gotten you over.)

Don't be put off by the descriptions in the reviews of the 'tall' Auditor. His head is exactly 10 feet off the ground, and the Mouth is 8 feet off the ground. But the effect is such that sizes and distances in the dark are augmented. Nor is her mouth as 'scarlet' as they say; that's journalese.

Am tired but delighted that the foursome came off so well. I mean the work. Will be free after middle of December. Going to Russia in the spring, and hope to stop off. Let me hear from you, at least to know if you've gotten material from us. Take care of yourself.

Best,
[Alan]

1. *Our Town* opened at the Arena Stage, Washington, D.C., 15 December 1972.

Paris
3.12.72

Dear Alan

Thanks for yours of Nov. 24. Congratulations to all. I had an offensive letter from Cronyn dated Nov. 16 to which I replied briefly. This ends our correspondence as far as I am concerned and discourages me from writing to his wife, to compliment her on her *Not I*.[1]

. . . .[2]

Forgive more now.

Affectionately
Sam

1. The incident is described by Deirdre Bair, 527–528. SB replied: "Any comments I may have to make on the production will be made to the director of the production, Alan Schneider." Passing the letter on to AS, Cronyn wrote: "To Alan from H.C. with a touch of the forelock."
2. SB still has dental trouble.

Paris
9.12.72

Dear Alan

Today your letter of Nov. 30 forwarded by Royal Court. I leave here on 15th and start rehearsing 18th.

Have received masses of material from L.C., Grove and other sources.[1] Again congratulations to you all—I know what a rough time it's been.

Thanks for offer of help in London. Shall not fail to consult you if in need.

Look forward to seeing you in the Spring.

Love to Jean & the children.

Best always
Sam

1. "L.C.": Lincoln Center.

December 9, 1972

Dear Sam,

Your card of Dec. 3 received here, operating on precise principles of Murphy's Law, i. e. it arrived the day after I had cabled you saying I hadn't heard from you. Thanks.

The mystery of the non-answered phone calls continues. I have now developed a habit of waking exactly at 5 o'clock local time, which according to my operatives is 11 in Paris. I go through a daily routine with the local representatives of the Bell telephone company, most of whom have never heard of Paris, France, and speak English with various overtones of unintelligibility. The conversation before KEL-8311 rings should be recorded—and probably is. Have you changed your phone? Are you answering at a different time? Have you not been in Paris? I tried Ussy (which no one here admits exists) several times also, not to mention poor Oscar Lewenstein's secretary, who doesn't actually want to admit that you exist, although I did manage to learn that NOT I will go into rehearsal next week. (I gather with Billie Whitelaw, bravo, she's marvelous; and Albie Finney[1] doing KRAPP, ditto.) Is KEL-8311 the same as 535-8311? What am I doing wrong? Your letter came from Paris so you must be there part of the time.

Sorry about Hume's letter. I knew nothing of it until afterward when he told me he had written something off to you and had not heard. Then he showed me your responding card. I appreciate your understanding thought. The whole business of his ad-libbing has completely simmered down, at least every time I've seen the show, which is still once or twice weekly. Last time was Thursday when we had special matinee for National Theatre Conference, association of theatre directors, who loved it and gave both performers standing ovation. We had sort of symposium afterward at which silly questions asked and unanswered. Hume has colossal ego, I'm afraid, which comes from deep insecurity. He tends to go off deep end and then regret it. Jessie is just frightened. She was frightened when she first read NOT I, though deeply moved, was frightened that she could not learn it (which she couldn't at same time as HAPPY DAYS), frightened she would not be good—she is marvelous, and I'm trying to get her voice on tape so that you can at least hear her, if we can sneak it all past the unions—frightened no one would respond to the play, etc. etc. Finally, she stopped all the psychologising and probing and just did it.

Responses continue to come in, mostly favorable one way or other. I have continued to remind Lincoln Center press dept. to send you all reviews as they come in, and assume you have been getting them. We are absolutely sold out, tickets impossible to get, and could run all season—but Cronyns have other engagement (previously committed) and are tired out. Plan is to map out tour of colleges in fall of next year. Run at LC ends Dec. 17,[2] probably last show in Forum, you've been reading about their financial troubles, sad to say.

Assume you've read Gottfried's review. He's married to Bert Lahr's daughter and has been out to get me for years. I was amused that the two instances he seized on to prove how I was betraying your intentions had to do with 'adding' business of bringing tape recorder in; and also getting Jessie to race through NOT I instead of dwelling on each word and moment. But he couldn't deny that he was impressed with the play.[3]

Sam, I just wanted to talk with you, share something of the whole experience with you because it has been wonderful though difficult and complex. Main thing is that the new play came off, and I am most grateful. Do hope all goes well in London.

Talked with Jackie who's rehearsing O'Casey. He hadn't seen the plays yet but promised to go this week. Seems in tense state and unsure of future plans. I invited him to do something at Arena next year, and hopeful can pin him down. His KRAPP tape remains with N. E. T., which continues to re-show the *Beginning to End*,[4] and then say that they can't do another Beckett for a while. NY Library of Performing Arts wants to do film record (just as stage plays) of the Festival, but union regulations preventing.

Take care of yourself. Would love to hear from you and find out where I might talk with you in next weeks. Love from Jean and all of us.

[Alan]

1. Albert Finney (b. 1936), English stage, film, and television actor, joined National Theatre Company in 1965; associate director, Royal Court Theatre (1972–1975).

2. *Happy Days* and *Act Without Words I* closed after 16 performances and 17 previews; *Krapp's Last Tape* and *Not I* closed on 16 December 1972 after 15 performances and 19 previews.

3. In his review, "A Beckett premiere," Gottfried said that AS "blundered" in his staging of *Krapp's Last Tape*, "befouling the play with directing business such as having Krapp lug the tape recorder in and encouraging Hume Cronyn to tremble, wheeze, shuffle and otherwise 'act'"; he "mutilated this exquisite and touching farewell to love. Beckett's trust of Schneider was never more misguided." Of Jessica Tandy's performance as Winnie, he said that she read the speech "feverishly" so that the performance became an emotional rather than a verbal experience. She should have been allowed "to vary her

tempo and timbre more often." Nevertheless, he concluded, her performance was "magnificent." *Women's Wear Daily*, 22 November 1972.

4. "N.E.T.": PBS, WNET-TV, New York, *Beginning to End.*

Paris

14.12.72

Dear Alan

Thanks for yrs. of 9.

Have not been very attentive to reviews and did not notice Gottfried's. I have passed them on to Lindon.

Start work in London next week feeling confident in Billie Whitelaw.

Alarming cutting from *N.Y.T.* (I think) about Grove's action against Random.[1] Very grieved for Barney and do hope it works out for him somehow.

Love to you all.

Sam

1. *NY Times*, 21 November 1972. Grove Press filed suit seeking to dissolve a five-year agreement with Random House under which Random handled sales, promotion, and distribution of Grove books and asking one million dollars in damages for alleged destruction of thousands of Grove Press books. Barney Rosset charged Random House with ineptness and with destroying Grove Press's relationships with authors and said the Press would fail unless it was free to seek distribution arrangements with another publisher; it had debts approaching four million dollars.

December 30, 1972

Dear Sam,

Assume you're in London and heavily involved with Royal Court proceedings,[1] though with time out on occasion to visit that nice pub down the King's Road. Thanks for your cards, duly received when I got home from Washington and OUR TOWN. Not directing anything for a month, and glad of it.

A cable from someone at Royal Court asking how we did lighting for NOT I. I asked our lighting designer to explain in detail. Basically, a type of lamp used for lighting paintings (in galleries or private homes), very small and powerful; we had it focused down to sort of oval shape so as just to hit mouth. In order to hide light source entirely, we built a 'box' unit, rolled on with Jessie standing at one end, sticking out of it; completely closed in and covered with black velour so as to be invisible. The lamp was inside and clamped down, focused on the mouth, but still requiring a stagehand rolled in with it to move it a fraction as Jessie's head, though also clamped down, moved a fraction. I'm sure all this information already transmitted in much more technical manner.

Oscar Lewenstein also wrote to me. I gather everyone is pleased and excited, and I'm sure all will be well. Billie Whitelaw is superb, and should be marvelous in the part, especially with you there helping her. Also Albie Finney. My gosh, the British are lucky to have so many good actors always available.

Thought for a moment I might get over to London next week and surprise you by suddenly appearing on the scene, but this is not to be. Someone who is putting Ted Whitehead's[2] ALPHA BETA on, either Broadway or off-Broadway, suddenly rang me up and asked me if I would be available because they were having some sort of difficulty with whoever was to direct. I said I liked the play and would be able to do it if they made the decision right now; and stressed the need of casting it well, with superb British actors (like Finney who did it in London). Anyhow, they have now stalled almost two weeks, and I feel there is just not enough time, so I cannot get involved, and I won't be coming to London to look at a few British actors, which I was hoping to do. Just as well, I suppose, I need time to unwind and be with the family and read a bit and listen to some music.

OUR TOWN enthusiastically greeted at the Arena; after all these years, it still lives on. Talk of a possible European tour for it in the fall, I'll believe it when it happens.

Plans now solidifying for college tour of KRAPP–NOT I in the fall, starting with a couple of weeks at the Arena (the smaller theatre, regular proscenium stage,[3] you'll be pleased to know) where we'll build a simpler version of Jessie's box to tour. Will let you know as plans develope.

In meantime, take care of yourself, hope things go well in London, best wishes for New Year, and always. Love from us all.

Affectionately yours,
[Alan]

P.S. Seeing Jackie in PLOUGH AND STARS next week, and will be talking with him. I've offered him prospect of doing Vladimir in GO-

DOT at Arena next season, and he wants to but reluctant to commit self to actual dates. We'll talk about it.

1. Rehearsals of *Not I* with Billie Whitelaw and *Krapp's Last Tape* with Albert Finney (see letter of 5 November 1972, n. 1, and letter of 14 January 1973, n. 2).
2. Edward Anthony Whitehead (b. 1933); *Alpha Beta* had opened at the Royal Court Theatre, 26 January 1972, with Albert Finney and Rachel Roberts.
3. Kreeger Theatre.

January 6, 1973

Dear Sam,

Saw Jackie last night as Fluther in O'Casey's PLOUGH AND THE STARS. He was just lovely. And I wanted to let you know.[1]

Talked to him backstage right after the performance and told him I had been watching him every moment from the second row, when he had lines and when he was just listening—which he does superbly. He gave a truly classical performance. Eileen O'Casey, whom I knew in Torquay when I used to visit Sean there back in 1949, was in the audience and came up on stage afterwards to hug him.

Then the critics came out this morning and, while praising Jackie highly, lambasted the play and/or the performance. Enough to make you cry.

Anyhow, wanted to share my feelings about Jackie with you.

How are things in London?

Had lunch with Tom Bishop, who says he's going to see you in Paris in a couple of weeks.[2] Nice chap. I believe he saw NOT I a couple of times, so he'll be able to tell you about our version, if you'll still be wanting to hear anything about it.

I'm eating my hat thinking of you all working away in London. Wish I were there to watch.

Take care of yourself.

Regards and good thoughts from us all.

[Alan]

1. Opened at the Vivian Beaumont Theater, Lincoln Center, 4 January 1973, closed 10 February 1973.
2. Thomas Walter (Tom) Bishop (b. 1929), born in Vienna, author, editor, translator, producer; Professor of French and Comparative Literature, New York University; ed. with Raymond Federman, *Beckett, L'Herne*, no. 31, Paris, 1976; organized *colloques* and festivals in New York and Paris for SB's seventieth and seventy-fifth birthdays.

London
14.1.73

Dear Alan

Thanks for your letters and news.

Things have gone fairly well here—though Finney miscast in *Krapp.* Billie W. magnificent. Shall wait over to see them after the opening (16th), then with relief depart. Good response so far—previews packed. Some difficult moments with Page (for him too no doubt), but pleasant atmosphere mainly. He's leaving soon for N.Y. to do a TV play about The *Pueblo* pirate ship[1] and perhaps you'll be seeing him.

. . . .[2]

Love to you all
Sam

1. *The Pueblo Incident,* by Stanley R. Greenberg, directed by Anthony Page, a dramatization of the capture of an American spy ship, 1968, by North Koreans, was shown on ABC-TV in April 1973.

2. SB apologizes for this "wretched scribble."

January 15, 1973

Dear Sam,

Just want you to know that I am thinking of you, and wondering how the NOT I previews are going.

Nary a word from London, and nothing in our papers yet. But I would assume by the silence that you are *in medias res.* Would love to know a bit if you manage a few minutes. I'm not sure when opening date is.

Are you still there? How is Billie? And Albert Finney? Everything and anything.[1]

Things here quiet and full of infinite detail, signifying very little. I'm preparing to do Gorki's ENEMIES at the Arena, reading Montaigne, trying to write a few articles, seeing my family.

Saw Jackie and discovered he hadn't come to see NOT I or any other of the plays, sad to say. Too busy and too tired, I guess. I understand but I sure am disappointed. Jackie has made a great personal success with the O'Casey, though the play and production were greeted unevenly. Not quite clear what his plans are. I keep getting reassured by the Public Service TV station here that they want to put on his TV *Krapp* we did so long ago, but it's not been on yet.[2]

Anyhow. Would love to see what you and the Royal Court have done with the Mouth and the Auditor, and would love to hear how you feel about it now that you've seen it.

Take care of yourself.

Best,
Alan

1. AS has not received SB's letter of 14 January 1973.
2. WNET, New York; AS's TV *Krapp* has never been shown on either commercial or public television to date.

Paris
27.1.73

Dear Alan

Thanks for yours of 15.

Glad to be back here. Pleased with work in London. Billie marvellous. Great set by Jocelyn. Spot technique excellent. Astonishingly well received even by—no names! Finney quite miscast but not too bad. That's the nutshell.[1]

Saw Kent Carroll a moment yesterday.[2] Turning down Mostel *Godot* film offer needless to say. Kent said you & Barney were to see Gregory's *Endgame* quite scandalously bad by all accounts.

Getting on now with arrears of translation. Ancient prose painful to go back on . . . .[3]

Madeleine & Roger Blin went to see the show in London. Former now asking for it in French. Can't imagine it working on that ice.[4] But suppose must try.

Love to all
Sam

1. *Not I* and *Krapp's Last Tape* opened at the Royal Court Theatre, London, 16 January 1973, directed by Anthony Page, designed by Jocelyn Herbert. Billie Whitelaw (Mouth), Brian Miller (The Auditor). Albert Finney (Krapp). SB virtually directed *Not I*. His amended script for *Krapp's Last Tape* included many of the changes made at the Schiller-Theater Werkstatt, 1969. Reviews: *Sunday Times*, 14 January 1973; *Times*, 17 January; *The Guardian*, 17 January; *Daily Telegraph*, 17 January; *Observer*, 21 January.
2. Kent Carroll, editor, Grove Press; cofounder of American publishing firm Carroll and Graf.
3. *Premier amour (First Love)*. SB says when he will be at Ussy and in Morocco.
4. A pun on the theater's name, Palais de Glace, but it did not play there.

January 30, 1973

Dear Sam,

Just this afternoon heard the news about Jackie, and find it almost impossible to believe.[1] Saw him opening night of the O'Casey, and spoke with him only a few days ago. We had been talking about possibility of him coming down to Arena in Washington next season to play Vladimir.

And now he is gone, all of him. The smile, and the crinkly eyes, and all those lovely stories. I always wanted to know him better than I did; but during the TV KRAPP I did get to know him a bit.

What else can I say. I know how much you meant to him and how much he meant to you. Nothing will make his going easier to accept.

We shall all help Gloria all we can. There's a service on Thursday, and I'll be there. I'm sorry that you won't be there, but I understand— and so would Jackie.

Take care of yourself. Jean's thoughts and mine are with [you].

[Alan]

p.s. I called Barney to tell him.

1. Jack MacGowran died in New York, 29 January 1973.

Feb. 13, 1973

Dear Sam,

Back in Washington once more (rehearsing Gorki's ENEMIES at Arena), after quick trip on 'day off' to New York.[1] Sorry to barge in on you in Ussy yesterday, but both Barney and I much disturbed *vis-à-vis* the Gregory ENDGAME production, and not sure what to do. We went last week, and shocked to see self-indulgent travesty, determined to be 'different' for sake of being different.[2] Gregory, who is talented and has strong avant-garde following, did another production of the play some 5–6 years ago at Philadelphia, where he had a theater group, and then at Yale. I wrote to you about it at the time.[3] He had Nelson Eddy and Jeannette MacDonald singing NAUGHTY MARIETTA and then winding down as curtain went up.[4] Rest of production used various dialects, Negro, Jewish, Puerto Rican, etc. and some vaudeville business, but stuck pretty much to the text. When I spoke to him afterwards, he said this was the way he saw the play; he was free-ing it from a rigid adherence to your directions. . . . He obtained the rights via S. French,[5] with all of us believing because of letter French had that you had seen him in Paris last summer and had agreed because you had been aware of his status and reputation; he is trying to follow in Peter Brook's footsteps as experimenter and guru. (Doesn't hold a candle to Brook!) Anyhow, I was disturbed when I heard reports last fall about what new production was like. I am in peculiarly vulnerable position because there is an entire cabal of avant-garde critics who feel that I have mesmerized you into some sort of permanent possession of your works, this cabal led by Martin Gottfried, who is married to Lahr's daughter, and John Lahr, Bert's son. They have on occasion been most vicious in their attacks on me. When GODOT off-Broadway, received favorable response, they were literally beside themselves and determined to wrest you away from me, not that I felt I had any hold on your works apart from your willingness to let me direct your plays, and your trusting me to more or less carry out your intentions. Gottfried has at times been so insultingly devastatingly vindictive that I have had to hold myself back from taking action, of whatever kind.

You may remember that about a year ago, Joe Chaikin did an END-GAME with his Open Theatre. While I disagreed with much of it, I could understand and respect it. (Judith saw it with me.) I was very nervous about the Gregory version, but felt it was not in my province to oppose it. But the production takes such liberties with your text (extra words, sounds, grunts, songs, elongations, repetitions) and with your directions (the ashcans, the old people, everybody)! Every homosexual joke is pulled out of the bag and included. Sure, there are laughs but not one moment of reality or feeling, of characters in a situation. And so on. Kerr, who actually is not a fan of the play, is accurate in his observation, as is Tallmer. It's just clever, tricky, & superficial. [handwritten from "It's"]

What to do? Barney considered legal action immediately, an injunction, sue-ing, everything. Everything is difficult, even though they have clearly tampered with your text. He doesn't want to focus additional attention. He has tried to reason with Gregory, who won't budge. Gregory feels I am influencing Barney to oppose the production; in fact, I feel he has said this to Barnes of the TIMES. Which is one reason why Barnes' review may be so defensive in tone, and so clearly inaccurate. Even Gottfried said the production was abominable—and no way to win your favor. The main thing is to protect the play and you. But how, except to keep it from going on in the first place? How to know you had not given approval? Please let us know how you feel about the situation, and whether you have a strong feeling in any direction. Too bad to involve you in this sort of thing, but the theatrical climate here always seems to get poisoned in this way. We are writing to the TIMES, but that doesn't really mean anything.[6] And whatever legal action that may prove necessary. But you understand why I am trying to advise Barney to move cautiously and only with your approval. I wish Gregory had served the play in any way, but he hasn't, even though Barney [handwritten sentence, ending missing]

Sam, I know all this is most disturbing to you; and I wish I could spare you from the matter. Actually, a lot of people will see the production and some of them will like it. Maybe we should all just let it run out its course; but I gather since talking with you that after an independent run until April, it is then scheduled to go into repertory with Gregory's free adaptation of ALICE IN WONDERLAND, which gained him great attention last year—although I felt it was an interesting acting and directorial exercise and no more. Certainly not a play. The trouble here is that he is now working with a text, a much different situation, and treating it as though it did not exist. Barney is sending you, I believe, a report by John Beary,[7] (who did HAPPY DAYS in Dublin) who took detailed notes on what Gregory had done . . . .

Wrote to Billie Whitelaw to congratulate her.[8] And I hear from all sorts of people (including John Gielgud) how marvelously it was done in London. Can't locate Tony Page, and he has not gotten in touch.

Trust you get away to Morocco next month, and from all this. Take care of yourself. [handwritten last sentence]

[Alan]

1. Opened at the Arena Stage, Washington, D.C., 16 March 1973.

2. *Endgame,* directed by André Gregory, opened 8 February 1973 at New York University School of the Arts. Gerry Bammam (Hamm), Larry Pine (Clov), Tom Costello (Nagg), Saskia Noordhoek Hegt (Nell). The stage was a small hexagon; the audience sat in wire-meshed chicken coops. The "decoration," according to Walter Kerr, "includes cockcrows, halloos, clucks, brrs, burbles, bugle sounds, imitations of automobiles and rockets, screeches, machine-gun rat-a-tat-tats, interpolated 'yucks' to express disgust . . ." Reviews: Clive Barnes, *NY Times,* 8 February 1973; Walter Kerr, *NY Times,* 11 February; John Lahr, *Village Voice,* 15 February; Edith Oliver, *The New Yorker,* 17 February; Harold Clurman, *The Nation,* 26 February; Martin Gottfried, *Women's Wear Daily,* 9 February. Gottfried said the production was a "travesty of one of the great plays of our time," all the more regrettable "because it is desperately important to break Alan Schneider's hammerjack on staging Beckett and this will only strengthen it."

3. Letter missing.

4. Nelson Eddy (1902–1967), Jeannette MacDonald (1901–1965).

5. Samuel French, Inc.: for many years the leading licenser of plays, founded by Samuel French (1821–1898), published *Waiting for Godot,* 1957.

6. This letter did not appear.

7. John Beary directed *Happy Days* at the Eblana Theatre, Dublin, opened 30 September 1963. Marie Kean (Winnie), O. Z. Whitehead (Willie).

8. Playing in first London production of *Not I* at the Royal Court Theatre (see letter of 27 January 1973, n. 1).

Paris
20.2.73

Dear Alan

Thanks for yours of 13.

I wrote to Barney advising to let *Endgame* run its [?] calvary at N.Y.U. but to prevent any further presentation. I don't know what action this may call for, depending I suppose on terms of contract with French. I would certainly back any proceedings to above effect. My work is not holy writ but this production sounds truly revolting & damaging to the play. I find it hard to understand how French, on strength of Gregory's assurances alone, could issue a license without consulting Grove. Surely this is enough to justify our demand that the production shd lapse after N.Y.U. run.

This of course is happening everywhere all the time and, as I wrote to Barney, if not to me in N.Y. till now only thanks to you.

Love
Sam

May 1, 1973

Dear Sam,

Thanks for your letter,[1] delighted you are going to be in Paris and able to see me on May 11. I'm arriving sometime that morning, and taking off for Moscow Saturday the 12th. Will be at L'Aiglon, and expecting you at 7. Thanks.

Lots to tell you.

Went to benefit for Tara Monday evening.[2] Sad occasion. Most of Jackie's friends there, and I believe they raised considerable amount. Various objects also auctioned off. I bid on small sketch of you by

Avigdor, and got it.[3] Don't know whether it came from Jackie or from you.

Saw Barney, in good shape; and things seem to be OK at Grove. New edition of EVERGREEN with LOST ONES, which I'm bringing along for you.[4]

Long to see you. Jean sends her love. Vickie about to take off for college. Is that possible?

Ever,
[Alan]

1. Missing.
2. "Tara": Gloria and Jack MacGowran's daughter.
3. Avigdor Arikha's drawing of SB's head was subsequently donated by Jean Schneider to the Lincoln Center Library.
4. *Evergreen Review,* 96 (Spring 1973), 41–64.

July 11, 1973

Dear Sam,

Back home from my travels to Moscow, Dallas, Washington—and about to take off for Kansas City, heaven help me for another session with the younger generation.

Did you get my card from Moscow? Had a marvelous trip, hospitality most pure, and some excellent theatre. Lots of discussion about Beckett over there. The Minister of Culture[1] asked me why I chose to direct your plays; I told her in a few well-chosen (I hope) sentences. Most of the theatre people are very aware of your work—GODOT has been published in a magazine[2] some time ago—but prevented from putting it on by official edict. Actually, at the Theatre Congress one day, a young directress from some theatre in Estonia crept up to me and handed me a photo of a production of KRAPP, which her theatre had done.[3] She was very proud of the fact and told me to tell everyone that the Soviets did indeed do Beckett. They'll do all of them once the wraps are off.

At a committee session which I chaired, we got involved in a question of your 'humanism' or 'anti-humanism', hah! Barrault and I, he most eloquently, spoke of your work as being the most human we know; but the East-bloc people didn't think you were 'dialectical' enough. Those two tramps shouldn't have just waited for Godot, they should have fought a revolution to have him appear. Such nonsense. As I told that Minister of Culture (?), they will yet come to you.

Also saw a young Rumanian chap, David Esrig,[4] who had been working on a GODOT project for years and then had it called off. He said he had met you in Paris some time back. Or perhaps Berlin, was it? He's most discouraged at the moment.

Will be more or less in charge of Arena's fortunes next season, living in Washington most of the time, Jean joining when she can. We're opening with the Tandy-Cronyn NOT I–KRAPP for a few weeks, at start of their college tour. Am also taking a long-range option on GODOT for Arena to do if not next season the one after. Much interest in that one from all sorts of quarters, including various people who want to do it with all-female cast, dammit. Not I!

Saw Bettina in London briefly on way back and she's fine, livid about a few things that are going on. Barney reasonably well, Judith away somewhere. I've just read FIRST LOVE, which I found absolutely lovely; although I do wish NOT I could be published all by itself, at least the first time.[5] News here is that Gregory has been trying like mad to reach you to get permission for French tour.[6]

Enjoyed seeing you, even for an instant, and hope not too long until next time. Trust you get back to your favorite Morocco soon. Take care of yourself. Jean and kids send their affectionate regards.

[Alan]

1. Minister of Culture: Yekaterina Alekseevna Furtseva (1910–1974).

2. M. Bogoslovskoi, "V ozhidanii Godo: Tragikomediia v 2-kh d," *Inostrannaia literatura*, 10 (1966), 165–195.

3. May refer to a production at the Estonian Drama Theatre, Tallinn, in 1973. Juri Jarvet (Krapp).

4. David Esrig (b. 1935), like Ciulei, was forced to work in exile for some time, and subsequently returned to Bucharest.

5. *Premier Amour*, 1970, trans. by SB, *First Love*, 1973, 1974.

6. Gregory's proposed tour did not take place.

Paris
[?]17.7.73

Dear Alan

Thanks for your good letter of July 11. Also for your card from Moscow.

Can't remember meeting Esrig.

Had a letter from Estelle Parsons about all-female *Godot* with Shelley Winters.[1] Declined.

No sign from Gregory thank God.

Spend time up and down between here and Ussy. Morocco again probably early September.

No other plans. No new work though keep trying. Translation of *Not I* rotting on siding. Madeleine pained—patient.

Reavey passed through on way to Dubrovnik where Jean is having a production at "Marin Držic" Theatre.[2]

Had a drink with Tom Bishop, wife & son. He said Gregory had damped his fireworks.

Love to you all
Sam

1. Estelle Parsons (b. 1927), Shelley Winters (b. 1922).
2. "Jean": Jean Reavey; theater called after Marin Držic (1508–1567), the Yugoslavian dramatist who wrote pastorals and comedies in the Croat language.

July 31, 1973

Dear Sam,

Please forgive the more than usually bad typing, but I am in unfamiliar country—Kansas—and unfamiliar typewriter.

Heard from Viveca,[1] who is working as a waitress this summer back home, that there's a note from you. Thank you. Will be reading it when I get back in a couple more weeks, when the new play I'm directing here at the university, a dramatisation of the life of cartoonist James Thurber, is finally on.

Just wanted to respond to a recent message from Barney. He tells me that ENDGAME will be playing in Paris though not at the Festival.[2] I do hope that you go to see the production, painful as it might be for you to do so, because I believe you should judge for yourself ultimately. Please understand why I'm saying this. I gather that Gregory or his supporters have been calling you all sorts of names, including 'Fascist' because of your unwillingness to permit the Festival production. Such stupidity and viciousness should not bother you though I am sure it does; which is why you have given permission for the Paris production.

It's just too bad that the matter goes on and on.

Certainly agree with you about the all-female GODOT idea. Seems as though everyone here is always looking for a 'gimmick' instead of sticking to the text of something.

Trust you are well and either have been back in Morocco or will soon be going back there because I know how much you like that part of the world.

Will be going back to the Soviet Union with OUR TOWN late in September but since we are all flying together on a chartered flight direct from NY to Moscow, I shan't be stopping off this time. When I see you next, I'd love to fill you in on details of the situation there. Did I tell you that someone from a small theatre in Estonia had come up to me at the Conference one day and whispered that they had done KRAPP?

Take care of yourself. Jean and David send their love.

Best wishes.

Ever,
[Alan]

1. The Schneiders' daughter, Vicki.
2. André Gregory tried in vain to bring his production to the Bordeaux Festival.

August 21, 1973

Dear Sam,

Back from the wilds of mid-America, Kansas City to be exact, to find your letter—thank you—and wanted to drop you a bit of a line before you took off for Morocco.[1]

Was lecturing and directing a play at the University of Missouri, rather a progressive school, especially for that part of the country. And Kansas City reasonably pleasant and attractive. Main thing is that family was with me and we saw a bit of each other for a change.

Play was a dramatisation of James Thurber's life, cartoon sketch and a bit of a change.[2] They did six plays in repertory in 16 weeks.

Cronyn and Tandy about to take off on college tour of KRAPP and NOT I. Intense interest from all the schools, including Missouri—which, unfortunately, won't be seeing the plays because too far West. We're going back into rehearsal this week, opening Toronto September 4 for two weeks, then three weeks at Arena, and on. Changes in NOT I text received and noted.

I saw Oscar Lewenstein on my day in London, and he told me how pleased they all were at the Court about the production of NOT I there. Tried to reach Billie Whitelaw, but she was off somewhere.

Will be going back to the Soviet Union at the end of September with our Arena company to do OUR TOWN and INHERIT THE WIND.[3] We'll be flying in a chartered plane direct, so won't be able to stop off. When I see you next, I'll fill you in with details of my two trips, both fascinating and depressing. Did I tell you that when I was attending the Congress of the International Theater Institute, and Barrault and I were arguing passionately against the official Soviet policy of 'not allowing' any Beckett plays because they were too 'pessimistic' and 'non-ideological', someone from a small theater in Estonia came up to me and whispered that they had done KRAPP, and to tell you that 'we know him here'. Indeed, they do, and are only waiting for the moment when they can do all the plays. I tried to get to that Estonian theater but they would not let me have a visa to go there.

Barney has kept me in touch with your recent messages. I do hope that, painful as it may be for you, you do get to see ENDGAME in Paris so that you will be able to judge for yourself.

Had a drink with Tom Bishop, who told me he had seen you recently, and in good shape. Hope to see Barney out at Easthampton this weekend. Talked with Judith, who expects to be going to Europe this fall but not sure when.

Take care of yourself. Will write to you from the USSR. Jean and kids send love. Vicky off to college and scared to death; David wants to fly airplanes. We shall see what tomorrow shall bring.

All the best.

[Alan]

1. This is a revised version by AS of the July 31st letter marked "Not Sent."

2. *Jabberwock* by Jerome Lawrence and Robert E. Lee opened at the Missouri Repertory Theatre, Kansas City, 9 August 1973. James Grove Thurber (1894–1961), American writer, artist, cartoonist.

3. AS first directed Thornton Wilder's *Our Town* at Arena Stage, Washington, D.C., 16 March 1953; *Inherit The Wind* by Jerome Lawrence and Robert E. Lee premiered 21 April 1955, but AS was directing it for the first time.

November 18, 1973

Dear Sam,

Back almost a month from the hegira, and traveling somewhere almost daily ever since. Forgive my not writing to you sooner.

A tremendous experience although when anyone asks me if I 'enjoyed' it, I have to say that isn't the word. 'Experienced' or 'endured' maybe. The USSR is a self-contradictory country in ways which make the USA or even France seem terribly unilinear. Some day when we meet I'll go into detail. For the moment, let me say that we were a huge 'success' in the sense of being greeted and welcomed and admired and applauded and gazed at. They were swept away by OUR TOWN, Wilder's cosmic vision being something they had never seen or heard but recognised the moment it was presented to them. INHERIT THE WIND was a lesser animal, more agit-prop, and more prop than agit, which they knew from their own examples of the genre.[1] But in both cases, they really liked our actors, their 'humanity' and informality. We mingled easily with lots of theirs, in homes and in theaters and all sorts of places. It was good, and none of us will ever forget.

I felt especially pleased when three different theaters, including the staid old Moscow Arts invited me to come back next year and direct a play for them, in Russian, with their actors. Don't know if I will, but it's nice to be asked.

And they know you over there. Even though they haven't done much, apart from that 'underground' production of KRAPP in Estonia, about which I heard a bit more. Everyone asked me about GODOT, which they really want to do if only their stupid cultural censors would let them. What are they afraid of? The lack of dialectical materialism? And one gal interpreter asked me to tell her about NOT I, which I did in great detail. But when I suggested sending her the script, she recoiled in horror because it was not something she was anxious to get in the mail. Too bad I didn't have a copy, she would have swallowed it up if only I could have handed it to her in person. What a system!

Anyhow, glad to be back, once more working on a new play at

Arena, and actually more or less in charge of the theater this year.[2] The double-bill went well here, I assume you got the reviews and program because I asked them to send everything to you even before we took off for USSR.[3] And the tour is evidently going well, though I haven't actually seen the notices. Either I or Barney will send on to you when we get them.

Have been sort of invited to the Abbey to direct next year, and would love to go if they really mean it. Will be over to see you in any case some time in summer. A tough year, between Boston and Washington, but hope to get through it. In spite of Watergate, war, and whatever.[4]

Trust you are keeping well, had a good holiday in Morocco, and are up to something. Will Billie be doing NOT I again? All the best, and we're all thinking of you. Even the Russians.

[Alan]

1. Propaganda theater, named after the Department of Agitation and Propaganda formed in the Soviet Union, 1920, to promote the party line; the term covers a range of political attitudes. Arena Stage players at the Moscow Arts Theater, then in Leningrad under the Soviet-American cultural exchange program (see "Americana in Moscow," *NY Times*, 8 October 1973).

2. *Tom* by Alexander Buzo opened 14 December 1973. AS was Acting Producer at Arena Stage, Washington, D.C., 1973–74.

3. The double bill was *Krapp's Last Tape* and *Not I.*

4. "Watergate": the name used to refer to the scandals surrounding President Nixon and his administration, and Nixon's resignation on 9 August 1974; the Watergate Complex was where the break-in of the Democratic National Committee Headquarters took place, 17 June 1972.

Paris
8.12.73

Dear Alan

Thanks for yours of Nov. 18.

Good to have such good news of your tour.

A friend of a friend going in with German edition of the plays had it taken away from him.

Still haven't translated *Not I.* No news of Billie. Figures & cheques from Asmus[1] via Barney. Seems to have done pretty well.

Gregory's antics announced here but no sign of him so far.

Same ill-starred work now to be seen with puppets in a Montparnasse café-théâtre.[2]

Not I in Schiller Werkstatt performed by Brecht's daughter! Well, they say, just 30 minutes. *Du Lieber!*[3]

Strick doing *Krapp* with Pat for Irish TV with *The Evils of Tobacco*—an adaptation of the *Modest Proposal*.[4]

Nothing new in sight. Cleaning up old odds & ends. Winding up? I fondly ask.

Love to you all
Sam

1. Walter D. Asmus (b. 1941), SB's assistant director for many productions; published "Practical Aspects of Theatre, Radio, and Television: Rehearsal Notes for the German Premiere of Samuel Beckett's *That Time* and *Footfalls,* at the Schiller-Theater Werkstatt, Berlin," trans. Helen Watanabe, *Journal of Beckett Studies,* 2 (Summer 1977).

2. The Daru Company performed *Endgame* with puppets in the Théâtre Manitout, Paris.

3. *Nicht Ich* opened at the Schiller-Theater Werkstatt, 26 October 1973, directed by Ernst Wendt, designed by Johannes Schultz, trans. by Erika and Elmar Tophoven. Hanne Hiob (Mouth), Heinz Rabbe (Auditor). Running time for Billie Whitelaw was sixteen minutes. "*Du Lieber!*": Good God!

4. Joseph Strick (b. 1923), American producer, director, writer. This production of *Krapp's Last Tape* did not take place. "*Modest Proposal*"(1729): a satire by Jonathan Swift (1667–1745).

January 14, 1974

Dear Sam,

Briefly, forgive please.

Thought you might be amused at the enclosed. KRAPP has now become part of our political heritage. Wonder if Nixon has read it.[1]

Been working with Elie Wiesel on a play of his we're planning for Arena in April.[2] Marvelous man, in despair about everything—as we all are at the moment. No light at the end of the tunnel.

Vickie off at college, unbelievable. David working on computers and radio-controlled planes and such mysteries. Jean struggling to keep us all together and heads above all waters. My Mum struggling to keep dignity intact.

Lunch with Barney this week. Gather they're managing.

Did Gregory ever do the show either in Paris or elsewhere?

Have just been told I can spend a month at the Rockefeller Villa and Research Center in Como from last half of August. Jean and I hope to be over via Paris if inflation doesn't overtake us.

Trust you are reasonably well. Take care of yourself.

Love from us all,
[Alan]

P.S. Just heard about Serreau.[3] Do you have his wife's address (and name). I'd like to write her a note. Met her briefly when in Israel in 1966.

1. *Watergate Classics.*
2. Elie Wiesel (b. 1928), Rumanian-born French educator, author, survivor of Auschwitz and Buchenwald, determined to bear witness to the Holocaust; awarded the Nobel Peace Prize, 1986. *The Madness of God (Zalmen; ou La Folie de Dieu)* opened at the Arena Stage, Washington, D.C., 3 May 1974.
3. Died 23 May 1973.

February 17, 1974

Dear Sam,

Finally stopping long enough in my journeys between cities to tell you of my session in Toronto last week, where I participated in a Beckett-Joyce Seminar with a few friends of yours: Ray Federman, Vivian Mercier, Alan Simpson. Hugh Kenner was coming but prevented by snowstorm, which I just missed flying up fom Washington. Lots of talk, good cheer, and even a drink or two whenever we managed to get off the campus. We missed having you with us. And Donald Davis was there too, and we exchanged some memories of our first Krapp. Jean and I stayed with him in Toronto, and he'll probably be writing to you if he hasn't already. Some of the talk was, of course, awfully academic, but some of it simple enough to mean something. I really liked Ray Federman, whom I had never met, and enjoyed what Mercier had to say about your being Irish.[1]

Everybody all over the place is talking about you, and you'll just have to get used to it. There's another sort of Seminar in April in North Carolina, on to which I'm going to pop in briefly, and another big one in Wisconsin which has asked me along but I can't because I'll be in rehearsal with Elie Wiesel's play at Arena. And so on. I believe Stanford

University wants to have an entire summer session in 1975 dealing with your work. Ruby Cohn will be there, and I'm going to direct one of the plays, I hope. Also, Arena at the moment is planning to do GODOT next season. We have an excellent company from which to cast it.

Am rather enjoying 'producing' the season while Mme. Fichandler is theoretically on leave of absence, although dashing around among three cities, Boston, New York and Washington is driving me batty. Will only be directing two plays but seeing to all the others. Right now, we have ARTURO UI on,² not bad, and in rehearsal (with a Rumanian director) with LEONCE AND LENA by Georg Büchner which has never been done over here. Fascinating material and work by the director.³

Thanks for your note giving me Danielle's name and address.⁴ I have written her. Also wrote to Billie Whitelaw some time back. I heard via someone that she wanted to answer me but couldn't read the return address. Quite possible with my handwriting.

Spoke with Tom Bishop before we went off to see you. Wants me to do an article on Working with Beckett. As does *Theatre Quarterly*, which had Jackie's piece in it a while back.⁵ Told him I wasn't sure I'd have the time, and I didn't know how you would feel about that.

Looks as though Jean and I definitely over to Rockefeller villa on Lake Como (to do some writing) in August, and both of us hopeful we'll see you before or after. Everyone who sees you in Paris tells me you're looking well, but your letters seem a bit down to me. Trust you are as well as possible considering the state of everything. Don't know where it's all going to lead, but in the meantime we go On. [*sic*]

Both Vickie and David want to be remembered, and Jean sends her love. We think of you always and wish you well. Take care of yourself.

Ever,
[Alan]

1. A James Joyce–Samuel Beckett Symposium was held at York University, Toronto, 8–10 February 1974. Ray Federman (b. 1928), Professor of Comparative Literature, SUNY-Buffalo; published *Journey to Chaos*, 1965, the first full-length study of SB's fiction, and, with John Fletcher, *Samuel Beckett: His Works and His Critics, an Essay in Bibliography*, 1970. Vivian Mercier (1919–1989), Irish-born academic, *Beckett/Beckett*, 1977. Alan Simpson (1921–1980), Irish director; cofounder, with Carolyn Swift, of the Pike Theatre Club, Dublin; *Beckett and Behan and a Theatre in Dublin*, 1962.

2. Zelda Fichandler (b. 1924), founder of the Arena Stage with Edward Magnum (b. 1913); Brecht's *The Resistible Rise of Arturo Ui (Der aufhaltsame Aufstieg des Arturo Ui)*, 1941.

3. Georg Büchner (1813–1837), German dramatist. The Rumanian director Liviu Ciulei (b. 1923) made his American debut with this production at the Arena Stage Theatre.

4. In his letter of 20 January 1974 SB gave information about Serreau's two wives, Geneviève and Danielle (née van Bercheycke), and added: "No sight or sound of Gregory in Paris. I don't know if he went to Powonderland."

5. "Jackie's piece": interview with Richard Toscan, "MacGowran on Beckett," *Theatre Quarterly*, July-September 1973, 15–22.

Paris
27.4.74

Dear Alan

Please forgive delay in answering yours of Feb. 17. You sound devastatingly active. Don't overdo it.

Just back from 3 weeks of foul weather in Morocco. Here even worse. Result filthy cold.

It's good news you'll be over in August. I'll certainly be around then, Paris-Ussy, and we must arrange to meet without fail.

Very poor *Godot* revival here in a small theatre—Théâtre de Plaisance, Rue du Chateau. Very young group.[1] Blin seems to have lost all interest. So plays in Paris area now available to all comers.

Had some good letters from Barney & good news of him from Tom Bishop here at the moment with his wife. Shall be sending him soon (to Barney) belated translation of an old prose text (1946?).[2]

I'm committed to directing *Godot* for the Schiller next December & January. Shivering in advance. With Held as Pozzo and all others actors I have worked with. Supposed to be "helping" with London *Happy Days* about the same time! Madness.

Not yet succeeded in translating *Not I*, largely for want of trying, but not altogether. The Bishops enthusiastic about new Barrault setup, Gare d'Orsay.[3] Haven't seen it. They had a colloquium at Récamier with a number of the [?]tenors, disrupted last day by a young man in bathing costume, gas mask and sabre, on behalf of Artaud's infuriated ghost.[4]

Love to you all
Sam

1. The revival of *En attendant Godot* opened 3 April 1974 at the Théâtre de Plaisance, directed by Thierry Destraz, designed by Jacques Salmon. Jacques Salmon (Estragon), Thierry Destraz (Vladimir), Jean Chevrin (Lucky), Jacques Desmoliers (Pozzo), Michel Estève (A Boy).

2. "old prose text": *Mercier et Camier*, 1970, trans. by SB, *Mercier and Camier*, 1974.

3. The Compagnie Renaud-Barrault opened at the Théâtre d'Orsay, a famous, disused railway station, in 1974; the Bishops, Tom and Helen.

4. Antonin Artaud (1896–1948), French director, actor, poet, artist, advocated a return to myth and magic in the theater, cf. *Le Théâtre et Son Double*, 1938; also founded the theater of cruelty.

June 17, 1974

Dear Sam,

How thoughtful of you to send me the new book![1] It greeted me as I walked in the door fresh from Paris and Washington. You're just incredible.

Even though the visit was fleeting, glad to get a glimpse of you—and in such good form. Don't remember when we've seen you looking so well.[2] Whatever's going on inside certainly doesn't affect your exterior. And glad your eyes are letting you read even the small print. You might need to do that some time if and when you get tangled up with film producers.

Spoke with Barney this morning, and he tells me the film project is off. At least for now. He is quite sad about it because he feels it would be important to have a permanent record of a *Godot* production. If it would be that, that's one thing; if, however, it would become transmuted into something quite different—both through the camera medium and through the confusions and rivalries of stars seeking to overpower each other, that's something else.

Anyhow, you should decide what is best for you and not worry about or be affected by others' feelings or needs in the matter.

Just glad that Jean and I managed an evening with you, even with all the other matters going on. Jean was most pleased, and so were the kids when we told them about the meetings. You wouldn't recognize them.

The production of HORATIO (Horatio Alger's life) I had to get back for is now in previews and getting slowly formed into shape for the opening on Wednesday.[3] After that I can take a bit of a breather as far as any theatre productions are concerned. Have been supervising nine of them since the fall, two of which I actually directed myself; and I don't care if I don't come near the theatre again. At the end of the summer will be doing the TV MADNESS OF GOD, and then on to Italy. With a little luck, I'll be dropping by on the way but will give you plenty of advance notice.

Delighted you are writing, and looking forward to reading THAT TIME when you have a ms., if you wouldn't mind. I'll get MERCIER AND CAMIER from Barney. Also pleased you have completed French version of NOT I,[4] and look forward to hearing about Madeleine's performance. Sorry I didn't get to the theatre in the railroad station. Next time.

One small matter, you may have noticed. Grove accidentally put Hume Cronyn's name in as the Figure in NOT I instead of Henderson Forsythe. I have called it to their attention, and am apologising to Henderson. He will understand. Had I seen the galleys earlier, I would have noticed it.

Take care of yourself. Thanks for everything, including your understanding and great warmth. I cannot tell you how grateful I am to you for your kindnesses on all fronts. Jean sends her regards, and to Suzanne.

All the best,

[Alan]

1. *First Love and Other Shorts*, 1974: *First Love, From an Abandoned Work, Enough, Imagination Dead Imagine, Ping, Not I*, and *Breath*.

2. SB, Barney Rosset, and AS met in Paris on 11 June, at L'Aiglon Hotel, where AS usually stayed.

3. By Vasile Alecsandri (1811–1890), Rumanian poet and playwright.

4. *Pas moi*, 1975, *Not I*, 1973, 1974.

Paris
10.7.74

Dear Alan

Thank you for your good letter of June 17. It was great being with you both again. I wish it could have been without the film business.[1]

My summer plans are Paris-Ussy till end of August, most of September away. Hope we may work out something on your way to or from Italy.

Gave *Pas moi* to Madeleine & Roger. Opening about mid-March. With Chabert in *Krapp*.

Have been working hard at *That Time.*[2] First draft finished. I had enormous difficulty and must leave it now to cool off. Don't know quite what to think for the moment but not too dissatisfied.

Forgive more. Feel emptied.

Love to you all
Sam

1. Henry Weinstein suggested that a film should be made of *Waiting for Godot,* but SB did not agree. There were many such suggestions, including one from Ingmar Bergman's agent, to which SB responded that he did not want Godot "Bergmanized" (see letter of 27 January 1973, n. 1).
2. Written in English, June 1974.

August 13, 1974

Dear Sam,

As usual, the best-laid plans . . . . .

Had expected to be writing to you a few days from now, from Como. To make a date to phone you and ask when it would be most convenient for us to pop up to Paris to see you . . . .[1]

Have just spent some weeks on TV taping and editing of Wiesel's MADNESS OF GOD. Horrendous experience because not enough time on anything, but the results so far reasonably satisfactory. We finished editing the first act as of middle of night Sunday. Hope to finish Act Two in October.

Yesterday, Ruby Cohn's new book about you arrived (had ordered it weeks ago from the publisher, Princeton Press)[2] and I have not been able to put it down. Have you seen it? I'm looking forward to spending some time with her next summer at the Stanford Beckett Festival.

Starting my teaching chores at the State University of New York, nearby, the end of September, and expect to be working on a number of scenes with the kids. Including COME AND GO, ACT WITHOUT WORDS II, perhaps PLAY, as well as portions of GODOT and END-GAME. Not for public consumption, although we'll probably do a performance or two for the Theatre Department after a few weeks. Would you mind if I worked on ALL THAT FALL? I've never directed that one but have always wanted to.

Assume you are still going to Germany to do GODOT there this fall, after a holiday in Morocco. Wish I could see you there. Judith tells me you are in good shape. She also asked me to remind you that there is a filmed version of our off-Broadway 1971 GODOT production, with fixed camera, in the archives of the NY Public Library Theatre Collection. Not to be seen except on special request by scholars. But at least a record of a contemporary GODOT production. I gather Peter Hall is doing another one, with Dustin Hoffman?, at the National this fall, and is hoping to persuade you to let him film it.[3]

The past week mad with news of Nixon, and no one really knows what's next. Expect that we are all relieved to get him out, whatever Ford brings.[4] In the meantime, I'm worried about the Russians.

Really sorry we won't see you for a while; but will keep you posted on how Jean is and future plans. Take care of yourself. How's THAT TIME coming? Would love to read it. Best to Suzanne. Do have a good holiday. Write. [handwritten from "Would"]

[Alan]

1. AS explains that these plans have to be abandoned because Jean has to have an operation and will be unable to travel for a while.

2. *Back to Beckett*, 1974.

3. Dustin Hoffman (b. 1937), American stage, film, television actor; this idea never materialized.

4. After the resignation of President Nixon, 9 August 1974, Vice-President Gerald Ford (b. 1913) was sworn in and served until 20 January 1977.

Paris
1.9.74

Dear Alan

Thanks for yrs. of August.

Fond thoughts to Jean. Do hope all went well. Let me know.

Thanks for *Watergate Classics*.[1] I so hate the hue & cry, however obnoxious the quarry, that I'm sorry to be there.

Haven't seen Ruby's book.

All That Fall is really for radio only. It has been tried in some out of the way theatres, in the dark & with faces only lit on [word illegible], but not much point in that. Oliviers want to "dramatize" it and were very insistent, but I held out. I think better leave it where it belongs.[2]

German *Godot* (Berlin) in Dec./Jan. alas. Shiver at the thought. *Happy*

Days London with Hall and Dame Peggy for 3 weeks Oct./Nov. Have been working out a Winnie that should suit her. French *Not I (Pas moi)* with Madeleine mid-March 75. She'll have her work cut out. I'll do a *Krapp* with Pierre Chabert to go with it. Far too much theatre for my liking. No doubt the final bout.

Haven't looked at *That Time* since completing first draft a month ago. Still a little to be done but not much. Hope to get it to you before the year is out. Feel it shd. be kept apart from *Not I*, i.e. the two never be included in same programme. Mutually damaging.

Know nothing about Hall's *Godot* with Dustin. The Film-Theatre gang will be at me again in London. Hope to withstand again.[3]

Off to Tangier day after tomorrow and after a spell there probably on south, driving. Not much zest to stir.

Love to you all, hoping for good news of Jean before long.

Sam

1. *Watergate Classics:* a comic revue that satirized President Nixon and the White House, parodied Lucky's speech in *Waiting for Godot,* and *Krapp's Last Tape;* opened at the Yale Repertory Theatre, 16 November 1973, *Yale/Theatre* Special issue 5 (1974), ed. Jonathan Marks.

2. In a letter to Barney Rosset (27 August 1957) SB was adamant that *All That Fall* was a "radio text, for voices, not bodies." He was opposed to any kind of adaptation for the stage; its quality, he said, depended on its *"coming out of the dark."* In the same letter he defined *Act Without Words* as primitive theater: it could not be made into a film.

3. Keep Films (see letter of 24 April 1967, n. 4).

Tangier
14.9.74

Dear Alan

. . . .[1]

There is no acceptable way of staging the radio plays in my opinion. Perhaps you could work on them on their own terms, i.e. record them with sound effects. Sorry to be so unhelpful. I have a bee in my bonnet about mixing media.[2]

Finding out things about *Godot* I'm glad I never knew. Making a good few cuts in 1st act. Some in 1st of *H.D.* also.

Sky & sea satisfactory here, but high wind day after day. Back in

Paris beginning of Nov.[3] Hope to see you in Europe when Jean is quite strong again.

Love to you all
Sam

Had a line from Andreas Brown to say the printing of *All Strange Away* (the fragment for Gloria) under way at last.[4]

1. SB commiserates with AS on Jean's having to undergo surgery.

2. AS wanted to do an evening of short pieces with students at the State University of New York at Buffalo, including the radio pieces which he was willing to do behind a screen or in pitch blackness.

3. In October SB expects to be in London rehearsing *Happy Days* with Sir Peter Hall and Dame Peggy Ashcroft.

4. A limited edition with illustrations by Edward Gorey, 1976; Andreas Brown owned the Gotham Book Mart, New York. "Gloria": Jack MacGowran's widow, for whom SB waived performance royalties as he had done for *Beginning to End.*

Berlin
6.1.75

Dear Alan

Thanks for yr. card from Geneva.

Sorry to miss you in Europe.

My phone now—& for years past—only works for outgoing calls. Sad state to be reduced to but essential to semi-survival.

Beginning the unequal struggle here with *Godot* for the Schiller opening scheduled for March 3. Then back to Paris & to Madeleine in French *Not I*—opening March 20 approx. [in right margin]—with yet another *Krapp* with Chabert (good young French actor who played Pinget's *L'Hypothèse* a good few years ago now). All this on top of 3 weeks with Dame Peg & Hall in London in Oct.[1] Look forward to breathing again in April and waving the stage goodbye.

Holding up *That Time* for the moment for a number of reasons. When I let it go it will be for you & McWhinnie at the same time.

Do hope Jean quite well again and the children in good form.

All the best of 75 & love to you all.

Sam

1. SB attended rehearsals for three weeks (13 October to 4 November) of Sir Peter Hall's National Theatre production of *Happy Days*, directed by Hall, designed by John Burry. Dame Peggy Ashcroft (Winnie), Alan Webb/Harry Lomax (Willie). Hall's production opened at the Liverpool Playhouse, Liverpool, 26 November 1975, transferred to Old Vic Theatre and then to the Lyttleton Theatre of the National Theatre, London.

Berlin
11.2.75

Dear Alan

Thanks for yours of Jan. 30 & good news of Jean.[1]

We open here March 8. Held (Krapp–Pozzo) walked out on us after a fortnight, pretending bad health. Replaced by Karl Raddatz.[2] I'm sick & tired of theatre & of *Godot* in particular. To have to listen to these words day after day has become torture. Then without respite more theatre in Paris with Madeleine & Chabert till late March. Then goodbye to theatre for me as far as directing goes. *That Time* I hope to get to you by end of April. Unseld, director of Suhrkamp Verlag, wd. like to present a single performance (in German) in Frankfurt in October on occasion of their Jubilee (20th anniversary of foundation by Suhrkamp when he left Fischer) and this may be possible.[3] In England first performance next year at Royal Court in a season of my plays again on occasion of their 20th anniversary (April 75 I think). I'll be meeting the recently appointed new artistic directors Robert Kidd & Nicholas Wright in Paris in April to discuss it. Billie is back at Court with *Not I* and Fugard's *Statements* etc.[4] Don't know what to think of our production here but fear no great things are to be hoped. No fault of the actors all good. Herm a remarkable Lucky, most moving.[5] Enough about all that.

So glad to hear about your shack by the sea. Much peace & happiness to you there.[6]

. . . .[7]

Tired, so no more for now.

Love to you all
Sam

1. Letter missing.
2. Karl Raddatz (b. 1912).
3. Siegfried Unseld; Verlag S. Fischer, SB's other German publisher; the performance in Frankfurt did not take place.

4. The revival of *Not I* opened 29 January 1975, directed by Anthony Page, designed by Jocelyn Herbert. Billie Whitelaw (Mouth), Melvyn Hastings (Auditor). Accompanied by Athol Fugard's *Statements After an Arrest Under the Immorality Act*, 1974, directed by the author. Scottish director Robert Kidd (b. 1943), and South African director Nicholas Wright (b. 1940), appointed joint Artistic Directors, Royal Court Theatre, 1975.

5. Klaus Herm (b. 1926), performed in *That Time*, 1976, *Play*, 1978, and the radio and television plays *Ghost Trio* and *. . . but the clouds . . .*, 1977, under SB's direction.

6. AS has bought a beach property in Amagansett, New York.

7. SB mentions Hans Lietzau, who had an accident in London.

March 4, 1975

Dear Sam,

Arrived home from Boston over the weekend to find both your cards.

Sorry you're having such a tough time with GODOT this trip. I know how much you were looking forward to Berlin. I do hope all has gone well since Raddatz joined the cast—I have seen him several times and found him extremely versatile. In any case, just wanted to wish you the best of luck on the production, safe return, and good wishes with Madeleine's NOT I. You are certainly running the gamut.

About the other matter, I didn't know Alex Hawkins was writing to you about me otherwise I would have sent out warnings in advance. He's a pleasant chap, a graduate student at TUFTS near Boston, and I've met with him several times. He knows more about my past at the moment than I do. If he does get to Paris—when?—and you are there and not too averse, I have no objection to your talking to him about me.[1] Although why he wants to write a book around my nefarious career is not entirely clear—except that it has something to do with the rise and fall of the American theatre in the 60's.

I wish I were coming over myself to see you but that seems highly unlikely this year. I'm at Arena doing two new plays, which will take me until the summer;[2] then to Stanford with Ruby C. for the Beckett summer there. I'll be doing GODOT with students, and wishing I had Raddatz. And you there.

Just finished that article on working with you for Tom Bishop's French anthology.[3] Will get it xeroxed and send on to you in case you would like me to change or omit something.

Jean coming along but still taking it easy. I'm just tired, and wish I could sit somewhere and not do anything. We hope to get to the shack in April.

Best to you. Think of you always.

[Alan]

1. Tufts University; SB had written to ask AS if it was "okay" to talk with Hawkins.
2. Preston Jones (1936–1979), *The Bradleyville Texas Trilogy*, premiered at the Dallas Theater Center in 1974.
3. Bishop with Raymond Federman, eds., *Samuel Beckett, L'Herne*, Paris, 1976, in honor of SB's seventieth birthday. AS's "article": "'*Comme il vous plaira*' *Travailler avec Samuel Beckett*," 123–136; other contributors included Jérôme Lindon, Richard Seaver, A. J. Leventhal, Ludovic Janvier, Roger Blin, Eugène Ionesco, George Reavey, Robert Pinget, John Calder, John Fletcher, Peter Brook, and Ruby Cohn.

Paris
23.3.75

Dear Alan

Thanks for your letters.

. . . .¹

Berlin wasn't too bad in the end. We were nearly there. There will be a film of a performance, purely documentary, no *adaphatrôce*.²

One day off when I got back, then at it again in that raileray station. Usual resistance to only correct *Not I*. Tired struggling. Chabert having difficulty with *Krapp*, but I have the feeling he may bring it off. We open April 8.³

Then goodbye to all that. Ussy alone with the larks. Then probably Tangier again.

Having trouble in the odd spare moment with *That Time*. Text & idea more or less okay but not yet the image.

Tom Bishop sent me the text you saw & Barney doesn't like. It seems all right to me. If I were a philosopher I'd be a pessimist. But as I'm not how can I be?

Saw Ruby Cohn in Berlin. She was in on last rehearsals. Now she is here. Rick Cluchey was also in Berlin. In on all rehearsals. Did *Haute surveillance* for the Forum.⁴ Now in London I think.

Love to you all and I hope *à bientôt*.

Sam

1. SB will not give an interview about AS unless AS approves.

2. Ten years after its German premiere at the Schiller-Theater, and with almost the same actors, *Warten auf Godot* opened at the Schiller-Theater, 8 March 1975, directed by SB, assisted by Walter D. Asmus, designed by Matias, trans. by Elmar Tophoven. Horst Bollmann (Estragon), Stefan Wigger (Vladimir), Klaus Herm (Lucky), Karl Raddatz replaced Martin Held (Pozzo), Torsten Sense (A Boy). *"adaphatrôce"*: a pejorative pun? (adaptation plus atrocious?)

3. *Pas moi* and *La Dernière bande* opened at the Théâtre d'Orsay, Petite salle, 5 and 8 April 1975 respectively, directed by SB, designed by Matias. *Pas moi*: Madeleine Renaud (Mouth). *La Dernière bande:* Pierre Chabert (Krapp). Used most of the changes made for the Schiller-Theater Werkstatt production with Martin Held, 1969.

4. Rick Cluchey (b. 1933), American director, dramatist *(The Cage)*, became involved with theater after he saw the San Francisco Actor's Workshop production of *Waiting for Godot*, 1957, while serving a life sentence at San Quentin State Prison for armed robbery. Paroled in 1966 after twelve years, as his interest in theater, and in SB, continued, he founded the San Quentin Drama Workshop, directed and acted in *Krapp's Last Tape, Endgame, Waiting for Godot,* and plays by Pinter, Genet, and O'Neill. Cluchey was invited to Berlin to direct Genet's *Haute surveillance (Deathwatch)*, a prison play, at the Forum Theater. SB at the time was directing *Warten auf Godot* at the Schiller. Seeing that Cluchey was ill and had financial difficulties, SB arranged for him to stage-manage his *Godot* even though Cluchey did not know German.

April 27, 1975

Dear Sam,

. . . .[1] You know, I'm scheduled to do GODOT at Stanford (with students) in August, hope leg will heal in time. Did you hear about some off-off-Broadway group saying it was going to do ELEUTHERIA (in English!) next fall?[2] I wanted to see Mabou Mines (Lee Breuer's group) do PLAY and COME AND GO, but was in Washington.[3] Gather they did good job. Have my doubts whether will get over to Paris this summer, but who knows? Also wish I could see the London HAPPY DAYS, which looks and sounds good.[4]

Take care of yourself. Haven't sent you my article because I'm still working on it, but will soon as I get out of hospital. Jean sends her love.

[Alan]

1. AS had an operation for a torn ligament in his right knee. *Waiting for Godot* opened 12 August 1975 at Stanford University, California.

2. Written in French, 1947, published posthumously in Paris, 1995, and as *Eleutheria*, New York, 1995, London, 1996.

3. Mabou Mines, an avant-garde company founded in 1970 by JoAnne Akalaitis, Lee

Breuer, Philip Glass, Ruth Maleczech, and David Warrilow; named after Canadian min-
ing company and village settlement where the group rehearsed. "Mabou Mines Performs
Samuel Beckett" opened at Theater for the New City, New York, 21 October 1975, directed
by Lee Breuer (see letter of 5 March 1971, n. 1). *Play* performed by JoAnne Akalaitis, Ruth
Maleczech, and David Warrilow. *Come and Go* performed by Ellen McElduff, Ruth
Maleczech, and JoAnne Akalaitis. *The Lost Ones* performed by David Warrilow, Ellen
McElduff, Linda Wolfe, and Bill Raymond. Breuer (b. 1937) joined Mabou Mines, 1970,
New York Shakespeare Festival, 1982, and earned three Obies for staging and adapting
SB's plays.
    4. Sir Peter Hall's National Theatre production.

Paris
4.5.75

Dear Alan

    Thanks for yrs. of April 27. Very very sorry to hear of your trouble.
Hope op. over now & well over and mending begun. Do keep in touch
& let me know how it goes.

    Nothing of interest here. No plans beyond Ussy now & then &
Morocco in June. In a jam—unless mistaken—with *That Time,* but have
been too tired to get after it seriously.

    We must prevent *Eleutheria* at all costs. A Quebec group was giving
extracts from *Endgame* here, played by women, without permission. We
stopped it.[1]

    Bon courage, cher Alan, *ce n'est qu'un mauvais moment à passer.*[2]

Love to you all
Sam

    1. Extracts from *Fin de partie (Endgame)* opened 27 March 1975 at the Théâtre du
Lucenaire, Paris.
    2. *"Bon courage . . . ce n'est qu'un mauvais moment à passer":* courage, the nightmare will
only last a short spell.

Ussy
30.5.75

Dear Alan

So glad to have good news of your knee. Hope you had a good spell in your shack.

Here past fortnight fitfully fiddling at *That Time*. Know at least now what *can't* be done to it. Can't quite part from it yet. But soon.

Morocco soon till late July—old bones creaking for warm sand.

Love to you all. Be quite well again soon.

Sam

[handwritten]

Alan Schneider
c/o Dept of Drama
Stanford University
Stanford,
California, 94305
July [27], 1975

Dear Sam,

Thought you'd be interested in my progress—or lack of it—here.[1] Arrived two weeks ago to find The Beckett Festival in full swing, saw *COME and GO* and *PLAY* that first evening. Both very college-level productions but spirited and well-intentioned. Since then, have seen *Endgame* (very good visually but acting not so good) and versions of *Cascando, Breath, & Act Without Words II*. Ruby has probably sent you full reports. I've been sitting in on her Seminar and have seen her several times for lunch & dinner. I like her immensely and am pleased to have gotten to know her a bit more. As to my own *Godot* production here, I was most disappointed by the talent or rather non-talent available—but I was fortunate enough to corral one of our Arena Stage pros (vacationing in California) to play Gogo—& he has lifted the level of the cast considerably.[2] The other three are kids, hard-working and willing. I'm trying. We shall see.

Ruby let me see a xeroxed copy of *That Time*, and I am bowled over. It's beautiful, fascinating, difficult and stays with me. Full of questions; which I won't ask—yet. Except that I can't figure out (nor can Ruby) what that first column of figures on left means. Would really appreciate your sending me a copy direct with whatever comments or suggestions you have. The xerox is hard to read, & Ruby won't let me see hers. When I get back to NY, with your permission I'd like to explore possibilities for production. Has Barney seen it? I've let *no one* look at the xeroxed version. P.S. Found a first edition of *Endgame* in bookstore here!!!

My knee, I'm glad to say, is much better. Full mobility and very little pain or stiffness. I swim every day in the pool here, the sun shines, and it's almost like a holiday. I do hope Morocco was refreshing for you; you needed a real breather. Jean (with me) and kids (elsewhere) are all fine and glad to have me out of the NY-Washington grind for a while. Love from all of us. *Godot* opens on Aug 12. I'll keep you posted.

Best,
Alan

1. Stanford University.
2. Howard Swift (*alias* Howard Witt).

Paris
8.8.75

Dear Alan

Thanks for yrs. of July 27.

So glad to have good news of your knee.

Touched to think of those kids having a go, but sorry you have to suffer it in such massive doses. Shall be thinking of you on the 12th (opening of grouse-shooting).[1]

The text I gave Ruby is not final. The figures in the margin refer to break-down of continuity—order in which fragments occur and number of same intervening before resumptions. This has been reorganised.

The delay in parting with it is due to misgivings over disproportion between image (listening face) and speech and much time lost in trying to devise ways of amplifying former. I have now come to accept its remoteness & stillness—apart from certain precise eye movements, breath just audible in silences and final smile—as essential to the piece & dramatically of value. The chief difficulty, A B & C being the same voice, will be to make clear the modulation from one to another, as between attendant keys, without breaking the flow continuous except where silences indicated. I feel that dissimilar contexts and dislocation in space—one coming to him from left, a second from above, third from right—should be enough to do it. If not the effect will have to be assisted at level of recording. I do hope we may meet and talk about it—& all the rest.

In England it will be for Pat with Donald McWhinnie directing, if he accepts (he has not read it). First performance at the Royal Court in their season next Spring. I wrote some time ago to the new directors to say I supposed they would have no objection to my following my custom of releasing new work simultaneously to you, to London & to German translator, leaving the world first to take care of itself. I have had no answer yet. If they ask for world first I can hardly refuse. In any case the final text will depart in the three directions before the end of this month.

That Time should never figure in the same programme with *Not I*.

Enjoyed suspended animation in Tangier. Great swimming. Lost touch completely with writing and no sign so far of its recovery.

No plans for months to come beyond the Paris-Ussy to & fro. Usual bits & scraps of self-translation to catch up on, no new work in sight.

Love to you all
Sam

1. Opening of *Waiting for Godot* at the Beckett Festival, Stanford University.

Paris
17.8.75

Dear Alan

Sending you today same mail final *That Time* as final as I can get it.[1] Could go on fiddling but sense it's time to part. Point of view realization it's all knife-edge & hair-breadth. Hope we may somehow meet & go through it as we did *Not I*. If not shall do my best on paper. But not till I have your reactions. Have sent copies to Barney, Royal Court, Pat, Donald, Faber, etc.

Love to you all
Sam

1. *That Time*, 1976.

Aug. 21, 1975

Dear Sam,

Back from lotus-land once more, and glad to see the rain. It's been a long time, two and a half months too long. We're off for a week or so at the shack, looking at the seagulls and whatever else comes over the horizon.

GODOT really came off well. Hard to believe, but the 'kids', most of whom were graduate students, really came through. Especially Estragon (Howard Swift, who was in actuality, Howard Witt of the Arena Stage company, who was spending some time with his girl in San Francisco until I corralled him.) He was the most touching (vulnerable) and yet comic GOGO I've yet had—including our old friend Bert—and I'm really pleased. If only I could get him at Arena! We opened to one preview on Monday, August 11, and worked our way up to something really worthy of you by Friday or Saturday. Ruby was there both nights, and she may be making her own report. Also, I have asked the U. to send you notices, the poster, and programs of the entire Festival. It was a hectic summer, what with a Beckett bill every weekend, Ruby on Tuesdays, and GODOT topping it all off at the end. The play keeps opening up for me, and I was most pleased to have done it, even with a largely student cast. They were willing to listen and respond; and, in spite of all sorts of technical difficulties mostly caused by lack of crew, it looked marvelous. No hiccuping moon.[1] I'll see if they'll send on a photo or two when they turn out. In meantime, this is my fifth GODOT and I feel I'm getting into stride.

Thanks for your letter which greeted me on arrival. Glad you had a quiet time in Tangier. Appreciate your comments of THAT TIME, which I've been quietly reading and re-reading since Ruby let me look at the copy. Grows on one. And I don't think you have to worry about juxtaposition of figure and voices. Should be very effective if voices can be orchestrated properly. I want very much to do it, but haven't been back long enough in NY to have definite plans. My first choice would be the Lincoln Center's FORUM, where we did NOT I, but not clear if and when they are available. I am pursuing. There are a couple of other theatres interested, including Arena Stage. I am also thinking about actors, and have had a thought about Donald Davis, who did original Krapp. He has an excellent voice and can modulate into three parts very well, I think. As far as premiere is concerned, I think you are right to let it take its course. But if Royal Court insists on world first, do let me know and I will hold off. On the other hand, I'm prepared to go ahead full steam of getting production, with your approval to be sought on place and player. I'm sure there will be no problem, and I have time this fall or winter. Also, I will make sure that I can fly over to see you beforehand when we get some definite plans because I would indeed like to talk over the whole thing. Main question is what should go with it. For example, PLAY. (I heard Mabou Mines troupe has done excellent production, and we might be able to get them; or I could do new one.) Or another KRAPP. Or bill of short pieces, including COME AND GO, ACT, which have not really been seen in NY. Will keep after this. Expect to see Barney this weekend, but won't show script unless you have already sent him copy.

Jean and family fine, my knee practically healed in mobility though still occasional stiffness. The year looks mixed but at least I'll be home more often: Juilliard, a new trilogy on Broadway in the spring (plays of small town in Texas, but metaphor of American decline),[2] OUR TOWN again at Arena in repertory, hopefully THAT TIME. I feel positive about own life, negative about state of universe. Trying to do some writing, harder than directing. Missed seeing you this summer, but hope to rectify mistake before end of year. Acquired first edition (English) of ENDGAME which I'll bring over for you to sign, good excuse for trip. No other news at moment, but will pass it on to you as it arrives.

Enjoyed meeting Ruby and pleased to have gotten better acquainted. Everyone here sends love and hopes you are well. I have just reread MERCIER AND CAMIER and now going back into trilogy.[3] Gets better each time.

Best, always,
[Alan]

1. "hiccuping moon" refers to an earlier production of *Waiting for Godot;* corrected here.
2. *"The Texas Trilogy": Lu Ann Hampton Laverty Oberland, The Last Meeting of the Knights of the White Magnolia,* and *The Oldest Living Graduate.*
3. The "trilogy": *Three Novels: Molloy, Malone Dies, The Unnamable,* 1965.

September 1, 1975

Dear Sam,

Attached, as you may note, was composed last spring but am only now getting up nerve to show it to you.

Various people want to publish it in English (French version going into Édition de *L'Herne*) though I have not shown it to anyone. Will do so if and when you approve of contents.[1]

THAT TIME text greeted me upon return this weekend from shack in country, and I have read it half dozen times. Basic reaction is that it is extremely powerful, terribly moving, and terribly delicate. Balance and level of three tones need very careful handling. Please forgive me if I wait to let it soak in before I badger you with detailed comments and questions. I am fascinated by it; and, as I mentioned upon that first reading of Ruby's copy, can't get it out of my mind. Not that I want to.

Will let you know about progress with people at Lincoln Center (the Forum).

Saw both Barney and Dick Seaver—together!—over the week, both in good shape. My knee continues to give me full mobility though occasional reminders of its existence. Jean is well and happy to be home. Will be writing again soon in detail.

[Alan]

1. "'Any Way You Like, Alan': Working with Beckett," *Theatre Quarterly*, 5.19 (September-November 1975), 27–38; "'*Comme il vous plaira*': Travailler avec Samuel Beckett," Beckett, *L'Herne*, no. 31, Paris, 1976, 123–136.

Ussy
10.9.75

Dear Alan

Thanks for yours of Aug. 21 & Sept. 1. Your piece on me is fine and most moving. All thanks. There is one slight mistake, p. 9. paragraph 3. The inference is to *Joyce* (in *Our Exagmination*), not to Proust.[1]

Still no answer from Court re world first. Shall let you know as soon as I hear.

Other odds & ends to show you if you come over. Do hope you make it.

Feel sure we've all had enough of *Krapp* for the moment.

Thanks again and best to you all.

Sam

That Time

Speaker (listener) shd use exactly same voice & tone for 3 sets of memories. Only means of differentiation those suggested in note.

1. SB contributed "Dante . . . Bruno. Vico . . . Joyce" to *Our Exagmination round His Factification for Incamination of Work in Progress*, 1929; *Proust*, 1931.

Samuel Beckett
38 Boulevard St. Jacques
Paris, 14
France

30 Scenic Drive
Hastings-on-Hudson
New York 10706
USA
Nov. 15, 1975

Dear Sam,

Have started to write a half-dozen times to let you know about hopes and plans for THAT TIME, but as usual they have been changing daily or even hourly—so I thought I should wait until all the dust, until all my dust, had settled. At least the present crop of dust. As I believe I mentioned immediately after my first reading, I felt that the Forum— where we had done the Festival—was the most suitable choice. This was now under the control of Joe Papp, who had sponsored Jackie's program. I called Joe, who said he'd be interested in any play by Beckett, though he would like to read it before committing. Yes, the theatre would be available in January, which was also a good time for me. Then weeks went by during which I heard nothing from Joe. In the meantime, I found out that Edward Albee had written a new one-act and was looking for something to pair it with. This seemed like an interesting idea, 15 years after KRAPP and ZOO; so I sounded out both Albee and Richard Barr, both of whom responded immediately although not entirely happy to share the producing with Joe Papp. On the other hand, when I brought up the idea of doing the plays at the Cherry Lane, they both felt that off-Broadway was no longer possible economically. On the other hand, their idea of doing the plays on a 'commercial' basis on Broadway seemed wrong to me; individually or collectively the two plays needed an institutional base guaranteeing a fixed even though perhaps limited run. In the meantime I got to Joe Papp, who was having his own problems because his entire year's plan for doing five new young American playwrights on Broadway had been aborted; I got Joe and Barr together, and they tentatively agreed that a Beckett-Albee double bill at the Forum in January would be fine.

Then I read the Albee play, an hour-long one-act called LISTENING, and wasn't wild about it. Then Papp read it and wasn't enthusiastic either. Then because of Papp's Broadway changes of plans, he had to move all his productions around, and the Forum became unavailable, either in January or the discernible future. Then a theatre in Buffalo, which had done the premiere of Albee's BOX-MAO-BOX some years back, said it would do the double bill. I wasn't keen on 'trying out' THAT TIME in Buffalo because I felt it should be done directly in New York somewhere. I went to see a production of some group named Mabou Mines doing an evening of COME AND GO, PLAY, and THE LOST ONES (assume you had heard about this) which had gotten excellent notices. Directed by Lee Breuer. Somehow, I thought this might be moved up to the Forum with THAT TIME, or elsewhere if the Forum continued to be unavailable. Then I went to see that production and was not impressed. PLAY was both unintelligible and unfunny, and badly acted; COME AND GO, reflected through a mirror, was heavily stylised and grotesque; only THE LOST ONES, actually a one-man reading of the text illustrated with miniature figures came off—and I'm not sure how you would have felt about such a 'dramatisation'.

Anyhow, if you can follow all this, we are back at the beginning. Except that I have asked Donald Davis to play in THAT TIME if and when; and he is anxious to do so. His face and voice are both quite right, in my opinion. The question now is where I go from here, but I am still staying with Joe as well as looking in other directions. Perhaps you have now heard from the Royal Court about their plans. But it is not the premiere that I am so much after as suitable auspices and a companion piece. I will keep you posted on further convolutions and permutations of confusion.

Spent this morning with Earl Kim, listening to him play his Beckett-pieces-set-to-music, which I understand you have approved.[1] They are lovely. The idea is to have six or eight musicians, two singers (I think) and Vanessa Redgrave.[2] I am trying to get it done at the Juilliard School, though there is some question of their willingness to accept outside performer. I like Earl very much. [handwritten after "there" in right margin]

The rest of life continues its mad way. I'm about to do a tour of Elie Wiesel's MADNESS OF GOD, which I did at Arena two years ago. In the spring, I do what we call the Texas Trilogy, three full-length plays about a small town in Texas, a new middle-aged author who writes very well. In between, I teach once a week at Boston, once a week in New York, and walk around Juilliard, where I am still slated to take over the Drama Division next fall . . . .[3] Take care of yourself. All the best. Jean sends love. [handwritten from "plans"]

[Alan]

1. Earl Kim (b. 1920), American composer, academic.

2. Vanessa Redgrave (b. 1937), English actress, daughter of Sir Michael Redgrave, joined RSC in July 1967, Academy Award for *Julia* (U.S., 1977).

3. A few personal family details here.

Paris
23.11.75

Dear Alan

Thanks for yrs. of 20th.

Sorry you have had all that trouble for nothing.

Pleased to hear Davis accepts the part.

No hurry about *That Time*. Perhaps hold it up till I have something to go with it. There are two theatre fragments, written in French circa 1960, which on rereading after translating for Faber seem to me perhaps performable. Still to make up my mind.[1] Also have nearly completed a short piece (15 min.) for Billie Whitelaw.[2] So best hold it.

Barney did not trouble to acknowledge receipt of *That Time* sent same time as yr. copy. Strange I grant you.

. . . .[3]

Love to you all
Sam

1. "two theatre fragments": *Theatre I* and *Theatre II (Fragments)*, published in *Ends and Odds*, 1976, 1977.

2. *Footfalls* (see JK, 616–617).

3. SB is about to go to Ussy, then to Morocco.

March 27, 1976

Dear Sam,

Forgive my longer-than-usual silence. Went into rehearsal for the Elie Wiesel play in mid-December (THE MADNESS OF GOD) and since then seem never to have emerged from the depths. MADNESS has been on the road and then opened a couple of weeks ago in New York[1] to reasonably good notices though business has been only fair—largely because everyone who wanted to see it has already seen it on TV, where it has played three times. Rehearsals on my Texas Trilogy (three full-length plays chronicling a small town in West Texas and, metaphorically, the decline and fall of the American dream 1950–1970) have been going on since before MADNESS got to New York, and I am just beginning to see the shape of things. We go off to Washington and the Kennedy Center in a couple of weeks, and then, maybe, Broadway. We shall see.[2]

Barney just sent me FOOTFALLS, which I love, and in which Billie W. will be superb. Wish I could see it and her. When do you open at the Court? Seems increasingly more difficult to know anything about anything anywhere. I know you're going off to London for rehearsals in April, and I wish you well. Would love to get over somehow to see the double bill,[3] but not sure how long it is playing, or whether I'll be finished here in time. We open the first week in May, but I may have to hang on depending on how matters progress. Also, I'm doing a play at Arena for its Bicentennial Repertory Season.[4] But if the double bill is on in June, I could possibly get over to London—and Paris—for a spell.

Have I your permission to move ahead on a production here of THAT TIME and FOOTFALLS for next season, hopefully in the fall? I'd try Joe Papp and the Forum Theatre again, but there are other possibilities. Donald Davis might be available, and I'd ask Rosemary Harris—if you approve. In any case I'd love to do them somewhere.

Someone gave me the latest *Theatre Quarterly* with the article on you directing GODOT in Berlin, as well as my piece. I hope you didn't mind it too much. One especially good photo of you, which I shall look at whenever things get too awful here.[5]

Seems to have been years since we've met. Life rushing by, and the grey blur outside getting more and more impenetrable. Haven't seen Barney or Judith or anyone. Jean OK, and kids thriving somewhere, Vickie 21 and David 17. My mother living with us, and fading each day, very sad to watch. Am hoping to retire to the seaside for the summer, and hoping to survive long enough to make it. Miss you and hope you are well. Word trickles back that you are in good shape. I want to come and see for myself.

Take care of yourself. All good wishes.

[Alan]

1. Opened at the Lyceum Theatre, New York, 17 March 1976.

2. *The Texas Trilogy* opened at the John F. Kennedy Center for the Performing Arts, Washington, D.C., 22 April 1976.

3. "double bill": *Footfalls* and *That Time*.

4. Wilder's *Our Town*.

5. Walter D. Asmus contributed "Beckett Directs *Godot*," *Theatre Quarterly*, 5.19 (September–November 1975), 19–26 (see letter of 1 September 1975, n. 1).

Long Sutton
17.4.76

Dear Alan

Many thanks for letter & birthday card. Good of you to think on me in my extremity.

Writing you from Jocelyn's place in the country. Great peace after the Paris hullaballoos.[1] Have just been talking on the phone to Donald & Billie, arranging to start work next Tuesday. Shall also see the Schiller *Godot* boys that evening. They open next Thursday for 10 performances. It will be a job adapting the production to Royal Court stage.[2]

Congratulations on your appointment to Juilliard School and more power to your work there.[3]

Of course go ahead with *That Time* & *Footfalls* as you judge best. They open at the Court, with *Play*, May 20th (previews 18th & 19th) for a first series of 12 performances. It would be great if you could come over. I'll return to Paris May 21.

I have not seen the *Theatre Quarterly*.

I keep well . . .

Love to you all
Sam

1. SB's seventieth birthday; Jocelyn Herbert's "place": Long Sutton, near Basingstoke, England.

2. The Royal Court Theatre mounted a Samuel Beckett Festival in honor of his seventieth birthday. SB attended final rehearsals. The Schiller-Theater production of *Warten auf Godot*, in German, directed by SB, designed by Matias, same cast as 8 March 1975, opened

21 April 1976. *Endgame,* directed by Donald McWhinnie, designed by Andrew Sanders, opened 6 May. Patrick Magee (Hamm), Stephen Rea (Clov), Leslie Sarony (Nagg), Rose Hill (Nell). *Play and Other Plays* opened 20 May: *Play* directed by Donald McWhinnie, designed by Andrew Sanders, with Anna Massey (First Woman), Penelope Wilton (Second Woman), Ronald Pickup (Man); *That Time* directed by Donald McWhinnie, with Patrick Magee (Face and Voice); *Footfalls* directed by SB, with Billie Whitelaw (May), Rose Hill (Mother's Voice). Both *That Time* and *Footfalls,* designed by Jocelyn Herbert, were premiere productions.

   3. AS succeeded John Houseman as director of the Drama Division of the Juilliard School's Theater Center at Lincoln Center (see Louis Calta, "Schneider Gets Post at Juilliard," *NY Times,* 17 February 1976).

May 10, 1976

Dear Sam,

Back from Washington for a minute to receive your letter, thank you. Also your regards via Suria St. Denis,[1] whom I saw briefly at Juilliard. The Texas trilogy opened one right after the other in Washington a week ago, very favorably received, and I'm dead tired. Tomorrow I start putting Arena's OUR TOWN back into the repertory. Then, if I'm still alive I hope to do nothing but sit out at the shack all summer and look at the sea.

Unfortunately, since OUR TOWN opens on May 23, I won't be able to get over to London while you are there. I'm still hanging on to a slight hope that I could get away (from the Texas confusions, and my home situation) early in June. Could you ask the Court to send me a schedule of how long and when THAT TIME and FOOTFALLS will be playing there? Just in case. And if I do get to London, I'll come home via Paris. Although I'm just not sure because there are too many variables.

. . . .[2]

Otherwise, I have just been trying to get by, day by day, and longing for a respite. Sorry that I haven't been and won't be in New York to see Madeleine, who has had a great success here with the Duras play, DAYS IN THE TREES.[3] I did get an invitation to a reception for her, but was in Washington.

Looking forward next year to the Juilliard adventure, though not entirely sure how long it will go on because they are, like everyone else, having severe financial problems; and there is a serious question whether the Drama Division can find the means to go on. I do enjoy working with young people; and I look forward to staying in one place for a while instead of going everywhere looking for work. They want me to continue my directing, but I can be a bit more selective.

Haven't seen Barney for some time but will be spending some time with him this summer, I hope; we are actually only a few miles away. Off-off-Broadway flourishing, including several productions of your work, including a stage version of CASCANDO.[4] Hope to get to one or more in June, in which case I'll be able to report any reactions. I'm pursuing the possibility of the double bill at the Forum in the fall; depends on Joe Papp's plans, theatre availability, and the usual uncertainties.

Best wishes for the Court season. Do forgive me for not being there. I'll be keeping fingers and everything else crossed. Regards to all involved.

Jean sends her love.

[Alan]

1. Suria Saint-Denis, wife of Michel Saint-Denis (1897–1971), French-born, worked at the Old Vic Theatre, became General Artistic Adviser for Royal Shakespeare Company under Sir Peter Hall in 1962.

2. AS gives an account in two paragraphs of his mother's deteriorating mental and physical condition.

3. *Des Journées entières dans les arbres,* adapted by Marguerite Duras from her short story of the same title, 1954, opened at the Ambassador, New York, 6 May 1976, directed by Jean-Louis Barrault, a Compagnie Renaud-Barrault production.

4. Subtitled "A radio play by Samuel Beckett," opened by Mabou Mines, 12 April 1976, directed by JoAnne Akalaitis; won an Obie Award. *Cascando:* Frederick Neumann (Opener), David Warrilow (Voice), Thom Cathcart, David Hardy, Ellen McElduff, William Raymond (Voices), Ruth Muleczech (Radio Voice), Jeremy Leggett (Announcer), music by Philip Glass. SB described it as a play about a character called Woburn who never appears; written in French, 1962, at the request of Marcel Mihalovici, published in 1963, trans. by SB, *Cascando* in *Evergreen Review,* 7.30 (May–June 1963), and in *Play and Two Short Pieces for Radio,* 1964.

London
13.5.76

Dear Alan

Thanks for yours of 10.

Below schedule of performances:

May 24 through June 3 – Triple bill
June 4   "   June 9 – *Endgame*
June 10   "   June 19 – Triple bill
June 21   "   July 3 – *Endgame*

Rehearsals of new plays going well. Billie will be wonderful again. Pat re-recorded *That Time* today. Successfully. *Endgame* doing well.

Love to you all
Sam

June 14, 1976

Dear Sam,

Just a brief note to let you know that I shall not be coming over to see the plays at the Royal Court, sorry to say. Had asked Jocelyn Herbert, whom I saw over here two weeks ago, to arrange tickets for both bills; had gotten my airplane tickets; was going to cable you to find out if you would be able to see me in Paris. Then everything happened. First of all, my mother's condition has worsened appreciably and we have had to put her in a hospital . . . .[1]

Secondly, my trilogy of plays, now running in Washington has suddenly had its run extended until September. They have been increasingly well attended, and now it seems definite that they will be coming to New York some time in the fall. On the other hand, with 'success' comes problems; actors are complaining not only about other actors but about the text. Generally, the good family feeling which produced the good things in the first place is threatening to disappear; so both the playwright and the producer feel I should be there as much as possible to hold everyone's hand. I'm about to take off for another couple of days as soon as I finish this.

Anyhow, so it goes. Am most disappointed because I was practically there and hoping to surprise you. Well, have hopes that the Court will do another Beckett Season, and I can make it then. Really want to see them in their native habitat.

Developments here: Joe Papp's current play at the Forum has been extended, and he is reluctant to make definite future commitments, altho I continue to pursue him about the double bill, or even making it a triple with PLAY. With your permission, I will also see if Arena Stage might not be interested. You know that Jackie played there, and everyone loved him.[2] I feel much at home there. And in control. [handwritten after "him"]

When are you going to Morocco, and when back? Very little else to report except that I have seen Barney, who tells me you were in great shape last time you met. Forgive my non-appearance this time, and I shall look forward to the soonest. All the best from all of us.

Ever,
Alan

["Ever" and "Alan" handwritten]

1. AS describes his mother's deterioration.
2. *Jack MacGowran in the Works of Samuel Beckett.*

August 13, 1976

Dear Sam,

Nice lucky number of a day,[1] so I thought I'd bring you up to date a bit.

Just spoken with Marty Fehsenfeld, one of your staunchest fans, who has returned from a European summer that included meeting you at the Court during rehearsals. She is putting together a book on BECK-ETT AT WORK.[2] I gather you know about it. They're trying to get a photo of you directing Billie Whitelaw on the cover.

Marty tells me you are soon off to the Schiller to direct the German version.[3] I trust you've had a decent rest this summer because I know how hard you work in rehearsal, and how much it takes out of you. All the best on it. Wish I could get to see you and it in Berlin but have my doubts whether I'll ever get away.

Still working on the Texas plays, commuting to Washington where the Trilogy remains at the Kennedy Center until we open in New York the end of September. Seems an eternity since we went into rehearsal in February. I did get a couple of weeks at the shack during July, but both sun tan and rest cure have already worn off. We shall see . . . . .

The news is that Arena Stage's Zelda Fichandler wants to do PLAY and OTHER PLAYS this season, assuming you approve. (The play that Joe Papp has in the Forum has been a great commercial success, so he doesn't know when or if the theatre will be free.) I'd like to do it down there if we can work out suitable cast and time. As I told you, I have already approached Donald Davis. I'd try to get Rosemary Harris but not sure of her availability. She is on tour with something. In any case, I would appreciate your reaction to doing it in Washington. I'm sure after that we could get it to New York, if you so desired.

Have seen Barney couple of times but spring and summer have been mostly taken up with 'Texas' plays. Jean and kids are fine, the latter fully grown and totally mysterious, rarely visible to the naked eye. My mother is steadily weaker, and not sure how long she will last. She is close by in a nursing home. We try to make her as comfortable as possible, and Jean is positively devoted.

Haven't been over to Europe in more than two years, a new indoor world record. But have hopes that somehow will get over this year in between Juilliard efforts. In the meantime, I miss you and hope you are in good form.

Fondest regards. And look forward to hearing from you about whatever you're doing. All send love.

[Alan]

1. SB was born on the 13th (April).
2. McMillan and Fehsenfeld, *Beckett at Work in the Theatre: The Author as Practical Playwright and Director*, 1988.
3. *Damals (That Time)* and *Tritte (Footfalls)*.

Aug. 16, 1976
[handwritten date and salutation]

Dear Sam,

Having just written to you a few days ago, I have opened the NY TIMES to discover that George Reavey had died.[1] I am most sorry to hear this, and I know that you must feel especially saddened by the news.

Although I did not know him very well, George was always generous and kind to me, an enthusiastic theatre-goer, and a real gentleman.

I haven't been able to reach Jean Reavey yet, but I'm sure she will be in touch with you. She told me all about that awful attack on George last year; that must have weakened him tremendously.

We are all thinking of you.

[Alan]

1. George Reavey died on 12 August. In 1975 he had been mugged in New York.

September 1, 1976

Dear Sam,

Have written to you twice with no answer, which is not your usual, and was beginning to wonder if you were OK. But today spoke with Barney who has just received your note about going off to Berlin. So I understand you must be busier than usual and concentrating on next directorial chore.

Writing again because as of yesterday Arena Stage and I—subject to your approval—have worked out plan and schedule for doing a two-and-one-half week run of PLAY and OTHER PLAYS. Rehearsals month of November, production running from first week in December till just before Christmas. Cannot run longer no matter what because they have another show on tap. But they do have this time free in their smaller theatre, where Jackie played and also the Cronyn-Tandy NOT I etc. program, which is about the same size as the Court. I am most pleased because the New York situation is increasingly difficult to tie down and predict. Should the plays go well in Washington, of course, there will always be interest in bringing them into some New York theatre. But we shall see when the time comes.

In the meantime, I am beginning to think of the cast. I mentioned Donald Davis to you, and am trying to see if he is available. I am also pursuing the possibility of luring Pat Magee, though I gather his one-man Beckett show is booked pretty solidly through the season. I don't know whether Billie Whitelaw could or would come, or whether we could afford her. Unfortunately, Rosemary Harris is out on tour. I am trying to get Jane Alexander and/or Frances Sternhagen,[1] who played W1 here originally. No thinking yet beyond that, and until I get your blessing.

Really excited and hopeful that I can get over to Berlin to watch you either in rehearsal or production. Could you tell me, as soon as possible what your schedule there is, when you start, when you open, and etc. I'm opening the TEXAS TRILOGY Sept. 21–23, so probably could not make it until after that. But I do want to come over to see you and perhaps even watch you work. Not even sure which plays you are doing but presume THAT TIME and FOOTFALLS together with something else, PLAY no doubt. Please write.

[Alan]

1. American actress Jane Alexander (b. 1939), appointed chairman of the National Endowment for the Arts, 1992; Frances Sternhagen (b. 1930), Obie Award, 1965.

> Akademie der Kunste
> 1 Berlin 21
> Hauseateaweg 10
> [c. mid-September, 1976]

Dear Alan

Thanks for yours of 1st here today.

We open here Oct 1st & next day I leave for London to work with McWhinnie on a new TV play.[1]

Here we are doing just the 2 plays, *That Time* & *Footfalls,* the former with Klaus Herm (Lucky), the other with a good young actress named Schmahl. Rehearsals began a fortnight ago & are going fairly well.[2]

Whatever arrangements you make for the plays are in advance okay with me.

Forgive my not having written earlier. I have been tired and confused.

Do hope you make Berlin.

Love to you all
Sam

1. *Ghost Trio,* "A play for television," original title *Tryst,* written in English in 1975, published in *Ends and Odds,* 1976.
2. *Damals (That Time)* and *Tritte (Footfalls)* opened 1 October 1976, directed by SB, assisted by Walter D. Asmus, trans. by Elmer and Erika Tophoven. *Damals:* Klaus Herm (Voice and Face). *Tritte:* Hildegard Schmahl (May), Charlotte Joeres (Mother's Voice).

September 28, 1976

Dear Sam,

Just wanted to catch you before the Friday opening to wish you all good things. I'm sure you've worked very hard.

Am only sorry that the school here prevented me from coming on Friday. Juilliard has just opened, as has my new play which is struggling to survive the *New York Times* review.[1]

Assume you got my telegram, I plan to come to Berlin to see both GODOT and FOOTFALLS.[2] Then, hopefully, if you are in London, I can spend some time with you with my usual questions. If you are back in Paris by the 10th of October, then I'll come to Paris instead. Just let me know where you will be as of that Sunday.

In the meantime, all the best from both Jean and myself.

[Alan]

1. Clive Barnes's review of Preston Jones's first play of the "Trilogy," *Lu Ann Hampton Laverty Oberlander:* "Preston Jones's 'Texas Trilogy' Opens With Portrait of a Loser," *NY Times,* 22 September 1976; according to one review the *Trilogy* was "sadly unappreciated."
2. AS probably means *That Time*, not *Waiting for Godot*.

October 28, 1976

Dear Sam,

Seems impossible that I've been back two weeks. Forgive me for not writing sooner, but things here unusually brisk. Or should I say as usual?

We're all cast, and starting rehearsals on PLAY and OTHER PLAYS on November 8. Donald Davis you know; the two girls are unknown to you, but Dianne Wiest, who plays Billie's parts, is in my opinion the best actress of her generation in the American theatre (she's around 35), has played many roles with Arena, and scored a triumph as Emily in OUR TOWN. The other actress is Sloane Shelton,[1] whom I've had in a couple of plays, and who has just been highly praised in an off-Broadway production of a new play, THE RUNNER STUMBLES.[2] I am extremely happy to have them both. We are all looking forward to the work.

Have been holding technical meetings with my designer, Zack Brown, and my lighting designer, William Mintzer. Billy has been talking with Duncan Scott of the Court, and we are rigging up some version of their lamp for PLAY. The rest of the technical matters will be handled pretty much as they were at the Werkstatt.

Our meeting was very helpful, as per usual, although much too brief a time with you. Would have wanted just to be with you longer, but I know you were tired, and anxious to get out to the country and then home. Really appreciate your holding up your plans for me. Also very much helped by some notes I received from that Marty Fehsenfeld and Dougald McMillan, who watched the Royal Court rehearsals, and did some talks with Dougald and Billie. One thing I didn't ask you was whether there was any change in your thinking about the makeup in PLAY. You still want their faces more or less to match the urns? And you prefer no changes in the sequence the second time around.

Saw Harold in NY before he went back. His play—like mine—is closing this week. But he seemed to be recovering from his recent bout with whatever he had, and expects to be back again for another directing chore in a few weeks. I told him if he went on like that I'd start writing plays. His new lady Antonia is quite attractive, but I do feel sad about Vivien.[3]

Do hope you are feeling well and recovered from your own siege of theatre-work. Presume you are soon off to North Africa. I shall keep you posted on our progress or lack of it. And perhaps when we get them I can at least send you some photos. There is a great deal of advance interest at the Arena and in Washington about the plays. We shall see.

The Texas Trilogy closes after 6 weeks. Believe it or not, the box office is taking in $70,000 weekly, and that's still not enough to keep the three plays running. It's crazy. I'm determined never to do another Broadway production.

All the best.

[Alan]

1. American actresses Dianne Wiest (b. 1948), May in *Footfalls* and W1 in *Play;* Sloane Shelton (b. 1934), Mother's Voice in *Footfalls.*

2. *The Runner Stumbles* by Milan Stitt.

3. Pinter's "play": *No Man's Land.* Vivien Merchant (1929–1982), English actress, married Harold Pinter; they were later divorced. Lady Antonia Fraser (b. 1932), writer, divorced Hugh Fraser, MP, married Pinter, 1980.

Paris
18.11.76

Dear Alan

Thanks for yours of Oct. 28.

Yes, faces same grey & texture as the urns. No change in order 2nd time round. But light a little less ("when first this *change*") & voices correspondingly lower.

Am invited by Lietzau[1] to direct it in the Werkstatt next season. Hesitating.

Have submitted a new TV piece to BBC to replace their very poor film of *Play*.[2]

. . . .[3]

Letter from Harold today. He left for N.Y. a few days ago to direct *Otherwise engaged*.[4]

Good being with you in London. May you be over again soon.

Love to you all
Sam

1. Hans Lietzau (1913–1991), Barlog's successor as General-Intendant, Schiller-Theater, 1972–1980.
2. SB submitted . . . *but the clouds*. . . in place of *Play* (see SB's letter of 27 December 1976, n. 1).
3. SB and Suzanne have had flu, cannot travel; he will meet Gloria MacGowran soon.
4. By Simon Gray (b. 1936), English dramatist, director, actor.

November 24, 1976

Dear Sam,

Thanks for your card. Came just as we were about half way through rehearsals—and gave us all a bit of a feeling that you were there.

Actually, work has been proceeding reasonably well. Sometimes, I'm pleased with PLAY, sometimes with FOOTFALLS; harder to tell about Donald Davis and THAT TIME until we get elements together. We did record his voice today, all day, and I think you would like the three separate qualities. Hard to define exactly but we did A, B, C on three differing microphones, and the separation was quite distinct. Donald, I'm sure, has a voice tone quite different from Pat's; but we did listen to Pat's MALONE tape just to hear what you originally liked when you

wrote KRAPP for him. I also spoke with Jocelyn last week about getting the Royal Court to send us Pat's THAT TIME tape if possible, but
it has not yet arrived. Anyhow I shall let you know how things are
going in Washington. We start previews on Dec. 3 and open on December 8.

The other two plays, as I say, move ahead, sometimes one more than
the other. We did have a kind of run-through without any technical
elements before a few of our Juilliard students this afternoon, and they
seemed to hold quite well. The girl playing May, Dianne Wiest, is
excellent. She also does W2. We have worked very hard to carry out
your instructions, and have all benefitted by my seeing the plays and
talking with you. Dianne and Sloane Shelton (Mother) make an excellent combination of voices; and Pierre Lefevre—whom you may
know—one of our instructors here, who saw the run-through today,
was much impressed with the casting and performances in both plays.
Pierre was associated with Michel St. Denis at Strasbourg for many
years.[1]

Actually, next week is going to be vital because we shall be in Washington getting into the urns, and working out the lighting and all the
technical problems. For the moment, we are in good shape though not
yet 'there'. Running times seem to be approximately what they were
for the two plays I saw in Berlin, and PLAY is played very fast but with
your desired changes in volume. All three actors have been most loyal
to your directions and extremely cooperative in all respects. I don't
know if our man on the Light is as good as Duncan Scott but he seems
to be doing fine.[2] We did talk with Duncan to get his ideas about the
mechanism, but we are using something slightly different, more like a
camera on a swivel. It works fine and very quickly from one to the
other.

What else? the *New York* TIMES magazine section people called me
about having a gentleman named Alan Levy, who is based in Vienna,
come to Paris to do an interview with you. I know Alan and like him
very much. He wrote the first really sympathetic piece about the Miami
GODOT many years ago,[3] and I was most grateful to him. If you are up
to it and give me the word, I'll give him your address. I think he might
be in Paris sometime after the first of the year . . . Have been seeing
Barney, who seems OK, Harold and his NO MAN'S LAND (Harold
very tired and not well). Tom Bishop. The kids home for Thanksgiving
tomorrow, and I'm thankful. They all send their love. Oh, yes, I met
Martin Segal,[4] who's trying to help us raise money for Juilliard.

Jean sends regards; will write from Washington. [handwritten in right margin]

Ever,

A

1. Pierre Lefevre, American director, actor; trained at the London Theatre Studio under Michel Saint-Denis and George Devine; member of Old Vic Theater Center, 1947–1954; director, Strasbourg School of Centre Dramatique de l'Est, 1955–1970; a member of the Juilliard School drama faculty since 1971.

2. Jack Milligan.

3. "The LONG Wait for Godot," *Theatre Arts*, 40 (August 1956), 33–35, 96.

4. Martin Segal (b. 1916), member of the Board of Directors, Lincoln Center for the Performing Arts (1973–1987).

December 12 (My 59th birthday!)
Hastings-on-Hudson

Dear Sam,

Finally home, in one piece, slept out. We opened on Wednesday last; and in spite of the unanimously good press, I think you might be pleased with our version of PLAY and OTHER PLAYS.[1] I have enclosed the press so far and sent on some photos under separate cover, just to give you an idea. Sure you'll be hearing from some others. Barney and Tom Bishop going down this week, Ruby also, I believe.

PLAY went absolutely fine, and looked much like it must have in London. I talked with Rosemary Harris about various matters, including some of your comments to the actors that time, the makeup, etc. Our three actors did nobly, and I was completely pleased. The audience laughed throughout the first half of the first time around, and listened in absolute silence the second time. Lighting and all the technical problems took a bit of doing, as usual. Our man-on-the-light, Jack Milligan, was marvelous, knew the entire text by heart, and ran the light as though he had been born with it in his hands. We took about 18–19 minutes for the entire play (twice through the text).

THAT TIME very difficult because of problem of lighting head properly and still achieve absolute blackout. We tried three or four positions of light before finding proper one, on what we call first pipe at about 45 degree angle in front of actor, but higher and farther away than in Berlin. Because of size of proscenium, etc. (By the way, we tried light in

PLAY from underneath but couldn't get it far enough away to miss the curve of the urns, so we finally also did it from above, where it 'shared the actors' space' but was able to light up faces without spilling onto back blacks.) Donald's voice held audience listening for the 21 minutes, without any interruption (I was especially pleased because our sound man cut out all the breaths that Donald had had to take in recording), and the three voices, quite differentiated in tone and sound quality, flowed from speaker to speaker. We held the volume down to the absolute minimum; one or two people complained a bit during the previews that they couldn't hear; but we kept playing around until we got it all just within auditory level. Mesmerizing. I must admit that I would hold my breath each night.

In FOOTFALLS, I don't suppose Dianne was up to Billie, but we tried hard and I was pleased with her at the end. General visual effect quite powerful, and the voices, including Sloane's, carefully worked on. Really chilling. I had a time with the chimes, but Marty Fehsenfeld, who had watched your rehearsals in London and who sat in with us for a few days, told me about your version, and we tried to approximate, with ever-increasing echoes. This one got to be my favorite, and I can hardly tear myself away from it, including when I'm asleep.

Anyhow, glad it came off well, slightly exhausted, and just sad because you not able to see it. Most grateful to you for the chance to do the triple-bill, and for all your help and understanding along the way. There's talk, of course, about doing it in NY, and we shall see. But main thing is that we've done it here. I'm sure that Zelda or Tom[2] would have written to you, but are shy. I'll keep you posted. Trust all well. Jean sends her love.

[Alan]

1. SB's *Play and Other Plays (Play, That Time, Footfalls)*, the American premiere of *That Time* and *Footfalls*, opened at the Arena Stage, Kreeger Theatre, Washington, D.C., 3 December 1976, directed by AS, designed by Zack Brown. *Play:* Sloane Shelton (First Woman), Dianne Wiest (Second Woman), Donald Davis (Man). *That Time:* Donald Davis (Face and Voice). *Footfalls:* Dianne Wiest (May), Sloane Shelton (Mother's Voice). Reviews: Richard Coe, *Washington Post*, 9 December 1976; David Richards, *Washington Star*, 9 December; Clive Barnes, *NY Post*, 10 December; R. H. Gardner, *Baltimore Sun*, 12 December.

2. "Zelda or Tom": the Fichandlers.

Arena Stage
Sixth and M Streets, Southwest,
Washington, D. C. 20024
December 27, 1976

Dear Sam,

Not entirely sure where you are at the moment, but have a feeling you are in London. Not having heard from you in response to my various letters, before and after the opening in Washington, I assume you're not in Paris. In any case, I do hope you are well.

Reaction to the Arena production continues to be good. Yesterday's *New York* TIMES had another piece quite favorable.[1] I continue to reassure you that in spite of all the good notices, I was reasonably pleased with the production—and felt that you might have been. I have asked the Arena people to continue to send you all the reviews, and shall check to see that they do so.

Have been in touch with Barney, who has not been well. He is also pleased with the response. We may be spending New Year's Eve out at the Shack at Amagansett.

And I've just been reading through both ENDS AND ODDS, and FIZZLES. Just lovely. I'm so glad you let them be published. Someday I'd like to do both *Theatre I* and *Theatre II*, if you have no strong objection.[2] Also, I loved *Ghost Trio*, and looking forward to seeing BBC version of both that and NOT I.[3]

Letter from Ruby C., who was unable to come East for the Washington performances.

And so on.

Enclosed a poem I've just unearthed.

And all good wishes and thoughts to you from all of us.

[Alan]

1. Mel Gussow, *NY Times*, 26 December 1976, compares the American production with the one at the Royal Court Theatre in April.

2. *Ends and Odds*, 1976, includes *Not I, Footfalls, Ghost Trio, Theatre I, Theatre II, Radio I,* and *Radio II; Fizzles,* 1976; *Foirade: Fizzles,* bilingual edition with French trans. by SB, 1976.

3. Broadcast 17 April 1977.

Paris
27.12.76

Dear Alan

Many thanks for your good letters of Nov. 24 & Dec. 12. Fond wishes for its having been a happy birthday.

I give interviews less than ever. Apologies to Alan Levy.

So glad Triple Bill went well. Gratitude and congratulations to you & all.

Just back from London working on a new short TV piece with same team as for *Ghost Trio*.[1]

Do hope 77 won't grind by without our meeting again.

Much love to you all
Sam

1. "new short TV piece": *". . . but the clouds . . ."* "A play for television," written in English, October-November 1976, published 1976, 1977. *Shades: Three Plays by Samuel Beckett. Ghost Trio* and *. . . but the clouds. . .* with the BBC film of the Royal Court Theatre's *Not I*, rehearsals from 30 September–5 October 1976, filmed 6 to 8 October at BBC Film Studios, Ealing, and broadcast 17 April 1977. SB was so pleased by Billie Whitelaw's performance in *Not I* that he said the telecast was more effective than the stage play. He attended rehearsals and supervised production closely. The "same team": produced by Tristram Powell, directed by Donald McWhinnie, Anthony Page, SB. Billie Whitelaw (Female Voice [V]), Ronald Pickup (Male Figure [F]), Rupert Horder (the Boy).

Paris
6.1.77

Dear Alan

Thanks for yrs. of Dec. 27 with poem which I liked.

Not sure theatre Fragments are worth doing. Shall have to decide one way or the other.

Returning to London soon to see final cut of *". . . but the clouds . . ."*, second TV piece too late for inclusion in Grove vol., but in time for Faber's due in March.[1]

A letter from Tom Bishop very impressed by your production.

Love to you all.
Sam

1. "Grove vol.": *Ends and Odds,* 1976 [omits *. . . but the clouds . . .*]. *". . . but the clouds . . .,"* published in Faber's *Ends and Odds,* 1977.

April 3, 1977

Dear Sam,

Just returned from Brooklyn, where I saw GODOT again and talked with the actors. Jean too, she for the first time and enjoyed hearing it in German. Now she wants to read it in German, and I am looking for a copy.[1]

It was beautiful. Even though this time I knew what to expect. Horst and Stefan were like parts of one person. And Raddatz was even more human and understandable than he had been in Berlin last October. Although the stage was not as large as at the Schiller, the space was excellent, very clean and spare. The audience most responsive. Sorry I wasn't able to be at the opening, to which I was formally invited by the Berlin Now people. Was to go to Washington for the weekend to serve on a Theatre Panel giving out money for the National Endowment for the Arts. At the last minute, I discovered I was exhausted (too much going on the past weeks and months) and stayed in bed; but too late to change GODOT plans. So I came to the final performance Sunday.

Actually, I must have had the flu because I feel better already. Everyone has it, and Jean with a bad cold, which didn't affect her enjoyment. You won't believe it but tonight we are celebrating—a bit ahead of time—my daughter Vickie's 22nd birthday. April 5, 1955. She's about to graduate from college and very worried about getting a job. . . .[2] David will be 18 on April 9, and has a scholarship (partial) to Yale. To study Math and Physics, thank the Fates, not theatre. Very serious type, and hardly ever talks. But lots going on inside. He and I are going on a round-the-world trip this summer, basically to Australia but stopping off in various exotic places along the way. Hoping to meet up with my Jean in London in middle of August—and if you're in Paris early in September or so to pay you a visit. Last time we met, you promised me a page of one of your manuscripts, and I'm coming over to collect it.

Lots of your plays being done all over the place. GODOT in Los Angeles, evidently well done, and they want to televise it. I think Barney intends to let them. A good cast. So long as they just do the play and not make a film of it.[3] The ENDGAME here at the Roundabout not good, but am hopeful of one that Joe Chaikin is doing at Princeton sooner.[4] Will let you know. Talk of PLAY and OTHER PLAYS coming off-Broadway with Washington cast; I'll tell you if that's really to happen. THAT TIME has gone well in Toronto, I hear.[5] Grove finally corrected the typo of "word, words" in the original GODOT, and I'm delighted.[6]

Have had reasonable year. No directing since Washington trio except for a CHERRY ORCHARD I did with Juilliard graduates, with which much pleased. The other ORCHARD, much acclaimed at the Lincoln Center, strikes me a bit like the mustache Dali painted onto Mona Lisa.[7] Enjoying the kids at the School, spending more time at home, trying to write, getting out to Long Island on weekends. Barney OK but busy, Judith wrapped up in the baby. My cousin from Moscow over here for several months on visit, and quite a handful. Not sure about Jimmy Carter but keeping fingers crossed.[8] Miss you and think of you often. I know you don't like birthdays, but hope you won't mind my wishing you a good one. Take care of yourself. Best to Suzanne. And look forward to seeing you this summer.

[Alan]

1. Text of the Schiller-Theater production, 1975. This New York production had the same cast and was brought to New York by Goethe House and the West German government as part of a five-week arts festival called "Berlin Now Festival" (see letter of 11 February 1975, n. 2). Opened at Lepercq Space, Brooklyn Academy of Music, 29 March 1977, closed 3 April.

2. Brief comment about his daughter's difficulties in getting a job as a teacher.

3. Los Angeles Actors' Theatre, produced by Gwen Arner, directed by Ralph Waite (b. 1928), designed by Robert Zentis. Donald Moffat (Estragon), Dana Elcar (Vladimir), Bruce French (Lucky), Ralph Waite (Pozzo), Rico Williams (A Boy).

4. *Endgame* opened at Roundabout Stage Two, New York, 27 March 1977, directed by Gene Feist, designed by James Grant. Gordon Heath (Hamm), Jake Dengel (Clov), Charles Randall (Nagg), Suzanne Shepherd (Nell). *Endgame* opened at the Murray Theater, Princeton, 4 May 1977, directed by Joseph Chaikin. Daniel Seltzer (Hamm), Christopher McCann (Clov), Charles Stanley (Nagg), Shami Chaikin (Nell).

5. There seems to have been no production of *That Time* in Toronto at this period.

6. In the Grove Press first edition Vladimir's line read: "Word words. *(Pause.)* Speak." Now emended to "Words, words," echoing Hamlet's reply to Polonius. POLONIUS: "What do you read, my lord?" HAMLET: "Words, words, words" (2.2).

7. *The Cherry Orchard*, directed by AS, opened at Juilliard Theatre Centre, New York, 24 February 1977. Salvador Dali (1904–1989), Spanish surrealist artist. The "other *Orchard*," produced by Joseph Papp, directed by Andrei Serban, opened at Vivian Beaumont Theater, Lincoln Center, 17 February 1977. Andrei Serban (b. 1943), Rumanian director associated with Yale Repertory Theatre, 1977–1978, where he replaced Alvin Epstein, then with Repertory Theatre at Harvard and La Mama E.T.C.

8. Jimmy Carter (b. 1924), President of the U.S., 1977–1981.

Paris
10.4.77

SAMUEL BECKETT

Dear Alan

Thanks for yrs. of April 3.

Glad Schiller *Godot* went well. Had now traditional collective card from cast sounding pleased. Perspiring over French translation of *That Time – Footfalls*. Hopeless thankless chore. Off to Morocco at last tomorrow week. Then late May through late June Stuttgart for TV plays. Then I don't know. Quietly Paris—Ussy I hope—and the prospect of seeing you & giving you ms inscribed with my love. Have received finally invitation to direct *PLAY* for Schiller in the Fall. Feel I've had Berlin. Attempts to get going on something new in vain. Just a few rhymes in French. Wish I could do an Atropos all in black—with her scissors.[1]

Love to you all
Sam

1. "Atropos": one of the Three Fates in Greek mythology.

Paris
14.5.77

SAMUEL BECKETT

Dear Alan

Many thanks for coloured card and remembrance of deplorable occasion.[1]

Back from 3 weeks in sunny windswept Tangier & off again in a few days to do TV plays in German in Stuttgart.[2]

Nothing of interest to tell. Endless invasion, endless mail, no work apart from a little self-translation *(Footfalls)* and some gloomy French doggerel.

Hope all well with you & yours & that we may meet again soon.

Love, to you all
Sam

1. "deplorable occasion": SB's seventy-first birthday.
2. *Geister Trio (Ghost Trio), Nur noch Gewolk (. . . but the clouds . . .)*, produced by Dr.

Reinhart Müller-Freienfels, directed by SB, designed by Wolfgang Wahl for both, camera Jim Lewis, with the BBC 2 *Not I* in a program titled *Shatter,* Stuttgart SDR, broadcast 1 November 1977. *Geister Trio:* Irmgard Foerst (Female Voice [V]), Klaus Herm (Male Figure, [F]), Mathias Feil (Boy). *Nur noch Gewolk:* Klaus Herm (M1), Cornelius Boje (Man's Voice [V]). SDR version, twenty-nine minutes; BBC version, twenty-one and a half minutes (see letter of 27 December 1976, n. 1).

Tangier
16.8.77

Dear Alan

Yr. letter of Aug. 2 here yesterday. Hope you got my cable. Post to & from here quite hopeless.

Very disappointed we can't meet. We return to Paris 25th. Then 29th I go to Berlin to direct *Krapp* with Rick Cluchey (Krapp) at the Academy Theatre. Designer a man you have worked with he says, Richard Riddell.[1] It's not going to be easy.[2]

Back Paris late September. Then I hope Paris/Ussy for a spell, apart from a hop to Stuttgart early October for a TV detail.[3] Unless I'm landed with *Footfalls (Pas)* at Théâtre d'Orsay.

Having a good rest here, swimming & lazing. No new theatre in sight. Working on & off at a prose piece to keep me company.

Love to you all & *à bientôt* for God's sake
Sam

1. Richard Riddell was a Ph.D. candidate at Stanford University when AS met him in 1975; designed SB's production of *Krapp's Last Tape* in Munich; later Associate Director of ART; currently chair of the Program in Drama at Duke University.

2. Opened at Akademie der Künste, 27 September 1977, as part of the *Berliner Festwochen,* directed by SB, designed by Richard Riddell. Rick Cluchey met SB at Stuttgart when SB was directing the television plays. They agreed that *Krapp's Last Tape* would be performed, in English, during West Berlin's annual Autumn Arts Programme. Cluchey would play Krapp, and other members of the San Quentin Drama Workshop would take charge of the lights, the sound booth, and stage management. This production adopted most of the changes from the Schiller-Theater Werkstatt (1969) production. For a fuller account of this production see Ruby Cohn, *Just Play: Beckett's Theatre,* 1980, chap. 12, "Beckett Directs," 230–279.

3. See letter of 14 May 1977, n. 2.

September 7, 1977

Dear Sam,

Taking a chance on this reaching you in Berlin. Have just heard from my old friend Rick Riddell, who is much excited with his KRAPP venture with you. I wish you well.

Am home again after the various gyrations on various continents; and quite content to be at rest apart from my sadness at not having met with you at either end of the summer.[1] Couldn't reach Billie while I was in London, though I did have a pleasant evening and drinks with Duncan over at the Royal Court.[2] A lovely fellow!

Latest news here is that Manhattan Theatre Club, a very enterprising off-Broadway group, has now more or less finalised plans to do the trio we did down at Arena last year, that is PLAY and OTHER PLAYS. I insisted on same cast, that is Donald Davis, and Dianne Wiest and Sloane Shelton—and we have evidently gotten the three of them free of all other engagements in December, so we'll be doing the plays then, I trust and hope. Will keep you posted.

All sorts of interest in all your plays, almost daily a new offer, I understand, keeps Barney busy. Do I understand that you're still reluctant to let *Theatre I* and *II* be done, because that's what I've said to Barney. Or have you changed your mind?

Didn't see the TV GODOT back in July, and have heard both sorts of reactions.[3] The only thing that worried me was that after telling us they were going to reproduce the stage version, which was supposed to be most interesting, they went off into a desert and shot it. Perhaps pressure from those eternal TV types. Anyhow, it doesn't matter. The play goes on.

I had a terrific idea while in Greece this summer: To do GODOT in the theatre at Epidaurus, and at the same time do ENDGAME right in Agamemnon's Tomb at Mycenae, a perfect setting. Have you ever been there? Of course, I'm just day-dreaming.[4] . . . .

Really had hoped to see you, so had dozens of things to talk with you about. Sorry I can't just take off like Ruby and show up in rehearsals. I'm back in harness at Juilliard and trying to get the year organised. Also doing a bit of work at Boston University. Just put David into Yale last weekend, and seeing Vickie go off to work each day trying to earn enough money to move away from us. Lonely prospects. We may try to sell the house and get a smaller one, the taxes here are mad. But Jean OK and glad to be in one place again. My mother wasting away, almost doesn't recognise me. We try to make her comfortable but hard to know what to do.

Escape to the Shack when possible, like tomorrow morning.

All good thoughts and wishes to you, and to the two Ricks.[5]

[Alan]

1. In letters dated 23 May, 27 June, and 2 August, AS said he hoped to see SB in Paris on his way to Australia where he was conducting a Directors Workshop during the month of July on the plays of SB. SB tried to get back from Stuttgart in time, but delays in the production made that impossible. AS returned to New York in early August for final technical rehearsals of *Mother Courage*, which was going on tour. In mid-August he conducted a theater tour of graduate students from the University of California to London, Stratford, and Paris, but was unable to meet SB, who was away.

2. Duncan Scott, in charge of lighting at the Royal Court Theatre.

3. Shown 29 June 1977, PBS, WNET-TV, New York, Theater in America, the production taken from the Los Angeles Actors' Theater, same cast as in letter of 3 April, n. 3, except for Todd Lookiniand (A Boy); the location: the Mojave Desert.

4. Ancient Epidaurus, on the east coast of the Argolid, has a well-preserved, acoustically effective Greek amphitheater. Agamemnon, King of Mycenae, led the Greeks in the siege of Troy.

5. Cluchey and Riddell.

Berlin
24.9.77

Dear Alan

Thanks for yrs. of 7 conveyed by Richard Riddell. Glad to hear of plans for *3 Plays* at Manhattan T. C. We open here Sept. 28. We have rehearsed under difficult conditions—limited access to stage, inadequate technical equipment, little help from Academy staff etc. The team has done a good job none the less and Rick is an impressive Krapp, in spite of having to play the part, in this very strict & stylised production, clearly against his temperament. At the moment unfortunately, so close to the opening and with many adjustments still to be made, he has a severe feverish cold & yesterday had to interrupt rehearsal. But turned up this morning a little better. I return to Paris on the 29 and look forward to a long rest from theatre.

Ruby was here 10 days & took off for home & teaching yesterday morning. I am more or less committed, I regret to say, to directing *Play* for the Schiller Werkstatt about this time next year. I'm seeing Lietzau tomorrow *à ce propos*.[1] Then the following Nov. a new production of German *Eh Joe* in Stuttgart with an actor named Bennent whom I have not seen. Then probably Spring 79 *Happy Days* with Billie at the Royal Court. I am told the American TV *Godot* was quite awful. I was not consulted about this.

I do hope next year will not pass without our meeting again.

Much love to you all.
Sam

1. "*à ce propos*": regarding this.

November 23, 1977

Dear Sam,

Started rehearsals today. PLAY and OTHER PLAYS. A five week run at the Manhattan Theatre Club, a rather enterprising off-Broadway outfit, on 73rd Street, under direction of a young producer, Lynn Meadow. We are basically repeating the Washington production. The designer and all the technical elements are the same. And all the actors would have been the same and were until a week ago when the girl playing W2 and May ducked out on us very suddenly and unexpectedly (and without even the decency to ring me up) in order to take the leading role in another play.[1] So I've had to replace her, and have, with another relatively young actress but one in whom I have a great deal of faith. She played Varya for me in last year's CHERRY ORCHARD, and I thought she was the best I'd ever seen in that role. Her name is Suzanne Costallos. I saw a number of actresses but no one whom I admire or trust more. Shall keep you posted. We have three weeks of rehearsal, including one week to get the technical stuff right, then some invited audiences starting on Dec. 12; official audiences on December 15, and critics invited for Dec. 18, Sunday. Will play five weeks and is on the subscription series of the theatre. I believe they also plan to show FILM a few times during the run. We are starting at 9 p.m. each evening.

The theatre itself is very small and intimate, totally black walls; so our blackouts should be more possible to accomplish. Also size helps us with vocal needs. There'll be other problems, I'm sure, but at the moment do not know what they are. I have a stage manager different from Arena's, and also a girl doing the light in PLAY. We're already calling her 'Sam'. Donald Davis and Sloane Shelton, the other two actors from the Arena production, send you their regards and good wishes. I'm sure they will be fine.

Other things. My main concern at the moment is my mother who has been sinking steadily now for some weeks. . . .[2] Very difficult for me to deal with this daily without cracking up. The other night, I sat by her and watched her for some hours; and her head on the pillow seemed to me the exact replica of THAT TIME, and I kept hoping that at least she might have some memory to accompany her loneliness but I don't think so. The doctor tells me the brain cells are dying, more and more each day. What an ending for my sweet lovely generous gracious mother. But nothing to be done, as some poet said.

. . . .[3] But I would love to see you, lots to talk about. Delighted to hear Brooklyn Academy to do GODOT. Not sure who is to direct, they want you to come. Have talked to Barney but not seen him. Jean and I at the shack on the beach last weekend, and it seems like Brittany. Wish you could see it. Hope you are well and rested. Had a good chat with Rick Riddell but longing for news that you are well and taking it easy for a change. At least, easier.

[Alan]

1. Dianne Wiest.
2. Brief comment on his mother's decline and its effect on him.
3. AS says he expects to be in London on another theater tour in January 1978 and hopes they can meet 14–15 January.

Ussy
4.12.77

Dear Alan

Did I answer yrs. of Nov. 23? Can't for the life of me be sure. In case not this just to say Jan. 14–15 fine for me. And to send you all best wishes for *Play* & *O.P.* at Manhattan Theatre Club.

All news when we meet. Looking forward.

Love to you all.
Sam

December 9, 1977

Dear Sam,

Would have written earlier, but my mother's condition has been steadily worsening; she died on Monday evening last (Dec. 5) while I was rehearsing FOOTFALLS, and I left rehearsal to go to the hospital. Jean was with her.

. . . .[1]

The plays progress. We have been having technical rehearsals all week, and progress each day. Last night was the best, PLAY and FOOT-FALLS positively breathtaking. We are still working on balancing levels in THAT TIME, keeping it flowing, and getting light on Donald's face and off of everything else. The new girl, Suzanne, is just fine.

We have previews this week, and open officially on the 18th, next Sunday.

I am sixty on Dec. 12. Can't believe it. My mother was 84. Or 85?

Will you be in Paris on January 14–15, so that I could come over from London to see you? It's been too long.

Am hopeful reaction here will be as favorable as in Washington. The shows look good, and I feel they are what you wanted. We shall see.

Let me hear from you.

Best.

[Alan]

1. AS reflects on his mother's death: "I am having a hard time getting through it."

Paris
16.12.77

Dear Alan

Yours with sad news today. But as you say better so. My affectionate sympathy to you & Jean & the children.[1]

You will have received mine from Ussy to say your Jan. dates fine with me and how keenly I look forward to them.

Thanks for good news of renascent triplets & warm greetings to players & all involved.

If I decide to release *Theatre Fragments 1 – 2* for pro. production I would of course first offer them to you. Have written Grove to this effect.

All when we meet next month.
Bon courage, dear Alan.
Love to you all & best in 78

Sam

1. Answers AS letter of 9 December 1977.

December 19, 1977

Dear Sam,

Well, we opened last night. Sorry you were not there (even though you would not have come) because it was the best show we ever gave. Audience response very good, especially observable in PLAY; but their silence during THAT TIME and the tension which FOOTFALLS created also very clear. The reviews this morning very good. The TIMES, which is of course most influential, excellent; the POST fellow, who was recently the TIMES critic and had already commented favorably on the shows when done in Washington, even more so—from a certain point of view. The horse-racing paper, the NEWS, which in the past has dismissed every play of yours, liked PLAY and hated the other two. I think the same chap reviewed PLAY when done originally—and hated it. Par for the course.[1]

The new girl, Suzanne, came through quite well; and her performance last night was really taut. Everyone cannot believe she is a recent Juilliard graduate. Tom and Helen Bishop there, and seemed to like it. Jean Reavey there a few nights ago; she will probably be writing to you. Ruby Cohn is supposed to be seeing it, but have not heard from her. Barney most enthusiastic. The others will be coming. Have not heard from Dick Seaver. Judith is coming; her baby taking her time.

You would like the theatre, very small and dark and quite unpretentious. Only problem is that noises outside tend to seep in; and I am always running around trying to stop someone or something from making noise. Very tough with the occasional pigeon that tends to gurgle a bit on matinee days from the alley.

Have enclosed the reviews so far, and the piece I wrote for the Sunday TIMES of yesterday.[2] More when forthcoming; and will bring everything along when I show up in Paris on January 14. Assume that we shall meet.

. . . .[3] The main thing is that I get a chance to see you and tell you everything about the production, and other matters.

It has been so fast, so direct, so deep an experience, I cannot begin to tell you all. And in the middle, actually while I was rehearsing FOOT-FALLS, the news from Jean that my mother had died. I can never forget your plays anyhow; but I shall never forget these two because the image of the head in THAT TIME was my mother's on her pillow in her last days; and, of course, the other play has reverberations of every kind from my own words and thoughts with her. I was not able to tell my mother in her last days what I was doing because she was not capable of any awareness; but the time we did them in Washington, she was still conscious and able to understand a little. She always knew when I was working on Beckett, and she always wanted to see and know more of your work.

Am fine, tired but relieved; and happy for a three-week vacation from school, and then London. We have just also opened Wedekind's SPRING AWAKENING at Juilliard, with a Rumanian director I brought over, with much acclaim.[4] So it has been a hectic schedule. But everyone tells me I look OK, and maybe I'll begin to believe them one of these years. See you in Paris. Let me know when convenient for you.

[Alan]

1. Opened 18 December 1977, Manhattan Theatre Club, New York, produced by Lynn Meadow, directed by AS, designed by Zack Brown, lighting by William Mintzer. *Play:* Sloane Shelton (First Woman), Suzanne Costallos (Second Woman), Donald Davis (Man). *That Time:* Donald Davis (Face and Voice). *Footfalls:* Suzanne Costallos (May), Sloane Shelton (Mother's Voice). Reviews: *NY Daily News*, 18 December 1977; Richard Eder, *NY Times*, 19 December; Clive Barnes, *NY Post*, 19 December. On 2 January 1978 SB replied: "Thanks for yrs. of Dec. 19. Bravo all."

2. "I Hope to Be Going On With Sam Beckett—And He With Me," *NY Times*, 18 December 1977.

3. The preceding lines deal with hotel and travel arrangements.

4. Frank Wedekind (1864–1918), German dramatist, actor; *Spring Awakening* was adapted earlier by Edward Bond and produced at the National Theatre, London, 1974. The "Rumanian director": Liviu Ciulei.

January 20, 1978

Dear Sam,

Back home, just making it on the wings of a blizzard, and hasten to tell you how much I enjoyed our meeting, and to thank you for your kindness and hospitality.

As well as to let you know that I managed to reach Billie, and had a good talk with her. Turned out that I had the wrong number for her, and also that she had been busy taping some children's TV show, and had not been home during the day for some time. In any case, I did talk with her, and she was glad to hear that we had met and that you were well. Very warm and friendly, and I was pleased to have gotten to her. She was busy at the Studio, otherwise we would have met. We shall.

My friend, Danny, rhapsodic about meeting you.[1] I hope you didn't mind. He was responsible for my being in Europe at all, and I thought you would like meeting him. He is quite a talented and bright teacher and director, and very well liked by his students. Ruby met him when he was watching rehearsals of GODOT at Stanford two summers ago.

PLAY et al has closed here, mourned by all. Evidently houses were pretty full right up until closing, but we were not able to extend further because the actors all had other engagements. Glad it went well.

Thank you for your willingness to let me try *Theatre I* and *II*. I shall investigate proper auspices, actors, timing, etc. Feel we should perhaps wait a bit, but I would love to try one or the other or both. Will keep you posted.

Always glad to catch glimpse of you, and have a bit of a chat, brief as they tend to be. You looked in good shape, and I do trust you will be having a rest in Ussy and then on to Morocco. Great time of the year to do so. We have had some 16 inches of snow here; driveway and roads completely closed, I shall have to walk to the station for at least a week. But it's lovely and crisp, and I don't mind. Jean glad to have me back. David back at Yale, so no matter. And Vicki always intrigued at the idea that I have seen you. She is teaching kindergarten classes and not too badly.

Have not spoken with anyone here, yet, but will give them your regards.

One thing I meant to tell you about my mother. Her father's name was Samuel; and by Russian custom her father's name became her middle name, so she was always Rebecka Samuel—which lent additional interest on her part to my knowing you.

What is the name of the restaurant you took us to? It has one of the most delicious menus I have ever encountered. And I thank you again for taking us there.

Take care of yourself, have a good time in Morocco, and all the best.

[Alan]

1. Danny Labeille, then at Cuyahoga County Community College, Parma, Ohio, later Head of Drama Faculty, State University of New York at Buffalo, asked SB to write a play to be included in the celebrations at the university for SB's seventy-fifth birthday, 1980 (see letter of 20 June 1980, n. 1).

Tangier
18.2.78

Dear Alan

Thanks for yrs. of Jan. 20.

Greatly enjoyed our meeting as always. I had a note from yr. friend Danny, but have mislaid it & cannot reply. Please thank him when you see him. It was a pleasure to have him with us.

The restaurant is "Les Iles Marquises" in the Rue de la Gaieté, opposite the old Bobino music hall.

Went to a couple of *Godot* rehearsals before leaving. Still in a mess but Aumont & Roussillon should be good. (D.& E. respectively). Opening at Odéon in three days from now.[1] Have *Pas* in my head well in advance. Look forward to working with Delphine Seyrig.[2]

No news of Rick except indirectly from Ruby who says he has had his oral surgery in Berlin and may stay on in Germany.

Here nearly a fortnight now and as much to go. Marvellous weather. Got out of icy Paris just in time.

Continue dubious about the two theatre *Fragments*. Certainly no hurry. As & when you please. Have given them to Asmus for Germany, but nothing arranged so far as to when & where production. Have not yet released U.K. rights.

No new work. Prose begun at a standstill. Mind going very silent.

Hope you haven't been too hard hit by NY blizzards.

Love to all.
Sam

1. *En attendant Godot* opened at Odéon-Théâtre de France, 21 February 1978, directed by Roger Blin, designed by Matias, with actors from the Comédie Française. Jean-Paul Roussillon (Estragon), Michel Aumont (Vladimir), Georges Riquier (Lucky), Francois Chaumette (Pozzo).

2. Delphine Seyrig (1932–1990), French actress, born in Lebanon, admired Blin and SB and in 1952–53 became one of the financial backers for *Waiting for Godot* in its world premiere, 5 January 1953.

13.4.78

Dear Alan

Many thanks for kind wishes & remembrance.[1]

Pas etc. opened 2 days ago. Seems to have gone well. Delphine very good.[2]

Off to Ussy next week at last. Need it sorely.

Buried in mail. So no more for now.

Love to you all
Sam

1. "remembrance": usual birthday greetings card.
2. *Pas (Footfalls)* and *Pas moi (Not I)* opened at Théâtre d'Orsay Grande salle, Paris, 11 April 1978, directed by SB. *Pas:* Delphine Seyrig (May), Madeleine Renaud (Mother's Voice). *Pas moi:* Madeleine Renaud (Mouth).

Monday, June 5, 1978

Dear Sam,

Sitting out here at Amagansett, watching the water and feeding the seagulls and trying to recover a bit from the last three months at Juilliard, which have been mad, harrowing, and almost entirely concerned with raising money—something I'm constitutionally incapable of doing. Just beginning to breathe.

Saw GODOT on its opening night.[1] Walter, whom I saw all too briefly a couple of times, has probably told you all about it by now. He did an excellent job at reproducing the physical form, but had trouble with the actors. They were unable or unwilling or both to make what they were doing seem organic; and they were so different physically and emotionally from the German cast that very often the actual impression of what they were doing turned out to be quite different even though the movement or gesture was identical. Sam Waterston (Vladimir) was the most effective and consistent, and had moments which were beautiful, even though his presence was not nearly so impressive as that marvelous tall brooding German actor whose name escapes me for the moment. Pozzo was also effective, especially in the first act. Lucky seemed miscast to me (Walter disagrees), a bit too well-fed, and I felt his speech was more broken-up than I had remembered in your production; but he was always interesting. Estragon, I'm afraid, was just not up to it in any way. He was the one I was worried about, and? I gather the one with whom Walter had the most trouble. It's too bad that the Brooklyn people foisted that actor on the production because there were others who could have done it much more effectively. Walter went through the second battle of the Marne on this one and deserves every decoration available.

Critics, as usual, split; and it doesn't matter. The physical production looked fine, and audiences very responsive. I'm sure that the differences of opinion will continue. Barney hasn't been yet. He was due to see it with me last Wednesday, but the torrential rain—which delayed opening time—kept him away. (He's just recovering from bad bout with bleeding ulcers, and hasn't been himself for some time, now recovering.) I managed to swim out across the Brooklyn Bridge.

Have also been reading D. Bair's book on you, as has Jean, and not entirely sure how I feel about it.[2] Sometimes I wonder where she got her information and how much she has made up. But I cannot deny that I'm enjoying knowing more about you when you were growing up, and before we met. I just hope that the book doesn't disturb you too much.

. . . .[3] Expect to take things easy this summer, no major travels. Walks along the beach, lots of reading, and maybe a start on a book of so-called memoirs, which various people and even publishers have been urging on me. So far, have written the title: Ashes and Sparks, or I Want My Son To Be a Stagehand.

Plans, as usual. We are re-doing a production of Wedekind's SPRING AWAKENING, which we did at Juilliard last fall, which caused a great stir. Directed by a Rumanian I brought over.[4] Under Joe Papp's auspices. A possible Broadway show in the fall, something I brought back from Australia. Have strong doubts whether it will ever get on. In September, will be directing Anouilh's *ANTIGONE* for a national tour. And so on.⁵ [handwritten after *"Antigone"*]

Rather enjoying the Juilliard grind except for the financial squeeze.⁶ The kids make me feel very positive about the future of the theater, something that Broadway and off-Broadway do not. General political picture, especially the Russians, worries me. Have been invited to direct over there but don't want to go. At the moment, don't want to go anywhere except into the water which is outside the window, and which happens to be too cold (until July). I have been taking up biking, and now go into the village, 4 miles each way, every morning to pick up the NY TIMES.

Trust you're enjoying some sort of rest before everyone descends on you this summer, and you're off to Berlin again. Or London. Think of you often and wish you well. As does Jean. If there's a chance that I'll be coming over I'll let you know in time. Not likely.

Oh, yes, I think I told you that during last winter's storm, the house next to us floated off and hit right into us. It's still there. [handwritten after "next" and into right margin]

Take care of yourself, and best to Suzanne. [handwritten]

[Alan]

1. *Waiting for Godot* opened at Lepercq Space, The BAM Theatre Company, Brooklyn Academy of Music, Brooklyn, New York, 25 May 1978, produced by Jack Garfein and Frank Dunlop, directed by Walter D. Asmus, based on SB Schiller-Theater production of 1975, designed by Carole Lee Carroll. Austin Pendleton (Estragon), Sam Waterston (Vladimir), Milo O'Shea (Lucky), Michael Egan (Pozzo), R. J. Murray, Jr. (A Boy). Reviews: Richard Eder, *NY Times*, 1 June 1978; Clive Barnes, *NY Post*, 1 June; Douglas Watt, *Daily News*, 1 June; Howard Kissel, *Women's Wear Daily*, 1 June; Holly Hill, *Wall Street Journal*, 6 June; David Sterritt, *Christian Science Monitor*, 12 June; Martin Gottfried, *Saturday Review*, 22 July.
2. *Samuel Beckett: A Biography*, 1978.
3. Preceded by brief comment on family matters.
4. "Rumanian": Liviu Ciulei.
5. AS had directed Brecht's *Mother Courage* with The Acting Company, American Place Theatre, 5 April–19 April in repertory. Anouilh's *Antigone* (1946), September 1978 with The Acting Company.
6. AS was director of the Juilliard School's Drama Division (1976–77, 1978–79).

August 1, 1978

Dear Sam,

Hadn't heard from you since my last letter a month ago, and was wondering if you were OK. Probably, you've taken off or are about to take off for Morocco. I do hope all those delays we're reading about involving French airports won't get in your way too much.

This has been a patched-together summer. Jean's blood pressure has suddenly shot up, and she has been on medication and trying to take things a bit easier; but so far not much in the way of positive results, and we are both a bit concerned. The student production of SPRING AWAKENING has had a successful run under the auspices of the Public Theater, and I am about to start on Anouilh's ANTIGONE for a nationwide tour with a young company of ex-Juilliard graduates.

Tom Bishop is arranging a Beckett Festival at New York U. in the fall, and has asked me to take part.

How was the Paris GODOT?

And when are you going to London again?

Doesn't seem as though I'll be coming over again this year, but with the changing tides, I'm never sure. Would really love to see you.

Take care, have a good holiday, and do let me hear from you when you can. Best to Suzanne.

Ever,
[Alan]

[early to mid-August 1978]

Dear Alan

Thanks for yrs. of June 5 & Aug. 1. Forgive my not having written. Rather hard pressed, what little left to press, with researchers & mail.

Off to Tangier tomorrow for 4 weeks. Then a week in Paris. Then a month in Berlin to direct *Play*, Walter assisting & directing, to go with it, *Come & Go* on his own. He came recently to Paris & related his N.Y. adventure. Seems to have pulled through well, Gogo notwithstanding. He is now in Copenhagen directing *Endgame* in Danish![1]

Blin's *Godot* revival did well, both at Odéon & Comédie Française. I kept aloof, just saw a couple of rehearsals. Also big success in Avignon directed by Tchech Klecja (forgive spelling) with Bouquet, Rufus & Wilson. But sounded pretty clownish interpretation.[2]

Nothing much of interest to tell. We jog along much as usual. Reedition of French poems in Fall with some recent doggerel. Also my translation at last of *That Time (Cette fois).*[3]

. . . .[4]

Absorbed in *Play* at the moment. That past from me there will be a new *Eh Joe* for Süddeutscher Rundfunk in Stuttgart (Jan. 79) with Bennent[5] of whom I know only that he looks about right for it. Still hopes of *Happy Days* with Billie next summer, at Court or perhaps Riversdale Studios,[6] but nothing firm so far.

Ruby in London with her theatre group. She may come to Berlin towards end of rehearsals.

Had a letter from Abeille.[7] . . .

So sorry Jean is poorly . . . .

Don't seem to have heard from Barney for years.

Do hope we may meet next year. My purse is yours in Paris, if that wd. help. With my old heart point five.

Love, dear Alan
Sam

1. *Slutparti (Endgame)* opened at Bristol Music Centers Teater, Copenhagen, 18 September 1978, directed by Walter D. Asmus, designed by Herbert Wernieke. Morten Grunwald (Hamm), Ove Sprogoe (Clov), Tommy Kenter (Nagg), Lily Weiding (Nell).

2. *En attendant Godot* was presented as part of the Festival d'Avignon, at la Cour d'Honneur du Palais des Papes, 16 July 1978, directed by Otomar Krejca (b. 1921), assisted by Alena Sluneckova, designed by Krejca and Yves Cassagne. Rufus (Estragon), Georges Wilson (Vladimir), Jose-Maria Flotas (Lucky), Michel Bouquet (Pozzo), Fabrice Luchini (A Boy). *Godot* was also part of the 1979 Festival d'Avignon with a slightly changed cast: Andre Burton (Lucky), Patrick Donnay (A Boy).

3. "French poems": *Poèmes suivi de mirlitonnades,* 1978; *That Time,* 1976, trans. by SB, *Cette fois,* a limited edition of 100 numbered copies, 1978.

4. SB has met Tom Bishop, Calvin and Joacim Israel, "and others."

5. Heinz Bennent (b. 1921).

6. Riverside Studios, London.

7. Danny Labeille.

October 7, 1978

Dear Sam,

Just a word to wish you well on the production in Berlin, and to tell you that I'm still in one piece and thinking of you.

Just finished staging Anouilh's ANTIGONE for the Acting Company (mostly Juilliard graduates) and now getting the school started up. Saw Tom Bishop this week about the festivities at the end of the month. Will be hectic. Just sorry that I won't have any productions on.[1]

There's an off-off-Broadway ENDGAME which has just started[2] (apart from Tom's arrangements with Mabou Mines et al) and I expect to see it soon and pass on a reaction. . . .[3]

When all quietens down, perhaps I can try to get THEATRE I and II on. Subject to your approval.

Wish I could visit with you and watch a few rehearsals. How I envy Ruby's mobility, no curse it. Give her my regards.

A chance that I might come on one of those student hegiras to London in February, in which case I will try to sneak over to Paris. And I'm trying to get Billie for a show that may or may not go on here.

Take care of yourself. I hope *alles geht gut.*[4]

Yours, always,
[Alan]

1. "the festivities": "Beckett Festival" at New York University, 20 October–4 November 1978, directed by Tom Bishop, then Director of the Center for French Civilization and Culture and Chair of the Department of French and Italian, New York University. Schneider's television films were shown: *Eh Joe* with George Rose and Rosemary Harris, 24, 25, 30, 31 October and 1, 3, 4 November; *Waiting for Godot* with Zero Mostel, Burgess Meredith, Kurt Kaznar, and Alvin Epstein, 21, 24, 25, 28 October and 1, 4 November; and *Film* with Buster Keaton included in the daily noon to 10 P.M. viewing. AS also participated in a round table discussion on Beckett's dramatic works, moderator Tom Bishop, Monday, 23 October, 8 P.M. in the Elsner-Lubin Auditorium, the Loeb Student Center. Other participants were Edward Albee, Lee Breuer, Ray Federman, Israel Horowitz, Phillipe Sollers, and Susan Sontag.

2. Directed by Mitchell Engelmeyer, opened at Squat Theater, New York, 5 October 1978, and played through 22 October as part of the "Beckett Festival." The Mabou Mines productions included *Come and Go*, directed by Lee Breuer, *Mercier and Camier*, directed by Fred Neumann, *Fizzles* 1, 4, 7, dramatic reading by David Warrilow, and *Not I* with Ellen McElduff.

3. Followed by a paragraph about family matters.

4. *"alles geht gut"*: all goes well.

Paris
24.10.78

Dear Alan

Thanks for yrs. of Oct. 7.

Spiel went well in Berlin & assistant Asmus did a very good job on *Kommen u. Gehen*.[1] Also did a lot of work with Rick & his San Quentinites on their *Endgame*, now running in London with his *Krapp* at the Open Space Theatre, with much success to judge from what he told me today when I phoned him.[2] From London they go to Lancaster University for a couple of performances, then to Bonn, then perhaps London again & later Copenhagen & Zurich. They are a gallant band—very likeable.

. . . .[3]

Meeting with Stuttgart TV team in a few days re new production of *Eh Joe* in January with Bennent whom I don't know. *Happy Days* with Billie seems certain now for next year (Royal Court), simply remains to fix date, late Summer probably. She has just opened in West End in a new play by Simon Gray.[4]

Apart from some recent French doggerel, incorporated in a reedition of the poems, no new work & none on the way that I can see. Tired of the old rigmarole.

. . . .[5]

Good that Jean is better. . . .[6]

Love to you all
Sam

1. *Spiel (Play)* opened 6 October 1978, directed by SB, assisted by Walter D. Asmus, designed by Hans Bohrer, trans. by Erika and Elmar Tophoven. Hildegard Schmahl (W1), Sibylle Gilles (W2), Klaus Herm (M). *Kommen und Gehen (Come and Go)*, directed by Walter D. Asmus, opened same time with same designer. Christine Prober (Flo), Charlotte Joeres (Vi), Karin Remsing (Ru).

2. Presented by the San Quentin Drama Workshop in association with the Goethe Institute and the Berliner Festspiele, *Endgame* and *Krapp's Last Tape* opened at Open Space, London, 18 October 1978. *Krapp's Last Tape* with Rick Cluchey, directed by SB, designed by Richard Riddell. *Endgame* directed by Rick Cluchey in consultation with SB, designed by Gerhard Trimpin, John Lovell and Rick Cluchey, lighting by Bud Thorpe for both. Rick Cluchey (Hamm), Bud Thorpe (Clov), John L. Jenkins (Nagg), Terri Garcia Suro (Nell).

3. SB comments on how he is: "filthily tired."

4. Simon Gray's new play: *Molly.*

5. SB mentions possible travel plans in December.

6. SB comments on David Schneider's health.

December 23, 1978

Dear Sam,

Thinking of you as the old year passes by, and wishing you well. Wish Jean and I could have a drink with you to celebrate, but afraid that no matter how hard I tried I couldn't arrange things so that I could get over there to surprise you.

Seeing Ruby in a few days at some sort of do for the Modern Language Assoc., and I'm sure she'll fill me in on your plans and whereabouts. Peter Hall paid us a visit at Juilliard a week ago, and told me you were definitely coming over to do HAPPY DAYS with Billie at the Court. I'll sure try to get to that one.

Peter gave me a copy of Harold's newest, which I read and rather liked—tho I gather it got a very mixed response in London.[1] Haven't heard from him lately. . . .[2]

Have had a reasonable fall and heading into winter with various prospects and confusions, as usual. Juilliard is a huge granite boulder in the roadway but I manage to travel down various roads. Just after the New Year, I shall be going down to the Arena in Washington once more to direct Michael Weller's new play, LOOSE ENDS. He's the fellow who wrote MOONCHILDREN a few years ago, which I did in Washington with great success and then brought to New York where it soon closed. This one is about young couples in the Seventies, and the difficulty of commitment to any kind of enduring relationship. He's very talented, somewhat Chekhovian, and catches the American rhythm better than anyone I know. I must say that whatever happens, I am looking forward to getting to work on it and away from the daily problems of Juilliard. I guess I prefer the process of directing to any other activity I've encountered.

. . . .[4]

Almost got to direct a play by Brian Friel on Broadway, but after working on it for more than a year with the author and management, had the play yanked away by the agent and given to another management which got James Mason, who wanted a different director. Par for the course.[5]

Have been trying to read the Bair book, and find its tone and general inaccuracies maddening. She's gotten all sorts of things wrong, including some of the stuff she had managed to pull out of me. Sad she's put you through that whole thing.

Want to wish you the best of whatever for the New Year. And hoping we may meet in it.

Take care of yourself. Jean sends love. And to Suzanne. [handwritten from "we"]

[Alan]

1. *Betrayal* opened at the National Theatre, 15 November 1978.
2. AS reports on Pinter's family matters.
3. Weller's *Moonchildren,* 1971; *Loose Ends,* opened 2 February 1979.
4. Comments on family matters follow (two paragraphs).
5. Brian Friel (b. 1929), Irish dramatist; the Friel play, *Faith Healer,* directed by José Quintero, opened at the Longacre Theatre, New York, 5 April 1979.

Parkhotel Stuttgart
14.1.79

Dear Alan

Glad to have yours of Dec. 23 with good news of you all.

Haven't read the Bair book.

Here for a remake of *Eh Joe* with Heinz Bennent in the part. Not enjoying it. Old hat. Assisted by the faithful Asmus.[1] Soon over, then a breather Paris/Ussy before starting in on *Happy Days* with Billie Whitelaw to open at the Court late June, rehearsals beginning early May.

Good spell in Tangier over Xmas into 79 far from the feasting.

No work apart from translation of *That Time* & some French doggerel. Acute perception of mental bluntening. Final paradox.

Do hope we can meet again this year.

Love to you all
Sam

1. *He Joe (Eh Joe)* shown 13 September 1979, Süddeutscher Rundfunk, SB assisted by Walter D. Asmus, camera Jim Lewis.

March 21, 1979

Dear Sam,

Spring finally here, and none too early. Snow and cold much too long, though not quite as bad as last year, when the shack in Amagansett got hit by the one next to it! Looking forward to the summer and the beach, and being away from the city. Jean hardly goes in any more, too ugly and too dangerous.

The die has finally been cast at Juilliard. Have resigned as Director of the Theater Center, and leaving as of the end of the term in June. No more pain and anguish running a school, four years was enough of that![1] Actually, life changing in a variety of ways. The Michael Weller play, LOOSE ENDS, turned out well at the Arena in Washington, and now coming in for a run at the Circle in the Square in New York, with some rewrites and some cast changes. A lovely quiet play about young people in the Seventies trying to stay together and having difficulties making a commitment to each other.[2]

Have been offered and am accepting a part-time Professorship of Drama at the University of California in La Jolla; a new and fairly non-academic professional theatre training program, located in one of the most beautiful sections of the USA. I'll be there October-November and then again January-February, thus missing the winter months and all that snow and ice we've been tangling with. The rest of the year, will go on being a director, which has been not so easy with my hours and chores at Juilliard. So it shouldn't be too bad. And I'll be on the same coast as Ruby, and may be seeing more of her, at least in the winter. Will be teaching an Advanced Directing course, and a Graduate Seminar dealing with your plays.

. . . .[3]

Have been re-reading THEATRE I and II, and wondering if you still would let me find a theatre for them next season. Perhaps also to have a go at them with the students at California some time. I meant to see THE OLD TUNE, which was done off-off-Broadway here, but was still in Washington when it opened.[4]

Trust you are well. Soon, I know, you'll be in London working with Billie. Wish I could come, both for rehearsals and to see the performance; but will be deep in LOOSE ENDS until middle of June. And London has gotten so expensive. Will be anxious to hear how it all goes. And would like to see you this year somehow. Regards and good thoughts from all of us. *Plus ça change, plus la même chose.*[5]

[Alan]

1. AS resigned after four years (Mel Gussow, "Alan Schneider Resigns as Head of the Juilliard Theater Center," *NY Times*, 3 March 1979) to become Professor of Drama and Head of the Graduate Directing Department at the University of California in San Diego in 1979.

2. Opened at Arena Stage, Washington, D.C., 2 February 1977; Circle in the Square, New York, 6 June 1979.

3. The following two paragraphs deal with the problem of owning a big house now that the children have left and AS is in California for part of each year; after fifteen years the Schneiders sold their home in Hastings-on-Hudson and moved to East Hampton.

4. *The Old Tune* (Robert Pinget's *La Manivelle*), English text by SB, played at the Ensemble Studio Theater, 21 February–11 March 1979, directed by David Shookhoff, with David Margulis and Stefan Gierasch. Review: *NY Times,* 6 March 1979.

5. *"Plus ça change, plus la même chose":* the more things change, the more they remain the same.

Ussy
29.3.79

Dear Alan

Many thanks for yours of 21. Good to have all your latest. Sounds good to me . . .

Here for the first time since Nov. to find the little house un-heated through the awful winter. Back to Paris tomorrow to clean up before leaving for London April 22 to start rehearsals with Billie next day. Hoping to get Ronald Pickup, but I fear unlikely because of some big film offer.[1] Deep in the play these past months, eyes & ears. A nervous Billie came to Paris, but is calming down now. We open June 7.

Talk of a remake of *Eh Joe* (BBC) with Rick & Billie—in the vague future. Rick having a thin time in Berlin, but has managed a few engagements through Germany & the group is together again.

Let me brood a little longer on the 2 *Fragments.* They'll be yours in the end for sure.

Look forward to seeing Barney again before leaving for London—after what feels like many years. Wish I could say as much for you—Jean. . . . .[2]

No new work, but feel like yet another go—perhaps when this last theatre job is out of the way.

Love to you all.
Sam

1. Ronald Pickup (b. 1941), English actor.
2. SB had some lung trouble early in the year.

June 23, 1979

Dear Sam,

Delayed much too long in writing to you, please forgive. I had wanted to wish you all the best for your Royal Court opening, and lo and behold I discover through this week's NEWSWEEK that you have already opened.[1] A favorable notice and a lovely picture of Billie holding up the umbrella. So my good wishes will have to turn into congratulations.

Reason didn't write before was that I was in rehearsal myself, with Michael Weller's new play, LOOSE ENDS, which I did during the winter at Arena. (He wrote MOONCHILDREN, which I also directed some years back.)[2] About young people and their problems with their new-found freedoms. Very Chekhovian and sad but ringing very true in terms of younger generation. Reviews and audience response generally OK, and we are doing well. But I was finishing up Juilliard at the same time, and also beginning process of moving books and things out to East Hampton. So lots of 20-hour days and not enough time to do anything else. House looks like the fourth act of CHERRY ORCHARD, books and paintings all over the place. But morale good as we set out for new adventure; and Jean can hardly wait. The house has been a tremendous physical burden on her the past few years, and the smaller one we are moving into will be more manageable.

Went with Barney couple of nights ago to see the HAPPY DAYS at the Public with Irene Worth, whom I know well. She is a marvelous actress, and does some fine things. Quite different, I gather from Billie's (and Ruth White's). Barney liked it bit more than I, but then, of course, I am somewhat prejudiced by the past. Serban's production was more or less scrupulous. I had feared that he might get really carried away as he did with THE CHERRY ORCHARD at the Lincoln Center, but he didn't. And the setting, though a bit ornate, was an attempt to do what you asked for. As was the entire production.[3]

I wish I could see Billie, but with the summer getting into July, and the movers coming in a couple of weeks to move the furniture out, I don't think I'll get East of East Hampton. We spend nights out at the beachhouse because there's no place to sleep at the other place, and walk along the beach and feed the sea gulls and think of how much you would like it—rough and primitive and elemental as it actually is.

Do hope you are relaxing a bit after the ordeal. Rehearsals no matter how much you enjoy the performers, are always arduous, and I know how hard you work. Don't mean to intrude either, just wanted you to know all well though slightly askew for a while. You know about Barney and Christine. Both of them feeling the effects, but both realise it's best for all concerned. I gather you spent some time getting photo-graphed with your small namesake.[4]

Life here getting increasingly concerned with the gas shortage, though we've managed so far. Not sure whether it'll get better or worse. Vickie starting to drive across the country towards California next week, and nervous about running out somewhere. We won't go out until end of September, hoping to look at the waves and listen to them the whole month of August, if nothing gets in the way. New address, by the way, is 41 Gingerbread Lane, East Hampton, Long Island, New York 11937. But here until July 15, and the mail will get forwarded in any case.

Do take care of yourself, get a good holiday, and think of us now and then.

Best to Suzanne. [handwritten from "Best"]

[Alan]

1. Jack Kroll, *Newsweek,* 18 June 1979.

2. *Loose Ends* opened at Arena Stage, Washington, D.C., 2 February 1979; *Moonchildren,* 1971–72 season. Rehearsals lasted six weeks. *Happy Days* opened at the Royal Court Theatre, 7 June 1979, directed by SB, designed by Jocelyn Herbert. Billie Whitelaw (Win-nie), Leonard Fenton (Willie). For this production SB worked with the more authoritative of the two notebooks he had prepared for the 1971 production at the Schiller-Theater Werkstatt.

3. In his review Kroll compares SB's *Happy Days* at the Royal Court Theatre with Billie Whitelaw and Andrei Serban's production at the Public/Newman Theatre, New York, with Irene Worth. *Happy Days,* presented by the New York Shakespeare Festival, Joseph Papp, producer, opened 7 June 1979, closed 26 August, directed by Serban, designed by Michael Yeargan. Irene Worth (Winnie), George Voskovec (Willie). Irene Worth (b. 1916), American actress.

4. Barney Rosset was getting divorced; one of the children was called "Beckett."

Ussy
6.7.79

Dear Alan

Thanks for yrs. of June 23.

Billie had difficulty with 1st act, but seems to have mistressed it in course of run. 2nd very good. Last night June 31. Yesterday & today BBC TV recording.[1] Relief to have it over. No more directing for me.

Great peace here. Wd. gladly stay for the duration.

. . . .[2]

Remake of *Eh Joe* laid on for Rick & Billie (BBC) next May. Director Donald McWhinnie. Shall be around if I can. If not no matter.[3]

Godot at National at last coming Fall. No details. Vague talk of Scofield.[4] Young Vic *Endgame* about same time.[5]

. . . .[6]

Can imagine yr. upheaval. All my wishes for many happy years in new home.

Love to you all
Sam

1. *Happy Days*, directed by SB and Tristram Powell, broadcast on BBC 2, 13 October 1979, a film of the Royal Court Theatre production, 7 June.

2. SB will go to Tangier in August.

3. Did not take place.

4. *Waiting for Godot* was not produced at the National Theatre until 1987; Paul Scofield (b. 1922), English actor.

5. Coproduced by the San Quentin Drama Workshop and the Goodman Theater, Chicago, *Endgame* opened at the Young Vic, London, 29 January 1980. Same cast as at Open Space, London, October 1978, except Alan Mandell (Nagg).

6. SB comments on Barney Rosset.

November 13, 1979

Dear Sam,

Just heard via Marty Fehsenfeld about Con, and I hasten to write.[1] Just to let you know that you are always in my thoughts and heart. I believe that I met Con once during an evening with you at the Shakespeare,[2] and I never really knew him in any personal way; but I know how much he meant to you, and you to him. That remains.

Haven't written since arriving in this sunlit wasteland[3] (except for that little postcard with the two shoes). Have been at it night and day: getting used to the new place and ways, teaching and directing a new play with the students (which just opened), and looking for some place to stay when we come back next year—if we decide to come back. It's very pleasant in many ways. Natural beauties of ocean and sky, eucalyptus everywhere, very friendly natives, general relaxation galore, and my morning 30 laps in the swimming pool even though it's November. Outside of that, there's an overall laxity and absence of intellectual stimulation in the social existences of the collective citizenry that both Jean and I are having some difficulty adjusting to. I'm happy enough at the University, where the students, talented and untalented, are immensely eager. But Jean, apart from frantic house-hunting for the future, has very little life or friends of her own.

Actually, I have spent an entire term with the third-year graduate acting students working on your plays. They are very interested and work very hard; and I get pleased once in a while. And their favorite short play is FOOTFALLS. Next term, I shall be teaching a literature course for upper division students dealing entirely with your plays. Looking forward to that. It will be a small class, really a seminar. I've spoken to Ruby up at Davis, and may get her to come down once to talk to us. And I'm hoping to get Martin Esslin to send me some BBC materials.[4]

My major responsibility here is to deal with the graduate directors, of whom there are six. They are a varied but rather impressive group, one of them replete with ten years of experience in the German theatre, and has seen all your productions in Berlin. I enjoy this very much, especially when they evidence progress on one front or another. Am taking one of them along with me to New York in December, when I am supposed to be directing Edward Albee's new play, THE LADY FROM DUBUQUE, which he asked me to direct—ending a ten-year separation. The play is quite beautiful, with the usual ambiguities. It doesn't seem to me to have a chance commercially, but I hope we can do it with some degree of dignity. Irene Worth is playing the lead.

Don't miss New York itself as much as I'd hoped, or Hastings as much as I'd feared. But the absence of decent theatre, French films, and worthwhile conversation is hard to take. On the other hand, I love the weather, the swimming, and the general informality. Jean is less sure, and would rather be closer to the East and particularly to East Hampton, where we consider our home to be, and where most of my books and all of our worldly goods continue to stay.

Hoping to see MERCIER *et* CAMIER in New York when we get back early in December.[5] Have heard varying things. Joe Chaikin doing another ENDGAME,[6] and there's a GODOT playing off-off-Broadway, but I know nothing about it. I'm still hoping that at the right time you'll let me do THEATRE I and II. Haven't heard much from Barney lately, but I gather Grove is holding its own.

The Iranian thing is getting us all down, and I am fearful of various consequences, not only economic ones.[7] The world seems to continue its toboggan slide towards disaster. I hope that I'll make Vienna in April to do a Ruth Draper[8] program there, in which case I'll surely stop off to see you. Will let you know. Take care of yourself. Jean sends her love.

[Alan]

p.s. Mrs Jacob Bronowski here, and says she and her husband knew you in Paris a long time ago.[9]

1. A. J. ("Con") Leventhal (1896–1979), one of SB's oldest friends in Dublin and later Paris.

2. "the Shakespeare": a pub.

3. University of California at La Jolla.

4. Ruby Cohn, Professor of Comparative Drama, University of California at Davis; Martin Esslin, now Professor of Drama at Stanford University.

5. SB novel, written in French in 1945, adapted and directed by Frederick Neumann for Mabou Mines, presented by the New York Shakespeare Festival, opened at the Public Theatre, 25 October 1979. *Mercier and Camier:* Frederick Neumann (Mercier), Bill Raymond (Camier), Terry O'Reilly (Waiter/Officer of Law and Orde), Harvey Spevak (Musician and Quinn), Honora Fergusson (Helen), David Neumann, Chris Neumann (children), David Warrilow (Storyteller and Watt); music by Philip Glass. Reviews: Mel Gussow, *NY Times*, 26 October 1979; William A. Raidy, *Plays and Players*, 1979. *Mercier et Camier*, 1970, trans. by SB, *Mercier and Camier*, 1974.

6. *Endgame* opened at the Manhattan Theatre Club, 1 January 1980, closed 10 February 1980, directed by Joseph Chaikin, designed by Sally Jacobs. Daniel Seltzer (Hamm), Michael Gross (Clov), James Barbosa (Nagg), Joan MacIntosh (Nell).

7. Tension between the U.S. and Iran increased when on 5 November 1979 revolutionaries seized sixty American hostages and held them in the embassy in Tehran.

8. Ruth Draper (1889–1956), American actress, famous monologist.

9. Jacob Bronowski (1908–1974), Polish writer, art historian, government official.

December 22, 1979

Dear Sam,

Hadn't heard from you in such a long time, was wondering if you were OK, or whether I had said or done something to upset you. I gather from several sources, specifically Daniel Labeille that you are about to take off for Morocco; and I just wanted to establish contact before you took off.

Am in East Hampton as of a week ago, ostensibly getting ready to go into rehearsal with a new Albee play, THE LADY FROM DUBUQUE. But almost at the last moment, they have not been able to get all their money, so I am now sitting around and chewing my fingernails. I had already gotten the Univ. of California to extend the time at which I had to be back by two weeks, but now it does not seem as though the play is going on at all. With the cast and staff all hired and sitting around hoping but with very little hope. Including Irene Worth, who so recently was doing HAPPY DAYS at the Public.

In the meantime, I've been unable to make plans for doing much of anything else, just in case we did go into rehearsal at the last minute. Last Wed. started out to see the Warrilow performance of the *Monologue* to discover that it was not playing that night.¹ Expect to go this week one evening. Also to see the new ENDGAME if it goes into previews on time. MERCIER AND CAMIER is not on any more, I believe.²

Danny has been telling you about the TV project next spring (1981). I gather you have given approval for Lee Breuer and myself to direct one of the shorter pieces each, with all rehearsals open to the theatrical community, lots of discussions along the way, and the whole affair to be recorded, process and product, on TV. I have qualms about the whole thing, especially doing everything in front of a group of eager onlookers, but since so many of your good friends are involved, including Ruby and Martin Esslin and Calvin Israel—and you have evidently approved all—I went along with Danny. As you know, I am extremely anxious to direct *Theatre I* and *II* in New York, at the right time and under the right auspices. My California commitment is only 20 weeks, in two 10-week stretches; the rest of the time I am not only free to direct but encouraged by the University to do so. This spring I expect to be in Vienna working on a Ruth Draper program, then to some sort of Conference on training directors in Warsaw. Hope I can somehow find the time and funds to stop over in Paris some time in May. It's been too long that we have not seen each other, and I long for a glimpse of 'le petit Sam'. Will provide ample warning.

Like the outdoor life out West, swim daily and drive past the ocean; but miss the inner turmoil of New York. Everything changing. Barney hardly visible or accessible, everyone somewhere else. Jean and kids reasonably well, luckily. I'm about to sign a contract with a publisher (Viking?) to write a book; whether I'll ever get it written is another matter.³ Jean and family spending Christmas out here. She loves it, and would be content to stay here year round. Can't afford that yet, sorry to say.

Think of you and wish you well, now and always. Just wish we could see each other. Have a good holiday, take care, and just let me know how you are. Best to Suzanne.

[Alan]

1. *A Piece of Monologue,* written in English, 1979, for David Warrilow; the first American production opened at La Mama E.T.C., New York, 18 December 1979, directed by David Warrilow and Rocky Greenberg. David Warrilow (Speaker). Published in *Kenyon Review,* Summer 1979, and *Rockaby and Other Short Pieces,* 1981.

2. Closed 25 November 1979 after thirty-nine performances.

3. *Entrances,* 1986.

Paris
1.1.80

Dear Alan

Many thanks for your letter of Nov. 13.

Forgive my long silence. No excuse. Just going silent.

Glad you're finding La Jolla bearable. I hope it leaves you reasonable time for professional theatre. Good to know you'll be directing Albee's latest. My warm regards to Irene Worth. I'm told she was an excellent Winnie.

. . . .[1]

Perhaps you will have seen David Warrilow at La Mama Annex. Good account of his performance in *N.Y.T.* Gussow.[2]

. . . .[3]

Put a stop to the prose piece *(Company)* after 3 years onning and offing. French translation due soon from Minuit. Am holding on to the original for the moment.[4]

Very absorbed past month in new work. Prose in French. Concocted also a crazy TV piece for Stuttgart.[5] Haven't sent it out either.

Saw Rick on his way through to Porto Rico via London. He was to have played *Krapp* there in the University Theatre but it fell through. He is due to open with it this month in Chicago.[6] No date yet from Tristram Powell for remake of *Eh Joe* (BBC) with Billie Whitelaw & Rick. Probably May or June. McWhinnie directing.[7]

Last season for Barrault Company at Théâtre d'Orsay. They now move to the Palais de Glace, Champs Elysées. Madeleine opens their season there with *Happy Days.*[8] Haven't seen them for a long time.

. . . .[9]

You know how dubious I am about the 2 *Fragments.* I gave very hesitating permission to Walter Asmus to direct them in German. That was last May at the Thalia Theatre in Hamburg.[10] Since when I haven't heard from him! To you I wd. like to suggest the following: that you investigate them with your students at UCSD Theatre and then if you really feel they are worth it on from there. Strictly only if! For me they are abortions. But I suppose what is not? More or less.

Fond wishes to you all for the ton of bricks now upon us. Look forward keenly to seeing you again in April after so long.

Love to all.
Sam

Not sure where you are I send this to old address.

1. SB has not heard from Barney Rosset.

2. Premiere production of *A Piece of Monologue* opened 18 December 1979, directed by Warrilow and Rocky Greenberg; Mel Gussow (b. 1933), American drama critic, review appeared in *NY Times,* 19 December 1979; *Conversations with (and about) Beckett,* 1996.

3. SB refers to A. J. (Con) Leventhal's last illness; he and Suzanne did not go to Tangier this year.

4. *Company,* 1979; *Compagnie,* 1980.

5. "Prose in French": *Mal vu mal dit;* "crazy TV piece": *Quad,* "Ballet for four people."

6. Cluchey's production entitled *"Beckett Directs Beckett: Krapp's Last Tape* by Samuel Beckett who directed, with Rick Cluchey," opened at the Goodman Studio Theater, Chicago, in repertory, 10 January–3 February 1980, designed by Richard Riddell, lighting by Bud Thorpe. Rick Cluchey (Krapp). Reviews: Glenna Syse, "The flawless beat of Beckett's distant drummer," *Chicago Sun-Times,* 11 January 1980; Linda Winer, "'Krapp's Last Tape' records futile realities of life, death," *Chicago-Tribune,* 11 January; Valerie Scher, "From South Side to San Quentin to Samuel Beckett," *Chicago Sun-Times,* 17 January; Barbara Brotman, "Cluchey: Beckett's Alter ego, From sheets to the stage," *Chicago-Tribune,* 24 January.

7. Did not take place.

8. *Oh les beaux jours* was not performed at the Palais de Glace in 1980, but opened with Madeleine Renaud 19 May 1981 at the Théâtre Rond-Point, Petite salle, to which the company moved.

9. SB had an evening with Ruby Cohn at Christmas time.

10. Asmus directed *Fragments I & II* at the Thalia Theatre, Hamburg, in May 1979. Ralph Schermuly (A), Ulrich Kuhlmann (B).

2.1.80

Yours of Dec. 22 just received.

I know nothing of the TV project you describe. Who is Danny & to whom can I have given permission?[1] It has always been my intention, if I decided to release these *Fragments,* to offer them to you. If what you will have read above holds, you may tell all concerned that I am opposed to this TV project and cannot okay it without proof that I have unwittingly done so in a moment of more than usual senility. When I last saw Ruby it must have been clear to her that I had come to no decision in the matter.

So sorry your Albee jeopardized.

Perhaps Danny is Labeille. If I see him as seems probable I'll dot the i's.

Love again.
Sam

1. In any event Daniel Labeille could not get financial support for his TV project.

Paris
5.1.80

Dear Alan

I hope you will have received my letter of a few days ago in spite of its having been sent to Scenic Drive for want of your present address in Hastings given me today by Daniel Labeille. As a result of my conversation with him the position is now quite clear. They may use any stage material of mine for their TV project *except the 2 Fragments*. These are therefore yours alone if you want them and are not opposed to the suggestion made in my last letter. Namely that you should first investigate them with your students in San Diego and embark on a professional production only if as a result you are fully satisfied they are worth it. Which as you know I greatly doubt.

Daniel was most understanding and I am relieved the misunderstanding is now removed.

Good news that the Albee is under way at last.[1]

All best, dear Alan, & love to you all
Sam

1. *The Lady from Dubuque.*

April 20, 1980

Dear Sam,

Much too long since the last time (not counting the card) and many apologies.[1] Winter and now the beginning of spring have rushed by, with a new life and environment to cope with, floods rampant and earthquakes imminent (a couple came tiptoeing in, without noticeable damage). Somehow managed to get through the year. We've bought a rather nice small house set on a mountainside overlooking a lake that resembles Como, and are quite pleased about that. If one is living in California, the scenery should at least be Californean; and this is, actually more like Italy or Switzerland. Jean is quite happy here, at least for six months at a time; though now longing for the simple joys of East Hampton, to which we shall soon be more or less returning.

I say more or less because actually I have just discovered that I'm going to Warsaw for some sort of conference on the training of young directors. I shall be there May 13–17, and was hoping that I could stop in Paris for a day or two on the way back to see you. I'll be leaving Warsaw on the morning of Saturday, May 17, and arriving in Paris midday. Unless you will be in Ussy, perhaps we could have dinner that evening, or on Sunday. If you could let me know if you are free, I'll make plans accordingly. . . .[2] Would really love to see you, as we haven't talked in such a long time.

Plans for the rest of the summer remain, as always confused. I may or may not be directing *Loose Ends,* the play I did in New York last year, in Los Angeles. *Loose Ends* was supposed to be done in London at the Hampstead Theatre Club, but they could not raise the money. I may or may not be going to Vienna to do a Ruth Draper program there. I may or may not be rehearsing a new play for New York. All I know is that I'd rather be sitting on the beach in East Hampton working on the book I am finally writing, contract with Viking Press and all, a book that is supposed to retrace my meanderings through the American theatre. Have been working on it fairly steadily for a while. Hard work.

Have heard from several sources that COMPAGNIE is lovely, and am looking forward to the English version. Am also hoping that you'll write another play for me to direct. I gather that you have just done something or will be doing something in Stuttgart.

Jean and the kids are fine, and send their love. Vicki is in L.A. working in the admissions office of some college there. David is finishing his junior year at Yale, in geophysics, whatever that is. . . .[3]

Hear via Ruby and Dan Labeille that you are in good shape. Trust that such is true, and I am longing to find out for myself. Do let me hear from you whether the timing will suit you. In the meantime, all the best.

[Alan]

1. In a postcard dated 20 April 1980, SB thanks AS for the usual birthday card.
2. AS explains that he will be "moving around," gives two addresses to which SB may write, one in Hastings-on-Hudson, the other in Warsaw.
3. Brief personal comment about David Schneider.

28.4.80

Dear Alan

Yours of April 20 just.

This in haste to say alas I can't be in Paris at the time you indicate. I shall be in London from May 7 to 23, working on *Endgame* with Rick & Co. before they bring it, & *Krapp,* to Abbey Peacock for 10 perform-ances.[1] Could you not stop off in London instead? I'll be staying at the Hyde Park Hotel, tel. 235 2000. Am writing to same effect to yr. Warsaw address in case this doesn't reach you before you leave.

Love to you all.
Sam

1. The San Quentin Drama Workshop presented by the Goodman Theater of Chicago opened with both plays at the Peacock Theatre, Dublin, 26 May, and ran until 7 June 1980. Directed by SB at the Riverside Studios, London, 7–22 May, assistant director Gregory Mosher, costume and sound Teresita Garcia Suro, lighting Bud Thorpe. *Krapp's Last Tape:* Rick Cluchey (Krapp). *Endgame:* Rick Cluchey (Hamm), Bud Thorpe (Clov), Alan Man-dell (Nagg), Teresita Garcia Suro (Nell).

May 29, 1980

Dear Sam,

Back home, and finally crawling out of bed, where I've been almost from the moment of landing with a bad chest cold. Much better now.

Really enjoyed seeing you in London and watching those rehearsals. Assume the show has opened in Dublin and doing well. And I expect to see them either at the Goodman or when they get to the West Coast. But good to see you actually at work, and with Rick—whom I had not seen for some years.[1]

Hope you will be getting somewhat of a holiday now. Actually, I thought you looked good, not as tired as last time. But I know how much the work takes out of you.

Came back to find Ruby's new book waiting for me.[2] Haven't gone through it all yet, but seemed in her usual good form. I assume you'll be seeing her this summer in Paris.

Appreciate your willingness to let me work a bit on *Theatre I* (and perhaps *II*) with the students next fall. I'll have a go with them when I get back. I'm sure they will be most excited, and I have a couple who might be reasonably well cast. In any case, will keep you posted. Sorry, but that other letter is probably batting around somewhere between coasts.

Telephone call from Danny Labeille. They didn't get all the money for the TV project next spring yet, but he is still optimistic that something can be done.

I rang Tom Bishop during my all-too-brief stay in Paris. Spoke with Helen. I gather he's cooking up something for next year also.

Am sending you that Yeats notebook from here. Sorry that I didn't have sense enough to bring it along. But after batting it back and forth, and wondering how you'd respond, I settled on the NY photo book.[3] Trust the mails will allow it eventually to arrive.

My Editor just rang me to tell me that he read the few pages I left with him the other day, and approves. Have decided that writing is much harder than directing, and wonder whether I'll last the course. But will try.

Good to have gotten a glimpse this time, and now I can look forward to the next. Take care of yourself. And I'll keep you posted. Best to Suzanne. Jean sends hers along too. She's glad to have me in one place for a change.

[Alan]

1. On his way back from Poland in May, AS saw SB rehearsing the San Quentin Drama Workshop at the Riverside Studios, London.
2. *Just Play: Beckett's Theater*, 1980.
3. "Yeats notebook": perhaps *Memoirs*, 1972; "NY photo book": unidentified.

Paris
20.6.80

Dear Alan

Thanks for yrs. of May 29. Also for Yeats book which looks of great interest.

So glad you were able to stop off in London. May it not be too long before we meet again.

Relieved to have cleared up *Theatre Fragments* situation. Hope to have a short piece soon for Danny Labeille's project.[1] Shall send you a copy at same time.

Off next week to Aosta Valley for a few weeks . . .

Not much news from Dublin, but it seems to have gone well.[2]

Love to you & Jean
Sam

1. *Rockaby,* written in English, 1981, 1982. Labeille wanted to have it included in the celebrations for SB's seventy-fifth birthday at the State University of New York at Buffalo, which had commissioned the work.

2. SB refers to Cluchey's production of *Krapp's Last Tape* and *Endgame* at the Peacock Theatre.

August 21, 1980

Dear Sam,

Worthwhile? It's super. And I'm thrilled at the thought that you would like Irene and myself to do it for Danny's do next spring.[1] Danny just sent me the script, which arrived the same morning I tracked down Irene in California, where she was on a brief holiday. She and Danny had dinner a night ago and talked over the project. I was supposed to be with them, but unfortunately have had a bout of some intestinal something which laid me up. However, I had an idea which they seemed to like, and I hope you might too. Danny was concerned that *Rockaby,* being relatively short, needed something else to fill up an evening for the performances in Buffalo. I suggested the idea of Irene doing *Footfalls,* and recording her mother's voice. I think we could work out the timing problem even though the Mother was on tape. Irene and Danny both thought that *Rockaby* and *Footfalls* would make a terrific evening. Would appreciate your thoughts on that subject.

Oh, yes, Barney also involved in conversations. Danny and he had lunch, and Barney told him he plans to publish *Rockaby* in conjunction with its stage premiere. Assume you and he will be discussing this.

All this was a most welcome surprise, since I knew nothing until Danny told me you had written a new piece. Stan Gontarski also keeps telling me that you are writing something for him in Ohio next spring. We're just not letting you alone.

I think *Rockaby* is lovely; very musical, and quite different from the other short plays you've written in the past few years. I look forward to working on it with Irene—and with whatever lighting man we can rustle up. Haven't really had time to study it, so won't say anything now except that I am delighted. Thanks, Sam.

The summer has gone, and not sure where. Apart from swimming a lot, and trying to write a few chapters on my so-called memoirs, I've had the usual constipated time trying to get a Broadway show on. We're supposed to go into rehearsal in a couple of weeks, then try-out in Houston, Texas, then if it goes all right to open in New York in December, when my teaching chores in California will be over. So, as usual, I'll be in two places at the same time for a while. Although if I don't get better fast, I'll not be able to go into rehearsal.

Trust you have had a decent summer, not too interspersed with visiting Americans and other nationalities. When are you going to Düsseldorf? Ruby is the source of all news about your doings and whereabouts, but she's not always easy to get hold of.

Jean fine, and enjoying East Hampton. Viveca working away in California and, apart from her man-less state, enjoying it. David starts on his last year at Yale. Geo-physics, whatever that is. He's awfully serious.

Rather looking forward to San Diego and some sort of order for a while, after the disorder of getting a show together here. We shall see. I'll keep in touch.

Best,
[Alan]

1. May refer to a missing letter (see JK, 663); "it": *Rockaby.*

Ussy
5.9.80

Dear Alan

Thanks for yrs. of Aug. 21. So glad you like *R*.[1]

I feel dubious about *Footfalls* as companion piece, especially with recorded voice as you suggest, because 1) Tiresome duplication of same device, 2) Problem of 2 voices in *F.* 3) Extreme difficulty of coordinating inflexible recording with steps. I don't want to upset your plans but wd. much prefer one of the *Fragments* if *R*. alone is not enough. I had no idea that a full evening was required.

I go to Stuttgart (not Düsseldorf) for prelim. talks late April or May & again in June for the shooting.

I have not promised anything to Gontarski, except that I wd. do my best.[2] Which in vain so far. I feel drained as dry as an old herring bone . . . .[3]

I fear my last letter to you went astray, addressed half to L.L. & half to Hampton.

Affectionately to you all.
Sam

1. "*R*": *Rockaby*.
2. Stanley E. Gontarski (b. 1942), American academic, founder of the SB *Newsletter*, 1978, now editor of the *Journal of Beckett Studies* (founded 1992), Florida State University, Tallahassee; planned celebration of SB's seventy-fifth birthday at Ohio State University. Gontarski, *The Intent of Undoing in Samuel Beckett's Dramatic Texts*, 1985; ed. *On Beckett: Essays and Criticism*, 1986, and *The Beckett Studies Reader*, 1993.
3. SB reflects on his "mental weariness."

Ussy
14.9.80

Dear Alan

Have heard from Irene, pleased with the piece. Intends to make it funny. I hope she doesn't succeed.

I have the feeling you made light, in your last letter, of your health problem. Do tell me how you are. All my fond wishes for rapid & complete recovery.

Love to you both.
Sam

San Diego: Department of Drama
UCSD Theatre
La Jolla, California 92093
October 2, 1980

Dear Sam,

Your second (first) card just arrived, and I hasten to answer both. Actually, between dealing with some kind of intestinal disorder which started at the end of the summer, and coping with the beginning of the academic year, I have not been in as close touch with either Irene or Dan as I might have been. I knew nothing of her letter or comments to you about ROCKABY.

Have spoken with Dan several times since receiving your letters. He and I are both determined to do only what pleases you in terms of this project. I thought he had explained to you that he was trying for an entire evening, though the composition of the evening, apart from ROCKABY, had not yet been determined. Agree with you about the FOOTFALLS problem; we'll forget about that alternative. Irene had ideas about repeating some of the musical pieces she had done with Earl Kim[1] at Harvard a year or so ago, or perhaps reading some of your verse. We didn't like either idea. We thought of ENOUGH,[2] and have asked Irene to read it. What would you think of that as a companion to ROCKABY? You suggested one of the *Fragments*. Problem there is getting two additional actors and diluting Irene's solo presence, or at least dominant presence.

I'd just as soon just do ROCKABY alone, but evidently since the State University people need to play it four nights, charging admission, they feel it is too short by itself. I suggested some sort of discussion afterward (which they'll probably have anyhow) could be extended a bit.

Anyhow, we are eager for your thoughts.

I gather from Danny and from Irene herself that she is very eager and enthusiastic. Her agent, of course, keeps putting up road blocks of various more-commercial opportunities. In the end, all will be settled.

Spoke with Ruby last week, who brought me up to date a bit about you. She seems in fine spirits.

Barney finally sent me a copy of GODOT, 59th printing, which had corrected the original typo on the second half of page 33, in which Vladimir said "Word words". I remember Herb Blau many years ago explaining it to me. I'd been trying to get Grove to have it changed for almost 20 years. Now it has, and I feel a personal sense of accomplishment. Hope you don't mind.

About my physical state. I'm OK . . . .[3] I'm waiting a while until I have a little time to myself, probably December, just before I get back to New York for a month to do GODOT for The Acting Company, Juilliard graduates who tour the country in repertory. Please don't worry about me, feel fine, swim daily, and enjoy my teaching out here. Jean also fine, gardening like mad.

Have written to Rick, not a peep in return. Hope to see them when they get to West Coast. Alan M.[4] will tell me. Trust you are well. Sorry to disturb you about the ROCKABY venture. Do let me know exactly how you feel about it all.

[Alan]

1. Earl Kim (b. 1920), professor and composer, wrote *Earthlight* to a pastiche text by SB.

2. *Enough,* SB short story written in French, 1965, published as *Assez,* 1966; *Enough,* 1967.

3. AS has had an "intestinal virus."

4. Rick Cluchey's San Quentin Drama Workshop was touring with *Krapp* and *Endgame;* Alan Mandell (Nagg), actor, business manager for the Blau/Irving San Francisco Actor's Workshop, 1956–1965.

Ussy
20.11.80

Dear Alan

Thanks for your reassuring letter of Oct 2 & please forgive tardy reply . . . .[1]

I heard from Danny & replied I had no further thoughts for second part of programme but nothing against *Enough*. He spoke of a "dramatic reading". I don't know what that is. Finally I leave it to you, Danny & Irene. Whatever you decide will be okay with me.
. . . .[2]

Brief retreat here ends this week. Have advanced towards its overdue end a short piece in French. Mere prose. Shall now try yet again to concoct something for Stan's do in May. Scant hope.
. . . .[3]

Stuttgart late Spring for a crazy TV piece. My last on stage or set. Have decided I can't take on *Godot* with San Quentin outfit & must now write sadly to Rick to that effect. No news from them since they left London. Martha saw their cramped *Endgame* at the Goodman.[4]

Much love to you both.
Sam

1. SB hopes AS is recovering.
2. SB will meet Herbert Mitgang.
3. Barney Rosset is getting married to Elizabeth (Lisa) Krug.
4. "Beckett Directs Beckett: *Krapp's Last Tape/Endgame*," opened at Goodman Studio Theater, Chicago, 25 September 1980, ran until 19 October 1980; directed by SB, assisted by Gregory Mosher. Same casts as in London and Dublin. Reviews: Richard Christiansen, "Beckett's vision of death full of life," *Chicago Tribune*, 26 September 1980; Glenna Syse, "Goodman's two Beckett plays compelling and complex," *Chicago Sun-Times*, 26 September 1980.

November 28, 1980

Dear Sam,

Not sure whether you are in Paris or in Germany, but decided to write anyhow before taking off for a month in New York, where I shall be directing GODOT for The Acting Company (that's the touring group of young actors, mostly from Juilliard, with which I have been associated). I'll be there until we open the tour on January 4, at Dartmouth College. Then back for another ten weeks here until East again for ROCKABY.

Haven't heard from you since my letter at the beginning of this month.[1] Though I have heard from various people, including Dan Labeille, Ruby, and Tom Bishop.

Dan tells me you have OK'd the idea of Irene reading ENOUGH with ROCKABY. I think it will make an interesting program, and that she will be very fine. I know you had an idea about Rick doing KRAPP or ENDGAME; but that would have made the evening something quite different even if it were financially feasible, which I gather from Labeille it wasn't. This way, we have an evening of one actress, very concentrated and unified. I am going to meet the technical people from Buffalo while I shall be in NYC, and will go into some detail with them. Then, if it is OK with you, I am hoping somehow to get to Paris for a few days in mid-March just to sit down with you and get some of your ideas about how you'd like it done. Not sure about that yet, but am trying to arrange schedule, finances, etc. Will keep you posted.

I did get to L.A. last week to see Rick's last performance. It was filled to capacity. I had not ever seen him except in that rehearsal session in London last May. The audience really liked his Krapp, and so did I. The ENDGAME seemed to me somewhat uneven, and I missed Alan Mandell as Nagg. But, again, the response was enthusiastic, and I understand the reviews were favorable.[2] Rick was very involved after the performance, but I did manage to get a few words in backstage. Not clear what happens to the tour now. I believe they are taking a bit of a well-earned holiday.

As per your permission, I did get to work a little on *Theatre I,* and the students found it very challenging. Can't say that anything we did was ready for a public, but at least I got to know the text somewhat better. Would like to continue next term, either with the same students or with two of the faculty members who are actors. One of them has been touring KRAPP around the California colleges for some years now, and does very well. There is great interest all round.

Received invitation from Stan Gontarski to do something in Ohio in May. He's not sure what. I'll try to be there. Harold Pinter wants me to direct HOTHOUSE off-Broadway in the spring, and I have accepted. Will know more about plans when I speak with the producer in NY.

Hope you are well. Worried a little when I didn't hear from you, but everyone reassures me as to your state of being.

Jean sends her love. I'll write again from New York.

[Alan]

1. Missing.
2. They opened at Schoenberg Hall, U.C.L.A., 17 November 1980, for three performances. Same cast as in letter of 28 April 1980, n. 1, except Alan Mandell (Nagg) replaced by John L. Jenkins. Review: Dan Sullivan, "Beckett: His Minus Is A Plus," *LA Times,* 19 November 1980.

3.12.80

Dear Alan

Thanks for yours of Nov. 28.

I thought I had answered your previous letter. Forgive me if I didn't.

Dan Labeille speaks of a "dramatic reading" of *Enough.* I don't know what that means.

I have not heard from Rick since they left England. The second-string Nagg is not good. They want me to do *Godot* with them, but I can't. My directing days are over. It grieves me to disappoint them.

I don't go to Stuttgart till April for a few days to set the thing up. Then back in June to do it. Very tricky little piece.

Good news that you may be over in March.

Have nearly finished the latest lucubration. In French. Mere prose. Next job translate it.[1]

We keep fairly well. Perhaps Tangiers again in Janvier.

Have offered enclosed playlet to Gontarski for his May days.[2] For you too of course if you deem it worthwhile.

Love to you both
Sam

1. "mere prose": *Mal vu mal dit.*
2. *Ohio Impromptu.*

December 23, 1980

Dear Sam,

Just received your letter addressed to Rimini Road in Del Mar, California! Thanks for trying to reach me, elusive and unplaceable as I seem to have become. Actually, forget about Rimini. That was a rented place, no longer in any way connected. I now have two addresses: . . . .[1]

At the moment, I am ensconced in a temporary pad in Hastings-on-Hudson while I rehearse the Acting Company's touring version of GODOT, which opens at Dartmouth College on January 5, and tours hither and yon all the way through '81, we hope. The kids are young, mostly Juilliard graduates, but talented and most willing. The problem, as always, is the amount of time for rehearsal; but I am trying. Will send you some pictures and reviews as they come out.

Spent some time this month with Danny Labeille and his various cohorts, and hope to get a session in with Irene since she has just opened in her BORKMAN.[2] She has been very well received. Danny is planning a trip to Paris very soon, and I will supply him with a few specific questions about ROCKABY, though I am also hoping to come see you in Feb. or March before embarking on rehearsals. Mostly about rhythm of rocking chair in relation to lines; and some things about the lighting.

Saw Stan Gontarski two days ago, and he gave me IMPROMPTU, which I liked more than much. I think my spring working out so that I can direct it. And we are going to talk with David Warrilow about doing it, subject to your liking the idea. We will need a look-alike of sorts. I haven't read it enough to ask any questions yet, but will. In meantime, I'm delighted that you wrote it, and that it will be done. I was going to do Pinter's HOTHOUSE off-Broadway, but Harold, after asking me, has evidently decided on some other director. No reason given. I shall be doing Wilder's OUR TOWN at the Guthrie in the summer; and then, perhaps, a new Bob Anderson play. In the meantime, I shall be back in California with my students.

I do hope to see you for a few hours in the early spring, and will let you know the moment my application for a grant to do so gets a response. I gather from everyone who has seen you, especially Tom Bishop, that you are OK, not going to North Africa any time soon, and are busy working. Good.

We have had a family reunion this Christmas, full of both joys and sadnesses. My son, David, is about to graduate Yale and is very happy as a geo-physicist, whatever that is. May be at Berkeley graduate school next year. My daughter, Viveca, is rattling around Los Angeles, one job after another and not very sure what she wants to do or be, or where. Jean, happily, is much better. Has lost some weight and looks terrific. We are all a bit at loose ends with our various geographical dispositions, but trying to find our way through the confusions. I miss the house in Hastings, Jean is relieved to be rid of it. My fistula situation both better and worse; I shall certainly have to have an operation but am trying to hold it off. Not serious.

Wish you all that is possible, and think of you always.

[Alan]

1. One in Escondido, in the San Diego valley, California, the other in East Hampton, New York.

2. *John Gabriel Borkman* by Ibsen (1828–1906) opened at Circle in the Square, New York, 18 December 1980.

11.1.81

Dear Alan

Thanks for yrs. of Dec. 23.

Had a long talk with Danny this morning & hope I answered questions to your satisfaction. Won't go back over it here. But do hope you can get over in the Spring. I'll be in Stuttgart from April 12 for a few days. Otherwise almost certainly in Paris or Ussy.

Glad you liked Ohio piece. David would be fine. Table shd. be slightly tilted.

Have been working. Finishing a French text, about *Company* length, then English translation, infernal job.[1]

. . . .[2]

Have had to break the news to Rick that I'm through with directing.[3] I couldn't face another *Godot*. He has been having a tough time with one thing & other including family. Hard to have to add this disappointment.

Much love to you all
Sam

1. "French text": *Mal vu mal dit*, 1981; trans. by SB, *Ill Seen Ill Said*, in *The New Yorker*, 5 October 1981, 48–58.
2. SB may go to Morocco, glad to hear that AS is well.
3. Cluchey wanted SB to direct *Waiting for Godot* for his San Quentin Drama Workshop's proposed tour of Australia.

February 15, 1981

Dear Sam

What a week! Walked into Irene Worth's dressing room one week ago Friday to be greeted by her announcement that she couldn't do the play in Buffalo. She's gotten an offer to do a film, needed the money, etc. Couldn't we postpone? I rang Danny immediately to let him know and to suggest trying to get Billie. Was sure you would approve.

As it turned out and via various transatlantic phone calls, Billie has now accepted, and Danny just rang to let me know that it seemed definite. I was waiting to let you know.

Can't tell you how delighted I am finally to be meeting Billie and working with her. Won't go entirely into detail, but basic plans thus: Will be flying to Paris to see you as of Monday, March 23—assuming you will be there—for couple of days, then to London, to start rehearsals with Billie on March 27 through April 3. On April 4, we all fly (including Danny, who will be in London with us) to Buffalo, where we will do final rehearsals, opening April 8 as planned. Will do recording at BBC.[1] If it turns out to be possible for you to spend any time at all with us at rehearsals in London, so much the better. Will await your word on this. We'll have rocker made in Buffalo, may get wig and dress either in London or Buffalo as things seem to allow us. I am most pleased by all this; and although have not yet spoken to Billie, I know she will be most amenable to whatever arrangements and ideas. She has already said that she will learn all of ENOUGH by heart, so that will give us more flexibility as to how to do it. And when I'm with you in Paris, we can talk about everything in copious detail.

That also includes OHIO IMPROMPTU. I saw David Warrilow in New York also, on Saturday week; and he will be doing it in Columbus. Only question yet unsettled at moment is who will do other role. David suggests Tom Bishop, a look-alike of sorts but not an actor. The two actors who really look exactly like David (i.e. Ellis Rabb and Sydney Walker) are not available.[2] I'm not sure about Tom but will see him this weekend when I go back to New York, this time to audition students for out here next year. Seem to be commuting across the continent. But we can talk about this one as well. I do hope this time will prove convenient for you. Longing to see you and talk.

I hope to be staying at the Hotel de la Paix as L'Aiglon has gotten too expensive. Will get travel agent here to book me. Expect to get in morning of March 24. Perhaps we could meet that evening. Let me know if that is OK with you. I'll be in California until March 13, then back to East Hampton.

Saw Barney and Ed de Grazia in New York also (it was a busy time!). Ed is involved with some sort of opera version of NOT I. Not very clear from the tape we heard.[3] Saw Lee Breuer at some theatre Conference recently. He's to bring COME AND GO and LOST ONES to Paris in autumn.[4]

Everything else OK although life a bit hectic. We enjoy our Italian lake in California but miss New York and Hastings house. Vicki leaving L.A. to work in a school in New York, and David graduating from Yale end of May, and then off to work the summer in Denver; he's a geo-physicist, whatever that is. Then maybe to graduate school. Jean well, and I'm fully recovered. Excited about the two new pieces,[5] and about working with Billie after all these years. Take care of yourself. Let me hear if dates suit you.

[Alan]

1. Whitelaw replaced Worth as (W) in *Rockaby*, play opened as planned; her voice recording (V) done at BBC. She also gave a reading of *Enough* (see letter of 2 October 1980, n. 2).

2. *Ohio Impromptu* requires two male actors as similar in appearance as possible. Ellis Rabb (b. 1930), founder and artistic director, Association of Producing Artists Repertory Company, 1960; Sydney Walker (b. 1921), actor.

3. Ed de Grazia (b. 1927), lawyer, experimental playwright, general counsel to Grove Press; "opera version": the Theater Chamber Players gave two performances of the opera version of *Not I*, a monodrama for soprano and tape, composed by Heinz Holliger, at the Kennedy Center, Washington, D.C., 31 May and 1 June 1981. Phyllis Bryn-Julson sang the main part. AS advised, produced by Dina Koston, directed by James Herbert.

4. For the Festival d'Automne, Paris, in October organized by Tom Bishop and Michel Guy.

5. "two new pieces": *Rockaby* and *Ohio Impromptu*.

Paris
24.2.81

Dear Alan

Yours of Feb. 15 today.

. . . .[1]

I would not go to London.

Billie asked me to call her and give her an idea of how I felt the text should be spoken. This I have done and am to call her again next Sunday. Hope you don't mind this encroachment.

I doubt if she'll be able to get *Lessness* by heart.

With identical black greatcoats and long white hair the likeness should not be too difficult to achieve.[2]

Looking forward greatly to our evening together.

Love to you all.

Sam

1. SB will meet AS at the Hôtel de la Paix on March 24.

2. SB apparently is confusing *Lessness (Sans)*, another prose piece, with *Enough*. The "likenesses" refer to the two characters in *Ohio Impromptu*.

April [18], 1981

[Dear Sam,]

Finally back home and to a typewriter, and hastening to tell you of the experience these past weeks with *Rockaby* and Billie. You have probably heard already from a variety of people. I can only say that it has been one of the most satisfying periods of rehearsal I've ever had. And getting to work with and know Billie a little has been beyond words, at least my words. She is the rarest and most generous of persons, devoted entirely to you, a consummate craftsman, patient, warm, and a delight to be around. To my last day, I shall treasure each moment we spent together. And the memory of Billie, sitting in that rocker during rehearsals putting her thumbs up in the air in answer to my question: Are you all right, Billie? is something that will always be with me. I'm only sorry that I won't be rehearsing with her tomorrow. And I quite understand how close the two of you have become.

The production came off well. Not only have the reviews been favorable—trust you have received the ones so far published—but the general audience response has been excellent. They have sat fascinated and mesmerized during *Rockaby*. The contrast with *Enough* is a good one.[1] The tape Billie made in London is superb, a real piece of music. The costume and the wig were, in our opinion, fine—we sent you some photos from Buffalo. The rocker worked beautifully, although we had to work on it each day to make sure that it did. (Believe it or not but Billie's actual weight and balance would affect the operator's control.) And the lighting, on which we had to work a great many hours, turned out very well. The whole thing ran just under 15 minutes; and, of course, timing varied only a few seconds from performance to performance depending on Billie's reactions. How true and right your instincts and demands were on this one. And I'm only sorry that you were not able to see a rehearsal.

As you know, we rehearsed in Billie's home, just about three hours daily when she didn't have a matinee. We started off with the tape, trying to get it just the way you had sounded the words to her. After about three days, we made a tape in a studio in Soho, very technically competent place but with various thumping noises which came from street digging somewhere. Billie was remarkably patient, never lost her patience with the problem, and somehow managed to work around the noises. We made various takes, worked all day, and edited another day while she had her matinee. The quality and rhythm is excellent, and Danny will send you a copy as soon as possible. We then worked on the rocker, though the rehearsal rocker we had was not very easy to manipulate, and Billie would get a bit dizzy if we worked too long, so we didn't, and waited until Buffalo. In between, we worked on *Enough* whenever we could. We had a period table with a podium, and Billie, very informally would either stand behind it, or move about the table, sometimes sitting on it. She looked fine, herself, and the contrast of light and dark (in *Rockaby*) was a good one for the audience.

We all flew over together, Billie quite comfortable in First Class. She wouldn't sleep, as we urged her, but worked on *Enough*. Then Buffalo, and four long hard days of technicals, trying to spare her energies as much as possible. Naturally, as always, the technical problems—lights, tape source, rocker, getting Billie out in the dark, etc.—were dealt with one by one. We opened on Wed. playing through last Saturday, then on to New York and La Mama to repeat. La Mama less equipped than Buffalo, but we brought everything with us, and had everything set up within one day for Billie to come in at 3 the day we opened (on Monday, your birthday). Played Monday, Tuesday, Wednesday, off on Thurs., and once more set up at the College in Westchester for tonight.[2] I left for East Hampton immediately after performance. Tired, a bad cold but feel fine, exhilarated, mad about Billie. Dan has been most helpful and hard-worked through it all. Saw great deal of Ruby, Martin E., Marty in Buffalo. You've probably heard from them all. Thank you, thank you, Sam, for the opportunity of doing this one, with Billie. You were with us all the time. And thank you for *Rockaby*.

My touring *Godot* opens in rep with two other Acting Company shows next week,[3] and then on to *Ohio Impromptu* for its May 9 performance. Saw David Warrilow, who is very ill with some sort of intestinal disorder and found another actor who looks much like him (Rand Mitchell) and whom I know. Next week, I'll go after the wigs and the coats. And will keep you posted on our rehearsals when we get going.

Barney brought up a few copies of the book, and I assume he has sent you some. He seemed quite pleased over the proceedings. Tom Bishop trying to get Billie to agree to come to Paris, but she doesn't yet know her RSC[4] schedule. I shall continue to be in touch with her.

Trust you are OK. And that Stuttgart goes well. Take care of yourself. Jean adds her love. My typing is worse than normally. Please forgive.

[Alan]

P S Filming also went well, & Billie got quite used to it as we went along.[5] [handwritten]

1. *Rockaby* and *Enough* opened at the Center for Theatre Research, State University of New York at Buffalo, 8 April 1981. Review: *Buffalo Evening News*, 9 April 1981.

2. After the Buffalo opening, 8 April, the plays opened at La Mama, E.T.C., New York, 13 April, and State University of New York at Purchase campus, Westchester County, 16 April 1981. Reviews: *NY Daily News*, 15 April 1981; *NY Post*, 16 April; *NY Herald-Tribune*, 18–19 April; Robert Brustein, *New Republic*, 9 May.

3. Opened at The Acting Company, Public Theatre, New York, 22 April 1981, directed by AS. Richard S. Iglewski (Estragon), Richard Howard (Vladimir), Paul Walker (Lucky), Keith David (Pozzo), Johann Carlo (A Boy). The other plays were Carlo Goldoni's *Il Campiello: A Venetian Comedy* and Shakespeare's *A Midsummer Night's Dream*.

4. "RSC": Royal Shakespeare Company.

5. Refers to AS's *Rockaby Documentary*, TV film of his 1981 rehearsals with Billie Whitelaw at her home in Camden Square, with the Buffalo opening as "the climax to his film," produced by Daniel Labeille, Donn A. Pennebaker, and his wife, Chris Hegedus. See also *Billie Whitelaw . . . Who He?*, 1995, chapter 7, "Rockaby," for Whitelaw's account.

Paris
22.4.81

Dear Alan

Thanks for your telegram from London, your kind birthday card and your letter of April 18.

I have not seen the press.

I called Billie last Sunday, just after her return. She was very pleased & grateful to you all for your solicitude.

Enthusiastic account from Ruby. Others from other quarters all favourable.

Thank you again, dear Alan, for the excellent & meticulous job. I realise how difficult technically it must have been, especially with so little time and the different stage conditions. Have a proper rest now before the Ohio headache. To Dan also congratulations & thanks.

The few days in Stuttgart were not very satisfactory. I'm quite lost in TV technicalities & shall never write again for that medium.

Returned to Paris to an avalanche of mail from which I am only beginning to emerge, far from unscathed.

My only desire for weeks to come is to sit quiet contemplating my old friend, empty space . . .

I'm wondering how, in the *Impromptu*, to make the book visually effective. So far can only see the largish format & black binding & hear the faint thud of its being closed at the end.

Much love to you both.
Sam

May 16, 1981

Dear Sam,

Forgive the week's delay in telling you about how OHIO IM-
PROMPTU went in Columbus. We did it last Saturday,[1] I took the plane
to New York for our first family reunion in almost a year, then went off
on Sunday to Minneapolis where I am now in rehearsal with Thornton
Wilder's OUR TOWN.[2] Living in a motel room there, sans typewriter,
learning the names of my actors and getting used to a play with a cast
of over 25.

I think the play went very well. Audience response was excellent,
even from those who had not read the text beforehand. Ruby seemed to
like it, and Jim Knowlson,[3] and John Calder. Barney, unfortunately,
could not come at the last minute. The visual image was very strong.
The two men completely alike in the coats and wigs (which I was,
luckily, able to have made without charge by the best wig-maker in
New York.) There are some laughs, not entirely expected by me, related
to L's knocking, wanting R to go back in his reading.[4] I am not aware of
any reviews, but Gontarski has promised to send you and me whatever
comes out.

David was splendid. Through rehearsals and in performance. His
voice is strong even at a low volume and expressive. He was suffering
from hepatitis through some of the rehearsals, but managed to get
through it all. We rehearsed in his flat, a fifth floor walkup, over a two
week period. It took several days to organize the costumes and props.
The other actor, Rand Mitchell, is an old friend of mine from several
previous productions. I chose him because of his close resemblance to
David. And, in addition, he applied putty to his nose to shape it exactly
like David's. When they finally turned and looked at each other and we
saw their faces, the effect was startling. And I must say that in rehearsal
on occasion, I would think that one of the actors was actually the other.
I think you would have been pleased with the general impact of the
performance. Very pure. Direct. Strong image of black and white. The
white table strongly lit, the two mirror-figures, blackness around.

The whole process was, of course, not nearly so satisfying as that of
ROCKABY. Apart from missing Billie, what we didn't have this time
was any kind of organization. Stan had not a clue about how a play is
put on, nor did he prepare us in any way for the actual rehearsal
situation in Columbus. He's actually in the English Dept. at a University branch 80 miles away.[5] The Theatre Dept. simply had us thrust on
them, without warning, without budget, and without understanding

that they were themselves deep in productions of their own, one of them GODOT (a student performance, much too overdone in all aspects). We had no production staff (I finally drafted Marty Fehsenfeld to help me in rehearsals), no budget, no adequate communication with anyone outside of ourselves. The only reason it came off so well was that David and Rand and Marty and I banded together for warmth and somehow managed. Even getting on the stage to rehearse in Columbus became a problem; we finally were able to work it out.

I do hope that you will allow us to go on with OHIO, as there is great interest in it in various New York quarters. Manhattan Theatre Club, La Mama, Public Theatre. David would like to do it here, if you agree. And, of course, Tom Bishop continues to want to do it in Paris. He'd very much like to do ROCKABY there, too but Billie will not be available. I gather Tom wants to use Billie's tape and have another actress in the rocker; but I told him I didn't know how you (and Billie) would feel about that.

Tired after the past month, and longing for a time without anything; but that will have to await the opening of OUR TOWN early in July. In meantime, I'm in [missing] . . . for a big Acting Company benefit, and a day at the little beach place, where I spent today walking along the shore, looking at the sand, feeling the reeds, and feeding our pet seagull, Susie. You would love it out there, not a sign of human habitation, not a sound except the sea. Jean and I feel most at peace there. And we shall have two months there in July and August before heading back to California.

Thanks for your letter after ROCKABY. I feel most grateful to you for the chance to work on these two plays, and especially to meet and be with Billie. I adore her. Do hope you are getting some rest, some time by yourself.

My son graduates from Yale next Sunday, then off to Colorado to prospect in the mountains. Cannot believe any of that is happening. Vicki working and happy in New York. Jean glad that soon I'll be with her. She sends her love.

[Alan]

1. Premiere production, 2:00–3:00 P.M., 9 May 1981. The conference was called "Samuel Beckett: Humanistic Perspectives," presented at the Ohio State University, 7–9 May 1981, as part of the SB Symposium and 75th birthday celebrations. *Ohio Impromptu,* directed by AS: David Warrilow (R), Rand Mitchell (L). Other performances included David Warrilow in *A Piece of Monologue, Footfalls* with Rosemary Pountney, and the student production of *Waiting for Godot,* 9 May. Pountney attended SB's rehearsals with

the San Quentin Drama Workshop in May 1980; see *Theatre of Shadows: Samuel Beckett's Drama 1956–76*, 1988.

   2. Opened at Guthrie Theatre, Minneapolis, 13 July 1981.

   3. James Knowlson (b. 1933), SB scholar, biographer, and friend, editor and critic at Reading University, where he founded the Samuel Beckett Archive, now the Beckett International Foundation, and where he holds a chair in French.

   4. In *Ohio Impromptu*, as R (Reader) reads, L (Listener) sometimes knocks on the table "angrily," sometimes "gently."

   5. The Ohio State University, Lima campus.

Paris
27.5.81

Dear Alan

   Thanks for yrs. of May 16. and again for your splendid handling of the 2 productions.

   Happy of course for resumption of the *Impromptu* in New York.

   Tom writes that both you & Billie accept the *Rockaby* scheme for Paris. In that case it is okay with me.[1]

   I wish I could look forward to seeing you during the Festival here, but I shall have ingloriously fled.

   I listened a few days ago to Billie's tape. Great.

   I go to Stuttgart next Sunday for the TV production. Preliminary talks were discouraging and I have not much zest for the job.[2]

   Then late June back to Aosta valley.

   Have a good rest after *Our Town*.

   Love to you all.
   Sam

   1. Agreement on "the *Rockaby* scheme" for Paris was not firm, as the following letters reveal.

   2. Under the title *Quadrat 1 & 2*, shown at Süddeutscher Rundfunk (SDR), 8 October 1981, *Quad*, directed by SB, produced by Dr. Reinhart Müller-Freienfels, designed by Wolfgang Wahl, camera by Jim Lewis. The same production, entitled *Quad*, was shown on BBC 2, 16 December 1982. Helfried Foron, Juerg Hummel, Claudia Knujpfer, Susanne Rehe.

June 16, 1981 [handwritten]

Dear Sam,

Just wanted you to know what was going on here with myself and the Paris ROCKABY.

Tom Bishop had given me the impression that Billie in no way objected to our doing the play without her but with her tape, and that you 'approved'. Subsequently, I received a letter from Billie in which she said that she 'felt very strange about being cut in half', but that of course as the actress, she would not stand in our way—especially if you and I 'approved'.

I rang Billie yesterday and had a long talk. It was clear to me that she was not happy about having her tape used without her. I told Tom this and said I felt that I did not want to repeat the production in this manner, without her but using her tape. If Tom wanted to use another actress and make a new tape, that would be up to you and to him; but I felt I could not do the play again at this time without Billie.

Tom evidently spoke to Billie today. His interpretation of her attitude is that although 'she feels strange', she does not want to stand in our way. My own interpretation remains, however, that Billie's unhappiness at having the tape used without her own physical presence is considerable. I cannot see myself contributing to that unhappiness. Nor is it fair to put Billie on the spot like this.

The whole thing is now so complicated and confused that all the pleasure of doing the original is being dissipated. Tom wants me to do the OHIO, as before, and we are evidently moving in that direction. He also wants me to do EH JOE with Warrilow and Helen Bishop, and I assume from what he says that you know about this and 'approve'.[1]

I love ROCKABY and I am devoted to Billie. And I also feel reasonably sure that you, yourself, are not entirely happy—even though you said it was 'Okay' with you—about our using her tape without her. Therefore, I have had to come to my decision. I hope you understand.

The work here continues. I shall be glad when it is over and I can have a few months to myself.

I do hope that things went well in Stuttgart. Your last letter sounded a bit down. You should be feeling better when you are back and out in Ussy again. Take care of yourself. My regrets at burdening you with all this, but I knew that you were seeing Tom and I wanted you to have my version very clearly.

Jean adds her love.

Alan [handwritten]

P.S. Glad you liked Billie's tape.

1. Helen G. Bishop, actress, wife of Tom Bishop.

Paris
23.6.81

Dear Alan

Yours of June 16 yesterday.

The first I heard of semi-Billie *Rockaby* was in a letter from Tom dated May 14. He spoke of it as "Alan's plan" which "Billie & I endorse wholeheartedly . . . We are dearly hoping that you will find this compromise acceptable." Hence my acceptance. Not to disappoint you all.

On receipt of your letter I called Billie. "If you all want it go ahead." That much heartedly.

I saw Tom & Helen yesterday evening. Of course now it's off. And the new production on, with Helen directed by David.

Don't let all this misunderstanding spoil your memory of work with Billie.

I had forgotten about *Eh Joe* with David & Helen. I understand it was staged in New York some time ago with her voice & another actor. I must have okayed it for here.

We leave for Courmayeur tomorrow. A little eternal snow will be a pleasant change, to which to lift up the eyes.

Much love to you all.
Sam

August 6, 1981

Dear Sam,

Don't know whether you are yet back in Paris, but I have been walking along our beach in Amagansett a number of times the past couple of weeks; and each time I think of you and know that you would enjoy its bleakness and very elemental feeling. No one, nothing. Just pebbles and the sea. Jean and I love it. And we wish often that you could come here one day just to see and feel it yourself. ["yourself" handwritten]

Enjoying the break from directing; though we haven't gone anywhere, and I have had to go into New York once or twice to find a new Pozzo for the Acting Company's touring *Godot,* which will be going on again in the fall. In fact, they'll be playing in the San Diego theatre in which my University puts on its productions. They are young, mostly Juilliard graduates, but the Vladimir and Estragon are quite good and work well together.

Have gotten myself into a kind of routine in which I get up, go out for the *Times,* then spend the next 4 or 5 hours working on so-called book, the memories of things gone past. Have about 200 pages and now up to my first Broadway play. Whenever I read it, sounds bloody awful and long-winded, but the editor I have at Viking keeps encouraging me. I send him the chapters as they come out. We shall see. Jean wants me to call it *Nothing to be Done,* but the publisher has other ideas.

I also swim daily, walk along the beach, bike down the out-of-way roads, and see a few people—including Barney, who is building his new house and life at the moment.

Tom Bishop continues to make plans for us to go to Paris on various projects for the Festival d'Automne. You know I'm not doing the non-Billie *Rockaby,* which seems to have just started rehearsals. I will re-do *Ohio,* pretty much as before I assume, with same actors. Later this month, I'll be rehearsing *Eh Joe* with David Warrilow and Helen B. Not quite sure how to do this on stage—although Helen did it with a British actor named Jack somebody a few years ago. Have been thinking a bit about how to get some equivalent of the closing-in camera from TV. What would you think of having some sort of lamp hanging directly over Joe's face when he's sitting on the bed, and then continuing to increase the lighting on his face more and more (perhaps even lowering the rest of the room a bit) so that we would see his face more and more intensely? Would appreciate your response to this one . . .

Also, a favor. Anticipating somewhat. Billie has spoken to Danny about her doing *Rockaby* in London some time when she gets free of present commitments, with me. We've also spoken of her doing it for a run in NY if and when; there's all sorts of interest. Whatever happens to Helen B. in Paris, I hope you won't give her the NY rights yet until we see whether indeed Billie could do it. Or another major actress whom we would both like. Please forgive me for mentioning this at this time. I really want to work with Billie again.

Trust you are feeling OK after your holiday, and not being besieged by too many visiting Americans this summer. I know you won't be there when I come in Oct., shall miss seeing you. Take care of yourself. Jean adds her love once more.

We'll be here until we go back to La Jolla early in September for another round with academia.

[Alan]

Ussy
12.8.81

Dear Alan

Thanks for yrs. of Aug. 6.

I have always thought *Eh Joe* peculiarly TV & do not remember ever having consented (if asked) to its being staged.

I like your idea. But nothing can replace the cycling in to maximum CU. Could possibly the voice seem to move in towards him?

Re *Rockaby* it goes without saying that you & Billie have priority in London & N.Y. or any other area of your naming. Or, if Billie not available, you & another actress chosen by you.

. . . .[1]

Love to you both
Sam

1. SB comments on his mental state; mentions travel plans.

September 3, 1981

Dear Sam,

Your letter of August 12 at hand, and I hasten to reply.

About the matter of "permission" to do *Eh Joe* for the stage. Before I ever embarked on this, I had reassurances from Tom Bishop and Helen both you had at least consented, if not approved. I saw a version in which Helen did the Voice some years ago at N.Y.U. and was told then that you had OK'd it. Nor would I have started on this one had I not been told over and over again that you knew all about it.

We've had several rehearsals, with David Warrilow and Helen, and I feel that there is some validity to the stage version. David is excellent, and Helen is doing very well. Her voice, especially when we do it in French—as we are now doing—is most persuasive. I feel pretty good about the way it's going to sound, and David will look.

What I am not at all sure about is what the Pompidou Centre will provide in way of setting and lighting, and am prepared to give battle to get what I need in the way of a door, a window and a cupboard, with the proper drapes in each case. We are prepared to borrow the walls from the American Centre on Raspail if not forthcoming from the French. We have sent all our requirements ahead.

I know you won't be there, and that will be sad, not to see you. But quite understand. I have a little something for you which I shall leave in your mailbox or with someone.

And I am only sorry that you won't see David (and Rand Mitchell) in OHIO IMPROMPTU, which if done as well as we first did it in Ohio should be to your liking. Nothing to be done.[1] . . .

You know that I'm putting in a new Pozzo into our touring GODOT, which the young people of the Acting Company (formerly mostly from Juilliard) have been touring since last winter. I'm going to Houston on Tuesday to open it at the Alley Theatre there. And in December, I hope to do PLAY and OTHER PLAYS (KRAPP and COME AND GO) with the same group for touring. This fall, I shall continue with THEATRE I and II with my California students, hoping that something may yet emerge for me to tell you about.

I'm glad QUAD came off better than you anticipated and I'm looking forward to seeing it.

The summer draws to a close. I've written some 250 pages on my so-called memoirs, and am now up to PENNYPACKER, my first Broadway show in 1953.[2] Sad to leave East Hampton and go back to Calif., though should be OK once we get there. Both Vickie and David fine, send their regards. The beach house remains, a refuge from everything.

Hard to believe that the war started 42 years ago today.

Glad you're at Ussy. Expect good things.

Ever
Alan

P.S. Thanks for the words about a NY *Rockaby*. I gather from David that Helen's OK. [handwritten]

1. AS is in Paris rehearsing SB productions for the Festival d'Automne.
2. Liam O'Brien's *The Remarkable Mr. Pennypacker* opened at the Coronet Theatre, New York, 30 December 1953.

> Hotel Pont-Royal
> 7, rue de Montalembert
> 75007 Paris
> Tel. 544.38.27
> Telex 270 11 3
> Oct 23 [1981]
> [date and remainder of
> letter handwritten]

Dear Sam,

Before departing these lovely rain-soaked streets, just a word or two. Little is left to say. *Ohio* went very well, David and Rand enriched by experience. David's reading most moving. *Dis Joe* still belongs on TV screen, its close-up unmatchable. But we tried, and the light growing on Joe's face plus the steady, growing presence of her voice gave some sense of movement. *Rockaby* was just not the same. Helen tried and did better than, perhaps, expected. But she's nowhere near Billie. While the technical matters (lights & rocker) lacked the previous precision. But the play is very powerful, & held them. Hope your Morocco stay OK. I'll write in detail from Calif. All my thanks for your patience with all of us.[1]

Alan

1. Festival d'Automne: *Premier Amour* opened at the Théâtre Gerard Philipe, Saint-Denis, 26 September 1981, directed by Christian Colin; *Oh les beaux jours* opened 29

September at the Théâtre du Rond-Point, directed by Roger Blin, with Madeleine Renaud and Gerard Lorin; *Textes pour rien* opened 2 October at the Théâtre de la Tempete/Cartoucherie, directed by Jean-Claude Fall; *Texts for Nothing* and *How It Is* opened at the Paris American Centre, directed by Joseph Chaikin; *Krapp's Last Tape* opened 5 October at the Centre Georges Pompidou, produced by the San Quentin Drama Workshop, directed by SB, with Rick Cluchey; *Le Dépeupleur (The Lost Ones)* opened 6 October at the Théâtre du Rond-Point, produced by the Mabou Mines, with David Warrilow, together with *Come and Go*, with JoAnne Akalaitis, Ruth Maleczech, and Ellen McElduff, both directed by Lee Breuer; *Ohio Impromptu* opened 14 October at the Centre Georges Pompidou, directed by AS, with David Warrilow (Reader), Rand Mitchell (Listener), together with *Rockaby*, directed by David Warrilow, with Helen G. Bishop; *Compagnie* opened 20 October at the Théâtre des Quartiers d'Ivry, directed by Daniel Zerki, with Roland Jacquet; *Dis Joe (Eh Joe)* in French opened 21 October at the Centre Georges Pompidou, directed by AS, with David Warrilow (Joe), Helen G. Bishop (Woman's Voice), together with *A Piece of Monologue* directed and played by David Warrilow; *Fin de partie* opened 26 October at the American Center, directed by Sandra Solov, with Pierre Chabert, Henry Pillsbury, Raymond Segre, and Sandra Solov. A number of actors and critics took part in discussions of "SB and Literature" and "SB and the Theatre" in the Grande salle du Centre Pompidou on 7 and 8 October. Videos of SB's works were shown in the Petite salle from 15 to 25 October (see JK, 672).

Paris
8.11.81

Dear Alan

Thanks for yrs. from *2 Magots*.[1]

Back a week tomorrow after 5 in Tangier. Bright sun & high wind all the time.

Have not read anything about the Festival. Great accounts from friends of *Ohio I*. Thanks & congratulations again.

Forgive this poor scrawl. Nothing in my head but wordless confusion.

Love to you both.
Sam

1. "2 Magots": Les Deux Magots, Paris brasserie.

Friday, November 13, 1981

Dear Sam,

Your favorite date, though I had planned to write much earlier. Got back from Paris a couple of weeks ago with a severe cold, nose and throat, from which I am just recovering. Also a very bad left knee, painful and stiff, variously diagnosed as arthritis, cartilage, and even gout! This getting slowly better, happy to say; but for a while I have even been unable to go swimming—which is only activity making California bearable . . .

Didn't know when you were coming back but hear via Greg Mosher who hears via Rick that you are now in Paris.[1] I sure hope the weather is better now than it was during those two weeks I was there. I have never been so cold or so wet. Maybe it's just the contrast with all this sunshine.

You have probably heard from everyone about the Festival, our part and the others. Seemed to me all sorts of things going on, and your name and countenance everywhere. I came in time to see the Mabou Mines doing COME AND GO (which I'd seen in NY) and David W's playing THE LOST ONES in French. Sorry to have been too late for Madeleine, would have welcomed seeing her in HD once more. And I was able to catch Joe Chaikin doing TEXTS over at the American Center, very impressive.[2] Also, evenings with Ruby and Barbara on those rare occasions when I wasn't discussing light cues or other technical matters with the French stagehands at the Beau Bourg.[3] They were a group of their own!

No one has sent me any reviews, and I'm not even sure there were any; but the audience response to our two evenings (ROCKABY and OHIO; JOE and MONOLOGUE) was excellent. As I said in the note I mailed in Paris, David (and Rand) were even stronger and surer than they had been originally in *Ohio*, David's voice—even for those who weren't too familiar with English—absolutely mesmerizing. The double image at the end is especially powerful. I hope some of the photos come out for you to see. About Helen in ROCKABY, I'm not entirely objective, memories of Billie always filtering through. But the response at the end was very strong. I am looking forward eagerly to seeing the Pennebaker TV version, and hope you will also. This should give you a reasonable idea of how we did it in Buffalo back in April. In EH JOE the impression of movement given by increasing the light on Joe's face and bringing the voice closer was there; but there was no substitute for the camera's insistent and steadily increasing closeup. Was able to see Barrault's version (along with a flock of other film and TV pieces) shown alongside the Exhibition, and liked it very much. Also watched QUAD several times, and much moved, especially by the slower section. Want to work on that as a stage piece with some of my students here—no audience—would you mind?

As I told you, I nipped over to London to see Billie, who was in fine shape, though unhappy about her aborted plans with the Peter Nichols piece,[4] and wanting to work. She's anxious to do ROCKABY again over here (as well as in London). I told her I'd go anywhere anytime to work with her again. All sorts of rumors of London plans, with and without her. I took liberty of ringing Curtis Brown to say that they had better not give London rights to any management or actress without consulting you. I gather that both Royal Court and Riverside[5] interested. Over here, I got in touch with several off-Broadway managements to see what I could set up for Billie in the spring. The Manhattan Theatre Club is definitely interested. Then Greg Mosher rang me up to say that Goodman was. So we are trying to set up something in combination. A double bill of ROCKABY and OHIO.

Have informed Billie. There's many a slip in our theatrical cups, but I do think this will happen—if Billie is willing to come, which she gave me every indication she was. And I'll keep you posted on progress.

Rest of life continues. Can't believe this is middle of my third year here. Still enjoying the teaching and the students, though not the California atmosphere or artifacts. Jean also feels out of water here. I've received an attractive offer from Stanford, where Martin is, and trying to find a way of accepting it. Main problem is that I must sell the house, which seems to be impossible at the moment. Every day brings hope and then dashes it. So we are a bit at sixes and sevens at the moment. What else is new? Back to NYC in two weeks to spend December working with Acting Company on another touring bill, this time PLAY, COME AND GO, and KRAPP. All young actors as with the GODOT, which is still touring and which has had very good response. And then into 1982. Trust your Morocco trip restful, and that all the Americans have departed, leaving you to yourself for a while. Jean sends love, & so do I. My knee's much better, truly. (And *no* gout!) [handwritten from "that"]

[Alan]

1. Gregory Mosher (b. 1949), American director, producer, Goodman Theatre, Chicago, 1974–78, Artistic Director, 1978.

2. Joseph Chaikin's solo performance was adapted by him from SB's *Texts for Nothing* and *How It Is.*

3. Ruby Cohn; "Barbara": probably Barbara Bray, BBC producer; Bray, "The New Beckett," *The Observer,* 16 June 1962; "Beau Borg": Centre Georges Pompidou.

4. Peter Nichols (b. 1927), English dramatist. Whitelaw starred in his *Passion Play,* 1981, Royal Shakespeare Company.

5. Riverside Studios.

Paris
20.11.81

Dear Alan

Thanks for yrs. of Nov. 13.

Sorry you had such an uncomfortable time in Paris and returned groggy to the States. Hope all quite well again now.

Herewith the press I have received. I send it on I confess unread. Friends' accounts on the whole very positive. Tom very pleased.[1] Again gratitude & congratulations to all.

Heard from Billie, she seems keen on American tour, including Chicago. Do hope it comes off. BBC approached her re possibility of a TV *Rockaby.* I said OK with me if you & she are in favour.

Can't see *Quad* on stage. But by all means have a go.

. . . .[2]

Have been trying to write a short piece to eke out Rick's *Krapp,* instead of impossible combination with *Endgame.* In vain so far. When I saw him in Paris he gave me his tentative *Krapp* video made in Chicago recently. Good things, but more loss than gain.

Great if you could get to London to work again with Billie. She wrote very highly of your direction. "He has eyes & ears everywhere," and she's not that easy to please. I'd come along & get in your way.

Off to Ussy in a day or two. Haven't seen it since June. I hear that silence—from here.

Keep well. Love to you both.

Sam

Forgive watery ink. Japanese "sailor." Marvellous little pen.

1. Tom Bishop. Reviews: Colette Godard, *Le Monde,* 8 October 1981 (about *Premier Amour*); Bernard Dort, *Le Monde, edition speciale;* Guy Scarpetta, *art press,* 51 (September 1981) (interview with David Warrilow).

2. SB comments on Tangier: "tedious and restful."

November 27, 1981

Dear Sam,

Suddenly occurs to me that I didn't give you the telephone number for Suzanne Jenkins, from whom the stones came.[1]

Please forgive me.

Departing in the morning—Jean's birthday—for New York City for a month, and a turn with PLAY and OTHER PLAYS (in this case, KRAPP and COME AND GO). If the Acting Company can meet its budget, which they think they can.

Anything you would like to tell me about how you'd like me to do COME AND GO would be much appreciated. Or the other two.

Will be in touch.

Yours,

[Alan]

P.S. Still working on getting Billie over in the spring, but things, as usual, going up and down on that.

1. AS gives Suzanne and Paul Jenkins' addresses in New York and Paris.

Paris
11.12.81

Dear Alan

Thanks for yrs. of Nov. 27.

. . . .[1]

I see *Come & Go* very formal. Strictly identical attitudes & movements. The getting up, going, return, sitting, whispered confidence, shocked reaction (sole colour), finger to lips, etc. the same for all 3. Absent one not wholly invisible. Same toneless voices save for "Oh!"s. Stiff, slow, puppet-like.

Rick's *Krapp* about right for me.

Play: Fast flow. Chief problem spot (eye). Operator shd. know by heart text & order of *répliques*.[2]

But, dear Alan, do them your own way.

Do hope Billie project comes off.

Love to you both.

Sam

1. SB has written to Suzanne Jenkins.
2. *"répliques"*: cues (retorts).

                                                        Paris
                                                        15.12.81
                        Samuel Beckett
Dear Alan

To a question re possible revival of *Rockaby* in N.Y. with Helen Bishop I have replied that you and Billie have priority & that you must be consulted.

Best
Sam

                                                December 24, 1981
Dear Sam,

Just been walking on the sand near my beach-house, alone with the gulls and the wind. Thinking of you and how much you would like this place. Not a soul around, hardly a sign of human habitation, just the shore line and the stones. Lovely! Very warm today, at least for the season, though they tell us there'll be a sprinkle of white for the Christmas tomorrow. Love it out here when no one is about.

Spoke with Barney a couple of days ago. He's just dug the hole in the ground for his new house. Very different from the place you saw, and on the other side of town, very near us, a farm house and feeling. Expect to see some of him this summer.

Your letter to the Acting Company arrived just as I wasn't getting into rehearsal. They didn't get the money they needed.[1] So at practically the last minute, everyone had to be told. Sad. But nothing to be done. The general theatre situation is bad here. Broadway booming with crap and awful prices. Off-Broadway not much. And off-off-Broadway and the Regional Theatre suffering from lack of suitable subsidy. Reagan has withdrawn a big chunk.[2] And the private companies are not coming through. So everyone is having a tough time. We hope that the project will be possible at another time. But right now, nothing is certain except the disappointment of the director and the actors. Thanks for all your thoughts on the plays.

The good news, on the other hand, is that Joe Papp is definitely interested in doing a double-bill of ROCKABY and OHIO IMPROMPTU this spring, probably in May, when his theatre is free. Have spoken with Billie and with David, and they are both interested. Billie especially keen to come over, and I'm hoping that all will be well on this one. Joe's theatre, the Public, where Jackie did his show, is the perfect place; and Joe has just had a recent hit, with PIRATES OF PENZANCE,[3] so he is in the chips still and will be until May. I have spoken with Billie several times, and she is clearly excited about coming over. I've just told all sides to work it out, and I'll be there. You know that Alan Mandell plans to do the two plus FOOTFALLS, with Bea Manley, in L.A. And there are all sorts of plans in all sorts of other places. Barney tried to keep me informed. I do hope we'll get your approval of the Public Theatre plans.

Instead of rehearsing, I've spent the weeks here seeing people, seeing some plays (mostly awful) and reading. Jean happy to be East, and we are seeing both our kids for the holidays. Then back to Nirvana-land for another ten weeks. After which I shall be here (as of early March) until September. David Warrilow showed me a long and mostly favorable piece from the Frankfurter ZEITUNG on the Paris festivities, but I have not seen anything in the French press.[4] Tom Bishop said we got all sorts of attention, but I have been unaware of it. Maybe the Beau Bourg people will eventually send me something.

Had dinner with Marty last week, and about to embark on reading her book (if I can lift it.) And I hope to see or talk with Ruby Cohn while she's in NY. Take care of yourself. Thanks for everything. And Jeannie and Vickie and my David join me in wishing you all good things.

Hope to see you in the New Year. [handwriten from "my David")

[Alan]

1. For AS's projected *Play and Other Plays* (*Krapp's Last Tape* and *Come and Go*).
2. Ronald Reagan (b. 1911), U.S. President 1981–1989.
3. Comic opera, 1879, by William Gilbert (1836–1911) and Arthur Sullivan (1842–1900).
4. George Hensel, "Beckett, Beckett, und warum kein Ende? Neue Theaterstücke, Prosastücke, Bruchstücke beim Pariser Herbst-Festival," *Frankfurter Allgemeine Zeitung*, 31 October 1981.

January 9, 1982

Dear Sam,

Back in California for a couple of months, and trying to pick up my 'other life'. This double existence has its confusions.

As usual, hoping for something definite to tell you about spring plans. But, as usual, everything keeps changing almost daily. So I figured I could at least share the present moment with you.

Phone call from Greg Mosher at the Goodman. Equity turned down application for Billie to play there in ROCKABY. The League of Resident Theatres, of which Goodman is member, has specific contract with Equity 'forbidding' use of aliens, though exceptions have been made in past on occasion. They will appeal—so none of us has yet told Billie.

Phone call from Joe Papp at the Public. Yes, they are going ahead with plans for double bill of ROCKABY and OHIO in May. Yes, they have to get approval of Equity, but this can be done by putting everyone on Broadway contracts though Public Theatre is technically off-Broadway. No, Joe has contacted neither Billie or David Warrilow with definite arrangements, but he will. So, I'm hoping that one will go through. We're talking about a 4–6 week run at the Public; and Billie is quite happy about idea (have talked with her twice via phone) as is David. Also Rand Mitchell.

Phone call from Alan Mandell, and more to follow. He's in rehearsal with triple bill in Los Angeles and full of questions for me. Trying to help him. Bea Manley should be OK. And I'll go up to see it. Sorry wasn't able to be more active at the beginning, but Alan got started while I was in NY.[1]

In NY, by the way, you know that the Acting Company, denuded of funds, was not able to go into production with PLAY and other two, notes for which were generously provided by you in your last letter to me.[2] Maybe later in the year; although the Reagan Administration cutting Arts funding has begun to affect all sorts of theatres all over the place.

Talked with Ruby on her return from London. I think I told you that I have had an offer from Stanford University, on an even more flexible arrangement than I have here; so I am tempted but not sure about moving again. Martin Esslin is there on similar deal. Saw lots of Marty, Barney's new house in East Hampton, all 8 and 3/4 hours of NICHOLAS NICKLEBY.[3]

In February, with your permission, will be working on an in-house (no public) workshop version of QUAD with one of my graduate directors. Just to see how the actors cope with it, and how it looks on a small stage. Percussion and all. I saw the TV version while at Beau Bourg and found it mesmerizing.

Ruby tells me you are in good shape after Morocco. Wish I could see you. Maybe sometime during the year. In the meantime, all good wishes of the season, and take care of yourself.

Jean sends love.

[Alan]

1. "triple bill": "Three By Beckett" (*Rockaby, Ohio Impromptu, Footfalls*), directed by Alan Mandell, with Martin Beck, Alan Mandell, Beatrice Manley, Bea Silvern; opened at Los Angeles Actors' Theatre in repertory, 23 February 1982. Beatrice (Bea) Manley, character actress and a founding member of the San Francisco Actor's Workshop, m. Herbert Blau.
2. AS is thinking of SB's letter of 11 December 1981.
3. Mobile Showcase presented the lengthy TV version of the novel by Charles Dickens, *The Life and Adventures of Nicholas Nickleby*, 1838–1839.

4.2.82

Dear Alan

Thanks for yrs. of Dec. 24.

About a fortnight ago I sent you c/o Acting Company the Paris press sent to me by Tom, on Festival productions. Unread. Sorry you haven't received.[1]

Public Theatre project fine with me. Do hope it comes off. *Footfalls* to boot, with Billie, perhaps then too?[2]

Struggling with impossible prose. English.[3] With loathing. To think writing was once pleasure.

Suggested to Billie she redo *Happy Days* some happy day, with you.

Love to you all
Sam

1. AS said he had not received the press clippings (see letter of 13 November 1981).
2. Joseph Papp hoped to produce *Ohio Impromptu* and *Rockaby* in May with Billie Whitelaw.
3. "impossible prose": *Worstward Ho*, 1983.

Paris
6.2.82

Dear Alan

Thanks for yrs. of Jan. 9 & news of various projects.

Heard from Alan Mandell saying you had been most helpful.

Rick chafing in P.R.[1] Have tried in vain to devise a companion piece to his *Krapp.* Talk now of his using *Theatre Fragment 1,* playing the cripple. Problem of direction.

Quad can't work on stage. But no doubt interesting for students, gymnastically.

. . . .[2]

Have translated *Rockaby* & *Ohio I* not too traitorously. But *Piece of Monologue* more than my French can chew so far.

. . . .[3]

May we meet again this year.

Love to you all
Sam

1. "P.R.": Puerto Rico, home of Cluchey's wife, Teresita del Suro.
2. SB has seen Tom Bishop.
3. SB hopes to go to Ussy.

Paris
9.2.82

Dear Alan

Yours of Feb. 3 this evening.[1]

You may use enclosed if you think it can help.

I don't think it would serve the cause at this stage for me to threaten no New York *Rockaby* unless with Billie.

Nothing new since my last. . . .[2]

Love to you both
Sam

[The "enclosed":]

I have the highest opinion of Billie Whitelaw as interpreter of my work.

Her performances in *Happy Days* and *Footfalls,* directed by me at the

Royal Court Theatre, London, were admirable. Her *Not I*, both stage and TV, an unforgettable technical achievement.

She has an uncanny rapport with my theatre and sense of its requirements.

Rockaby was written for her. The play needs her.

I am grieved at the refusal of Actors Equity to authorize her appearance in New York. I would regard a reversal of this decision as a favour to me and to my work.

Samuel Beckett
9.2.82

[signature both handwritten and typed]

1. AS letter "Feb. 3" missing in which he may have suggested the threat: "no New York *Rockaby*" without Billie Whitelaw.
2. SB comments on how he feels and hopes "we may get together this year."

Paris
16.3.82

Dear Alan

Thanks for yrs. of March 7.[1]

Did not know about BBC *Rockaby*.[2]

Talk of it at the Royal Court. I said OK if you directing. So that should be on if you can make it, whatever happens with N.Y. "Equity."

I remember Hauptle very well. He was very helpful with Berlin Rick *Krapp*. I liked him.[3]

Both of us have been a bit shaky. Much better now.

Yes, high time we met again.

Love to you all
Sam

1. Missing.
2. SB saw the BBC *Rockaby* film in December 1982 when Daniel Labeille took him to the BBC studios to see it (JK, 664).
3. Carroll Hauptle, technical assistant with the San Quentin Drama Workshop.

Friday, March 19, 1982

Dear Sam,

We lost.

The Equity arbitrator, for reasons not yet clear to me because Joe Papp has not passed on a copy of the report to me, ruled against us. That means we cannot use Billie in the play over here. Madness!

I think the whole affair demonstrates a kind of blacklash over the granting of permits during the past year or so to a great many alien performers.

This also means that the Public will not be doing ROCKABY in any form, as Joe feels he cannot do the play with any other actress since he made such a strong argument for having Billie. He is almost as upset as I am, although in a different way.

I haven't told Barney yet, but will.

Just got back from California and am in Hastings for a few days, still unpacked, trying to recoup my forces and morale. The other play which I was supposed to do prior to ROCKABY has gotten neither its money nor its theatre; it is now scheduled for early fall although I have my doubts. So it goes, always, in the American theatre.

I guess I'll retire to East Hampton and work on my book. And try to find a way of somehow getting to see you this spring. Will let you know.

Am desolate that we won't be having Billie. And I'd still like to consider the possibility of the double bill (ROCKABY and OHIO) at another theatre; Joe won't do it without Billie. At this point, I find it hard to think of any other actress.

After I get unpacked and organised, I'll write again. In the meantime, my apologies for not being able to deliver on this one. Great sadness here.

Hope you're OK, not too besieged, and writing.

Jean sends love.

[Alan]

Paris
4.4.82

Dear Alan

Thanks for yrs. of March 19 with the sad news. Hope you'll be able to do it with Billie in London, Royal C. or Riverside, some day.

Finished translating *R., O. I.* & *Mon.* Last especially difficult. Finally did a free shorter version & called it *Solo.*[1]

Wrote a short act in French *(Catastrophe)* for a group gesture toward Václav Havel,[2] for next Avignon Festival.[3] Not yet translated.

. . . .[4]

Have a good rest. All best for your book.

Love to you both
Sam

1. *Rockaby, Ohio Impromptu, A Piece of Monologue*, published in *Rockaby and Other Short Pieces*, 1981; published in French as *Berceuse, L'Impromptu d'Ohio*, and *Solo* in *Catastrophe et autres dramaticules*, 1982.

2. *Catastrophe*, dedicated to Václav Havel; "group gesture": AIDA, the International Association for the Defense of Artists, asked SB among other writers to contribute a piece as part of "Une Nuit pour Václav Havel." Václav Havel (b. 1936), Czechoslovakian playwright and eventually president of his country; a strong opponent of the political power then prevailing in his country, he was still a prisoner in 1982.

3. "Avignon Festival": July 1982, devoted to drama, begun in 1947 by Jean Vilar.

4. SB hopes to get to Ussy.

April 5, 1982

Dear Sam,

Believe it or not, today is my daughter, Viveca's, 27th birthday, reminding me of L'Aiglon and those so-romantic days. We're going to have a bit of a do with her in Hastings this evening.

Have been dashing around this week, Washington to see the opening of TWELFTH NIGHT by the young Acting Company (which did GODOT, and was prevented by budgetary problems from doing KRAPP and PLAY last December—we hope to do it next year); then Minneapolis to see AS YOU LIKE IT;[1] I'm directing ROOM SERVICE, a classic American farce, there this summer.[2]

Spoke with John Calder in New York about ten minutes before he took off for London last week. He had just seen you a few days previously. He told me about your words concerning the Royal Court. Am most grateful. As it happens, I am free, rhapsodically interested, and would make myself very available if the Court could indeed fit it in this spring. I'm sure Billie would also find a way. When I saw her back in October, she wanted very much to do it there. Anyhow, I gather John is talking with Max Stafford-Clark;[3] and I'll talk with him when he gets back. Maybe we can work things out.

Having been foiled in our efforts to get ROCKABY and OHIO on at the Public here, it would be satisfying to get the two on in London. I haven't said anything to Billie about this (except in relation to the defeat at the Public) but will the moment I know that something might happen.

John also told me you had completed a new short piece in French. Anxious to read it, if and when.

Thanks for words about Carroll Hauptle. We're trying to get him. Do you remember Richard Riddell, who did lights on the Berlin KRAPP? He's on our faculty at Univ. of California, and a wonderful guy. He's doing ROOM SERVICE with me.

Jean is well and radiant at the idea of being EAST for six months. We have finally sold our Escondido house (bought with the University's money) and will take a little apartment near the school when we get back in the fall. In the meantime, Jean has fixed up a tiny pied-a-terre in Hastings on the assumption that I would be working in New York all spring—a Broadway show, and ROCKABY and OHIO at the Public. Hah! But the pied-a-terre is lovely (and inexpensive) even though the terre outside has been very shaky.

Hope fervently that the London hopes will materialize into plans, and that I shall get to see you this spring. In any case, I shall try.

Good to hear that you and Suzanne are both better.

Will stay in touch.

Best from us all,
[Alan]

1. At the Guthrie Theatre, with David Warrilow.

2. *Room Service* by John Murray and Allen Boretz opened at the Cort Theatre, 19 May 1937, for 500 performances, directed and produced by George Abbott; scheduled for the Guthrie Theatre summer repertory season, 1982.

3. Max Stafford-Clark (b. 1941), English director, producer at the Traverse, Edinburgh, 1966–1970; in 1979 moved to the Royal Court Theatre where he succeeded Stuart Burge, 1977–1979, and Oscar Lewenstein, 1972–1977.

13.4.82

Dear Alan

Thanks for yrs. of April 5 & for your kind card & remembrance.

I do hope you may direct Billie in London. Some time ago I told *Spokesmen* that was my wish & thought I mentioned it to you in a letter at the time.[1] Provided you don't run foul of their "Equity."

I know Richard Bailey. He was with us on Berlin *Krapp* (sound). Now in L.A. [handwritten in margin]. Don't remember Riddell.

Havel piece not yet translated from French. Scheduled, with pieces by other writers (Frisch, Dürrenmatt, Ionesco, Miller, Wiesel etc.) July 21 in Avignon.

Have a good rest from the west.

Hear Warrilow excellent in *A.Y.L.I.*[2]

Love to you all
Sam

1. "Spokesmen": SB's London agent.
2. "A.Y.L.I.": *As You Like It.*

May 13, 1982

Dear Sam,

Was about to write to you about a letter I just received from Max Stafford-Clark at the Royal Court when the phone rang, and it was Peter Hall from the National asking me if I'd be available to do ROCK-ABY with Billie in September. Am sure it's all your doing. Of course, I am and will be, and will be delighted if it actually works out. Peter said something about a very simple "early evening" production. I explained that the physical production was "simple"—just a rocking chair—but that the lighting required was very specific. We didn't talk that much detail, but I gather someone from his staff will be ringing me. And I'm going to call Billie to see how much she knows about all this.

What I don't quite understand is the Royal Court's position. At John Calder's suggestion—he had evidently been talking with them—I wrote to Max to say that I'd heard they were going to do ROCKABY and OHIO, and that I'd be very interested in being considered as director. Max's reply indicated that they were indeed going to do the two plays but not until early 1983. He also added that "although I would be enthusiastic about the possibility of you repeating your production with Billie Whitelaw I would prefer to use one of our own actors in the other play." I don't suppose he had yet read OHIO to realise that two actors were involved.

Anyhow. There's a certain amount of activity after the lull; and I shall look forward to something. Maybe I'll know more after I talk to Billie.

Thank you so much for all your efforts on this, Sam. I cannot tell you what it means to me. After the Equity turndown here, I had been going through a sort of dark tunnel, wondering whether the American attitude toward almost everything was ever going to rid itself of its confusion and stupidity. The theatre scene over here now is so awful I can hardly bear it. I have walked out of more shows in the past few weeks than ever in my life. And tearing down those two lovely theatres, the Morosco and the Helen Hayes, to make way for a hotel is a perfect example of greed triumphing over everything else.[1]

There is a chance that David Warrilow might be doing OHIO and, I think, MONOLOGUE while he is at the Guthrie Theatre this summer working on MARRIAGE OF FIGARO.[2] I shall be there at almost the same time directing an American period piece called ROOM SERVICE; and we plan to work together. I assume David has told you about this possibility.

I hear you have written a new play in French for that benefit for Havel et al. Would love to read it, especially when you get to the English version. Such another short piece might be useful either with ROCKABY or OHIO, depending on the situation. Have no idea of number of characters or subject matter. I'm still hoping to direct David in OHIO in New York when a suitable occasion arises. Although it's very hard to see anyone other than Billie in ROCKABY.

Anyhow. Jean is happy as two larks, being back East, and working for the East Hampton Historical Society. I'm slowly progressing on my "memoirs," reading lots of plays, and trying to cast a new Russian play for possible Broadway production. The kids are fine. If anything happens at either end of London, I'll be coming over to see you. Maybe I can get there in any case. Best regards, [handwritten from "happens"]

[Alan]

PS. Did you hear that Barney had a new baby girl—Chantal? Lisa is fine. [handwritten]

1. The Morosco Theatre on West 45th Street opened in 1917; the Helen Hayes Theatre, formerly the Fulton on West 46th Street, named after Helen Hayes (1900–1993), opened 21 November 1955; present Helen Hayes, 240 West 44th Street.

2. By Pierre-Augustin Beaumarchais (1732–1799), French playwright.

Ussy
22.5.82

Dear Alan

Thanks for yrs. of May 13 here today.

A few days ago a letter from Sue Freathy of "Spokesmen" (my London agents) re plans for Billie to "do" *Rockaby* & *Piece of Monologue* at the National. Either she does not know the latter is for an act*or* or there is a suggestion that Billie shd take it over. I have requested enlightenment. In my reply I also said that I felt a commitment to the Court & would be sorry if the London premiere of these plays were not to be given there. Billie according to her agent, as reported by Ms Freathy, would prefer the National. John Calder told me some time ago that I would be hearing from Stafford-Clark. Nothing so far. The usual confusion.

I am now translating the Havel piece & hope to get it to you soon. It was written at the invitation of A.I.D.A. (Association Internationale pour La Défense des Artistes) as part of a tribute by various writers to Václav Havel for presentation in July at the Avignon Festival under the title *Une Nuit pour Václav Havel.* After which it would be available in English for London production. Very short, 15′ maximum. Two male parts (one mute), one female. Title *Catastrophe* (in the sense of *dénouement*).

. . . .[1]

Do hope London comes off for you & thus *à très bientôt.*

Love to you all
Sam

1. SB is returning to Paris, will see Alan Mandell and his wife.

Wednesday, June 9, 1982

Dear Sam,

Meant to answer your last letter sooner. But, as it happens, I have been for the first time in my life involved with some surgery problems, which are not yet settled.

. . . .[1]

In the meantime, The Manhattan Theatre Club, where we did PLAY AND OTHER PLAYS a few years back, remember?, is interested in a double bill of OHIO IMPROMPTU and Pinter's FAMILY VOICES. (This to avoid the ROCKABY problem with Billie.) I'd prefer to wait for your new short one to go with OHIO and David W. How do you feel about these various possibilities?

I saw a rough cut of the ROCKABY film that Pennebaker did, and it's very fascinating.[2] Billie is just lovely and comes through in a most human way. You understand, I'm talking about the entire process of preparation, not just the performance.

Afraid I'm not thinking much about anything other than my water works at the moment. Just wanted to establish contact with you. We should be staying in Hastings until things settle dust, at least all my dust. Jean is wonderful but also feeling the strain.

Trust you are well. I'm actually not as bad off as I sound, just did not expect this.

[Alan]

P.S No word about a London ROCKABY from either place. [hand-written]

1. AS has had a minor operation and needs another.
2. *Rockaby* TV documentary, filmed in 1981, available in New York Public Library, Theatre Collection (Lincoln Center) (see letter of 18 April 1981, n. 5).

Ussy sur Marne
20.6.82

Dear Alan

Thanks for yrs. of June 9.

Sad to think of you having such a wretched time. . . .[1] May the second op. bring you lasting relief.

No news of Billie. I'll call her soon.

English *Catastrophe* nearly ready, so expect your copy soon. Presentation at Avignon tomorrow, by & with whom & what else I know not. Re Manhattan, your decision OK with me.

Here in outward peace last few days & I hope for another week.

Wish I could look forward to seeing you soon.

Bon courage, dear Alan, & love to all

Sam

1. SB has had a similar physical problem.

Ussy
24.6.82

Dear Alan

Herewith Havel piece.¹ Opening not June but July 21, Avignon Festival.

Do hope things are better with you. Let me have news of you soon.

Love to you both
Sam

1. *Catastrophe* published in *Catastrophe et autres dramaticules*, 1982, trans. by SB; *Catastrophe, The New Yorker*, 58 (10 January 1983), 26–27; *Index on Censorship*, February 1984.

July 11, 1982

Dear Sam,

. . . .¹

I read CATASTROPHE and much moved by it, on all levels. And really looking forward to working on it. Haven't done much yet, though I did speak to David Warrilow, who seems to be good casting for the Protagonist. (Haven't thought in detail about the rest of the casting.) Especially if we were to do OHIO on the same bill, that would be an interesting contrast of vocal and physical image. What do you think?

The Manhattan Theatre Club is definitely interested. We shall, of course, have to await David's availability; he's currently in Minneapolis at the Guthrie doing Beaumarchais. I was supposed to do ROOM SERVICE there following, but have had to withdraw. And I am sure Joe Papp at the Public would also be interested, depending on the availability of his theatre spaces. Will pursue as soon as I have a bit more energy. I know that Barney has a copy of CATASTROPHE, and will presumably be publishing it soon.[2] Have not yet reached him, as I came home only yesterday from my stay in purgatory.

Will also be writing to Billie to let her know I am back. She rang last week and spoke with Jean. Evidently the National wants to do ROCK-ABY for some sort of short run in December. I have told her and them that I shall make myself available whenever. They will probably change their minds about the date and everything else several times.
. . . .[3]

[Alan]

1. AS, now out of the hospital, thanks SB for his "notes and support"; "notes" are missing.
2. In *Collected Short Plays*, 1984.
3. In the following two paragraphs AS says how supportive his wife, Jean, was during his time in the hospital. They are now going to East Hampton to be near the ocean.

Paris
23.7.82

Dear Alan,
. . . .[1]

July 21 Havel night seems to have been a very mixed & muddled bag.[2] Saw a few depressing extracts on TV including a brief flash of the Protagonist all trussed up with screaming white bonds to facilitate comprehension. God knows what they did with the rest. This coming after a scandalous parody of *Godot* at the Young Vic.[3] Try to persuade myself I'm past caring.

Like your suggestion of doing it with David in conjunction with *Impromptu*.

I called Billie to be told she was on holiday with family. Shall try again next month. Hope it comes off at the National or elsewhere and that we may meet in December.

Wrote a short piece for Süddeutscher Rundfunk (Stuttgart) and am due there in October to set it up.⁴ Half committed for a contribution to next year's Graz Festival (Steirischer Herbst) but nothing in view.

Stuck in Paris . . . .

Love to you both
Sam

1. SB is relieved to hear of AS's recovery: "Health be with you from now on."

2. "muddled bag": On 21 July 1982 the Avignon Festival took the form of a tribute by several writers to Havel, entitled "Une Nuit pour Václav Havel," and included *Aubade* by Alfred Simon, *Un Moment de Refus* by Elie Wiesel, *La Chaloupe* by Victor Haim, *Je pense beaucoup à vous* by Arthur Miller, *Une Chaise* by Jean-Pierre Faye, *Visite* by André Chedid, and *Catastrophe* by SB, directed by Stephan Meldegg. Gérard Desothe (Director, D), Stephanie Loik (His female assistant, A), Pierre Arditi (Protagonist, P).

3. *Waiting for Godot* opened 15 July 1982, directed by Ken Campbell, designed by Bernard Culshaw. Jonathan Barlow (Estragon), Andy Rashleigh (Vladimir), John Sessions (Lucky), Don Crann (Pozzo), Robert Packham (A Boy). Reviews: Irving Wardle, "'Waiting for Godot' Young Vic," *Times,* 16 July 1982; James Fenton, "Children of the Revolution," *Times,* 25 July.

4. *Nacht und Traüme* (Night and Dreams), written at the invitation of Dr. Reinhart Müller-Freienfels, in *Collected Shorter Plays,* 1984.

East Hampton (prior to
California sojourn)
September 13, 1982

Dear Sam,

Here I am again, again.

Wanted you to know that I had finally heard more or less definitely from the National Theatre in London, and that it looks now that ROCK-ABY will be going on in December, opening on December 9 and playing four times a week for an indefinite period. Every time someone calls me, it seems to be a different person; but they do seem to have concluded matters with Billie and her agent, and I expect to be there also.

Billie is off somewhere filming and evidently unreachable by phone, but I have written to her, and will try to talk with her when I get to California at the end of this week. I'm off for another ten-week session, which ends conveniently just in time for me to get to London for rehearsals.

Would there be a chance of your coming over? (Don't answer now.

We can all think about it. But I'd love to have you there, and so would Billie, I'm sure.)

We're getting the chair and the dress and hat via Danny, who is having them shipped over. I have or will have the tape. Billie will be getting the same wig she had from the wigmaker in London. We will have a week's rehearsal on stage, which should be enough or more than enough. She will also do her reading of ENOUGH to start the evening. We will be playing at the Cottlesloe, the lovely small theatre, which will be housing some other setting in front of which we shall have to place black velour curtains. I assume that you know some of this from Billie.

Anyhow.

The summer has gone, I know not where. Have not been doing much of anything the past month except getting well, gaining back most of the twenty pounds I lost, swimming, and reading. Also walking around East Hampton with Jean, a lovely twilight occupation. I am most excited about the National prospect because I think Billie really wants to do it in London, and she will be superb.

About OHIO and CATASTROPHE at the Manhattan Theatre Club, they now seem a bit hesitant partly in terms of their schedule and partly because they think the evening will be too short. I don't agree. Joe Papp at the Public may be interested. In any case, I'm sure, we'll get it on in the right place, but I have to take David Warrilow's availability in strong consideration as I think he is especially fine for the two roles. Will keep you posted.

Oh, yes, am working on KRAPP, PLAY, and COME AND GO for the Acting Company tour, starting in January (after I'm back from London). That's the young group from Juilliard which did GODOT two years ago. Some excellent youthful talent.

Finally, the Goodman—still not certain of Equity's ruling re Billie—now tells me that they may try to import 'the National Theatre production' with Billie, of course. We shall see if they can manage that.

So it's a real Sam Beckett year for me. When was it not?

. . . .[1]

Saw Marty, who was full of her summer tracing your past. Hope you are well and writing. All the best from

[Alan]

1. A short paragraph about family matters follows.

Paris
19.9.82

Dear Alan,

I have tried repeatedly to write a short piece for Rick Cluchey, in sore need of help, for performance in Chicago at the Goodman. In vain. It now suddenly occurs to me that the part of the Protagonist in *Catastrophe* is what he needs, his strong point being massive presence, his weak point speech.

Would you have any objection to my offering it to him? Or even consider directing him yourself? I have not mentioned this to him and shall not till I get the clear from you.

. . . .[1]

Love to you all
Sam

1. SB hopes AS is fully recovered.

Solana Beach, Ca.
Sept. 25, 1982

Dear Sam,

Your letter of Sept. 19 sent to Gingerbread Lane received here. Now you have another address, one more exotic than normal, to deal with. Please forgive.

Have been thinking about the question posed about Rick.

Yes, I think Rick is suited for the Protagonist. What I'm not sure of is whether you are talking about a Goodman Theatre production, or the one planned in New York for next spring. You recall that I wrote to you about a double bill planned for the Manhattan Theatre Club, of OHIO IMPROMPTU and CATASTROPHE, with David Warrilow. And I said that I thought it an interesting idea that David would have all of the lines in OHIO and a totally silent role in the other play. I thought you liked the idea. And I have spoken about it several times with David— who is enthusiastic but still uncertain about his spring because of various possibilities at the Rond Point, I gather. Also the availability of Frederick Lonsdale.[1] I understand that he has promised to make himself available in the event that Lonsdale isn't, and that you know about this.

For the New York production, wherever and whenever, I'd still much prefer David Warrilow, and would like to wait for him. If you approve. For a Goodman Theatre production, I think Rick would be fine. And I would be most happy to be involved if that proves possible. The only thing that I would not want to happen is a Goodman Theatre production prior to one in New York, as that would affect us a great deal, both from the point of view of the theatre involved, and the attitude of the critics, etc. I do hope you allow me to do the American premiere in New York, with David W., as previously stated and planned. After that, whatever you feel about Rick, I would certainly concur.

Still have not heard in writing from the National about the December ROCKABY; but have spoken several times via phone with various people, and plans seem to be definite, or as definite as the National ever does anything. I wrote to Billie. And I have secured all the materials, chair, costume and tape from Danny without charge. My own services will be also without fee; I just want them to pay my fare and give me a minimal per diem so that I could survive a week or so in London. I plan to be there on Dec. 2, and will be staying with a friend.

California is OK once one gets there. We have a pleasant apartment, near the ocean, and equipped with a swimming pool. The group of actors I have this year is the best since I got here, the equivalent of any class at Juilliard. I am working on a variety of short scenes and pieces from your work; and I think you would be pleased. In fact, I have enough certainty of their talent to ask you if you would mind if I included CATASTROPHE among the materials with which we work. Only in class, no performances of any kind, public or private.

Jean and the kids are fine. And my plumbing seems to be functioning as of old. Glad to be back in my den again.

Take care of yourself. And I'll stay in touch. Hope to see you, either briefly in December or next spring at the latest. ["briefly" handwritten]

[Alan]

1. Théâtre Rond-Point, Paris; "Frederick Lonsdale": Michael (Michel) Lonsdale (b. 1931), French stage, film, television actor, appeared in many SB plays in Europe.

Paris
2.10.82

Dear Alan,

Thanks for yrs. of Sept. 13 & 25.

OK C. Rick perhaps later.

By all means C with your students.

I shrink from London. But if you can't come to Paris I'll try to make it.

Just back from Stuttgart TV prelims. Tired. So no more now.

Love to you all
Sam

November 3, 1982

Dear Sam,

Been waiting to get some tangible evidence from the National Theatre that I am indeed going to London, but they seem to take forever to do anything, including what was promised and agreed upon weeks ago. However, they did telephone, and I have talked to the Technical Director or Production Manager, one Jason Barnes, and to the lighting man, Laurence Creighton; and the two seem to believe we're actually doing ROCKABY, so I believe it also. The chair has arrived, but its mechanism not yet assembled. I have tried to tell them some of the needs and problems involved.

The main question I have is whether you might be there with us during the preliminary festivities. I hear rumors that you are, but not yet from you. I shall be arriving the morning of December 2. My understanding is that we have Dec. 3 and Dec. 7 to rehearse—but not in the actual space. We shall try to simulate conditions and deal with the chair, the lights, Billie's needs, etc. Then on December 9, we have the day in the space to run our final technical, before 'opening' at 6 o'clock that evening.

Billie will also be doing ENOUGH, opening with it as before and then changing into her makeup. I haven't spoken to her for a while, but I gather she is happy at the prospect of doing the project in London. We do not know how many performances are scheduled. If things go well, we could go past the December dates they now have marked down.

I'm flying directly to London from Los Angeles. Jean will be joining me via New York a couple of days later, and stay on until I go back after we have 'opened'. Since I was not sure whether you would be able to come to London, I was leaving myself open to the prospect of returning to NY via Paris and pop in on you. Jean also. Naturally, it would be wonderful and more productive if you could be with us in London even for a few days or for the December 9 finals. Just let me know, and I'll adjust my plans accordingly. I'll be staying with friends very near the Hyde Park.

Feeling fine, although I tend to get a little more tired a bit earlier in the evenings than I once did. Trying to take it easier, but that's not always possible. The term seems to have flown by. I'm not actually directing anything of a public nature until next term, but I did go to Japan for a week for some Conference and to meet a fascinating Japanese director, Tadashi Suzuki, who wants me to come to his theatre to direct, possibly ROCKABY with a very interesting Japanese actress, Shiraishi. I also spent some time with Takahashi, whom I believe you know, and who is most dedicated to your work.[1]

Have spent most of the term, believe it or not, with my acting students working on a number of the short plays, which they love. A rather nice COME AND GO, and also a stab at OHIO IMPROMPTU. Still trying to pin down the theatre and the dates for the double bill of OHIO and CATASTROPHE in New York in the spring. Will talk to you about it when I see you. The Goodman's plans keep changing.

Hope you are well and recovered from your TV chores. I've talked with Marty and Danny and Barney, but I feel cut off from most of civilisation out here, pleasant and sunny as it is. How much longer I can survive this bi-coastal existence is not clear to me. Jean in good shape, and looking forward to her first trip to London in years. Also to seeing you again.

[Alan]

1. Tadashi Suzuki (b. 1939), founder and innovative director of the Suzuki Company of Toga (SCOT); creator of the Suzuki Method of training actors. The actress Kayoko Shiraishi works with him. Yasunari Takahashi, professor of English Literature, Tokyo University, translated all of SB's dramatic works into Japanese; *Samuel Beckett*, 1971.

December 16, 1982

Dear Sam,

Sitting in East Hampton, looking at the ocean, and unable to believe that one week ago, I was at the National Theatre with you and Billie.[1]

Watched all three performances, including one last Saturday where an Irish fellow who had had too much to drink and didn't like his seat was muttering to himself occasionally. All three were packed. We worked with the light and the chair before each performance, and have managed to remove all squeaks and other noises; also, the light now seems to contain her face at all times. The audience's concentration and willingness to listen is remarkable. And Peggy Ramsey—whom you may remember as London's leading play agent—told me that she felt the tape was the most pure and beautiful recording she had ever heard in the theatre.

The response of the press has been, on the whole, quite favorable. All the reviews I saw with the exception of the GUARDIAN liked the performance, and found both the play and Billie intensely moving. The fellow on the *Guardian* preferred the short story, which he felt had some life in it, to the play, which seemed static to him.[2]

Spoke with Billie just before taking the plane, and she seems in good shape, happy enough. There's evidently been some talk about a possible transfer to the West End if and when—and assuming that there would be another piece to go with it. I did speak to David Warrilow, and he is thrilled at the possibility, although his Paris plans might interfere if, indeed, some such prospect were to loom in London. We're getting together next week to talk about all sorts of combinations and permutations. The only sure thing is that we plan to do OHIO with PIECE OF M. at the Goodman mid-January. With Rick.

Billie doesn't play again for a couple of weeks. By that time, I suppose, there'll be some decisions made about a future course.

All I can say for the moment is how happy I was to have you there, how grateful I am to you for your continual patience and understanding. I know how hard it was for you to leave Paris for us; that meant a great deal for both Billie and myself. And I was especially glad because you have never been around with me when I was working on a stage piece of yours. This was a bit different because we weren't starting from scratch, but at least you had a glimpse.

Hope Suzanne is better. And that you are not so tired. Perhaps you'll be getting away to North Africa soon. Before any more Americans descend upon you. I'm still planning to visit you in the spring, but that seems a long time away. As of Monday, I work on PLAY, KRAPP, and COME AND GO for two weeks. Then to California for a while. I've spoken to Barney about various things, and I believe he is writing to you. Or has.

Jean adds her love and thoughts. Take care of yourself. And again, again—thanks, Sam.

[Alan]

1. *Rockaby* opened at the National Theatre, Cottesloe Theatre, London, 9 December 1982, directed by AS. Also Billie Whitelaw's reading of *Enough*. *Rockaby* documentary broadcast on BBC 2, 15 December 1982.

2. Reviews: Michael Billington, *The Guardian*, 11 December 1982; Ned Chaillet, *The Times*, 11 December; Sir Harold Hobson, *TLS*, 17 December; *Sunday Telegraph*, 19 December; Russell Davies, *Sunday Times*, 19 December; Julian Barnes, *The Observer*, 19 December.

Ussy
22.12.82

Dear Alan

Thanks for yrs. of Dec. 18.

I did not thank you properly in London for the fine job on *Rockaby*, for your understanding of what was needed & pertinacity in getting it. *Gratias tibi.*[1]

I called Billie. She was off for a brief holiday before giving a few more performances over the new year.

I have not seen the papers, & don't want to, apart from a disdainful comment in the *Sunday Telegraph*. I understand Hobson had some wild stuff in the TLS, all his quotations wrong & casting *Enough* for 2 males. Perhaps he heard "Enough my old chest etc."

Got here today for perhaps only a brief stay.

Love to you all & thanks again. Look forward to a quiet evening with you in the Spring.

Sam

I heard from Barney upset about *New Yorker* affair.[2] I told him not to give it another thought. [written at head of letter, above the address]

1. *"Gratias tibi"*: thanks to you.

2. *"New Yorker* affair": Georges Borchardt, also SB's literary agent in New York, gave permission to *The New Yorker* to publish *Catastrophe* and *Ill Seen, Ill Said*.

January 21, 1983

Dear Sam,

Just back from Chicago and the Goodman and a fine experience, all too short, with Rick and David Warrilow. I felt a bit like Sam Beckett, ducking out before the opening (had to get back here to teach). But things went very well. I have just talked with Greg Mosher, and gather that the audience was most moved, the reviews quite ecstatic, and the performers pleased.

I did, as you know, just the OHIO IMPROMPTU. Rick and Helen worked on EH JOE. And David did his usual PIECE of M. I did talk with him about the running time, and I think he cut it down somewhat. Rick tried very hard and worked very hard in OHIO; he was most pleasant and cooperative, very aware that we had done the show before without him. He didn't resemble David as much as Rand Mitchell had, but the costume and wig helped a lot. I was actually going to cut the wigs down a bit, but didn't in order to hide the roundness of Rick's face—which contrasted with David's angularity. We didn't hide Rick's face, just changed its shape. He also put some makeup on his nose to make it seem a bit different.

The staff at the Goodman was extraordinarily helpful and efficient. And the time was well spent. They are playing for two weeks, and should have good audiences throughout.[1]

Oh, yes, Athol Fugard came to our dress rehearsal last Sunday, and was most appreciative. We had some small discussion with a group of University of Chicago students, and he spoke out as well.[2]

Spoke with Billie before the New Year, and she was in fine form. I was then involved in rehearsals of PLAY and OTHER PLAYS for the Acting Company (PLAY, KRAPP, JOE, and COME AND GO).[3] Had a trial run the first weekend in January in Dobb's Ferry, near Hastings, at a very posh girls' school. Went well, and audience most responsive, except for some technical problems with the tape recorder—which are now, I trust, solved. They're on tour nationally with the show, in repertory with PERICLES, TARTUFFE, and TWELFTH NIGHT.[4] I'll see them next at the Kennedy Center in Washington in early March. Then perhaps a short season in New York.

I now have David's availability in May, and am trying to arrange for a double bill of OHIO and CATASTROPHE. Perhaps at the Public. I'm hoping to catch Neumann's performance of COMPANY there in Feb. if it's still on.[5] I have to go to NY for two days to audition next year's students.

Fond memories of our days in London. Hope it wasn't too bad for you. Thank you for your last letter and Latin thoughts. Much appreciated. Jean joins me in sending love. Still expect to see you in May. Hoping to arrive for a few days on May 13.

Take care of yourself.

No word re possible London OHIO. [handwritten line]

[Alan]

1. "The Beckett Project," presented by the Goodman Theater of the Art Institute of Chicago, Goodman Theater Studio, ran in repertory 18–30 January 1983. *Ohio Impromptu,* directed by AS, lighting by Rocky Greenberg. David Warrilow (Reader), Rick Cluchey (Listener). *Eh Joe,* directed by Rick Cluchey, lighting/set by Kevin Rigdon. Rick Cluchey (Joe), Helen G. Bishop (Voice). *A Piece of Monologue,* staged by David Warrilow and Rocky Greenberg, designed by Greenberg. Warrilow (Speaker). Reviews: Richard Christiansen, "Goodman produces top-drawer 'Beckett Project,'" *Chicago Tribune,* 19 January 1983; Glenna Syse, "'Beckett Project' sharp, striking studies of nothingness," *Chicago Sun-Times,* 19 January 1983.

2. Athol Fugard (b. 1932), South African dramatist, actor, director.

3. *Play and Other Plays* in repertory with *Pericles, Tartuffe,* American Place Theatre, The Acting Company, 19 April–1 May 1983. *Play and Other Plays,* directed by AS, designed by Mark Fitzgibbons. *Play:* Libby Colohan (W1), Megan Gallagher (W2), Jack Kenny (M). *Krapp's Last Tape:* Richard S. Iglewski (Krapp). *Come and Go:* Margaret Reed (Flo), Libby Colahan (Vi), Megan Gallagher (Ru).

4. *Tartuffe* by Molière (1622–1673), the others by Shakespeare.

5. Frederick Neumann (b. 1907), director, actor, one of original founders of Mabou Mines; acted in a number of other SB works, *Cascando,* 1976, and the premieres of *Theater I* and *Theater II,* 1985; staged *Mercier and Camier,* 1979, and *Worstward Ho,* 1986; knew SB for forty years. *Company,* produced by Joseph Papp, the New York Shakespeare Festival/Mabou Mines, directed by Neumann, Public/Other Stage, New York, 16–30 January 1983. Neumann (The Performer), Honora Fergusson (She).

Paris
1.2.83

Dear Alan

Thanks for yrs. of Jan 15.

I heard from Greg, with a few reviews. They all seem pleased.

. . . .[1]

Remake of *Film* on its way here. Producers Damien Pettigrew / Gaspare di Caro. Coproducers FR 3 (France), CBC (Canada) & PBS (U.S.A.) Actor Klaus Kinski. Cameraman Raoul Coutard, Godard's cameraman.[2] Shooting in Paris next month. I said I would not take part, but could be consulted. Pettigrew (not the *Rockaby* P.) knows my work and seems anxious to do a faithful job. Barney in agreement.

. . . .[3]

Still incapable of work. Shall call off Graz[4] if I continue so much longer—as seems likely.

Don't fail to come in May.

Love to you both
Sam

1. Barney and Lisa Rosset were in Paris.
2. Jean-Luc Godard (b. 1930), French film director (*Le Petit Soldat,* 1960; *Une Femme est une Femme,* 1961); Klaus Kinski (1926–1991), Polish actor.
3. Ruby Cohn had been ill.
4. Graz Autumn Festival.

April 2, 1983

Dear Sam,

Sitting in East Hampton once more, California a distant memory. Don't have to go back until end of September.

. . . .[1]

Jean and I went out to the beach house, closed all winter, and walked along the water. Not a soul. Kept thinking how much you would like the feeling of the place. Not quite Morocco, but completely primitive, elemental, true. We love it, and can't wait to get it organised so that we can spend some time there this summer.

After the usual uncertainties, I'm really coming to see you in May. Arriving in Paris the morning of Friday, May 13! and staying until that Monday, when I'm off to London and Reading for a few days. I have not made my hotel arrangements yet because this has all just happened, but will try again for Hotel de la Paix on Raspail. I do hope my timing is OK for you, and that we'll be able to meet. How about dinner that evening? Or Saturday? or Sunday? Or whenever. I do want to see you. It seems so long since December 9.

Was supposed to have started rehearsals on a new play for Broadway as of this Monday; but almost at the last minute, it has been postponed, not clear for how long. It was to have opened on May 5. Right now, it looks as though we may do it at the Kennedy Center in Washington, with rehearsals in June or July. I'm supposed to go to the Guthrie Theatre in Minneapolis in August to do John Osborne's THE ENTERTAINER, but that may be changed too. The general state of the American theatre at the moment is more precarious than ever.[2] Reagan is out to kill the arts as well as everybody.

At the end of this month, the Acting Company comes into New York for a two-week season, which includes PERICLES, TARTUFFE, and PLAY and OTHER PLAYS *(Krapp, Come and Go, Eh Joe).*[3] As of June, there is a strong possibility that OHIO and CATASTROPHE will be done by the Writers and Directors Theatre (off-Broadway) for 4–6 weeks—if I can get David Warrilow committed, and proper guarantees by the theatre, etc. Hoping will know more by the time I see you.

Jean and I celebrated our 30th anniversay a week ago. Vickie is 28 this week, and David 24. Seems like yesterday when it all started. They all send you their fond regards. And if you don't mind, I'd like to add a word to Suzanne . . . .[4]

Au revoir, mon chèr Sam, I hope to see you in about a month. Please let me know if this is OK with you.

Ever,
[Alan]

P.S. Went swimming out here yesterday, and my locker number turned out to be 113. A good omen.[5]

1. Two paragraphs follow, the first about the beach house in Amagansett, the second about flight plans to visit SB in Paris.
2. In fact Broadway theater was in its worst slump in ten years, with theaters standing empty, gross receipts down, the U.S. suffering a national recession.
3. 19 April–1 May 1983 (see letter of 21 January 1983, n. 3).
4. AS attached a letter in French to Suzanne; he and Jean hope to see her and SB in May.
5. "A good omen": a joking reference to the date of SB's birthday, the 13th of April.

Paris
20.5.83

Dear Alan

In haste to let you know Graz has no objection to American premiere of *What Where*. Shall mail it to you early next week.

Washington problem solved. . . .[1]

Love to you both
Sam

1. "Washington problem solved": (see letter of 1 June 1983, n. 2). SB wanted to send money to his cousin in America, but since money could not be transferred at that time from France, he intended to sell a manuscript of *Waiting for Godot*; however, a way was found around the difficulty.

25.5.83

Dear Alan

Herewith translation of Graz piece.[1]

They have no objection to an American production prior to theirs.

I have sent a copy to Barney.

Peter Hudson (*Endgame* director) very remorseful at having received you so inadequately. He says he panicked.

Love to you all
Sam

1. *Quoi où (What Where)*, written for the 1983 Graz Autumn Festival in Austria.

June 1, 1983

Dear Sam,

Your script arrived this morning. I was waiting to write to you until then.

Fascinating and marvelously theatrical. We have time and even enough actors, but deadlines on publicity, program, etc. making schedule very tight. We open June 15. Question of order of three plays needs to be decided before time to think. We were going to do OHIO and then end with CATASTROPHE. If three plays, with two intermissions, should end with CAT or WHAT WHERE.

Donald Davis as Voice of Bam, David Warrilow as Bom, others as we can. By the way, combination of Davis and Warrilow in CAT is excellent. Also, the Assistant, Margaret Reed, from Acting Company COME AND GO.

Problems with the management, as usual, about money for props, costumes, etc., but Barney and I united in the good fight.

By the way, is there not a misprint on page 1 of WHAT WHERE at bottom? Surely, it is "Bam *alone at 3 head haught*" just before last five lines on page? Bom enters top of page 2. Please tell me if I'm wrong.¹

Thousands of other things to say, but I want to get this letter off to you. Glad to have seen you. Worried about you. But glad you settled Washington business with Barney of GODOT ms. You know that Jim Knowlson and I rang Lindon from Reading on May 18. Heard then that French government had relented or whatever.²

The Polish director's production of the *Fragments* impressed me much, as did he and his scene designer.³ Really well performed and most faithful. I think he is talented fellow. The English production of ENDGAME did not, I'm afraid, nothing personal re director's lack of response to me or whatever it was. Clov and Nagg were OK, but Hamm and Nell inadequate as actors. Hamm all on one note, sorry to say.⁴

Will write again when we get through pre-production crises and confusions. Right now, I have high hopes for the actors, costume designer, and lighting person; worried about management delivering on time and as promised. What else is new?

Take care of yourself. Thanks for getting script to us in time. Will do everything I can.

Best,
[Alan]

1. Bam is alone.
2. See letter of 25 May 1983, n. 1.
3. "Polish director": Jacek Gasiorowski (b. 1950); "scene designer": Ewa Biejat; *Fragments: Theatre I* and *Theatre II* opened at Lucenaire Forum, 17 May 1983. Martin Trevieres, Jacques Dumur.
4. *Endgame*, directed by Peter Hudson, opened at Tai Théâtre d'Essai, 13 April 1983. Nick Calderbank (Hamm), Christian Erikson (Clov), Robert Barr (Nagg), Judith Burnett (Nell).

Thursday, June 9, 1983

Dear Sam,

Have just put the phone down after your call. Delighted to hear your voice. This was actually a perfect time for you to telephone. You can almost always reach me at this hour. Sorry I wasn't in last Friday when you called but I had to go to Washington on some kind of conference.

Things are progressing. The actors are in fine shape, and I am most pleased with my cast—Warrilow, Davis, Mitchell, and Margaret Reed and Daniel Wirth, whom you do not know—.[1]

Technical problems galore, but we are gradually overcoming them. OHIO is in the best shape; but even then—because the stage is so small—we have to keep working on the lighting. I have shortened the wigs. The table is exactly like it was at the Goodman, top slightly slanted so that everyone in the audience can see it. The stage floor rises a little at the Harold Clurman Theatre but not that much.

CATASTROPHE seems to work very well. Bare stage. Awful-looking chair for the director; grandeur and bad taste. The movements of the Assistant are what we have been mainly working on. David Warrilow is superb as the Protagonist; and the effect at the end is very strong. We are still working on location and volume and quality of Director's voice from the stalls after he leaves the stage. Running time somewhere over ten minutes, I think.

WHAT WHERE the main concern because it's just starting. The moment I put the phone down I remembered I wanted to ask you if you had any preference on the color of the megaphone. At the moment, it's gray—like the robes. We are also working on the wigs. The four figures look very much alike, though Davis' girth is a bit more than the others. We are trying to hide this through the four robes being a bit full. I think I understand what you mean by 'reduction' in BAM's voice, and will work on it by time we get our final tape. Lighting the main problem, so that the entrances at N, W, and E work the way you want them. The stage is smallish; and, of course, the scenic arrangements of walls, drapes, etc. for the other two plays have to be taken into consideration. But the technical staff here is a good one and very anxious to do the work the way you want it.

Only problem is that the management got into some kind of hassle with the actors about their contracts right at the beginning, and it has not been entirely straightened out. Actors in the off-Broadway theatre are so minimally paid that it's always hard for them to realise that the Press Agent and Company Manager (unionised!) get more than they do. I told Jack Garfein (our producer) right at the start that I wanted no fee.[2] If the show runs six weeks and starts to break even, then I will get what actors get. That's fine with me because I'm subsidised for all my nefarious activities by that university out west, as you may remember. But I want the actors to feel that Jack is not exploiting them, and that takes a bit of doing. Please don't concern yourself about it. Normal American theatre confusions. No wonder you won't come to visit us.

Jean fine, in East Hampton. We're having audiences starting Saturday, and then opening on Wednesday, June 15. Will talk with you afterwards. Many thanks. (Also to Graz Festival; we'll do what you want on that.) Do hope you're OK. I also wanted to ask you how your cousin's operation went. Please excuse hasty tone of this letter. Trying to get it off before I head into town for rehearsal. All the best.

[Alan]

1. The Harold Clurman Theatre and Lucille Lortel presented *"Samuel Beckett Plays"*: *Ohio Impromptu, Catastrophe, What Where,* 15 June 1983–15 April 1984 (394 performances), produced by Jack Garfein, directed by AS. *Ohio Impromptu:* David Warrilow (Reader), Rand Mitchell (Listener), succeeded by Alvin Epstein and Daniel Wirth. *Catastrophe:* Donald Davis (Director [D]), succeeded by Kevin O'Connor, Margaret Reed (His Female Assistant [A]), succeeded by Leigh Taylor-Young, David Warrilow (Protagonist [P]), Rand Mitchell (Luke, in charge of the lighting, offstage [L]). *What Where:* Donald Davis (Bam, Voice of Bam [V]), succeeded by Kevin O'Connor, David Warrilow (Bom), succeeded by Alvin Epstein and Daniel Wirth, Rand Mitchell (Bim), Daniel Wirth (Bem). Reviews: Douglas Watt, *NY Daily News,* 16 June 1983; Mel Gussow, *NY Times,* 21 and 31 June; Clive Barnes, *New York Post,* 21 June; Humm (Richard J. Hummler), *Variety,* 22 June; John Beaufort, *Christian Science Monitor,* 27 June; Alisa Soloman, *Village Voice,* 28 June.
2. Jack Garfein (b. 1930), Czechoslovakian-born American producer, artistic director at the Harold Clurman Theatre; this was the second time AS had directed for no fee (see letter of 25 September 1982).

June 19, 1983

Dear Sam,

Excuse the thin paper; have a feeling the envelope will be full of reviews. Would have sent this earlier, but for some reason, the Barnes review kept getting delayed.

We are doing well. The show of three one-acts, unusual as it is, seems to have attracted lots of attention and interest; and from the time of our first audience one week ago, we have had good or reasonably good audiences. As you can see, the reviews are the usual mish-mash, but generally favorable; and we gather many of the weeklies even more so. Will send rest on to you as soon as they are out.

Wish I could really tell you something about the three plays. OHIO pretty much as before, but benefits from the small space, the concentration, the lighting. CATASTROPHE, we have worked on very hard; and I think it comes off well. The technical problem is to make sure that David's head is in the light at the end. If he moves a quarter of an inch, of course, it isn't; and he has to be very very careful. The effect at the end is stunning; and when I saw the show last, it really moved me. David is superb; and I just hope he stays with us. We are doing very good business—enough so that maybe Jack Garfein can increase the actors' salaries, I hope—and should run a while. Also Donald. And I think you would find Maggie Reed as the Assistant very 'ballet-like' indeed. We have found that Donald's live voice unseen at the back of the very small house works better than having him coming through a loud speaker. WHAT WHERE, most people keep wanting to interpret on the literal political level—I think it may suffer from coming after CATASTROPHE. But it is lit very well, costumed as you asked, and played with simplicity and great power. People keep asking me to lift the volume of the megaphone and to make the lights brighter; but I have done it the way I think you would have wanted it, and will keep it that way.

Thank you for calling on Thursday. We were all most pleased. As I told you, Barney came to the opening and was very impressed and affected. Various other people.

The technical problems were, as always, quite present throughout. Especially in a small theatre where we had constantly to balance the amount and direction of the light with the amount of light which spilled on to other things. That is, for example, from the megaphone onto the floor and to the actors. We worked on this for days, and finally solved it about 90 per cent. Light, unfortunately, doesn't stop when it hits an object or person; it flows on around them and past them. We were always trying to see something and *not* see something else—the black curtains, the brick walls, etc. Eventually, we did fairly well. OHIO is well lit and yet floats in a black void. CATASTROPHE takes place on a really bare stage with only a chair and a plinth. And WHAT WHERE is exactly the way you asked for; the actors literally appear from the black void outside. We don't even see the black wire holding up the megaphone. But it took time.

Hope you are feeling a bit better than you were that weekend we met. And glad that you were able to solve the matter of your cousin without involving GODOT ms.

Think of you all the time, and even dream of you. David Warrilow and Donald and all of us miss you and wish you were here to see the three plays. But we do understand. Take caRE OF YOURSELF [*sic*]. I shall stay in touch and keep you informed as to what is happening. The note about Graz got printed as an insert and will be put into the next edition of the program.[1] I have written to them also.

Thanks again for letting us do these plays. I cannot tell you what they mean to me.

[Alan]

1. AS inserted this acknowledgment in the program: "The Graz Autumn Festival in Austria, for which *What Where* was written, has kindly waived its rights to the world premiere in order to make the Harold Clurman Theatre's production possible."

June 24, 1983

Dear Sam,

Two weeks since our very first audience, and a million years! Finally, no reviews, just a few thoughts from me to you. It was a wonderful and difficult rehearsal period. Wonderful because of Warrilow and Davis and the others, and your texts, and the work, and the feeling that we were doing something special. And it really came off, all three portions in their very different ways. OHIO we knew was OK, and David W. has grown and deepened; one of the critics said his 'hand sighed' when it came down off the book, and it did. CATASTROPHE, we worked on a great deal; to get the proper tone from Donald, the proper 'ballet-like' movement from the Assistant, the proper lighting (it is very difficult for David to keep holding his head all through the show in exactly the right place for the light to hit his face at the end; more difficult than in the urns or in NOT I, where the actor is held rigid or confined.) We actually found it was better to light him from below, more controllable and dramatic, the light closer to him and confined without any spill. We tried the Director's voice in the back of the house, the middle of the house, other parts of the house over a speaker; and finally had him, unseen by the audience, with his live voice coming from the back of the house, which is small enough to suggest that the front row of the larger house is where he is. For WHAT WHERE, apart from getting what we felt was the proper tone and rhythm thruout, the main problem was lighting. The rectangle lit dimly so that they came into it from blackness. The megaphone lit so that its shadow would not spill on to the floor or to the actors. Eventually, I think, we were able to achieve what you set for us. Suzanne Jenkins (who took the *ROCKABY* photos) came and shot some pictures one night while the regular photographer was shooting the photos for the press—which are mostly bad because she kept putting on more light; and they are absolutely lovely; as soon as they are printed up from the contacts, I'll send you a set. This will take a couple of weeks, as I am off for Denver for some Directing Workshop I got myself into.

Difficult because off-Broadway tends to be schlocky at best. There's not enough time, not enough money, not enough people. (Our Stage Manager, Chuck, not only runs and calls the show from the light booth, but has to run down during each interval to change the set, arrange the curtains, get the actors ready, and practically wash out the shirts.)[1] Jack Garfein is calming down a bit, but before we opened, he refused to spend a nickel on anything without copious and furious discussion; he wasn't paying the actors much; but he was paying the production staff nothing; they were working for the credit and the "experience." It's better now that we are practically selling out the 100 seats every night. We should get a decent run—if we can keep the actors, especially David W.

Donald already has to go back to Canada around the end of July—but we knew that when he came. David has a film he's doing in August, so he may be off for a week and a half; then he'll be back. We are now looking for another actor to replace Donald; possibly a fellow named Moultrie Patten, who believe it or not played Pozzo in Chicago in the late 1950s for the Second City troupe. I thought of Rick, but he's doing GODOT, I've been told. And I'm not sure whether David W. and he would get along this time after the Chicago experience. Never an easy moment in this business. David W. will play BAM; we'll do a new tape. [last sentence handwritten]

I'll keep sending reviews as they come in. Surprisingly enough, with the exception of John Simon and VARIETY, they have been sympathetic or favorable or more than that.[2] Wed. night, we had a large group of students, and the actors and I answered questions. Very perceptive. I'll keep in touch. Really glad it came off for you. Hope you are OK.

[Alan]

1. "Chuck": Charles Kindl was stage manager at the Harold Clurman Theatre, New York.
2. Review in *Variety* by Humm (Richard J. Hummler), 22 June 1983.

July 5, 1983

Dear Sam,

Much touched by your phone call yesterday. Really pleased to hear your voice as well as the good news from Washington and Paris.

I've been away a week, so not completely caught up. But I'll be coming in this week to see the production again. And then to put in the replacements.

Kevin O'Connor, who is replacing Donald Davis on July 17, is a fine actor whom I've known a long time. He will be somewhat different, but has a definite power of his own.[1]

David, of course, will be fine as BAM; and I would have used him in that role in the first place except that I was trying to split the evening more evenly between Warrilow and Davis. We will be making a new tape sometime soon. I think you will find Davis' tape properly 'reduced' as you once put it. And his voice was fine. But so will David's be.

I gather business continues. Matinees are about half full, but the weather has been murderous, and people go somewhere where they can be outside. But if we get through the Fourth of July season—and we have—things should pick up with tourists and general theatre people, all of whom want to see the plays.

Jean and I are fine. She's happy to have me with her for a while. My daughter, Vickie, has just gotten engaged; and my son, David, has just gotten his Master's from Berkeley, and a job nearby in New Jersey. It's a lot better than last year at this time when I was just about to get out of the hospital.

Will send you the photos of CATASTROPHE and WHAT WHERE as

soon as I can get them from Suzanne Jenkins. Also more reviews as they come out, and I find out about them.

Take care of yourself.

Best,
[Alan]

1. Kevin O'Connor (b. 1938), actor, director, producer.

July 16, 1983

Dear Sam,

Couple more for you to look at.

A hard week. Blazingly hot. Donald Davis leaving; and we rehearsed Kevin O'Connor, who will be fine. Going in on Tuesday, 19th.

The problem has been David. He's leaving also to do a film starting August 1. We knew that, and were going to have the understudy, Dan Wirth, play his parts for two weeks . . . .[1] I think, since he can only come back a few weeks before he would have to go off again on his European tour, that the best thing is to replace him after his film assignment. To that end, we have approached several actors, including Alvin Epstein—the original Lucky over here, you may remember, who also played Clov for me. Alvin is interested. We shall see what happens—particularly to David. I'll keep you posted.

Business continues very good, after the Sunday ad last week. We are even beginning to get an advance. You know the theatre is only 99 seats, but that still means we have an audience. If we can survive the heat (and our cast problems), we should get a decent run.

The rest of life continuing. I swim daily, think of you every time I walk into our beach house. I expect to be starting on a Broadway venture, THE WAR AT HOME[2]—if the producer gets the needed money—around the middle of August.

Am reading a lot: T.S. Eliot, Tolstoi, and some new spy novels. Jean sends her love. We hope it's not as hot where you are.

[Alan]

1. Brief comment on David Warrilow's health.
2. By the American playwright James Duff (b. 1956).

San Diego: Department of Drama
USCD Theatre
La Jolla, California 92093
August 1, 1983

Dear Sam,

This was the week that was. I thought you should know that David Warrilow is now out of the show . . . . The understudy, Dan Wirth, went on and did nobly. We have been preparing him, rehearsing him, and making sure he was ready for whatever—for some time . . . .[1]

Dan will play it for about a week, and then we get Alvin Epstein, who unfortunately is not available at this exact moment. Dan is, of course, much younger (30ish) but extremely intelligent and sensitive. His OHIO IMPROMPTU is really quite effective. And we've had to get him a wig for CATASTROPHE with tufts of gray hair. It takes him some time to makeup each night.

Sad as it has been to see David leave, the general morale back-stage has improved. Because it has been most difficult to have the normal chit-chat and camaraderie in the face of his pain. I shall keep in close touch to see how he is doing, and let you know. He told me this week that he had had a letter from you but had been unable to reply.

The enclosed article appeared yesterday, ironically just as David was leaving. It seems not bad, and should help business, which has been continuing amazingly. We tend to sell out or almost sell out each night, although matinees are about half full. The theatre is small, but it's good to have it full. The interesting thing to me is that the audience is so varied, young people, ordinary middle-aged people, and some older people. More of a general audience than a specialised one, which we had at first.

About Mel and his powers of observation: That look of the Protago-nist's was always one of cowing the audience, shaming the audience, making the applause stop. How Mel ever got the 'supplication' idea, I don't know. David's eyes literally glowed like coals, and sometimes even knowing the play as I do and seeing it over and over again I would recoil in a kind of terror from that look. Mel continues to want to find a political base in WHAT WHERE, as do many others, who feel more comfortable with it.[2] My daughter, Vicki (your 'niece'), who is getting married in the spring, loved it and was quite moved. Seems a long time ago when she was toddling around the L'Aiglon.

Saw the new JOURNAL OF BECKETT STUDIES with Billie in

ROCKABY on the cover.[3] Called her a few days ago, and she was in good form, rehearsing at the National with a new Christopher Hampton play.[4] Our producer here thinks he can get her over here in the Harold Clurman because Equity has no jurisdiction over theatres with less than 100 seats. I told him to make sure before we led her down the garden path again. There's talk of Donald Davis doing CATASTRO-PHE in Toronto in the spring. Also, of his doing KRAPP again after all this time. Heard from Pennebaker that the ROCKABY TV film will be shown on Public Television in the fall.

Barney publishing WHAT WHERE in the new Evergreen, you know. I see him almost every week out here. Fred Jordan saw the show and seemed to like it.[5] I'm trying to get Dick Seaver. Wish I could come and see you again this fall, but going back to Calif. for the fall term before coming back to NYC in December to stay.

Jean surviving the summer but thinks I'm working too hard. If I didn't, I'd fall apart. . . . Thinking of you and wishing you well. I'll keep in touch about David and the rest of us.

[Alan]

1. Comment on David Warrilow's health in the two places in this paragraph indicated by ellipses.

2. Mel Gussow, "Beckett Distills His Vision," *NY Times,* 31 July 1983.

3. *Journal of Beckett Studies,* 8 (Autumn 1982).

4. Christopher Hampton (b. 1946), English dramatist, born in the Azores; the new play: *Tales from Hollywood.*

5. *What Where* was published as one of "Three Plays" in the *New Evergreen Review,* 98 (1984), 39–51 (pp. 47–51 specifically). The other two plays were *Ohio Impromptu* and *Catastrophe,* all included in *Collected Shorter Plays,* 1984. Fred Jordan was Senior Vice-President and Senior Editor, Grove Press, at this time.

August 13, 1983

Dear Sam,

Great to hear your voice this morning!

Can't believe it's exactly three months since I saw you in Paris and we talked about the three plays.

Enclosed, a couple of more bits that might interest you.

Alvin Epstein going in on Tuesday, and I'll let you know how he's doing. No one is like David, and each one has his own individual strength. The main thing is that the plays hold up on their own, and the audience is quite content to sit there listening to your words.

The summer has gone. I still don't know if I'm going to be in rehearsal with THE WAR AT HOME or not. They don't have all the money. I'd love to come to see you again in September before heading back to California, but I don't think that's going to be possible. When I know Jack Garfein's Paris dates and address, I'll let you know.

Thank you for telephoning. Not as good as being with you, but it does give me a feeling.

All the best.

[Alan]

August 22, 1983

Dear Sam,

Was going to write last week, but wasn't sure whether you might call. Things are moving along. David Warrilow is improving, and should be coming back to himself in a few weeks. We hope he'll be able to take over when Alvin has to leave, the end of Sept. Alvin went in one week ago. He is still finding his way in OHIO, but is very effective in CAT, and doing well in WW. David was, of course, very special; but Alvin has his own quality and tone; and the audience seems to respond. We are still doing decent business, a little off during the extremely hot spell last weekend, but holding up.

Lots churning on all fronts. Gordon Davidson[1] of the Mark Taper Forum, a Los Angeles non-profit theatre, where I have almost worked many times, is now pursuing Barney for the rights to all your plays in order to do a Beckett Festival in the spring. Gordon is a decent producer-director, and we are good friends—he'd like me to direct some of the plays—but I'm not sure it's a good idea to do all the plays at once. Also, Jack Garfein, our current producer, retains the rights, including touring for the 3 we're doing right now. How do you feel?

Jack Garfein is currently in Europe and will be in Paris between Sept. 3 and 7. He wants to talk to you, about a Beckett Festival in New York in the spring. Also wants to do all the plays, and is even talking about getting Billie over to do ROCKABY. I have explained all the Equity business, but he claims that since his theatre is under 99 seats, he can get her. I'm not sure. Nor do I entirely trust Jack in terms of some of his ideas and plans. I told Billie I would not approach her and make her go through all that again until and unless I was *sure* we could get proper permission. If you feel like seeing Jack, he can be reached via Carolas Frankqui; 8 Cité D'Angoulème, Paris 75011. The phone there is 70–38–67. (There is another phone where messages for him could be left: 32–25–23.) Forgive me for bothering you with all this. And if you do meet with Jack please take everything he says with several grains of salt. Like all NY producers, he is an 'operator'.

My Broadway show has been postponed once again; not enough money. I am dashed a bit but what can one do? Harold Pinter has asked me to do his three new plays off-Broadway in the spring; we shall see. I have three weeks before taking off for California, and for a minute I thought that I could come over to see you. But the trouble is that not only am I now racing an already-past deadline with my book for Viking; but we have found a nice little carriage house very close to Hastings, which we have decided to rent in place of our East Hampton abode. We have to move everything; and I am trying to pack as much as I can before I go to CA so that Jean can do the rest. The move will enable us to consolidate East Hampton and Hastings into one place; and we shall still have the beach place to stay in when we come out here. All very mad and confusing but after it's done, we'll be relieved. We have been too scattered the past few years.

. . . .[2]

Hope you are having a little time to yourself. Jean joins me in wishing you all the best. I'll write again.

[Alan]

1. Gordon Davidson (b. 1933), director, artistic director, producer.
2. AS gives David Warrilow's address.

Paris
25.8.83

Dear Alan

Thanks for yr. letters, excellent photos & other enclosures.

Heard from Graz. Premiere of *What Where* (with *Catastrophe*) Sept. 23.[1] Also programmed *Krapp*. Shall see [?]Langurith here next week.

Had dinner with Ruby at the *Iles*[2] . . .

Chabert pleased with progress. Opening Sept. 15. Especially with combination Lonsdale–Barrault in *C. & Ohio*.[3]

. . . .[4]

The Arikhas moving to N.Y. in a few days. They'll go to the plays & hope to see you.

Stifled with visitors. Don't know when I'll get back to Ussy. No work in train or in sight.

Do hope you get over before Ca.

Love to you all
Sam

1. *Katastrophe (Catastrophe)* and *Was Wo (What Where)* opened at Theater im Malersaal, Graz, 23 September 1983, directed by Kurt Josef Schildknecht, designed by Hans Michael Heger, German trans. by Elmer Tophoven. *Katastrophe:* Walter Kohls (Director [D]), Petra Fahrnlander (His Female Assistant [A]), Alexander Holler (Protagonist [P]), Peter Hegelmann (Luke, in charge of the lighting, offstage [L]). *Was Wo:* Rainer Hauer (Bam, Voice of Bam [V]), Armin J. Schallock (Bom), Horst Klaus (Bim), Dietrich Schloderer (Bem).

2. "the *Iles*": Closerie des Iles.

3. *Catastrophe,* directed by Michael Lonsdale, opened at the Compagnie Renaud-Barrault's new theatre, Théâtre du Rond-Point, Paris, 15 September 1983, in a triple bill with *Berceuse (Rockaby)* and *L'Impromptu d'Ohio,* directed by Pierre Chabert, designed by Jean Herbin-Pierre Didelot. *Catastrophe:* Michael Lonsdale (Director [D]), Catherine Sellers (His Female Assistant [A]), Jean-Louis Barrault (Protagonist [P]), Dominique Ehlinger (Luke, in charge of lighting, offstage). *Berceuse:* Catherine Sellers (Mouth). *L'Impromptu d'Ohio:* Michael Lonsdale (Reader), Jean-Louis Barrault (Listener).

4. SB says Madeleine Renaud is well.

"Not sent" [handwritten]
August 28, 1983

Dear Sam,

Wasn't sure I should write you this letter, but decided I had to.

Barney just rang me to tell me that they were selling xeroxed scripts of the three plays at the theatre for some exorbitant sum. I had no idea. Barney was livid, and I don't blame him. Another in a series of actions taken by the producer, Jack Garfein.

All through the summer, I have had to be ambivalent about what has been going on. On the one hand, the three plays are doing well, and should be running for a while; and Jack keeps talking about future Beckett projects. On the other hand, we have had problems all along with his refusal to pay the actors properly, with his lack of taste on various matters, including the advertising, the posters, the payment of royalties to you, etc. etc. I have been torn right down the middle because he has a theatre and a long-range plan, and a desire to do your plays; and on the other hand, I find him just grabbing on to what he has found to work commercially and exploiting everyone and everything.

As my last letter suggested, I do not feel that a Beckett Festival is such a great idea for the spring, or that Garfein is capable of getting it on in a way that does not cheapen or jeopardise the entire idea. I have been reluctant to say this to you because I did not want to stand in the way of the plays getting on. But in my opinion—and, I believe, in Barney's—putting on the entire canon of plays at the moment in a tiny off-Broadway theatre, where getting the proper actors for the entire range of plays will prove even more difficult than getting the actors for the current plays, where Garfein will be constantly cutting corners and standards unless I watch him every moment, is not a good idea. It will cut across our present audience and attention. It will not necessarily be done the way it should be done. And I'm not going to be able to be around watching it every moment, which I've had to do on these shows.

Garfein talks a good game, but when the chips are down, he is always trying to get by, make do, operate, and chisel. I have had to fight him every step of the way on the present threesome; and the fact that they have come off as well as they have is only because the plays are marvelous, and the actors have stuck it out with me. They would have quit a dozen times because of what Garfein was doing or not doing.

Even if he were the finest and most idealistic producer in the world, I would be worried about doing so many Beckett plays at once in NY. Los Angeles, where they have only rarely been seen, is one thing; but the New York critics and public have to be approached with some sense of the past. It is, of course, up to you; but I beg you if and when you meet with Garfein, to understand that he is basically interested in making as much profit as he can while giving as little as he can.

By the way, are you doing GODOT in Paris with Rick and Bud? And are they really going to Australia and etc.? Marty keeps telling us various things, and I am not entirely sure where her flights of fancy take over. [handwritten from "things"]

Forgive this letter,
Alan

P.S. David Warrilow continues to improve. [handwritten in left margin]

Not *Sent*
[handwritten heading with "Not" scratched out]
[revised version of letter of same date "not sent"]
August 28, 1983

Dear Sam,

Wanted to write to you once more before you saw Jack Garfein—if you are seeing him.[1]

Lots been happening, most of it people climbing on the Sam Beckett bandwagon. And I'm beginning to get a little worried.

I told you that Jack wants to do a Beckett Festival in the spring. And I have already told him that I did not think it was such a great idea doing every single Beckett play ever written all at once. Especially in NYC, where people and critics have seen all of them several times. In Los Angeles, where Gordon Davidson has the same idea, at least they haven't been seen as much. But to saturate the audience with all the plays at once will, in my opinion (and, I believe, in Barney's) not only hurt the present three, but will flood the market in a wrong way. Everybody and his brother has been besieging Barney to get rights to one or more of your plays because the present three have proven so successful. Many of these would be done with poor or inadequate performers, directors and spaces. You know about Marty wanting to do HAPPY DAYS in December. I'm not even sure about that one, but I know that you feel indebted to her and want her to have a chance. But I do not really know about her as an actress except what I saw of her at Stanford some years ago, which was not exactly reassuring.

What I guess I'm trying to say very badly is that I think Barney should be very leery of handing out the rights to your plays wholesale; and that not too many of them should be done all at once. Not that I'm always qualified to make judgments, but I do try to consider the talent and the motives involved. People should want to do your plays because there is someone special involved, not just to make money or get attention.

Barney told me that Jack was selling our xeroxed scripts at the theatre for a very high price. I had no idea, and will attempt to have this stopped immediately. I know we had been hoping that the three plays could be published while we were running, so that the people who wanted to buy copies could do so. I am sorry to learn about the scripts themselves being sold.

David Warrilow is improving, and we are hopeful that he will be able to come back to us when Alvin leaves. Alvin is improving steadily, and the audiences are responding to him. I see the show about once a week.

We have definitely gotten our "carriage house" on the Hudson, in Irvington, just above Hastings, familiar territory. I'm starting to pack my books, but poor Jean will have to do most of the moving, since I have to take off for California in three weeks. In between, I'm getting an honorary Doctor of Fine Arts at Williams College, one of USA's oldest universities. All your fault. We are happy to be consolidating East Hampton and Hastings into one place, but the process will be horrendous the next few months.

Are you doing GODOT in Paris with Rick and Bud?[2] And are they really going to Australia, and on Australian TV? Marty keeps telling us various things, but I am not always sure what's real and what isn't. I do hope you are OK, and having some time to yourself. Seeing Tom Bishop at the plays tomorrow and will find out how you are. Take care.

All the best

[Alan]

1. AS's letter of 28 August 1983 crosses SB's letter of 25 August 1983.
2. "Bud": Bud Thorpe.

Sept. 4, 1983

Dear Sam,

Your letter arrived yesterday, for which many thanks. I'm glad you liked the photos; and I have told Suzanne Jenkins.

Last night, I spoke with Avigdor Arikha from backstage. He had just seen the show, and was talking with Alvin. My stage manager called me, as he does almost every night I'm not at the theatre. He seemed to like the evening. He has an exhibition opening next week, and we are going to try at least to meet.

David is improving steadily. I spoke with him a couple of days ago at the clinic, and he is sounding his old self. He should be out in a week or two. And then we are hoping that he will replace Alvin when Alvin has to go back to his other commitment. Will let you know. I think he may have written to you.

Tom Bishop also saw the show last week, and his reaction to me was most enthusiastic. Perhaps he will let you know how he felt.

I wish I could say that I can make it to Paris prior to California . . . .[1]

I contemplated flying to you on the 13th and returning on the 16th, but that's really too hectic, apart from all the other problems. I'd love to see you and to see Barrault and Lonsdale. I'm sure they will be fine. But neither my time nor my energy seem sufficient. ('seems sufficient'?)

Please forgive and understand. Nothing would give me greater pleasure than if I could just take off, even for a day, to see you and the plays. I just cannot stretch the moments. I do promise that I shall be in Paris early in the next year.

Haven't yet heard whether you saw Jack Garfein. I'm sure he will tell me all about the meeting, if there was one, when he gets back. Thanks for understanding.

I'm hoping to hear your voice once more before I take off for California. I'll be in East Hampton most of the time until Sept. 14 when we have to go back to Hastings to deal with the moving business. I do hope you are not too besieged with everybody—and I'm sure you are.

All the best.

[Alan]

1. AS describes his difficulties in arranging his schedule which is complicated by moving house from East Hampton to Irvington, near Hastings-on-Hudson.

October 13, 1983

Dear Sam,

Too long since I last wrote and we last spoke, but my daily chores at both sides of this continent have gotten in the way for a while. I've been here almost a month now, getting started with the new term and beginning to rehearse another production, this time Wilder's OUR TOWN, with the students.[1]

The Harold Clurman Theatre seems far away, but it actually isn't.[2] My stage manager calls me two or three times a week to report on the production. I have spoken several times with David Warrilow, who is back and in fine form. I am paying a sneak visit to NY tomorrow for the weekend—to attend some sort of conference—and will see the show, hoping and trying to make sure that no one knows I am there until after the show, when I shall come backstage and be met with incredulous looks. Things are going well. Jack Garfein rang me last week to tell me several things, including that we are doing the best box office business we have ever done. Going into the fall, of course, we have not only schools but the general NY theatre audience. And our word-of-mouth must be very good because people are still coming.

The actor situation is as follows. David is back and doing well, according to all reports. I shall judge for myself tomorrow night. Kevin O'Connor, who took over as the Director when Donald Davis left, has left us for another show. But Alvin Epstein, who took over for David and was with us for 7 weeks, had to go away to do a previous commitment. He will be back in a few weeks. In the meantime, the Director is being played by a fellow named Daniel Wirth, who is an ex-student of mine here, and who did well in David's role before we got Alvin. (Are you following all this?) Then Alvin will come back, and we have decided to try alternating David and Alvin as the Protagonist and the Director. This will keep us until the first of the New Year, when both actors have to leave for other commitments. We haven't thought that far ahead, but we shall. Assuming we are still running, which we might be. I shall try to keep you at least even with us in the news of who is playing whom? I feel very good about Alvin and David alternating. In the meantime, we have also lost our Assistant, and are trying to find a first-rate actress to take the role for a while. You must understand that off-Broadway salaries are so low that people always have to take off to do a film or TV role to stay solvent.

In the meantime, more news: Edinburgh is definitely taking us in August, hopefully David and either Donald or Alvin.[3] Then, perhaps, into the West End if they will allow us. We are also thinking of a national tour for 1984–85! The best news is that Jack G. informs me that Equity will now allow Billie to play ROCKABY; this in return for our Edinburgh visit with American actors. I have informed Billie and asked her when she is free and whether she is interested. Los Angeles is still talking about a Beckett Festival in the spring. Garfein and I are exploring various possibilities in NY. Alan Mandell tells me he is wanting to name one of his new theatres after you, and wants me to do the opening production sometime in 1985. I told him I was not sure I would still be in the land of the living, but that I would be honored. And so on.

Will try to reach Barney in my fleeting hours in NY. Jean is still there trying to get our new place into shape for me when I come back for the long stretch in Dec. I do hope to see you as early as possible in the New Year, and will let you know when I can come. It was just impossible early in Sept. Even though I would have given anything to see the

Barrault-Lonsdale version. Are they still on? Did you see them? How are you?

All the best,

[Alan]

1. At University of San Diego, California, opened 10 November 1983.
2. Where *Ohio Impromptu, Catastrophe,* and *What Where* were playing.
3. Edinburgh International Festival of Music and Drama, held annually from mid-August to September since 1947. *Ohio Impromptu, Catastrophe, What Where,* and *That Time* opened 13 August 1984, had been directed by AS, designed by Rocky Greenberg. *Ohio Impromptu:* David Warrilow (Reader), Rand Mitchell (Listener). *Catastrophe:* Donald Davis (The Director [D]), Leigh Taylor-Young (His Female Assistant [A]), David Warrilow (Protagonist [P]), Rand Mitchell (Luke, in charge of the lighting, offstage [L]). *What Where:* Donald Davis (Bam, Voice of Bam [V]), David Warrilow (Bom), Rand Mitchell (Bim), Daniel Wirth (Bem).

November 20, 1983

Dear Sam,

Two more weeks in California, then back to the familiar confusions of the East.

Wanted to bring you up to date about a number of things. Thanks much for your last note.[1]

The plays are still running, going into the sixth month. We now have David and Alvin alternating, as that was the only way we could keep Alvin through those dark days back in August when we were not sure of David's return. He is completely recovered now, and better than ever as the Reader and the Protagonist. He is also fascinating as the Director when Alvin plays the other role. The two have a certain amount of rivalry, which is both good and bad. David leaves us again to go to the Guthrie Theatre after Jan. 1; we are hoping that Alvin will stay on. Depending on how the shows are doing. We also put in a new Assistant, an actress from films and TV mainly, named Leigh Taylor-Young.[2] I flew in last weekend to work with her. She is just marvelous, the best ever, and has given everyone a welcome bubble of renewed enthusiasm in the middle of the David–Alvin situation. I shall see her again when I get back on December 3—for nine months or, maybe, forever, if I decide I can afford to go on without coming back to Calif.

The big good news: Equity seems to have reversed itself on Billie, and we have been in negotiation with her to come over to do ROCK-

ABY, in the theatre right next door to the Clurman,[3] for 4–6 weeks in February–March. Evidently, the contract is now being negotiated. Billie will be free from her National Theatre chores after Feb. 4, and I shall probably come over to London after January 15 to work with her—as well as to see you. We are planning an evening of ROCKABY, FOOTFALLS, and either the reading of ENOUGH, or—hopefully— something short that you could write for her to do. I know there is not much time, and you may be disinclined or not able. But if there is anything at all that might be possible for Billie, she and I and everyone would indeed welcome it.[4]

More on ROCKABY. Evidently, the TV that Pennebaker did will finally be shown in New York next week some time. Danny also told me that Penny is planning to show the film in some sort of two-week theatre run in the near future. I am not at all happy about that, for various reasons, and told Danny that I felt this was not in the original agreement. But he says it is not in his control. So there we are. I just hope it does not affect Billie's live presence with us in February.[5] Billie talks also about Japan's interest in ROCKABY. Someone from Tokyo saw the three plays at the Clurman two weeks ago, and wants to take them to Tokyo. You know that the Edinburgh plans for August are getting fixed. And so on.

Mabou Mines is re-doing COMPANY. Marty F. keeps trying to get HAPPY DAYS on at the La Mama with her in it, around Christmas. Not definite.

Jean has not been out here at all this term, and I am desolate. She is totally involved in getting our new living quarters ready in time for us to move in by the time I get back. We will exchange the house in East Hampton for the place in Irvington, which is the village right next to Hastings. We will be sharing a French-style chateau on the Hudson with two other families. Lovely and pleasant and close to New York. So we'll have just that and the beach place. I'll send you all addresses and phone numbers when I have them. I miss not hearing your voice once in a while. I'll be at the Hastings number or in Cal. in the discernible future. [ending missing]

[Alan]

1. SB's "note" missing.

2. Leigh Taylor-Young (b. 1944), in *Catastrophe* (see letter of 13 October 1983, n. 3).

3. The Writers and Directors Theatre.

4. SB evidently responds that *Still* might be substituted for *Enough*.

5. Pennebaker *Rockaby* Documentary was not broadcast by PBS, WNET-TV, New York, until 23 July 1984.

                                                                Dec 17 plus [handwritten]
Dear Sam, [handwritten]

Been trying to write this letter since your phone call.

Wanted to reassure you about ALL STRANGE AWAY. I talked to the fellow and to Barney and to everybody; and I hope you can stop concerning yourself about the matter. Someone at Grove Press (not Barney) did indeed transmit permission to him without the qualifying clause about the plays at the Harold Clurman. He did go ahead on that assumption. I have explained it all to Garfein. The La Mama presentation will take place in January; and whatever effect it has on our run at the Clurman will just have to be faced. Sorry that Gerald whatever his last name is got you so involved in the issue. It's done, it will be done. And the main thing is that the actor who is playing the role is evidently quite good and will do your text justice.[1]

We are still going on, considerably affected by the pre-Christmas slump but still there. David has to go off to the Guthrie for another sting (HEDDA GABLER), so Alvin will be playing Reader and Protagonist regularly. For the Director, we shall have either Donald Davis back for a while, or Kevin O'Connor, who originally succeeded him. We are also losing our Assistant, and will probably go back to the original actress. So it goes on. Amazingly.

Spoke with Billie, and looking forward to going to London and Paris in a month. I expect to arrive in Paris the morning of January 18, see you that day and go off to London probably on the 19th. I shall have a week or so with Billie, then back to New York. Will give you exact times and location as soon as it is definite. I'll try the Hotel de la Paix once more.

Billie is quite excited about coming to New York for a proper run. She is only anxious about having the audience see her somehow as she is and not just in her makeup and costume for ROCKABY and FOOTFALLS. She quite understands your feeling about ENOUGH. No one is happy about the EH JOE idea for a number of reasons. She's offstage. We need another actor. And it does not really satisfy her desire for something with a strong age and character contrast. Let's think about this one a bit more.

Jean and I are happily if not completely ensconced in the new place, which is very close to the old Hastings house. We feel we are home. And for the first time in five years I have everything in one place. We shall probably sell the East Hampton house this spring—but hang on to the beach.

I am just about to start rehearsals for the Acting Company again (John Houseman's ex-Juilliard group)[2] with something called PIECES OF EIGHT, which I did last year at the University. Eight short one-acts by modern authors, including your COME AND GO. Plus Pinter, Albee, Ionesco, Stoppard, Ring Lardner and a couple of others. An interesting evening. No play longer than 15 minutes. We open on tour January 15, after which I come to London.[3]

Marty will soon be in NY for her HAPPY DAYS, which I shall see. And there is a showing of your TV films at NYU next week to which I have been invited. New York is ablaze with Beckett, and I think it's about time. Hope you don't mind the naming of the theatre. I know you wrote Jack.

Thinking of you and hoping you're OK. An intriguing favorable review of WORSTWARD HO by Hugh Kenner last Sunday's TIMES.[4] I'll ask Barney to send it to you. Take care of yourself. We think of you always. And I'm looking forward to seeing you very soon.

Jean sends her love. Our best also to Suzanne.

[Alan]

1. Gerald Thomas, a Brazilian-Englishman, adapted and directed *All Strange Away*, opened at La Mama, E.T.C., 10 January 1984, with Ryan Cutron. Thomas staged the piece again, opening 23 September 1984, with a different actor, Robert Langdon Lloyd.

2. John Houseman (1902–1988), actor, director, producer; founded Mercury Theatre (1937) with Orson Welles; Artistic Director (1956–1959) for the American Shakespeare Festival; Director of the Drama Division, Juilliard School's Theater Center, 1965; founded the City Center Acting Company in 1972.

3. *Pieces of Eight*, "Eight modern one-act plays presented with one intermission": *The Unexpurgated Memoirs of Bernard Margendeiler* by Jules Feiffer, *The Black and the White* by Harold Pinter, *The Tridget of Greva* by Ring Lardner, *The Sandbox* by Edward Albee, *The (15 Minute) Dogg's Troupe Hamlet* by Tom Stoppard, *Come and Go* by SB, *Foursome* by Ionesco, and *I'm Herbert* by Robert Anderson, had opened at the University of California, San Diego, 10 February 1983.

4. "Ever Onward. Worstward Ho," *NY Times Book Review*, 18 December 1983.

Sunday, January 29, 1984

Dear Sam,

Finally! Back home, after Paris, London and Iowa City! I left Billie in London on Thursday and flew directly, via a half-night in New York, to Iowa to see *Pieces of Eight* on tour.

Just heard about Roger Blin.[1] I can only offer you my sincerest sympathy and thoughts. I know what he meant to you and how you must feel. Nothing I can say will be of the slightest solace. But I want you to know that I am thinking of you and hoping that you will summon the strength, as you always have, to go on.

Sorry that our meeting was so brief, but I did appreciate even those moments, as always. Great to see you and to share some words. I got off the next morning to London in a snowstorm. I assume you saw Barney, and I'll talk with him when he gets back.

Billie was wonderful. A bit frightened of coming to New York but very much wanting to. We rehearsed in her place. She had been doing some work even before I arrived on FOOTFALLS, and had recalled most of it. We're both sorry that the Royal Court has lost Jocelyn's dress; but we shall do the best we can over here to duplicate it. The other dress is also mysteriously lost somewhere; but a fellow in the National's costume department who is very fond of Billie found us one in their storage depot which is quite beautiful and suitable—very much like the original—and we shall be adding some sequins over here. Billie tried it on and was happy. I lugged it back together with her wig, so all is well on that score. The chair arrives from Buffalo tomorrow, and we start the endless process of getting it to rock smoothly and without making obvious creaks. Rocky Greenberg is doing the lighting for both shows, so all will be well on that side. The theatre is very small but should be OK. I will keep at everyone to make sure we do you justice.

Jocelyn had just returned from America and seemed to be very busy, so we did not see her. I did talk with Robbie,[2] but unfortunately it was not possible to get him over here to help us.

Sorry about Billie's insistence on ENOUGH. She liked STILL,[3] but felt unable to tackle a new piece on top of the other two. She also wanted to contact the audience directly in order to make the contrast clearer between her two characterizations and herself. She was actually terrified of embarking on something totally new to her. Both she and I hope that you will understand and not think too harshly of either of us.

Business at the Clurman has been up and down.[4] Alvin Epstein has left, and a young man, Dan Wirth, once a student of mine, is playing the Reader and the Protagonist. He is quite good, and getting better with confidence. We are all looking forward to the day when there will be six Beckett plays side by side with each other on 42nd Street. Will try to take a photo of the outside as well as production pictures.

Plans for the future continue. We are going to Los Angeles in March for a week for a combined OHIO, CATASTROPHE, and ROCKABY. Garfein and Frank Dunlop continue to talk about Edinburgh,[5] and I spent some time in London with Max Stafford-Clark at the Court and Ian Alvery at the Warehouse.[6] As always, everything is a question of who finances what. Will keep you posted.

Jean sends her love. She is happy in our new place and busily preparing for Vicki's March wedding. With a little luck, I'll get through the spring and will be seeing you this summer. Take care of yourself and do . . . [ending missing]

[Alan]

1. Died 21 January 1984.

2. Robbie Hendry, stage manager for all SB productions at the Royal Court Theatre.

3. *Still*, a brief prose work written in 1972, a limited edition of 160 copies published in Milan, 1974; also in *Signature Anthology 20*, 1975, *For to End Yet Again and Other Fizzles*, 1976, and *Yet Again and Other Fizzles*, 1976 (see letter of 20 November 1983 and n. 4).

4. The Harold Clurman Theatre; Epstein had replaced David Warrilow in *Ohio Impromptu*.

5. Jack Garfein and Frank Dunlop produced *Waiting for Godot* at the Brooklyn Academy of Music in 1978; SB refused to direct, Walter Asmus did (see letter of 5 June 1978, n. 1). "Edinburgh": Festival, August 1984; Frank Dunlop (b. 1927), English director, directed Edinburgh Festival, 1984–1991.

6. Ian Alvery, producer at the Warehouse Theatre, London.

Friday morning,
February 17, [1984]

Dear Sam,

Getting this off to you at once. Hope you got my cable, which I sent right after the opening.

All went very well, and the response has been most favorable all around. The three dailies are included. I gather that some of the weeklies are already clearly positive. I'll keep forwarding them to you.[1]

The main thing is that Billie was just splendid, like a piece of exquisite music, and the evening is a total triumph for her—and you. Even the weather did well for us by holding off all dampness for the preshow festivities out in front when we unveiled the new name and marquee.[2] Representatives from the Mayor, both senators—including Patrick Moynihan[3]—people from the Theatre, Billie (who spoke of Pat Magee and Jackie, Jameson's and Guinness), and myself reading your gracious telegram to us. We stopped traffic on 42nd Street for a half hour.

The combination of FOOTFALLS and ROCKABY really works, building to a tremendous intensity, not a squeak in the audience throughout. And I must confess that they seem to enjoy the contrast with her reading of ENOUGH, which she is doing very simply.

Everyone was there, and you will probably be hearing from most of them: Avigdor and Anne, Barney, Tom B., Marty . . .

I'm sure we will do well at the box office, and that Billie can stay as long as she cares to or can. And I am so pleased for her success after all the difficulties and delays which that stupid actors' union of ours interposed.

Wish you well with your London venture.[4] Sorry that Billie and I are not there to hold your hand. We shall be thinking of you. Take care of yourself and, please, don't do any more than you can. Jean joins me in sending love.

[Alan]

1. *Rockaby, Footfalls,* and *Enough* opened at the Samuel Beckett Theatre, New York, 16 February 1984, produced by Jack Garfein, directed by AS. *Rockaby:* Billie Whitelaw (Woman and Voice). *Footfalls:* Billie Whitelaw (May), Sybil Lines (Mother's Voice). *Enough:* Billie Whitelaw. Mel Gussow interview with Billie Whitelaw, *NY Times,* 14 February 1984. Reviews: Frank Rich, *NY Times,* 17 February 1984; Clive Barnes, *NY Post,* 17 February; Douglas Watt, *Daily News,* 17 February; Ron Cohen, *Women's Wear Daily,* 17 February; Richard Corliss, *Time,* 27 February; John Beaufort, *Christian Science Monitor,* 1 March; Jack Kroll, *Newsweek,* 5 March; Sylviane Gold, *The Wall Street Journal,* 13 March.

2. The "Writers and Directors Theatre" on West 42nd Street was renamed the Samuel Beckett Theatre.

3. Senators: Daniel Patrick Moynihan, elected 1976; Alfonse D'Amato, elected 1980.

4. On 17 February SB went to London to "supervise" Rick Cluchey's San Quentin Drama Workshop production, "Beckett Directs Beckett," before their tour of Australia. After their 13 March opening in Adelaide the three plays, *Waiting for Godot, Endgame,* and *Krapp's Last Tape,* went to Sydney, Melbourne, and Canberra. Review: Peterrt Smark, "'Godot' Reconsidered," *World Press Review,* June 1984, 68.

Hyde Park Hotel
Knightsbridge
London SW1Y 7LA
28.2.84

Dear Alan

Thank you for yrs. of Feb. 17 received only today, & enclosures.[1]

Thank you also for yr. cable.

I saw Avigdor yesterday. He gave me a good account of the opening ceremony and brought other reviews.

Delighted to hear of Billie's great success. And I know how much we both owe to you for your direction.

Please thank Billie for her telegram & note of Feb. 21 & enclosures. Also Jack Garfein for his telegram.

It has been a harrassing time here & I am very tired & confused. The San Quentin *Godot* is now presentable with very good moments.

I return to Paris day after tomorrow, i.e. earlier than I intended. Suzanne is not well & I must get back.

Love to you both & to Billie. And again thanks & congratulations.

Sam

1. SB's recorded last letter was 25 August 1983, but he and AS have communicated by telephone.

March 2, 1984

Dear Sam,

Just spoke with Billie, who tells me she rang the Hyde Park yesterday, and you had checked out. Not clear whether you are elsewhere in London, in Paris, or off to Stuttgart. I hope the days with Rick and GODOT are at least behind you . . .

Presumably by this time you are aware that the ROCKABY evening is the most sought-after theatre event of the season. All hell is breaking loose. We are selling out at the Samuel Beckett Theatre (!), turning away hundreds on weekends. We are the talk of the town, and Billie has been absolutely besieged by newspaper and TV people; she has had hardly a moment to herself. I gather that Avigdor and Marty have shown you the reviews; others are still coming out. There have, of course, been some negative ones, but none in a major newspaper. I'm getting the theatre to gather an entire set for you, and will send them all on eventually.

I cannot entirely explain what has happened. You did see Billie at the National. Here it has been, somehow, deeper and more moving than ever, a combination of the plays, her work, the theatre, and the timing. The combination of FOOTFALLS and ROCKABY, which we worried about (Billie concerned about being 'an old hag' twice in a row; she was kidding), turned out most effective. The audience is left absolutely riveted on her face. And Billie has found depths and intensity—in that tiny theatre—which leave an unforgettable image. Our lighting is the best ever; so is her makeup; the chair works better than anywhere; the sound of the tape is beautiful. An actress named Katharine Hepburn was there two days ago, and said she had never heard such quiet in a NY theatre.[1]

In the midst of all this acclaim, Jack has been putting enormous pressure on Billie to move the show to a larger theatre. First, he wanted to do it on Broadway, but my strong objections plus a realisation of the economics involved have finally discouraged him. Now he wants to take it to the Theatre de Lys (now called the Lortel after its owner, and our co-producer), which is 299 seats in Greenwich Village, close to the Cherry Lane. It is a suitable theatre, and I would not have minded starting there because its intimacy and warmth is very evident. But to move our production now would still be risky, both in terms of reproducing the intangible something we seem to have at the Samuel Beckett (!) and in discombulating Billie, who is torn back and forth. I myself want to stay where we are. But Jack, of course, sees a potential of making much more in a theatre more than twice the size we are in now. He would also pay Billie more. But, as we both say, we are not in the business of doing Beckett plays to make money. Anyhow, Jack is in Europe for a few days, but the pressure will return when he comes back. I don't know actually how long Billie will stay. We could run a long time at the Beckett.

Hope you are not too exhausted. And I wish I could see you. May be in London in May to do a new American play at the Hampstead Theatre Club.[2] In the meantime, starting on Pinter's OTHER PIECES at Manhattan Theatre Club.[3] Too much going on at one time. But ROCKABY is lovely, and I'm only sorry that you cannot see it here. I'm sure Billie joins me in sending all love and good thoughts to you.

Let me hear from you when you can. In the meantime, there are six Beckett pieces (seven if you count COME AND GO, which will play a week in my PIECES OF EIGHT with the Acting Company)[4] lighting up off-Broadway.

Best to Suzanne.

[Alan]

1. Katharine Hepburn (b. 1909).

2. James Duff's *The War at Home* opened at the Hampstead Theatre, London, 13 June 1984, and as *Home Front* in New York, 2 January 1985.

3. *Other Pieces* (*Victoria Station, One for the Road,* and *A Kind of Alaska*), directed by AS, opened at the Manhattan Theatre Club, New York, 3 April 1984.

4. *Pieces of Eight* opened at the Public Theatre, New York, 8 March–11 March 1984, seven performances, produced by Joseph Papp, "conceived and directed" by AS.

Index

Beckett's works appear alphabetically under their titles;
other literary works are listed under author entries.
SB = Samuel Beckett; AS = Alan Schneider.

MW01166352

Journalism
Today

Journalism Today

A CHANGING PRESS FOR A CHANGING AMERICA

David Shaw

Harper's College Press
A Department of Harper & Row, Publishers
New York / Hagerstown / San Francisco / London

Portions of the Introduction to this collection originally appeared in **New York** Magazine (copyright © 1976 by the NYM Corp.; reprinted with the permission of **New York** Magazine). Portions of Chapter 15 ("A Personal View: Of Obscenity, Timidity and Hypocrisy") are reprinted with the permission of the **Southern California Review of Journalism** and **Forum** magazine, where they originally appeared.

ALL OTHER material in this book is reprinted with the permission of the **Los Angeles Times,** where it was originally published during the years 1974 through 1976 in substantially the same form. © **Los Angeles Times.**

Everything in this collection has, however, been edited, expanded and updated to yield the greatest possible benefit to readers interested in the function and performance of the American press today.

Sponsoring Editor: William Eastman
Project Editor: David Nickol
Designer: Emily Harste
Production Supervisor: Kewal K. Sharma
Compositor: Maryland Linotype Composition Co., Inc.
Printer and binder: The Maple Press Company

**Journalism
Today**
A CHANGING PRESS
FOR A CHANGING AMERICA

Library of Congress Cataloging in Publication Data

Shaw, David, Date—
    Journalism today.

    1. Journalism—United States—Collected works.
I. Title.
PN4867.S46   071'.3   77-1738
ISBN 0-06-160435-6
ISBN 0-06-160432-1 pbk

For Bill Thomas

Contents

Journalism
Today

Introduction

I have been a professional journalist ever since four days after my sixteenth birthday, when a company that published a weekly newspaper and a monthly magazine hired me as a janitor—then promoted me (my first morning on the job) to a reporter and (six months later) to editor-in-chief.

Actually, I first began writing for publication—for my junior high school newspaper—when I was thirteen, and I was first paid for writing when I was fifteen, covering my high school football and basketball teams for $1 a game and a $15 gift certificate at the end of each season. But I don't really count that as "professional" journalism experience, despite seeing—even then, in a dim, adolescent haze—that it was a necessary prerequisite to Becoming A Newspaperman.

Except for a few brief years—say, between the ages of seven and ten, when I was absolutely certain that I was destined to become the third-baseman for the Dodgers—I always wanted to be a newspaperman. Although my father assured me, with the certitude born of parenthood, that I would "never make any money doing that," I was unalterably convinced that journalism was my one true calling. It was exciting, glamorous, important: an opportunity to write, learn, travel, meet famous people and, hopefully, contribute something to society.

Thus, when I turned twenty and—still in college—took a full-time job as a reporter with the *Huntington Park Daily Signal*, a small daily newspaper in the suburbs of Los Angeles, I was not the least bit surprised to find, first-hand, that the general public shared my lofty, almost awe-struck view of the press: The *Daily Signal* published a regular feature

1

not atypical of most daily newspapers then—"Man in the Street"—and each day, one of the paper's young reporters would visit one of the local shopping centers with the paper's lone photographer, and proceed to interview (and photograph) shoppers and passersby. We would ask each person the same question—either on current events or on social behavior—and the next day, six one-paragraph answers (and six one-inch-square photographs) would appear in the *Daily Signal*.

As the youngest and most eager member of the staff, I drew the "Man in the Street" assignment several times in my first few weeks with the *Daily Signal*, and what the project lacked in creative challenge, it more than compensated for in ego-gratification; people saw us coming from blocks away and ran up to us breathlessly, virtually begging to be interviewed and photographed. Or, if we came on some shoppers unawares, they began squealing with delight and exultation the instant we identified ourselves: "Oh," they would screech, "you're newspapermen, from the *Signal*," and only my cunning postulation of that day's question—perhaps, "Do you think it's all right for a girl to ask a boy out on a date?"—prevented a full and immediate swoon at our very feet.

But that was in the summer of 1963—before Selma and Watts, before Berkeley, before Tet and My Lai and Saigon, before Watergate, before placards, demonstrations, riots, mass murders and assassinations, before runaway inflation, crippling energy crises and massive street crime, before Charles Manson and Spiro Agnew.

Few people romanticize reporters anymore. Fewer still welcome their requests for interviews and photographs. The "man in the street" today is far more likely to sneer, curse or just stalk angrily away than he is to greet a reporter with wide eyes, open arms and a warm heart.

The role and function of the press has changed dramatically since 1963, and, to most of the general public, it has been a change for the worse. Reporters are no longer thought of as reliable and trustworthy observers and commentators but as partisans, *provocateurs*, collaborators, enemies.

Simply by reporting what happened—and reporting in great and gory detail—the press frightened and infuriated large segments of the American public. No one wanted to hear that blacks were being discriminated against, starved, beaten, murdered—and that those atrocities were taking place daily, in large measure because of the bigotry (or, at the very least, the callous and careless indifference) of society at-large. Nor did people want to read that they also discriminated against Chicanos, old people, women and—worst of all—their own children. And when all these disadvantaged people finally decided to fight—actively, angrily, sometimes violently—for their rights, the news became more than discomfiting, it became threatening, in every sense of the word. To right most of the wrongs would take, among other things, massive infusions of tax money. Those higher taxes, many in the middle-class felt, would threaten their own standard of living. But if the redress did not come quickly or fully, there was the greater threat of armed insurrection—of protest marches, riots, bloodshed.

Still, the greatest threat of all was neither financial nor physical but moral. The socio-political upheavals of the 1960s and 1970s were, perhaps more than anything else, a challenge to the values and principles by which most of society had lived for generations: bras, crewcuts, shoes, respect for your elders, obedience to authority, the Protestant work ethic, know-your-place, stand-on-your-own-two-feet, school-is-a-place-to-learn, my-country-right-or-wrong, obey-the-law, good-girls-don't-do-that. All these symbols and standards and homilies—however trite and however hypocritical—had helped form the matrix of our civilization. Now, suddenly, all were under attack on every side, and, in their place, the unheard of: America is fighting an immoral and illegal war. The president of the United States is a crook. Marriage is unnecessary at best—and repressive at worst.

And who was reporting all these challenges—each new issue, each new charge, each new onslaught? The press, of course. And not just the morning newspaper, which could, if its presence became too annoying, be ignored or canceled, but virtually every periodical—daily, weekly, monthly and quarterly, whether delivered to the porch or in the mailbox or merely sighted on the newsstand or in the supermarket. Even more pervasively, it was all on the radio—the clock radio that signaled the start of each new day, the car radio on the way to work, radios in the office, the garage, on the beach. . . . And, most maddening of all, television—the ultimate escape—became the ultimate oppressor, reporting in full, grisly color just before dinner and again before bedtime what the blacks, browns, women, students, marchers, soldiers, politicians and muggers had done that day. Vietnam became the living-room war, Watergate a national soap opera, the SLA-Patty Hearst shootout a prime-time cops-and-robbers show: "Kojak" with real bullets—and real bodies.

Many people blamed the press for these problems. If the press ignored the "troublemakers"—be those "troublemakers" Martin Luther King or Mario Savio or Gloria Steinem or George McGovern—the trouble itself would all go away. Instead—or so it was argued—the press provoked further unrest, created instant heroes, provided both a rationale and a reward for dissidence and destruction. There were, of course, instances of excess, carelessness and irresponsibility on the part of the press. But these were the exception. It was precisely the policy of benign neglect that so many now urged upon the press that had created and, for so long, had fed the furies now unleashed. The public, like the ancient Greeks, wanted to kill the bearers of ill tidings; if anything, they should have censured the bearers for having taken so long to deliver so urgent a message.

The press, however, did more than merely report what was happening;

breaking with generations of tradition, the press was not only looking, listening and reporting, but asking, demanding, probing, pursuing, investigating, doubting. Thus, the press, like the dissidents, became a skeptical challenger of the status quo: further fuel for the fires of public disenchantment.

But public perception of the press is only one factor in the equation. The actual performance of the press in the 1960s and 1970s is, perhaps, the more significant factor, for the press has become—individually, collectively and institutionally—more skeptical, more iconoclastic, more determined to look beyond the superficial Who?/What?/When?/Where? to the causative How?/Why?

This is not to say that analytical/investigative reporting sprang, full-blown, from the fevered brow of Woodward and Bernstein. Or from the hyperfervid imagination of Norman Mailer. Or David Halberstam. Or Tom Wolfe. Or Neil Sheehan. Or . . . Reporters have always been, by temperament and by profession, a curious, doubting lot. There have been good investigative journalists for as long as there have been good newspapers. But until the traumatic events of the 1960s and 1970s, these reporters were all too rare; most reporters simply asked the wrong questions of the wrong people at the wrong time—and were too easily satisfied with the wrong answers. Or, to be more charitable—and, perhaps, more accurate—too many were content with asking too few questions. Not that all of today's reporters are paragons of diligence and perspicacity; the majority of the nation's press corps still plods along, uninspired and uninspiring, asking the same old questions of the same old sources—when they think to ask any questions at all. But there are more reporters than ever before asking the difficult questions, looking beneath the surface, demanding to know the reasons and causes and motivations behind the day's events: their editors (and their readers) want it, insist upon it.

In a sense, the events themselves have precipitated this metamorphosis. Race riots, a losing war, a White House scandal and an end to the era-of-plenty required careful, thorough explanation. But this is not the first time in American history that complex occurrences have presented themselves to the American press. What made the complexities of the 1960s and 1970s unique was the existence, this time, of an educated press—reporters and editors who, like the rest of society, had more formal schooling, more intellectual training, a greater ability to understand and analyze the day's news. Then, too, there was television, one of the most influential and pervasive forces on contemporary culture. By covering the day's major stories quickly and graphically, television made it necessary—and possible—for newspapers to modify their essential news-gathering function. Newspapers had to do what television news programs did not do: explain and interpret causation, rather than merely show results. No newspaper story or photograph could possibly achieve the direct, dramatic impact of television footage during a riot in the streets or a war in the jungle—or an earthquake in the city, for that matter. Newspapers had to scrutinize and criticize and analyze and synthesize. Nor was this an altogether unnatural (or uncomfortable) burden; a few of the country's better newspapers had already begun moving in that direction, and television just accelerated the process. Moreover, by providing the general public with at least the bare rudiments of the day's news, television created a glimmer of enlightenment and, in some, an appetite for more information. In a sense, then, television and newspapers became rather more complementary than competitive. In fact, television actually became a vital element in the self-perpetuating events of the 1960s and 1970s. A student demonstration in Berkeley, for example, might be expected to have minimal impact when it appears as a three-paragraph story on page seven of the *Milwaukee Journal*. But when it appears on television—in full, screaming color—students at the University of Wisconsin see it, sympathize with it, identify with it, emulate it. Now, it's a page-one story in Milwaukee. And, if the same thing happens—*i.e.*, when the same thing *did* happen—on campuses and in cities all across the United States, it became a genuine national phenomenon, demanding explanation in not only the major daily newspapers but in the newsweeklies and the monthly and quarterly journals as well.

There have, of course, been many other forces responsible for the changing American press. Most significantly, in Vietnam, it was the steady accumulation of misrepresentations and falsehoods. Most reporters like to feel, with Ernest Hemingway, that they have "a built-in shit detector," and when they discovered, belatedly, that they had been lied to, again and again and again, they became enraged. In the better reporters, that rage translated itself into a cynical refusal to accept the official version of anything less demonstrable than sunrise or tide changes. Out of this— and out of similar experiences covering peace marches, campus protests, race riots and government corruption at home—came a whole new approach to reporting. No longer would the press simply ask the general or the police commander or the university president or the White House press secretary "What happened?" Now, the press sought out the dissidents themselves. It was a more difficult job. The dissidents, at first, were neither as accessible nor as professionally articulate as the "officials." But, in time, they, too, learned the new rules, and they, too, issued public pronouncements which were often every bit as pompous, self-serving and inaccurate as the official statements themselves. Which, of course, made it that much more difficult to ferret out the truth—and that much more likely that the press would emerge with its skepticism of all appreciably heightened.

This skepticism has, at times, assumed epidemic proportions, and it has, at times, led to an excess of missionary zeal in the press—especially in the immediate post-Watergate period when, it seemed, the fall of Richard Nixon and the revelations about John Kennedy's promiscuity and the FBI and CIA assassination plots rendered every individual and institutional act a fit subject for journalistic disparagement.

But, these occasional excesses notwithstanding, the press appears to have learned well the lessons of Vietnam, Berkeley, Watts and Watergate. The best reporters and the best newspapers now, more often than not, look for cause, as well as for effect; they look at yesterday and tomorrow, as well as today. Whether writing profiles of Hollywood stars, *exposés* of corporate corruption or campaign-trail accounts of a political candidate's progress, they ask more questions—more intelligent and probing questions—of more people at more levels of society than was customarily their wont a generation ago.

Still, the general public—the ultimate beneficiary of an aggressive and skeptical press—remains uneasy (if not downright hostile) amid this transformation. Their once-predictable newspapers are no longer as comfortable—or comforting—as an old pair of shoes. They bring, instead, unsettling news. Thus, the gap between press and public has grown larger.

It was, in part, to help bridge this gap that I received, in the fall of 1974, a message as enigmatic as it was peremptory:

"T.H.E. wants to see you. Now. He'll explain why."

"T.H.E." is Bill Thomas, the editor of the *Los Angeles Times*, where I have been a reporter for the past eight years. Journalistic bureaucracies not being appreciably more penetrable than governmental bureaucracies, the number of people between us in the normal chain-of-command is positively legion. There are, at the very least, one managing editor, two assistant managing editors, a metropolitan editor, three assistant metropolitan editors and a partridge-in-a-pear-tree. That, perhaps, is why my immediate superior, the metropolitan editor, had taken to calling Thomas "T.H.E."—as in *the* editor—to distinguish him from lesser mortals with more complex corporate titles.

Thomas had summoned me to his office three or four times previously over the years—always to suggest a particular story assignment he thought uniquely suited to my skills and interests (and always letting me know that in advance, through the proper chain-of-command). Not this time. All the metropolitan editor would say was that Thomas did *not* want to talk to me about a specific story.

What he did want to talk about, it turned out, was a new job for me at the *Times*.

I had never before been given a specific job at the *Times*; I had, in fact, assiduously avoided even the faintest hint of specialization throughout my reportorial career—specialization being, for me, just another term for straitjacket. I didn't want to be a "political writer" or an "education writer" or even an "investigative reporter." As a man of catholic tastes, convinced that patience is the most over-rated of the virtues, I had always insisted on remaining free to range from subject to subject—writing on teenage drug use, black militancy, the paramilitary right, urban sprawl, supermarket merchandising, gambling, court reform, the sexual revolution, violent crime, football, poverty, corruption. . . . I generally spent anywhere from three weeks to three months on a project, traveling wherever the story took me, spending whatever money was necessary and writing 4,000 to 6,000 words on it—all virtually unheard-of freedoms on most newspapers.

Now, Thomas wanted me to write in the same exhaustive fashion on the American press.

"The one thing the press covers more poorly than anything else," he told me, "is the press." That was, he said, one explanation for our diminished credibility—and circulation: We don't tell our readers what we do or how we do it. We don't admit our mistakes unless we're virtually forced to under threat of court action or public embarrassment. We make no attempt to explain our problems, our decisions, our fallibilities, our procedures. . . .

The idea of writing about the press *in* the press was not an altogether new concept, of course. For several years now, both *Time* and *Newsweek* have had press/media sections to report on the latest trends and *causes celebres* in the Fourth Estate. Moreover, the *New York Times* already had a reporter specifically assigned to write much the same kinds of stories—just as other reporters are assigned to write about the environment, science, the courts. The *Washington Post* and a few other papers had even appointed ombudsmen—a staff member whose exclusive responsibility it is to respond to (and evaluate) readers' complaints about the paper and to write internal memos and, periodically, a story or column about some specific error or oversight the paper had been guilty of.

But the job Thomas envisioned for me was unique—neither beat reporter nor ombudsman; he wanted me to write about the press as I had written about other subjects—to provide long, thoughtful overviews on broad issues confronting the press today, to analyze, criticize and make value judgments, to treat my own newspaper as I would any other, to write as if my stories were to appear in some other publication (say *Harper's* or *The New Yorker*).

My stories would not be buried on page 19, as press stories customarily were in the *New York Times.* Nor would they be on the op-ed page as they usually are in the *Washington Post.* Like most stories I had written at the *Times,* they would generally appear in the upper left-hand corner of page one—and I would have the freedom to use that forum as I saw fit: I would not be prevented from criticizing my own paper. All Thomas asked of me was that I apply the standards of good journalism to my criticism—that I be "more responsible reporter than shrill critic."

"We don't want you to sound self-righteous, making judgments from

Mt. Olympus," he said. "Second-guessing everyone with 20-20 hindsight would be self-defeating—for you and for us."

I agreed. But I gathered that there was considerable resistance to my new assignment; other editors were not exactly clamoring for the appointment of someone to publicly criticize their work—and certainly not someone as outspoken as I had always been, both verbally and in a local journalism review. Perhaps that's why Thomas offered the assignment to me personally; others might have done so somewhat less enthusiastically. In fact, it was Thomas' persuasive salesmanship—combined with the opportunity to put my typewriter where my hypercritical mouth had always been—that convinced me to take the job and to temporarily abandon my role as a renaissance man.

When I said I would accept the assignment, Thomas offered one additional cautionary note:

"I hope you have a lot of friends outside the newspaper business." He grinned mischievously. "By the time you're through with this job, you may not have many left inside it."

Actually, it hasn't turned out that way. I've been writing about the press for two years now—on subjects as disparate as White House coverage, police-press relations, sportswriting, invasion of privacy, political polls and the Patty Hearst case—and all my friends at the paper have remained my friends . . . despite my having criticized both of them rather severely in print. (One friend, a news editor, I took to task for his judgment in playing a particular post-Watergate story on Richard Nixon with a big headline on page one; he seemed hurt, but in subsequent dinner engagements with our respective ladies, he has yet to sprinkle cayenne pepper on my *soufflé Grand Marnier*. The other friend, a reporter, I criticized for being a bit too cozy at times with the police department; his only complaint was with my physical description of him in the story: he telephoned the morning it ran and said, "God damn it, Shaw, I'm not 'burly'.")

But if my friends have remained my friends, my detractors have also remained my detractors—and their number has never been slight (owing, I assume, to my abrasive self-confidence—or, as another writer once described it—my "prickly congeniality"). Worse, I suspect that those colleagues whom the pollsters might have been inclined to call "undecided" have since found themselves decided indeed.

In one story, for example, I was considering at some length the influence (if any) of film critics on moviegoers, and I suggested that Charles Champlin, the *Los Angeles Times'* film critic and entertainment editor, gave favorable reviews to far too many movies. He was, I quoted another critic as saying, "the Will Rogers of film criticism; he never met a film he didn't like."

Champlin was not pleased; I was told that he wrote a four-page memo to Bill Thomas taking exception to my theories. Even his 15-year-old daughter got into the act; she wrote me a note, assuring me that her father was "one of the most highly respected critics by people actually involved in movie-making." Champlin said nothing to me personally, though I did notice him pivot away from me in the hallway the next afternoon with a move that would have done O.J. Simpson proud. A few days later, he seemed about to make the same move again, then thought better of it, approached me and said, rather gruffly, "We must talk about all this some time, David—rationally."

But it was Jean Taylor, an associate editor at the *Times*, who howled the loudest about my film critics piece. Or so I heard. She never came to me directly, and Thomas insulated me from her wounded squeals by refusing to pass them along. But she is the paper's highest-ranking woman editor, in charge of the paper's feature and entertainment sections— among other things—and she let it be known, in no uncertain terms, that she thought I had been both cruel (to Champlin) and disloyal (to the *Times*), if not, indeed, to her personally.

You can imagine what she had to say, then, when my next story examined newspaper best-seller lists—the *Los Angeles Times'* best-seller list also falling within her corporate purview. My well-documented conclusion to that story: best-seller lists are often a sham—haphazard, imprecise, even dishonest; the *Los Angeles Times* best-seller list, I wrote, was "less valid" than most—and I provided several irrefutable examples. Taylor's reaction: moral outrage. How, she asked several people, could I possibly write such a story when the *Times* was striving so mightily to produce a good, viable, independent book section for the first time in the history of the newspaper? Even the publisher heard about my alleged disloyalty this time. But, again, Taylor said nothing to me directly, and neither the publisher nor Bill Thomas passed along her warm words of wisdom. Clearly, they did not want me to feel intimidated; I was free to pursue my appointed rounds (although, the next time I saw Taylor, when she was delivering the first copies of a new tabloid insert she was overseeing for the paper, she told me—with a wince-*cum*-smile—"I hope you're going to give me at least two weeks before you start shooting at me on this one.").

The story that caused the most discussion in the *Times'* offices involved a somewhat more notorious woman than Jean Taylor, though—Patty Hearst. Hearst was still at-large in the spring of 1975 when a 31-year-old ex-convict named Michael Casey walked into the *Times* city room and told reporter Dave Smith that Patty might be willing to talk to him. Smith had known Casey casually for four or five years, and—preposterous though it sounded—he was inclined to believe Casey's story that Hearst, disguised by plastic surgery, had been helping with the evacuation of Vietnamese refugees in Saigon; she now hoped, Casey said, that if she told the world (through the *Los Angeles Times*) of her heroic humanitarian efforts, federal authorities might offer some leniency in exchange for her surrender.

Smith took Casey's story to his editors, and they decided Casey should be interrogated thoroughly by a special task force of four reporters and an editor assigned specifically to investigate the Hearst kidnaping and its aftermath. Casey passed the test easily, pouring forth trivial details the *Times*' team was convinced that no one but they (and someone close to Patty) could possibly know. The reporters checked Casey out with a few other sources, and their editors finally decided that the only way they could actually prove if Casey was (or wasn't) telling the truth was to send two reporters to Southeast Asia with him. The three men flew first class to Hong Kong, as per Casey's instructions, and checked into the Mandarin Hotel—at $50 per day, per person—also as per Casey's instructions.

Over the next several days, there were secret meetings with "Patty's contacts," promises of meetings with Patty herself, whispered telephone calls, warnings not to mention Patty's name "or else you'll blow the mission"—even a side trip to Bangkok for a purported rendezvous with Patty.

At one point, the increasingly skeptical *Times* reporters gave Casey two questions to ask Patty to prove he was really in contact with her. Only she, they said, would know the answers; they had gotten both questions and answers from Patty's cousin in San Francisco. That afternoon, with the two reporters in his hotel room, Casey received a telephone call. He kept saying, "Wait a minute, wait a minute; I can't remember the code." Then he scribbled something down on a piece of paper, hung up, rewrote it—translated it?—and handed the paper to the reporters. On it were the correct answers to their two secret questions. The reporters were ecstatic. Euphoric. Everyone shook hands and whooped with joy and jumped up and down on the beds.

But Patty Hearst was not, of course, in Hong Kong—nor in Bangkok. (Casey, it seems, had asked a friend to call Patty's cousin in San Francisco, pose as a *Times* reporter, and ask what the questions and answers were "one more time, just to make sure we have them right.")

By the time the disgusted *Times* reporters were ordered home by their editors, the wild-goose chase had cost the *Times* about $15,000 in salary, air travel, telephone calls, hotel bills and other assorted expenses (including a rented Rolls Royce limousine and some clothing Casey bought in the Mandarin Hotel and charged to the *Times*).

It seemed like a good opportunity for me to do an offbeat story on various media hoaxes through the years. I wrote it—for page one—and mentioned several pieces of evidence that should have rendered Casey's credibility questionable to our editors and reporters from the very first.

Casey had, I wrote, a "previously demonstrated unfamiliarity with the truth," and I wondered, in my story, if the *Times* should, perhaps, have "investigated Casey—and his story—more carefully" before financing the trip to Hong Kong.

The reporters involved in the story told me they thought I had dealt fairly with them. But not all the editors were so sanguine about my published observations, and Thomas subsequently told me he had put the story in the paper "over a few dead bodies."

It was not the first time he had encountered such resistance: the story I had finished just before the Hearst hoax had detailed the success of suburban newspapers in the Los Angeles area, and I had made the mistake of submitting it and asking that it not be run until I returned from a month's vacation abroad. Generally, no one who would not routinely see my stories is given an opportunity to see them before they are published—especially not reporters and editors directly involved in what I am writing about. But this particular story, lying around the office for the month I was out of the country, found its way to the *Times* promotion department and, ultimately, to executives concerned with the paper's success as an advertising medium. They immediately yelped that my story would provide the suburban papers with valuable ammunition in the continuing marketplace struggle for advertising dollars; I had, after all, pointed out in the story that the suburban papers did a better job than the *Times* in covering local community news—and I had quoted one source as saying that a particularly successful suburban paper, the *Valley News*, "does its job so well it's damn near chased the *Times* out of the Valley."

My story survived intact, but a few months later, when I wrote about all-news radio and pronounced it "the broadcasting phenomenon of the last decade," the *Los Angeles Times* marketing research department quickly produced a 19-page study for use by the paper's advertising staff, rebutting my story and arguing—with statistics, charts, graphs and rhetoric—the supremacy of the *Los Angeles Times* as an advertising medium. But this, too, was an indirect protest. No one in advertising called me to complain. No editor told me to be more careful in the future. I didn't even see a copy of the 19-page study until a friend passed it along—several weeks after my story had been published with nary a comma changed.

There have, however, been a number of uncomfortable personal encounters on my media stories—all, alas, pointing to one sad truth: many newspaper reporters and editors are not one whit better than politicians, crooks, businessmen, athletes, doctors or lawyers when it comes to dealing with the press; they are guarded, suspicious and quick to tell me "No comment" or "I was misquoted" or "I was quoted out of context" or "I didn't realize I was being interviewed" or. . . .

Nor do newspapermen suffer criticism any more gladly (or graciously) than others. In fact, when I wrote an article for *New York* magazine late in 1976, describing my experiences in covering the media for the *Times*, the shrieks of outrage positively shattered glass in many *Times* offices. In that story, I identified, by name, various reporters and editors who had objected to some of my stories. How could I be so cruel? many of my colleagues wondered. And the people I named . . . well, they yelped so indignantly that one person who liked my story would only tell me so behind closed doors. "I'm sorry I can't defend you publicly," he said, "but we are not dealing here with rational people. They're hysterical. I have enough problems of my own without adding to them by defending you."

It was all, I thought, decidedly ironic: newspapermen regularly issue clarion calls for full disclosure, public accountability, and honest criticism, but they yelp self-righteously the instant those standards are applied to them.

My first experience with this phenomenon came on my second media story—a piece that argued "newspaper polls on political races seriously distort and undermine the electoral process."

For this story on the press' use—and abuse—of political polls, I interviewed more than 60 politicians, pollsters, newsmen and social scientists. One reporter whom I did *not* interview was Ken Reich, the man who devises, coordinates, supervises and helps to conduct the *Los Angeles Times*' own political polls. Those polls, I found—and subsequently wrote —"are not especially reliable in predicting elections" and carry "an aura of mathematical precision that their methodology does not justify." I wanted to discuss my findings with Reich, but when I asked for an interview, he declined most haughtily. Were I from the *New York Times*, he said, he would be happy to accommodate me; that not being the case, he would have a brief written statement ready for me in an hour.

Ten minutes later, he handed me his statement:

"I think it is incestuous for one reporter from the *Los Angeles Times* to interview another reporter from the *Los Angeles Times* for a story to be published in the *Los Angeles Times* about polls being conducted by the *Los Angeles Times*."

Reich wasn't the only one who saw my media assignment in these terms. About a year later, for my piece on film critics, I put in a call to Pauline Kael. No, she said, she would not consent to an interview; it would, she insisted, "be rather incestuous for one journalist to interview another." (I subsequently interviewed Judith Crist on this selfsame story, and when Crist asked if I had spoken with Kael yet, I repeated Kael's demur. "Huummpph," Crist snorted. "Since when does *she* consider herself a journalist?")

Others in the press didn't even bother to invoke the "incest" argument to avoid being interviewed by me. While researching my story on best-seller lists, for example, I telephoned Harvey Shapiro, editor of the *New York Times Book Review*. He wouldn't even come to the telephone; he directed his secretary to tell me he didn't want to talk to me. (John B. Oakes, editor of the *New York Times* editorial page, did the same thing on another of my stories.)

But my favorite response to an interview request came from another *New York Times* editor, one I wanted to speak with about the increased use of off-the-record stories from unnamed sources during and, especially, in the immediate aftermath of Watergate. I was looking into the possibility that such stories, in all the media, had resulted in the publication of some highly speculative reportage, of dubious origin and credibility.

The *Times* editor said he would be delighted to consent to such an interview—on one condition: that it be off-the-record.

(I should point out that not all *Times* editors were so difficult; I probably interviewed at least eight or ten who were extremely cooperative—and none more so than the publisher, Arthur Ochs Sulzberger. When I telephoned Sulzberger to arrange an interview for my story on the future of the daily newspaper, I was put through to him on my first call, without either delay or secretarial inquisition about my identity or the nature of my business. Sulzberger allowed me to select the time for our interview, personally ushered me into his office at precisely the appointed hour, spent 90 minutes with me and never once evaded a question or said, "No comment." In contrast, on that very same story, I telephoned Stan Cook, the publisher of the *Chicago Tribune*, nine times over a ten-day period—usually at specific times arranged by his secretary —and he was never available to speak with me . . . although I did have several pleasant chats with *two* secretaries, an executive assistant and what sounded like an escapee from the local idiot farm.

Even some of the journalists who did speak with me gave me a royal run-around worthy of Ron Ziegler. One suburban newspaper executive spent half our lunch telling me how courageous he was in fighting for freedom of the press and freedom of speech and how he always said what he thought, "and if I'm fired, I'm fired." But he spent the other half of our lunch asking me not to quote him on a variety of comments so trivial and innocuous that I could barely stay awake as he droned on. At one point, I asked him when his newspaper had shifted from twice-a-week to three-times-a-week publication. His brow furrowed. He glanced furtively over both shoulders—simultaneously (a feat I had never seen anyone but Richard Nixon accomplish before). He scooted his chair closer to the table, bent conspiratorily toward me and whispered, "We're still just chatting, right? I mean, you're not taking notes yet, are you? This is still off-the-record?" I stared dumbly ahead. He leaned even closer: "1953." Then, having delivered himself of so sinister a burden, he leaned back, smiled . . . and knocked his fork clattering to the floor.

The next day, I interviewed the man's boss—the publisher of the paper. He quickly sought to intimidate me. He was, he said, "very close" to *my* publisher. They had attended the same university and their daughters had made their debut into society together and my publisher's wife had personally invited his wife to join an organization whose name he uttered with an air of hushed reverence: the Amazing 400.

I recognized the name as belonging to some blue-ribbon social group or other, but I manufactured my most ingenuous expression and asked, "Isn't that the new low-cholesterol diet?" He rocked back in his seat at such heresy, but I pressed on: "No, I'm sorry. It's the name of a road race they have every year down in North Carolina, isn't it? No? A chain of Southern motels then? A British rock group? A. . . ."

It was not one of my most productive interviews.

But my most controversial media story, without question, was a piece on the evolution of sportswriting from a pastiche of batting averages and locker-room clichés to a probing, literate form of journalism, concerned as much with the sociological as with the statistical.

Ironically, as things turned out, the genesis of that story was the dissatisfaction I had heard voiced about the *Los Angeles Times* sports section during the year I had spent writing my first book, *WILT: Just Like Any Other 7-Foot, Black Millionaire Who Lives Next Door*. Most of the local sports fans I had encountered in that year had complained that the *Times* had drifted too far away from prompt, thorough, knowledgeable coverage of the day's activities in the major sports and toward offbeat features and sociological studies. Instead of sending a sportswriter on the road with the city's professional basketball team, for example, the *Times* was assigning sportswriters to do stories on rodeo clowns, sports in prison, and the psychology of channel swimming.

Starting with that bias, I began reading regularly the sports pages of more than 30 daily newspapers. Then I began interviewing people around the country. What I found was that the most progressive sports sections were trying to expand their readership—to reach the casual fan, as well as the committed fan; to reach women, as well as men; to reach backpackers and weekend tennis-players, as well as diehard baseball and football enthusiasts—to reach people who might be interested in the relationship between sports and society, as well as in the relationship between pitcher and catcher.

And what newspaper was doing the best job of bridging this gap? The consensus, to my utter amazement, was the *Los Angeles Times*. I reported the good (?) news to Bill Thomas.

"You can't write that," he said, "It'll look self-serving."

I countered: "If everyone said we were the worst, you'd let me use it."

He nodded.

"Well then. . . ."

I got no further. Reluctantly, he agreed.

He should have known better. So should I.

Between praising my own paper and suggesting that sportswriting, on the whole, was better today than in previous generations, I managed to offend the entire sportswriting fraternity. A columnist in San Francisco wrote in his paper that I was a "ninny." Red Smith spent an entire *New York Times* column trying to demonstrate that I was "uninformed." Roger Kahn, Dick Young, Bob Lipsyte—all chimed in with snide comments, in print, about my story having been both inaccurate and self-serving.

Perhaps the harshest criticism came not in a column but in a letter— from Jim Tuite, the sports editor of the *New York Times*. I had inter- viewed Tuite for my story and had quoted him—among others—as saying the *Los Angeles Times* had the best sports section in the country. I had also quoted one of his own sportswriters as saying news executives at the *New York Times* didn't much care if their sports section was good, just so long as it wasn't so bad that it would "embarrass the paper."

"Being a sportswriter on the *New York Times*," I wrote, "is like being Raquel Welch's elbow."

Tuite denied the quote I had attributed to him and said the quote I attributed to his sportswriter was "suspect" because I had not identified the sportswriter by name. Tuite's letter was filled with such words and phrases as "distortions," "innuendo," "self-serving," "highly subjective," "snide" and "highly biased." I wrote back, recalling for Tuite the specifics of our conversation in his office and insisting on the accuracy of my reportage. I also assured him I had quoted his sportswriter accurately, and said, "You and I both know that his comment is hardly original, and his sentiment widespread in your department. One need not possess the perspicacity of Albert Einstein (or even Albert Finney, for that matter) to realize that he asked to remain unidentified in my story to avoid the ill will of his superiors—a phenomenon you may not be entirely un- familiar with yourself."

About a year later, James Michener's book *Sports in America* was pub- lished. In his chapter on the media, Michener wrote that "the best sports pages in the nation right now appeared in the *Los Angeles Times*." There it was: confirmation—vindication—from an unbiased, unimpeachable source. But it was too late. The damage had been done.

Never mind that I had begun my research on sportswriting with a bias *against* the *Los Angeles Times*. Never mind that I had not even men- tioned the *Times* until almost two-thirds of the way into my story. Never mind that I had deliberately included in the story twice as much criticism as praise of the *Times* sports section. I had committed the un- pardonable sin: I had praised my own paper *in* my own paper. It is not a mistake I have made again. I have, in fact, carefully avoided doing certain stories, simply because I knew that some element of those stories would make the *Times* look good. (I have eschewed favorable mention of *Newsday*, which is owned by the *Los Angeles Times* parent company, for much the same reason: in my sportswriting piece, I had spoken well of *Newsday*, and that, too, was perceived by some as disingenuously serving to burnish the *Times'* corporate image.) But I have continued to write stories that contain so many unfavorable references to the *Times* that one editor who both likes me and respects my work once groaned in exasperation, "Christ, Shaw, aren't you ever going to say anything nice about us?"

Because my stories generally deal with broad issues, rather than isolated situations, I rarely devote more than a small portion of any story to the *Times* (or any other single newspaper). When I have mentioned the *Times*, though, I have criticized the paper (as I have other papers) not only for specific factual inaccuracies but for wrongheaded editorials, the use of fraudulent photographs, irresponsible and speculative reporting, sensationalism, a potential conflict of interest, poor news judgment. . . . These criticisms *have* been specific—and, when appropriate, have included the names of the staff members involved. I have also written critically about subjects that might be regarded as sacred cows: In a story on the influence of newspaper editorial endorsements on the way people actually vote, I quoted one source as saying the *Times* endorsements in years past had been given to Republicans so regularly that they were as ineffectual as they were predictable. In fact, I wrote, the *Times'* support of California Attorney General Evelle Younger (a close friend of *Times* publisher Otis Chandler) was so predictable that "if Younger ran for God, the *Times* would run an editorial saying he was 'well-qualified for the position'." I also quoted, in that same story, another source who said the *Times'* decision in 1973 to abandon its policy of "routinely" endorsing candidates for president, governor, and senator was made "primarily to save the Chandler family the inevitable embarrassment of one day having to break a lifelong Republican tradition and endorse a Democrat for president or governor."

Another story was similarly sensitive: In evaluating the development of op-ed pages in the nation's leading newspapers, I concluded not only that the *New York Times* op-ed page was clearly "the best in the country"—and that the *Los Angeles Times* op-ed page was "not sufficiently abrasive or exciting"—but I quoted the first editor of the *Los Angeles Times* op-ed page as saying he had quit the job largely because "several articles he solicited were killed for 'political reasons'." He had felt like a "lackey," I wrote, and he had found the experience "humiliating."

Several editors were somewhat less than enchanted with reading those comments in a page-one story in their own newspaper, but—*comme d'ordinaire*—the story was neither screened beforehand by those involved nor censored in any way by anyone else. A year later, when I was working on a story on the future of the daily newspaper, I was told that someone did, indeed, want to read the story before it was published: That "someone" was the publisher himself, and friends suggested that if I concluded the daily newspaper had no future, he might reach the same conclusion about me. But he changed his mind and the story ran without his having read it. Not that he—or Bill Thomas—personally agreed with all my findings. But, then, Thomas at least hasn't agreed with my findings in several stories. He has, on occasion, assessed my judgments as "horse-shit." He is, understandably, no fonder of my disagreeing, in print, with his policies, editorials and theories than others on the staff are of my criticizing *their* performance. All of which makes, at times, for rather awkward working conditions. There have even been a few instances in which I've had to compromise on a passage or two because Thomas felt— usually quite rightly—that I had either been too turgid in my prose or too shrill in my pronouncements. He has not, however, reneged on his pledge to give me complete freedom in my job—and that is certainly not because he feels any discernible personal affection for me. Even though I respect him more than any man I've ever known, except my father, ours is strictly a business relationship. We've never gone out to-gether for lunch or dinner or a drink; we've rarely visited each other's homes; even in the office, we've never discussed anything that was not at least peripherally related to the paper. (I might prefer it otherwise, but since he has not shown the slightest inclination toward friendship, I have thought it presumptuous for me to make the first such step.)

Nevertheless, despite mounting criticism of my work from some editors (and reporters) who just don't understand what Thomas hopes to achieve with my stories, he has not weakened in either his resolve or his commitment. He and I have even won a convert or two in the office: the man who agreed to be interviewed (and was so candid) in my story on op-ed pages was Ken Reich . . . the same man who had so snidely refused to be interviewed for my earlier story on political polls.

1 / Public Figures, Private Lives

Names make news.

It is, perhaps, the oldest axiom in the newspaper business—older even than newspapers themselves.

Thus, reporters scurry to their typewriters to tell their readers of every step (or misstep) taken by President Ford and Frank Sinatra and Jacqueline Kennedy Onassis and Joe Namath.

By extension, it seems, the children of public figures also are considered public figures, and the press responds accordingly—with stories about the rodeo-riding antics of Steve Ford and the social and academic progress of Caroline Kennedy and . . .

But what happens when the child of a public figure behaves in a fashion that does not necessarily reflect credit upon his (or her) celebrated parents?

Is it a legitimate news story when Doris Day's son files for divorce? Or when Spiro Agnew's son is arrested as a peeping Tom? Or when United States Senator James Abourezk's son is given food stamps? Or when Los Angeles Mayor Bradley's daughter or Pennsylvania Senator Hugh Scott's daughter or Jerry Lewis' son is arrested on relatively minor drug charges?

Many respected newspapers all across America printed these stories—but only because the stories involved the offspring of celebrities; stories on divorce, suicide, voyeurism and routine drug cases are rarely published if they involve the children of truck drivers and waitresses and bank tellers.

18

But many editors are beginning to wonder if such celebrity stories constitute an unwarranted invasion of the privacy of both parent and child—an implicit public chastisement of the parent for the sins of the child, as well as a public humiliation of the child for the celebrityhood of the parent.

Given the increasing independence and rebelliousness of the children of the 1960s and 70s, is it fair of the press to hold a parent publicly responsible for his child's behavior—especially if the "child" is already an adult, living an autonomous life away from home?

Doris Day's son was 34 when he filed for divorce. Spiro Agnew's son was 28 when he was arrested. Senator Abourezk's son was 22 when he was given food stamps. Mayor Bradley's daughter and Jerry Lewis' son were both in their 20s when they were arrested. Senator Scott's daughter was 41, married, divorced and eight times a mother when she was arrested.

Senator Scott's daughter? Hadn't she—hadn't they all—earned their own identities by then? Didn't they deserve to be judged in their own right, not merely as public extensions of their parents? And didn't their parents have the same right?

"What the press did to my daughter was obscene," says Scott. "One paper ran five different stories on her, and they all seemed to imply that I should still be exercising parental control over her and be responsible for her."

Many would argue that this is the price of both parenthood and celebrityhood—the sacrifice a public figure must make in exchange for the perquisites of fame: the money and power, the special treatment and continual ego gratification that inevitably accrue to (and, almost inevitably, are sought by) those in the public eye.

But exacting the price of privacy from the celebrity himself is one thing; should the press (and the public) also exact that price from the celebrity's offspring?

Abourezk thinks not. The stories about his son were, he says, "grossly unfair." Young Abourezk was living away from home; he was legally entitled to food stamps; he was not claimed as a tax deduction by his father—and he was caring for a 16-year-old Indian child (a fact omitted from the original story, which appeared in the *Washington Post*).

Charles Seib, ombudsman for the *Post*, agrees with Abourezk. The story was, he says, an invasion of the son's privacy and "an unwarranted embarrassment of the father . . . the urge to expose gone wild."

Sometimes, of course, a public figure almost seems to invite public embarrassment by the very nature of his private behavior—or by the inconsistency between his public words and his private behavior. Thus, a public figure who publicly bemoans the disintegration of the nation's moral fiber probably ought to be held publicly responsible for his own profligacy and debauchery.

(There has, for example, been much criticism of the French press of late for largely ignoring the story of a prominent Roman Catholic Cardinal who died in a prostitute's apartment . . . after many years of championing priestly celibacy.)

But if it is not the public figure himself who strays but his child—as, say, in the case of Agnew's son—is it proper for the press to succumb to this easy target practice and to penalize the child for the preachments of the parent?

Many editors think not. So do many public figures—and a number of private individuals with no vested interest in the matter.

A Beverly Hills psychiatrist who specializes in treating the children of celebrities says many of these children deliberately misbehave—"the more outrageously the better"—simply to compete with their parents for attention.

Does the press, by reporting this behavior, unwittingly contribute to a syndrome of continued bad behavior—either by rewarding it with attention or by forever stigmatizing the child and creating a severe psychological trauma that makes future misbehavior all but inevitable?

Does the press exacerbate what already is a difficult life for many of these children? Is that a partial explanation for the chronic trouble in which many offspring of celebrities seem to find themselves?

Bradley's daughter has been arrested several times—for drunkenness and for traffic violations and for possession of drugs and for resisting arrest.

The sons of United States Senator Alan Cranston and California State Treasurer Jess Unruh also have been arrested several times, mostly on similarly minor charges (Cranston's son was also arrested once on a more serious charge, but he is convinced that incident never would have happened had he not been a senator's son, and the jury—which acquitted him in little more than two hours—seemed to agree.)

Did press coverage of these otherwise unnewsworthy events contribute to the continuing problems of these offspring?

Bradley thinks so—and he bitterly resents it.

"It's grossly unfair to the child," Bradley says. "In the long run, the public figure himself doesn't really suffer significantly. I've never heard of anyone losing an election because of what his child did. But to make the child a target of public scorn and derision leaves permanent scars on the child.

"They feel they've let down their parents and they're embarrassed in front of their friends and it makes recovering and leading a normal life that much harder."

What of the argument that a public figure who cannot raise his own children properly cannot be trusted to execute the duties of public office properly either?

"Bunk," says Bradley—and many agree, including Ronald Reagan, who cannot generally be expected to come riding to the rescue of such ideological antagonists as Bradley, Cranston and Unruh.

"In today's world," Reagan asks rhetorically, "how many people do you know in your own circle who have done everything they possibly can as parents, only to have their children go wrong? It's a tragedy that can befall anyone today.

"It hasn't anything to do with the man's discharge of his public duties."

If the offspring's behavior *is* in some way related to his parent's position, though—a conflict-of-interest case, for example—Reagan and other critics agree that it should be reported.

In contrast, it also is generally agreed that improper but not illegal behavior—what Wes Gallagher, longtime president of Associated Press, calls "just your typical kid's mischievous escapade"—should not be reported.

But there is considerable disagreement—among public figures and newspaper editors alike—on the propriety of reporting cases that do not fall in either of these categories.

Bradley and Reagan say no story should be published unless the act of the offspring is so heinous or so notorious that it would be a legitimate story regardless of the identity of the parent of the perpetrator.

Thus, newspapers were bound to cover the fatal stabbing of Lana Turner's boyfriend by her daughter back in 1958—and the sex perversion conviction of Loretta Young's son in 1973 after a grand jury investigation into the making of homosexual movies featuring young boys.

These stories surely received greater news play than they would have had the individuals involved not been the offspring of celebrities, but given the lurid circumstances of both cases, that probably was unavoidable.

Many journalists insist, however, that the very visibility of public figures obliges the press to similarly report any violation of the law—or any other misdeed that makes the public record—no matter how trivial.

"That," says one Eastern editor, "is our job—to record the day's events, the news. Our only responsibility in that regard is to avoid sensationalism—big, splashy headlines and unsubstantiated charges."

Many in public life reluctantly agree.

"I had a doctor friend whose son was arrested in the same kind of case as Alan Cranston's boy," says former California Governor Edmund G. (Pat) Brown. "There was no story on him, but there sure as hell was one on Alan's boy, and I just don't know what you can do about it.

"That's the risk you take when you go into public life. There really isn't any way to avoid it."

Moreover, says Cranston's son, Robin, the public figures themselves must sometimes share the blame for the attention focused on their children.

"My brother and I were taken out on the campaign trail when we were very young," he says.

But young Cranston readily admits there are also undeniable advantages to being the child of a celebrity; for example, he is now working in a law firm whose partners he met through his father's political activity.

Jerry Lewis's son, Gary, has been in a similar position: His career as a rock singer clearly benefited, in its embryonic stage, from his father's identity. But his arrest for possession of drugs was widely publicized for the same reasons.

"You can't avoid it," Lewis, the father, says. "We all have egos. That's why we're celebrities. We can't accept all the good stories and then tell the press, 'No, you can't write any bad stories about us.'"

In fact, says former United States Senator John V. Tunney, himself the son of a famous father (former heavyweight boxing champion Gene Tunney), the implied threat of adverse publicity can sometimes help a celebrity's child.

"When I was growing up, I knew that anything I did would be in the papers," Tunney says. "I had to accept that as the natural result of being my father's son. I knew that if I got into trouble, I would bring disgrace to him and everything he stood for.

"That knowledge acted as a brake to some of my youthful excesses."

Art Linkletter says he told his children at an early age that they had "money and security and a chance to go to the best schools and camps. They wouldn't have to work in cafeterias and deliver newspapers at 5:30 in the morning like I did.

"But they had to pay a price, and the price was that anything they did would be scrutinized by the press and the public, and any wrong move could hurt me and my career. I'm not sure I would have been willing to accept that myself if I'd had that choice as a kid, but they didn't have the choice; the choice had already been made for them."

When one of Linkletter's daughters jumped to her death from a sixth-floor window after taking LSD, he gathered his family around him.

"This time, I told them they did have a choice," he says. "I said we could either do the traditional Hollywood clamup and say it was a private matter, or we could use Diane's death as a platform to help others who might have the same problem.

"With all the benefits we'd enjoyed from being a celebrity, I felt we had the responsibility to help others. They agreed."

Thus, fighting drug abuse has become a crusade for Linkletter, and he feels he cannot justifiably object to continued newspaper stories about his own daughter's tragic death "any more than I could object to other stories about my family life throughout a television career based on talking about families.

"When you commit yourself to the limelight, those are the rules of the game. It comes with the territory."

But what of public figures who do not wish to turn their family tragedies into public platforms?

That question is, of course, but the tip of an increasingly prominent journalistic iceberg—the whole question of where the press ought to draw the line in reporting on the private lives of public figures.

A special subcommittee of the ethics committee of the American Society of Newspaper Editors has met to discuss this very problem. They could reach no decision. Almost every case, they decided, had to be judged on its own merits.

At another meeting, Ralph Otwell, managing editor of the *Chicago Sun-Times* and chairman of the editors' ethics committee, presented 10 actual and hypothetical cases involving public figures to 130 people in the media and the law. He asked his listeners to decide which stories should be printed and which ignored. Disagreement was widespread on almost every case.

"There just aren't any rules to go by," Otwell concluded.

Perhaps the only consensus—the only rules—involve good taste, judgment and restraint: The press should be more sensitive to the entire issue of privacy and not respond automatically to the indiscretions and misadventures of the sons and daughters—and husbands and wives—of public figures (and of the public figures themselves, for that matter).

Is it really necessary to report that one of former President Richard M. Nixon's cousins is on welfare—and that another has gone bankrupt? Or that the aunt of Jacqueline Kennedy Onassis has been threatened with eviction? Or that Senator Edward M. Kennedy's wife has a severe drinking problem?

Some of the arguments that apply to stories on the offspring of public figures might apply here as well: If the individual's activity is not especially heinous, if it is not related to the position held by his famous kin, and if it would not be a story except for the relationships to that kin, perhaps it should not be a story, period.

"You expect that kind of sensationalism in the *National Enquirer* and the *National Tattler* and the movie fan magazines, but not in responsible daily newspapers," says Dale Olson, a press agent who represents many Hollywood stars.

But sometimes a story in one of the sensationalist publications is picked up by the "responsible" press. That happened in 1976 with a *National Enquirer* story based on interviews with two patients in the same alcoholic rehabilitation center where Kennedy's wife, Joan, was being treated.

The story quoted these patients as saying Mrs. Kennedy told them she'd been an alcoholic for "at least four or five years." The story also contained several other embarrassing disclosures about Mrs. Kennedy and others in the Kennedy family.

The Associated Press refused to use the story.

"We didn't think her problems had anything to do with her husband's job in the Senate," says the AP's Gallagher.

United Press International did use the story, though.

"It was a borderline case," admits UPI President Rod Beaton, "but we felt we had a responsibility to our subscribing papers. It was up to each newspaper editor to exercise his own judgment about using it in his particular paper."

Beaton now has doubts about that decision. So does Jim Bellows, editor of the *Washington Star*, which gave prominent play to the story—and drew a furious letter from Mrs. Kennedy's sister-in-law, Eunice Kennedy Shriver, in response.

Mrs. Shriver's letter—also played prominently in the *Star*—accused the paper of "violating every canon of honorable journalism." The story, she wrote, was "notorious, malicious [and] inaccurate," and *Star* editors should feel "deep shame."

Bellows now admits publication of the story was "a mistake." Most editors agree. The story, they say, had absolutely nothing to do with Kennedy's public responsibilities, was not a legitimate news story in its own right and ought, therefore, to have been ignored.

In fact, many say, that same yardstick ought to be applied to stories on the private behavior of public figures themselves—although politicians may be held to a somewhat more exacting standard than other celebrities, simply because of their public responsibilities—and because "politicians are generally inclined to preach morality in one form or another, so their morality then becomes the public's business" in the words of Norman Cherniss, executive editor of the *Riverside Press-Enterprise* and long active in national newspaper organizations.

But Jess Unruh, among others, thinks politicians ought not to be so judged.

"Except in rare instances," Unruh says, "the press should only cover those things that directly affect a public servant's public service.

"Does a guy drink? Yes. Does he make a public disgrace of himself when he's drunk? Yes. That's a story. Does he have to go off and dry out for a week or two? Yes. That's a story. Is he so unbalanced that he can't discharge his duties? Yes. That's a story. But if the answers to those questions are no, it's not a story."

But Unruh admits he is "not being very realistic," and he says "he's willing to live by the rules of the game.

"Sensationalism is what gets readers," he says, "and that's what the newspaper business is all about, regardless of what you journalists like to think and say about it."

Some editors insist, however, that they are only providing what their readers want—interesting news about famous people—and there is, indeed, ample evidence of this appetite, as witness the rampaging popularity of *People* magazine and of the *National Enquirer* and other supermarket tabloids.

The *Washington Star* even has a gossip column ("The Ear"), which seems to have become the most popular feature in the paper and now also appears in 60 other papers across the country.

In fact, gossip has become so pervasive that *Newsweek*, *Esquire* and *New York* magazines all published cover stories on the subject in rapid succession in 1976.

British gossip columnist Nigel Dempster explains the gossip phenomenon thusly:

"We live in a banana-peel society, where people who are having a rotten, miserable life—as 99.9 percent of the world is—can only gain enjoyment by seeing the decline and fall of others . . . They see that those who obtain riches or fame or high position are no happier than they are. It helps them get along."

But many see this invocation of the public's "right" (and zeal) to know as an irresponsible journalistic rationalization.

"The public interest is not the prurient interest," says *New York Times* columnist William Safire. Just because some people enjoy the misfortunes of others—a perverse pleasure the Germans call *"schadenfreude"*—is no reason for newspapers to try to satisfy that longing.

Tunney calls this kind of journalism "keyhole reporting," and says it is often as spurious as it is tawdry. Recently, he says, he had dinner in Washington with his ex-wife and his child; the next day, there was a slyly suggestive story in the papers about his having been seen out late "with a belle and a babe."

Even when such stories are accurate, though, Reagan feels they ought to be eschewed as "the basest sort of gossip-mongering."

"Gossip has always been around," Reagan says. "That's why we gossip over the back fence. But the press doesn't have to cater to the worst in us."

Gossip has, indeed, "always been around"—in newspapers and out. But beginning with Congressman Wilbur D. Mills' public cavorting with stripper Fanne Foxe in 1974, there seems to have been a resurgence of it in the public prints—"a return to yellow journalism" in the words of Agnew.

In one nine-month period, there were widespread stories on:

- Betty Ford's comments about the likelihood of her daughter having a premarital affair.

- The alleged lack of intimacy between former President Nixon and his wife.
- The rumored philandering of former President John F. Kennedy.

In some instances, such stories can be justified. Kennedy, for example, purportedly had an affair with Judith Campbell Exner at the same time she was also consorting with a prominent Mafioso—and at the same time the CIA was plotting with the Mafia to assassinate Fidel Castro. Moreover, this evidence came to light during a Senate investigation of the CIA.

That, obviously, is a story—a significant story.

But what of Kennedy's other "affairs"? Are they the proper subject for newspaper speculation now, 13 years after his death? Even if true, is Kennedy's sex life now relevant to his presidency?

"What possible benefit is there in probing Kennedy's private life?" asks Agnew.

Some members of the press think these stories are merely a conscience-stricken overcompensation for the adulatory treatment the press generally gave Kennedy while he was alive.

But Lewis Lapham, editor of *Harper's*, thinks they serve a far more useful purpose. He suggests that Kennedy's purported liaisons are clear evidence of an "emotional weakness that apparently goaded Kennedy into seeking ceaseless proof of his omnipotence."

Might not that same weakness have been at least partially responsible for the Bay of Pigs, the Cuban missile crisis and the beginning of our war effort in Vietnam?

Moreover, Lapham asks, "If it was in Kennedy's nature to make himself vulnerable to his sexual confusions, then perhaps he also made himself vulnerable to the more ominous seductions that glimmer around the brilliant light of the presidency.

"He was surrounded by flatterers and camp followers; many of them were knowledgeable men who could speak in honeyed voices about the advantages of the occasional assassination in small and distant countries."

That, surely, is the public's business.

Jack Landau, chairman of the Reporters Committee for Freedom of the Press, offers essentially the same argument in defense of stories about Nixon's alleged drinking and sexual estrangement.

"It crystallizes the picture of a man completely alone, isolated from friends and family," Landau says. "You can make a strong case that all these things contributed to his psychological state of mind, which led up to Watergate and what happened afterward."

There is, no doubt, an element of truth in that line of reasoning. But such theories may also lead to dangerous syllogisms.

"Bob Haldeman and John Ehrlichman and most of the other men

around Nixon led exemplary private lives," says Unruh, "and look what they did with their public jobs and the public trust."

Both Unruh and Pat Brown, two of Nixon's oldest and most bitter foes, think reportage of his alleged sexual estrangement from his wife reprehensible.

"There must be 15 million marriages in this country where there's no sex any more," Unruh says. "That doesn't necessarily mean the man won't be able to do his job at the office right."

If a public figure is not fulfilling his public responsibilities, Unruh and Brown and others say, there will be sufficient evidence of that failure elsewhere, without the press "resorting to speculation and innuendo and gossip about his private life."

Even Lapham admits that: Nixon's shortcomings were "plainly visible on the public record . . . for more than twenty years," he says.

And yet the beat of gossip journalism throbs on. Why?

Some press critics see the renascent interest in gossip as escapism, as part of what Alexander Cockburn, writing in *New York* magazine, calls a "spirit of triviality lurking in the bosom of the average newspaper reader . . . now blazing up more fiercely than ever before [after] the dark clouds of the Vietnam war, of Watergate, of the recession."

But there is more to the phenomenon than mere escapism. In a sense, it is an overreaction to the disillusionments of Vietnam and Watergate, "a Watergate tic" in the phrase of the *New York Times'* Arthur Gelb. Newspaper editors and reporters are more skeptical of public officials than ever before, and neither personal nor official conduct is beyond the pale of their scrutiny. Public officials are no longer sacrosanct; they are seen as suffering from the same human shortcomings as the rest of us— perhaps more so. Newspapermen want to expose those shortcomings, and citizens seem to want to read about them.

Moreover, after being told for so long that the FBI and CIA were the embodiment of all that was good and just and holy and that the war in Vietnam was a gallantly altruistic struggle against brutal Communist aggression and that Watergate was just "a third-rate burglary," many in the media and the public alike have now fallen victim to a pervasive cynicism. They see dishonesty and venality and corruption everywhere they look.

Charles Seib of the *Washington Post* calls this attitude "an aggravated instinct for the jugular." *Time* magazine calls it "predatory journalism." Pat Brown and Spiro Agnew call it "bloodlust." Other politicians liken it to the frenzy of crowds who used to watch lions devour Christians in ancient Rome.

"The public has come to look with suspicion on all politicians, to assume we're all guilty of some wrongdoing," says Tom Bradley, "and the press is both responding to and contributing to this attitude. It's gotten out of hand. There's an excess of zeal on the part of the press to appeal to the ghoulish appetite of its most cynical readers."

Although most editors say vigilance and healthy skepticism are long overdue, they do admit it has become egregious in many cases. Balancing investigative vigilance-cum-missionary zeal with journalistic responsibility is now "the single most difficult issue facing the press," says *Los Angeles Times* editor William F. Thomas. "It's the one thing all editors talk about and try to find an answer to when they get together."

In today's climate, editors admit, a minor official may make an honest mistake—or a stupid one—on a relatively trivial matter, and newspapers will accuse him of all manner of sinister misdeeds. Watergate made heroes of the press—Woodward and Bernstein up there on the silver screen, toppling a government, winning a Pulitzer Prize for their paper . . . and more than a million dollars for themselves; "Woodstein Envy is now rampant," says *Newsweek*. "Scarcely a reporter in the country is now immune to fantasies of heroic achievement—and epic remuneration."

Warns Melvin Mencher of the Columbia University School of Journalism:

"Every little paper in the country and every reporter on the beat is going to want a scalp."

While these characterizations may be a bit hyperfervid, they are more accurate than many journalists would care to admit, and in the grip of this trenchcoat psychology—goaded on by competitive pressures—some reporters and editors are more likely to print stories of dubious credibility, origin and significance than they might have a decade ago.

Thus, the *Los Angeles Times* has given page-one play—and a screaming street-edition headline—to an Associated Press story about Admiral Thomas Moorer, retired chairman of the Joint Chiefs of Staff, having taken just one free trip to a Rockwell International hunting camp. The *Times* also gave page-one play to a story by its own Washington bureau about Internal Revenue Service Commissioner Donald Alexander's decision to delete from federal tax returns a question dealing with foreign bank accounts.

Although both stories carried a clear implication of official wrongdoing by the respective parties involved, no specific examples of malfeasance were provided, either in those stories or subsequently.

The *New York Times* published a similar story about a possibly illegal $2,000 union-fund contribution to then-Congressman Gerald Ford. But there was no evidence the transaction ever took place—and the story admitted as much.

Another example:

The *Washington Post* published a story saying two of the three largest banks in the United States had been "placed on a super-secret list of problem banks" because of "inadequate" capital. But the list, it subsequently turned out, was more than two years old and had never really warranted a level of concern even remotely approaching the apocalyptic tone of the *Post* story.

There are similar examples available from almost every big-city newspaper in America in the last few years—if only because the suddenly glamorous field of investigative journalism is now glutted with more reporters (experienced and otherwise) than ever before, all digging, digging, digging, whether in the interest of public service or self-aggrandizement or, as in most cases, a perfectly understandable blend of the two.

The congressional sex scandal of 1976 is perhaps the best—worst?—example of this phenomenon. The scandal began with the disclosure by the *Washington Post* that powerful Ohio Congressman Wayne Hays was paying a sexy blonde named Elizabeth Ray $14,000 a year in federal funds solely to serve as his sexual playmate. That was a genuine—and valuable—*exposé*: the alleged misuse of the taxpayers' money. But the Wayne Hays/Elizabeth Ray story sent reporters scurrying like berserk bloodhounds for their very own stories of lust and avarice in the hallowed halls of Congress. Almost every day, it seemed, some new story broke involving some new congressman and some new blonde (or redhead or brunette).

When the *Cleveland Plain-Dealer* headlined a story that Congressman Charles Vanik had on his payroll a woman who had once been convicted of prostitution and who had not shown up for work in months, the *Cleveland Press* followed with a story saying the woman had also been arrested for larceny and conspiracy. The *Plain-Dealer* story was accurate, albeit—on even the most cursory examination—hardly the sort of stuff of which Pulitzer Prize entries are made: The woman's prostitution conviction had occurred eight years before Vanik had hired her; she had a history of psychiatric illness; she had been kept on the payroll (out of "compassion") at the minimum salary so she would be eligible for hospitalization benefits. But if the *Plain-Dealer* story was flimsy, the *Press* story was downright feeble: the woman had never been arrested for either larceny *or* conspiracy; it was a case of mistaken identity.

It is precisely this sort of "mistake" that many editors (and some politicians) see as the inevitable by-product of excessive journalistic zeal. What frightens these editors (and politicians) is that such errors—whether involving public figures or their offspring, public venality or private indiscretion—could ultimately prove destructive both to a free press and to a free society.

They fear that if newspapers do not exercise responsibility and good judgment, the public, when it tires of cynicism and disillusionment, will not raise much of an outcry should censorship be imposed from above by government officials embittered at having their every motive impugned.

Ralph Otwell, chairman of the ethics committee of the American Society of Newspaper Editors, also fears that excessive invasions of privacy and unproved accusations of wrongdoing could drive good people out of public life.

"A public figure has to expect to take a certain amount of heat," Otwell says, "but there has to be a limit or the best people will just decide it's not worth it."

Former Senator John Tunney shares this fear: "With everyone in the press automatically assuming that anything a politician does he does for venal purposes, you create a greater division between the governors and the governed, a mutual hostility that leads to irresponsibility on both sides—a sense of frustration for the public official and a disenchantment with the democratic process for the public at-large. When that happens, you destroy people's confidence in their elected officials and public institutions, and you lay the groundwork—you make people susceptible —for someone to come riding in on a white horse and saying he'll singlehandedly make things better again.

"That, inevitably, means authoritarianism, not democracy."

2 / Patty, Squeaky and Sally: One Kidnap, Two Assassination Attempts

September 5, 1975. Lynette (Squeaky) Fromme, a follower of convicted mass murderer Charles Manson, is arrested in Sacramento after an assassination attempt against then-President Gerald Ford.

September 18, 1975. Patricia Hearst, newspaper heiress-turned-kidnap victim-turned-machine-gun-toting revolutionary, is arrested in San Francisco after a 19-month cross-country odyssey.

September 22, 1975. Sara Jane Moore, would-be radical and part-time FBI informer, is arrested in San Francisco after an assassination attempt against Gerald Ford.

Within a period of 17 days (and a radius of 100 miles), three events of national, if not international interest—each with its own, uniquely bizarre twist—exploded upon the public consciousness.

Press coverage of all three events was immediate and exhaustive, and criticism of that coverage was subsequently substantial.

For the most part, critics questioned whether such saturation coverage tends to glamorize and glorify would-be assassins and terrorist kidnapers, thereby inciting more assassinations and kidnapings by unstable individuals seeking similar notoriety.

That is, of course, a valid concern. But it obscures several other, equally valid questions raised by press coverage of the assassination attempts and, especially, of the Hearst case.

Among these questions are:

- Did the press, in a fit of adrenal and competitive zeal, overreact to the events, covering them so heavily that speculative, spurious, even contrived stories were often published?
- Did the press, in that zeal, jeopardize the rights of the accused to a fair trial?
- Did the newspaper most intimately involved in the Hearst case, the Hearst-owned *San Francisco Examiner*, suffer a conflict of interest that compromised the integrity and credibility of its coverage of the case—and, concomitantly, affected its coverage of at least one of the assassination attempts?

None of these is a new question for newspaper editors. Overreaction, speculation, conflict of interest and the fair trial-free press controversy have long troubled responsible newsmen everywhere. But rarely have these issues been focused so intensely on one shattering series of events in so close a chronological and geographic proximity.

Ironically, these questions come at a time when the American press is undergoing a metamorphosis that would almost seem to have rendered such questions moot.

Newspapers, in recent years, have generally drifted away from sensational, crime-and-violence coverage into more serious and responsible reportage—commentaries on changing life-styles, analyses of major social problems, investigations of governmental and corporate wrongdoing.

But press coverage of the Hearst arrests and of the two assassination attempts prompted at least one editor to suggest, unhappily:

"Maybe we haven't come quite as far as we like to think we have."

Many other editors find this self-appraisal a bit harsh—at least insofar as the *quantity* of coverage is concerned. It is almost impossible, these editors insist, to publish too much about an attempt to assassinate the president. That is not, they say, a crime story in the traditional sense of the term. It is a socio-political story about the ultimate act of dissidence—of violence—in a democratic society.

In a sense, the Hearst case was also "far more than a crime story," says one newsman who made a careful study of press coverage of that story and of the two assassination attempts.

"Christ, it's a once-in-a-century story," says Murray Olderman of the Newspaper Enterprise Association. "It's a story that has it all."

Says a reporter who covered the story:

"It's got sex and violence and money and politics—everything from mere titillation to real questions about corporate power and violent revolution in America."

That the Hearst case is, indeed, more than "a crime story" can be seen in its treatment by media not characteristically associated with sensationalism.

The *New York Times*, for example, made the arrest of Hearst and William and Emily Harris the lead story in its next day's paper, beneath a large headline and accompanied by another page one story and a page one picture—treatment the paper generally reserves for the fall of a major foreign government.

The Hearst story remained on page one of the *New York Times* for the next five days—as it did in most major American newspapers.

In the San Francisco Bay Area, the arrests and their aftermath dominated the media even more thoroughly. That was to be expected. The Hearst family lives there. The kidnaping took place there. The arrests were made there.

Still, there is some reason to question the pervasive extent to which that story dominated Bay Area newspapers.

In Oakland, for example, coverage of the case became such a regular feature in the *Tribune* in the weeks after the arrest that stories were accompanied by what is known as a "standing head" ("Patty Hearst Update"), a device normally used only for such daily features as syndicated columns and crossword puzzles.

In San Francisco, the *Examiner* devoted the first five full pages of its paper to the Hearst story the day after her arrest. No other story appeared on those pages. The next day, the story still occupied the entire front page —at a time when other newspapers were giving front-page play to such stories as:

- The recommended discharge of an Air Force sergeant who made his homosexuality a *cause celebre*.
- The smallest increase in the national cost of living in more than three years.
- The swearing-in of Portugal's new coalition cabinet after months of civil turmoil.

The Hearst story remained the lead story on page one of the *Examiner* for eight of the next nine days, interrupted only by the September 22 assassination attempt on President Ford. Even the assassination attempt lasted only one day atop the *Examiner* front page; the very next day, the lead story was on the affidavit Hearst's lawyer had filed with the court, claiming she had lived in a "perpetual state of terror" for 19 months.

The Hearst story remained on the front page of the *Examiner* for 19 of the first 20 days after her arrest—and it stayed somewhere in the paper for 24 consecutive days, disappeared for one day, then reappeared virtually every day for the next month.

The *San Francisco Chronicle* also permitted the Hearst story to dominate its front page, albeit less dramatically. The story led the *Chronicle* for nine of the first 14 days after the arrest, and it remained on the front page for 13 of those 14 days.

All this Hearst coverage in both San Francisco papers came during a hotly contested mayoral campaign that all but disappeared from the papers for days at a time.

Nonetheless, Abe Mellinkoff, city editor of the *Chronicle* for 29 years before becoming associate editor, snorts in derision at the suggestion that San Francisco papers overplayed the story.

"It was a great story," he says. "It was the topic of dinner table talk everywhere I went. It sold papers like mad. The only way to cover a story like that is to go looking for new angles every day."

The Hearst story did, indeed, sell newspapers. The *Examiner* printed 14,000 copies of an extra edition the afternoon Hearst was captured. Only 15 were returned.

But a story must be justified by more than circulation figures and reader titillation—just as the coverage itself must be judged qualitatively and not only quantitatively.

In this instance, a qualitative analysis clearly shows that haste, competition, carelessness, sensationalism and the quest for "new angles every day" often led the press into publishing stories of dubious credibility and, on occasion, stories of demonstrable inaccuracy.

When Fromme was arraigned, for example, she told the judge:

"The gun is pointed. Whether it goes off is up to you all."

But most newspapers, relying on erroneous wire service reports, left the word "all" off the end of that sentence, thereby giving readers the impression that Fromme had threatened the judge personally, whereas she had actually been threatening the entire corporate/political establishment.

Time magazine offered its readers an even more ominous story in its September 15 coverage of the Fromme case. *Time* said more than 100 Manson family members were "fanned out in communes up and down California." But dozens of official and unofficial sources familiar with the Manson clan subsequently scoffed at that assertion as absurd.

In its coverage of the next assassination attempt, the *Los Angeles Times* published a lengthy, front-page profile of accused assassin Sara Jane Moore, describing her as "a blue-blood Southerner . . . from a wealthy West Virginia family [with] . . . mining, lumber and political interests."

But Moore came from a modest family, not a wealthy one. And her family's only contact with mining was her grandfather's job as a bookkeeper for a coal company.

A week later, the *Sacramento Bee* also printed an erroneous story—this one on Hearst. The *Bee* story—accompanied by a picture and spread all across the top of page one—purported to disclose an apartment in nearby Carmichael in which the *Bee* said William and Emily Harris were "believed to have lived . . . for at least a month" before the robbery of a Carmichael bank.

But the Harrises never lived in that apartment.

The *Philadelphia Inquirer* printed a seemingly erroneous story on the Hearst case, too. The *Inquirer* said, on October 2, that the FBI had found Hearst by monitoring the mail of the father of two people linked to the SLA.

But the father, Martin Soliah, said the FBI didn't have to monitor his mail because he had voluntarily told the FBI where to find his son.

Many other stories that appeared dubious—if not downright erroneous—when they were published cannot be properly evaluated yet, simply because no one yet knows everything about the three cases involved.

Was Hearst's conversion voluntary? Or was it induced? Or coerced?

Was her arrest the result of determined police work? Or was it blind luck?

Was the affidavit her attorneys filed about her ordeal an honest account of her experience? Or had the attorneys prepared her defense months before her arrest?

Did Fromme really want to kill President Ford? Or was she just trying to draw attention to herself? Or to Charles Manson?

Was Moore acting out of personal frustration? Or radical commitment?

All of these conflicting theories—and dozens of others—were propounded by various newspapers. No one—not the FBI, and perhaps not even the three women themselves—knows all the answers. Maybe they will never be known.

But if it is difficult to determine which stories were demonstrably erroneous, it is less difficult to determine which may have been speculative, spurious or contrived.

When a story like the Hearst arrest or an assassination attempt breaks, the adrenalin begins to flow in most reporters—and in their editors as well. If these newsmen are working in a competitive situation, fighting to be first with each new detail and nuance—as most newsmen are, in one fashion or another—that adrenal flow may occasionally becloud good judgment and undermine restraint.

This was especially true of the Hearst story, with its irresistibly exotic accumulation of unanswered questions.

"You want to be first," admits Bill German, executive news editor of the *San Francisco Chronicle*. "We haven't been able to really explain the main story—what the hell happened to Patty?—so we've been exploring cul-de-sacs of information, looking into every nook and cranny of the story, and we've overdone it a few times."

Says Dave Felton, an editor at *Rolling Stone*:

"There just haven't been all that many good, solid, breaking developments, so what you got was a bunch of reporters racing around, trying to find something, anything, to keep the story alive every day."

One example of such reportage was a *Chicago Daily News* story that said federal authorities feared Hearst faced "the threat of violence—even another kidnaping—by splinter radicals."

But the story contained not the slightest proof of this "threat."

A *Daily News* reporter had simply asked an FBI spokesman if Hearst might be kidnaped again, and the spokesman had replied, "Sure, it's a possibility. There's always a possibility."

On the basis of that—and similar interviews with defense attorneys— the *Daily News* published a 10-inch story, at the top of page two, beneath the headline:

"Officials Fear Patty Periled by Radicals"

The *San Francisco Examiner* published several stories that may also be viewed as what one reporter terms "the journalism of contrivance"—and what the *Examiner's* own editor calls "journalism on the run."

Among these was a page-one story saying that law enforcement authorities were test-firing guns found in the homes where Hearst and the Harrises were arrested to see if those weapons matched weapons "used in a number of major crimes in California, including the assassinations of two policemen."

(Larry Kramer, the reporter who wrote that story, later admitted he was "really reaching" for a new angle, and that such test-firings are routine procedure.)

The *Sacramento Bee* published a similarly speculative page-one story saying, "Bill and Emily Harris . . . and possibly Patty Hearst may have come face-to-face with Sacramento law enforcement officers last spring, but eluded capture in their dilapidated hideout . . ."

The story, subsequently reprinted elsewhere, told of a murder investigation—unrelated to the Hearst case—and suggested that since the murder had taken place "only yards from the structure" inhabited by Hearst and the Harrises, detectives working on the murder case must have visited the Hearst/Harris home in the course of routine, door-to-door investigation.

But the story did not say the detectives had, in fact, "come face to face" with all three fugitives. It merely implied such a confrontation could have taken place, simply because the police and the fugitives were in the same place at the same time. (Subsequent stories indicated the police did interview Mrs. Harris but not the other two.)

In the same vein, what one editor calls "one of the most atrocious examples of speculative journalism I've ever seen" was published by *Newsweek.*

A *Newsweek* map showing Hearst's "known stops" and "possible stops" as a fugitive indicated she may have visited Idaho, Oregon, Alaska and Canada.

But no one was quoted as having seen her in any of those places, and the only support *Newsweek* offered for these claims was the comment, "Underground sources . . . suggest that Patty could have" visited these places, presumably because other radical fugitives may have done so.

The use of unnamed sources always has been a difficult problem for the press, and *Newsweek* was not the only publication to have its credibility on Hearst coverage questioned because of its reliance on this device.

The *New York Post* published a story saying Hearst had confessed to several crimes and had agreed to testify against the Harrises in exchange for immunity or special treatment.

The story was based on "sources familiar with" Hearst's interviews with court-appointed psychiatrists. But when prosecution and defense attorneys vehemently denied the story, it seemed—at best—premature and speculative.

Newsday, a suburban New York newspaper, also published several "exclusive"—and questionable—Hearst stories based on the comments of unnamed sources. One began:

"Patricia Hearst made an attempt to give herself up two days before the fiery shootout in which six members of the Symbionese Liberation Army were killed last year, according to a well-known radical attorney."

Hearst's attorneys categorically denied that story, too—even though it could, if true, enable her to tell a jury she had wanted to surrender to authorities, but became frightened by the shootout and thought she, too, would be shot if she tried to do so.

Some journalists are as critical of the press for what they call "unnecessary" stories as for speculative and spurious stories.

"Did we really have to print each new clue that might tie Patty to the Carmichael bank robbery?" asks one *San Francisco Chronicle* editor. "Did the *Los Angeles Times* really have to print all those details on the sex life of the SLA? Or were we all just catering to the lowest tastes of our readers?"

Says John Burks, a former *San Francisco Examiner* reporter now with television station KQED:

"The problem with the way the press covers a story like Patty or the assassinations is that they don't try to place it in any meaningful, historical context. They don't relate it to what's going on, say, in South America, where they also have assassinations and political kidnapings.

"Instead of giving their readers information that would enable them to understand why students become activists or terrorists, they present each of these events to their readers as a series of unrelated, totally amazing events.

"When Patty was busted, every reporter I knew was chasing around, looking for inane, meaningless details like, 'Is Patty's red hair more auburn or more carrot-colored?' and 'Were Bill Harris' tennis shoes Pumas or Adidas?'

"It was the same when she was first kidnaped. I worked at the *Examiner* then, and I tried to interest them in some books and movies that would help them understand radical thought and political kidnaping. They weren't interested. Editors may talk a lot about how they're giving the story a lot of space because it's not just a crime story, but they're sure covering it exactly as if that's all it were."

The *Examiner* was, of course, in a sensitive position from the moment the kidnaping story broke, simply by virtue of being owned by Hearst's father, Randolph Hearst. The *Examiner* did not even report the kidnaping until the *Oakland Tribune* did so, and in the early weeks after the kidnaping, the *Examiner* appeared as much a captive of the SLA as was Hearst herself.

Examiner reporters did not pursue leads on the identity of the SLA kidnapers, but lengthy SLA communiques were printed in full in the *Examiner*, and nothing was published that could in any way jeopardize Hearst's life—all, seemingly, at the behest of Randolph Hearst.

The situation, says *Examiner* reporter Carol Pogash, was "horrible."

"We were told to cool it. When there was violence in the food program (a free-food-for-the-needy project demanded by the SLA), Randolph Hearst came and told us to try and minimize the violence." He feared for his daughter's life, Pogash said.

When tape recordings were released with "Tania" proclaiming her conversion to the SLA, the *Examiner* published an article quoting a specialist in political revolution as saying her conversion "does not mean she reached that conclusion through her own free will and of her own volition." The *Examiner* also published a story quoting another expert as saying she may have been brainwashed; the story ran beneath the headline:

Look at Patty with Caution, Charity—Expert

When SLA members robbed the Hibernia bank of $10,000, the *Examiner* story ran beneath the headline:

Guns Point at 'Tania' in Bank.

Not until the fifth paragraph did the *Examiner* mention that the FBI was considering "the possibility that she was a willing participant," and even then, the story did its best to cast doubts on that interpretation.

The *Chronicle* followed much the same pattern—its publisher having both a personal and a business relationship with Randolph Hearst; the *Chronicle's* story on the bank robbery did not even mention that Ms. Hearst was in the bank until the fifth paragraph.

One *Chronicle* editor defends both papers for withholding the original kidnaping story and treading lightly thereafter as "what we've always done to safeguard the life of any kidnap victim," but one *Chronicle* reporter, Tim Findley, quit in disgust over the handling of his kidnaping-related stories, and morale at both San Francisco papers was extraordinarily low in those early weeks after the kidnaping.

After the arrests, however, both San Francisco papers covered the story fully—the *Examiner* even more so than the *Chronicle* (in part, editors admit, to avoid charges of a second cover-up).

The *Examiner*, in fact, scored more exclusives on the story than any other newspaper, in or out of San Francisco, except *Rolling Stone*. Nevertheless, its coverage—inevitably viewed through the prism of its Hearst family connections—came in for considerable criticism.

Reg Murphy, editor-publisher of the *Examiner*, was pilloried for acting as a spokesman for the Hearst family—providing other media with the family's official comment on certain developments and, on one occasion, calling what amounted to a press conference to report the family's denial of a *Newsday* story.

But Murphy says he only acted in response to inquiries from newsmen unable to reach the Hearsts themselves.

"Usually, I had the good sense to refer them to the Hearst attorneys," he says, "but sometimes, I tried to facilitate their jobs for them by getting the answers directly. Reporters have always helped other reporters this way."

Murphy and the *Examiner* have also been criticized for making "unethical" use of information available exclusively to them through Hearst family contacts. The *Examiner* was the first newspaper, for example, to have the affidavit filed by Hearst's attorneys.

Murphy and reporter Steve Cook, who wrote the affidavit story, deny they obtained the affidavit through Hearst connections. But Murphy says he would see nothing wrong with that if it had happened.

"I'd do anything I could, legally, to get a story," he says. "When you've got the best sources, you use them."

But the most serious charge levied against the *Examiner* after the arrests was that its coverage of the Hearst case seems designed to create a sympathetic climate for her—to portray her as a victim, as a poor, young girl reunited with her family after a terrible ordeal, rather than as a possible suspect in two bank robberies and one murder, among other things.

"The *Examiner*," several reporters said at the time, "is part of the defense team."

There have been several stories that would seem to lend credence to this criticism—beginning with a story written by Murphy himself the day after the arrest. It began, "Patty Hearst came home again last night."

Headlines on other *Examiner* stories included:

- "The public has Patty all wrong, lawyer says"
- "Patty's plight 'like Three Faces of Eve' "
- "An Opinion: Why don't they give Patty Hearst a chance?"
- "Mrs. Hearst: 'They treat her like a caged animal' "
- "Patty falling apart and must leave jail, her lawyer says"

The *Examiner's* own reporters have criticized their paper for its handling of a *Rolling Stone* account of the first seven months of Hearst's odyssey.

That story, which said Hearst was a willing convert to the SLA, was held out of one edition of the *Examiner*, then played on page two in subsequent editions. But when Jack Scott—generally believed to have been the primary source for the *Rolling Stone* "inside story"—denounced the story, the *Examiner* led the next day's paper with his comments.

"The way that was handled was wrong. It annoyed me," says Larry Kramer, an *Examiner* reporter who wrote many of the Hearst stories.

Examiner reporters also are said to be upset that editors vetoed a proposed story showing the inconsistencies between the affidavit Hearst attorneys filed and Hearst's own comments in taped SLA communiques, in the *Rolling Stone* story and in a jailhouse conversation with a friend.

But the *Examiner* was also the first newspaper to publish several page one stories damaging to the Hearst defense—including one linking Hearst to a bank robbery and murder in Carmichael, and another (based on fragments of an SLA manuscript) describing her as "an eager student of her SLA mentors."

In effect, the *Examiner's* coverage was as schizophrenic as the paper's staff was uncertain.

Reg Murphy repeatedly told his staff to handle the story "just like any other story," but as reporter Carol Pogash admits, "Sometimes, that's easier said than done."

In addition to the normal factors involved in news judgment, some *Examiner* staffers may not have been able to avoid, at times, being influenced by how their readers would perceive their stories—and by how the Hearst family would react to them.

They must also have been concerned with the impact of their stories on any future trial of Hearst and the Harrises.

The *Examiner* was not, of course, the only paper required to take into consideration the fair trial versus free press issue—with Hearst and the Harrises and with Fromme and Moore as well.

Not surprisingly, however, most editors denied that press coverage of these cases could have jeopardized the legal rights of the accused.

Reg Murphy of the *Examiner*, the victim of a celebrated kidnap himself, says he knows from personal experience that the impact of press coverage on potential jurors is "greatly exaggerated."

"By the time a case goes to trial," he says, "readers just don't remember that many specifics about what they read."

The Angela Davis case, Murphy and others say, is a good case in point. Davis was the subject of a great deal of unfavorable publicity before her trial on charges of supplying the weapons used in the 1970 Marin County courthouse shootout. But the state's case was as weak as the media speculation was damning, and she was acquitted.

"You shouldn't underestimate a juror's intelligence, and you shouldn't overestimate his memory," one lawyer says.

These three cases were unusual, moreover, in that there were so many witnesses and so much evidence already available to law enforcement that none of the trials were typical guilt-or-innocence trials.

Paul Avery, who covered much of the Hearst case for the *Chronicle*— and for a book—said before the trials:

"It's not a question of 'I didn't do it. I wasn't there. It's a case of mistaken identity.' These trials will be determined by the medical testimony, by questions of intent and mental capacity."

But that was precisely the area the media concentrated on in all three cases. Might such speculation on the state of mind of Hearst, Fromme and Moore have jeopardized their respective legal defenses?

Many editors grudgingly acknowledge this possibility—however remote—but they tend to regard the question much as they regard charges that coverage of the cases could incite similar acts of violence.

"It's one of the dangers of living in a free society with a free press," Murphy says, "but the alternative—secrecy and suppression—is a far worse danger. Look at what the conspiracy theorists have done with the other assassinations. Can you imagine what a field day they'd have, the national paranoia we'd see, if we didn't print everything we can find now, regardless of the effect?"

Most fairly recent accusations that press coverage could incite imitative violence began with the appearance of Squeaky Fromme on the covers of *Time* and *Newsweek* after her attempt to assassinate the president. That exposure, critics said, glorified Fromme.

But Roy Fisher, dean of the School of Journalism at the University of Missouri, thinks such press critics confuse reportage of actual violence with entertainment featuring fictional violence.

"The kind of TV shows that have four or five corpses in a 30-minute period do cheapen life and distort our standards," Fisher says, "but to suggest that the press shouldn't report in detail on a major kidnaping or assassination attempt is to ask the press to sweep everything unpleasant under the rug. That's crooked journalism."

Although there may have been some media excesses that could be said to have jeopardized the rights of the accused—or to incite unstable minds to violence—no clear evidence to support either contention has yet been advanced by psychologists or sociologists who have studied the relationship between press coverage and human behavior.

In fact, a Marquette University psychologist made a study of the Hearst case late in 1975 and concluded that pretrial publicity probably does not strongly influence jurors in criminal cases.

Nor has anyone yet advanced a reasonable alternative to present coverage that would avoid these potential excesses without simultaneously compromising the media's right to inform and the public's right to be informed.

There is, however, general agreement among newsmen and critics alike that society *would* benefit from a greater exercise of restraint and responsibility in the media to prevent the publication of the kinds of speculative and spurious stories that abounded in the immediate aftermath of the Hearst arrest and the two assassination attempts. Even once the trials were underway, newspapers continued to print dubious stories —often permitting themselves to be used as pawns in the courtroom struggle between defense and prosecution. Leaks from both sides were as plentiful as false leads had been during the first few weeks after the Hearst kidnaping—and the press rushed them into print.

If press coverage *does* incite violence or influence potential jurors, withholding stories of questionable credibility should reduce that effect. But even if press coverage has no such effect, that restraint would, at the very least, spare the community from yet another onslaught of sensationalism and misinformation.

That alone, most editors concede, would be a valuable public service.

3 / Political Polls: Use and Abuse

There is a growing feeling among sophisticated poll-watchers across the country that newspaper polls on political races seriously distort and undermine the electoral process.

The manner in which polls are now published can adversely affect fund raising, media coverage, staff morale, campaign strategy and voter turnout. The polls can also help perpetuate incumbencies, discourage young and relatively unknown candidates for office and even influence government policy on controversial issues.

Were it not for the published polls, many responsible critics say, Houston I. Flournoy—not Edmund G. Brown, Jr.—might now be governor of California. And Hubert H. Humphrey—not Richard Nixon—might have been elected president in 1972.

In 1974 alone, these critics say, polls were largely responsible for the outcome of elections in Massachusetts, New Hampshire, Ohio and Maine, as well as in California.

To diminish the undue influence of the polls, critics propose a whole range of reforms governing the timing, content, structure and publication of political polls. These suggested reforms include:

- No polls should be published more than three or four months before an election.
- No polls should be published within the last 10 days before an election.
- Pre-primary polls should either be abandoned altogether or greatly modified.

- Polls should concentrate more on voters' general attitudes toward the candidates and on the major issues of the day, rather than on what many call "the foolish horse-race question of who's ahead by how many points."
- Polls should be published in the same manner as any other story submitted to a newspaper—subjected to rigorous analysis by trained political writers and published with the appropriate qualifying comments and disclaimers, rather than be treated as an exact science and published almost word-for-word as the pollster writes them.
- Polls should include a much more careful analysis of probable voter turnout and what is now called the "undecided" vote.
- Political writers should be given at least a rudimentary training in the methodology and interpretation of polls so they and their readers can more fully understand the results (and limitations) of polls.

Among the more extreme reforms proposed by those interviewed for this study were the licensing of pollsters and the creation of a governmental or quasi-governmental agency to conduct polls or, at least, to monitor them.

Although several attempts have been made, both statewide and nationally, to regulate polls by law, almost all of the more than 60 politicians, pollsters, newsmen and social scientists interviewed prefer voluntary controls, imposed by newspapers and pollsters themselves.

Even the most vigorous critics of polls do not want polls prohibited— a few, in fact, deny that they exert any influence at all on elections—but almost everyone interviewed insisted that substantive, often drastic, reforms are necessary immediately.

These critics cited the increasing impact of the mass media, the gradual breakdown of traditional party loyalties and the enactment of campaign financing reform as major reasons for prompt action.

New York and South Dakota have already passed laws requiring pollsters to fully disclose how and when their polls are taken—and who finances them—but that disclosure (supported by all responsible pollsters) is generally felt to be but a small step in the right direction.

"I think you would have real First Amendment problems if you tried to do much more than that by law, though," says Jess Unruh, long a power in the California Democratic Party. "Besides, if you try to control them by law, you just leave the public at the mercy of the private polls, the self-serving polls commissioned and financed by candidates and then leaked to the press anyway.

"The press already does a pretty good job of discounting the private polls. Now they have to do something about their own polls—the Field and Gallup and Harris type polls; with their stamp of credibility and scientific accuracy, they can be an instrument of the devil the way they often mislead the public and influence the outcome of elections."

Among unsophisticated critics, the most frequent complaint about polls is that they tend to create a bandwagon psychology—that voters, seeing a particular candidate running ahead in the polls, will vote for him so as to be on the winning side.

A companion criticism involves underdog psychology—that voters, seeing a particular candidate behind in the polls, will vote for him out of sympathy.

Dr. Joseph Klapper, former professor at Stanford and Columbia universities and now director of social research for CBS, has made the most exhaustive study of these phenomena, and his conclusion is that the bandwagon/underdog syndromes have been vastly overstated.

"In most elections," Klapper says, "there is generally about a 1 percent bandwagon effect and a 1 percent underdog effect, and they cancel each other out.

"People tend to make their voting decisions, not because of what the polls say, but because of how their family and friends and close associates vote or because of their social background, their party affiliation or their feelings on the issues and the personalities of the candidates.

"In fact," Klapper says, "most studies show that people very often aren't even aware of what the polls show."

After the 1960 presidential election, Opinion Research Corporation conducted a poll that would seem to confirm Klapper's thesis. ORC interviewers asked voters whom they had voted for, and who the polls had said would win.

The percentage of voters who said they did not remember what the polls had said was almost identical among both Nixon voters (65 percent) and Kennedy voters (64 percent). The percentage of voters who said the polls had shown their man would win was exactly the same (27 percent) among both groups of voters.

Most responsible poll-watchers agree with Klapper on the absence of any significant bandwagon or underdog influence by the polls.

George Gallup, Jr. is fond of pointing to the one election in which pollsters took the most criticism—the 1948 Dewey-Truman race—as a direct contradiction of the bandwagon theory.

"Thomas Dewey was way ahead in the polls," Gallup says. "If people had wanted to vote for a winner, they would have voted for him and he would have won by a landslide. Instead, he lost."

"Simple logic," adds pollster Burns Roper, "suggests that if polls created a bandwagon effect, they would necessarily always be wrong. They would always under-measure the winner."

Other pollsters cite other races to make the same point:

- In 1962, Richard Nixon led Governor Edmund G. Brown, 56 percent to 44 percent, early in the California gubernatorial race. Final vote: Brown 52.6 percent, Nixon 47.4 percent.

- In 1965, Governor Frank Clement led Howard Baker, 50 percent to 30 percent, early in the Tennessee senatorial race. Final vote: Baker 55.7 percent, Clement 44.3 percent.
- In 1966, Frank O'Connor led Governor Nelson Rockefeller, 56 percent to 29 percent, early in the New York gubernatorial race. Final vote: Rockefeller 44.8 percent, O'Connor 38.3 percent.

There have been similar results in recent years in Texas, Ohio, Oregon, Maine, Oklahoma, Georgia and North Carolina, among others. If a bandwagon psychology were operative, the front-runners in all these races should have won big. But all lost.

There is equally compelling evidence available that the underdog theory is also fallacious. In the two most one-sided presidential elections in recent history—Lyndon B. Johnson's 1964 rout of Senator Barry Goldwater and Richard M. Nixon's 1972 rout of Senator George S. McGovern —the two losers received just about the number of votes the polls said they would.

Both ran far behind in the polls, from the beginning of the campaign until just before Election Day, with no discernible switch of sympathy votes to them as underdogs.

Although it seems clear the polls rarely have a direct influence on *whom* a voter votes for, the polls can help determine *whether* a voter votes at all.

In the 1974 California gubernatorial race, all the polls showed Edmund G. Brown, Jr. with a commanding lead over Houston Flournoy.

Even the last poll gave Brown a seemingly insurmountable lead of eight percentage points less than a week before the election.

But Brown won by less than three percentage points, and there is general agreement in both the Brown and Flournoy camps that had the election been two or three days later, Flournoy would probably have won.

There are several reasons for the surprising narrowness of Brown's victory, but one theory provisionally accepted by both camps as a partial explanation, is that many Democratic voters—not especially enamored of Brown and not much more enthusiastic about the rest of the Democratic ticket—just did not vote on Election Day; given the lead the polls credited Brown with, they were confident he could win without their votes.

(There is also, of course, an equal likelihood that potential Flournoy voters stayed home, too, convinced by the polls that their man couldn't possibly win.)

But the direct impact of a given poll on a given voter in a given race is only one demonstration of the influence of the polls. Of far greater significance is the influence of the polls on the "four M's" of political campaigning—money, media, morale and momentum.

There are, essentially, two kinds of people who give money to political candidates—contributors and investors (or, in the words of campaign film maker Charles Guggenheim, "idealists and pragmatists").

Contributors ("idealists") give money almost solely because they sincerely believe in the candidate and/or in his ideology; they expect little, if anything, in return for their money, and are only minimally influenced by the candidate's prospects for victory.

Investors ("pragmatists") give money primarily because they expect something substantial in return—personal access to the candidate, ego gratification, business contacts, political favors; they often support the candidate the polls say is likely to win, regardless of their own personal and ideological preferences.

"The big contributors like to know where their man stands," says Leonard Hall, former chairman of the Republican National Committee. "Just like the bettor at the $2 window, no one likes to put his money on a loser."

Here again, the 1974 Brown-Flournoy race in California is a good case in point.

Stu Spencer, who served as consultant on the Flournoy campaign, says his candidate's poor showing in early Field polls (which are financed by major newspapers and television stations in California) seriously undermined his fund-raising capabilities.

Flournoy trailed Brown by eight percentage points the week after the June primary and by 14 percentage points in a poll released August 22.

"That August 22 poll dried up all our contributions, just like that," Spencer says, snapping his fingers.

"It wasn't until early October, when our own private polls showed Hugh starting to make a move, that the money began to come in again. By then it was too late.

"I figure that poll cost us $500,000 in contributions. As close as things turned out, we could have bought enough TV time with that money to win the election."

Brown strategists agree.

They learned the value of the Field Poll in the primary, they say, and they capitalized fully on that knowledge against Flournoy.

"In the primary, the conventional wisdom was that Jerry would ultimately fold," says Richard Maullin, who was in charge of polling and fund-raising for Brown. "Every time a new Field Poll came out showing Jerry's lead holding up, I'd package it up and run around the state saying, 'See how good we're doing.' That kept the money coming—and it hurt Flournoy."

Says another Democrat:

"Flournoy had to spend too much of his own time raising money to counter this. If he'd been running better in the polls, he could have left the fund-raising to his staff and spent his own time campaigning. In a close election like that, one or two more campaign tours through the state probably would have won it for him. The polls killed him."

Flournoy certainly isn't the only political candidate to have lost big contributions because he was running poorly in the polls. Congressman William Green of Pennsylvania, who ran unsuccessfully for mayor of Philadelphia in 1971, recalls a newspaper poll stalling his fund-raising just at the moment his campaign was beginning to gather momentum. Green had been endorsed by the governor, and had raised $40,000 in one weekend; then, on Monday, a new poll came out, showing him running behind.

"I didn't raise a dime that Monday," Green says, "and I didn't raise a dime Tuesday or Wednesday or Thursday either."

Perhaps the best example of this phenomenon came in the 1972 California Democratic presidential primary race between Senator George S. McGovern and Senator Hubert H. Humphrey.

Humphrey had trailed throughout the campaign, but his aides felt he was gaining dramatically in the final week or so. Then, two days before the June 6 primary, the final Field Poll was released. It showed Humphrey 20 points behind.

"It was like turning off the water tap with one flick of the wrist," says Joe Cerrell, Humphrey's California campaign manager.

"We not only couldn't get any contributions, we couldn't even collect the money that had already been pledged."

But when the votes were counted, McGovern won by only 5 percent.

To this day, Cerrell and many others in and out of the Humphrey campaign are convinced that that final poll defeated Humphrey.

"If it had been more accurate," Cerrell says, "we would have raised more money, spent more money and we would have won. If we'd won California, there are a lot of people who say we would have won the nomination—and the election."

Staff morale and campaign strategy, like fund-raising, are also affected by the polls.

A candidate who is running well ahead in the polls may grow overconfident, complacent, lazy.

Charles Guggenheim says that's what happened to John H. Glenn in his 1970 Ohio senatorial campaign against Howard Metzenbaum, to Robert Casey in his 1966 Pennsylvania gubernatorial campaign against Milton J. Shapp, and to Frank Lausche in his 1968 Ohio senatorial campaign against John J. Gilligan.

Glenn, Casey and Lausche all let huge poll leads lull them into feelings of false security that greatly reduced their campaign effort—and all ultimately lost.

There is some evidence that Jerry Brown also fell prey to the complacency syndrome in 1974. Running well ahead in the polls, he decided, late in the campaign, to give some of his own campaign funds to other Democrats on the statewide ticket. Insiders say Brown also neglected to concentrate as much as he should have on getting out the Election Day vote, confident he would win, regardless of the turnout. Those decisions almost defeated Brown.

But the effect of polls is far greater on the morale and strategy of candidates who trail than on those who lead.

If the trailing candidate begins to recover dramatically in the polls—as, for example, then-President Ford did in 1976, slashing Jimmy Carter's lead from 33 points to a virtual dead-heat by Election Day—the effect can be galvanizing, the shift in momentum all but irreversible; suddenly, amid seeming disaster, everything appears to be going right.

More often, a poor showing in the polls can demoralize the campaign staff, traumatize the candidate and prematurely terminate the campaign effort. In a phrase, the loser's staff gives up, for, as Mervin Field says, "volunteer effort thrives better on hope than on desperation."

Joe Cerrell still vividly recalls what it was like at Humphrey head-quarters when he first heard about that last poll showing Humphrey 20 points behind McGovern in 1972.

"We all went into shock," he says. "When I came back to the head-quarters at 10:30 that night, everyone was either gone home or one drink short of being drunk. You run on adrenalin in a campaign anyway, and the poll cut off our adrenalin, as well as our money. Everything ground to a halt. The election wasn't till Tuesday, but the campaign was over. It was devastating."

Says Jess Unruh:

"When a candidate is running way behind in the polls, he has to start off every day giving himself a big pep talk, convincing himself he can really win. Then he has to give the same pep talk to his staff and volunteers, and then, again, to the fund raisers and contributors. By the time he gets to the people he should be talking to—the voters—he's exhausted."

Josiah Spaulding, who ran unsuccessfully for attorney general in Massachusetts in 1974, is one of several politicians who cited the impact of the polls on the media.

Spaulding was a Republican in a Democratic state, and he was running against a well-known Democrat (Francis Bellotti) in a Democratic year. Not unexpectedly, the early polls showed Spaulding far behind—as much as 19 points behind in late September. He urged his volunteers to keep working, though, and within a couple of weeks, he thought he was beginning to gain momentum. He was certain the next newspaper poll would show him moving up.

Instead, it showed him trailing by 21 points.

"That made it impossible for me to run a good campaign," Spaulding says. "Not only did I have to cancel some TV and newspaper advertising because I couldn't raise any money, but it became a real effort just to pull my troops up again and again. We all got discouraged."

The day before the election, the polls showed Spaulding had dramatically forged two points ahead. "But it was too late," he says. "You can't buy ads and mount a campaign in two days."

Spaulding, who eventually lost by less than one percentage point, blames the polls for his defeat—and he thinks early polls like those in his race tend to become self-fulfilling prophecies.

"The polls say you're way behind, so the media and the fund-raisers and big contributors react accordingly," he says.

"In my race, every time I went into a new town to talk to the local newspaper, they'd wave the *Boston Globe* poll at me and say I didn't have a chance."

In the 1972 New Hampshire presidential primary, Senator George McGovern was not even considered much of a factor before election day; a *Boston Globe* poll six weeks before the election showed him with just 18 percent of the vote, to 65 percent for Senator Ed Muskie. But when McGovern pulled 37 percent of the vote—to 46.4 percent for Muskie—it was hailed as a great "victory" for McGovern, the beginning of his inexorable drive for the Democratic nomination. Had it not been for the polls, McGovern would have been perceived as a loser in New Hampshire, and his campaign might never have gained the public credibility provided by his having "defeated" the pollsters.

But many primary voters are "genuinely uncommitted and therefore express preferences which may be shallow or volatile when they're interviewed by pollsters," says William Shannon of the *New York Times*.

Even George Gallup, who—like most pollsters—tries to minimize the impact of polls, says primary election polls can be misleading because "the task of eliminating nonvoters . . . is more difficult . . . the last-minute statements and events are much more likely to influence voters [and] . . . the party machine can exert its greatest power."

In primaries, especially primaries with a relatively large field, the media must decide early which are the major candidates, most deserving of serious daily coverage. Too often, critics say, that decision is made (or, at least, guided) by the polls.

"The play and the amount of space and time the media gives a candidate is almost directly correlated to his standing in the polls," complains Fred Dutton, a Washington attorney who has worked on campaigns for Robert Kennedy and Edmund G. Brown.

"That's more true in California than anywhere else," says Pat Cadell, a political pollster who has worked for Democrats in 47 states.

"I've never seen a press corps—especially TV—so geared to polling as they are in California. It becomes a chicken-and-egg syndrome. If the polls say you aren't a major candidate, you can't get good news coverage. But if you don't get the coverage, you can't become a major candidate."

"That," says William Matson Roth, "is what I mean by polls becoming a self-fulfilling prophecy."

Roth, who ran unsuccessfully for the Democratic gubernatorial nomination in California in 1974, never polled more than 6 percent.

"In many ways," one Democrat says, "Roth was an ideal candidate that year. He was big on environment. He was a new face. He was bright and articulate. But the polls never gave him a chance to get going."

To some extent, that is true. But several men close to Roth admit he did not have a chance, regardless of the polls. In his case, they say, the polls just confirmed the obvious—that he was not (and never would be) a major candidate.

There have, moreover, been several candidates who ran very poorly in the early polls and still won.

McGovern, for example, began with only 2 percent in the national polls in November, 1970, and never rose above 7 percent until he won the Wisconsin primary in April, 1972. Three months later, he won the Democratic presidential nomination. Jimmy Carter made a similarly meteoric rise in 1976.

Hugh L. Carey in New York, James Longley in Maine and David Boren in Oklahoma all polled less than 5 percent early in their respective gubernatorial races in 1973. All won in November.

But these men are exceptions.

In many ways, in fact, the race between Carey and Howard Samuels is a good example of the role polls play in a campaign—and of the often misleading and inadequate nature of newspaper polls.

The early polls showed Samuels ahead, 47 percent to 7 percent.

But Carey's private polls also showed one more figure: Samuels' name recognition was 93 percent, Carey's 8 percent.

"What that meant," says Frank Goldsmith of Oliver Quayle Company, "is that only half the people who knew about Samuels actually liked him enough to vote for him—47 percent of his 93 percent name recognition. Those numbers showed us Samuels was vulnerable."

Most men in Carey's position would have been unable to mount a respectable campaign after such a poor poll showing. They would have been denied both media coverage and big campaign contributions.

But Carey had a wealthy brother who was able to finance the campaign until Carey could establish his own momentum and begin to rise in the polls and to attract media coverage and other financing.

"Some people say money buys votes," says political media specialist

David Garth, one of Carey's top strategists. "Strictly speaking, that isn't quite so. What money buys is access and recognition. Then it's up to the candidate to translate that into votes.

"If he's no good or has nothing to say or turns people off personally, all the money in the world won't get him elected."

That, some people say, is why William Roth (in last year's California Democratic gubernatorial primary) and Norton Simon (in his 1970 United States Senate race against George Murphy) were both unable to mount good campaigns, despite spending a considerable amount of their personal fortunes.

"What money does for a relatively unknown candidate," Garth says "is give him a chance, no matter what the early polls say. But with the new campaign spending limits, that could be all over. A candidate like Carey might not be able to challenge a well-known person like Samuels in the future.

"Campaign spending limits are supposed to be reforms, but that's not always true. They can help perpetuate incumbencies and discourage new, young, relatively unknown candidates whose only hope of getting exposure is by spending money."

That is especially true in primaries, where the influence of established political organizations is often so great.

For that reason, among others, many people think pollsters and newspapers should agree not to conduct or publish preprimary polls—certainly not six months or a year before the primary, as most do now.

Daniel Yankelovich, who conducts polls for *Time* magazine and the *New York Times*, is one who takes this view.

Yankelovich, almost alone among the major pollsters in acknowledging the impact of polls on elections, tries to avoid conducting primary polls himself and favors their outright elimination.

"They're not very reliable and they tend to have a disproportionate influence on the campaign," Yankelovich says.

David Broder, political columnist for the *Washington Post*, says the media have "a great responsibility to treat preprimary polls more carefully and not give them great prominence."

Broder also thinks polls, whenever published, should place greater emphasis on the mood of the electorate—the voters' views on the issues and the candidates—rather than just on whom they say they're going to vote for.

That is a sentiment echoed almost unanimously among the people interviewed for this study. In fact, most of those interviewed tended to blame the media more than the pollsters for the undue influence polls have on elections.

Although polls are occasionally inaccurate, methodology has become sufficiently sophisticated that most reputable polls have an excellent record in general elections.

(Gallup, for example, has been off an average of only 1.2 percentage points in national elections dating back to 1952.)

It is not the accuracy of the polls that concerns most pollwatchers; it is the content and use of the polls. What often appears, after the election, to have been an inaccurate poll was actually an incomplete or incorrectly interpreted poll.

Early polls on the New York and California gubernatorial races, for example, might have seemed more accurate had news stories on them included an analysis of the relative softness of the commitment of the Brown and Samuels voters.

The same was true of the polls and the 1976 United States Senate primaries in California. The polls showed then Senator John Tunney with a rapidly dwindling lead of only eight percentage points over Tom Hayden in the final days of the Democratic campaign. But Tunney won comfortably, by 21 percentage points. In the Republican primary, the polls showed S. I. Hayakawa with just a four-point lead over Robert Finch. But Hayakawa won by twelve points. Pollster Mervin Field's explanation for having misjudged the races so badly: Hayden was relying heavily on the youth vote, and "they just don't turn out; a candidate who has the young voter suffers on Election Day—as much as 10 percent." On the Republican side, Field decided, in retrospect, that voters "had not been paying much attention to the race and decided at the last minute, 'Why not Hayakawa?'"

On rare occasion, of course, the pollsters cannot measure the most important factor in a given race. That's what happened in the 1969 Tom Bradley-Sam Yorty mayoralty race in Los Angeles. The last poll, three days before the election, showed Bradley 17 percentage points ahead. But pollster Don Muchmore—hampered by his own methodology and by the reluctance of his poll respondents to be honest about their racial attitudes —had been unable to accurately gauge the intensity of the antiblack feeling directed at Bradley.

Yorty won by more than 6 percentage points.

Most often, however, critics agree that newspapers, not pollsters, are to blame for incomplete or seemingly inaccurate polls.

Editors, preoccupied with the horse-race standings of the candidates, are generally unwilling to give their pollsters sufficient money and space to analyze issues, voter turnout, the undecided vote and the intensity of the voters' commitment to various candidates.

"There is a tendency among newspapers to spend just enough money on polling to get one good story, but not enough to get a really good poll," says campaign consultant Doug Bailey.

Joe Belden—who runs the oldest of the state polls, the Texas Poll—thinks last-minute election polls are especially nefarious, and he no longer conducts them for any of his newspaper clients.

Cynics point out that Belden's decision may stem from his own disastrous experience in incorrectly predicting a Waggoner Carr victory over John Tower in the 1966 United States Senate race, but many agree with his position.

Former California Governor Edmund G. Brown is one.

"Newspapers shouldn't publish any polls within the last 10 days before an election," he says. "They don't really contribute anything important that late, and they can cause irreparable harm."

This is particularly true of telephone polls—which, to meet deadlines, is how most last-minute polls are conducted (in contrast with most mid-campaign polls, which are generally based on personal interviews).

Telephone polls are not as accurate as personal-interview polls because a respondent can more easily evade a question or refuse to cooperate on the phone. More significantly, no one has yet devised a reliable means of correcting the telephone polls for a built-in bias and imbalance that occurs because most people without telephones tend to be poor, young, under-educated, black or brown and live in small towns or in the South.

The potential for harm from these last-minute telephone polls is greater now than ever, many say.

"The high rate of political realignment, the decomposition of traditional party loyalties, the role of image and the media, the high level of fluidity of events—all these things give last-minute polls far more impact than they used to have," says Vince Breglio of Decision Making Information, a national Republican polling concern headquartered in California.

Although some newspapers may modify or even abandon their use of last-minute polls, the news value of "who's ahead?" polls at various stages of the campaign makes it highly unlikely that these will be forsaken entirely in favor of the issues and mood-of-the-electorate polls. There does, however, seem to be some potential for improvement and compromise.

Eliminating or greatly modifying preprimary polls would be a good first step, most poll watchers agree.

Early in 1975, for example, Gallup released a poll on contenders for the 1976 Democratic presidential nomination. Because the front-runner in the poll, Alabama Governor George C. Wallace, received only 19 percent—and because Wallace also finished on top of the "most unacceptable" candidate rankings (with 29 percent)—the basic thrust of the Gallup story was that no candidate was a "clear first choice."

But most newspapers played the story the way the *New York Times* did. Its headline was "Wallace, With 19 Percent, Leads in Poll Of Democratic Candidates in '76."

Sophisticated poll-watchers say this sort of distortion and oversimplification is a disservice to pollsters and public alike—and is too often typical of the manner in which newspapers report polls.

"It's much easier to take a poll for a newspaper than for a candidate, and that just shouldn't be," says pollster Pat Cadell, who was one of Jimmy Carter's chief campaign advisors. "Sure it would cost the paper more for a really good poll, with someone on the staff to properly interpret it, but the paper would get its money's worth.

"Instead of just getting one short story on who's ahead, they'd get a full survey—25 pages of questions and answers on a whole range of voter attitudes toward the candidates and the issues. Then the press could really tell the public something of value."

Alan Rosenthal of the Eagleton Institute, which conducts the New Jersey Poll, condemns newspapers for "printing our numbers without the flesh and blood of reportorial analysis."

Pollster Mervin Field said newspaper editors "should look carefully at what we give them, call us, ask questions, demand more information. Most of them just print what I give them—and complain it's too much!"

Polls, most critics say, should be given to the appropriate specialist on a newspaper staff, and he should analyze it, solicit comments from the candidates involved and write the story himself, perhaps including the pollster's track record in previous elections and any circumstances that might mitigate against the accuracy of this particular poll.

In the case of the August 22, 1974, Field Poll on the California gubernatorial race, for example, it would have been instructive to point out that Flournoy's poor showing might well have been attributable, in part, to the polls having been conducted in what his campaign manager calls "the worst week in the history of the Republican Party"—the week of congressional impeachment hearings and the resignation of Mr. Nixon.

Pollsters insist their polls are not predictions but snapshots in time. Expecting a poll to accurately predict the outcome of an election, pollsters say, is like expecting a horse-race photo taken at the quarter-pole to match one taken at the finish line. This is certainly true. But when the polls do prove accurate on Election Day, the pollsters want everyone to know about it. Gallup, for one, produces tables and press releases attesting to his accuracy.

Sophisticated poll-watchers say newspapers should tell their readers, in the appropriate poll stories, when the polls have been right or wrong in the past. They should also include a brief explanation of the methodology and limitations of the polls, and should prominently provide the statistical margin of error—generally 4 percent in a typical random sample of 1,500 voters (which is what Gallup, Harris, Field and most reputable pollsters use; any larger sample is statistically unnecessary). Doing all this would help demystify the polls.

Newspaper polls should also make a far greater effort to evaluate voter turnout and undecided voters.

Some pollsters have devised elaborate series of questions to determine who actually will vote, and whom a voter who claims to be undecided will eventually vote for.

These questions—called "screens" by pollsters—deal with issues, interest in the election, previous voting record and general attitudes toward the candidates.

Again, using these screens costs money and takes time and space.

Most polls inaccurately forecast the outcome of the 1976 Presidential election precisely because they did not use such screens. As a result, they severely underestimated Jimmy Carter's strength. The final Gallup Poll, for example, gave Mr. Carter 46 percent, the final Harris Poll gave him the same and an NBC-*Los Angeles Times* poll gave him 41 percent. All three polls showed a relatively high percentage of undecided voters. But most of these "undecideds" ultimately voted for Mr. Carter, and he wound up with 51 percent of the vote.

One of the few newspapers that has occasionally been willing to make available the money and space for screening the undecided vote is the *Boston Globe*. The *Globe* spent almost $100,000 on polls in 1974, and regularly devoted more than 1,500 words to presenting each poll. (The *Los Angeles Times*, in contrast, pays Mervin Field $15,000 per year and rarely publishes poll stories longer than 500 words.)

The *Globe* poll was remarkably accurate in the 1974 primary, largely because of this commitment—and because pollster Irwin Harrison developed screens to forecast voter turnout and to intelligently allocate the undecided vote. (In the Democratic gubernatorial primary, for example, Harrison's polls gave Michael Dukakis only a 34 percent to 32 percent lead over Robert Quinn, with 29 percent undecided, based on the respondents' own estimates of their likelihood to vote. That's a close, unpredictable race. But when Harrison applied his screens, he reduced the undecided to 11 percent and gave Dukakis a 55 percent to 34 percent lead. That's a runaway. Final vote: Dukakis 50 percent, Quinn 42 percent —a solid victory, albeit not a runaway.)

In the general election, however, the *Globe* did not pay enough attention to the undecideds and the turnout, largely because Executive Editor Robert Healy didn't think it was necessary in light of the state's historically high voter turnout—75 to 80 percent.

The turnout was only 64.7 percent, the lowest in Massachusetts since 1917, and the *Globe* poll was off in several races.

Healy promises a complete review of *Globe* polling procedures, but he rejects any suggestions that the paper abandon polls altogether.

"You're always going to have someone on the paper analyzing and predicting the outcome of elections," he says. "Better to have it done scientifically, with polls, than have your political writers doing off-the-wall predictions."

But when a newspaper runs a poll the way most papers run them at present, they purport to be scientific projections—and, as Healy readily admits, the paper's credibility is on the line.

Gene Roberts, executive editor of the *Philadelphia Inquirer*, says that is one reason his paper publishes no state or local polls.

"You not only run the risk of undermining your credibility," Roberts says, "you also inject your paper as a partisan force in the campaign. Whoever's trailing in the polls has to attack the polls—and the paper that publishes them—to maintain his own viability."

Nevertheless, Roberts says he, like Healy, is reevaluating his newspaper's policy on polling. "Polling is here to stay," he says.

William F. Thomas, editor of the *Los Angeles Times*, is also reevaluating his paper's approach to polling.

"Polls are not an exact science, and we should quit acting as if they are," Thomas says.

Certainly, whatever claims pollsters make to theirs being an exact science are seriously undermined by such incidents as the conflicting polls conducted by George Gallup and Louis Harris in late 1975: In a hypothetical race between then President Ford and Senator Humphrey, Gallup found Ford holding a 51 percent to 39 percent lead—a runaway. But Harris found Humphrey holding a 52 percent to 41 percent lead—also a runaway. The credibility of the polls was further undermined in the summer of 1976 when successive Gallup polls showed Jimmy Carter's lead over then President Ford jumping from 17 points to 33 points, then dropping to 23, then to 10 and then jumping again to 15 points—all within two months' time. Public opinion just doesn't fluctuate that wildly, certainly not in the absence of war, depression, riots, scandal or some similarly cataclysmic event—none of which were even remotely on the horizon at the time.

That, as Thomas says, almost makes a mockery of the pollsters' claims to be engaged in an "exact science."

"I'm troubled by the harm polls can sometimes cause in an election," Thomas says, "and I think we can do something to mitigate that effect by developing new guidelines."

In the 1976 elections, many in the media did just that—concentrating more on voters' attitudes than on their candidate preferences. The *New York Times* and CBS News jointly conducted a series of attitude polls on the mood of the electorate, and NBC, the *Washington Post*, *Time* and *Newsweek* did similar, albeit less exhaustive polling. Nevertheless, most polls still concentrated on the question "Who's ahead?" In fact, only about eight percent of all polls published from the New Hampshire primary to Election Day in November asked mainly about issues, according to a study by the National Council on Public Polls and the Gannett Urban Journalism Center of the Medill School of Journalism at Northwestern University.

Many critics think the media should develop its own polling capacity.

Phil Meyer, a reporter specializing in social science survey research, has already done that for the Knight newspapers.

A few other papers, the *Washington Post* and *Los Angeles Times* among them, have also begun to use reporters as pollsters.

The *Post* polls are essentially issue-oriented, mood-of-the-electorate surveys which generally minimize precise numbers and candidates' standings. The *Times* surveys include both issue/mood reports and a numerical analysis of voting preferences.

But the *Times* polls are not taken by the random sample method preferred by Gallup, Harris, Field and most reputable pollsters; it is the consensus of most politicians and pollsters that the *Times* polls are not especially reliable in predicting elections.

The mood/issues interviews with voters add a valuable dimension to conventional campaign reportage, most feel, but attempts to forecast the election result lend the *Times* polls an aura of mathematical precision that their methodology does not justify.

The *Times* polls have generally been accurate, but after they incorrectly forecast a one-sided Brown victory in the 1974 gubernatorial election, reporter Kenneth Reich—who devises, coordinates and helps conduct the polls—admitted the shortcomings in his methodology. He plans to seek guidance from experts at University of California at Berkeley who also work with the Field Poll.

As Reich's concern—and the comments of other editors—clearly indicates, many newspapers are actively trying to improve their polling procedures. Some may decide to do their own polls (as the *Los Angeles Times* and the *Washington Post* do). Some may hire an independent pollster (as the *Boston Globe* does). Some may use an outside specialist in issue and attitude polling (as the *New York Times* does). Some may use a combination of two or more of these techniques (as a few already do). Some may demand—and more carefully use—far more detailed polls from the conventional pollsters (as most pollwatchers think all newspapers should do).

But however the polling reforms are effected, it seems certain that those reforms are as inevitable as they are necessary.

4 / The Press and the Police

Alfred E. Lewis. For 35 years, he covered the police beat for the *Washington Post*. In 1972, he covered the Watergate break-in.

Bob Woodward and Carl Bernstein talk about Lewis briefly in their book *All the President's Men*. Lewis was, they say, "something of a legend in Washington journalism—half cop, half reporter, a man who often dressed in a blue regulation Metropolitan Police sweater. . ."

Half cop, half reporter.

For generations, that was the role of the typical—the stereotypical—newspaper police reporter. Many—perhaps most—were even more than half cop; their loyalties, their interests and their instincts lay with the police, not with their newspapers. The police sweaters they occasionally wore—and the police badges they often carried—were but outer displays of their inner allegiances.

Not surprisingly, the police came to look on the reporters who regularly covered them—and on the press in general—as part of the police department . . . as "cops without guns" in one reporter's apt phrase. The police and the reporters grew to like each other, to trust each other—when necessary, to cover up for each other.

A cop beating a suspect? The reporter ignored it; after all, he figured, the guy probably deserved it. A reporter drunk at the wheel? The cop ignored it; after all, he figured, he might find himself in the same situation someday soon.

But over the last 10 or 15 years, relations between law enforcement and the press have undergone a drastic, often traumatic change. Once founded on mutual trust and common objectives, these relations have foundered on the shoals of mutual suspicion and downright hostility amid the socio-political upheavals of the 1960s and 1970s.

Like the ancient Greeks, who killed messengers bearing bad news, many in law enforcement tend to blame the press for reporting the protests of longhairs, antiwar demonstrators, student radicals and black militants that began in the 1960s.

These dissidents challenged and attacked the very traditions and values and institutions the police identified with and felt sworn to protect; by providing a public forum for the dissidents, most police felt, the press made law enforcement's job more difficult—and, often, actively sided with the dissidents, against them.

"We used to be the heroes, the guys wearing the white hats and riding the white horses," says Lieutenant Dan Cooke, press officer for the Los Angeles Police Department.

"In the 1960s, all of a sudden, we became bad guys; the media had nothing but pictures of us busting skulls with nightsticks.

"They made us look like a bunch of corrupt, obnoxious, brutal, overbearing bastards."

"The media," says Los Angeles Police Chief Edward M. Davis, "has a distinct liberal bias. They're lopsided on the funny-farm side."

Although Davis speaks more harshly of the press than most in law enforcement are willing to do in public, there is considerable evidence that he is saying what many are thinking—a bit exaggerated at times, perhaps, but generally reflective of the prevailing law enforcement view of the press.

That doesn't mean that police-press relations are now in a constant state of open warfare. There are, in fact, many instances when the press and law enforcement still do cooperate:

- When the Zodiac killer was sending letters to the *San Francisco Chronicle* a few years ago, the newspaper readily agreed to a police suggestion that some portions of his letters not be published, in hopes that the Zodiac would get angry enough to write more letters—and, perhaps, give police a clue to his identity.

  ("We were in bed with the *Chronicle* on the whole case," says Police Inspector Bill Armstrong.)
- In the immediate aftermath of the Patty Hearst kidnaping, San Francisco newspapers withheld stories identifying and examining the Symbionese Liberation Army because editors, police and the Hearst family feared publication of that information might jeopardize Patty's life.
- In 1975, the *Los Angeles Times* published a psychological profile calling the Slasher—the then-unknown killer of nine men in two months—

"sexually impotent . . . a jackal, an animal who hides in the dark and preys on weaklings and cripples."

The reporter who wrote that story did so knowing that the police had carefully and deliberately chosen those words, hoping they would so infuriate the Slasher that he would call or write to defend himself—and perhaps unwittingly give a tip to his identity.

A few weeks later, the same reporter learned exclusively that a suspect in the Slasher case was in custody; he withheld the story for 10 days in exchange for a Police Department promise that he could break the story 24 hours before the formal press announcement of the arrest—which would not be made until police felt they had enough evidence to seek a formal murder complaint.

(A radio station subsequently learned of the arrest and broke the story first.)

The Slasher, Hearst and Zodiac cases are unusual—and increasingly rare—examples of police-press cooperation. But even they raise serious ethical questions about the often conflicting roles of the press and the police . . . a conflict that is at the heart of police-press friction.

Suppose, for example, that the Zodiac had been so enraged by the *Chronicle's* refusal to print his letters in their entirety that, rather than write another letter, he had killed another person?

Suppose the Slasher had also responded with murderous rage to the sneering psychological profile of him that ran in the *Times?*

Moreover, given the widespread uneasiness over the Slasher in Los Angeles, might not an earlier *Times* story saying a suspect was in custody have enabled some people to sleep—and walk the streets—more easily?

In the Hearst case, might the SLA have been flushed from hiding—maybe even seen and reported to the FBI—more quickly if the public at large knew who and what they were?

Did the press, in all three cases, allow itself to be used by the police to perform what is essentially a law enforcement function?

The reporters involved in the Slasher and Zodiac cases—Bill Hazlett in Los Angeles and Paul Avery in San Francisco—think their actions were fully justified . . . that the apprehension and successful prosecution of a murderer take priority over full and immediate newspaper disclosure of the facts in the case.

But Tim Findley, one of the *San Francisco Chronicle* reporters who covered the Hearst case, was so distressed by his editors' handling of his stories that he quit his job.

"I have a responsibility to the public, not to the police," Findley says. "That may sound contradictory, but they're not the same. It's our job to inform; we're neutrals in this war."

It is, of course, a measure of the changing nature of police-press relations, that questions on the propriety of cooperating with law enforcement are even raised on these—and other—stories.

At one time, it was assumed—taken for granted—that the police and the press were on the same side:

"We all wanted the bad guys in jail, so the streets would be safer for the good guys," as one longtime police reporter says.

Ironically, the problems between law enforcement and the press today can best be summed up by a line originally attributed to black militant Eldridge Cleaver:

"If you're not part of the solution, you're part of the problem."

In earlier generations, before the polarization and fragmentation of the 1960s, that was an easy line to draw. The "problem" was the "bad guys"—robbers, rapists, murderers and the like. The "solution" was for the police (the "good guys") to arrest and imprison them to safeguard the streets for the citizenry (the other "good guys").

But in the 1960s, when the police began to deal not only with traditional crime but also with sociopolitical unrest—with ghetto riots and antiwar protests and campus demonstrations—the traditional societal consensus about "good guys" and "bad guys" and "problems" and "solutions" began to break down.

Merely by fulfilling its constitutional and societal obligation to report the news of the day, the press enraged many in law enforcement. In this war, police felt, there was no room for neutral observers; if the press was not willing to be part of the solution—to defend the police—the police decided the press was part of the problem.

There were times, of course, when some elements of the press were not neutral—when reporters *did* allow their support for the dissidents to influence their reportage, when television news crews *did* instigate demonstrations for the benefit of their cameras.

There were also instances when some in the press naively allowed themselves to be manipulated by dissidents—and when heavy news coverage of protests virtually guaranteed other protests. (FBI Director Clarence M. Kelley thinks the "evidence is impressive" that certain kinds of antisocial behavior are "born of, and nurtured by, their own publicity.")

But these were isolated exceptions, not the general rule, in the responsible media. The press' real shortcoming in covering social unrest, many critics feel, was in failing to make the same effort to understand the police that they made to understand the dissidents.

There were profiles of dissident leaders and analyses of the dissidents' objectives, police complain, but few thoughtful stories on what the police were going through at the same time, under great pressure.

Moreover, where once the invariably sympathetic police reporter was just about the only reporter who dealt with the police, police had to deal with a new breed of reporter in the tumultuous 1960s.

The new-breed reporter was generally younger, more skeptical, often more liberal, and he asked questions and wrote stories that sometimes made law enforcement look bad—stories that included charges of police brutality and racial discrimination.

But these new reporters rarely knew much about how law enforcement officers thought and functioned, and the police rarely knew much about how the new reporters thought and functioned.

Thrown suddenly together, generally in crisis situations—with the reporter often looking and thinking and talking more like the demonstrators than like the police—it was not surprising that hostility and suspicion became the order of the day.

The press wanted answers; the police wanted support. The two were seldom compatible. The police, accustomed to dealing primarily with criminals whom no one listened to or sympathized with, interpreted this seemingly sudden change in press attitudes as tacit approval of, if not conspiratorial alliance with, the demonstrators.

The police were equally resentful of another, similar reportorial change: For the first time, reporters were not just taking the police department's word for what happened in a given incident. Just as reporters, in the 1960s, began to ask blacks and poor people and consumers what they thought, rather than automatically accept the Establishment view as gospel, so reporters also began to ask dissidents and demonstrators what they thought, rather than automatically accept the police view.

To the reporter, this was fairness—getting "the other side," getting "both sides"; to many in law enforcement, this was incitement, if not bias.

When some newspaper columnists and editorialists and some television commentators did agree with dissidents on some points, the police felt further embattled.

In Los Angeles, there was at least one major confrontation every year, from 1965 to 1971, in which the media posed serious questions about police conduct:

- After the Watts riot in 1965, the widely publicized McCone Commission report said "a resentment, even hatred, of the police" was "a fundamental cause" for the riot.
- In 1967, an antiwar protest at the Century Plaza Hotel erupted in violence, and the media—for perhaps the first time in Los Angeles—gave widespread attention to charges that police overreaction helped trigger and prolong the violence.
- In 1970, when two Mexican nationals were mistakenly killed by police

officers—and again when newsman Ruben Salazar was fatally shot by sheriff's deputies—the media called for thorough investigations of law enforcement actions in the incidents.

At about the same time that law enforcement was being questioned—and criticized—over these events, they were also finding their methods increasingly criticized and restricted by Supreme Court decisions on search and seizure, confessions, evidence and lineups.

"The language in some of those court decisions was downright offensive and insulting to the police," says District Attorney Cecil Hicks of Orange County, California.

More important, wrote the late Judge John C. Bell, Jr. of the Pennsylvania Supreme Court, the police thought these decisions limited their ability to do their job properly—and that only made them feel still further isolated, even more besieged by forces from without.

By frequently providing editorial support for the court decisions, the press became the focal point for police frustrations and resentment.

"Police have traditionally led a fairly incestuous existence," one reporter says. "In the 1960s, they turned even more inward. It was a kind of self-protective thing. Now they eat only with each other and drink only with each other and party only with each other.

"That's made them more paranoid and more suspicious of everyone else—especially the press—than ever."

But there has always been a tendency for those in law enforcement to think of themselves as the thin blue line between order and chaos—and to resent criticism of any sort.

Even an old-time police reporter like Ed Montgomery of the *San Francisco Examiner,* a man so in sympathy with the police that he wears a police tie-bar (and incurs the scorn of many colleagues), has felt the wrath of the law on those infrequent occasions when he has criticized the police.

Montgomery once almost singlehandedly saved an innocent man from Death Row by disclosing that law enforcement officers in Los Angeles had "deliberately suppressed evidence favorable to him.

"The guys working that case hated me after that," Montgomery says. "One guy in particular would never talk to me again."

As criminologist A. C. Germann puts it:

"To many police, THE mortal sin is for anyone . . . to question or criticize the police."

Even as far back as the 1920s and 1930s, police thought the press discriminated against them by "glamorizing" notorious criminals—just as they would later accuse the press, with greater hostility, of discriminating against them by "glamorizing" radicals in the 1960s.

"People tend to identify with the heroes the media creates," says Lieutenant James Robenson of the Pasadena (California) Police Department. Whether the "heroes" are John Dillinger and Al Capone or Mario Savio and Eldridge Cleaver, Robenson says, "it makes law enforcement's job that much rougher."

Although the turmoil of the 1960s was unquestionably the biggest single factor in the souring of police-press relations, those relations were already beginning to change, long before Watts and Berkeley and Century City.

In the old days of journalism—when crime news was big news—a good story was not a protest march but an ax murder, and the men who wrote those stories were reporters who covered the police on a daily basis. They ate and drank and fished and partied with the police, and when police went on a raid or a stakeout, their reporter friends went with them.

The police trusted the reporters not to jeopardize their operations— and not to make them look bad when the operations were over. The reporters trusted the police to see that they did not get hurt—and to give them first crack at the big stories when they broke.

There was great camaraderie between police and reporters then, and old-time police reporters still regale their younger colleagues with wild tales about their friends on the force.

One reporter for a major daily newspaper in the Midwest still jokes about the press room at police headquarters being "the only place one could get a drink on a Sunday night." Cops and reporters alike used to gather there to drink and play cards and swap stories.

"I used to take dates there," the reporter says.

The same reporter remembers telling a cop over a drink one night that he had been robbed twice.

"He walked into the other room and came out with a sawed-off High Standard .22-caliber revolver with the serial numbers filed off," the reporter says. "He tossed it in my lap and said, 'Next time, kill the bastard.'

" 'Wait until he starts to take off,' the cop explained, 'then shoot him in the back. Get his gun and throw it away, then get his hand all over your gun and tell the police it was his and you took it away from him.' "

Reporters were equally helpful to law enforcement in those days.

One East Coast police officer who was threatened with dismissal after reporting to work drunk every day for a week kept his job only because the local police reporter interceded with the chief on his behalf.

In another city, a delegation of reporters once made the same effort for an officer involved in a drunken driving incident. He, too, stayed on the job.

The reporters—his friends—pretended it had never happened.

Old-time police reporters even went so far as to help police solve crimes—and apprehend criminals.

Ed Montgomery, a reporter for the *San Francisco Examiner* since 1945, once found the bodies of a Santa Rosa couple buried in the basement of their murderer's home—at a time when the couple's friends (and police) thought the couple was vacationing in Mexico.

Bill Hazlett, who covered law enforcement in Wichita, Denver and Long Beach before joining the *Los Angeles Times* in 1970, once had a stickup man call him to confess five or six robberies. Hazlett turned him over to police.

On another occasion, police deputized and armed Hazlett and several other reporters to help them look for a man who had killed a Highway Patrol officer.

This "teamwork" probably would not occur today, for a variety of reasons—not the least of them being that, as newspaper sensationalism has given way to a more sober and responsible brand of journalism, the role of the police reporter has diminished considerably.

Crime stories are rarely accorded the big, splashy, page-one play they once enjoyed—the *Los Angeles Times*, for example, didn't put the Slasher story on page one until he'd killed for the *seventh* time—so well-connected police reporters are no longer as valuable to their papers as they once were.

An extraordinary crime story can still dominate the media, of course— a Charles Manson case, a Patty Hearst kidnaping, mass murders like those involving Juan Corona and Charles Whitman and Richard Speck.

But these stories are the exception now. The media concern themselves more with politics and pollution and poverty than with murder and mayhem, and even when there is a spectacular crime, it, too, is often as much sociopolitical phenomenon as pure crime—the Manson and Hearst cases being ideal examples of that.

Moreover, the shift from straight cops-and-robbers journalism to stories of greater sociopolitical concern has almost coincided with a shift from straight news accounts—"just the facts, ma'am" as Sergeant Joe Friday would say—to a more analytical, interpretive brand of reportage.

It is this combination of new methodology and a different concept of what makes news that has contributed most significantly to the metamorphosis of police-press relations from warm friendship to, in many cases, enmity.

In many ways—directly and indirectly, wittingly and unwittingly, politically and logistically—television has also played an important role in the deterioration of police-press relations.

Veteran newspaper reporters speak with fondness of the days, 15 or 20 or 30 years ago, when they could go to the scene of a murder or a fire or a train wreck, wave to the officers on duty and walk as close to the bodies as their eyes and stomachs would permit.

A reporter with a pencil and a notebook and, maybe, a camera gave the police no problems—especially since the reporter usually knew from long experience precisely what he could and could not do if the integrity of the crime scene were to be preserved intact for police investigators and technicians.

But now, in the age of what has been called the "one-ton pencil"—the television reporter, with his cameraman and soundman and their heavy equipment and, seemingly, miles of electrical cords—police are quicker to close access to the immediate area of a crime or disaster.

"The cops don't want 15 TV guys stomping through the blood and kicking the bullets all over the goddam room, so they don't let any of us in," grumbles one old-time police reporter.

There is, obviously, an element of sour grapes in this complaint, but police themselves say TV—and radio—sometimes place an additional burden on them at a crime or disaster scene because TV and radio crews are invariably in a hurry.

Being first is the name of the electronic media game—much as it was the name of the newspaper game in the all-but-bygone days of special editions and "Exclusive" headlines.

Police now find themselves besieged by radio and television newsmen jamming microphones at them and flashing hot lights on them, demanding information, often before the police themselves know or understand what has happened.

Invariably, that hell-bent rush for the first tidbits of information strains relations—and relations are often further strained when that hell-bent rush results in stories that are irresponsible, incomplete, distorted or downright inaccurate.

The police see their function as essentially that of capturing criminals; the press sees its function as essentially that of informing the public. Sometimes, there is a seeming conflict between the two.

Take the hijacking of a school bus with 26 children aboard in central California during the summer of 1976: The children and their bus driver were buried alive for 17 hours by their kidnapers. Finally, they dug their way to freedom. Police thought the kidnapers might return if they did not know their victims had escaped, so they quickly and quietly took the children away and posted a stakeout crew. Would the press cooperate, they asked, by withholding news of the safe recovery of the children? The press refused; its responsibility was information, not apprehension— to tell the world that the children had been found, unharmed, and reunited with their parents. Thus, a potential opportunity for the quick capture of the kidnapers was lost, and the police blamed the press. When probing reporters subsequently learned details of the preliminary police investigation in the case, their newspapers printed stories on these leads. Again, the police became angry. The press, they said, was jeopardizing their investigation and aiding the kidnapers. Early news reports on this dramatic story were, moreover, filled with errors—most notably the inaccurate tale of how FBI agents and deputy sheriffs had rescued the children by storming the quarry in which they had been entombed (actually, the bus driver and some of the children had clawed their way to safety and had then sent for the police).

This kind of error—in newspapers, as well as in the electronic media—is one of the biggest continuing complaints law enforcement has against the press.

Sometimes, the press makes these mistakes because of haste and carelessness; sometimes, the press makes mistakes because the police make it difficult, if not impossible, for the press to learn the facts.

Either way, especially in a big case, the mistakes are magnified, and the press' reputation for accuracy and responsibility is irrevocably sullied.

In the Manson case, for example, *Time* magazine said one of actress Sharon Tate's breasts had been cut off by her murderers; the *Los Angeles Times* said another victim, hair stylist Jay Sebring, was found with a black hood over his head. Neither story was true, but both—and many others, equally inaccurate—were picked up and repeated, all across the country.

Most reporters react defensively to accusations of inaccuracy, but Paul Avery of the *San Francisco Chronicle*, who is certainly not regarded as a friend of the police, said he was "appalled" by the number of media errors he encountered in researching a book on the Patty Hearst case.

"I'd never gotten that deeply into any one story before," Avery says. "By the time I was through, I could sympathize with the police some when they complain about our mistakes."

Says Ralph Darton, police chief in suburban Lynwood, California:

"If I had a buck for every time I've seen mistakes in a newspaper story about a case I personally knew something about, I could retire right now and not have to wait until I'm eligible for my pension."

But if media inaccuracy irritates law enforcement, what law enforcement regards as media bias absolutely infuriates them.

Although television—visual, immediate, pervasive—especially enrages them in this regard, most members of law enforcement generally tend to think of the media (radio and television, newspapers and magazines) as a single entity, and what one reporter or cameraman does can often further damage (or help repair) police/press relations.

That is one reason the FBI, in the last few years, has hired press relations agents in many large cities to open channels of communications between the FBI and the press and to establish one-to-one relations with individual newsmen.

With the same objective in mind, the Los Angeles Police Department and Los Angeles County Sheriff's Department—both of which have had press relations officers for several years—now frequently invite members of the press to speak to their officers in classroom situations.

Proximity and familiarity can sometimes conquer prejudice, and it is hoped that by exposing the press and law enforcement officers to each other in academic and informal settings, rather than crisis situations, they can begin to understand each other's problems—and to avoid foolish and self-defeating misunderstandings.

In 1975, for example, Los Angeles Police Chief Ed Davis became angry when he learned that a sketch of a black suspect in the Slasher murder case had not been used by the press at the same time a sketch of a white suspect was used. Davis was especially upset because he knew—and the media did not—that his homicide investigators had the black suspect in custody. (He was eventually convicted.)

"Typical" media bias in favor of the blacks had prompted withholding the black sketch, Davis charged.

But investigation disclosed that the black sketch had not been used for a far different reason: A high-ranking officer in the police department had ordered it withheld from the press at the last minute because, at that time, homicide investigators had decided the black man was not involved in the Slasher killings.

By the time of Davis' outburst, the homicide officers had changed their minds completely; the black man was now a prime suspect. All that was explained to Davis, and another potential police-press conflict was narrowly averted.

Before this incident, Davis had often publicly criticized the *Los Angeles Times*—and had become embroiled in several letters-to-the-editor controversies in the paper—over stories he felt were unfairly critical of his officers.

But no public flurry of charges and counter-charges flew over the Slasher sketch, in part because Bill Hazlett, the reporter who covered the Slasher case, had already built considerable rapport and credibility with law enforcement by covering them, cultivating them and, among other things, speaking regularly to classes of police officers and sheriff's deputies.

Hazlett, a burly former combat infantryman who looks, talks and often thinks like a cop, has covered law enforcement for 12 years and has taken advanced academic courses in several areas of police work and crime reportage. He also numbers several police officers, FBI agents and district attorneys among his close friends.

There are some reporters, in fact, who think Hazlett is too close to law enforcement, too much like the old-time police reporter, too willing to be used by law enforcement when flattering stories are needed to justify budget requests or to deflect public criticism.

But Hazlett, whose stories helped convict more than 70 Denver police officers in a 1961 burglary ring scandal, says of his dealings with law enforcement:

"It's a tradeoff. You give them a little, and they give you a little. The key is to make sure you never compromise your primary responsibility—

which is to the paper and the public, not the police. A paper's got to have at least one guy who speaks the cops' language these days, though, or we'll never get anything from them."

That Hazlett speaks the cops' language is obvious almost from the moment he appears before one of their training classes. At one such session—attended by 24 Los Angeles police sergeants—Police Commander Pete Hagen, the department press officer, spoke first on the need for better police-press relations. But the sergeants were openly skeptical, and when Hagen mentioned a train wreck of some years past "when some of our officers hit some reporters over the heads with their flashlights and threw them over an enbankment," the sergeants whooped with glee.

Then Hazlett took the podium, speaking in a voice that is a cross between a hoarse bullfrog and a slide trombone.

When one sergeant complained, "Your retractions never undo the damage of your original errors," Hazlett agreed: "That's right. Just like when you make a bum arrest; you release the guy, but it never erases the original arrest, does it?"

All around the room, heads nodded and sheepish grins broke out.

Hazlett admitted that the press makes mistakes, and he criticized the few reporters who permit their prejudices to distort their reportage. He also tried to explain, briefly but precisely, just how the writing, editing and selling functions of a newspaper operate.

Within 45 minutes, the sergeant who had led the cheers for the police who had attacked reporters with their flashlights, said:

"I've been on the force nine years, and this is the first time I've seen a reporter in a classroom setting. Maybe we should get them when we first come on the force so we can try to understand and sympathize with each other."

Many in law enforcement agree.

There are, however, other steps that could also be taken to rebuild police-press relations, and with the streets and ghettos and campuses now quiescent, many people think the time is right for law enforcement and the press to calmly consider several of them.

"Police and reporters are almost all much better-educated now than ever before," says Deputy Police Chief William Keays of San Francisco. "I think they can get along better than ever."

That may well be so, for if police are more defensive now, many are also not only better educated but more sophisticated, more aware of their responsibilities, less likely to think and act like the unthinking, billyclub-wielding rednecks they have often been depicted as being.

Among the other suggestions for improved relations made by police and reporters are:

- Police should try to recognize that the press is an independent agency, not an arm of law enforcement, and that press scrutiny and/or criticism of law enforcement does not mean the press is siding with dissidents or criminals against law enforcement.
- The press should take extra care to get both sides of every story, to avoid sensationalism, to exercise responsible judgment and to use precise, rather than potentially pejorative or inflammatory language.

  (Police are almost as sensitive to the nuances of language as some writers are; that's why the policeman's billyclub has gradually metamorphosized, first to a "nightstick" and now to a "baton.")
- Police should not try to be editors or reporters; they should neither try to conceal nor to direct the flow of news but should let the press decide what is and is not news.
- The press should assign better reporters to cover the police, rather than routinely assign—as many do—either the youngest man on the staff or old-timers on the verge of retirement.

  ("The police reporter," complains former United States Attorney General Nicholas D. Katzenbach, "is thought of not as an expert craftsman, but as a colorful fellow who talks in underworld slang and fixes parking tickets.")
- Police officials should make it a matter of policy to be available to answer questions fully and honestly, rather than answering defensively or hiding behind a "no comment" or behind recent court decisions protecting the accused's right to a fair trial.
- The press should recognize that some information may occasionally have to be withheld temporarily, to avoid compromising either an ongoing investigation or the legitimate rights of the accused.

(A gag order imposed on Chief Ed Davis in the Los Angeles Slasher case is a good case in point. Press interest in disclosing that a suspect was in custody may be justified on the grounds that such disclosure would quiet fear that the Slasher was still at large; but identifying the suspect by name before formal murder charges were filed could, as the court order pointed out, unfairly jeopardize the suspect's right to a fair trial in an unrelated case for which he was already in custody.)

But the major point raised by police and reporters alike in discussing police-press relations was the need for each side to try to get to know the other, to try to understand the function—and problems—of the other.

Mutual understanding, it is generally agreed, is clearly in the best interests of both the police and the press, and of the public that is ultimately served by both.

5 / The Influence (?)
of Editorial Endorsements

William Mason, a sociologist at Duke University, has developed a modest little formula for calculating the impact of newspaper editorial endorsements—among other factors—on the way people actually vote:

$$Y_i = B_1R_{1i} + B_2R_{2i} + B_3R_{3i} + B_4R_{4i} + B_5I_{1i} + B_6I_{2i} + B_7A_i + B_8P_i + E_i$$

David Garth, a New York-based media consultant who specializes in political campaigns, expresses his theory on the same subject a bit more succinctly:

"Newspaper endorsements don't usually mean a damn to anyone."

Between these antipodal views—one precise and positive, the other visceral and negative—political arguments have long raged. But rarely has the influence of newspaper endorsements been subjected to any thorough, systematic analysis. Such an analysis has now been made—based on more than 40 interviews and on examinations of scores of election returns and a dozen studies of voter behavior and mass communications.

The major findings:

- In the vast majority of elections, newspaper endorsements tend to have considerably less influence than has been generally assumed by politicians, newspapermen and the public alike.

- Insofar as endorsements have any impact at all, they are far more likely to reinforce and crystallize existing predispositions than to persuade any voter to change his mind on a given candidate or issue.
- The influence of endorsements is waning with each election, as the impact of television grows, as voters become more sophisticated and independent, as traditional party allegiances continue to dissolve, as our society becomes more pluralistic and as newspapers themselves become less predictably partisan.

One additional factor mitigating against the influence of endorsements is that the voters most likely to read them are the very people whose intelligence, tenaciously held political views and access to other sources of information render them the least likely to be converted.

In fact, most studies show that fewer than a third of all newspaper readers read the editorial pages at all, and while that percentage undoubtedly increases significantly at election time, studies also have shown that most readers still haven't the slightest idea whom their papers endorsed.

(One Ohio study, for example, showed that 65 percent of the citizenry did not even know who had been endorsed for governor.)

Despite all these factors, there remain certain kinds of elections in which newspaper endorsements can play an important, even a critical role.

Most often, if a newspaper endorsement is to have any effect on voting behavior, that effect will be greatest in races of low visibility, for local, nonpartisan office, in campaigns with few issues and little controversy. Or, as former Presidential Press Secretary George Christian puts it:

"The more important the race, the less important any newspaper endorsements will be."

Thus, it is widely agreed (and election returns show), newspaper endorsements can be most influential on races for judgeships and local school boards—and least influential on races for president, governor, senator and, in most large cities, for mayor.

Similarly, newspaper endorsements may—under certain circumstances —help carry (or defeat) a complex, technical, relatively obscure ballot proposition but will have little if any impact on the vote for such controversial, widely publicized propositions as those involving fair housing, obscenity, capital punishment and school busing.

"What it really amounts to," says Nelson Rising, who has directed campaigns for former United States Senator John V. Tunney of California and Mayor Tom Bradley of Los Angeles, "is that the more interested an individual voter is in any given race, and the more sources of information he has—the more he sees about the campaign on television and hears about it on radio and talks about it with friends and reads about it in the newspaper and in campaign literature—the less likely he is to be influenced by how any newspaper editorial says he should vote."

Additionally, it would seem, whatever influence a newspaper endorsement does exert is most likely to be exerted:

- In a close race.
- In primary, rather than general or runoff elections.
- In cities with a monopoly (or virtual monopoly) newspaper.
- In elections in which the vast majority of newspapers take the same position.
- In behalf of a candidate whose age, race, religion, relative obscurity or other characteristics require the imprimatur of legitimacy and credibility by some respected institution.
- In behalf of a candidate whose personal or partisan affiliations are traditionally opposed by the newspaper now endorsing him.
- Against an incumbent or otherwise Establishment-oriented candidate.

"Another point a lot of people overlook is the influence a local daily paper can have on its readers as opposed to the influence a big metropolitan paper has on *its* readers," says campaign consultant Bill Roberts.

"The local paper is seen as part of the community, as having the reader's best interests at heart," Roberts says. "But a big-city paper is seen as an intruder, an impersonal business with its own corporate interests at heart. Many people will look at their endorsement and then vote just the opposite for that very reason."

Charles Winner, who directed Vincent Bugliosi's campaign for Los Angeles County district attorney in 1973, says today that two local newspaper endorsements cost his candidate that election.

"The *Los Angeles Times* endorsed Joe Busch, but Vince still carried the city of L.A. by 90,000 votes," Winner says. "What killed him were the Busch endorsements in the suburban Long Beach and San Gabriel papers."

Bugliosi, who lost the countywide race by only 10,000 votes, lost Long Beach alone by more than 20,000 votes—and he lost the San Gabriel Valley by an even greater margin.

But there is some evidence that even strong local newspapers are losing their influence. Until fairly recently, for example, it was widely agreed that in Long Beach, the endorsement of the *Independent, Press-Telegram* was—in the words of campaign consultant Joe Cerrell—"the absolute single most critical factor in any local race from school board to Congress."

Several of the paper's candidates have lost—and lost badly—of late, though, most notably Travis Montgomery, who was endorsed in three separate editorials during the final week of a special City Council election in 1975 . . . and ran fifth, beaten 5 to 1 by the eventual winner.

"Our endorsement just doesn't carry the weight it used to," concedes Executive Editor Miles Sines. "People have more sources of information these days, and they're more skeptical of all the press."

A statewide survey conducted last year in California would seem to confirm Sines' view. Voters in the survey were given a list of individuals and organizations and asked which would be most likely to influence them in an election. The three newspapers in the survey—the *Times* and the *San Francisco Chronicle* and *Examiner*—all ran well behind consumer advocate Ralph Nader, Tom Bradley, the League of Women Voters, the Sierra Club and Common Cause.

Nonetheless, all these generalizations about the influence of endorsements are just that—generalizations, not eternal verities. All are subject to change, contradiction, exception and challenge, for in any given election, several of these generalizations may come into direct conflict with each other.

Newspaper endorsements are generally credited with the most influence, for example, in races for judgeships—campaigns in which little money is spent, little publicity is available and most voters are presumed willing (and sufficiently concerned) to trust the judgment of a respected newspaper.

But in 1970, when the *Los Angeles Times* and most other newspapers endorsed Judge Alfred Gitelson for reelection, he was soundly beaten— the victim of widespread resentment over his decision that busing should be implemented to integrate Los Angeles schools.

"The problem for most judges in a campaign is that the people don't know enough about them," says Bill Roberts. "In Gitelson's case, they knew too much about him. Busing blew him right out of the water, and there was nothing any newspaper endorsement could do to help."

In contrast, it is universally agreed that newspaper endorsements rarely have even the slightest influence on how people vote for president —the one race on which most voters have the greatest amount of available information, the greatest exposure to the candidates themselves, the deepest personal and ideological feelings and the most tradition-bound voting habits.

Thus, Franklin D. Roosevelt won four landslide victories, despite the overwhelming opposition of the nation's daily newspapers, and Harry Truman, John Kennedy and Jimmy Carter all won Presidential elections despite similar press opposition.

But many people in politics thought newspaper endorsements could have had a significant influence on the 1976 Democratic presidential primaries.

"There's a big field of candidates with largely undefined images," said Stuart Spencer, who was political director of then President Ford's campaign committee.

"Most people don't have any real commitments to any one of the candidates yet. If the *New York Times* and two or three other key papers all came out strongly for one candidate very early, before everyone's feelings begin to crystallize, it could make a big difference."

For different reasons, Robert Healy, executive editor of the *Boston Globe*, is convinced that his newspaper's endorsement of Senator George S. McGovern was largely responsible for McGovern's 1972 victory in Massachusetts—the only state he carried against Richard Nixon.

Many knowledgeable politicians and journalists agree with Healy, if only because, in 1972—when most of the nation's newspapers were still virtually ignoring Watergate as a political issue—the *Globe* endorsement accused the Nixon administration of "burglary . . . spying, lying . . . laundering [money] . . . scandal," and said Nixon had surrounded himself with "too many men of questionable integrity, self-serving advisers whose last concern seems to be the protection of the American people."

Thus, the *Globe* endorsement was effective not only because the *Globe* is the dominant voice in the state, taking a position in opposition to most of the nation's newspapers, but because it did so in clear, uncompromising terms.

"It's not who you endorse but how you endorse them that counts," says Eddie Mahe, executive director of the Republican National Committee.

"Most endorsements either just list a bunch of names or they say, 'Both these candidates are honest, capable men with good records, but old Joe is just a little bit better, so you should vote for him.'

"Those kind of endorsements don't influence anyone. To influence a voter, an editor has to get a ballsy editorial writer—the meanest, toughest son of a bitch in the backroom—and have him write that the other candidate is a rotten, no-good bastard, and the paper's candidate is a saint come down to earth to save the human race."

But few major newspapers take so jaundiced a view of campaigns these days, and their more evenhanded approach is a major reason for the declining influence of their endorsements.

In previous generations, newspapers were a powerful—often the most powerful—influence in many political campaigns. But the American press was more fiercely partisan then; newspapers didn't just endorse a candidate in an editorial—they routinely slanted their news coverage in his favor as well.

Endorsed candidates received not just an endorsement but a blessing. Stories and pictures on an endorsed candidate's most routine activities would flood the news and society pages. His opponent would either be ignored or—in the most egregiously partisan papers—subjected to snide innuendos and accusations of the most heinous and scandalous sort.

A few newspapers still cover politics in this fashion—some more subtly than others—but most of these are smaller, local newspapers. Most modern, big-city newspapers at least try to be fair in their news columns, and their endorsements have thereby become little more than formal expressions of editorial preference—a journalistic bark without the rabid bite of earlier years.

There are some exceptions to this rule, of course—the most visible being the anachronistic *Union Leader* in Manchester, New Hampshire, where publisher William Loeb regularly prints vitriolic page-one editorials beneath such headlines as "Jerry Is a Jerk!" and "Kissinger the Kike."

One recent Republican survey showed more than a third of the people in New Hampshire "always or usually" agree with Loeb's editorial position—compared with only 11 percent who "rarely or never" agreed—a finding that was given further credibility, it would seem, when Ronald Reagan, running with Loeb's vigorous backing, ran strongly in the state's 1976 Republican presidential primary.

Although most of today's voters are too sophisticated to be influenced by the kind of blatant bias promulgated by Loeb and his predecessors, it was the unanimous—and vehement—conclusion of political people interviewed for this study that most newspapers still, however inadvertently, tend to help one candidate at the expense of another in most daily campaign news coverage.

"It continues after the election, too," says Los Angeles County Supervisor Kenneth Hahn.

"A newspaper seems to have a stake in a guy they endorse. I'm sure that's why the *Los Angeles Times* has been so reluctant to print much of anything unfavorable about Tom Bradley."

Most editors deny any such bias, during or after a campaign, but few political campaign officials are persuaded by their demurs—especially not in the heat of a campaign.

"The news columns are far more important than the editorial endorsements," says Stuart Spencer, "and the guys who write the headlines are far more important than the guys who write the news stories *or* the endorsements.

"Campaign coverage, day in and day out, is what influences voters, far more than any endorsements."

Spencer's comments were echoed more frequently than any other single sentiment by politicians interviewed for this study in every part of the country, and several Los Angeles area campaign consultants cited the *Times'* coverage of the 1973 city attorney's race as a classic example of the power of news stories over endorsements.

The *Times*, which endorsed incumbent Roger Arnebergh in the race, published more than 30 major stories on the Arnebergh-Pines campaign— most of them prominently displayed. The extent of the coverage lent credibility to the 33-year-old, relatively unknown challenger, Burt Pines, as a serious candidate, not just a young upstart.

Pines won.

"You give me a choice between all those news stories and an editorial endorsement, and, hell, I'll take the news stories any day," says Charles Manatt, chairman of the California Democratic Party.

In fact, precisely because of the news coverage of the Arnebergh-Pines race, almost every local campaign consultant interviewed for this study incorrectly remembered the *Times* as having endorsed Pines—and all agreed this "endorsement" was critical because television showed so little interest in the city attorney's race.

Television has, of course, become a dominant force in influencing voters, both in terms of daily campaign coverage and in diminishing the impact of newspaper editorial endorsements.

In most major races—and even in some minor races—television enables the candidate to carry his campaign into the voter's living room and bedroom. The voter can see and hear the candidate himself; no longer will he blindly heed a newspaper endorsement telling him how to vote.

"Candidates still get all excited when they get a newspaper endorsement," says campaign filmmaker Charles Guggenheim, "but that and 25 cents will buy you a cheap cigar today. I believe in the sign Bobby Kennedy had in his campaign headquarters:

'Politicians Read Newspapers
Voters Watch Television'

"Newspaper endorsements are old politics," Guggenheim and others say. "Television is new politics."

(Ironically, virtually everyone agrees that television endorsements themselves have almost no impact on how people vote. "I love to have some dreary TV vice president endorse my opponent," says one campaign consultant. "By law, they have to give my guy equal time; I just get Lorne Greene or someone like that to go on the same station and endorse my guy, and we come out way ahead.")

There are many in politics who say the voter has never been as independent of newspaper influence as he is right now—a circumstance they attribute almost as much to Watergate as to television and to changes in the press and in society itself.

"It may be only a temporary thing, but for a few years or so, I think a lot of voters are going to look a little more carefully at the candidates and the issues and pay less attention to our endorsements," acknowledges Dick Tracy, editor of the *San Gabriel Valley* (California) *Tribune*. "They're skeptical of everything—including the press."

There is, however, a tendency for history to run in cycles and for circumstances that seem unprecedented—even apocalyptic—to be merely echoes and foreshadowings of generations past and future.

In 1910, for example, Francis Leupp wrote about "The Waning Power of the Press" in America, and concluded that the election of a new mayor in New York over the vigorous opposition of most of the city's daily newspapers proved that "in our common-sense generation, nobody cares what the newspapers say."

That may, indeed, be true again—still?—in 1976, but newspapers were extraordinarily influential in the generation after Leupp's premature obituary, and there are some in politics who insist the influence of newspaper endorsements has not been diminished by Watergate either.

Russell Hemenway, national director of the Committee for an Effective Congress, thinks editorial endorsements are "critically important now when disillusionment with the political process is so high."

But even Hemenway admits that endorsements are not generally as influential as they were 20 or 30 years ago.

"Today," he says, "it's not so much the direct influence of an endorsement on voters that counts. It's what use the candidate makes of the endorsement—reproducing it in his campaign literature, using it to raise money and to build his prestige and credibility and to influence other people and organizations to support him."

Endorsements are also valuable, Hemenway and others say, in helping to build morale among campaign workers—"to give your troops the buoying up, the periodic psychological boost they need" in the words of Tom Bradley.

But Hemenway's organization involves itself only in races that seem to be closely contested—perhaps 60 or 70 of the more than 400 congressional races every election year—and it is in these races, he and others say, that newspaper endorsements are most effective.

"The doctrinaire Democrat or Republican is beyond conversion," Hemenway says. "We're after the swing vote—the undecided voter and the ticket-splitter. Those are the people we—and newspaper endorsements —can influence."

Most people in politics agree that newspapers rarely influence more than 3 percent to 5 percent of the vote in any given election—and seldom even that much—but in a close race, those few votes can be critical.

Of course, in a close race, any factor can be considered critical. A candidate who wins by a small margin can give anyone credit for his victory—a newspaper, his tailor, the left-handed vote, his mother-in-law . . .

Nevertheless, interviews and analyses have disclosed several races in recent years in which newspaper endorsements do seem to have played a vital, perhaps determining role on Election Day.

Perhaps the single characteristic all these elections had in common was the endorsement of the winning candidate by a newspaper that traditionally opposed him or his party or ideology.

"Most newspaper endorsements are predictable," says Vincent Bugliosi. "Like, the *Times* has always endorsed Evelle Younger [the California attorney general]. If Younger ran for God, the *Times* would run an editorial saying he was 'well-qualified for the position.'"

But people expect most such endorsements, and are not generally influenced by them.

It's when a newspaper makes an unexpected endorsement, diverging from its historical pattern, that it can have a significant influence—and then, it can exert that influence even in a major statewide or national race in which endorsements are customarily of negligible value.

In the 1970 race for California superintendent of public instruction, for example, the traditionally conservative *San Jose Mercury-News* first endorsed conservative incumbent Max Rafferty, then withdrew its endorsement, accused Rafferty of a "sordid . . . campaign characterized by smear and innuendo" and endorsed his opponent, Wilson Riles, a black.

Rafferty, who had carried the San Jose area by a 2½-1 margin in 1966, lost by a 2-1 margin in 1970. The reporters who covered the campaign—and who buzzed for weeks about the *Mercury-News* switch—are convinced the switch was largely responsible for Riles' victory in San Jose and may even have had a ripple effect throughout the state.

In the 1974 gubernatorial primary in New York, the *New York Post*—with a readership predominantly liberal, urban and Jewish—achieved a similar effect by endorsing Hugh Carey, a Brooklyn Irish Catholic.

"There's no question that endorsement helped Carey win," says David Garth, his campaign media consultant. "It gave him credibility with a large bloc of voters who might otherwise have been hostile—or indifferent—to him."

Daniel Patrick Moynihan benefitted from a similar endorsement in the 1976 Democratic primary for the United States Senate seat from New York. Both Congresswoman Bella Abzug and former United States Attorney General Ramsey Clark were more liberal than Moynihan, and either might well have expected the endorsement of the *New York Times*. Instead, the *Times*—in an editorial written personally by Publisher Arthur Ochs Sulzberger, over the vehement objection of his own editorial page editor—enthusiastically endorsed Moynihan. He defeated Abzug by 1 percent of the vote, and it would be difficult to find any knowledgeable New York politico who would not agree that the *Times'* influence—especially with its Jewish readers—was not decisive.

This theory is supported by several studies of "against-the-grain" endorsements, as well as by the research of sociologist George Lundberg, who has concluded that newspapers with a homogeneous readership—like the *Post's*—have a greater influence over their readers than a newspaper with a more heterogeneous readership.

For this reason—and because of its greater reputation and readership—Garth says, the *New York Times* exerted an even greater influence over voters in the 1970 United States Senate race among Democrat

Richard Ottinger, Republican Charles Goodell and Conservative Party candidate James Buckley.

Ottinger was ahead in the polls with about a month to go in the campaign, but then the *Times* endorsed Goodell. Both Goodell and Ottinger were liberals, battling for essentially the same vote, and that endorsement—by the most influential liberal paper in America—almost certainly siphoned enough votes away from Ottinger to enable Buckley—with less than 40 percent of the total vote—to squeak through to victory by less than 2 percent of the more than 2 million votes cast; Goodell ran a distant third.

Moreover, says Cliff White—Buckley's campaign manager—Buckley further benefitted from the endorsements of almost 30 other, smaller papers in every major city in New York except Buffalo.

"Buckley was a third-party candidate," White notes, "and third-party candidates don't generally do well; the voter sees them as splinter candidates, not really serious. But all those endorsements gave Buckley credibility."

Sometimes, however, the withholding of an expected endorsement can be as effective as the bestowing of an unexpected endorsement.

California politicians say that's what happened in the 1970 United States Senate race between incumbent George Murphy and challenger John Tunney.

"The *Los Angeles Times* has almost always endorsed Republican candidates for high office—especially if they're incumbents," says Joe Cerrell. "Even if a Republican had two heads, he usually got the *Times'* endorsement."

But the *Times* did not endorse Murphy (or Tunney) in 1970, and many voters saw that as a repudiation of Murphy. Tunney won the election—after making widespread use of a *Times* editorial published six months earlier, charging Murphy with having "violated the trust reposed in him by the people of California" and having "forfeited the privilege of representing California in the Senate."

Campaign strategists offer dozens of other examples of newspapers crossing partisan or ideological lines or breaking with tradition to make (or withhold) an endorsement in a close election and seemingly swaying many voters in so doing:

- In the 1970 United States Senate race in Missouri, Democratic Senator Stuart Symington was endorsed by the generally conservative *St. Louis Globe-Democrat*. He was reelected by only 5 percent of the more than 1 million votes cast. His opponent's campaign consultant insists Symington would have lost without that endorsement.
- In the 1974 United States Senate race in Pennsylvania, Republican Senator Richard Schweiker was endorsed by the city's most influential

black newspaper. He was reelected, with 45 percent of the city's black vote—the best showing ever made by a Republican in those precincts. His campaign consultant says the black votes were "absolutely crucial."

• In the 1975 mayoralty race in San Francisco (ostensibly a nonpartisan race), Democrat George Moscone was endorsed by the traditionally Republican *Examiner*. He won by 4,300 of almost 200,000 votes cast. Campaign consultant Sandy Weiner thinks the *Examiner* endorsement "may have been the determining factor in the election."

But as persuasive as the evidence is in all these cases, they are isolated instances, involving special circumstances—exceptions to the rule that most newspaper endorsements do not influence many voters.

In the 1976 United States Senate race in California, for example, the *Los Angeles Times* broke with its Republican tradition and endorsed Democratic incumbent John Tunney in *two* strongly worded editorials. Tunney lost anyway. Moreover, in that 1975 San Francisco mayor's race, both the *Examiner* and the *Chronicle* had endorsed Diane Feinstein in the primary. The *Examiner*, in fact, had endorsed her early and often— two months before the election and again three weeks and one week before the election. But she finished third and didn't even make the runoff.

Traditionally, in San Francisco, newspaper endorsements have relatively little influence. The city is compact, its voters sophisticated, its sources of information many and varied, its newspapers predictable and—in the words of one longtime campaign consultant—"too frivolous to be respected."

In contrast, there are other cities in California in which newspaper endorsements have somewhat more influence, either because the newspapers exercise virtual monopolies (as in San Diego, San Jose and San Bernardino) or because they are widely respected (as with the *Riverside Press-Enterprise* and the *Bee* papers in Sacramento, Fresno and Modesto).

"The *Sacramento Bee* probably has more influence on its readers than any other paper in the state," says Don Bradley, a campaign consultant in San Francisco. "It's a good paper, widely respected, with predominantly Democratic readers who generally agree with its predominantly Democratic endorsements.

"If you're a Democrat and the *Bee* doesn't endorse you, it raises serious questions about your credibility; you're in real trouble."

But even papers like the *Bee* don't always fare well with their endorsements—in part, because most newspaper endorsements are not made until the final week or so of the campaign, when it is too late to influence either voters or campaign contributors.

Contrary to popular assumption, several independent studies have shown that 65-75 percent of the electorate has made up its mind on most major races before the formal beginning of the campaign; the two most definitive studies of voting behavior in America show that fewer than 5 percent of the electorate actually changes its mind in the course of a major campaign.

Voters are, however, less decisive—and, presumably, more susceptible to last-minute influence—on races for lesser offices and on ballot propositions, even controversial propositions.

Five weeks before the November, 1972, election, for example, public opinion polls showed that more than 75 percent of the California electorate was either unaware of or undecided on propositions for marijuana legalization, obscenity control and tax reform.

But newspapers throughout the state editorialized strongly against all three—and all three were resoundingly defeated. Did the unanimity of the press contribute significantly to those defeats?

"We probably pay more attention to newspaper endorsements than anyone else in the business," says Doug Bailey, a Washington, D.C., campaign consultant, "and we're convinced that mass press endorsements can be the single most influential factor with the undecided voters. It helps create a real bandwagon effect, a sense of irresistibility and inevitability about your candidate. After all, no matter what criticisms the voters have of any one paper, they know *all* the papers can't be wrong or biased."

Bailey says one of his most effective radio campaign ads consisted of an announcer just reading, in a monotone, the names of 24 newspapers that endorsed Senator Charles Percy—a tactic other campaign consultants say can be even more effective in a less-publicized race.

"People just won't take time to find out enough about a lot of the bottom-of-the-ticket offices and the less important ballot propositions," says Bill Roberts. "They don't even look at their sample ballots until the night before. They trust the paper on those things. They figure the paper has more time and experience and knowledge than they do. When all the papers say vote 'Yes' on one of those propositions, it's a cinch to win."

Revenue measures—school bond and tax proposals in particular—were once regarded in the same light, but the campus protests of the 1960s and the economic recession of the 1970s have rendered such propositions almost as emotion-charged (and made voters almost as resistant to editorial influence) as racial and sexual issues.

On non-emotional, non-revenue issues, however, most politicians say their poll-watchers report a great number of voters carrying newspaper sample ballots into the voting booth with them—presumably to vote as the newspaper recommends. Several veteran campaign managers say they even follow this practice themselves.

But pollster Mervin Field believes the influence of newspaper endorsements has been overstated, even on these lesser races.

"Most of the unpublicized ballot propositions should never be on the ballot anyway," Field says. "They're just technical, pro forma adjustments that would pass anyway, no matter what the newspapers recommended."

Although an examination of election returns tends to contradict Field in most instances, the returns do support his general contention that newspapers are often wrongly given credit for influencing the outcome of specific elections.

Many politicians, for example, say the *Los Angeles Times* endorsement of Tom Bradley for mayor in 1973 gave Bradley a credibility and legitimacy in the white community that he, as a black man, would not otherwise have had—and could not have won without.

But the *Times* also endorsed Bradley in 1969, when higher racial tensions and his own lower profile should have made this stamp of credibility even more valuable. Yet Bradley lost in 1969—largely because of those racial tensions and his own campaign mistakes, but also because incumbent Sam Yorty used the Bradley endorsement and the *Times'* long and well-known anti-Yorty campaign to galvanize public hostility toward the media.

"Actually," Field says, "it was a case of overkill. Yorty made the *Times* a code word for all the anger the people felt against the press in general. He ran against the *Times*. And he won."

Many people in both Bradley's and Yorty's camps agree with this analysis—and they point to other races in that same election year as proof that endorsements are not especially influential.

The Los Angeles Community College Board of Trustees was created that year, and the trustees' campaign was precisely the kind of race in which endorsements should have been influential—a large field (133 candidates) running for seven new and relatively obscure positions, in a race with little media attention or campaign spending.

The *Times'* endorsement said 19 of the 133 candidates were acceptable. But 12 of those 19 didn't even make the runoff election, and of the seven who did, only three were ultimately elected.

"It's pretty hard to convince me the *Times'* endorsement had an overwhelming influence on that race," says Charles Manatt, one of the original 133 candidates. "I had their endorsement, and I finished 50th."

Even in judgeship races, where newspapers are presumed to have the greatest influence, that influence is not always incontrovertible.

The man who wrote the *Los Angeles Times'* editorial endorsing Joan Dempsey Klein for Superior Court in 1974 is convinced that endorsement propelled her to victory. But two years earlier, in a similar Superior Court race, the *Times* endorsed James Nelson. He lost.

Thus, virtually every generalization about the influence of newspaper endorsements is open to exception, and the only logical conclusion that can be drawn after an exhaustive study is that in most elections, most endorsements will have little, if any, impact.

It is precisely because endorsements are of such dubious value that the *Los Angeles Times*, in 1973, abandoned its policy of "routinely" endorsing candidates for president, governor and senator.

The *Times* said then that "wide public exposure of the candidates for the top three partisan offices makes our judgment on these dispensable; our readers have more than ample information on which to make up their minds."

Times editors also felt that readers "find it hard to believe that this newspaper's editorial page endorsements really don't affect the news columns."

Most people in politics tend to agree with both those explanations. But they still disagree with the new endorsement policy.

"It's an abdication of journalistic responsibility," says Mayor Tom Bradley. "A newspaper owes it to its readers to periodically evaluate all the candidates and issues, and an endorsement in any race is just that— a barometer of the paper's views at a given point in time."

One *Times* editorial writer—echoing the sentiment of many politicians —says the new policy was "designed primarily to save the Chandler family the inevitable embarrassment of one day having to break a life-long Republican tradition and endorse a Democrat for president or governor." (*Times* editors scoff at this charge.)

Although no other major American newspapers (except *Newsday*) have recently formalized a policy of nonendorsement in specific races, many editors—including those at the *Boston Globe, Chicago Tribune* and *Washington Post*—are increasingly convinced that selectivity of some sort is necessary for both political effectiveness and journalistic responsibility.

In 1932, the *Editor and Publisher* poll of Presidential endorsements showed only 7 percent of the nation's daily newspapers making no endorsement. By 1972, the figure was up to 23 percent. In 1976, it was 26 percent.

Says one of these newspapers, the *Wall Street Journal*:

"We don't think our business is telling people how to vote."

Philip Geyelin, editor of the *Washington Post* editorial pages, thinks newspapers should endorse only in local races with which they are thoroughly familiar or in national races involving special circumstances —and even then, only with extreme caution.

"If you endorse early in the campaign, you place a burden on your reporters because the politicians and the readers perceive them as no longer being totally objective, as reflecting your editorial position," he says. "If you endorse late in the campaign, it doesn't really have any effect, so you're just indulging in a pretentious, presumptuous and largely meaningless exercise."

Geyelin says the *Post*, which made no presidential endorsements from 1956 to 1972, came under considerable pressure to endorse Senator George McGovern in 1972 after having played so instrumental a role in exposing the Watergate scandal. But *Post* editors had almost as many misgivings about McGovern as they did about Nixon.

"I think our editorials made it clear that we preferred McGovern, who was at least a decent, honest man," Geyelin says, "but he had so many shortcomings, we couldn't quite bring ourselves to formally endorse him.

"I know it would have been bolder to take the plunge, but that was one time I just didn't think there was any water in the pool."

In 1976, the *Post* relented—sort of; again, the editors had little enthusiasm for either candidate. But the *Post* endorsed Jimmy Carter in a tepid editorial that concluded, "If this doesn't strike you as much of an endorsement, well, that's fine. It isn't meant to be. Not being in the business of manufacturing or marketing candidates, we offer no warranties."

6 / The Op-Ed Page

The *New York Times*, a journalistic institution almost as well known for its gravity as for its quality, has given prominent play in recent years to such uncharacteristic exercises in whimsey and frivolity as:

- A lawyer's account of why he enjoys eating at McDonald's.
- A purported exchange of letters between a 9-year-old boy and several famous politicians.
- The genealogy of Alfred E. Newman, the nonexistent character created by *Mad* magazine.
- Excerpts from a children's cookbook.
- Andy Warhol's explanation of why he began dyeing his hair gray before his 25th birthday.

All these stories ran on the *New York Times* op-ed page—literally, the page opposite the editorial page—sandwiched among stories written by United States senators, Pulitzer Prize-winning poets, foreign diplomats and university professors, as well as by housewives, construction workers, businessmen and people on welfare, unemployment and Social Security.

The opening of the op-ed page to this diversity of authorship—and, inevitably, of subject matter, literary style and reader interest—is a relatively new phenomenon in American newspapers; until the last five years or so, Sunday book and music reviews and a few skimpy letters to the editor were about all that most newspapers published by writers other than their own reporters or syndicated columnists.

"We've finally realized there are a lot more things in this world than newspapers traditionally pay attention to," says Anthony Day, editor of the *Los Angeles Times* editorial pages. "For too long, our op-ed page presented a terribly narrow range of argument—all those boring columnists saying the same thing, day after day, week after week, year after year.

"Our op-ed page was too dull, abstract, official, impersonal and predictable."

The *Los Angeles Times*, more than most papers, did experiment from time to time with outside contributions, but the *New York Times* was the first major paper to make a total commitment to the regular daily publication of outside work.

The *New York Times* spends more money, devotes more space and has a larger staff for its op-ed page than does any other paper, and its op-ed page is generally regarded as the best in the country. But over the last few years, the *Los Angeles Times*, *Washington Post*, *Boston Globe* and *Chicago Tribune* have also opened their daily op-ed pages to a wide range of outside contributors—many of them previously unpublished amateurs—whose topics and viewpoints have ranged from the trivial to the heretical and from the scholarly to the scandalous.

Even poetry and essays, two literary forms heretofore all but ignored by the nation's major newspapers, now find an occasional home on the op-ed page in these papers. Other newspapers—the *Milwaukee Journal*, *Minneapolis Star* and *San Francisco Examiner* among them—have also, to varying and lesser degrees, opened their op-ed pages to outside contributors who may range from poets to plumbers.

In most newspapers, the evolution of the op-ed page has been accompanied by a substantial increase in the space devoted to letters to the editor—a confluence of events that is by no means coincidental.

Amid the socio-political upheavals of the 1960s and 1970s, many editors began to feel that their newspapers should provide a more thorough and diverse discussion of the increasingly complex and controversial issues of the day.

Even with the publication of a wide array of columnists, stretching all across the political and ideological spectrum, it was felt that there was a certain insular—if not downright incestuous—quality to most newspaper opinion pages.

"Syndicated columnists all tend to write about the same subject on the same day with the same Washington correspondent's point of view," says Philip Geyelin, editor of the *Washington Post* editorial page.

"We wanted to introduce some new voices on our op-ed page, people other than professional journalists, who might have some interesting things to say about what was happening in our society."

Many of these new voices have been experts, specialists, academicians, scientists. But, increasingly, the new voices have also included the common man—and woman—describing personal feelings about (or personal experiences with) a given issue or incident.

Newspaper editors realize that press coverage of the bitterly divisive issues of the past 15 years has left many readers skeptical of—and hostile toward—the media, and they hope to bridge this credibility gap by publishing more articles (and letters) from these readers.

Some editors see the development of the op-ed page as but one stage in a continuing evolution of the opinion pages.

"I think it presages a totally new attitude on the part of newspapers," says Gene Roberts, executive editor of the *Philadelphia Inquirer*. "In time, I think we'll become less institutionalized, more open, more accountable, especially on the editorial page itself.

"Instead of just unsigned editorials, speaking for the newspaper as an institution, we'll have signed editorials—by individual staff members and outsiders as well," Roberts says. "Then we can have genuine debates, maybe two editorials on different sides of the same issue."

Most newspapermen trace the origins of today's still-changing op-ed page to the *New York World* of the early 1920s. The *World's* op-ed page was essentially a cultural offering, but its inclusion of some political columns, along with movie and theater and book reviews, is generally thought to have been the first regular publication of a full page of commentary in a major American newspaper.

Over the decades that followed, other papers began to publish op-ed pages, most of them featuring syndicated columnists writing on primarily political issues. On Sundays, many major papers began to devote one entire section to a review and analysis of the week's news—with outside commentary often supplementing staff-written and syndicated material.

Through the 1960s, as the complexity and contentiousness of the day's events seemed to grow, newspapers began experimenting with occasional outside contributors in the daily paper as well, striving for what one editor calls "rapid expert analysis on developing stories."

At the *Los Angeles Times*, for example, such "expert analysis" was published about twice a week from July, 1967, to September, 1969, most of it under the bylines of such prominent academicians as Sidney Hook, Philip Kurland, Edward Teller, Bruno Bettelheim and Hans Morgenthau.

At about the same time, the *New York Times*—which published its own columnists on a regular schedule, but used no syndicated material—initiated serious discussions about developing an op-ed page.

Twelve newspapers had ceased publication in New York since 1900—five of them since 1949—and *Times* editors felt an increasing responsibility to provide their readers with a more diverse spectrum of opinion than their own generally liberal columnists then offered.

"We talked at length about an op-ed page once or twice a year for several years," says Harrison Salisbury, the *Times'* Pulitzer Prize-winning reporter who ultimately served as the first editor of the *Times* op-ed page.

"Jurisdictional disputes were what delayed the page," Salisbury says. Two editors each wanted control of it, and a third didn't want the page to exist at all.

Finally, on September 21, 1970, in a decision that was as much a matter of corporate economics as civic responsibility, the *New York Times* introduced its op-ed page.

"We knew we had to do something to attract the readers of the old *Herald-Tribune* [one of the last of the New York papers to fold]," Salisbury says.

"We'd also signed new union contracts that cost the paper a lot of money that spring. We had to raise advertising and subscription rates to offset this, and Punch Sulzberger (the publisher) decided it would be a good time to give the readers something extra for their extra money."

The *Times'* own columnists were moved from the editorial page to the op-ed page, to be complemented by two or three outside contributions a day.

The *Times* pays $150 per outside story—more an honorarium than an actual fee really, since most of the prominent people who write for the *Times* could command five or 10 times that amount from other publications.

Times editors hoped that the prestige of writing for the *New York Times* would compensate authors for their time—and that is exactly what has happened, despite some early consternation by Salisbury.

"We decided to have an ad on the page most days," Salisbury says. "One reason, obviously, was the money it would bring in. Another reason was that I thought it would help keep the page in touch with reality, prevent it from becoming an ivory tower.

"But, frankly, without the ad, I was afraid we wouldn't get enough stories to fill the whole page every day. I was haunted by the idea that I'd wake up one morning and have nothing to put on the page."

That apprehension, Salisbury now admits, was "incredible naivete on my part. We wound up getting 200 unsolicited manuscripts a week."

Almost from the day of its inception, the *New York Times* op-ed page has been something of a status cachet in many social, political and intellectual quarters. Prominent people from around the world have sought assignments from the op-ed page, and it has become, on most days, precisely the controversial and provocative "intellectual marketplace" Salisbury hoped for from the beginning.

In the second month of the page's existence, Salisbury published an open letter, written by a Southern physician to his college-bound son, urging the boy to avoid campus demonstrations. If the boy were to be killed in a campus protest, his father wrote, "Mother and I will grieve, but we will gladly buy a dinner for the National Guardsman who shot you."

More than 300 letters came in attacking the doctor.

A year later, a brief, four-paragraph excerpt reprinted from the British magazine *The New Statesman* brought the *Times* op-ed page an even greater avalanche of angry mail. In that article, author J. B. Priestly argued, tongue firmly in cheek, that most Britishers' preference for brown eggs over white eggs clearly demonstrated the superiority of British civilization to American civilization.

"We got so many letters of protest, I thought we'd have to fight the Revolution all over," says one *Times* editor.

In January, 1974, Salisbury retired, and Charlotte Curtis, formerly editor of the paper's family/style section, assumed the editorship of the op-ed page.

Curtis had, she said, two basic objectives: "To get more ordinary people, rather than famous people, writing for the page, and to broaden and lighten the spread of the page."

Salisbury had relied too heavily, some critics felt, on big-name contributors who did not always have something important to say.

"A dull piece by a famous person is still a dull piece," says one editor.

Curtis made public her desire for pieces reflecting "the experiences and perceptions of people living ordinary lives away from the East Coast," and in response to her plea, unsolicited manuscripts received by the op-ed page have now increased to 300 a week.

Only a small fraction of those are good enough or original enough to be used, and Curtis estimates that 85 to 90 percent of the published op-ed pieces are assigned by her or by one of her two full-time assistants.

The *New York Times* op-ed page, like those in other papers, also makes regular use of excerpts from noteworthy speeches and from articles printed in other, often technical or esoteric magazines, but Curtis' op-ed page is somewhat less issue-oriented than Salisbury's was—in part because of her personality and her commitment to modify the page, in part because of the quiescence of Vietnam, the campus, the ghetto and Watergate.

The *New York Times* op-ed page remains, however, the most cerebral of the nation's op-ed pages, containing not only some of the best writing published in any paper but also dealing regularly in pure, abstract ideas, independent of any current issue, as discussed by many of the most discerning intellectuals of our time.

Some critics think the page is too cerebral at times—"dull" and "turgid" are the words one editor applies. Others think it is too frivolous.

"The page was more vital, more provocative, under Salisbury," says Robert Healy, executive editor of the *Boston Globe*. "The page gives me a good surprise once in a while now, but it just isn't as consistently serious as it used to be."

Sometimes, the lightheartedness of the *New York Times* op-ed page is both contrived and counterproductive—as when a well-reasoned, statistic-filled article on the federal government's "ferocious neglect" of rural America was published beneath the playful headline "Nix Pix of Stix as Hix."

More often, however, offbeat headlines and stories and large, stylized, often surrealistic illustrations on the op-ed page serve as an effective antidote to the stolid, somber quality of much of the *New York Times*. Once, for example, almost half the op-ed page was devoted to a story on flower-smuggling; the bold illustrations and eye-catching headline ("Flower Smuggler, Drop that Pistil!") probably lured several readers who might otherwise have neglected what proved to be a fascinating tale.

Curtis is aware of the criticism that her page is sometimes too frivolous, and she says John Oakes, when editor of the editorial page, occasionally made that charge himself. "He calls my softer pieces '*True Confessions*' or '*Readers Digest*' pieces," she says.

Nevertheless, the only story Curtis has published that she wishes, in retrospect, she had not published was a deadly serious attempt by a Southern conservative to equate the "persecution" of Richard Nixon with that of Jesus Christ.

"I think now that piece was tasteless," Curtis says.

Despite such lapses, most editors speak of the *New York Times* op-ed page with considerable envy and enthusiasm. They are far more critical of other op-ed pages—especially of the *Washington Post* op-ed page.

"I get the feeling the *Post* editors just dump in anything they have, then write a dull head [headline] for it," says Ed Hawley, editor of the *Chicago Tribune* op-ed page.

"I don't remember anything on the *Post* op-ed page ever attracting my attention," says another op-ed page editor. "That's pretty bad."

The *Post* began its op-ed page about the same time as the *New York Times*, although the *Post* really treats its facing editorial and op-ed pages as a single entity, sandwiching columns and outside contributions between editorials on the extreme left and letters on the extreme right.

Because Washington is the quintessential political town, the *Post* continues to run more political columns—syndicated and by *Post* staffers—than most papers. That leaves less room for op-ed page pieces than either the *New York Times* or *Los Angeles Times* run.

The *Post*, more often than not, publishes only one outside piece a day, and editors make an effort not to permit politicians to write that one piece too frequently.

"We feel they already have access to our news columns," says Philip Geyelin, editor of the *Post* editorial page.

Still, *Post* editors see politicians on the Washington cocktail party circuit, and op-ed page stories are frequently a byproduct of these casual meetings.

Geyelin once met former Senator William Fulbright at such a party, and when Fulbright began talking about a recent trip he'd taken to the Mideast, Geyelin asked him to write an op-ed page piece on the experience. Fulbright did so.

Although the *Post* op-ed material is often political, the paper has published an intriguing—if rarely compelling—variety of stories, including, in one month:

- A Christian scholar's explanation of "the vitality of religion in a supposedly scientific age."
- An American motion picture director's comparison of British and American television, based on their respective coverage of the Wimbledon tennis tournament.
- A Washington attorney's account of a small, experimental college in Phoenix.

Other op-ed pages around the country have also produced an uncommon diversity of stories.

The *Chicago Tribune* op-ed page has been part of a continuing trend away from the singlemindedly conservative image the paper had for decades, and now, on any given day, the most interesting story in the paper may well appear on the op-ed page.

One 1975 piece argued that people in underdeveloped countries too often blame "demons and black magic," rather than international politics and economics, for overpopulation, food shortages and other problems of daily life.

Another piece, written by an Irish playwright, used the occasion of the death of an old Irish revolutionary leader, Eamon de Valera, to talk about de Valera's impact and philosophy.

The *Tribune*, which publishes outside contributions four or five times a week, also publishes a weekly "Speak Out" column by one of its readers and a twice-weekly column written by a local construction worker.

The *Boston Globe* publishes three or four outside pieces a week on its op-ed page, many of them designed to ventilate a local controversy.

The *Globe's* page was, in fact, born—and has continued to develop—in direct response to a series of conflicts in Boston: antiwar protests, a caucus of black elected officials, a feminist sit-in at the paper, anger in some white neighborhoods over the *Globe's* support of busing, complaints by local Arab leaders that the *Globe* was pro-Israel.

Anne Wyman, editor of the *Globe* editorial pages, says she wishes she had more space available for outside contributions, "but we've got too damn many fixed columns."

Most editors have similar problems, and they're reluctant to run their syndicated columnists less frequently, for fear the columnists will take their columns to a competing paper instead.

"That's where you guys at the *Los Angeles Times* are lucky," says one editor. "You don't have any real competition in L.A. You don't have to run the columns three or four times a week, and there's really no place else for them to go if they don't like it."

The *Los Angeles Times* has, indeed, drastically reduced its use of syndicated columnists; few run more than once a week now, and most run far less often than that, thereby enabling the *Times* to publish two or three outside pieces a day on its op-ed page.

Most *Los Angeles Times* op-ed page pieces are assigned by the op-ed staff, and only three or four of the 75 or so unsolicited pieces that come in every week are generally published. Whether assigned or unsolicited, outside contributors are generally paid $150 each, the same fee as the *New York Times* pays.

Although the *New York Times* and *Los Angeles Times* have made greater contributions than any other newspapers to the use of outside material on their op-ed pages, there are many differences between the two pages. Among these are:

- The *Los Angeles Times* permits its own staff writers to contribute to the op-ed page, and places no formal limit on the number of articles an outside writer may contribute. The *New York Times* prohibits its staffers from writing for the op-ed page, and limits outsiders to two pieces a year.
- The *Los Angeles Times* op-ed page appears five days a week, and is merged, in effect, with the "Opinion" section on Sunday; the same staff, for the most part, produces both "Opinion" and the op-ed pages. The *New York Times* op-ed pages appears seven days a week, and is produced by a staff wholly independent from Sunday's "The Week in Review."

Unlike the *New York Times*, which runs one large ad on its op-ed page about four times a week, the *Los Angeles Times* prohibits advertising on its op-ed page.

"An ad would reduce the space available for stories, and it would be a commercial intrusion on one of the pages that, like the editorial page itself, should be free of that," says Anthony Day, editor of the *Los Angeles Times* editorial pages.

But the most substantive differences between the op-ed pages of the *New York Times* and the *Los Angeles Times* are in philosophy and content.

Los Angeles Times editors admit their page is less intellectual than the *New York Times'*, but they say that is deliberate.

"We have different papers and different audiences," says Peter Bunzel, editor of the *Los Angeles Times* op-ed page. "I think that for our readers, we have enough reportage on social issues on the news pages and enough pontification from the columnists.

"I'd like the op-ed page to provide something that does not exist anywhere else in the paper. I'd especially like us to give our readers a clear feeling of what it's really like to live in Southern California.

"I want personal experience pieces, stories that tell how it feels to drive the freeway and to suffer a death in the family and to be out of work."

Thus, in one three-week period, the *Los Angeles Times* published accounts of:

- What a patient's death meant to a switchboard operator in the hospital.
- What a Monrovia police officer remembered about his great-grand-mother.
- A politician's bad experience with her doctor.
- A grocery clerk's encounters with customers who were angry about rising food prices.

On the broader social canvas, op-ed page pieces have also ranged from a Catholic educator's ruminations on Governor Brown's seminary training to a discussion of the public policy implications of earthquake predictions to an excoriation of those who would misquote the Bible to condemn homosexuality.

The *Los Angeles Times* also likes contrapuntal dialogue on its op-ed page, often pairing articles representing divergent viewpoints on the same issue—feminism, welfare, the Mideast, rapid transit.

Some critics think the *Los Angeles Times* op-ed page still contains too narrow a range of opinion and too little trenchant social commentary.

Kenneth Reich, now a *Los Angeles Times* political reporter, served as the *Times'* first op-ed page editor in 1972, and he thinks the page is not sufficiently "abrasive or exciting."

"We seem to have a great reluctance around here to run pieces that represent truly new and different ideas," Reich says. "Our editors seem afraid that the paper will be perceived as lending credibility, if not actually support, to any far-out idea that's expressed on the page."

Reich asked to be relieved as op-ed page editor after only six months, largely because he felt he was often prevented from doing the job he was hired to do—that of bringing truly divergent ideas into the paper. Several articles he solicited for the op-ed page were killed for "political reasons," he says, and he found it "humiliating; I felt like a lackey when I had to tell some guy we couldn't run his piece, even though I personally thought it was a very fine, responsible piece."

Reich admits he was "never temperamentally suited to be an editor anyway, though," and he says his superiors probably "heaved a sigh of relief when I quit."

Times editors scoff at Reich's charges that op-ed page stories were killed for political reasons and they agree he was ill-suited to the job (although they do think he got the op-ed page off to "a good start").

"The whole idea of the op-ed page is to bring in ideas we don't necessarily agree with," says Anthony Day. "We often reject pieces because they repeat something we've already said or because they're poorly written or inconsistently argued, but never for political reasons."

Because so many contributors to the op-ed page have never before written for a newspaper—or for any other publication—op-ed page editors frequently must work long hours helping them shape their stories.

"Authentication is also a big problem for us," says Peter Bunzel. "How can we be sure that a guy we never heard of before is writing a true story? That's especially difficult with personal experience pieces."

Bunzel has yet to run a piece he now wishes he had not run, but he does admit to "ex post facto reservations" about a short piece on poets and poetry by Rod McKuen.

"Perhaps we dignified the author's simplistic notions about poetry and the role of poets by using it," Bunzel says.

In publishing the McKuen piece, the *Times* appended an editor's note that said, in part:

"In submitting this article at the *Times'* request, the author described himself as follows: 'Having sold more than 10 million books of poetry in hard cover in the past 10 years, Rod McKuen is considered not only the best-selling poet of all time, but the best-selling author writing in any medium in hard cover . . .'"

One letter-writer took the *Times* to task for this "immature treatment," and Bunzel himself admits, somewhat shamefacedly, that he used that editor's note because he rather enjoyed seeing McKuen, "a celebrated fellow . . . sort of make a fool of himself in public."

The *New York Times* encountered far more embarrassment—through no apparent fault of its editors—with a frivolous op-ed page piece of its own in mid-1975.

The piece purported to be an exchange of letters between Martin Bear, a 9-year-old San Francisco boy visiting a relative in New York, and Senators Edward Kennedy, Jacob Javits, Hubert Humphrey and James Buckley, as well as New York Congresswoman Bella Abzug and Mayor Abraham Beame (to whom Martin Bear sent a dime because "I heard that you need money").

In a typical exchange, Martin wrote to Humphrey:

"I saw you at our temple in New York. You were late and you never stopped talking. How come you talk so much?"

Humphrey's response, in part:

"One of the nicest things about being a United States senator is getting letters from young people like you. It's a great satisfaction to me to know that I have so many fine young friends . . ."

Martin's exchanges with the other politicians were equally charming and equally amusing, and all the politicians' letters were genuine.

But there is no such person as Martin Bear. He was a figment of the creative imagination of a young lawyer in a prominent Wall Street firm. The lawyer wrote the letters, then signed the "boy's" name.

Times editors were sufficiently embarrassed by this hoax to apologize to their readers and to the politicians involved. But their embarrassment must have diminished considerably with time because, eleven months later, during the Democratic convention in New York, they asked the lawyer if "Martin" might again have "something to say" to the politicians. He did, indeed.

In an open letter to Jimmy Carter, published in the *Times* the day Carter was to be nominated for president, "Martin" offered Carter several pieces of unsolicited advice. Among them:

- "Get Congress to put Smokey the Bear on Mount Rushmore."
- "Try not to bang your head all the time like President Ford does. It looks stupid and it probably hurts."
- "Don't eat yogurt. I ate yogurt last week and threw up. If you throw up on television, you're in trouble."

7 / Hoax!

It all began on a chilly Monday morning in mid-May of 1975—three months after Patty Hearst had been kidnaped (and four months before she would be arrested)—when a 31-year-old ex-convict named Michael Casey walked into the city room of the *Los Angeles Times*. Casey could, he told *Times* reporter Dave Smith, arrange for an interview with the fugitive heiress.

Casey said Patty, disguised by plastic surgery, had been helping with the evacuation of Vietnamese refugees in Saigon, and she hoped that activity would show both her contrition for past acts and her potential for future humanitarian works.

Perhaps, he hinted, if all this became known, authorities might offer some leniency in exchange for her surrender.

The story seemed unlikely, but Smith had known Casey casually for four or five years, and the two had established a certain mutual trust and rapport.

Casey had first come to the attention of the *Times* in 1970, when another *Times* reporter, William Drummond, had been writing about racial unrest in Soledad Prison.

Casey, who had been in and out of correctional institutions most of his life, was in Soledad then for passing bad checks. A white radical with a glib tongue and a winning manner, he had become a mediator of sorts between black inmates and prison authorities, and he had offered to help Drummond with his story.

Several months later, Smith was working on a story about violence, and

—recalling Drummond's praise of Casey—he contacted him for an interview.

"I was immediately captivated by him," Smith recalls. "He seemed genuinely concerned about prison reform and other social issues, and he seemed really devoted to his family."

Smith was so impressed, in fact, that after two visits and several letters, he wrote to state parole authorities on Casey's behalf.

But Casey had also piqued Smith's professional interest: he said he had been imprisoned, in part, because—as a free-lance war correspondent in Vietnam in the 1960s—he had discovered the true story behind the My Lai massacre. He said he had documents implicating General William Westmoreland and other high Pentagon figures in the mass murder and the subsequent coverup.

Although Casey never produced those documents, he and Smith remained in occasional contact after his release from prison in 1971, and in 1974—after working sporadically on prison reform—Casey took a job with Boys Town in Omaha.

Boys Town was then trying to recover from an embarrassing series of newspaper stories showing that vast amounts of money were being collected and very little was being spent on the boys. Casey was hired as director of special projects for the new Boys Town administration.

He lasted nine months.

Boys Town said he was fired for taking 31 confidential files, without permission, to negotiate a television series on Boys Town. Casey says he was fired because he was sincere about wanting to change conditions for the boys, and Boys Town officials were not.

"They just wanted me for window-dressing and the cocktail circuit," he told Smith, and he tried several times to persuade Smith to expose Boys Town.

Then, on March 14, 1975, Casey called Smith to say that a former fellow-inmate from Soledad had just given him a private New York telephone number—and hotel room number—for Randolph Hearst, Patty's father.

Casey hinted that Patty might be willing to talk to Smith, and he said —somewhat cryptically—that someone else, an attorney, had called Hearst at that New York number earlier in the day to tell him that something he had said that day was "OK with Patty."

Smith, mystified and on his way to another assignment, relayed the information to Jerry Belcher, another *Times* reporter—one who had written a book on the Hearst kidnaping and who would soon be named to a special, four-reporter *Times* team that would ultimately spend more than three months investigating the Hearst case.

Belcher, who had worked for Hearst's *San Francisco Examiner* before joining the *Times*, dialed the New York number, and immediately recognized Hearst's voice. Hearst told Belcher he had, indeed, been called as Casey said, but he didn't know who had called him or what comment the man had been referring to.

Neither Smith nor Belcher nor Hearst knew what to make of the day's events, but a few weeks later, Casey again called the *Times*—this time intending to tell Smith that his ex-inmate friend now thought he could arrange an interview with Patty. But Smith was in Phoenix on another story when Casey called, and Casey left only part of the message with someone else at the *Times*. Even that much didn't reach Smith until the next day—by which time Casey was on his way to Southeast Asia.

Then, in mid-May, Casey returned. He had been working with Vietnamese refugees in Saigon and on Guam and Wake Island, he told Smith. He had talked to Patty twice. He could take Smith to her.

Smith was intrigued by Casey's story, but he knew he couldn't sell it to his editors by himself.

"I have a reputation around here for hanging around with flakes," he says. "People seem to think, 'Well, Smith can write OK, but he don't always think so good.'"

Smith was not a member of the *Times'* Patty Hearst team, so he invited the team to meet Casey. Sporadically, over the next two weeks, all four members of the team questioned Casey, probing for inconsistencies in his story. Lee Dye, an assistant metropolitan editor assigned to supervise the team, joined the interrogation sessions four times.

Dye had been to Vietnam himself, and he was impressed by Casey's knowledge of the people and politics and geography of Saigon—and by the *Time* magazine credentials Casey carried.

Dye was also impressed by Casey's intimate knowledge of the Hearst case—of trivial details Dye thought no one but his reporters (or someone close to Patty) could know.

"He said things and knew things that to this day dumbfound me," Dye says.

The Hearst team had reason to believe, for example, that Patty had met secretly in eastern Canada with Stephen Bingham, the fugitive attorney accused of smuggling a gun to George Jackson in San Quentin just before Jackson was killed by prison guards in an escape attempt in August 1971.

The Hearst team had also been told that a young woman wearing a red bandana had been seen with Emily Harris, another SLA fugitive, in Baja, California.

"Casey knew about the meeting with Bingham," Dye says, "and he also mentioned that Patty was often wearing a red bandana."

But every time Casey mentioned these and other details about Patty, he did so in a "casual, off-handed way—just throwaway lines," Dye says. "He didn't seem to be trying to sell us or convince us of anything."

In fact, Dye and Smith both say, Casey seemed for more interested in talking about the Vietnamese refugee problem and in persuading the *Times* to expose Boys Town than he did in arranging a meeting with Patty.

But Casey did say he could arrange a meeting with Patty in Hong Kong.

Skeptical, Dye asked Bob Kistler, another of the Hearst team reporters, to call someone at Soledad for a rundown on Casey. Kistler made the call and gave Dye a glowing memo on "Gus"—the code name Kistler assigned to Casey.

Kistler's Soledad contact had "tremendous respect" for him, and "personally thinks very highly of Gus' guts, ability and insights," Kistler wrote.

Dye next asked Belcher to check with the Hollywood movie producer whom Casey had supposedly been talking to about a television series on Boys Town. The producer also spoke well of Casey.

At about the same time, Narda Trout—another member of the *Times'* Hearst team—was working on a story about the radical underground, and Casey said he could probably help her meet a couple of fugitive radicals. He suggested they talk about the arrangements while he drove to Camp Pendleton to see some Vietnamese refugees.

On the drive down, Casey told Trout about his work with the refugees —including a highly dramatic account of how he and a Vietnamese photographer for *Time* magazine helped boost one young Vietnamese girl over the wall of the American Embassy in Saigon on the final day of the evacuation.

Sure enough, at Camp Pendleton, Trout and Casey encountered both the photographer and the girl—who came running up to Casey, threw her arms around him and thanked him for saving her life.

Casey also took Trout—without clearance or credentials—right through the tight security in the refugee camp and directly into the tent assigned to former South Vietnamese Premier Nguyen Cao Ky. Casey even chatted briefly with Ky about refugee problems.

Casey's credibility was looking better each day, but still Dye decided to check with newspapermen in Omaha for their impressions.

"We got some negative feedback," Dye says, "but it was all nickel and dime stuff, mostly about writing bad checks and not paying his bills.

"Hell, that wasn't surprising. We already knew he'd been in prison for that. All his problems seemed to involve personal fiscal irresponsibility, and that didn't bother me because he wasn't asking us for any money."

At one point, Casey did ask Dye for $1,000 to cover his expenses in Hong Kong, but Dye had rejected the request, while assuring Casey that the *Times* would certainly pay his expenses if the *Times* sent a reporter with him to Hong Kong.

Casey said that arrangement was fine with him.

As a final check on Casey, the Hearst family was asked for three questions that could be put to Patty and that only she could answer.

Belcher got the questions—and answers—from Will Hearst, Patty's cousin, and Casey was given two of the questions—without the answers. He was told that if he could get Patty to answer them on the telephone, a reporter would accompany him to Hong Kong to meet her (and ask the third question, in person, as a final proof of her identity).

"She won't answer them," Casey reported back a few days later. "No one over there will say anything unless we go there. They don't want to take any chances."

It was time to make a decision.

Dye consulted his superiors, and it was decided that—skeptical or not —the only way the *Times* would know for sure if Casey was telling the truth would be to go to Hong Kong.

Belcher was the logical choice to go. He was, it was felt at the *Times*, the ranking expert on the case.

"It all sounded pretty bizarre," Belcher says, "but everything I'd encountered in the case, from the very beginning, had been so bizarre, so far out, that the more unbelievable something seemed, the more believable it really was."

But Casey wasn't happy with the choice of Belcher. He didn't know Belcher, he said, and his contacts told him Belcher was "too sympathetic to law enforcement.

"The word I get," Casey said, "is that except for a badge, he's a cop."

Casey wanted Smith—someone he knew personally and trusted politically—to come to Hong Kong, too. The *Times* agreed.

On May 28, Smith, Belcher and Casey flew first class—at *Times* expense —to Hong Kong. When they arrived they checked in—as directed by Casey—at the Mandarin Hotel ($50 per day per person).

While Casey was out "checking with my contacts," Smith and Belcher spent most of the day, Friday, preparing questions for the interview with Patty.

At 5 p.m. Friday, Casey called: "The meet is set for 7 p.m."

Smith and Belcher began to get excited—Belcher so much so that he couldn't eat dinner. But shortly before seven, their excitement gave way to what Belcher now calls "cloak-and-dagger paranoia."

Belcher called Dye in Los Angeles, and said that if he could find out where they were to meet Patty, he would write the location on a scrap of paper and leave it on page 50 of the novel *Watership Down* in Smith's hotel room—"just in case something happens to us."

But at 7 p.m., Casey called to say the meeting had been postponed until Saturday. In the meantime, he said, Smith and Belcher should find out how to get to Peng Chau; that, he implied, might be the site of the meeting.

Peng Chau, it turned out, was a lonely outpost about 20 minutes from Hong Kong by ferry, but before Smith and Belcher had determined that, Casey had called again to invite them to join him at the Hong Kong Press Club.

"The lady might drop by," he said, adopting the cryptic reference to Patty he would use—and encourage Smith and Belcher to use—throughout their stay in Hong Kong.

Casey told the two reporters he might be with other people when they arrived; if so, he said, they should not approach him but should wait for him to come to them.

"Mike was with four people when we got there," Smith recalls, "an American girl, a Chinese girl and two Chinese men."

When Casey left the group to join Smith and Belcher, he said the four were his contacts with Patty—"sort of a screening committee to look you guys over and make sure you're OK." One of the four, the American girl, was Patty's "closest friend in Hong Kong," he said.

Casey said he would introduce them, but he urgently cautioned the two reporters not to mention Patty's name nor even to hint at why they were in Hong Kong—"or else you'll blow the mission."

When Casey gestured, three of the four came over. The fourth, the Chinese man, remained behind—"looking," Smith says, "like a sinister heavy doing a Casablanca number."

Patty's "friend," Dinah Lee, recognized Smith's name from a *Times* story he had written about the University of California at Santa Cruz a couple of years earlier, and she told him she had studied there and at the University of California at Berkeley.

"She was," Smith says, "just the sort of girl you would expect Patty to have as a friend. Berkeley, Bevery Hills, the whole number.

"What was especially convincing," Smith recalls, "was that none of those people asked us why we were in Hong Kong. That's the normal question you would expect in that situation, but they seemed to know the answer without asking."

One of the Chinese men was a photographer, and he took photos of Smith and Belcher—"so Patty and the others can size you up," Casey explained.

Later that night, when they were alone, Casey told Smith and Belcher they "passed inspection"; tomorrow, he said, they would meet Patty.

But Casey called the next afternoon to postpone the meeting until 4 p.m. Sunday. His "main contact" had disappeared the day before the two reporters had arrived, he said, and "something heavy is going to come down in the States. Everyone is up-tight."

That same afternoon, a woman called and said the Sunday meeting was now being postponed "24 to 72 hours."

Something in the woman's voice prompted Smith to ask, cautiously but hopefully, "Are you the lady we came here to see?"

"Yes."

"Would you mind answering a couple of questions?"

"No."

Smith asked two of the questions they had been given by Will Hearst.

The girl didn't know the answers.

Smith hung up in disgust.

Belcher, who kept an informal journal of sorts throughout the trip, wrote then, "We are bitterly disappointed, dejected. Think our mission is kaput."

But when they stormed into Casey's room and told him what had happened, he seemed as baffled—and as angry—as they were. The woman, he said, was only supposed to deliver a message, nothing else. She was just a functionary. She knew nothing. Perhaps she had just become so curious, she had tried to bluff her way closer to the intrigue.

Smith and Belcher were somewhat mollified, but—having checked again with Dye in Los Angeles—they were growing increasingly impatient. They needed proof that Casey was, indeed, in contact with Patty, or they would have to return home, they said.

They told Casey to try again to get Patty to answer their two questions.

That was Saturday or Sunday night; no one seems to remember for sure. By Tuesday afternoon—with the 72-hour delay about to expire, and with no answers forthcoming from Casey—Smith and Belcher, encouraged by Dye, gave Casey an ultimatum:

"If we don't have hard evidence, we're leaving on the four o'clock plane tomorrow."

That afternoon, with Smith and Belcher in his hotel room, Casey received a telephone call. Belcher remembers Casey's end of the conversation clearly:

"He kept saying, 'Wait a minute, wait a minute; I can't remember the code.' Then he scribbled something down in code on a piece of paper, hung up, translated it and handed us the translation."

There were three words on the piece of paper: "Marma Lee" and "Anita."

"Marma Lee" was the correct answer to the first question—"What is the in-family name among the Hearst clan for Patty's grandmother?"

"Anita" was the correct answer to the second question—"What is the name of Patty's grandmother's sister?"

Smith and Belcher were euphoric. Everyone shook hands. Casey says they all whooped with joy and jumped up and down on the beds. Then they all went out for what Belcher calls "a very expensive dinner, to celebrate," and his journal entry at the time reflects their optimism:

"Now believe, almost without reservation, the project will succeed." They telephoned Dye. He, too, was elated.

Now it was just a matter of waiting for Patty to set the specific time and place for the rendezvous.

The next night, Belcher went to sleep early, and Smith decided to go to the Hong Kong Press Club. He bumped into Dinah Lee and one of the other contacts there, and they had dinner together and went dancing at the Godown, a popular Hong Kong nightclub.

This time, Smith says, both he and Miss Lee hinted around a bit—"very subtly, very obliquely, with no names and no specifics"—about their mission in Hong Kong.

When he returned to his hotel that night, he told Belcher he thought he had "scored some points for us; we all got along real well." He called Dye with the same report.

But when Casey learned of Smith's evening out, he became furious.

"Dave almost blew it," he told Belcher. "You guys weren't supposed to see those people without me. You weren't supposed to talk to them about anything."

The next day, Casey said Hong Kong had become "too hot for Patty"; she would meet them Thursday night in Bangkok. They should fly there and check into the Siam Hotel, and they would either be met at the airport or they would find a message waiting for them at the airport or at the hotel.

The two reporters checked with Dye, who was now convinced it was all a hoax. He told them to skip Bangkok and come straight home. The two reporters discussed the situation, then called Dye back to say they were going to "disobey orders and go to Bangkok."

They agreed it was probably all a wild-goose chase, they said, but having gone so far, they'd never be able to live with themselves if it ultimately turned out that Patty was waiting for them in Bangkok.

Dye wasn't persuaded, but he gave them the impression that they had his tacit approval to go to Bangkok.

"Mike said he'd have to stay behind in Hong Kong as a sort of hostage," Belcher says. "He was kind of John Garfield cool about the whole thing. We all took a Rolls Royce limousine out to the airport (a mere $10 in Hong Kong)."

While Smith and Belcher were on their way to Bangkok, Dye checked in with Will Hearst by telephone, and Hearst told him that someone claiming to work with Smith and Belcher had called him earlier in the week "to make sure they had those questions and answers right."

"I gave him the answers again," Hearst said.

Dye could barely control his anger and disappointment. Obviously, Casey—or a friend of Casey's—had called Hearst. That's how he'd gotten the answers.

Dye called his reporters in Bangkok, gave them the news and told them—rather firmly this time—to come back to Los Angeles.

The reporters had already decided to do just that, though, for no one had met them—or left any messages for them—in Bangkok. They had given up.

"Even when we got a wire from Michael a few hours later saying 'they' (meaning Patty and one of her friends) were en route to Bangkok by car and we should 'Keep the faith,' we knew it was all over," Smith says.

Smith and Belcher had to stop in Hong Kong overnight to make airplane connections to Los Angeles, and while there, they went looking for Dinah Lee and Patty's other "friends." In the Godown, they found the Chinese photographer—who was, Smith says, "dumbfounded when we told him what role Casey had assigned to him.

"He was just a young free-lance photographer, and Casey had asked him to take our pictures so we'd have souvenirs of the trip."

Dinah Lee and Patty's other "friends" didn't know anything about Patty either, Smith and Belcher learned. Just as Casey had told the two reporters not to mention anything about the mission to his "contacts," so he had told his "contacts" not to ask Smith or Belcher any questions about why they were in Hong Kong.

"Casey had told them we were two important American newspapermen on a big story," Smith says. "He told them several lives could be endangered if they asked us any questions."

With the pieces now beginning to fit into the puzzle, Smith and Belcher decided to leave the Godown. Then Casey showed up.

In the ensuing shouting match, Smith and Belcher accused him of being a "phony" and a "liar." He accused them of being "fools."

But he refused to answer any of their questions; from all reports, his demeanor could best be characterized as belligerent evasion. He insisted the Hong Kong mission was legitimate, and he even persuaded the local newspaper there to print a story across the top of page one the next morning, complete with his account of the episode . . . and a photo of him, Smith and Belcher.

To this day, Casey maintains that the *Times* reporters could have had the interview with Patty had they not been so "impatient and indiscreet."

Smith's conversation with Dinah Lee—during which Casey says Smith "screamed and pleaded to see Patty"—showed "the *Times* couldn't be trusted," he says.

The *Times'* Hearst team is convinced it was all a hoax. So is Smith. Certainly, not one shred of testimony was offered in Patty's trial—or in any related trial—that would provide even the vaguest hint of substantiation for Casey's tale. But no one has a persuasive explanation for Casey's motivation. Certainly, a free trip to Hong Kong was not his objective; he had obviously been to Southeast Asia and back at other people's expense many times. Nor had he seemed interested in money or personal publicity.

"I think he hoped to use this thing as a springboard to get us to do the Boys Town expose, maybe even give him a reporter's job," Smith says.

But if Casey knew all along it was a hoax, how could he expect anything from the *Times* when it all fell through?

"I think he really believed it was true himself once he got into it," Smith says. "I think he's delusional. Besides, I don't think he worries much about the eventual outcome of things. He likes action, constant action, excitement, the thrill of putting something over on a big organization. He likes to throw all the cards in the air and see how long he can keep them up there before they fall down."

In that sense, the compulsive hoaxer may have much in common with the compulsive gambler, for as Dr. Edmund Bergler writes in his definitive study, *The Psychology of Gambling*:

"When a gambler places his stake on a card or a color or a number, he is not acting like a person who has adapted himself to reality; he is 'ordering' the next card to win for him, in the complete illusion that he is omnipotent. Mentally, he has regressed to the earlier period in which he was, to all intents and purposes, omnipotent, that is, to infancy, when all his desires were automatically fulfilled."

It is this "fanatical belief in infantile megalomania," Dr. Bergler says, that explains the "mysterious thrill" gambling gives men—and may give hoaxers like Casey as well.

But whatever Casey's motivation, *Times* editors have hastened to assure Dye, Smith and Belcher that they need not feel embarrassed by their week-long wild-goose chase in Hong Kong—even though the misadventure cost the *Times* almost $15,000 in salary, air travel, transoceanic telephone calls, hotel bills and assorted other expenses (including some clothing Casey bought in the Mandarin Hotel and charged to the *Times*).

"We knew it was a longshot when we took it," says Metropolitan Editor Mark Murphy, who gave the final go-ahead for the Hong Kong trip. "We don't want this experience to inhibit us if we get a chance for another good story like it in the future."

Is it possible, though, that the *Times'* Hearst team and their editors, having already expended so much time, effort and money on the Hearst story, subconsciously lost their customary journalistic inhibitions, suspended their disbelief—in short, believed Casey because they *wanted* to believe Casey, wanted his story to be true?

Could the *Times* have investigated Casey—and his story—more carefully beforehand?

The *Times* could, for example, have checked with *Time* magazine to see if his credentials for them were valid—especially since he had once claimed to work for NBC in Vietnam, and NBC had denied it.

But that denial was contained in a series of articles published earlier in the year in the *Omaha World-Herald*—articles the *Times* did not ask to see until the Hong Kong mission was under way. Those articles also questioned Casey's credibility on such points as:

- He said he had a master's degree from the University of South Carolina (He doesn't.)
- He listed as a job reference one doctor he had worked with on prison reform. (The doctor said he hadn't been able to use the inmate inter-

views Casey had conducted because "the interviewing was not entirely reliable.")

- Casey said United States Senator John V. Tunney (D-Calif.) had intervened with Governor Ronald Reagan to obtain his parole from prison. (Both Tunney and Reagan denied any such involvement in the case.)

Early on, Casey had also told the most skeptical member of the *Times'* Hearst team, Ellen Hume, that he had pictures of Patty, taken in Southeast Asia. Hume spent three hours with Casey one afternoon, awaiting what he assured her was the "momentary" delivery of the pictures.

"They never came," she says.

Despite that—and even if they had known about Casey's previously demonstrated unfamiliarity with the truth—*Times* editors say they probably wouldn't have vetoed the Hong Kong mission.

"We knew the guy was no saint," Dye says. "But we knew all along that if anyone could lead us to Patty Hearst, it wasn't going to be Mr. Clean. It was going to be a guy like Casey, a guy with a questionable background and an uncertain character. We weighed all that, and we decided the story was worth the risk."

What it all comes down to, says Editor William F. Thomas, is that "in certain situations, we just don't have a very good defense against a kook who has no tangible personal motivation for giving us a phony story. You never know when some nut is telling the truth.

"It's just that kind of guy who sometimes tips you to a good, legitimate story."

(A historical note of interest. In September, 1945, Igor Gouzenko, a cipher clerk who wanted to defect from Russia, went twice to the *Ottawa Journal* with stolen documents that would ultimately lead to the uncovering of a vast Communist espionage network in North America.

(The *Journal* did not want to talk to Gouzenko, though. "I could see from the [editor's] expression that he thought I was crazy," Gouzenko said later, after turning himself in to the Canadian government instead.)

And what does Michael Casey say about all this?

He has sent the *Times* a bill for "consultant's fees" of $500 a day for his stay in Hong Kong.

Meanwhile...

It was a one-day sensation around the world.

On the night of July 7, 1953, three men were driving down Highway 78, just outside Atlanta, when they saw a flying saucer in the middle of the road.

Two tiny creatures scurried aboard, and the saucer whirred out of sight, turning from red to blue as it rose.

But one creature didn't board the saucer in time, and the three Georgians, racing toward the strange sight, ran him over in their pickup truck.

That, at least, was the story they told when they brought the dead creature to an Atlanta newspaper office that night.

The next day, the story appeared on page one of the *Atlanta Constitution*, under the headline:

Hairless Critter
Killed, 2 'Escape'

Newspapers everywhere picked up the story. More than 25 reporters and photographers deluged the three Georgians with questions. Two military officials also interviewed them.

But, the next day, scientists identified the creature as a rhesus monkey. The three men—two barbers and a butcher—had bought the monkey, killed it, cut off its tail and shaved it . . . all so one of the men could win a $50 bet that he could get his name on the front page of the Constitution.

Keeler McCartney was one of the *Constitution* reporters who worked on that story back in 1953, and even today, 22 years later, a note of sheepishness creeps into McCartney's rich Southern drawl when he talks about how "that little critter weren't nothin' but a shaved monkey."

McCartney's enduring discomfiture is not surprising. Newspapermen tend to pride themselves on being congenital skeptics, and to be hoaxed as McCartney and his colleagues were is both a personal and professional embarrassment.

But along with reportorial skepticism comes reportorial enthusiasm— even romanticism—a desire to write those few good stories that make all the false leads and routine assignments worthwhile.

Newspapers, like law-enforcement agencies, are constantly besieged by people with unlikely tales of intrigue, persecution and adventure. Most can be discounted after a brief question or two. Some require considerable interrogation and investigation. Always, there is the risk of wasting time, effort and money—of ultimately being made to look foolish.

There are those occasions, however, when such stories sound so good —and reporters want so desperately for them to be true—that their enthusiasm may becloud their skepticism; in their anxiety to believe the stories are true—and in their inability to prove otherwise, except by going along—they, and their publications, become vulnerable to a hoax . . . especially if the hoaxer is glib, persuasive and reasonably knowledgeable about journalists.

That's exactly what happened to Bill Shelton—and his editors—in 1960, when he was Miami bureau chief for *Time-Life*.

Fidel Castro had come to power in Cuba several months earlier, and, not long after, the commander of his revolutionary army, Major Camilo

Cienfuegos, had been reported missing on a flight from Camaguey to Havana.

When search parties failed to find Cienfuegos, he was presumed dead. Castro gave him a state funeral.

Then a soldier-of-fortune named Jack Youngblood came to Shelton with a proposal:

Cienfuegos was not dead, Youngblood said. He had discovered that Castro was a Communist—"a traitor to the revolution"—and he had fled Havana to recruit an army and "give Cuba back to the people."

Youngblood said he had flown Cienfuegos to an undisclosed location in Central America. Cienfuegos, he said, thought an interview in the American press could help him raise the money he would need to challenge Castro. Youngblood would take Shelton to him.

"At the time Cienfuegos was supposed to have been killed, no one knew Castro was a Communist," Shelton said. "So it made some sense—especially when Youngblood gave me a locket he said was from Cienfuegos and asked me to take it with a message to Andrew St. George, one of our photographers in New York.

"Cienfuegos had met St. George during the revolution, Youngblood said, and he trusted him. Apparently, Cienfuegos had been wearing this locket, or one like it, during the revolution, and he thought St. George would recognize it."

For his role in the rendezvous, Youngblood wanted $3,000—$1,500 in advance, $1,500 when the meeting took place.

Shelton was skeptical, but he delivered the locket and the message to St. George, checked Youngblood out with his local FBI contacts and asked his editors for advice.

"They told me to go ahead," he says. "It was going to be a great exclusive."

Shelton gave Youngblood $1,500, and the two of them flew to Montego Bay, Jamaica, chartered a plane and flew on to Port au Prince, Haiti, where they were to rendezvous with St. George for the final leg of the trip to Cienfuegos' still undisclosed hiding place.

But there had recently been an assassination attempt against Haitian ruler Francois (Papa Doc) Duvalier, and Shelton's arrival at the Port au Prince airport, in a light plane during a thunderstorm, attracted widespread attention from security guards and the press alike.

"The next day," Shelton says, "Youngblood showed me a note he said was from Cienfuegos, canceling the mission because of all the publicity."

A few weeks later, Youngblood came to see Shelton again. The meeting with Cienguegos had been rescheduled. This time, though, he wanted $5,000—$2,500 in advance, $2,500 when the meeting took place.

Again, Shelton queried his editors. Again, they gave him the go-ahead —and the money.

Shelton, Youngblood and St. George rendezvoused in New Orleans, then flew to a small town in Yucatan, Mexico.

"There was another guy on the plane who looked like a professional photographer, with all his equipment," Shelton recalls. "I kidded Youngblood about his going to Cienfuegos' press conference."

When they got to Yucatan, Youngblood received several messages he said were from Cienfuegos. One included a crude map. They set out for the rendezvous.

On the way, Shelton thought they were being followed. He ordered the driver to turn suddenly and park. Sure enough, a car roared by, carrying the photographer Shelton had seen on the plane.

They returned to the hotel, and—the next day—Youngblood said Cienfuegos was canceling this meeting, too; it wouldn't be safe with someone following them.

Shelton decided to do a little detective work.

"When I was all through," he says, "I found out that the photographer worked for a TV station in Miami. Youngblood had told him to follow us and he'd get a good story."

Shelton laughs, not altogether comfortably.

"Youngblood was just using that guy as an excuse to abort the mission. Cienfuegos was dead. It was all a hoax. But it cost *Time* about $7,000, maybe more."

The *Los Angeles Times* spent almost twice that much money on a similar hoax in 1968, in the immediate aftermath of the assassination of Dr. Martin Luther King, Jr.

On that occasion, a shady character who identified himself only as "Bob" told a *Times* editor and reporter that he had information on James Earl Ray, then a fugitive in the case.

"Bob" knew just enough about Ray, the shooting and related matters to persuade the *Times* he might, indeed, be able to lead them to Ray.

Based on "Bob's" information—gleaned during several barroom sessions—the *Times* sent one reporter to Kansas City, another to a small town in Tennessee, two to Florida and two to Memphis.

All "Bob" asked for was a plane ticket out of town when the story broke. The *Times* compromised and gave him a bus ticket.

But when the day came for all the pieces to fit together—for the FBI, alerted by the *Times*, to swoop down on the house in which "Bob" had said the murder weapon was concealed—it all fell apart.

"He told us the gun was hidden in a downstairs furnace," says Nick Chriss, on of the *Times*' reporters who worked on the story. "When the FBI got to the place, there was no gun and no furnace. I don't even think there was a downstairs."

No one at the *Times* ever saw "Bob" again.

When hoaxes are perpetrated by drifters like those involved in the

James Earl Ray and Camilo Cienfuegos cases—or even potential mis-
chief-makers like those involved in the Atlanta monkey hoax—it may be
easy, with 20/20 hindsight, to wonder why the journalists involved were
so gullible.

But what if the hoaxer is an investigator for the district attorney's office?

In the summer of 1974, a newspaper in Odessa, Texas, published a page
one story about a high-speed chase and the subsequent arrest of a 25-year-
old suspect in a narcotics ring.

The story was accompanied by a photograph of Tom Barker, a district
attorney's investigator, staring grimly at a cellophane package said to contain cocaine valued at $87,800. A 9-mm. automatic pistol lay nearby. Both
had been confiscated from the suspect, Barker told the *Odessa American*.

But the "suspect" was actually an undercover narcotics officer working
for the district attorney. Authorities had feared his cover was about to be
blown, so they had devised the phony narcotics arrest to give their man
renewed credibility with his underworld contacts.

In an editorial following disclosure of the hoax, the *Odessa American*
criticized Barker and his cohorts for having "tampered with one of the
public's most important and most cherished rights—the right to know.

". . . the press must not be manipulated at the whim of an enthusiastic
investigator or anyone else. For how will the newspaper, or the public,
for that matter, ever know for sure what is true and what is not true?"

Hoaxes are perpetrated on newspapers more often than their readers
might suspect—or their editors might wish to admit:

- In 1972, the *Chicago Daily News* ran a gushing feature story about a
25-year-old investment wizard who had parlayed $30,000 into $1
million. Less than a month later, the *Daily News* had to admit that the
"wizard" had hoaxed them; almost everything in the story was phony.
- Jack Nelson, now Washington bureau chief for the *Los Angeles Times*,
recalls getting an exclusive interview with baseball great Stan Musial
"back when I was just a young sportswriter." Nelson's newspaper gave
the story prominent play. But Nelson learned the next day that he had
talked to an imposter, not to Musial.
- Newspapers and television stations all across the country carried stories
in the early 1950s about a 26,911-word directive from the U.S. Office of
Price Stabilization, regulating the price of cabbage. What gave the
story unique human interest was an enterprising journalist's research
comparing that lengthy proclamation with the Ten Commandments
(297 words), the Bill of Rights (463 words) and the Gettysburg Address (266 words).

Why, some television commentators wondered aloud, when such profound and transcendent truths as these could be expressed so concisely,
did bureaucrats require 26,911 words to regulate the price of cabbage?

"There was no such order," says Max Hall, who worked for the Office of Price Stabilization and subsequently made a study of "the great cabbage hoax."

But to this day, Hall isn't altogether certain how the hoax began.

- In 1975, an ex-convict who had served time with Jimmy Hoffa in the Lewisburg federal prison, collected almost $10,000 from CBS by promising information about the location of Hoffa's body. The ex-con, Clarence Medlin, had no such knowledge. He was arrested.

- The Santa Ana (California) *Register* published an emotional story in 1967 on a 20-year-old soldier who served a 13-month tour of duty in Vietnam, then reenlisted for another six months "to continue defending the cause of freedom" and because he "couldn't forsake" the many friends he had made at the front. While on his second tour, the *Register* said, the soldier was trapped in a land mine explosion; the blast blew off one of his legs and severely damaged the other. Or so he said. Two days later, one of his Marine buddies said the damage had actually occurred in an automobile accident on a freeway not too far from the newspaper office.

- In 1972, veteran *Newsweek* journalist Karl Fleming, then discussing the possibility of editing his own weekly newspaper for wealthy business-man Max Palevsky, was tricked into spending $30,000 of Palevsky's money for an interview with a man who claimed to be in contact with Seattle skyjacker D. B. Cooper.

  This, too, was all a hoax—one that Fleming had unwittingly initiated by placing a newspaper ad asking Cooper to tell his story to him "with-out jeopardizing your safety in any way."

There have, however, been occasions on which newspapermen de-liberately hoaxed their own editors and readers.

In 1924, Sanford Jarrell wrote several page one stories for the *New York Daily News* about a 15,000-ton luxury ship lying off Fire Island. Jarrell wrote vividly of the drinking and gambling and partying aboard, and assured his readers, "This boat is neither rumor nor fiction." He had, he wrote, "passed Thursday night aboard."

But Jarrell had been aboard nothing more buoyant than his own imagination. There was no such ship.

More recently, in the summer of 1972, the *San Francisco Examiner* published a series of articles by reporter Robert Patterson, written—the *Examiner* said—from inside the People's Republic of China.

Patterson wrote with great detail and even greater enthusiasm about what he saw in China.

But the rival *San Francisco Chronicle* received a tip that Patterson had never been to China (only to Hong Kong), and when *Examiner* executives learned that the Chronicle was about to publish this information, they demanded that Patterson provide proof of his visit.

He couldn't.

The *Examiner* repudiated his series and fired him.

There are scores of other newspaper hoaxes that newsmen enjoy recalling, but perhaps the granddaddy of them all occurred more than 200 years ago.

On April 15, 1747, one of London's leading newspapers printed a courtroom speech which it said had been delivered in New England by a woman who was being prosecuted for the fifth time for giving birth to an illegitimate child.

The newspaper identified the woman as Polly Baker, and said she had been whipped and fined after her first four convictions. This time, however, she had spoken eloquently in her own defense, the paper said; she had claimed she was merely obeying "the first and great command of nature, and of nature's God, 'increase and multiply.'

"I have hazarded the loss of the public esteem, and have frequently endured public disgrace and punishment," the newspaper quoted Miss Baker as saying during her trial, "and therefore ought, in my humble opinion, instead of a whipping, to have a statue erected to my memory."

So persuasive was Miss Baker, the newspaper said, that she was acquitted—and, the next day, one of the judges married her.

This story—and Miss Baker's 1,100-word speech—were reprinted in at least five London newspapers over the next several days. By month's end, three British magazines had also told the story. So had magazines in Edinburgh and Dublin.

In July, when copies of the English magazines reached America by ship, newspapers in Boston, New York, New Haven and Annapolis published the story.

But there was no Polly Baker, no trial for bearing bastards, no courtroom speech, no acquittal, no marriage to a judge. The entire story had been a hoax—a figment of one of colonial America's most fertile imaginations, a man who was, among many other things, a newspaper publisher himself.

The hoaxer?

Benjamin Franklin.

8 / Covering the Nixon-Ford Transition

In the immediate aftermath of former President Richard M. Nixon's resignation on August 8, 1974, much of the American press—blinded largely by its hostility toward Mr. Nixon—did a generally inadequate and sometimes irresponsible job of covering the Ford Administration.

An analysis of leading newspapers, news magazines and wire services —along with several White House press briefings and almost three dozen interviews—makes clear a number of significant deficiencies in press coverage and attitudes during the first 50 days of Mr. Ford's presidency. The most important of those include:

- In the month between Mr. Ford's accession and his pardon of Mr. Nixon, the press was too gentle and uncritical in its treatment of the new president, frequently imputing to him many virtues that, in the words of Peter Lisagor, the late White House correspondent for the *Chicago Daily News,* "he didn't possess, we knew he didn't possess and he didn't even claim to possess."
- Press reaction to the pardon of Mr. Nixon was, in most cases, harsh, subjective and speculative, at times giving the impression that the act was, above all, a personal affront to (and a betrayal of) the press itself.
- Given the critical nature of other domestic and foreign problems, the press was often much too preoccupied with Mr. Nixon's mental and emotional health and, to a lesser extent, his status as a former president. In some aspects of that preoccupation, the press ran the risk of allowing itself to be used by Nixon friends and relatives determined

to create considerable sympathy for the former president, seemingly to help condition public opinion to accept the pardon from Mr. Ford.

- The widespread use of stories from unnamed sources—a practice long accepted in Washington (and, of necessity, intensified during the Watergate period)—resulted in the publication of several highly speculative stories of dubious origin and credibility.

Although those deficiencies can be documented, that documentation should not be construed as an accusation that the press did nothing right in its early Ford/Nixon coverage. There were, in fact, several instances of sound newspaper coverage:

The *New York Times* published a story on President Ford's friendship with "several of Washington's most powerful lobbyists." The *Washington Post* published an analysis of voter attitudes, including reaction to the pardon, all across America. *Time* magazine published an insightful and well-balanced essay on Mr. Ford's pardon decision seen in terms of "The Theology of Forgiveness."

Moreover, most leading news organs decided to ignore the most lurid and unsubstantiated rumors about Mr. Nixon's emotional condition (that he had tried to commit suicide; that Secret Service men had pulled him, unconscious, from the Pacific) and about the pardon (that Mrs. Nixon and their daughter Julie Eisenhower had flown to Washington to personally persuade Mr. Ford to act).

But good journalism was the exception, not the rule, during the first 50 days of the Ford Administration.

President Ford's month-long honeymoon with the press was not unprecedented, of course. It is customary for an incoming president to enjoy a brief period of bliss with the press, Congress and the public alike.

In fact, a strong case could be made that Mr. Ford's honeymoon was neither as extravagant as John F. Kennedy's nor as intense as Lyndon B. Johnson's—nor as long as Mr. Nixon's when he was first elected in 1968.

But Mr. Ford took office in the midst of one of the worst peacetime economic slumps in American history—a time for hard questions.

Of greater significance, none of Mr. Ford's immediate predecessors moved into the White House in the wake of a pervasive scandal that should, of itself, have taught the press anew to be wary of accepting uncritically any political leader.

But extravagant praise of President Ford came forth nonetheless.

When Mr. Ford was nominated to be vice president, almost every major news publication reminded its readers that he was intensely partisan, and recalled Lyndon Johnson's observations that Mr. Ford had played football too often without a helmet . . . and couldn't chew gum and walk at the same time.

And yet, as soon as Mr. Ford became president, all that was forgotten amid the celebration of his all-American goodness.

There is, of course, a tradition of what Helen Thomas, White House correspondent for United Press International, calls "wiping the slate clean; not mentioning what a new president has done or said before, giving him a chance to grow in office."

Moreover, it is understandable that after the deviousness and hostility of the Nixon years, the press—especially in Washington—would welcome the comparative openness and genuine friendliness of the Ford White House.

However, much of the press lost sight of its role as public sentinel.

The *New York Times* published a resignation day editorial that called attention to the new president's "dreary blandness" and "stolid conservatism," and warned that he was "a predictable, fierce, but amiable . . . partisan . . . [who] has gained no reputation for vision, imagination, creativity or compassion."

But in ensuing days, the *New York Times* joined the Ford bandwagon, praising his "straightforwardness . . . and humility," his "deserved reputation for decency, integrity and honesty," his "receptivity to new ideas" and his "frank, open manner."

The *Washington Post* said:

"A man who deals in so open and honest a manner with the American people cannot fail to retain their support."

The *Los Angeles Times* spoke of Mr. Ford's "honesty, candor, devotion to duty, a plain sense of right and wrong," and praised his "ready assumption of the powers of the presidency and his apparent willingness, even eagerness, to use them"—neglecting to warn that it was precisely Mr. Nixon's "eagerness" to use the powers of the presidency that led to Watergate.

Newsweek said Mr. Ford's "square-cut, straight-shooting political style . . . swept like a cornfield breeze through the Byzantine corridors of the Nixon White House."

Time praised Mr. Ford's "loyalty, honesty, diligence, patience, a fear of the Lord . . . political and legislative acumen," and suggested, "The new president seems to be very much what he eats: unpretentious, hearty, open-minded."

Even muckraking columnist Jack Anderson lauded Mr. Ford as "basically decent, inherently honest, without guile"—a man "who still would like his friends to call him 'Jerry'."

Such editorial praise was but one manifestation of the press' initially uncritical view of President Ford.

Another was that came to be known as "the English muffin theory of history," to use the words of columnist George Will. In essence, that theory held that any president who toasted his own English muffins for breakfast must be a different—and better—breed of politician than we were accustomed to.

The press' eagerness to ennoble Mr. Ford's homey touches can be demonstrated by the widespread use of a photograph showing President Ford toasting his own English muffin three weeks after the new First Family had moved into the White House.

The *Denver Post, New York Daily News* and *Pittsburgh Post-Gazette* all ran the picture on page one. The *Los Angeles Times, Cleveland Plain-Dealer, Chicago Tribune, Washington Post* (two pictures) and *San Francisco Chronicle* (three pictures)—among many, many others—gave the pictures prominent display inside.

There was only one trouble with all this: President Ford had prepared his own breakfast in his Virginia home during his first few days as president but once in the White House, the servants took over.

Both the Associated Press and United Press International stories that accompanied the pictures made the point clear—and said that the pictures had been staged in response to requests from photographers.

But neither the wire-service caption-writers nor scores of newspaper editors across the country paid any attention to the stories. The AP caption, which contradicted the AP story, said, in part: "The Chief Executive, who has always fixed his own breakfast, has not changed the habit." Most newspapers used some variation of that caption.

Whatever the cause of the widespread misrepresentation, it was clearly born of the press' desire to present the president as friendly, homey old Jerry.

The most obvious explanation for this desire is that Mr. Ford pledged an open, honest Administration, and the White House press was willing—indeed eager—to take him at his word.

When he appointed a respected member of their own club—J. F. (Jerry) terHorst, Washington bureau chief of the *Detroit News*—as White House press secretary, he added immeasurably to his already sizable instant reservoir of goodwill and credibility.

Another explanation for the Ford honeymoon is that many regulars in the White House press corps, having accumulated vast amounts of overtime during the prolonged Watergate coverage, simply went on vacation almost as soon as Mr. Ford took office.

That left coverage of Mr. Ford, in some instances, to reporters relatively unfamiliar with either him or the presidency—and, hence, unlikely to make too many waves.

(At the *New York Times* bureau in Washington, for example, White House correspondent John Herbers, investigative reporter Seymour Hersch, reporter James Naughton [who covered the House impeachment hearings] and news editor Bill Kovach all went on vacation.)

More important, those reporters and editors who remained on the job were overworked and emotionally drained.

"We'd all been wound up like springs almost 24 hours a day for more than a year," Kovach says. "We'd been up, night after night, editing all those Watergate transcripts. Now it was over. We couldn't get up to challenge Ford right away. You need enthusiasm to dig, and we just didn't have it. I'm only starting to get my enthusiasm back now."

But it was more relief than relaxation that accounted for the press' generally gentle treatment of Mr. Ford during his first month in office.

When you ask White House correspondents about their feelings after Mr. Nixon resigned, nearly all will insist that their feelings merely reflected what one calls "the great national sigh of relief."

But the point has been made before that the Washington press corps— and, in particular, the White House press corps—is the most insular and parochial of institutions. The reporters reflect nothing so much as themselves.

Not that there wasn't a general sense of relief that—in President Ford's own words—"Our long national nightmare is over." But the press helped create and reinforce that mood, and it was not just relief in the White House press room; it was euphoria—the word used over and over again by Washington reporters and editors.

Mel Elfin, bureau chief for *Newsweek,* drew a colorful analogy:

"It was like walking down the streets of London after the blitz . . . I stood on my balcony and watched that chopper taking Nixon away after he resigned, and it was like I was coming out of Buchenwald. In that mood, even a 35-cent hamburger tastes like steak."

It is almost impossible to convey to anyone outside Washington just how deep and intense the press' bitterness toward Mr. Nixon runs—and how pervasively, albeit subconsciously, that bitterness colors some of their perceptions.

Several writers have compared Mr. Ford to Harry S Truman, another Midwesterner who came suddenly to the presidency. But Truman succeeded one of the most popular leaders in American history; Mr. Ford— in the words of Jim Deakin, White House correspondent for the *St. Louis Post-Dispatch*—"was the luckiest president of them all; he succeeded the worst president in our history, the worst act ever.

"The press was so high on Ford not because he was Ford, but because his predecessor was Richard Nixon."

Although most reporters deny it vigorously, there also seems to have been a subconscious desire on the part of the press to show the American people they were not Jeremiahs and Cassandras—the "nattering nabobs of negativism" Spiro T. Agnew had called them.

"Everyone in the White House press room was acutely aware of the widespread public hostility toward them," says William Broom, Washington bureau chief for the Ridder Newspapers. "When Ford came in, they overcompensated."

That was especially true at the *New York Times*, says one senior news-magazine editor: "Their coverage reflected what I call the remorse of victory."

In an attempt to justify their easy acceptance of President Ford, White House correspondents tend to make two basic points—(1) that there was really nothing of substance to cover during the first month anyway, and (2) that everything Mr. Ford did in those first weeks was "right."

But there was something of substance to cover—President Ford's plans for the economy. And Mr. Ford did make at least two very important moves early in his Administration—nominating Nelson A. Rockefeller as his vice president and announcing his support of amnesty for deserters and draft-evaders.

Those moves coincided with the views of most leading editorialists, so the praise for Mr. Ford mounted.

In fact, when Mr. Ford announced that he would not be naming his vice presidential nominee as soon as he had originally intended, most of the press lauded his judicious deliberation, and printed, without challenge, his explanation that the delay was due—in UPI's words—"to the press of more urgent demands on the president's time."

One illustration of the press' perspective during this early period came in its coverage of Mr. Ford's first press conference. He said flatly at that time there would be no wage and price controls.

But most of the press chose to emphasize instead his remarks on the possible prosecution (or pardon) of Mr. Nixon—and the difference in press conference style between Mr. Ford and his predecessor (*Newsweek*: ". . . no grand entrance, no pan-cake makeup, no studio-style backdrop . . . a meaningfully open door").

Both the *Los Angeles Times* and the *New York Times*, for example, led their front pages the next day with the pardon/prosecution story. Both also prominently displayed page-one stories on the mood and style of the press conference. The wage-price story, though also on page one, was almost lost in the shuffle.

The White House press corps' preoccupation with (1) itself and (2) Mr. Nixon—both preoccupations born of Watergate—led to an egregious indifference to the larger issue of the troubled national economy.

David S. Broder, political columnist of the *Washington Post*, laments that attitude:

"There's a tendency in the press to filter out more of the complexities than we should, and to personalize things—to take the easy way out and talk about people, rather than deal with the complexities of issues and institutions."

But it was not just laziness that led many reporters to be more concerned with style than substance—more concerned with Mr. Nixon than Mr. Ford. It was, primarily, their hostility toward Mr. Nixon—and, thus, the day Mr. Ford announced his pardon, the honeymoon was over.

"The forces of retribution in the White House press room are stronger than anywhere else in the nation," says one highly respected member of the White House press corps. "People here wanted that son-of-a-bitch Nixon to get his just deserts."

It was almost as if the press realized it had gone too far in praising Mr. Ford, and now—betrayed by him—felt used and abused.

Throughout the 1960s, many editors say, the press had been criticized for reporting racial and campus unrest. Then came Agnew and Watergate and Mr. Nixon—and more criticism.

When Mr. Nixon resigned, the press felt a sense of justification. They were grateful. And Mr. Ford was the beneficiary of that gratitude. But when he pardoned Mr. Nixon, he deprived the press of their ultimate public vindication. They felt shortchanged, and they took it out on him.

The abrupt change in attitude toward Mr. Ford manifested itself the next day in the nation's editorial pages.

The *New York Times* called the pardon "a profoundly unwise, divisive and unjust act," and said Mr. Ford had "affronted the Constitution and the American system of justice . . ."

The *Washington Post* called the pardon Mr. Ford's "Bay of Pigs . . . an early and monumental blunder, born of miscalculation, ingenuousness and a considerable degree of self-indulgent and unpresidential impulsiveness."

The *Chicago Tribune* said, "Mr. Ford's announcement has left a sour smell all too reminiscent of Mr. Nixon's handling of Watergate."

The *Los Angeles Times*, by comparison, seemed mild and restrained, calling Mr. Ford's act only "a serious mistake."

Columnists really sailed into Mr. Ford, though.

Rowland Evans and Robert Novak said, "Mr. Ford has bloodied his young presidency."

Mike Royko, writing in the *Chicago Daily News*, said Mr. Ford had "brought a new dignity, solemnity and historic perspective to the old business of putting in the fix."

Mary McGrory, writing in the *Washington Star News*, accused Mr. Ford of a "sneak attack . . . a Pearl Harbor . . . leaving legal, moral and political devastation in his wake."

Joseph Kraft, in a syndicated column, harped on a theme that would come to haunt Mr. Ford—that he was adopting the tactics of his predecessor, a tactic Kraft called "government by bombshell."

Suddenly, all the prose about how different Mr. Ford was from Mr. Nixon vanished; all the metaphors and analogies, post-pardon, were Nixonian.

Reaction to the pardon was, to quote David Broder again, "an emotional backlash to a self-induced high. The press was betrayed, not by the real Gerald Ford, but by the mythical super-president created by the press' own artifice . . ."

Joe McGinniss, author of *The Selling of the President, 1968*, warned, in a column published on the morning of the pardon:

"Shaken and somewhat guilty" over its role in Mr. Nixon's fall, the press felt "the need to demonstrate . . . that there really is no murder in our hearts . . . In our lust for decent leadership, we are creating an idol whom, history suggests, we will eventually feel compelled to destroy."

"Eventually" came that very day—and the press never really let Mr. Ford forget his "betrayal." All the old jokes about his intellectual inadequacies were resurrected—but with a cruel new twist: the president was not only stupid but clumsy. Ford himself made possible these charges, of course—by falling on ski slopes and stumbling down the steps of Air Force One and getting his legs tangled in his dogs' leashes—but the press seemed to seize on these misadventures with an almost vengeful glee. For more than a year after pardoning Mr. Nixon, Mr. Ford had to contend with editorial cartoonists and night club comics virtually competing among themselves to see who could make him look like the greatest bumbler. Jokes like "The only thing between Nelson Rockefeller and the presidency is a banana peel" began circulating; *Washington Post* columnist Nicholas von Hoffman took to referring to the president as "President Klutz," "Mr. Ten Thumbs," "Great Flub-Dub" and "Old Bungle-Foot"; the most successful new comedian on the most successful new TV show—Chevy Chase on NBC's "Saturday Night"—made a regular routine of doing Jerry Ford pratfalls. It is not unreasonable to suggest that the cumulative (albeit subliminal) impact of all this ultimately helped to defeat Mr. Ford at the polls in November 1976.

Would the cruel jokes have flown quite so freely had Mr. Ford not pardoned Mr. Nixon? Probably not, although Jim Squires, Washington bureau chief for the *Chicago Tribune*, argues that Mr. Ford was lampooned because his physical and verbal blunders coincided with "a series of political and policy blunders that leave no doubt they're all being pulled off by the same guy." Nevertheless, there is reasonable cause for doubt that the ridicule would have been as pervasive—and, often, as gratuitous—had Mr. Ford not pardoned Mr. Nixon when and how he did.

But should the pardon have come as such a surprise—such a "sneak attack"—to the press?

Before he became president, the press called frequent attention to Mr. Ford's unyielding partisanship and his personal friendship and ideological kinship with Mr. Nixon. After he became president, the press hailed his decency and compassion.

Before he became president, Mr. Ford had consistently defended Mr. Nixon on Watergate, dismissing the scandal as "Democratic partisan politics," calling the House Judiciary Committee impeachment resolution a travesty and insisting, as late as the end of July, "I can say from the bottom of my heart the president of the United States is innocent."

After he became president, Mr. Ford said he thought Mr. Nixon had already "suffered enough"—and he sought $850,000 in federal funds to ease Mr. Nixon's transition to private life.

Taken as a whole, might not all this have indicated that Mr. Nixon's pardon was inevitable? What else would one expect of a decent, compassionate, partisan friend who did not think Mr. Nixon was guilty anyway?

Many in the press said it was not the pardon itself but its "precipitate" timing that surprised them. But if Mr. Ford was determined to pardon Mr. Nixon, would not decency and compassion dictate doing it sooner rather than later?

The Douglas Case

And what of Jerry Ford, the loyal, partisan politician who, as House minority leader, had sought to impeach Supreme Court Justice William O. Douglas, almost solely in retaliation for the Senate's refusal to confirm Mr. Nixon's nominations of Judges G. Harold Carswell and Clement F. Haynsworth, Jr. to the Supreme Court? Certainly such a politician could not possibly be oblivious to the advantages to the Republican Party of getting the pardon out of the way well in advance of the 1976 presidential elections.

All this could be dismissed as 20/20 hindsight were it not that some in the press very early had seen the possibilities for a pardon—perhaps even before prosecution could begin.

John Herbers, writing in the *New York Times* the morning after Mr. Ford's first press conference, said Mr. Ford "was leaving open the option of granting Mr. Nixon protection from prosecution or granting him a pardon.

"His statements, clearly leaning toward leniency for his predecessor, followed those of other Republican leaders. Taken together, they seemed designed to bring about a climate of public opinion in which some step could be taken that would spare the former president prosecution or a prison term."

Several in the press criticized Mr. Ford for not having prepared and conditioned the public to accept his pardon. But if he had prepared the public—and the press—with hints and leaks, he could have been accused of Nixonian orchestration of the news and Machiavellian manipulation of the public sentiment.

A case can be made, in fact, that the public had, indeed, been prepared —as John Herbers' story pointed out.

That story, combined with Mr. Ford's own statements and similar statements by both Rockefeller and Senate Minority Leader Hugh Scott (R-Pa.) to the effect that Mr. Nixon had "suffered enough" should have provided the necessary public conditioning.

So should Mr. Ford's amnesty announcement before the Veterans of Foreign Wars in Chicago. Leniency toward deserters and draft-evaders could be viewed, politically, as a necessary prerequisite to leniency for Mr. Nixon.

Most of the press was not listening then, though. The amnesty announcement, for example—undisclosed beforehand, a complete surprise to everyone—could have been attacked as "government by bombshell" just as readily as the pardon announcement would be attacked three weeks later.

But the amnesty statement came when Mr. Ford was still enjoying a honeymoon with the press—and it was a position most of the nation's leading newspapers agreed with.

"He did it in front of the VFW, a potentially hostile audience; that took some guts," says Aldo Beckman, White House correspondent for the *Chicago Tribune*, echoing the feelings of most of his colleagues.

Press reaction to the pardon announcement was, however, considerably more hostile than VFW reaction to the amnesty announcement.

Press speculation immediately put the most sinister interpretations possible on the pardon. A secret "deal" between Mr. Ford and Mr. Nixon was mentioned. So was pressure from Mr. Nixon's family, friends and former aides. And hints of some new, undisclosed "bombshell" in the White House tapes. And Mr. Nixon's mental and physical health.

Mr. Ford himself penciled into his pardon announcement a statement that possible Watergate prosecutions "hang like a sword" over our former president's head and threaten his health . . ."

That was cited as proof by many that Mr. Ford must have received some late, personal, vital, alarming intelligence on Mr. Nixon's health.

That was a reasonable interpretation. But what was not reasonable was that hardly anyone in the press even considered an alternative explanation.

One who did is Carroll Kilpatrick, White House correspondent for the *Washington Post*, who said:

"I think he penciled the health thing in not because it was so important, but just the opposite—as an afterthought. After all, from everything we've been able to learn about the long meeting he had the night before the pardon with the attorney he'd sent to San Clemente to negotiate with Nixon, Nixon's health was one of the last things he asked about."

Don Gormley, managing editor of the *Chicago Daily News*, also tended to take Mr. Ford at face valuue on the pardon:

"I think he just decided it was the right, decent thing to do, so he plunged ahead and did it, without really thinking it through. Remember, no one ever accused Jerry Ford of being smart."

But Gormley and Kilpatrick were rare exceptions. Most members of the press angrily accused Mr. Ford of Nixonian deception.

Again, as with the initial glorification of the new president, regulars in the White House press corps insist they were merely reflecting the national mood.

There is, of course, some merit to that, judging from surveys and letters to the editor that followed the pardon:

- The Gallup Poll showed that Mr. Ford's favorable job rating had plunged from 71 percent to 50 percent; the Phillips-Sindlinger Survey showed a drop from 53 percent to 36 percent.
- A *Chicago Daily News* poll showed that 77.4 percent of the paper's readers opposed the pardon.
- In the first week after the pardon, letters to the editor of the *Los Angeles Times* ran 23 to 1 against the pardon; letters to the editor of *Newsweek* ran 25 to 1 against the pardon.

But, once more, press reaction was at least as bitter as that of the public-at-large, for it was the press ("the long-suffering White House press corps," in the words of the *Washington Post*) that had been forced to deal directly, on a daily basis, with Richard Nixon and his palace guard.

Although the press—even the White House press corps—is by no means monolithic, there is a certain herd instinct that often overtakes them in times of crisis, and their first move in this crisis was to make Jerry terHorst a hero.

TerHorst had resigned as White House press secretary over the pardon, and he was saluted in print by many of his former colleagues.

"One of the worst things about the whole Watergate affair," syndicated columnist Garry Wills wrote, "is that not a single White House official resigned in protest at what was going on."

Wrong.

Attorney General Elliott L. Richardson and Deputy Attorney General William D. Ruckelshaus had both resigned rather than fire special prosecutor Archibald Cox.

While many in the press were transferring their admiration from Mr. Ford to terHorst, they were also—more significantly—transferring their antipathy from Mr. Nixon to Mr. Ford . . . or, more accurately, to Mr. Ford as the only available (if unwilling) surrogate for the secluded former president.

Almost instantly, the press became preoccupied anew with Mr. Nixon. At the president's next press conference and, more noticeably, at the daily

White House press briefings, questions about Mr. Nixon dominated the proceedings:

- Had Mr. Nixon's advisers persuaded President Ford to issue the pardon?
- How great a role had Mr. Nixon's physical or emotional health played in the decision?
- Why should Mr. Nixon get $850,000 to work in San Clemente?
- Why was a government courier plane flying briefing papers to San Clemente on a regular basis?
- Would Mr. Ford seek Mr. Nixon's advice on foreign policy?

The then-forthcoming economic summit got short shrift from reporters at the briefings. So did uncharacteristically bellicose statements by Mr. Ford and Secretary of State Henry A. Kissinger on Arab oil prices.

At the September 16 press conference, questions often came with what *Time* accurately called "insulting directness."

Nicholas von Hoffman, the acerbic columnist for the *Washington Post*, took the press to task for such questions as:

"Do you find any conflicts of interest in the decision to grant a sweeping pardon to your lifelong friend and your financial benefactor . . ." (Von Hoffman: "Is that a question or an insult?")

There were 20 questions asked at that press conference. Only two dealt with the just-disclosed CIA participation in an attempt to "destabilize" the government of Chile. Only one dealt with the economy. But 14 dealt, directly or indirectly, with Mr. Nixon.

There is no doubt the Nixon pardon is a major story of surpassing public concern. But in those proportions? At that length? With that edge of bitter sarcasm?

At a subsequent White House press briefing, on September 25, there were more questions asked on the courier plane sent to San Clemente— as one had been sent to Johnson when he left office—than on all other subjects combined.

The very next day, when former presidential aide Charles W. Colson made a not altogether astonishing request for a pardon himself, the *Washington Post* made that the lead story in the next day's paper.

(Many other papers either ignored or buried the story. It ran on page eight in the *Los Angeles Times*, for example, and—surprisingly—not at all in the *New York Times*.)

In many instances, a case can be made that the press' obsession with Mr. Nixon and Watergate clouded both its news judgment and its editorial perspective.

But other, perhaps more damaging shortcomings—speculation and the widespread use of anonymous sources—were visible in much of the press during the Nixon/Ford transition period.

The *Washington Post*, proud of having set the pace on Watergate, was also the first to report that Mr. Ford would retain General Alexander M. Haig, Jr. as White House chief of staff—according to what the *Post* termed "authoritative sources."

The *Post*, of course, was wrong. General Haig has since been relieved of his White House duties and given instead the NATO command.

But the *Post* also was the first to identify Donald Rumsfeld as Haig's successor in a story attributed to "sources close to President Ford." This time, the *Post* was right.

Do the two "exclusives" cancel each other out? Do you take a "win some, lose some" attitude with such stories? Was the *Post* being used as a trial balloon on the first story? Should either—or both—stories have been labeled as such? Or, perhaps, not run at all?

In recent years journalism has become increasingly more investigative, more interpretive, more subjective. Insight and analysis have augmented a dry recounting of facts often already known.

But there has been a concomitant growth in reportorial speculation and in the use of unnamed sources—"blind sourcing" or "sourceless" or "un-sourced" stories, in the argot of the newsroom.

Such speculation reached its apex—nadir?—many months later, with the publication of *The Final Days*. Authors Bob Woodward and Carl Bernstein, whose indefatigable perseverance and meticulous attention to detail had helped crack Watergate initially, now asked their readers simply to have faith in them as they wove tales of Mr. Nixon's heavy drinking, the breakdown of his sexual relationship with Mrs. Nixon and his near-hysterical paralysis in those final days before resignation. The book was written in the compelling narrative, "non-fiction novel" style (to use Truman Capote's phrase), with nary a word of attribution. This technique was necessary, the authors wrote in their foreword, to gain "information we would never otherwise have been able to obtain."

But freed of conventional journalistic constraints, they speculated on the state of Mr. Nixon's mind, reported his nervous mannerisms and re-lated his conversations—all without a shred of first-hand knowledge.

A certain amount of "blind sourcing" has always been unavoidable—especially in Washington, where bureaucrats at virtually every level are reluctant to be quoted by name, for fear of losing face, status, access and employment. Anonymity—or, at least, freedom from identification with unpopular or unofficial views—is a prerequisite to continued survival in the Byzantine corridors of power.

Some newsmen—Edwin Guthman, national editor of the *Los Angeles Times*, for one—believe "blind sourcing" was actually more prevalent in the Kennedy years than the Nixon years.

Like others who hold that view, Guthman—former press secretary to then Attorney General Robert F. Kennedy—attributes that to the press' respect and affection for the Kennedys and their aides.

But that is a minority view. Most observers agree that "blind sourcing" was necessarily more prevalent in the Johnson and Nixon years because both men, especially Mr. Nixon, ran a closed shop—and woe unto the government official who leaked anything the president did not want leaked.

When Watergate broke, "blind sourcing"—already institutionalized by tradition—became enshrined by imperative. Without "blind sourcing," Watergate might never have been fully disclosed; it was often the only way to get the news.

But as one editor reluctantly admits:

"Because of the competitive scramble on Watergate, there was a tendency to use stories less solidly sourced than previously, even in the most cautious papers.

"When one paper (the *Washington Post*) is regularly whipping another's (the *New York Times*) ass, the loser starts to get pragmatic. They find a way to use stories they might previously have been damned edgy about."

Says Jack Nelson, now chief of the *Los Angeles Times* Washington bureau:

"Watergate had a tremendous impact on sourceless stories. Reporters are now more likely to write them, editors are more likely to accept them and sources are more likely to insist on them."

'Off the Record'

Simply put, reporters are now more willing to let sources go "on background" or "off the record," without challenge, and that is but one of several indications that the press has fallen into bad habits.

Speculation over the reasons for Mr. Nixon's pardon and terHorst's resignation—and over the state of Mr. Nixon's mental and emotional health—was often irresponsible.

Despite the White House press' loudly trumpeted respect for terHorst's candor, for example, there was an almost universal refusal to accept his word that he resigned solely because he could not accept, on principle, Mr. Ford's pardon decision.

TerHorst admits he was misled on the story by Administration officials, but he insists that played no role in his resignation. Hardly anyone in the press believed him.

Nor did most of the press accept Mr. Ford's explanation that he pardoned Mr. Nixon more to heal the nation's wounds than out of any concern for Mr. Nixon's personal well-being.

Fair enough. Although Mr. Ford said at his first press conference that he would ultimately consider a pardon, he also seemed to say he would let the judicial process run its course first.

There are those close to Mr. Ford who say that is not the impression he wished to convey, and that one major reason for his abrupt pardon announcement was that he did not want that misconception to linger any longer.

But the press—misled by the seeming ambiguity of those first press conference statements and habituated to presidential duplicity under Mr. Nixon—could be forgiven, even praised for its skepticism.

There is some feeling among the White House press corps, in fact, that in pardoning Mr. Nixon, President Ford—in the words of columnist Mary McGrory—"did us all a favor by slapping us all awake . . . everybody is on patrol again, and that's where they ought to be."

It is one thing to be awake and questioning, though; it is another altogether to speculate wildly or to publish stories of dubious origin and credibility.

The single most controversial aspect of Mr. Ford's pardon decision was the extent to which Mr. Nixon's health was a factor in that decision.

The *New York Times* ran a page one story nine days after the pardon saying that Haig had been advised of the "alarming state" of Mr. Nixon's health, and had persuaded Mr. Ford to grant an immediate pardon.

The source for the story was identified only as "a longtime friend of Mr. Nixon" and "a former member of the presidential staff . . . in daily touch with affairs inside the Nixons' heavily guarded Casa Pacifica estate here [San Clemente]," thus giving the impression that the source had firsthand knowledge of Haig's role.

But when both Haig and Mr. Ford denied the story, the *New York Times* source said he remained convinced of its authenticity because it came from "very trustworthy sources"—a phrase that indicates his knowledge was second-hand, at best.

The *Los Angeles Times*, after publishing several stories casting doubt on the alarmist view of Mr. Nixon's health, published a story saying that Mr. Ford had pardoned Mr. Nixon "largely because of his concern about the former president's health, particularly his emotional condition."

The story suggested that anyone from Mr. Nixon's son-in-law, Edward Cox, to former Secretary of Defense Melvin R. Laird might have persuaded Mr. Ford to pardon Mr. Nixon.

But all sources for such suggestions were anonymous—"a longtime Ford associate," "one well-connected Republican," "a former political associate of Mr. Nixon," "a former White House staff member"—and the story itself was frankly speculative.

"The 60 column inches of copy," complained one *Times* reader, "clearly add up to a 'definitely maybe not'."

Meanwhile, speculation over Mr. Nixon's health continued to mount.

Many White House correspondents had felt for several months that Mr. Nixon was losing touch with reality, becoming mentally and emotionally unbalanced—to say the least.

But they did not feel they could say such things about a sitting president of the United States.

"There are some things one just doesn't say about a president," says Adam Clymer, who covered President Nixon for the *Baltimore Sun.*

"Once Nixon left the White House, we were freed from that constraint. It became a little more respectable to suggest that he'd gone bananas."

Concern with Mr. Nixon's physical health was, for the most part, justifiable, if only because it might have determined his availability to testify in various Watergate trials. But speculation over—and preoccupation with—his mental and emotional state seemed excessive.

Time magazine was perhaps the most blatant offender in this regard, linking Mr. Nixon's mental and physical health in a story quoting a Harvard psychoanalyst who had never treated Mr. Nixon, but who, nonetheless, was "willing to declare that Richard Nixon's phlebitis is psychosomatic."

The *Washington Post* published a story under the headline, "Nixon in Exile: Lonely, Depressed." It was typical of the stories many papers would carry, and it mentioned—in the second paragraph—"Secret Service men who out of his [Mr. Nixon's] hearing refer to him as 'the old man' and try to keep out of his way."

But White House staff members had often referred to Mr. Nixon as "the old man"—a not uncommon reference to one's boss—when he was at the peak of his presidential powers. Why should that affectionate and altogether normal term suddenly be made to seem a term of pity?

(And why should Mr. Nixon's walking, alone and unshaven, along the beach on a Sunday afternoon, be made to seem the aberration some newspapers, such as the *Post*, made it seem? Mr. Nixon had often walked the beach alone—and only a martinet, or an idiot, shaves for such an activity.)

The *Post* story also quoted "a friend" as saying Mr. Nixon was "terribly depressed."

Who wouldn't have been depressed in Mr. Nixon's position? He had just been stripped of his office, his prestige, his job and his honor. He was suffering withdrawal symptoms from what terHorst calls "the most powerful drug in the world—the presidency of the United States.

"They said Nixon looked like hell," terHorst said a few days ago. "Well, you should have seen me after I resigned. I looked like hell, too. And I felt like hell."

Bruce Herschensohn, a former Nixon aide, went on a television interview show shortly after Mr. Nixon's resignation, and—in response to a question—said he understood Mr. Nixon to be in "good spirits."

Herschensohn says the interviewer's response was, "Is that realistic?"

Mr. Nixon—and his surrogates—"couldn't win either way," Herschensohn complained, with some justification.

Two days after the pardon, the Associated Press was told that a member of the Nixon family wanted to make a statement on the former president's condition, without being publicly identified.

Mike Sniffen, a reporter/editor—since promoted to assistant news editor—in AP's Washington bureau, wrote the story, without identifying the family member by name, sex or relationship.

Sniffen's story quoted the family member as saying Mr. Nixon was "in a deep depression" that was not lifted by the pardon. "Emotionally," the family member said, "he's still way down and that's what bothers me even more [than the phlebitis]."

Sniffen says he is "absolutely convinced" the person talking to him was who he claimed to be, but he refuses to say how he confirmed this. Nor will he now identify the family member, even though the Knight newspapers the next day identified him as Edward Cox. Cox did not deny (or confirm) the report.

Reaction to the AP story varied considerably among the nation's editors.

Neither the *Washington Post* nor the *Chicago Tribune* used the story because of doubts as to its credibility.

Other editors were skeptical of the story for different reasons. Taken together with similar comments by David Eisenhower and several friends of Mr. Nixon, they saw the telephone call as part of a concerted campaign to create a climate of sympathy and compassion that would still the mounting furor over the pardon—and enable Mr. Nixon to avoid testifying at the upcoming Watergate trials.

"You put the weight and credibility of your organization behind the story when you use it," says Murray Gart, chief of correspondents for *Time*. "It becomes more than 'A family member says . . .' To the average reader, it's 'AP says . . . .' "

Adds Bill Kovach of the *New York Times* Washington bureau:

"Using a blind story that's so obviously self-serving is something we don't like to do. We don't want to be used."

Nevertheless, the *New York Times* published the AP story—on page 28.

(The theory at the *New York Times* seems to be that if a story is buried deep enough and does not actually carry a *New York Times* byline, it did not really appear in the *New York Times*.)

Other newspapers played the AP story much more prominently—the *Los Angeles Times* being the prime example. The *Los Angeles Times* made the story its main banner headline on page one of its early morning street-sales edition.

"Nixon 'in Pain' " the headline screamed. And, in slightly smaller type: "Relative Tells of 'Deep Depression'."

Jim Melton, the news editor who made the decision to play the story so big, said he did so mindful of the nature of a street-sales edition—"You're looking for something new, and you're generally going more for reader interest than importance."

Melton said he had someone at the paper call AP to try to confirm the authenticity of the story, and he was assured it was authentic.

"You have to have a certain amount of trust in the AP," he says.

That's what Lou Bosardi, executive editor of AP, also says.

When told that some editors were reluctant to use the story, Bocardi snorted, "To suggest that we didn't check the story out thoroughly is silly; we wouldn't have put it on the wire without 100 percent confirmation."

Moreover, Bocardi said, "I don't see any substantive integrity problem with the story. I don't think the specific name identification of the family member would have added significantly to the story, just like I don't see a great deal of difference between saying, 'Pentagon sources say . . .' and General William Glutz, Army chief of staff, says . . .'"

But most responsible journalists agree that relying on blind sources can lead to irresponsible speculation and to providing credibility for trial balloons and self-serving, vested interests. The practice can also tempt reporters to invent quotes, bend quotes and go looking for any source, no matter how far removed from the decision-making process, solely because the reporter knows he will say exactly what the reporter wants him to say.

That can be an especially dangerous temptation in the coverage of an administration—or an issue—the press has strong feelings, even hostilities, about.

9 / Film Critics

In 1975 the movie *Nashville* opened amid a crescendo of critical acclaim so deafening in its unanimity that it almost seemed to be heralding the coronation of a king or the canonization of a saint—if not, indeed, The Arrival Of The Messiah.

Judith Crist called the film a "brilliant and incomparable masterwork." The *New York Times* said it was "the movie sensation that all other American movies this year will be measured against." The *Los Angeles Times* likened the movie to James Joyce's *Ulysses*. So did Pauline Kael— who was so transported by *Nashville* that she proclaimed it, five months *before* it was released, as "a radical, evolutionary leap . . . the funniest epic vision of America ever to reach the screen."

Newsweek lavished upon *Nashville* a front cover, five pages of stories and pictures and more superlatives than you could shake a thesaurus at: "immensely moving . . . exhilarating . . . so wide-ranging and prismatic that one viewing is inadequate . . . powerful . . . epic . . . eloquent . . . smashing . . . extraordinary . . ."

But *Nashville* was not merely a cinematic masterpiece, the critics thundered; it would also be a commercial bonanza: "a work of art that promises to be hugely popular" (*Newsweek*); "this picture is going to take off into the stratosphere" (Kael).

Paramount Pictures, the distributors of *Nashville*, could not have been more pleased. Kael's review was reprinted, word-for-word, in newspaper and magazine ads and on flyers and billboards and posters and placards —in everything but skywriting and fortune cookies.

Paramount calculatingly opened the movie at two prestigious but very small theaters (combined seating capacity: 703) on New York's Third Avenue, the traditional launching pad for many a smash film.

"Our plan was simple," says Barry Diller, chairman of the Paramount board of directors. "We wanted to create a riot on Third Avenue—to open in two theaters that couldn't possibly accommodate all the people who would come rushing to see the movie after all those incredible reviews."

The turnaway crowds would, of course, further accelerate the sense of excitement the critics had already generated about *Nashville*, and as the movie opened in other cities, word would spread: Everyone would just *have* to see it. *Nashville* would become the all-time box-office champion.

Diller shrugs:

"It didn't happen."

Not that *Nashville* was a flop; the film has earned more than $8 million in domestic rentals on an investment of about $1.5 million—a profit that even the ghosts of Howard Hughes and J. Paul Getty would look kindly on.

But given its breathless critical reception, that is merely a drop in the box-office bucket—a tiny fraction of what Paramount and virtually everyone else involved with the movie had expected.

For all its ballyhooed brilliance, *Nashville* does not even appear on the list of the 200 biggest money-making movies of all time; in 1975 alone, 26 movies earned more money than *Nashville*—and four of the 26 were on the *New York Times'* list of the year's 10 *worst* movies (one of the "worst": *Jaws*, already the biggest money-maker in Hollywood history with more than $100 million in domestic film rentals).

Does all this mean that film critics have no more influence on moviegoers than, say, Raquel Welch had on the formulation of the Vatican Declaration on Sexual Ethics? Not necessarily. But in more than 50 interviews with motion picture executives, exhibitors, distributors, producers and critics, *Nashville* was cited again and again as the classic example of the dictum that critics can neither make nor break a movie—that all the critics' horses and all the critics' men cannot override word-of-mouth among the general movie-going public.

"Word-of-mouth." The "smell" of a movie. The "nose" of the audience. A "telepathic underground." Everyone in the industry has his own favorite phrase to describe the phenomenon, but all agree it is both omnipresent and incontrovertible.

"No one knows," says producer Stanley Kramer, "why two similar movies, with similar casts and similar advertising, can open side-by-side in Westwood, and from the first day, one will have long lines and the other will die.

"It's something that happens almost from the first minute the camera rolls. Somehow, the public gets a feeling very early about whether they want to see a certain picture or not, regardless of what the critics or the ads ultimately say about it."

But what about big-budget movies that open with massive advertising campaigns and much attendant publicity, only to receive uniformly hostile reviews and then perform disappointingly at the box office? Isn't there a cause-and-effect relationship between the critics' revilement of movies like *Gable and Lombard, Lucky Lady* and *At Long Last Love* and the public's subsequent reluctance to see them?

"Absolutely not," says Sherill Corwin, chairman of the board of the Metropolitan Theater chain and former president of the National Association of Theater Owners. "The paying customers find out those films stink at the same time the critics do and they pass the word."

Nor are captious critics likely to dissuade many people from seeing movies with such presold qualities as a well-known title (*The Exorcist*) or star (Robert Redford) or character (Billy Jack) or studio imprimatur (Disney) or gimmick (*Earthquake*) or subject matter (sex).

It is certainly no coincidence that of the 14 most successful movies of all time, seven were made from best-selling books, another was made from a hit Broadway play, another was based on a story that was a large cult favorite as a book and again as a play, another featured a burning skyscraper and two others starred both Robert Redford and Paul Newman.

"Almost all of them got terrible reviews," says Dan Polier, formerly the head film-buyer for the National General theater chain. "I remember when we opened *Sound of Music* in San Francisco, and the headline on one nasty review called it *The Sound of Mucous*."

He smiles the smile of the vindicated.

"Before long, we turned it into *The Sound of Money*."

The Sound of Music is now the fourth-biggest money-maker in motion picture history.

"If you think people who want to see films like these are going to change their minds because the critics pan the movies, you're crazy," Polier says. "The only question the audience has with those films is, 'How early do we have to get there to stand in line?' "

When one of these films becomes hugely successful, its success is self-perpetuating; it generates its own momentum. Many people who were not originally interested in *Jaws, The Godfather* or *Love Story*, for example, ultimately saw them simply to find out what all the excitement was about; it probably didn't make the slightest bit of difference that the critics loved *Godfather*, hated *Love Story* and were divided on *Jaws*.

Sequels to these films also seem virtually immune to critical venom, as do most action/exploitation films of the variety that feature Clint Eastwood, Charles Bronson or a gang of motorcyclists (or rapists) whose primary appeal is more to the drive-in crowd than to intellectuals.

Critics are, however, generally conceded to have considerable influence on the success of foreign and other specialized films—films with no known stars, small advertising budgets and, perhaps, a difficult and demanding style or subject matter.

"For those films," says Charles Champlin, entertainment editor of the *Los Angeles Times*, "the critic almost has to take the reader by the hand and tell him the movie is really worth the extra effort."

Without the critic to at least bring these movies to the attention of the moviegoing public, they just die. Examples abound, but *Alice Doesn't Live Here Anymore* is one of the best.

"It was a damn good movie, but how was anyone to know that unless the critics told them so?" asks Leo Greenfield, senior vice president in charge of worldwide film distribution for MGM. "There was no compelling reason to run down and see *Alice*. It didn't have any well-known stars or a big buildup. Hell, no one even knew it was around at first.

"But two days after it opened, I started hearing people say, 'Gee, I hear *Alice* is a great movie.' Where'd they hear it? It was only playing one small theater, and it wasn't even doing any business there yet, so their friends couldn't have seen it.

"I know where they heard about it. Chuck Champlin gave it a good review in the *Los Angeles Times*, and John Barbour raved about it on Channel 4. That's what got the movie started . . . Now it's earned more than $7 million."

With a movie like *Alice*, critics actually become an almost inseparable element in the entire word-of-mouth syndrome—a role that is uniquely crucial to the success of a film made abroad and shown in the United States with English subtitles.

Most foreign films have a narrow, limited audience—but an audience that is invariably well-educated, sophisticated and discriminating. Movie reviews tend to be read most avidly—and heeded most frequently—by precisely this kind of moviegoer, rather than by the common folks who, with other products, are generally more susceptible than the intellectuals to endorsements and testimonials, whether it's a newspaper telling them how to vote or a star athlete telling them what to eat.

"The lowbrow doesn't even read reviews," says John Simon, film critic for *New York* magazine. "The only way the critics can influence him is if he sees a quote from them in the ads: 'Best Movie I Ever Saw—Rex Reed.' Even then, it will only have influence if he doesn't happen to look at the paper the next day and see another ad for a different movie: 'Best Movie I Ever Saw—Rex Reed.' "

But the discriminating filmgoer may read several reviews and synthesize them for himself before deciding whether to see the latest offering by Claude Chabrol or Lina Wertmuller.

This is especially true in New York.

Max Laemmle, for example, owns ten Los Angeles theaters that show most of the city's foreign fare, and he routinely turns down offers by distributors to give those movies their American premiere.

"We don't have a built-in audience for foreign films in Los Angeles," he says. "No city but New York really does. Until the film opens in New York and gets reviewed in the *New York Times* and *Time* and *Newsweek* and the other magazines, hardly anyone out here knows about it."

Thus, the New York critics influence not only New York moviegoers but, indirectly, moviegoers elsewhere simply by creating a climate in which theater owners feel safe in playing a given movie.

This influence need not even be immediate; it can be cumulative: The critics praised Swedish director Ingmar Bergman for years, perhaps enticing a few more exhibitors to show his work—and a few more customers to see it—with each ensuing film. Finally, with *Scenes From a Marriage*, he had a big commercial success.

The influence of the New York critics is even more pervasive than that, though, for their impact is felt—at least subconsciously—by critics in other cities. If several prestigious New York critics all like (or dislike) a particular film, critics elsewhere may be inclined to accept and parrot their judgment.

The critic may, however, have his greatest impact on motion picture executives themselves:

If a movie opens and does poorly at the box office, the distributor may quickly close it—or, at least, stop promoting and advertising it. "Our tendency," says one studio official, "is not to throw good money after bad; we like to bury a loser in the vault in a hurry, forget about it and go on to the next one."

But good reviews from a respected critic or two may help convince the studio (or the distributor) to spend a bit more money to promote the film.

When *Last Tango in Paris* was ready for distribution in 1973, for example, there was some concern at United Artists about releasing it in the United States. *Tango* was an X-rated movie, with subtitles, a combination more likely to attract censors and lawsuits than mass audiences.

But Pauline Kael—in the words of one distributor—"had a double-orgasm over the movie" in her *New Yorker* review. She likened its opening to the first performance of Stravinsky's "The Rite of Spring" and said it would be a "movie breakthrough . . . the most powerfully erotic movie ever made."

Art Murphy, film critic for the movie trade paper *Daily Variety*, says Kael's review "legitimized the movie. Without her review, it might have been viewed as just a dirty movie with Marlon Brando, and we all feel a little guilty about seeing those kind of movies.

"She gave us our final absolution—a horny picture with artistic value, something for both the artsy-intellectual crowd and the people just looking for cheap thrills."

United Artists reproduced Kael's entire review in a two-page *New York Times* ad and in other newspapers around the country; *Time* and *Newsweek* both did cover stories on the film; what had been a dubious venture became, almost overnight, a $16-million hit—the most successful foreign-language film ever to play in the United States.

Nor is this kind of influence limited to foreign films.

Jack Lemmon says his good reviews in *Save the Tiger* helped persuade the distributors to push the film more vigorously than they had originally planned for what was essentially a small, difficult film. Similarly, Warren Beatty was able to use rave reviews from Kael and Judith Crist to virtually bludgeon Warner Brothers into wholeheartedly backing *Bonnie and Clyde* after they had all but dismissed it as just another gangster movie.

The same was true with Stanley Kramer's *It's A Mad, Mad, Mad, Mad World* and with Gordon Parks' *Leadbelly*.

But for every *Bonnie and Clyde* and *Mad, Mad World*—two of perhaps 50 pictures ever to earn more than $20 million each—there are dozens of movies like *Pretty Poison* and *11 Harrowhouse*.

Twentieth Century Fox was not much impressed with *11 Harrowhouse* when it was released in 1974, and neither, apparently, were the critics or the audiences. Then Richard Shickel wrote a rave review for *Time*. The producer took the review to the studio and convinced them his film deserved more support.

"It was like throwing money down a rathole" says one Fox executive. "The movie did nothin' the first time, and it did less than nothin' the second time."

Pretty Poison, also a Fox picture, was an even more frustrating case.

The studio did not think *Poison* was anything special, so it was opened citywide and drew so-so business. But the critics said it was a brilliant little film and chastized the studio for throwing it away in neighborhood theaters and drive-ins when, they insisted, it should have opened in exclusive, prestige engagements.

The studio followed the critics' advice, pulled the movie in, rereleased it "properly" and took out big ads apologizing for its initial error.

"The movie still didn't go anywhere," says Fox Vice President Jonas Rosenfield. "The public just didn't like it very much."

"Look," said Sheldon Ginzberg, who owns 30 theaters in a dozen different cities, "what it all boils down to is that all the critics can really do is give a certain kind of movie a chance. They can help people in the door the first week or two, but after that, the movie is on its own; it takes on its own life, its own identity; it finds—or doesn't find—its own audience.

"You can't make a movie with a limited audience appeal to a universal audience. *The Story of Adele H.* is never going to play to the same number of people as *Earthquake,* no matter what the critics—or the audiences, for that matter—say about it."

Adds an MGM executive:

"In a city like Charlotte, [N.C.] if a guy picks up *Time* and it has a sensational review on *Seven Beauties,* he's still going to flip to the next page and say, "Wonderful, we'll play bridge tonight."

There are any number of movies that fit this category—movies like *Hearts of the West* and *Fat City* and *The Magic Flute* and *Badlands*— much beloved by the critics, but utterly incapable of striking a responsive chord among the masses. Whatever the reason—subject, tone, cast, style —the movie lacks the chemistry that enables films like *Tango* and *Bonnie and Clyde* and *Alice Doesn't Live Here Anymore* to capitalize on the opportunities provided by the critics.

Some of these critics' favorites open with good business, then fall off as quickly as if an anchor were tied to them once word spreads among the general public. Other such films ultimately become cult films for the cognescenti. But most never even get started at the box office.

MORE magazine, in fact, analyzed the 1974 10-best lists of nine prominent critics and noted, almost in an aside, that not one of the lists had included even one of the year's 10 biggest money-makers. Does that mean the critics are too often out of touch with the mass audience?

Perhaps. But the critics and the audiences agreed on *Shampoo, Young Frankenstein, Dog Day Afternoon, Network, All the President's Men* and *Taxi Driver,* and even if these are rare exceptions, well, no one ever said artistic and commercial success are one and the same.

But what of the vast majority of movies that do not fall into either the small/art/foreign film category (in which the critics may have considerable influence) or the large/mass/exploitation movie category (in which the critics generally have negligible influence)? What impact, if any, can the critics have on the potential audience for all these other movies?

The answer, it would seem, is that for some films, some critics may have some influence on some moviegoers in some cities—some times.

Generally speaking, critics are far more likely to confirm and crystallize existing predispositions than to actually change anyone's mind; except in rare instances, few people who are determined to see (or to skip) a given movie are persuaded to do otherwise by what the critics say.

"I wanted to see *Missouri Breaks,* and I saw it, even though all the critics said it was a piece of crap," one studio executive says.

But the ambivalent moviegoer—the person who has no predetermined feelings about a particular movie or its cast or subject matter—may well be persuaded (or dissuaded) by the critics, especially if the critics are virtually unanimous in their judgment.

Sometimes, the studios find they cannot accurately convey to the moviegoing audience precisely what kind of movie they have—that

The Three Musketeers is really a funny movie or that *American Graffiti* is not just another teen-age movie of the *Beach Blanket Bingo* ilk.

In those instances, favorable reviews are enormously beneficial.

The same is true of what is known in the industry as "breakout" films —films that would seem to appeal to only one segment of the audience but which, with good reviews, can play successfully across a much broader spectrum.

A "black movie" like *Sounder* was such a film. So was a "Western" like *Blazing Saddles*. Or a "nostalgia film" like *That's Entertainment*. Or a "cops-and-robbers movie" like *French Connection*. Or a "rock movie" like *Tommy*. Or a "political movie" like *All the President's Men*.

All benefitted to some degree from laudatory reviews that made clear they were more than genre pictures. But the more successful the "breakout," the more difficult it is to determine precisely how great that benefit is.

Vincent Canby of the *New York Times* says that *The Godfather* probably would have earned $30 to $40 million—even if all the critics had hated it—simply because it starred Marlon Brando and was based on a best-selling book (and was both a good and a violent, crowd-pleasing movie).

But almost universal critical acclaim created a "breakout" for *Godfather*, luring in more than just the Brando-and-bloodshed fans and earning more than $85 million—second only to *Jaws* in motion picture history.

How much of the difference between $35 million and $85 million is attributable to the power of the critics—$10 million? $20 million? $30 million? No one knows for sure. But Canby, who thinks the power of the critics is often "vastly overrated," is convinced they made a significant contribution to the runaway success of *Godfather*.

"The critics" is, of course, a rather vague and amorphous term. So is "moviegoers." Which critics? Which moviegoers?

New York critics are not generally thought to have much direct influence, for example, on moviegoers in small towns, rural areas or even in most of the larger cities outside the two coasts.

Most movies are released in the big cities first, "and by the time they reach Waxahachie, Texas, or Hays, Kansas, whatever the national critics said has long since been forgotten," says MGM's Leo Greenfield.

Moreover, it is in the largest cities that movies encounter the most competition for the audience's leisure time. A potential customer in New York or Los Angeles may look at the reviews not only to decide which of perhaps two dozen movies he will go see, but also to decide if he will go to any movie at all—or whether he will go, instead, to a play, a concert, a baseball game, a museum, a beach party, a . . .

In the smaller cities, the potential audience is not only less sophisticated—and, hence, less influenced by the critics—but also less possessed of the luxury of choice that often makes critics valuable consumer guides; for these people, the choice is often between two movies and color television.

Nor are local critics in these cities especially influential. *Robin and Marian*, for example, did very well in Kansas City, but even though it received good reviews there, the ads in the local papers do not quote those reviews; *Time, Saturday Review* and three New York newspapers are quoted instead. (At just about the same time, *Taxi Driver* also received good reviews in Kansas City—but did poorly at the box office.)

There are a few cities in which individual critics have built a substantial personal following—Chicago and Washington, D.C., are the best examples outside New York—but even in those cities, the power of the critic is arguable.

For every movie the critics in those cities seemed to have helped succeed (or fail), there are even more that thrived despite their animosity or died despite their affection.

There is, however, no question that critics are more influential in New York than in any other single American city. New York is the media-conscious media capital of the United States, a city with a large, concentrated, sophisticated moviegoing audience—people who are exposed to as many as 15 or 20 newspaper, magazine, radio and television reviews of any given movie.

A favorable review by Vincent Canby in the *New York Times* can mean more to a movie than almost any other single review—in part because of Canby's own reputation for insight and evenhandedness, in part because of the prestige of his newspaper.

Critics like Judith Crist (*TV Guide, Saturday Review* and *Playgirl*), Rex Reed (the *New York Daily News-Chicago Tribune* Syndicate) and Jay Cocks (*Time*) all have far larger audiences than Canby, but none of the three is as widely respected as he.

Still, four stars—the top rating—from the *Daily News* can mean almost as much as a Canby rave; it is an easily identifiable symbol for theater ads in New York and elsewhere—the Good-Theater-Keeping Seal of Approval.

Because most movies, domestic as well as foreign, open in New York first, the New York critics—those who write for New York publications and those who write for national magazines based in New York—tend to be quoted more copiously in ads in other cities, thereby compounding their influence: First they provide the initial impetus (or impediment) for New York audiences; then, as advertising surrogates—assuming the distributors can find a favorable word or two in their reviews—they continue to provide momentum, in varying and lesser degrees, for audiences in other cities.

Knowing that, some studios will assiduously avoid opening certain kinds of movies in New York. They will open movies like *Ode to Billy Joe* in the South or in some other area where the critical and public reception is likely to be more favorable, rather than risk a hostile New York reception that could trigger a fatal, self-perpetuating cycle of failure.

There are two other major cities in which most movie people say critics can be rather influential with certain kinds of movies (and audiences)— San Francisco (because, like New York, it has a compact, sophisticated audience) and Los Angeles (because there is a great awareness of films here and a concomitant presumption that the critics, working in such close proximity to the industry, must have special insights on the merits or flaws of any given film).

But the reputation—and influence—of any one critic may vary considerably. Some critics are so busy trying to sell their own movie scripts to various studios that their critical objectivity can be seriously questioned. Others have become so friendly with certain directors that their reviews are as easy to predict as they are to ignore.

Pauline Kael, for example, has long been among the most respected critics in America. But her reputation now seems in at least temporary eclipse because she has become so ardent a champion of Robert Altman and a few other directors; she has, other critics say, lost her sense of perspective—and many moviegoers are presumed to be discounting her views accordingly.

Kael's unbridled enthusiasm for movies like *Nashville, Last Tango, Shampoo* and *Thieves Like Us* has become "hysterical and evangelical," complains one critic; she is drifting into "press agentry" says another.

The *Los Angeles Times*' Charles Champlin has been similarly castigated by his fellow critics. Champlin, says John Barbour of NBC and *Los Angeles* magazine, is "the Will Rogers of film criticism; he never met a film he didn't like."

John Simon of *New York* magazine is so appalled by Champlin's critical standards that he resigned in protest when Champlin, among others, was elected to the National Society of Film Critics.

Critics who praise too many movies too highly not only demean their art, other critics say, but they vastly diminish their influence on the moviegoing public.

They raise expectations that cannot possibly be fulfilled—and may actually backfire, says Stephen Farber of *New West* magazine. People read about how magnificent *Nashville* is supposed to be, and when they see it and it's good but not really all *that* good, they're disappointed; instead of encouraging their friends to see it, they warn them away. That movie suffers—and so does the critic's reputation; if he oversells his audience often enough, they'll begin to ignore him altogether.

But critics who consistently disparage movies may have their own credibility problem.

Through the first six months of 1976, for example, *Time* magazine reviewed 38 movies—and liked only 10 of them (26 percent). John Simon was even more difficult to please; of his 53 reviews, only five could reasonably be construed as favorable (9 percent). (Champlin liked 18 of the 31 movies he reviewed during the same period—58 percent—and even at that, he says he was more negative than usual.)

Distributors and exhibitors—whose obviously vested interest cannot be ignored—say the enthusiastic critics are considerably more influential than the naysayers.

"When a constructive critic writes about a movie, you can tell he loves movies in general and has some respect for the picture-making process," says exhibitor Sherill Corwin. "Most people who read reviews feel the same way. They listen to the critic when he likes a movie and then, when he really blasts one, they know it's gotta be bad.

"But these guys in the weekly magazines are so smug and patronizing and hostile and full of jokes at the movie's expense that I'm convinced most readers either read them for the fun of it and ignore their advice or do just the opposite of what the critics say they should do."

Says Jack Lemmon:

"Sometimes I get the feeling we're very lucky these guys are movie critics; otherwise, they might be snipers."

John Simon, in particular, is thought by most people in the industry (and by his fellow critics, as well) to be gratuitously cruel in his critical witticisms.

"He is," says Vincent Canby, "a fraud."

Movie critics who work for television are especially susceptible to the charge of pursuing self-aggrandizement through splenetic wisecracks.

"They're too busy trying to be sarcastic and cracking funny one-liners to give a movie a fair review," says Jules Landfield, division operations manager of the 400-theater American Multi-Cinema chain.

Thus, John Barbour will dismiss *Amarcord* as "*Our Town* with pizza" or *Lipstick* as "*Death Wish* in drag," and he'll say Paramount is considering charging $6 a ticket for *The Great Gatsby*—"$3 to get in and $3 to get out."

Canby says this is just "the nature of the medium; what can you say about *Barry Lyndon* in one or two minutes anyway? It's not criticism; it's entertainment."

In fact, Canby says, all critics—in print and on television—are "conned into a position where you almost have to love or hate something. Most people want a consumer's guide—yes or no, good or bad—not a thoughtful, measured analysis."

Judith Crist, who has reviewed movies for the "Today" show, as well as for several magazines and newspapers, says it's "far more difficult to provide shading and nuance on television than in print. If you give a mixed review on television, one-third of your viewers think you liked the movie, one-third think you hated it and one-third doesn't know what you said.

"You're almost reduced to just giving a thumbs-up or a thumbs-down."

Nevertheless, studies have shown—and print media critics grudgingly concede—that film critics on TV have the most influence. Gene Shalit of the "Today" show almost certainly influences more moviegoers than any other critic in the country today—in part because of the massive size of his audience, in part because of the intimacy of the medium, in part because he can show actual film clips from the movies, in part because of the personal following he has developed over the years and in part because he can provide viewers with a quick, simple, clever answer to the question "Should I go see this movie?"

Ironically, however, television is becoming a major influence on moviegoers at the same time the more intellectually oriented print critics are also gaining in influence.

There have always been a few superb film critics in this country—James Agee, Dwight MacDonald, Frank Nugent, Stanley Kauffman—but until the last 10 or 15 years, movies were not really taken very seriously at most daily newspapers (where film critics often wrote under puerile pseudonyms—Kate Cameron ["camera on"] in New York and Mae Tinee in Chicago, for example.)

But now college students are studying the cinema as a contemporary art form, and book-length collections of film criticism are rolling off the publishers' presses like so many Jacqueline Susann novels, and, in some quarters, film criticism has become an art (and an end) in itself.

"Movies are no longer the national habit," says Roger Ebert of the *Chicago Sun-Times*. "People go to see a specific film instead of just going to the pictures."

Thirty years ago, theaters sold almost 100 million movie tickets a week. Now, despite a population increase of almost 50 percent, movie attendance has dropped 75 percent—to less than 25 million tickets a week.

Free television and competition from other leisure-time activities have made the moviegoer more selective—and, on some films, the critic can aid in that selection. Studies have shown that many of the people who went (or would have gone) to movies 15 or 20 or 30 years ago now stay home and watch television. Those people who do go to movies regularly are better-educated than moviegoers of earlier decades—and better-educated than the habituees of television. (One recent study showed that 36 percent of the people with some college education attend movies frequently, as compared with 24 percent of the people with no college education and only 11 percent of the people who hadn't even completed high school.)

Moreover, although more than 70 percent of the nation's movie tickets are now being purchased by people under the age of 30, the fastest growing group of moviegoers is in the 25–39 age group—precisely the group most newspapers and magazines would like to capture. Thus, film critics are writing for a more enlightened—and, potentially, a more receptive—audience than ever before.

Still, no one knows just how much guidance these moviegoers actually accept, how much they either reject or ignore and how much filters, undifferentiated, into their decision-making process as what Paramount's Julian Schlossberg calls "just one of a dozen crazy elements in this crazy business."

Crazy business indeed.

It is difficult to measure the influence of the critics on the moviegoing public as it is to explain why a movie like, say, *Bye Bye Braverman*—a comedy about Jews in New York—should die at the box office in New York after just three weeks and then thrive in Kansas City for 22 weeks.

"No one can really say what makes any movie go in any particular town or at any particular time," says Ted Mann of the Mann Theaters. "We know that with a movie like *Love Story*, reviews don't mean a damn, and that with foreign films, they can mean life or death.

"But outside of that, about all we can say for sure is that any time a critic or anyone else says something good about your movie, it sure can't hurt, and anytime they say something bad, it sure can't help."

Two Critics

John Simon

Actor Jack Lemmon likes to tell the story of the New York City police captain who receives a note every week with the plea:

"Please stop me before it's too late."

The note, Lemmon says, is signed "John Simon."

Simon is the brutally acerbic film critic for *New York* magazine—a man so virulent in his hostility toward most films that another critic recently described him as a "Transylvanian vampire . . . his fangs dripping every week from fresh blood."

Simon's discomfiting forte is the venomous personal description of actors and actresses. A few samples:

". . . she looks like Mussolini in drag."

". . . [his] face looks like an armored car made, inexplicably, of meat."

". . . there may be uglier women in the world than . . ."

". . . a face, physique and personality that could deter a nympho-maniacal she-monkey."

". . . the thick lips of a heathen idol, the heavy legs and ankles of a Maillol nude and breasts like large but not quite solid gourds."

". . . [she] is fat and unattractive in every part of the face, body and limbs . . . When she climactically bares her sprawlingly tuberous left breast, the sight is almost enough to drive the heterosexual third of the audience screaming . . . into the camp of the majority."

". . . she is herself a perfect *menage a trois* in which lack of talent, lack of looks, lack of speaking voice cohabit blissfully. [The director] sensibly concentrates on her best feature, her legs, but he unfortunately can't wrap them around her face."

And what does Simon say to the widespread accusation that these are gratuitously cruel observations?

"No one," he says, "can possibly be as cruel to these people as history will be."

Judith Crist

Judith Crist—having reviewed movies for the NBC "Today" show, as well as for *TV Guide, Vogue, New York, Playgirl* and the *New York Herald Tribune*—may well be America's best-known film critic.

Crist is, she insists, "a populist critic," not an intellectual critic, and as such, she more often reflects the tastes of the mass moviegoing audience than do critics for the more highbrow journals.

Still, it is interesting to compare her list of the 10 greatest movies of all time with the list of the 10 biggest money-makers of all time.

The Crist list:

1. *City Lights*
2. *Rules of the Game*
3. *Citizen Kane*
4. *Grand Illusion*
5. *8½*
6. *La Guerre Est Fini*
7. *Tokyo Story*
8. *Cries and Whispers*
9. *War and Peace*
10. *The Maltese Falcon*

The money-makers:

1. *Jaws*
2. *The Godfather*
3. *The Exorcist*

4. *The Sound of Music*
5. *Gone With the Wind*
6. *The Sting*
7. *One Flew Over the Cuckoo's Nest*
8. *The Towering Inferno*
9. *Love Story*
10. *The Graduate*

10 / Sportswriters:
Look, Ma, No Decimal Point

Wherever sportswriters gather in New York, they tell the story about the time, many years ago, when Leonard Koppett was walking into the pressbox at Yankee Stadium, briefcase in hand.

Koppett's stories at the time were always heavily larded with statistics, and as he entered the pressbox, another veteran sportswriter, the late Jimmy Cannon, pointed to Koppett's briefcase, grinned mischievously and asked:

"Whatcha got inside, Lenny—decimal points?"

For too many years, a briefcase full of decimal points (and maybe a flowery adjective or two) seemed about all most sportswriters really needed to do their job.

"Meat and potatoes" sportswriting, it was called, and it consisted almost solely of scores and statistics—batting averages, shooting percentages, earned-run averages, running yardage, passing percentages . . .

But that was before television and the explosive growth of professional sports revolutionized sports journalism, before *Sports Illustrated* demonstrated anew that sportswriting and literacy were not necessarily incompatible, before the socio-political upheavals of the 1960s challenged and transformed sports—and the best sportswriting—as suddenly and dramatically as the rest of American society.

The times—and the nation's sports pages—they are a changin', and it is now no longer sufficient to write sports stories by the numbers . . . or by the cliches. The more sophisticated and literate reader of today's sports page wants to know more than *what* happened on the field. He

148

also wants to know *how* it happened and *why* (or why not), as well as what may have happened before (or after) the event, in the locker room, the courtroom, the boardroom and the bedroom.

Racism, drugs, sex, religion, gambling, exploitation, psychology, cheating, feminism, dress styles, violence, antitrust legislation—all these subjects, and many more, have been explored in detail on the sports pages in recent years.

Not that the revolution in sportswriting is by any means complete. Far from it. A careful reading of the nation's major newspapers shows most sports pages to be suffering from a kind of identity crisis these days, vacillating uncertainty between the old and the new.

There is, in fact, considerable resistance to the new school of sports journalism—from fans, from athletes and from longtime sportswriters themselves. These critics see the sports page forsaking its traditional role as an essentially escapist medium—a purveyor of information and entertainment—and becoming, instead, a forum for haughty cynicism and gratuitous sociology.

These criticisms are not without merit. Even the most *avant garde* sportswriters admit that in their zeal to eschew the old scores-and-statistics approach, they often have overreacted and provided a surfeit of offbeat, interpretive, sociological stories at the sacrifice of solid news and analysis of daily happenings in the sports world.

Nevertheless, the best sports sections are beginning to resolve the old versus new identity crisis, the better sports sections are at least aware of it, and it is clearly only a matter of time—and resources—before most of the others join the parade.

The most significant (and sometimes controversial) of these changes in newspaper sports pages include:

- Where once the athlete was romanticized, glamorized, even mythified, he now is analyzed, criticized, even condemned.
- Where once a sporting event was generally treated as seriously as a holy crusade, now sports are often dealt with lightly, humorously, even sarcastically or scornfully.
- Where once a sports personality story rarely included more than a superficial, sophomoric account of the athlete's heroic on-the-field exploits and, perhaps, a brief mention of his inevitably "lovely wife," now such stories try to probe the athlete's development as an individual, his relations with others (on and off the field) and his attitude toward a whole range of personal, political and psycho-social issues.
- Where once the sports pages contained some of the worst writing in the newspaper, now—on any given day—the best piece of pure writing in some very good newspapers might well be found on the sports pages.

- Where once baseball dominated the sports page, with scores, standings and statistics in season and trade rumors and hot-stove league gossip in the off-season, football and basketball now challenge for sports page supremacy, with tennis, golf and hockey being accorded increasing attention, along with such relatively obscure sports as rodeo, motor-cycling, martial arts, rock-climbing and river-rafting.
- Where once most sportswriters functioned as sycophantic "housemen" cheering on the local team in print, most sportswriters now have achieved a level of professional detachment, in print at least, and the rooter-as-writer is a dwindling breed.

But the biggest single change in sportswriting has been the coming of sociology to the sports page and the concomitant shift of the sports page away from its traditional image as the toy department of the daily news-paper—a sandbox peopled by the idiot children of journalism.

The transformation of the sports page has been more evolution than revolution, really, for there were a few good, serious sportswriters—precursors of the modern movement—as long ago as the 1930s.

Stanley Woodward, a legend even among contemporary sportswriters, assembled a brilliant staff at the *New York Herald Tribune* almost a half-century ago. His staff included men like Joe Palmer, Al Laney, Harry Cross, Cas Adams, Jesse Abramson, Rud Rennie, Don Stillman, Everett Morris, Kerr Petrie—and Red Smith, who is still, perhaps, the nation's most gifted sports stylist (and the winner of the 1975 Pulitzer Prize). But sports editors like Woodward, writers like Smith and staffs like the *Tribune's* were few and far between, and it wasn't really until the late 1940s and early 1950s that the first faint winds of change began to blow, even sporadically, across the nation's sports pages.

Although the *New York Post*—with sports columnists like Jimmy Cannon and, more importantly, Milton Gross and Leonard Schecter—pioneered the modern skepticism and irreverence towards sports, it was a young man in Philadelphia named Larry Merchant whom many credit with the more pervasive influence.

Cannon, Gross and Schecter, like Smith, were individual stylists whose influence was felt primarily by other individual stylists. Merchant's influence was more attitudinal than stylistic, and it ultimately affected entire sports page staffs.

Merchant, who was 26 when he became sports editor of the *Philadelphia Daily News* in 1957, began his new job determined to change the then-prevalent mode of sportswriting, as described by Schecter in *The Jocks*.

Sportswriters were, Schecter wrote, "so droolingly grateful for the opportunity to make their living as nonpaying fans at sporting events that they devoted much of their energy to stepping on no toes."

Their resultant prose, Schecter lamented, was "consistently bland and hero worshipful . . . pedestrian, cliche-ridden."

Merchant wanted sportswriters who were both writers and reporters —skilled, knowledgeable journalists who could give him the acerbic, trenchant, iconoclastic reportage he wanted in his sports section.

He began by hiring good men.

One, Jack McKinney, had been a music critic. Another, Joe McGinniss, would later become the author of a political best-seller (*The Selling of the President, 1968*).

But Merchant's most important acquisition was George Kiseda, a Pittsburgh sportswriter whose crusading columns against racism had forced the Army football team to forego playing Tulane in a segregated stadium in New Orleans.

That was in 1957, when sports pages were blissfully ignorant of racism, and the publisher of Kiseda's paper had ordered him to restrict his opinions to sports and forget about civil rights.

Exit Kiseda.

Kiseda quit several jobs over similar principles in those days—"he was more moralist than journalist," one friend says—and he became so disillusioned that in subsequent tours of duty with the *New York Times* and, now, the *Los Angeles Times*, he has contented himself with editing other writers' stories.

"I haven't written anything myself in four years except notes to the milkman," Kiseda says, with more than a trace of bitterness.

"I'm 47, and I just don't want to risk getting into those hassles again. Sports pages may have changed a lot, but not nearly enough for me. They've still got a long way to go."

Kiseda's self-exile from sportswriting is, Merchant says, "a terrible waste, even though I understand it. George was the best sportswriter in the country."

Many others agree, but then most of the men Merchant hired in Philadelphia were outstanding sportswriters—so much so that within two years after he took over, the two other Philadelphia newspapers also had changed sports editors and their styles of sports coverage.

Before long, news of what was happening in Philadelphia was heard elsewhere. Ultimately, several Philadelphia sportswriters—Merchant among them—moved to New York to spread the word.

"What we did may not sound all that radical now," Merchant says, "but back then, it was heresy. Instead of just reporting what happened, we criticized and analyzed and did personality pieces and asked questions that made athletes and coaches uncomfortable."

Sports, Merchant says, had been "a sanctuary from the real word." He thought it was time for reality to invade and illuminate that sanctuary.

Today, with pre-game and post-game interviews so much a part of routine sports coverage, it seems difficult to believe that less than 20 years ago, most sportswriters rarely talked to athletes at all. But that, indeed, was the case. Merchant, in fact, can still recall that when he researched a major controversy involving Joe DiMaggio, he couldn't find a single interview with DiMaggio in any of the New York newspapers.

"Sportswriters," Merchant says incredulously, "used to sit in the press-box, write their stories and go home. No interviews, no communication with the athletes, nothing."

There were, of course, exceptions—Dick Young of the *New York Daily News*, for example, covered the Dodgers so "ferociously" (to quote one of his admiring competitors) that manager Burt Shotton barred him from the clubhouse. But Young is a feisty, snarling fellow—as aggressive and independent as he is talented—and he would be an anachronism in any age. It was Merchant in Philadelphia, Gross and Schecter in New York and Stan Isaacs and Jack Mann on Long Island's *Newsday* who were promulgating the major changes in sports coverage.

It was during Merchant's five years as sports editor and four years as sports columnist in Philadelphia that most of the other forces that eventually changed sportswriting began to coalesce.

The first of these was the founding of *Sports Illustrated* in 1954.

When plans for *Sports Illustrated* were first being discussed, intellectuals inside the parent *Time-Life* organization scornfully referred to the proposed magazine as "Sweatsox" and "Jockstrap," and that attitude prevailed for the first six years it was published.

"We were," says senior writer Frank Deford, "ashamed of sweat, and we floundered, looking for an identity as a nonsports sports magazine."

"But we'd been created to fill a void," says Mark Kram, another *Sports Illustrated* writer. "We were supposed to do what the daily sports pages weren't doing."

Finally, in 1960, Andre Laguerre became managing editor of the magazine, and gave it both the tone and direction it retains to this day—a blend of sound reporting and imaginative writing on major spectator sports and offbeat leisure activities alike.

Thus, Kram has written a marvelously insightful profile of a ballet dancer, Deford has written a sensitive, lighthearted piece on a dead whale, and Dan Jenkins—author of the best-selling football novel *Semi-Tough*—has written ribald, flavorful accounts of pro football.

This blend of literacy and leisure is the continuing legacy of *Sports Illustrated*.

But television has had an even greater impact on contemporary sportswriting.

Just as a newspaper's front page can no longer merely report what a president said or how many people were killed in a fire, so a newspaper's sports page can no longer merely report the score and highlights of a football or baseball game.

The game—like the fire and the president's speech—is covered live and, later, summarized on television. The newspaper must probe deeper, look into the crannies and crevices of the event, critically examine its surroundings and its participants.

"We used to think a 2,000-word story and a page of pictures on a game was sensational," says Mel Durslag, sports columnist for the *Los Angeles Herald-Examiner* and other Hearst newspapers.

"That's nothing compared to what TV does, especially with instant replay. They slaughter us on pure news. Anyone who's really interested in a game can see the whole thing on TV and then watch the scores and highlights on the 11 o'clock news and hear them again on the radio in the morning."

Television's usurpation of the newspapers' traditional role has forced sportswriters (like other journalists) to take on a new role.

That has been both an opportunity and a challenge, for if it has freed the sportswriter from the mire of routine play-by-play coverage, it also has made his already-critical readers even more critical.

A reader of the front page may have his own opinions on politics, but he usually realizes he isn't quite as knowledgeable as the paper's Washington correspondent. But a sports fan, says Dick Young, "goes to to three games, and he thinks he knows more than all the sportswriters, players and coaches combined.

"He's a demanding reader," Young says, "and after watching the game on television himself, he's not going to take your word for anything just because you happen to write for some damned paper. TV just whets his appetite. Now he wants the real lowdown—and you better have it."

The runaway growth of television as a sports medium in the 1960s closely paralleled—and contributed largely to—the equally dramatic growth in professional sports themselves. Expansion has been the order of the decade. There are now 120 professional sports teams—four times the number in existence immediately after World War II.

Faced with so many more teams to cover (as many as 10 in some cities) and given no more space than they ever had, sports editors have had to reevaluate their priorities.

Many have opted to greatly reduce direct game coverage and emphasize instead the "softer" angles that television had already forced them to begin experimenting with.

At about the same time these changes were taking place, the social revolution of the 1960s also was under way.

Cassius Clay became Muhammad Ali—and a Black Muslim—and refused induction into the Army. Joe Namath boasted of having sex with girls the night before a big game. Other athletes protested, boycotted, insisted on wearing long hair, dressing more casually, having the right to determine the conditions of their employment.

Americans—sportswriters and non-sportswriters alike—had been accustomed to athletes in the Jack Armstrong mold. Clean-cut. Chaste. Patriotic. Modest. Obedient. Never mind that Babe Ruth was a drunken womanizer or that Bill Tilden "befriended" little boys. Such things just weren't mentioned in the see-no-evil, write-no-evil sports pages of generations gone by.

In the 1960s and 1970s, that all changed.

To Larry Merchant, Ali and Namath—and the early New York Mets —were "litmus tests" for the new school of sportswriting . . . and many sportswriters flunked the test.

They saw Namath as a profligate Pied Piper, leading innocent young men to moral ruin. They saw Ali first as an idle braggart and then as a traitor.

"They couldn't deal with either man on his own terms, as a representative of a new independence and self-awareness," Merchant says. Nor, he says, could they see the humor in either man—or in the Mets.

The Mets of the early and mid-1960s were "fun and games, not life and death," Merchant says. Rather than bemoan the Mets' inadequacies as a civic disgrace bordering on tragedy—as the older sportswriters in New York were wont to do—the new-breed sportswriters treated the Mets as an amusing diversion and "laughed sympathetically" with them.

If the new sportswriters—derisively dubbed "chipmunks" by one of their older brethren—were operating in a new arena, beset by new societal forces, they also were motivated by new stimuli.

Most newspapermen take up their profession because they are interested in writing or newspapers—or both. In time, they may develop an interest in politics or education or some other specialty, but they are essentially reporters, not political or education buffs. Sportswriters, however, have generally taken their jobs because they love sports.

As Glenn Dickey writes in *The Jock Empire*: "They remain convinced to the end of their working days that the best possible life is that of an athlete. It is too much too expect that you will get objective reporting from anybody with this set of mind."

Moreover, unlike other reporters, sportswriters are not generally—by instinct or by training—skeptical, questioning, probing. They have tended to shy away from asking the difficult question—and they have too often automatically believed, and written, whatever they were told.

Again, there have been exceptions. Many great newspapermen and novelists and writers for the stage and screen began their career as sportswriters—men like Ernest Hemingway, James Reston, Damon Runyon, Westbrook Pegler, Heywood Broun, Gay Talese, Jimmy Breslin, Paul Gallico, Ring Lardner and John Lardner.

Gallico, who wrote sports for 13 years (and has subsequently written, among other things, *The Poseidon Adventure*), wondered, when he wrote *Farewell to Sport* in 1938, why he and his colleagues never thought to ask so many important questions about sports and society.

The new-breed sportswriter—socially and politically aware, motivated more by his own curiosity and need to write than by a love of sports for sports' sake—is not so inhibited.

Many critics say the new school has gone too far. Their favorite example of this excess is the post-World Series interview in which New York Yankee pitcher Ralph Terry was interrupted by a congratulatory telephone call from his wife.

"Where's your wife?" a reporter asked.

"Feeding the baby," Terry replied.

"Breast or bottle?" asked the reporter.

Such questions appall Dick Young, a widely respected sportswriter whose basic approach is, nonetheless, old school. No intimacies or sociology for Young.

"I'm tired of this so-called in-depth crap where sportswriters ask a guy whether he wears jockey shorts or boxer shorts," Young snorts. "Too many of the young sportswriters forget they're reporters. They think they're university anthropologists or literary artists.

"They don't know enough about the game to tell the reader what's really going on out there. They forget the name of the game is still NEWSpaper."

Young's criticism is echoed by many, for sports is essentially a conservative establishment.

"The owners and the sportswriters reflect that conservatism, politically and in every other way," says Charles Maher of the *Los Angeles Times*. "Sports organizations are basically militaristic and authoritarian, and they cater to basically mid-America fans. That attitude rubs off on most sportswriters."

But some criticism of the new school of sportswriting is not simply the stubborn bleating of conservatives unwilling to change.

Jack Wilson, former sports editor of the *Philadelphia Bulletin*, and now editor of the *Bulletin*'s Sunday magazine, says, "Too many guys write out of the side of their mouth now.

"Sure, you have to kick a guy in the ass when he deserves it," Wilson says, "but you also have to pat a guy on the back when he deserves it, and too many of the newer sportswriters refuse to do that."

Jim Murray, whose *Los Angeles Times* sports column is syndicated in almost 180 newspapers, puts it more succinctly:

"Sportswriting used to be 80 percent 'Gee whiz!' Now it's 80 percent 'So what!' "

The single greatest criticism of the contemporary sports page is that the people who write and edit it are publishing so many offbeat stories, sociological studies and in-depth analyses that they no longer provide a satisfactory accounting of the day's major sports events.

The *Los Angeles Times* provides a good case in point, both because it is generally regarded as one of the most progressive of sports sections and because it has come under much criticism from readers, athletes and many of its own sportswriters for its innovations.

Jim Tuite, sports editor of the *New York Times*, once said the *Los Angeles Times* has the best sports section in the country. Many knowledgeable newspapermen agree—among them Larry Merchant.

"Most sports pages are dull, repetitious and predictable," Merchant says. "Not the *Los Angeles Times*. I've been to all the Super Bowl games, for example, and the one in L.A. in 1973 was the only time I've been able to pick up the local paper and read something I didn't already know."

Changes in the *Los Angeles Times* sports section—as in the rest of the newspaper—began in the early 1960s when Otis Chandler became publisher.

"Until then," says Mananging Editor Frank Haven, "we probably had the dullest sports section in the United States."

In 1961, the *Times* hired Jim Murray away from *Time-Life*, where he had written business, politics and entertainment as well as sports.

Murray's sports columns for the *Times* witty, critical, often only peripherally related to sports—set the tone for the new sports section. Other writers were added—younger writers, men with master's degrees and questioning minds and, generally, a sense of humor.

When William F. Thomas became editor of the *Times* in 1971, the shift in the sports section began to accelerate.

Thomas was determined to publish a sports section that responded to the challenges of television and a changing society, and he also wanted a sports section that would attract as many nonsports fans as possible.

Thus, the *Times* carried sports page stories on rodeo clowns, gun clubs, volleyball, playing in pain, the psychology of channel swimming, religion in sports and sports in prison.

The *Times* also published sports page interviews with such nonsports figures as novelist James Michener, theologian Norman Vincent Peale and television commentator Alistair Cooke. And every week, sports editorials and readers' letters fill two columns on page three of the sports section.

Clearly, the *Times* sports section has been patterned—in tone, in style and in content—after *Sports Illustrated*. No other sports section has gone as deep or as far afield as the *Times*. But not everyone is happy with these changes.

"The *Times* does a great job on the sociology and the features, but you stink covering the games—especially baseball and basketball," says one Philadelphia sportswriter.

"What the *Times* lacks now," says another sportswriter, "is a running commentary on the day's sports stories. You have Murray's one-liners and, a week or two later, an in-depth study. But the sports fan wants to know today what your guys think about yesterday's big game or big trade, and the *Times* no longer provides that."

Among the specific *Times* oversights and shortcomings mentioned most often by readers, athletes and sportswriters are:

- Not sending a sportswriter to cover the Muhammad Ali-Ken Norton fight in San Diego in 1973 or the NCAA swimming championships in nearby Long Beach or the UCLA-Maryland basketball game in Maryland or the USC basketball team in the Holiday Festival in New York—all in 1974.
- Not sending a sportswriter on the road regularly with the Los Angeles Lakers basketball team or the Kings hockey team (and covering the game by having a sportswriter in the office watch it on television).
- Being beaten by both *Newsday* and *Sports Illustrated* in covering the controversy surrounding Portland's Bill Walton, who played his college basketball in Los Angeles at UCLA.

"I just don't get enough sports NEWS in the *Times*," says Vic Kelley, director of sports information at UCLA since 1945.

Newspapers always used to publish what they called "second-day" stories on the Monday after a big Saturday game—comments from the coaches and players and an analysis of the game itself. Many of the more progressive sports sections, including the *Times*, rarely carry such stories anymore.

Bill Shirley, sports editor of the *Times*, says he does not have enough space or personnel (only 28 people, half the size of the *New York Times* sports staff) to cover games, provide analyses and do all the new, in-depth and offbeat stories he sees as the section's primary objective.

Critics say there should be a little less of the new and a little more of the old in progressive sports sections like the *Times*.

"Papers used to have too much beat stuff," says the *Times*' Mal Florence. "We had long game stories and then stories on every team every day. Some papers, like the *Herald-Examiner*, still do. That isn't necessary. But we don't have enough of it anymore. Neither do some of the other progressive sports sections."

Where are the other progressive sports sections?

By general consent, *Newsday*'s investigative sports reportage is second to none. *Newsday* has exposed a high school championship swimming team that used three students who enrolled with phony addresses. *Newsday* also investigated the death of a high school football player, the antitrust implications of new sports franchises and the use of drugs by athletes.

The *Boston Globe* is also in the forefront of the move toward more substantive and literate sports reportage, and the three Philadelphia newspapers, collectively, continue to command the respect of knowledgeable sportswriters everywhere.

The *Philadelphia Inquirer*, in fact, carries some of the best sports journalism in the country. It was an *Inquirer* sportswriter who first exposed the vastly inflated attendance figures announced by the World Football League, and it was another *Inquirer* sportswriter who wrote the most sensitive and incisive analysis of athletes who had adopted the Islamic religion.

(Like all sports pages, those in Philadelphia still surrender, on occasion, to the parochial fandom and starry-eyed excesses of earlier days. When the Philadephia Flyers won hockey's Stanley Cup in 1975, the *Daily News* headlined: "God Bless the Flyers"; the *Inquirer* headlined, on page one: "We've Got a Winner"; the *Bulletin* headlined, also on page one: "We're Number One!")

There are only a few other sports sections in the United States now actively moving toward the level of those already mentioned, among them the *Washington Post, New York Post, Chicago Tribune, Chicago Sun-Times, Miami Herald* and *New York Times*.

The *New York Times* has published several major sports projects—most notably examinations of gambling, college recruiting and the changing face of sports. But being a sportswriter on the *New York Times* is like being Raquel Welch's elbow, and as one sportswriter there put it:

"The higher-ups aren't overly concerned with our doing a great job. They just don't want us to do anything that would embarrass the paper."

The *New York Times* does have a few special problems—limited daily space for sports (one third less than the *Los Angeles Times*) and a tradition of covering such space-consuming events as dog and horse shows, yachting, sailing and British soccer. But those problems alone, it is generally agreed, wouldn't prevent the *New York Times* from publishing a much better sports section if its editors made such a commitment.

But with all the progress that has been made in sportswriting in the last 15 years, even the best sports sections clearly have a long way to go.

The sports page is now more sensitive than ever to the needs of blacks and women, for example, but there are still fewer than a half-dozen of each working full-time as newspaper sportswriters throughout the country, and coverage of blacks and, especially, of women suffers accordingly.

Similarly, today's sportswriters are considerably more skeptical and probing than their predecessors, but too many still have a tendency to avoid asking the tough questions, especially in Southern California, where the generally less frenetic lifestyle makes for a more casual attitude among all reporters. ("Walt Alston wouldn't last 20 years in New York, that's for damned sure," says one East Coast journalist.)

Three other areas of reform not yet complete:

- The quality of writing has improved so much that some sports books (most notably Roger Kahn's *The Boys of Summer*) are attracting respect from nonsports readers and critics. But too many sportswriters still rely on numbers and cliches.
- Most reputable sportswriters now avoid even the appearance of a conflict of interest by routinely refusing to accept gifts, free meals, free tickets and free transportation and lodging from sports entrepreneurs. But not all sportswriters are immune to such blandishments: Many Northern California sportswriters wear $295 digital quartz watches given to them for Christmas by the Oakland Raiders professional football team; some sports editors still accept free golf shoes at celebrity tournaments; some otherwise circumspect newspapers still promote their own sports events and suffer at least the appearance of a conflict of interest.

  (The *Los Angeles Times*, for example, sponsors a track meet, an auto race and an exhibition football game—with proceeds from all three going to charity. All three events are given far greater coverage in the *Times* than similar events the *Times* does not sponsor, and critics say the sponsorship of these events—however charitable and civic-minded the motive—puts the *Times* in a potential conflict-of-interest position should any controversy arise involving those events.)
- Many sports editors now rotate their writers, so that no one man covers a single team year after year. But most sports editors do not rotate the writers frequently enough to avoid an erosion of the writer's freshness and objectivity, most critics say. And no major newspaper has accepted the revolutionary concept of merging its sports and news staffs, so that a reporter might cover, say, the courts one day and a baseball game the next.

Some of the more progressive newspapers have, however, brought nonsports journalists into their sports departments. Dick Sandler, *Newsday's* sports editor, had been in straight news for several years. Jack Quigg, the *Los Angeles Times'* assistant sports editor, was an Associated Press news editor who had attended only three or four sports events in the previous 10 years—and hasn't been to one since joining the *Times* in 1972.

Men like Sandler and Quigg have brought a fresh approach and stricter newswriting standards to sportswriting—stripping sports copy of tired cliches and pushing sportswriters to cover new stories and to ask new questions.

Quigg, for example, often writes lengthy, detailed memos to *Times* sportswriters when he assigns a specific story.

Bob Oates, who covers pro football for the *Times*, praised one such memo for its "insight, detail and thoroughness." But many other sportswriters on the *Times* resent what they view as uninformed, preconceived and rigidly structured assignments.

Sportswriting today is in a state of flux, moving in one direction but still being tugged backward. Nevertheless, despite all the problems and uncertainties and shortcomings, the sports page today is markedly superior to its predecessors in almost every way, and it shows every sign of getting even better.

11 / Community Newspapers

Over the last 10 or 15 years, as the *Los Angeles Times* has expanded to include bureaus in seven American cities and 16 foreign countries, some local critics have asked, with increasing but generally good-natured sarcasm:

"So when is the *Times* going to open a bureau in Los Angeles?"

The implication, of course, is that as the *Times'* concerns have become more global—as the *Times* has become more a regional newsmagazine and less a traditional local newspaper—*Times* coverage of the more than 100 individual cities and communities in the Los Angeles-Orange County area has changed accordingly.

Times executives readily acknowledge that change.

Times readers in one small community, they say, are not especially interested in detailed news of another small community unless that news involves issues of area-wide significance. The *Times* now leaves most routine local reporting to community newspapers, and in the Los Angeles-Orange County area, these community newspapers have become what one publisher calls "a remarkable sociological phenomenon."

There are now 19 community dailies and more than 300 community weeklies in the area, and, increasingly, the reader's appetite for news of his community—for PTA news and high school football stories and coverage of civic clubs and municipal controversies and social affairs—is being satisfied by these local newspapers.

"The more a paper like the *Times* grows and prospers, the bigger the vacuum they leave, and the more a paper like ours can grow and succeed," says Jim Box, editor of the *South Bay Daily Breeze*, one of the most successful of the suburban dailies.

And yet, many suburban newspapers have severe problems of their own today—several of which have been exacerbated by the recession of the early-to-mid-1970s.

Between 1969 and 1976, seven suburban dailies in the Los Angeles-Orange County area either folded or were reduced to weekly publication. At least two other dailies are reported to be having acute financial difficulties, and almost all have effected major economy measures, ranging from the elimination of Saturday publication and Sunday magazine sections to the reduction of payroll through attrition, staff cutbacks, technology and tight controls on overtime.

Among the economic factors most seriously affecting suburban newspapers today are:

- The rapidly rising cost of newsprint, up 58 percent in one 37-month period. (Smaller newspapers, like other small businesses, are often less able than their larger competitors to absorb skyrocketing costs or to pass on those costs to their customers in the form of higher prices.)
- Advertising cutbacks by major retailers. (Broadway Department Stores, for example, have all but eliminated four major suburban daily newspapers from their advertising budget in one recent year.

    (Other department store and grocery store chains have made similar reductions, and as advertising rates continue to rise in both metropolitan and suburban newspapers, the suburban papers will be hurt more.

    ("In a recession," says Deane Funk, publisher of the *Santa Monica Evening Outlook*, "we're the first to get cut—especially with the proliferation of chain stores. The more outlets a chain has, the more saturation advertising they want. That means using the *Times*—or TV—more and community newspapers less.")
- A trend toward more advertising on radio and television by grocery and department store chains, whose ad revenue has long been the lifeblood of community newspapers. (These retailers were skeptical of television as an advertising medium until relatively recently, but Vons and Safeway officials estimate they now spend 25 percent to 30 percent of their advertising budget on the electronic media, almost triple the ratio of a few years ago. Some department store executives have made approximately the same change.)
- A loss of readership occasioned by a loss of advertising. (Studies have shown that community newspaper readers are almost as interested in reading ads as news—sometimes more interested. "Local ads and local news are really one and the same," says one suburban editor. Thus, when a suburban newspaper loses advertising, it sets off a dangerous chain reaction: lost advertising means fewer readers, which requires

lower advertising rates, which incurs further losses in readership and ad revenue, which . . .)

- A drift away from the two-newspaper household. (As newspapers raise their subscription rates to meet rising production costs, many families faced with their own rising costs—and with greater competition for their leisure time—are limiting their newspaper readership to the one paper that best serves most of their needs. That is more often a metropolitan newspaper than a suburban newspaper. Of the *Times'* more than one million subscribers, for example, 64 percent now read no other newspaper.)

Community newspapers face other problems as well these days, many of them having little or nothing to do with the current state of the economy:

- One public opinion survey taken for television shows that 65 percent of all Americans now receive most of their news from television. This poses a special threat to afternoon newspapers (which most suburban dailies are) because they must then compete with the evening news, as well as with dinner and family and social obligations, for the reader's time.
- Suburban readers are becoming more sophisticated, more demanding of their local newspapers. Faced with mounting costs and, in some cases, declining revenue, the suburban papers must, nonetheless, do a better and more thorough job of covering increasingly complex local issues.
- Many sociologists feel there is a growing sense of anonymity and alienation in our society that undermines the traditional sense of community most Americans once felt. ("It's awfully difficult to sell community news to people who aren't much interested in their community," says Tom Keevil, editor of the *Orange Coast Daily Pilot*.)

  The diminution of community identification is a special problem in sprawling, mobile Southern California.

  "I've lived in L.A. for 15 years," says one newspaperman, "and when I drive the freeways, I still don't know whether I'm in Garden Grove or Garden City or the City of Industry. How can I be interested in community news when I don't even know where my community starts or ends?"

Statistics make all too clear this blurring of community lines:

- Every day 82 percent of the people in the Los Angeles-Orange County area commute out of their immediate community to go to work.
- In the last five years, half the people in the area have moved at least once, and almost a third have moved more than once.
- In 1960, people living in single-family homes outnumbered apartment-dwellers by a slightly more than a 3 to 1 margin; today, the margin is

less than 2 to 1. Since apartment-dwellers tend to move more and participate less in their communities than do homeowners, that is a particularly ominous sign for community newspapers.

All this is not, however, to say the future is unrelievedly bleak for community and suburban newspapers. Several are immensely successful, and will continue to remain so. There are, in fact, many in publishing who think the prospects for the suburban press are brighter now than ever before.

Robert Weed, for example, publisher of the *Orange Coast Daily Pilot*, thinks contemporary alienation will ultimately lead to a rebirth of the communal spirit and a return to the traditional concept of community. Weed even thinks he is already seeing the first faint signs of this metamorphosis.

"A few years ago," he says, "if you asked anyone who lived in the L.A.-Orange County area where he lived, he'd usually say 'L.A.' Not now. If he lives in Newport, he'll say 'Newport' now. He'll even name the specific development in Newport—'East Bluffs' or 'Dover Shore.'

"I think that's a healthy sign for the suburban press."

Ed Dean, publisher of six weekly newspapers in the Torrance-Lawndale-Hawthorne area, agrees with Weed.

"I think we're going to see a new period of isolationism at home and abroad," Dean says. "Just as America is pulling back from foreign commitments, so individuals in America will pull back into their individual communities."

As this happens, many editors think, community newspapers will benefit from the skepticism and hostility many in the public have increasingly felt toward metropolitan newspapers and television networks for their coverage of civil rights, campus protests, crime, Watergate and other "bad news" over the past 10 or 15 years.

"In a polarized, 'us-and-them' society," says one editor, "I think people will see community newspapers as being on their side—the 'us' side."

There are also some editors who see television as helping, not hurting, the community newspaper.

"TV does the same job the big metropolitan papers do," says Bill Totten, managing editor of the *Huntington Park Daily Signal*. "They cover national and international news, and it's easier to get that on TV than in the paper. You just flick the switch.

"That'll hurt the big papers, not us. TV will never be able to cover purely local community news the way we can."

Like television, even a recession can be viewed as helping the suburban press in some ways.

Among other things, the economic squeeze accelerated long-overdue technological innovations for papers of all sizes—computer-set type, plastic engraving plates, lighter, narrower rolls of paper. These measures could help some newspapers reduce production costs by as much as 50 percent.

The recession also made shoppers more price-conscious, and most studies have shown that newspapers are far more effective than television or radio in selling goods by price.

"Television," says one major retailer, "is good for institutional commercials. You can sell your store name and you can sell convenience and service and variety. But it's damn hard to tick off a half-dozen prices in a TV ad and get anyone to remember them.

"As long as price is paramount, most of the retail advertising dollar is going to go into newspapers."

So who's right? Will television, the recession and the dissolution of the community weaken and undermine the suburban press? Or will television, the recession and a renaissance of the community reinvigorate and strengthen the suburban press?

The answer, at least in the Los Angeles-Orange County area, would appear to be that certain kinds of suburban newspapers will continue to do quite well, but that certain other kinds will almost certainly fail.

Small, independent, daily newspapers published in areas close to the central city, with little sense of community identity, will be in the most trouble.

That's one reason the *Hollywood Citizen-News* folded and the daily papers in Inglewood, Culver City, Monrovia and Alhambra are now weeklies. That's also one reason the circulation for the *Huntington Park Daily Signal* has dropped 20 percent in the last 15 years, and why the newspaper was recently sold by its longtime owners.

Some newspapers in cities with a strong, traditional sense of community also encounter problems if they're too close to the central city. Circulation of the *Pasadena Star-News*, for example, has dropped 10 percent in the last 15 years.

Even the *Santa Monica Evening Outlook*—long regarded as one of the better-quality suburban dailies, operating in an older city, rich in tradition and community identity—is not thriving as it once was.

After increasing its circulation by 50 percent, from 26,000 to 39,000, in the decade of the 1960s, *Outlook* circulation fell off after a mid-1973 increase in subscription rates, and it has never fully recovered.

"It's lucky we're a family-owned paper," publisher Deane Funk said in March, 1975. "We lost money here the last two months; if we had corporate offices back East, I might have been the first guy fired."

In many ways, the *Outlook* is an ideal example of the problems confronting one type of newspaper: its readers are generally among the better-educated, higher-income families—the same demographic pool from which a metropolitan newspaper like the *Times* usually draws.

Thus, 41 percent of all *Outlook* subscribers also take the *Times*—a higher duplication percentage than for almost any other suburban daily in the Los Angeles-Orange County area.

"Every time the *Times* raises subscription or advertising rates, a paper like the *Outlook* becomes more vulnerable," says one suburban editor. "If an advertiser or a reader decides he can't afford both papers, it's the smaller paper that loses out."

What most urban areas will ultimately have, says another suburban editor, is a "three-tier system of newspapers—a big metro, ringed in close by big chains of free weeklies and, much further out, by viable suburban dailies."

One exception to this might be the small, specialized community—the Leisure World or Marina del Rey, where small, independent weeklies prosper, run by owners/editors whose interest and concerns are essentially the same as those of their readers.

But the successful small newspaper is a dwindling breed.

"The day is long gone when a smaller community can support a daily newspaper," says Terry Donnelly, editor and publisher of the *Glendale News-Press*.

Newspapers that survive in suburbia will have to be "specialty publications," Donnelly says. "Our paper has one column of national and world news on page one, and the rest is local. It's the *Wall Street Journal* approach. Their specialty is business news; ours is local news."

Donnelly works for the Morris chain of newspapers, an organization that bought four dailies and nine weeklies from the Copley chain and folded two of the dailies and one of the weeklies within six months.

"Copley wanted to influence people," Donnelly says of his former boss, the late James Copley, an arch-conservative. "Morris wants to make money."

The trend toward chain ownership by people who "want to make money" is one means of survival in suburban journalism; in Southern California, chain ownership has almost become a way of life, especially for weekly newspapers.

In the mid-1960s, for example, the *Herald-American, Call-Enterprise*, Hicks-Deal and Rodgers & McDonald groups were all medium-size chains of weekly newspapers. Since then, Hicks-Deal bought the *Herald-American* group, merged it with the *Call-Enterprise* group and sold out to the Meredith Corporation, publishers of *Better Homes and Gardens*.

That merged group now publishes 24 newspapers with a combined circulation of 427,000 in southeast Los Angeles County and in the Hollywood-Wilshire area.

Rodgers & McDonald, meanwhile, sold some of their newspapers to the Copley chain (which also owns the *South Bay Daily Breeze* and other weeklies) and others to the Dean Newspapers (which now publishes seven weekly newspapers with a combined circulation of 184,000).

There are similar chains elsewhere in the Los Angeles Basin—among them the West Orange Publishing Company (five newspapers, 205,000 circulation, in West Orange County) and the Northeast Newspapers (eight papers, 100,000 circulation, in the Eagle Rock-Highland Park area).

"There has been a tendency around here," says Northeast Newspapers Publisher Oren Asa, "for the stronger neighbors to absorb the weaker ones."

This has also happened in the daily newspaper field, most notably in Orange County, where the *Times Mirror* Company now owns the *Orange Coast Daily Pilot*, the *Santa Ana Register* now owns the *Anaheim Bulletin*, the Scripps-Howard chain owns the *Fullerton News-Tribune* and Knight-Ridder owns West Orange Publishing Company which, until 1971, also included a daily paper.

This trend toward chain ownership—which, among other things, amortizes expenses and maximizes profits—has happened elsewhere in suburban America, too, of course, but the rapid, lucrative proliferation-cum-merger of weekly newspapers has been a publishing phenomenon unique to Southern California.

The weekly—alternately called a "shopper" or a "throwaway," and generally delivered twice weekly, on Sundays and Thursdays—is officially known as a "controlled-circulation newspaper" (i.e., the publisher guarantees his advertisers that he will deliver a specific number of newspapers each week, whether the readers pay for them or not).

Some weeklies that are delivered free today were delivered only to readers who paid for them in the 1920s, but during the Depression, many people canceled their subscriptions. Faced with shrinking circulation—and with advertisers unwilling to pay for such limited exposure—several newspapers experimented with free or voluntary-pay delivery, thereby guaranteeing advertisers more exposure.

That practice became truly widespread here during the post-World War II population boom, when new communities sprang up faster than existing newspapers could expand to serve them. Small, strictly local papers were created to help give new residents a feeling of belonging, a sense of community, in the strange, new land.

Retail outlets—especially grocery stores—opened almost as quickly as the new areas were settled, and they encouraged the founding of community newspapers to carry their advertising message in their immediate neighborhood.

In the 1960s and 1970s, as retail commerce became decentralized—as small "downtown" shopping areas increasingly gave way to regional shopping centers—suburban newspapers continued to grow, fed by a massive urban population exodus.

In the period from 1962 to 1975, suburban population increased 41 percent nationally; central city population grew only 2 percent. In the Los Angeles-Orange County area—almost 5,000 square miles, populated by almost 10 million people—there are now more than a dozen suburban areas that, individually, would be major metropolitan areas elsewhere.

The San Fernando Valley is more populous than Baltimore, the Santa Monica Bay area is more populous than Cincinnati, the Pomona-Foothills area is more populous than Washington, D.C.

"There's no media market like Los Angeles anywhere in the country," says Cal Gunnell, advertising manager for Safeway. "I've worked in Seattle, Denver, San Francisco and Dallas, and they can't begin to compare with the spread and diversity you have in the media here."

In most large cities, the major metropolitan newspapers are virtually unchallenged in the areas they circulate. In Chicago, for example, the three major dailies, combined, reach 78 percent of the homes. In Detroit, the figure is the same. In Houston, it's 71 percent.

But in the Los Angeles-Orange County area—admittedly a much larger metropolitan area—the *Times* and the *Herald-Examiner*, combined, reach only 43 percent of the homes (even though *Times* circulation has doubled in the last 15 years).

"In my area," says Orange County publisher Bernard Ridder, "the three big dailies combined—the *Times*, the *Herald-Examiner* and the *Santa Ana Register*—still miss about 40 percent of the homes. My weeklies miss only 15 percent."

The Los Angeles area is so fragmented, says a Los Angeles area publisher, that "people here tend to look on a paper like the *Times* as an outsider, an intruder.

"With a free weekly, they probably don't spend as much time reading the stories—or put as much credence in the stories and ads—but at least it's their paper.

"If they live in Van Nuys, they want a Van Nuys paper, a local paper—not an L.A. paper."

The *Valley News*, distributed in the San Fernando Valley, north of Los Angeles, is such a local paper.

The *Valley News*, which began publication as the weekly *Van Nuys News* in 1911, expanded to twice-a-week publication in 1927, to three-times-a-week in 1953 and to four-times-a-week in 1959.

In its early years, the *Valley News* charged its readers for their subscriptions. But to attract advertising with saturation coverage in the postwar period, the paper switched to a voluntary-pay system, and today, only about 25 percent of the 280,000 people who receive the *Valley News* pay for the paper.

Advertising revenue more than offsets that loss, though, and the *Valley News* is the envy of profit-conscious newspaper publishers—six different geographic editions, all bulging with advertising (although no one knows just how well the paper does financially, since its circulation is largely unpaid and its records are not public).

"It is," says Charles Aydelotte, former president of the California Newspaper Publishers Association, "the classic, outstanding example of community journalism."

Owned for more than 50 years by two pioneering Southern California families—the Mendenhalls and the Markhams—the *Valley News* was sold to the *Chicago Tribune* in 1973. But the Mendenhalls and Markhams have remained on the job, and the *Valley News* has remained the *Valley News*—seemingly covering every PTA meeting, every church potluck, every garden club luncheon, every Boy Scout banquet, every bowling league, every high school wrestling match, even reporting every lost dog, from North Hollywood to Chatsworth and from Woodland Hills to Tujunga.

"The *Valley News* is really still the old country weekly," says Roy Copperud, a journalism professor at USC. "Nothing is too trifling to be printed. Everything that happens in the valley gets shoveled in. If a cow craps in the pasture, it makes the *Valley News*."

Barbara Fryer, editor and part-owner of a small weekly in Seal Beach, calls this kind of newspaper a practitioner of "grab-you-by-the-arm journalism; the newspaper staff is in the community every day, where your readers can see you and talk to you and hold you personally responsible for what you print."

Another newspaperwoman calls this "name journalism, people journalism."

"When I worked on a weekly in Laguna Beach," she says, "my editor told me the way for a community newspaper to succeed was to make sure you printed the name of every person in the community at least once a year."

There are times when the *Valley News*—despite having to serve an often disparate "community" of more than one million people, spread over 260 square miles—gives the impression of just that kind of coverage.

The *Valley News* publishes two columns of national and international news on the front page, and fills the rest of the page with local news. The rest of the hefty newspaper package has a seemingly random mix of local news and world news scattered throughout—but with the emphasis so predominantly local that most of its valley readers and advertisers find the paper invaluable.

Almost two-thirds of the people who receive the *Valley News* take no other newspaper.

"We don't advertise in many suburban newspapers," says one major department store executive, "but the *Valley News* has such a pull in the community that we can't ignore it; we have to use it."

Says one envious publisher:

"The *Valley News* does its job so well it's damn near chased the *Times* out of the Valley."

That, says one *Times* executive, is "somewhat hyperbolic—*Times* circulation in the Valley is 150,000 weekdays and 180,000 Sundays, more than double the *paid* circulation of the *Valley News*."

In an effort to compete with newspapers like the *Valley News*—and to meet the changing needs of its own readership—the *Times* has, since 1952, added twice-weekly suburban sections to its newspaper. Each suburban section—there are seven now, plus a separate daily edition in Orange County—carries local news and advertising designed solely for the area in which it is delivered (the South Bay, for example, or the West Side or the San Fernando Valley).

In 1962, recognizing the potential represented by the burgeoning growth of the San Fernando Valley, the *Times* began publishing its suburban section there on a daily basis. In 1973, with that edition not doing as well as desired—and with press capacity needed elsewhere—the *Times* reduced publication of its San Fernando suburban section (actually two sections, West Valley and East Valley) to twice weekly.

The *San Gabriel Valley Tribune* has become almost as successful an exponent of suburban daily journalism as the *Valley News* has become of community weekly journalism.

The *Tribune* began, in effect, with the merger in 1955 of three weeklies —the *Baldwin Park Bulletin*, the *West Covina Tribune* and the *Covina Argus-Citizen*. The new daily formed by this merger had a beginning circulation of 14,000 in an area with a population of 746,000.

By 1965, the population of the San Gabriel Valley—east of Los Angeles proper—had grown to 1.1 million, and *Tribune* circulation had more than quadrupled, to 68,000. Today, the population is almost 1.3 million, and *Tribune* circulation is 80,000.

Population growth has leveled off now, but the *Tribune* expects to grow to 150,000 circulation—a growth fueled in part by diminished competition; with daily newspapers in Monrovia and Alhambra now retrenched as weeklies, and with increased subscription rates likely to cost the *Pasadena Star-News* even more circulation than it has already lost, the *Tribune* plans to seek readers north and west of its current base.

"If you plunked the *Tribune* down in the middle of Nebraska some place, it would be a major metropolitan newspaper in its own right," says one newspaper publisher.

But growth has given the *Tribune* some special problems—the same problems that have been felt by two newspapers in very similar situations: the *South Bay Daily Breeze* and the *Santa Ana Register*.

The *Breeze* was still a sleepy little seaside daily with barely 10,000 circulation in 1950. But when the population explosion hit the South Bay, the *Breeze* aggressively expanded its territory, and its circulation jumped accordingly—more than quadrupling, to 47,000, in 1966 and almost doubling again, to more than 80,000, today.

The growth of the *Register* has been no less remarkable. The paper has mushroomed from an essentially one-city, 53,000-circulation afternoon newspaper in 1959 to an all-day, seven-edition, 205,000-circulation county-wide giant today.

Most of that growth came during the 1960s, when Orange County more than doubled in population to its present 1.4 million.

But, ironically, as newspapers like the *Register*, the *Breeze* and the *Tribune* have grown, they have had to struggle to maintain the very community identity that is their *raison d'etre*.

"You can only stretch a rubber band so far before it snaps back and hits you in the face," says one suburban newspaper publisher. "That could happen with papers like these."

Editors at these papers are fully aware of their dilemma.

"When you get as big as we are," says *Tribune* Editor Dick Tracy, "there's a temptation to try to be all things to all readers. You want to give them enough national and international news, as well as local news, that they don't have to take any other paper but yours."

When the *Tribune* began publishing 20 years ago, it ran 70 percent local news. It now runs 50 percent local, 50 percent national and international news, says Publisher Al Totter.

"When we started, we thought we'd just be the second paper in the home," Totter says. "But reading habits have changed. With competition from TV and more leisure-time activities, most people have time for only one paper now."

In the *Tribune* circulation area, that one paper is often the *Tribune*. (As in every other area, executives in San Gabriel said the other metropolitan daily, the *Herald-Examiner*, was not a significant competitive factor in their operational planning).

The temptation to be the main newspaper in a given community—to "out-metro the metros" in one editor's phrase—is especially tempting during a recession.

"It's easier and cheaper to try to copy a paper like the *Times* than it is to hire your own reporters to go out and dig in the local community," says Larry Allison, former managing editor of the Long Beach *Independent, Press-Telegram.*

"Hell, we can get all that great material on the *New York Times* wire service for less money than it would cost us to hire one good local reporter.

"But when you fill your paper with wire copy, you don't have enough space left to cover the local news well. Then you lose the readers altogether because you can't realistically compete with the *Times* on the *Times'* terms."

Jim Dean, editor of the *Santa Ana Register*, puts the successful suburban daily's need for a continued emphasis on local news in more colloquial terms:

"We're like the girl who goes to the dance and knows she'd better dance only with the guy who brung her."

In a sense, the *Register* and the *Independent, Press-Telegram* are almost metropolitan papers in their own right, though, and they really have little competition from the *Times* in their home communities.

An overwhelming majority of the 138,000 *Independent, Press-Telegram* subscribers do not take the *Times*, and even a weekly *Times* suburban section in that area many years ago proved so unprofitable that it was discontinued.

In Orange County, the *Times* has expanded from a weekly suburban section in 1954 to a twice-weekly section in 1959 to a daily section in 1963 to a separate daily edition in 1968.

But *Times* Orange County circulation has grown only 18 percent since 1968, while *Register* circulation has more than doubled. Only a very small percentage of the *Register* readers also read the *Times*.

(In Long Beach and Orange County, those readers who do take the *Times* usually do not take the local papers—and they are also generally the higher-income, better-educated readers, indicating that even these two community papers draw from a somewhat different market than the *Times*.)

Nevertheless, as newspapers like the *Breeze* and the *Tribune* and the *Register*, among others, continue to expand to meet rising costs and to serve expanded populations, they do—like it or not—sacrifice some of their community identity.

The *Breeze*, for example, began as the *Redondo Beach Daily Breeze*. People there thought of it as their own local newspaper. But the *Redondo Beach Daily Breeze* is now the *South Bay Daily Breeze*, and it covers 16 incorporated cities.

"Some people in Torrance or Lawndale might still think of us as the Redondo Beach paper," says editor Jim Box. "If we don't really do a good job covering their individual community, we might seem almost as much an unwelcome intruder as the *Times*."

In trying to avoid that pitfall, several of the more financially successful suburban newspapers have, at times, taken on an almost schizophrenic personality—suffering an identity crisis of sorts.

They grew so quickly, they didn't have big enough reportorial staffs to generate the local material they needed to fill the space made available by vastly increased advertising lineage; just to get the paper out each day, they often seemed to shovel in almost any wire service copy that was available, no matter how trivial or obscure.

"We realized most of our readers didn't really care about the VD rate in Tanganyika," says Jim Box, "but sometimes, that was the only kind of story we had left to fill our inside pages."

In the last two or three years, as growth has declined and the recession has forced economy measures, this hell-bent race to fill the paper has abated somewhat, and newspapers like the *Breeze* and the *Tribune* are beginning to make the same strides artistically that they have already made financially.

The *Breeze* and *Tribune*, among others, have also been operating their own daily geographic zone pages and their own chains of free weekly shoppers, both to lure advertisers and subscribers and to help maintain the community identity that forged their initial success.

They have also tried to take a lighter approach to the news than the more serious metropolitan newspapers do.

"We operate on the feather-edge of taste sometimes," says Tom Keevil, editor of the *Orange Coast Daily Pilot*, which has grown almost 60 percent in the last 10 years and now publishes eight separate editions. "We don't do that to be salacious, but to try to stay as light and bright and breezy as possible, partially to compete with TV."

The bright-and-breezy approach manifests itself in a newspaper that is more feature than news in tone and more human interest than issue-oriented in its concerns.

That may be the journalistic wave of the future in suburbia.

12 / Dear Abby (and Ann and Carroll and . . .)

Dear Abby, Dear Abby,/You won't
believe this,
   But my stomach makes noises/
Whenever I kiss.
   My girlfriend tells me/It's all in my
head,
   But my stomach tells me/To write
you instead.
   (Signed)
   Noisemaker
     —From a folk song by John Prine

Every day, in virtually every newspaper in America, syndicated columnists like Ann Landers and Abigail Van Buren, Billy Graham and Norman
Vincent Peale, Carroll Righter and Sydney Omarr offer advice on life and
love and health and happiness to their millions of readers.

In most cities, these columns are among the best-read features in the
paper, day after day and year after year. Between them, Abby and Ann
Landers alone receive more than 2,000 letters a day. Almost everyone, it
seems, wants help, advice, guidance, counsel:

- A 69-year-old man who says "I still like the ladies" wants Abby to tell
  him how he can prevent his wife from hiding his false teeth every time
  he leaves home alone.

174

- A 16-year-old boy who claims to have suffered a double hernia from masturbation wants Ann Landers to tell him how he can avoid reinjuring himself in the future.
- A woman sends Sydney Omarr her husband's birthdate and a swatch of of his undershorts, and wants to know if Omarr can determine "astrologically" from these items if he is being unfaithful to her.

Other letter-writers want to know if incest is hereditary, if powdered reindeer horns are an aphrodisiac, if cremation jeopardizes reincarnation, if raccoons breed through the nose and gestate in the sinus cavity, if . . .

One woman even wrote Ann Landers to complain about "your holier-than-thou attitude toward husbands who give their wives a well-deserved belt in the mouth . . . A crack in the teeth can be a real tension-breaker . . . My husband hauls off and slugs me every few months and I don't mind."

The letter was signed "Real Happy."

But why ask these questions—or questions on etiquette, impotence, bed-wetting, alcoholism, child-beating, dieting or breast-feeding—of a newspaper columnist? Why not go to a doctor or a clergyman or a psychiatrist—or to a friend or relative?

What kinds of people write to a newspaper columnist for help on the most intimate of problems? What kind of society produces those letter-writers?

Skeptical readers think most of the letter-writers are either kooks or pranksters. They suspect, too, that the most amusing and outrageous letters are invented by the columnists themselves.

There are, no doubt, many kooks and pranksters who do write in. But a careful study of the columnists' mail makes it incontrovertibly clear that almost all of it comes from real people with real problems—and that none of it has to be concocted by the columnists.

As Ann Landers says:

"The notion that I have to fabricate letters in order to put together a lively column is absurd. A person would have to be psychotic to make up those letters . . . Nothing is so far out, or bizarre, that somebody, somewhere, won't do it—and write me about it."

Advice columnists are fond of saying that their mail comes from every segment of society—from men and women, young and old, rich and poor, urban and rural, intellectual and illiterate.

"I hear," Ann Landers says, "from construction workers, bank presidents, truck drivers, politicians, clergymen, school teachers, prostitutes, teen-agers, housewives, prisoners, artists, drug addicts, mental patients, doctors, lawyers—and I've even received a letter from an Indian chief."

Although the subject matter of the letters is as diverse as their authorship, more involve questions of love (i.e., sex/romance) than any other single topic. Questions of health and money matters (i.e., job and career) are the next most prevalent.

Suprisingly, this priority and predominance holds true whether the letters are sent to a Dear Abby or to a Sydney Omarr—and regardless of who the writer is. There are, moreover, several characteristics all these letter-writers seem to have in common, the columnists' assurances as to their normalcy and heterogeneity notwithstanding.

— The letter-writers are, for example, more often women than men.

"Because of our cultural conditioning," astrologer Omarr says, "most men don't think it's masculine to share intimate confidences or ask for help or admit to personal weaknesses. They feel it undermines their virility —especially if they have to admit they've been hurt by a woman."

Astrologer Carroll Righter says he, too, receives more mail from women than from men—and more from those born under the sign of Libra than under any other sign.

"Librans," he says, "like to analyze things, weigh them, look for corroborative judgments."

But specialists in human behavior find this theory self-serving.

Most people who write to newspaper columnists for advice are "essentially naive and simplistic, not analytical or critical," says Annette Baran, a psychotherapist and clinical social worker. "They're followers, not, leaders—relatively unsophisticated people with relatively limited interests.

"Generally, I would say they don't have much confidence in their own judgment," Baran says. "They tend to be in awe of important people and to invest these people with more authority and credibility than they deserve.

"They're lonely, but they're more passive, say, than the kind of lonely people who call the talk-radio stations and get into arguments."

Abby herself acknowledges that many of her letter-writers are "obviously lonely, just looking for someone who'll listen to their problems and respond to them. They've been reading me for so many years that I'm almost like a personal friend, someone they know and trust."

This unique—and sad—form of supplication-cum-communication is becoming more prevalent, sociologists say, as we become a more urbanized and technological society—a society in which isolation and alienation are pandemic.

Someone writes to a newspaper columnist about a problem, other people respond with advice or disagreement or descriptions of similar problems and for months to come a curious dialogue ensues among hundreds, sometimes thousands, of strangers.

"Partially because of our high mobility rate, we're a culture that no longer has very deep kinship ties," says Dr. Joyce Brothers, a psychologist and syndicated columnist. "People used to have relatives they could turn to for help. Now we often live far away from our relatives, and we don't live or work in any one place long enough to develop close, genuine friendships.

"When we need advice, there's no one to turn to."

Says Omarr:

"The saddest cases are the people who are so lonely they convince themselves I'm writing a personal message for them alone—even proposing marriage—through my column. One young woman, a nurse in the Midwest, has written me every day for a year. She sends me cigars and ties and candy and cakes, and she finds something in almost every column that she interprets as a direct answer to her."

The apparent failure of our social, political and religious institutions to cope with the complexity of contemporary society has also contributed to the popularity of the advice column.

Confused and disillusioned, many people turn to newspaper columnists as familiar, trustworthy, sympathetic figures who will provide simple, reassuring answers to difficult questions.

This may help explain one of the publishing phenomena of recent years —the burgeoning success of newspaper "how-to" columns, an outgrowth, really, of the more general advice columns.

"Money is tight, good professional advice is getting too expensive and the bureaucracy—both governmental and corporate—is increasingly unresponsive," says Christian Chenoweth, executive editor of the Field Enterprises Syndicate. "People are turning to their daily newspapers for help."

Faced with competition from television—and with reader disaffection brought about by their socio-political coverage and rising subscription costs—many editors are using these new, consumer-oriented columns to maintain and build circulation.

Thus, newspapers now offer columns not only on love and health and astrology but on beauty care, sewing, nutrition, automobile repair, animal psychology, bicycling, antiques, interior decoration, gardening, indoor plants . . .

But it is one thing to ask a newspaper columnist how to keep your philodendron alive; it would seem to be another matter altogether to ask Ann Landers how to keep your marriage alive.

The two may not, however, be all that different.

The connection, Dr. Brothers says, is that "we are a culture that seems to think there is a right answer for everything. We refuse to accept the fact that there are some things for which there are no answers."

Dr. Michael Franzblau, a Beverly Hills psychoanalyst whose mother is both a psychologist and a longtime advice columnist for the *New York Post*, thinks people who write to newspaper columnists are "very much like people who believe in magic—people who go to Lourdes or enroll in est.

"They want simple, instant, 'how-to' cures," he says. "They want someone else to solve their problems for them. They want to evade responsibility for their own actions and decisions."

But why shift that responsibility to a newspaper columnist? Why not seek professional help?

Why, for example, would a man who finds himself stimulated by newspaper advertisements for men's clothes ask Dear Abby if she thinks he has homosexual tendencies, rather than take that same question to a psychiatrist?

Why would a woman tell Ann Landers, rather than a marriage counselor, that she and her husband "watch a lot of TV and play gin rummy" because "he learned early in our marriage that I was not keen on sex, so he adjusted his sex appetite accordingly"?

Why would a man write to Omarr, rather than his clergyman, to say, "I have recently learned that my purpose in life is to work for God . . . I have strong reason to believe I am getting my instructions from the daily horoscope . . ."

One woman who has written several letters "on a variety of problems to a variety of columnists" says she has done so because "each time, I felt they were the only ones who would listen to me and understand me.

"My husband is always too busy watching football on TV," she says, "and my friends have their own problems to worry about. Besides, I couldn't talk to them about such personal things. A shrink or my rabbi? Come on. What do they really know about everyday life?"

Many other people, it would appear, are intimidated by professional therapists—by a genuine authority figure with imposing credentials and formal offices. Many more just cannot afford—or are unwilling to pay—a professional therapist: A 13-cent stamp is a manageable expenditure; a $60-an-hour psychiatrist's fee is not.

Moreover, says psychologist Chaytor Mason, most people don't see their problems as personal shortcomings, but as "the result of their having been unfairly manipulated by others—by a husband or a boss or a girlfriend.

"It might be difficult to maintain that position with a professional therapist—or even a friend," Mason says. "They might be judgmental. They might tell you you're wrong. But you can structure a letter to a columnist so that you seem right. The other person has no chance to present his side, so the columnist will probably be sympathetic to you."

On those rare occasions when the columnist is not supportive, his (or her) advice need not be heeded; advice given freely and anonymously is far easier to ignore than advice in which one has an economic and/or psychic investment.

Most advice columnists readily agree that it is less burdensome—both emotionally and financially—for someone to write to them about a problem than it would be to seek professional help. Sometimes, it is also just as efficacious, for although a columnist may print only four or five letters a day, some columnists—Abby and Ann Landers, for example—have several assistants who help them answer every letter that bears a name and address.

The columnists' published answers may often seem flip ("You need this guy like a giraffe needs strep throat"), but the columns are, after all, intended to entertain, as well as to inform and to advise. The vast majority of the letters that are answered are answered personally—not in the column—and the answers are based on Abby's and Ann Landers' consultation with a private network of doctors, psychiatrists, social workers, clergymen and other specialists.

The column, then, is but the frivolous tip of a substantive iceberg, and concern that the columnists may be dispensing ill-informed and potentially harmful advice is largely unjustified—unless, of course, one disagrees with the basic tenets of the columnists' philosophy (an altogether understandable position in many instances).

But most of the columnists' mail—80 percent in Abby's case—is unsigned, completely anonymous. These people will receive no personal response, and only the tiniest fraction of them can expect to see their letters—and the columnists' answers—in print. Why do they write?

Because, the experts agree, by writing anonymously, a person can get a problem off his chest, persuade himself that he has made a genuine effort to seek help and not have to worry that he will be embarrassed or disgraced or hurt by making his problems or mistakes known to his friends and family.

"It's tough for a man to tell a buddy he's impotent—or for a woman to admit to her next-door neighbor that she can't have an orgasm or that her husband never tells her he loves her," one psychiatrist says.

"Some people just can't talk about those things to someone they know —or even to a therapist or a minister. They're afraid of losing the friend or being laughed at or being called crazy or sick or rotten."

But Randall Phillips, former president of the Los Angeles Council of Churches, sees the letter-writer's plea as an excruciating ambivalence—as a desire for both anonymity and recognition.

"By writing to a columnist, you're projecting yourself—you're identifying yourself with someone important," Phillips says. "It satisfies a need for attention and ego-gratification without risking public exposure."

That may be why some people sign their letters, but insist their names not be used. It's as if they're shouting, "I'm me; I'm someone" but—having done so—they then want desperately to retreat into the safety of anonymity.

Columnists who have been writing for years say this scream for recognition has lately become increasingly shrill—and its underlying tone increasingly anxious and fearful.

"My mail has doubled in the past 10 years," says Ann Landers, "and in that time, I've seen people become much more uncertain and worried about themselves and our society."

Some of this concern is reflected in the very subject matter of the letters—far more questions now than eight or 10 years ago on violence, interracial marriage, homosexuality, drug use, abortion, religious cults, the generation gap, the economy, mistrust of government.

Letters these days are more often frantic pleas for help of any kind, rather than friendly requests for specific advice. One young man, for example, recently wrote Abby a two-page letter lamenting his having "completely lost all my motivation about school and life."

He was so depressed, he said, that he couldn't sleep or "get involved in anything anymore."

"I am really scared. What should I do? PLEASE help me."

But if today's letter-writers are more anxious, they are also more intelligent—and less inhibited—than ever before.

"The young people, in particular, are much more aware, more inquisitive, more willing to talk about things we used to be ashamed of," Abby says. "They're also much less willing to take my word for anything. They challenge me and demand proof and documentation."

Abby and other columnists say their younger correspondents also tend to be more humanitarian and less self-centered—a finding confirmed by sociologist Terry Smith Hatkoff in a recent study comparing lovelorn columns written from 1947 to 1951 with those written from 1967 to 1971.

In the earlier period, Hatkoff found that 59 percent of the letters written to the columnists she studied were written about "problems involving heterosexual relationships." In the later period, the figure dropped to 39 percent.

Hatkoff found a corresponding increase—from 16.9 percent to 35.8 percent—in letters of "a more general orientation" (i.e., letters not involving family, friendship or love affairs).

These shifts, Hatkoff suggested, represent "a change in the prevailing values of the society and an increase in its level of social awareness. As people in the society become more conscious of social movements, the effect may be to alter their central concerns."

But even with this dramatic change, most people still want advice on personal problems—and an astonishingly high number of these problems involve young people.

One girl wrote Omarr recently to complain that she was "touchingly naive about love . . . and life in general." She was 14.

Another girl wrote Abby to ask how she might persuade a younger boy to ask her out on a date. She signed the letter "Confused and Hopeless." She, too, was 14; the boy was 9.

A more poignant letter came to Abby the same day from a young boy who said, "I think I hate my brother because I can't keep from hitting him. What should I do?"

But Abby's favorite piece of correspondence came from a man of 33 who wanted to know if she thought he could win a $100,000 lawsuit he was planning to file against his parents for having violated his civil rights by having him circumcised as an infant.

Abby's reply:

"I don't know if you'll win your suit, but if you do, you should think of the money you get as being severance pay."

13 / City Magazines

In September 1975, *Philadelphia* magazine breathlessly told its readers where to find the best bagels in town. In November 1975, *San Diego* magazine told its readers where to find the best cookies in town. In January 1976, *Boston* magazine told its readers where to find the best coffee beans in town. In March 1976, *Cleveland* magazine told its readers where to find the best pizza in town. In . . .

Of such fare are fortunes—and publishing phenomena—now made.

Over the last 10 or 15 years, city magazines have begun dispensing consumer advice of this kind on everything from azaleas to zabaglione in virtually every major city in the United States—and in many not-so-major cities as well.

"After the 1960s, people realized they weren't going to save the world after all," says *Los Angeles* magazine editor Geoff Miller. "They decided the next-best thing was to try to make the most of their own lives, to try to solve the problems of rising prices and pressures in urban society.

"City magazines help them do that."

There are now almost 50 city magazines of one sort or another, and despite a few failures—most spectacularly, *City* magazine in San Francisco in 1976—the majority are thriving.

New York magazine—in a sense, the progenitor of the entire breed (though now really more a national magazine than a city magazine)—has a weekly circulation of almost 400,000. *New West*, which began publication in Los Angeles and San Francisco in 1976 under the aegis of *New York*, passed 250,000 bi-weekly circulation in less than a year.

Texas Monthly increased circulation by more than 80 percent in one year to more than 200,000 by the end of 1976. *Chicago, Los Angeles* and *Philadelphia* all have monthly circulations well in excess of 100,000.

After overcoming the initial reluctance of many national advertisers, city magazines are now equally successful in attracting advertising—despite a poor economy that has hurt most magazines.

Esquire, for example, dropped 28 percent in advertising in 1975. *Time* dropped 22 percent. *Playboy* and the *New Yorker* each dropped 14 percent. But city magazines gained an average of 10 percent, and *Chicago, Los Angeles, San Francisco* and *Texas Monthly* each gained more than 20 percent.

The gains continued in 1976, with all city magazines gaining an average of 17 percent, and one—*Texas Monthly*—gaining 48 percent!

Nowhere has the success of the city magazine been more evident than in Los Angeles.

In 1973, negotiations for the sale of *Los Angeles* magazine to *New York* magazine collapsed, in part because *New York* discovered that *Los Angeles'* announced circulation of 65,000 per month was actually—because of various promotional gimmicks—less than half that (a not uncommon circumstance for many city magazines until relatively recent).

But another buyer came along—CHC Corporation, a firm that publishes medical books and operates nursing homes; CHC quickly legitimized existing *Los Angeles* circulation, began an aggressive promotion campaign and increased both circulation and advertising so dramatically that today—after 15 years of either losing money or barely breaking even—*Los Angeles* is one of the fastest growing magazines in the country, with a 1975 profit of more than $300,000.

The sudden growth of *Los Angeles* has come despite the continuing success of two other local/regional magazines (*Westways* and *Sunset*) and the arrival, in 1976, of *New West* magazine. City magazines have been so successful, in fact, that when Australian press magnate Rupert Murdoch bought control of *New York* and *New West* (along with the *Village Voice*) in January 1977, he paid more than three times the per-share price the company's stock had been selling for.

New York is generally regarded as one of the best of the city magazines—along with *Philadelphia, Texas Monthly* and *Washingtonian*—but virtually all the city magazines share with *New York* what might best be described as a common absentee parentage; they have, their editors say, filled a partial vacuum left by the large daily newspapers.

Over the last 10 or 15 years, city magazine editors say, the preoccupation of the daily press with Vietnam, Watergate, civil rights and similar issues—and their competition with television for those stories—has diminished their concern for local news.

"If newspapers did their jobs properly in the local community, I'm not sure there would be room for city magazines," says Jack Limpert, editor of *Washingtonian*.

Some city magazine executives insist that their publications are strongest where newspapers are weakest in local coverage.

Both *Philadelphia* and *Texas Monthly*, for example, achieved their financial and journalistic success in part because of the void created by the general mediocrity and timidity of the daily press in their areas.

"The newspapers in Texas were just incredibly bad," says *Texas Monthly* publisher Mike Levy.

The same has been true in San Diego, where magazine profits are better than ever.

"When we started, the *Union-Tribune* was ultraconservative, to the right of Genghis Kahn, and they left a lot of news unreported," says Edwin Self, publisher of *San Diego* magazine.

"We were able to write about the issues they ignored—blacks and the New Left and the environment and even the arts. We also took a lot of liberal positions that made the Establishment—and some of our advertisers—pretty unhappy."

(*San Diego* magazine, its editorial courage and financial success notwithstanding, has never, however, been regarded as one of the better city magazines.)

Ironically, the city magazine success story has been written in an era when television was helping to write the obituary for such American institutions as *Life*, *Look* and *Saturday Evening Post*, as well as for many other mass-circulation magazines.

For a magazine to make money today, it must serve a special interest market. Sex is one such interest (as the success of *Playboy*, *Penthouse*, *Hustler*, *Playgirl*, *et al* indicates), but skiing, feminism, auto racing, photography or horticulture will do almost as well.

The key is to select a fairly narrow, clearly defined audience to whom articles on specific subjects and, more importantly, advertisements for specific products may be addressed—at a considerably lower price than television could provide.

"Our audience," says Seth Baker, president of the company that publishes *Los Angeles* magazine, "is the upper-middle-class homeowner, college educated, making $40,000 a year."

That audience—sophisticated, status-conscious, generally between their late 20s and early 40s—is a consumer audience, a prime audience for advertisers, an audience that buys liquor and new cars and stereo equipment and fine clothes.

But this is not an audience secure in its success; it is an audience of "the comfortable but not content" in the words of David Brown, former publisher of *Los Angeles*.

City magazines have tapped not just an audience but a neurosis—an audience increasingly anxious (if not, indeed, desperate) about the challenges, complexities and frustrations of the contemporary urban environment.

The "special interest" of this audience is, in one editor's apt phrase, "making it"—or, as *New York* founder Clay Felker puts it, "survival."

Crime, inflation, congestion and competition are the four horsemen of this audience's imminent apocalypse, and city magazines cater to those concerns—telling their readers how to protect their homes against burglary, where to shop for bargains, how to beat rush-hour traffic, where to go for psychoanalysis, transcendental meditation or crash-dieting.

Most people, it seems, read city magazines either to learn how to cope with their environment or to enjoy, vicariously, the success that others more wealthy and fortunate than themselves have had in so doing.

It's what David Brown calls "the F. Scott Fitzgerald syndrome, the kings and queens theory of journalism.

"What *New York* magazine does," Brown says, "is hold up the top 5 percent of New York society and say, 'See, read us and you can make it, too.'"

Thus, city magazines delight in publishing both gossip about the city's elite and such stories as "Power—Who Has It in Boston" and "Who's Got Clout in L.A." and "Making It in Washington" and "Philly's Ten Sexiest Women and Ten Sexiest Men."

City magazines also specialize in providing guides to the best of everything—the not-so-subtle implication being, "You, too, dear reader can now eat (or wear or sit on) that which has previously been available only to the true cognoscenti—the men and women of privilege and taste in our society."

By so doing, the reader gains not only instant status but the ego gratification—however superficial and ephemeral—of having, at last, bested his oppressive environment.

But city magazines often provide far more than this. At their best, they offer valuable guidance in selecting lawyers, therapists, private schools, children's camps, health salons, interior decorators, maintenance men, restaurants, late-night emergency help, weekend vacations . . .

On occasion, the city magazines transcend this service orientation and offer aggressive, provocative, investigative journalism of a quality generally available in only the best newspapers in America—and only sporadically in even these papers.

Washingtonian has exposed fraud and empire-building in local charities. *Texas Monthly* has taken a critical look at banks, airport safety, large law firms and the natural gas industry. *New York* has examined poor judges, the city's fiscal crisis and the financial relationship between the city's socio-political establishment and the Times Square porno district.

Philadelphia, the pioneer (and premier) muckraker among city magazines, has won major national awards for stories on rape, hunger, grand juries, diet drugs and the disadvantaged minorities, and has also published highly regarded exposés on a newspaper reporter who was blackmailing local businessmen, on the mistreatment of children by an organization created to care for them and on mismanagement of funds for the city's bicentennial celebration.

But this iconoclastic brand of journalism requires money, courage, skill, judgment and independence, and most city magazines—fearful of offending potential advertisers, and unable to attract talented staffs—wind up as little more than slick, visually impressive urban service and entertainment guides.

They are more likely to be civic boosters than skeptics, and they are all too often produced by the local chamber of commerce or some similar organization, rather than by editors and publishers with a commitment to journalistic excellence and integrity.

A few of the chamber-type city magazines—most notably, *Atlanta*—can sometimes compete with the better independent city magazines, but they are the exception. In fact, even some of the independent city magazines have occasionally made commercial compromises to fuel their growth.

One, *Los Angeles*, suffered until relatively recently from a shortage of newsstand outlets—especially in supermarkets. Then came a breakthrough: most supermarkets now carry the magazine. So what happened when one writer sent *Los Angeles* a not-altogether sympathetic story on "The Evolution of Los Angeles Supermarkets?"

She received a letter from the editors which said the story was rejected because, "Basically, the problem was a political one; we were concerned that doing the story might present us with some distribution problems since a majority of our street sales are in supermarkets."

The best city magazines have refused to play this game, but not all have lived to boast of their clear editorial consciences.

Seattle magazine, for example, drew considerable national praise in the six years it lasted. But several controversial articles—on homosexuality, racism, the Black Panthers and fraudulent used-car dealers—alienated so many advertisers the magazine had to fold.

"We were an antiestablishment magazine that had to rely on the establishment for both advertising and circulation revenue," says Peter Bunzel, who was the editor of *Seattle*.

Although city magazines, in their current incarnation, are a relatively new phenomenon, the genre itself dates at least from the founding of the *New Yorker* in 1925, if not from the first issue of *Golden Era* in San Francisco in 1849.

But *Golden Era* quickly tarnished, and the *New Yorker* became a national magazine (with more than 75 percent of its circulation now outside New York), and the gossip-sheets, high-society journals and chamber of commerce promotional magazines that sprang up in their stead during the booming 1920s collapsed in the depressed 1930s.

Philadelphia, which began shortly after the turn of the century as a chamber newsletter, was acquired in 1962 by Herb Lipson, son of the original publisher, and it is from 1962 that the success of the modern city magazine really dates.

Although the first of these new city magazines (*San Diego*) began publishing in 1948 and the second (*Los Angeles*) began in 1960, it was *Philadelphia* and—more significantly—*New York* that provided the commercial and journalistic environment in which a whole host of imitators eventually would flourish.

Philadelphia proved the viability of the city magazine format first, but *New York*—which began its independent life in 1968 after five years as a Sunday supplement to the now-defunct *New York Herald-Tribune*—attracted the most attention and received the most credit; *New York* not only did its job well, blending lively writing with distinctive graphics, but it did it weekly—and in the city that is both the media capital—and urban problem capital—of the United States.

Not that *New York* was without its critics. In the magazine's early days, when creating controversy often seemed more important to the editors than exercising taste or responsibility, *Newsweek* labeled it "a tedious collection of pop trivia"; the *Columbia Journalism Review* criticized it for "vulgar, superficial . . . stories"; the *Wall Street Journal* exposed one of its stories as a fraud; writer Jimmy Breslin denounced it for "boutique journalism" and quit contributing to it.

But even these critics helped contribute to the magazine's image as a daring innovator, a trend-setter, and more than a dozen hard-cover books —and at least twice that many other city magazines—had their beginnings in its pages.

To many—including its own publisher—the quintessential *New York* article appeared on June 8, 1970. Tom Wolfe took up most of that issue with a bitchily brilliant caricature of "limousine liberals" who attended a fund-raising affair for the Black Panthers at Leonard Bernstein's Park Avenue apartment.

The story had virtually all the elements of the successful city magazine story, and Clay Felker insists is was influential as well: "It killed radical chic," he says.

Whatever the accuracy of that claim—and there are many who would argue that Wolfe simply pulled the plug on an already hopelessly moribund patient—there is little question that *New York* is a trend-setter, a magazine of both local controversy and national impact—as likely to publish stories on war in the Mideast and gourmet food in France as on muggings in Manhattan and cheesecake in Brooklyn.

Because most city magazines publish strictly local stories ("That's why we're here," says one editor), they do not generally make interesting reading for people in other cities.

Apart from *New York*, the only consistent exceptions to this rule are *Texas Monthly* and *Washingtonian*.

Washingtonian is interesting almost anywhere because even its local stories almost inevitably involve national political figures. But *Washingtonian* has been severely criticized for largely ignoring the city's predominantly black population, and the magazine is now actively seeking to remedy that neglect—and, seemingly, to do more strictly local consumer service stories.

Texas Monthly is the unique story among all city magazines—actually a statewide magazine, only four years old, already challenged by fast-growing city magazines in both Dallas and Houston.

Texas Monthly is run by men and women in their late 20s and early 30s, with little or no previous journalism experience: The publisher is a graduate of the Wharton School of Business. The editor is a former assistant superintendent of schools. Two senior editors are lawyers.

But these men have brought a fresh, crisp approach to the magazine. They have attracted what is generally regarded as the finest group of writers now available to any city magazine. They generally give their readers a higher gravity/frivolity ratio than any other city magazine.

Still, for all its brash excellence, *Texas Monthly* is published in Austin, Texas, not New York, and it is *New York* magazine that continues to establish the trends in what one envious publisher calls "the titillating but still acceptable way of writing about what the Important People are talking about over lunch today—which usually means some aspect of money, power, politics, media or sex."

Esquire media columnist Nora Ephron describes this preoccupation as "the new porn," and says it is a manifestation of a "Let them eat cheesecake" philosophy. Magazines like *New York*, she says, "have taken food and home furnishings and plant care and surrounded them with just enough political and sociological reporting to give their readers an excuse to buy them"—much as early *Playboy* subscribers could claim to buy that magazine for its fiction or interviews.

But the *New York* formula has been remarkably successful in New York. It has been copied—sometimes slavishly—in other cities, and Felker himself tried to adapt it to Los Angeles with *New West*.

Herb Lipson, who built *Philadelphia* into perhaps the most widely respected city magazine in the country, has tried a similar transplant with the purchase of *Boston*, but despite more than doubling circulation there (to 55,000) in five years, *Boston* has never gained wide respect.

Lipson has had to function in Boston without the half-century of tradition his magazine enjoyed in Philadelphia—and without the uniquely perverse love-hate relationship Philadelphians have always had with their city.

Moreover, says Nancy Love, dispatched from *Philadelphia* to edit *Boston*, the presence in Boston of "a very good newspaper (the *Globe*) and two good alternative papers (*Boston Phoenix* and *The Real Paper*), made it very difficult for us to stake out an important area that no one else already had."

Lipson has tried exporting story ideas from *Philadelphia* to *Boston*— "Fifteen People We'd Rather See as Mayor" ran in both magazines—and he once went so far as to use virtually identical covers (and cover stories) in the two publications.

There was considerable speculation in Los Angeles early in 1976, just before Felker brought out the first issue of *New West*, about whether *New West* would be a similar carbon-copy of *New York*—and if it would be able to compete with *Los Angeles* magazine and the *Los Angeles Times*.

Felker was adamant on both points:

"I firmly believe that publications don't compete with each other," he said. "A publication creates its own unique audience."

The *Los Angeles* magazine audience is among the oldest (average age: 42), most affluent (annual income: $40,000) and most geographically centralized (essentially the upper-middle class and upper-class West Side and the well-to-do sections of the San Fernando Valley, although it has been broadening considerably of late).

Moreover, *Los Angeles* magazine has long been criticized for coddling these readers, for being too "soft"—for largely ignoring social, political and economic problems, and concentrating almost exclusively on consumer guides and on the good life in the Beverly Hills-Brentwood-Malibu-Bel-Air axis.

It is not surprising that a November 1976 *Los Angeles* article on automobile insurance rates selected for its "typical" insurance policy a "new Cadillac Seville."

Los Angeles has also published such stories as "A Connoisseur's Guide to Powder Rooms," "Is This LA's Erogenous Zone—The Joys of Sex in Century City" and a Christmas shopping guide that included a $44, solid-gold toothpick, a $650 teddy bear, a $5,000 birthday cake, a $150,000 car and a $3-million home.

In part because of such stories ("whipped cream—and artificial whipped cream at that," says one dissatisfied reader), most critics place *Los Angeles*—along with *New West*, *Chicago*, *Cleveland* and perhaps two or three other city magazines—in the second rank of city magazines, a clear drop in quality below the big four of *Philadelphia*, *Texas Monthly*, *New York* and *Washingtonian*.

But *Los Angeles*, like *Chicago*, now has burgeoning advertising revenues at its disposal, and substantial editorial improvements already are visible.

Los Angeles Editor Geoff Miller wants the magazine to continue to expand its geographic base and to move away from trivia toward "substantive investigative stories," but he says the magazine will not traffic heavily in socio-political pieces.

"People in L.A. lead very internalized lives," Miller says. "The city doesn't dictate to them the way it does in New York. They aren't forced to deal with the harsh realities of daily life in the big city, and they don't want to read about it."

Los Angeles magazine executives would appear to have at least three pieces of evidence to support this theory:

- A subscription renewal rate higher than any other city magazine (and second only to *National Geographic* among all magazines).
- A readership survey showing that the most popular features in the magazine are the restaurant, entertainment, vacation and shopping guides (and that fewer than half the readers have "much interest" in politics, social problems or economic issues).
- A survey showing that about twice as many readers of *Los Angeles* also read *Time, Newsweek, Sunset, Readers Digest, Better Homes and Gardens* and *TV Guide* as read *Esquire, Fortune,* the *New Yorker* or *Psychology Today* (and that so few read *Harper's* or *Atlantic* that neither is even listed among the 31 magazines surveyed).

New West editors saw this evidence more inviting than foreboding. They insisted that by doing their job skillfully and provocatively, they could create a readership as interested in socio-political issues as in gossip, consumer guidance and social climbing.

From their very first issue, with its cover photo of California Governor Jerry Brown and its cover story on "Who Is Shaping the Future of California?" they have set about doing just that. In addition to a regular political column, their early issues carried stories on mass murder, solar energy, nuclear power, the Patty Hearst trial, Senator S. I. Hayakawa, the holistic health revolution and increasing handgun sales. But *New West* did not neglect the trivial, the mundane and the entertaining; those same early issues carried stories on skateboarding, producer Robert Evans, Jane Fonda, the Beverly Hills Hotel, the Dodgers and the Angels baseball teams, classic cars, Palm Springs, horse-racing, the *Billy Jack* films, Hollywood trade papers—and, of course, the obligatory collection of movie and restaurant columns and how-to and where-to guides.

New West has expanded circulation, as well as editorial, horizons from those envisioned by *Los Angeles* magazine; not only has *New West* gone further into suburbia than *Los Angeles*, it has also gone into San Francisco—first with a four-page insert, then with a separate 32-page section.

"*Los Angeles*," sniffs *New West* Senior Editor Larry Dietz, is afraid to go outside Beverly Hills without pith helmets. They act like anything east of La Brea is darkest Africa."

Felker knows any new magazine is a risk, but he said he was prepared to spend $3 million on *New West*, if necessary, (reports are that he spent more than $4 million in the first year of publication alone), and while he confidently predicted "reaching the level of performance and success we want in a year or so," he also claimed to have "plans and budgets that go into the eighth year."

Many knowledgeable people think *New West* will succeed. But it will have to do so without Felker. He spent so much money getting *New West* off the ground—and paying *New West* and *New York* writers—that the parent New York Magazine Co. showed an operating loss of $229,000 for the last six months of 1976; angered and distressed, the board of directors sold control of the company in January 1977, and Felker refused to work for the new owner. He walked away from the magazines he had created.

Many critics had charged—even before the first issue of *New West* was on the newsstands—that it would be a carpetbagger, a magazine edited by New Yorkers for New Yorkers, a Los Angeles reprint of *New York* magazine.

Felker vigorously—splenetically—denied the charge. Although he did use columnists Richard Reeves and Dan Dorfman in both magazines and, on occasion, used a story in both magazines, most of the *New West* material (and most of the *New West* staff) has been home-grown in the West.

The three top editors at *New West*, Felker pointed out, have spent several years each in Southern California—and they are assisted by a full-time staff of nine, eight of whom are native Californians.

Several people who have had contact with the *New West* editors have, however, complained of a certain "Eastern arrogance" in their approach to the magazine.

This attitude may be best exemplified by Jack Nessel, executive editor of *New York* and an executive editor for *New West* before returning to New York after a few months.

"People in New York have a sense of identity about their city," Nessel said. "Same thing in Chicago and, God knows, in San Francisco. But not Los Angeles. We think *New West* can help create that identity and provide a definition of what Los Angeles is really all about."

Somehow, the idea of a New York editor—even one born and raised in the Los Angeles suburb of Long Beach—promising to impose an "identity" on Los Angeles seems unsettlingly presumptuous to many.

New West has generally managed to avoid the snide, mistaken perceptions about Los Angeles so typical of East Coast journalists, but they have stumbled a time or two: Early on, in back-to-back issues, they purported to present the definitive study of "A California Woman" ("Psychological Penalties of Being Locked Into Paradise") and "The New California Man" ("Passive Conquistador?"). Both pieces were ill-conceived, superficial, grossly inaccurate and glibly written. The piece on "A California Woman" was a vaguely stream-of-consciousness account of a "composite" California woman's tortured thoughts as she sat in her white Mercedes ("which she loves"), thinking *something's* wrong." The piece on "The New California Man" opened with a frantically narcissistic fellow indulging in a series of contortionist exercises and "minutely examining the small of his back with a magnifying mirror."

But such egregiousness notwithstanding, *New West* has generally presented the thinking reader with better material than has *Los Angeles*, and readers have been responding accordingly.

Using a variety of mailing and subscription lists—*New York* magazine itself has 16,000 subscribers in California, more than half of them in the greater Los Angeles area—Felker conducted a blitzkrieg promotional campaign that quickly brought him more than 150,000 subscribers. To his own astonishment, he also began selling 75,000 copies a week in Northern California six or seven months after his first issue.

Most of these subscribers are paying cut-rate prices, though—some as little as $6 a year (the regular price is $12)—and studies have shown that such subscribers are rarely as loyal as readers who pay full price. Come renewal time—at full price—they often say, "No, thanks."

There was, in fact, a considerable drop in newsstand sales after curiosity over the first couple of issues expended itself, and executives at *Los Angeles* gleefully attributed it to Felker's "ignorance about what sells that kind of magazine in Los Angeles—pretty girls and celebrity's faces on the cover, not skateboarders and Helen Copley [the publisher of the *San Diego Union-Tribune*, featured on the cover of the third issue of *New West*]."

If either aggressive promotion or a misreading of their potential audience ultimately kills *New West*, it won't be the first city magazine to have died amid much initial fanfare.

Fourteen city magazines have failed in Chicago alone—most notably the *Chicagoan*, begun in late 1973 by two local newspaper columnists, Jon Anderson and his wife, Abra (a Rockefeller heiress). The Andersons didn't last a year.

"We tried to do too much too quickly, and we couldn't fulfill our promises," Anderson says. "Too many city magazines are started like that —by newspaper people who don't know enough about the business. People need their daily paper, but you have to create an identity and a need and a habit for a magazine."

Perhaps the most spectacular failure among all city magazines was that of *City* magazine in San Francisco. Movie producer Francis Ford Coppola lost an estimated $1.5 million when *City* folded in 1976.

Like *Boston, City* found itself suffering from an identity crisis of sorts. *San Francisco* magazine and the two daily newspapers in San Francisco, though not widely respected, do provide adequate entertainment listings; the paper's Sunday *California Living* magazine and a good muckraking weekly, the *Bay Guardian*, had already staked out other areas that have been fertile for city magazines elsewhere.

City published rambling, self-conscious, often meaningless pieces that one staff member characterized as "masturbatory idiocy." The magazine, he said, was a "dinosaur of frivolity"—sensational, titillating but unsure of itself and out of touch with contemporary San Francisco.

Typically, the most talked-about piece in the magazine's brief life was a cover story by a woman writer: "Why Can't I Get Laid in San Francisco." But the content of *City* was not its only handicap. The office was always—in the words of staffer Rasa Gustaitis—"total chaos, a constant roller coaster ride, a strip mine." Names were constantly misspelled, credit lines were lost, stories were assigned but never turned in, entire issues were torn apart and reassembled on deadline and the graphics were so outlandish that one writer says the magazine seemed engaged in "an active conspiracy against the written word—a campaign to discourage readership."

Perhaps the best example of the frenzied turmoil that pervaded *City* offices was the $70,000, Rube Goldberg-like private telephone system Coppola had installed.

The system so infuriated *City* staffers with its random ringings and sudden breakdowns that many made all their calls from a corner phone booth—and one man in the art department ripped his phone from the wall and sawed the receiver in half: an appropriately symbolic gesture for a magazine designed to help its readers cope with the frustrations and complexities of urban life.

14 / All-News Radio

It's seven in the morning, and all over Los Angeles, people are awakening to the sounds of their clock radios—tens of thousands of them tuned to the fanfare of trumpets and xylophones that herald the beginning of each newscast on KFWB.

The KFWB theme lasts only 12 seconds, but it is clearly designed to give the impression that something V-E-R-Y B-I-G is about to happen. Nothing in the announcer's stentorian tones is likely to contradict that impression:

"This is KFWB Los Angeles . . . Group W . . . Westinghouse Broadcasting . . . serving Southern California . . . All news, all the time . . . You give us 22 minutes; we'll give you the world . . ."

All news? All the time?

In 1964, when KFWB's sister station, WINS, introduced the all-news concept in New York, most people in radio thought the station's executives were certifiably crazy.

"There was no way they could find enough news or enough audience to make it work," says Reg Laite, then a reporter for WINS' major competitor, WCBS. "They were out of their minds, all of them."

That was Reg Laite in 1964. But in 1967, Laite's own station went all-news, and in 1976, both WINS and WCBS were still all-news and Laite himself was the new director of all-news KFWB.

All-news radio is the broadcasting phenomenon of the last decade. In almost every major city where there is an all-news station, that station ranks at or near the top of the market in the two critical measures of radio success—audience size and advertising revenue.

WINS and WCBS rank in the top five among New York's 64 radio stations. Los Angeles' two all-news stations, KFWB and KNX, hold similar rankings in that area's highly fragmented, 73-station market.

In Philadelphia, an all-news station is the number one rated station in town. In San Francisco and Miami, the all-news stations are number two; in Chicago and Boston, they're number three.

But why is all-news suddenly so popular? Haven't people been complaining that they're tired of news, tired of reading and hearing about crises and shortages and riots and trials and wars and violence and . . .

"That," says George Nicholaw, general manager of KNX in Los Angeles, "is precisely the point. Look at the news we've had in the last eight or 10 years—Watergate, Vietnam, a man on the moon, the '68 Democratic convention in Chicago, women's liberation, the assassinations of Martin Luther King and Robert Kennedy . . .

"There's a growing awareness that what's happening in the world affects everyone directly today. Thanks to modern communications and transportation, the world is smaller today. Things happen faster. People want to know about them. They need to know about them."

Robert Mounty, general manager of the short-lived NBC all-news network, put it this way:

"If I'd walked outside my office 10 years ago and asked people what Saudi Arabia was, most of them would have thought it was some new kind of imported sportscar.

"But when King Faisal was assassinated [in 1975], people immediately wondered what that would do to the price of gas for their cars."

Most journalists, sociologists and psychologists who have studied the all-news concept tend to agree with Nicholaw and Mounty. To them, the success of all-news is born of insecurity and curiosity.

"It's part of a general social-psychological phenomenon," says Harold Mendelsohn of the University of Denver School of Communications. "Americans are now very anxious about knowing what happens the instant it happens. Deep in the recesses of their consciousness is the damn thermonuclear thing and the related fear that we must all be ready at an instant's notice for some tragic catastrophe.

"People constantly feel in imminent danger. Subconsciously, they're terrified that if they don't keep up, they'll be caught short."

To some in radio, that kind of theorizing is just so much psychological gobbledygook. They see all-news radio as simply the most convenient, most accessible form of news available to people who wish to remain informed.

"When you want water, you turn on the faucet," says Art Schreiber, general manager of KFWB. "When you want news, you turn on us."

The ratings, however, would seem to lend some credence to the theories of men like Mendelsohn, Mounty and Nicholaw.

All-news radio attracts its largest audience, for example, during what the industry calls "morning drive time"—from 5 or 6 a.m. to 9 or 10 a.m., when most people are waking up, dressing, eating breakfast and driving to work or school. The demand for news is so great during those hours that many stations with formats other than all-news shift to a three-or four-hour all-news block during that time.

It is not unusual, in fact, for the three largest audiences in Los Angeles radio during morning drive time to be KNX, KFWB and KABC—all of them then broadcasting news exclusively.

"Ours has become a rather frantic society," says Ken Draper, program director at KFWB. "There's something comforting about waking up each morning, turning to an all-news station and learning right away that everything's still OK, that we haven't been invaded by either the Russians or the Martians while you were asleep."

George Mair, former director of community service for KNX, thinks many listeners take an almost perverse delight in listening to all-news radio each morning.

"They're the same kind of people who go to the circus for the high-wire act or go to Ontario Speedway hoping to see a big crash," Mair says.

"They get a psychic pleasure out of a sense of impending disaster, an anticipation of tragedy, and they want to be in on it, part of it, the first to know about it."

Draper doesn't fully accept that explanation, but he does think people listen to all-news because they want to be the first to know something.

"It's socially advantageous," he says, "to walk into your office or meet some people for lunch and be able to say, 'Hey, did you hear Joe Busch just died?' or 'Hey, the Dodgers just blew another one' or 'Hey, I just heard that Cher is getting a divorce; she only got married nine days ago.'"

Psychologist Chaytor Mason thinks the ability to share that kind of "impersonal gossip" is especially appealing to those who feel "inadequate and overpowered in contemporary society.

"They're afraid to reveal themselves in conversation," Mason says. "They don't know what to say. So they chatter about news stories—the newer, the better. It makes them feel like they're on top of things, in control, one up on their otherwise intimidating peers."

There are, of course, almost as many theories about why people listen to an all-news station as there are listeners to all-news stations—if only because there are so many all-news listeners, cutting across so many demographic lines, that it is difficult to generalize. (Both KNX and KFWB, for example, consistently reach more than one million *different* listeners every week—a spectacular performance in a radio market as fragmented as Los Angeles.)

There are, however, a few common denominators in even the most diverse of audiences.

People tend to listen to all-news, it is generally agreed, because—as our existence becomes more specialized and compartmentalized—we seek at least the superficial knowledge in other areas that a brief but regular exposure to all-news radio can provide.

All-news radio also seems to offer listeners a sense of community in an otherwise amorphous and impersonal urban society—"almost like gathering around the old village well to exchange gossip," says Miriam Bjerre of KNX.

At its most basic level, all-news radio can be seen as simply providing company in an empty house or car—"the security or sexual attraction of one voice, talking directly to you, when you're alone" as one radio news executive sees it.

Trying to identify the precise appeal of all-news radio is almost as difficult as trying to pinpoint its origins.

The format seems to have had its tentative beginnings in Portland and San Francisco in the mid- to late-1950s. But it wasn't until Gordon McLendon brought all-news to XTRA in Tijuana that network executives began to see its potential.

XTRA was a renegade station of sorts, audible in Los Angeles and throughout parts of the Southwest, but Jim Simon—later the director of news and programming for KABC—can barely stifle his laughter when he recalls his early days with XTRA.

"We had two men to read the news," he says. "One guy looked exclusively at the AP tickertape; the other guy looked exclusively at the UPI tickertape. We took turns on the air, 15 minutes at a time. It was strictly rip-and-read—no rewriting, no checking, no individual enterprise."

The modern all-news stations are far more sophisticated—and far more expensive—than XTRA. KNX and KFWB each has a staff of more than 100, about half of them reporters, writers, editors and announcers.

Each station also has an annual budget of more than $4 million—more than almost any other station in town.

The NBC all-news network was also an expensive operation—a staff of 160, $10 million for start-up and first-year costs and an anticipated budget of $11.6 million annually thereafter.

Rates for the NBC News and Information Service varied with market size, but even in a city as large as Los Angeles, the annual charge was only $180,000—far less than the cost of running an independent all-news station, even including the station's additional costs for developing its own local news.

NBC provided up to 47 minutes of national and international news per hour, and local stations subscribing to the service had to fill in the balance with local news. Stations could, however, have taken as little as 28 minutes per hour if they preferred to use more local news—as many did during morning drive time, so they could repeatedly give the time, weather forecast and traffic conditions.

NBC began its all-news network in 1975, with plans to sell the format to 150 stations by the end of 1976. But fewer than half that number signed up, and network executives announced they would discontinue the service by mid-1977.

The NBC all-news service was thought to be especially attractive to small and medium-sized cities that neither produce enough local news nor generate enough advertising to support an independent all-news station. But NBC officials had also hoped to sell the service to enough large city stations, at higher rates, to both increase revenue and acquire prestige.

But the success of CBS and Westinghouse in most major markets thwarted NBC, and with no AM outlets in these markets, NBC had considerable trouble convincing stations in other markets that their all-news service would be good enough—or last long enough—to warrant the expensive and risky commitment to a new format.

Even the AM stations owned and operated by NBC were reluctant to make the switch—only WRC in Washington, D.C., did so—and NBC finally had to sell their service to FM stations instead. Thus, of the nation's ten largest cities, NBC had an AM all-news outlet in only two (Detroit and Dallas). In four others—New York, Chicago, Baltimore and Houston—NBC had to settle for FM. In the remaining four—Los Angeles, Philadelphia, San Diego and Cleveland—NBC had no all-news outlet at all, AM or FM.

For a while, NBC executives tried to brazen it out, insisting they preferred FM stations in some markets. But most people in radio scoffed at that as *ex post facto* rationalization.

"Given the nature of an FM signal," says one East Coast radio man, "even the most powerful FM stations fade in and out in certain cities. That's not generally conducive to building a regular audience with a new format."

Nevertheless, necessity could have been the mother of success at NBC, for adult listening habits are, indeed, changing. FM listenership has increased dramatically in the last six or eight years, and in one rating period, an FM station (WJIB-FM) placed number one in Boston, another (KBIG-FM) placed number two in Los Angeles and a third (WRFM) placed number three in New York . . . an unheard-of phenomenon just a few scant years ago, when FM audiences were so small, they almost thought of themselves as a cult.

What is happening, it seems, is a polarization of the listening audience. Just as many listeners want more news, many others want more music— and FM, with a far cleaner sound (in those areas where it is audible) and far fewer commercials, can provide that.

The dual evolutions toward FM and toward all-news are really the almost inevitable by-products of a shift from general-interest to special-interest radio programming that began with the rise of television.

"Too many people found they could get radio's brand of variety entertainment on TV," says Stanley Spero, general manager of KMPC in Los Angeles. "Radio programming had to become more specialized—jazz music, country music, personalities, talk and, now, all-news."

Many listeners perceive today's all-news stations as being almost identical from city to city, and it is true that there is a strong similarity among many stations; most, generally, are at their best in swarming over a big, breaking news story—a riot or an earthquake or a fire—when they can reach their audiences more quickly than either newspapers or television. But there are some clear differences among the various stations in their daily programming philosophy and performance.

KYW-Philadelphia, for example—a Westinghouse station—is generally conceded to have some of the best local news coverage of any all-news station, providing responsible, thorough reportage that often includes major interpretive and investigative efforts.

In contrast, WBBM-Chicago—a CBS station—fills the airways with four hours of often corny domestic banter surrounding the news each day during the time slot filled by Bob and Betty ("Mr. and Mrs. News") Sanders.

CBS and Westinghouse now compete head-to-head in three cities. In one—Philadelphia—the CBS all-news operation did not begin until 1975, and, despite significant strides, still has not caught up with Westinghouse's KYW. But in New York and Los Angeles, the CBS stations are generally thought to be superior to their Westinghouse competitors.

Los Angeles, because of its temperate climate and its reliance on the automobile, is a unique case. People drive farther to work—and to play—here, so they listen to the radio longer and more frequently. They also spend more time outdoors—working or relaxing in the yard or playing on the beach or in a park—where radios are the most convenient source of companionship and/or entertainment.

KFWB's Ken Draper, who devised the "You give us 22 minutes; we'll give you the world" format, calls radio in Los Angeles "a subliminal medium.

"Even driving 45 minutes on the freeway, from Woodland Hills to downtown, you'll be distracted by traffic or by your own thoughts. The same news story may come on the radio two or three times, but you'll really only hear it once," he says.

That, according to Draper, is the theory behind the 22-minute format on KFWB. Most stories are repeated at least twice an hour, and major stories are mentioned six times—once in the "headlines" that begin each 22-minute newscast, again in the body of each newscast.

KNX also repeats some stories within any given hour, but their repetition is less frequent—partially because of a difference in programming philosophy, partially because of the KNX commitment to use CBS network material at specific times every hour.

It is generally agreed that people seldom listen to any all-news station for more than 15 to 25 minutes at any one time, and the KFWB 22-minute format would seem to cater to that habit—and to give listeners the feeling that, at any time of the day, they're never more than a few minutes away from the day's big stories.

But the 22-minute format also would seem to discourage a longer listening span, and that may help explain why listeners tend to stay turned to KNX about 25 percent longer than to KFWB each day. KNX has been a consistent winner in the ratings war.

KFWB's sister station in New York, WINS, switched to the 22-minute format in January, but the CBS station there, WCBS, also has continued to win the ratings war.

The differences between the CBS and Westinghouse stations in New York and—especially—in Los Angeles have become more discernible under the 22-minute Westinghouse format.

KFWB is clearly more entertainment (rather than information) oriented than KNX, for example—seemingly aiming for a less-sophisticated, less demanding audience.

KFWB officials tacitly acknowledge this.

"When I joined KFWB," says Ken Draper, "I didn't think we were doing news for the people who pumped gas, only for the people who had white-collar jobs and made a lot of money. I think the entertainment value of news is the most critical. I think news can be exciting. In any survey I've ever seen, people put the desire to be educated at the bottom of the list of their priorities in deciding what radio station to listen to."

KFWB covers local news well and also provides listeners with generally sound national and international news and commentary from Westinghouse reporters around the world. Nevertheless, there is a certain tone, a certain feeling, about the overall programming that clearly reflects Draper's philosophy.

Sandwiched around the news are light features, whimsical essays and pun-filled weather reports. Even the news stories themselves are sometimes more frivolous than those on KNX. On one morning, a story about the development of pre-deodorized underwear was a major news story on KFWB—repeated six times every hour, all morning.

"KFWB is the top 40 of all-news radio," says one radio executive.

"It's the three Rs of all-news radio—rapes, robberies and wrecks," says Dick Casper, general manager of WINZ-Miami.

Perhaps that explains why, when the 1971 earthquake struck Los Angeles, listeners turned to KFWB by the hundreds of thousands. Their ratings almost tripled that day and the next day; KNX ratings increased only 25 percent.

"KFWB is like a tabloid newspaper, like the *New York Daily News*," says Jim Simon, formerly of KABC. "KNX is more like the *New York Times*. It's a news machine. It just keeps pumping out the news, more news than you could ever want to hear in your whole life."

KNX has tried to brighten its format in the last two or three years, but it is still a sober and more sophisticated—at times, even stodgy—dispenser of news. KNX blends network celebrities like Walter Cronkite, Dan Rather and Daniel Schorr into local programming that is generally serious-minded, seldom lighthearted, often featuring documentaries on such subjects as illegal aliens, women in prison, homosexuality, alcoholism, rapid transit and the energy crisis.

Not surprisingly, KNX generally scores heaviest with the better-educated, higher-income listeners; KFWB generally scores heavier with blue-collar listeners and minorities.

KFWB also is beginning to draw more successfully from younger listeners.

In Los Angeles, KNX and KFWB rank one-two among listeners in their fifties and older—listeners who generally have a greater interest and a greater stake in (and, concomitantly, a greater anxiety about) the day's events. But in one typical ratings period, KNX and KFWB ranked 13th and 14th among listeners 18 to 24—and they ranked 16th and 22nd among teen-agers.

KFWB hopes to change that with its brighter, lighter, tighter format.

But even with these differences between the two stations, the lines of demarcation still aren't completely clear, and both stations overlap considerably in all demographic areas.

Listener loyalty is, however, remarkably consistent. Few people who listen to KNX also listen to KFWB—and vice versa. There is less duplication between these two stations than between, say, any two rock stations or any two country music stations or any other two stations in town with similar formats.

There is general agreement that programming all-news is one of the most difficult jobs in radio, if only because—on most days—there just isn't enough interesting or important news to fill 24 hours. The result, often, is either contrived lightheartedness or trivia repeated *ad nauseum.*

"There's a basic, rhythmic dullness to the constant presentation of news," admits Dave Nelson, general manager of WCBS in New York.

"Not all news is interesting," Nelson says. "A lot of it is even depressing. It's difficult to walk the line between being credible and authoritative, providing good, solid, responsible journalism on the one hand, and still being bright, light and interesting on the other."

Nelson has managed that balancing act quite well, according to his peers; WCBS is generally regarded as the best all-news station in the country, with solid local, national and international news, good sports, business and weather coverage, special documentaries and perhaps the best all-news anchormen in the field.

KCBS-San Francisco is also well-regarded, as are both Los Angeles stations. But the all-news format everywhere has many critics—critics who see it as little more than a headline service, a superficial presentation of news blurbs to listeners not sufficiently sophisticated to appreciate the underlying significance of most stories.

Too often, these critics say, all-news stations seem to do too little with the resources available to them. Even on the best stations, there is too much repetition, too much routine, institutional coverage and too little interpretive or investigative or genuine human-interest reporting.

But that criticism, if not made carefully and specifically, can be both specious and spurious.

"There is a tendency," says Gordon Davis, former general manager of KFWB, "for people in newspapers to fault all-news radio for what it isn't, rather than for what it is. You shouldn't criticize all-news radio for not being a daily newspaper, any more than you should criticize a daily newspaper for not being a book. Neither is an adequate substitute for the other, but each does something the other can't do."

15 / A Personal View: Of Obscenity, Timidity and Hypocrisy

It was, perhaps, the most controversial (if not the most consequential) event of the entire 1976 presidential campaign: Jimmy Carter gave a lengthy interview to *Playboy* magazine, and in the course of that interview, he not only admitted that he had "looked on a lot of women with lust," he also used such words as "screw" and "shack up."

Screw?

Shack up?

A candidate for president of the United States saying "screw" and "shack up"? The howls of righteous indignation poured forth. Mr. Carter was accused of using "barracks language," "locker-room language," "*gutter language.*" It was bad enough that he had even granted an interview to a magazine like *Playboy.* (Never mind that at least two other presidential candidates, Senator George McGovern and California Governor Jerry Brown, as well as Albert Schweitzer, Princess Grace, Senator Charles Percy, Martin Luther King, Arnold Toynbee, Buckminster Fuller, Walter Cronkite and such card-carrying conservatives as Bob Hope, William Buckley and John Wayne had all previously been interviewed by *Playboy* without having either their sanity or their integrity publicly impugned). It was bad enough that Mr. Carter had admitted to having carnal thoughts about a few women. (Never mind that it was, for a politician, a uniquely candid admission of something almost every man has felt—and an admission made to allay fears that his religious beliefs would make him a rigid and unbending president). But to do all this and to say "screw" and "shack up," too, why, it . . . it . . . it was the most blasphemous of betrayals.

But large numbers of Americans didn't even know Mr. Carter had said "screw" and "shack up"; many newspapers—and radio and television stations (including the CBS and ABC nightly news shows)—either omitted the words altogether or substituted vague euphemisms for them. Walter Cronkite simply said Mr. Carter had used "words mild for *Playboy* but perhaps a little racy for Sunday school." The *New York Times* said Carter "used a vulgarism for sexual relations." Which "vulgarism"? The implication, to many, was that Mr. Carter had said "fuck"—a far more heinous sin than "screw" in the jaundiced eyes of those who would be offended by any such colloquial divergence from the King's English. The next day, apparently realizing they had perpetrated a misimpression on their readers, *Times* editors changed the reference to "a common but mild vulgarism for sexual intercourse." Why didn't the *Times* just print the damn word, rather than beat around the journalistic bush? A. M. Rosenthal, managing editor of the *Times*, said, "It was simply a matter of taste and style, *our* taste and style. It has been our policy not to use obscenities in the paper. It's a harmless little eccentricity of ours." A "harmless little eccentricity"? To put a story on page one and then report it imprecisely and incompletely—a story that generated nationwide debate about a presidential candidate's fitness for office?

Fortunately, not all newspapers were so timid. Many in fact, quoted Mr. Carter verbatim. That, I suppose, is a measure of how far the press— and society—has progressed from the embarrassingly unprofessional prudery of earlier years. As recently as 1963, when a Dallas police officer called Jack Ruby a "son of a bitch" just as Ruby shot Lee Harvey Oswald, most newspapers either excised the offending phrase or abbreviated it to "s.o.b." But everyone, on that dark weekend in Dallas, wondered about Ruby's relationship with Oswald and with the police: Did Ruby and Oswald know each other? Had the police invited Ruby to the station? Was he part of a conspiracy? Were they? What the police officer said to Ruby might have provided a clue—a clue most Americans were deprived of by the gratuitous moral guardianship of the nation's newspaper editors.

Although this linguistic puritanism *has* lessened over the past decade or so, the *New York Times'* tremulous treatment of "screw" makes it clear that the struggle for candor and clarity is far from won; there are still many words and phrases that many (if not most) newspapers are unwilling to use, regardless of the context of the language or the significance of the story. A classic example of this editorial timorousness occurred just a couple of weeks after the release of the *Playboy* interview with Mr. Carter: Secretary of Agriculture Earl Butz was quoted as having told singer Pat Boone that Republicans can't attract black voters "Because coloreds only want three things . . . First, a tight pussy; second, loose shoes; and third, a warm place to shit." This time a firestorm of controversy broke around President Ford. How, the Democrats asked, could he possibly have in his Cabinet a man possessed of such repugnant, racist views? It was, the Democrats chortled publicly, typical of the Republicans' insensitivity to blacks. It was an election-year crisis for Ford—only partially alleviated by Butz' resignation. Who will ever know how much of Mr. Carter's narrow margin of victory—and his overwhelming support among blacks—was influenced by that one event? But no daily newspaper in the United States except the Toledo (Ohio) *Blade* and the Madison (Wisconsin) *Capital Times* quoted Butz verbatim; all others either substituted blanks or ellipses for "pussy" and "shit" or they resorted to such euphemisms and circumlocutions as "a woman's sexual organ" and "defecate" or they said—as the *New York Times* did, in terms as sexist as they were imprecise—that Butz had uttered "obscene, derogatory and scatological terms" for "satisfying sex, loose shoes and a warm place for bodily functions." (At times, one felt as if it were all a game—or, perhaps, a crossword puzzle in a girlie magazine: "No. 19 down—A five-letter word for a woman's sex organ." Courageously, however, no editors dropped "shoes" from Butz' remarks and substituted "an article of footwear.")

Similar examples of this silliness abound:

- A Los Angeles Municipal Court judge was removed from the bench a couple of years ago for, among other transgressions, allegedly abusive treatment of law enforcement officers. On one occasion, it was charged, she capriciously ordered a government lawyer imprisoned and later asked the bailiff who had accompanied him to jail, "Did they look up his ass?" (a routine check for narcotics). The word "ass" was replaced with three dashes in press reports of the incident. The same judge was alleged to have become so angry with a police officer that she said, "I'm going to shoot his balls off and give him a .38-vasectomy." In the newspaper accounts of that incident "balls" was replaced with a long dash followed by "testicles" in parentheses.
- Just before the 1976 Democratic convention, Governor Philip Noel of Rhode Island spoke with columnist Jack Anderson about the problems of black teenagers being bused to white schools, then returning to the ghetto, "with a drunken father and a mother that's out peddling . . ." Newspapers said Noel used "an obscenity alluding to prostitution." Which obscenity? "Ass"? "Pussy"? The story engendered so much resentment among blacks that Noel, the temporary chairman of the Democratic national platform committee, could not seek the permanent committee chairmanship; a few months later, he was defeated in the primary in his bid for reelection to the governor's mansion. But no

newspaper quoted the offending word that helped destroy his political career.

- Not too long ago, on the front page of its Sunday entertainment section, the *New York Times* published a lengthy article about network censorship of movies that were bought for TV. The article began with a discussion of the search for a substitute for the word "twat" in the movie *Blazing Saddles*. The substitute word would have to be a one-syllable word, preferably one beginning with a "tw" sound so the viewer would not be jarred when he saw the actor's lips form one word on the screen, only to have a radically different, dubbed-in word come through his television speaker. At the time this article was written, CBS-TV executives seemed uncertain about whether to opt for "twerp" or "twivit" (the latter apparently having the advantage of ending in a "t," like "twat," but the disadvantage of having two syllables). The article was an unusually insightful commentary on the technological, commercial and artistic concerns involved in a crucial executive decision. Only one thing was missing from the *New York Times* article. Nowhere in the story did the word "twat" appear. "Twivit" and "twerp" were there, but no "twat." It was left to the reader to supply the word himself, either by using the powers of deductive reasoning or, if he had already seen the movie, by remembering that brief and relatively inconsequential bit of dialogue.

It could be argued, of course, that in none of these stories was the precise "obscenity" absolutely essential—that what mattered was not the exact word involved but Judge Cannon's behavior, Governor Noel's attitude and the television executives' technological dilemma. It could be further argued that the inclusion of any of the appropriate "obscenities" would alienate and offend more readers than such precision would warrant. But I don't think a writer should ever have to justify any word as "absolutely essential" or "worth the alienation of countless readers." The only test in word selection should be: "Is it accurate—is it the best word for the occasion?" The same test should be applied whether the word is "big" or "beautiful" or "balls."

When Norman Mailer interviewed Jimmy Carter for the *New York Times* Sunday magazine during the 1976 presidential campaign, Mr. Carter—trying again to reassure voters that he would not impose his religious and moral beliefs on them—said, "I don't care if people say 'fuck'." *Times* editors ordered the word "fuck" stricken. Mailer substituted ". . . ." and appended the comment. "He actually said the famous four-letter word that the *Times* has not printed in the 125 years of its publishing life . . ." But Mailer's story was 16,500 words long: were any of the other 16,499 words subjected to so rigorous an examination—and so tortuous a circumlocution? Of course not.

Not that I advocate the indiscriminate use of four-letter words—at least, no more than I would advocate the indiscriminate use of six- or eight- or ten-letter words. I don't want reporters capriciously dropping "fuck" into stories, any more than I want them capriciously dropping "fast" or "flashy" or any other word into stories. I don't want a reporter who's covering a speech or a demonstration to feel obligated to reproduce every "fuck you" or "bullshit" he hears, any more than I want him to feel obligated to cut those words (or to cut, or include, every "stupid" or "marvelous" or any other word). The art of journalism is, to a certain extent, the art of compression and selection—of elimination and illumination—and the reporter must weigh every word for its relevance to his particular story. I only want all words weighed on the same scale. There are contexts in which "stupid" is preferable to "dumb," contexts in which the reverse is true and contexts in which neither is appropriate. The same is true of "fuck" and "intercourse" and their synonyms. But if "fuck" (or any other "obscene" word) is the best word—whether it is used in a direct quote or not, whether it is absolutely essential or not—it should be used, without hesitation or equivocation.

The English language is such that certain "obscenities" are often the best—the only—appropriate colloquialism. I once quoted someone as saying a particular individual had "brains and balls." The editors changed "balls" to "guts"—my vigorous insistence on the crucial differences between the two notwithstanding. The same thing happened when I quoted a Black Panther as saying, "The white man's been screwing us for 300 years"; I could not convince my editor that neither "cheating" nor "exploiting" nor "oppressing" nor any other substitute carried the connotations and implications of "screwing." The word "bullshit" has been especially troublesome for me—and others—in this regard. I once quoted an architect's wife as fondly summing up her husband's bizarre tales of travel and conquest in these words: "Richard's the biggest bullshitter in the world." The sentence was edited out—even though my editor agreed with me that no substitute—"liar"? "con artist"? "phony"? "story-teller"? —conveyed precisely the shade of meaning as "bullshitter."

My editors at the *Los Angeles Times* told me "bullshit" was not absolutely essential to my story.

Bullshit!

That's merely a convenient subterfuge for their own timidity, for even when such words are "absolutely essential," most editors are afraid to use them. When J. Anthony Lukas, Pulitzer Prize-winning reporter for the *New York Times*, was covering the trial of eight radicals accused of conspiring to disrupt the 1968 Democratic convention in Chicago, one of the defendants, David Dellinger, looked up after a particularly disturbing bit of testimony and said, "Oh, bullshit!" The judge admonished Dellinger for "using that kind of language" in court, and revoked his bail for the duration of the trial. That, clearly, was "central to the day's events," as Lukas later wrote. But neither the *Times* nor any other newspaper quoted Dellinger.

"The editor on duty said he didn't think we could use it, and suggested I just say 'an obscenity'," Lukas says. "I objected, arguing that it wasn't, strictly speaking, an obscenity; that if we call it that, most people would assume it was something much worse; and that . . . we ought to tell our readers just what Mr. Dellinger had said." Lukas said his editor then suggested "we call it a barnyard epithet," and Lukas—frustrated—gave in.

He shouldn't have had to. I mean, here were two grown men, working for the newspaper generally considered the paper of record in the United States in 1970, trying to find some admittedly inadequate substitute for a word that had triggered the day's biggest news at one of the decade's most sensational and significant trials. Ridiculous! We're supposed to be in the business of communication, not obfuscation. Who are newspaper editors to edit history? No, not edit history; rewrite it and distort it.

It was not the first time editors had appropriated that role for themselves. Just two years earlier, during the Democratic convention itself, witnesses said Chicago Mayor Richard Daley became so incensed by what Senator Abraham Ribicoff was saying about Chicago police tactics that Daley leaped to his feet and shouted, "Fuck you, you Jew son of a bitch, you lousy mother-fucker, go home."

That outburst was certainly relevant to what was happening in the convention hall and outside in the streets; it was certainly relevant to what the young demonstrators were saying about the attitude Daley and the police and the Democratic establishment had toward them, toward minorities and toward all who criticized the status quo. But no newspaper in the country quoted Daley.

On rare occasion, an editor will defy this unwritten prohibition against "dirty words." The results, for him, are often catastrophic. I know. I was filling in for the city editor one night when I was working for the Long Beach (California) *Independent, Press-Telegram*, and I did not change a line in another reporter's account of a civil rights demonstration: "He told him to 'Get your black ass out of here.'" The next day, the regular city editor came back—and was promptly buried beneath a blizzard of memos from the front office. Our jobs—if not, indeed, our lives—had been jeopardized, the memos implied (his because he had foolishly trusted me, mine because I had been horrendously irresponsible). Ultimately, we both survived. Charles T. Alexander, editor of the Dayton (Ohio) *Journal Herald*, was not so fortunate.

In 1975, two Treasury agents had a bitter argument in Dayton. One said to the other: "Goddamn it, you are fucking with my family. You are fucking with my future . . . I'll kill you first." The man doing the talking then pulled a gun and shot the other man dead.

The *Journal Herald* printed the exchange verbatim, reasoning—

Alexander later explained—"We reported the story of a savage argument in which the obscene word was directly crucial to the outcome, a fatal fight . . . they were the last words of a man drawing his gun to kill a fellow agent and friend."

But the owners of the *Journal Herald* didn't quite see it that way. They had lost confidence in Alexander's judgment, they said. He resigned.

Editors and publishers who oppose the publication of "obscene" words argue that by printing them, they would appear to be sanctioning, perhaps encouraging, the legitimization of the words. My response to that line of reasoning is (1) Great! Maybe if we legitimize these words, they'll lose their capacity to offend, and we can quit playing charades with them, and (2) This legitimization is not, alas, likely to take place. Newspapers just aren't that influential. Besides, the press regularly reports rapes and robberies and murders, and their doing so isn't construed as approval of those acts; I detect no groundswell of support for legalizing rape.

Editors and publishers also argue—with a moral fervor that approaches frenzy—that "obscene" words must be kept out of the daily newspaper because young children will see them. This is perhaps the most specious of all anti-obscenity arguments. Most children who are old enough to read the daily newspaper have already encountered most variations of the most salacious four-letter words. In addition, there is absolutely no evidence that repeated, or even infrequent, exposure to such language is either offensive or corrupting. Those few children precocious enough to read the daily newspaper but too young, or too sheltered, to have been previously exposed to obscenity are even less likely to be irreparably damaged by such exposure. They wouldn't know what they were reading anyway; an "obscene" word would just be another arbitrary and incomprehensible configuration of letters.

In fact, the sheer folly of attempting to safeguard the morals of the young by eschewing obscenity in the press was brought home to me a few years ago when an elderly Californian lion named Frasier received considerable publicity after impregnating several lionesses. The newspaper photographs of Frasier showed him lying blissfully on his back, front paws curled, hind legs spread apart—with his genitals carefully airbrushed out.

When I showed the newspaper report on Frasier to Leonard, the ten-year-old boy next door, he gleefully read the story, then glanced a second time at the picture and, his face contorted with bewilderment and consternation, said to me:

"But, Mr. Shaw, what happened to his balls?"

What, though, of the "good taste" argument—the argument that even adults should be able to read the daily newspaper, free of the terrifying visual onslaught of four-letter words? That, too, is specious.

As Seymour Krim writes in his book *Shake It for the World, Smartass*, the "much-used and abused journalistic slogan 'good taste' merely enables the middleclass public [to] continue its hypocritical idealism in spite of facts which were quite different."

Leonard Shecter, formerly the sports editor at *Look*, made the point even more tellingly when he complained that the excision of words like "horny" and "bullshit" from his *Look* stories reflected "an elderly, prissy, mid-century middle-America, an America that, in fact, no longer exists."

I would argue, in fact, that the press' attitude toward "obscenity" is rather similar to its attitude toward sex itself: Just as newspapers try to safeguard the sensibilities of their readers by pretending certain four-letter words don't exist, so they pretend certain sex acts—preferably all sex acts—don't exist. It's the Victorian attitude, the concept that sex is a subject not fit for public discourse or acknowledgement, a subject appropriate only to the dark, dirty corners inhabited by perverts and degenerates. In this way, the press has helped perpetuate the hypocritical Puritanism that has stifled and repressed natural human sexuality and spontaneity in this country until so recently.

Thus, when Los Angeles police were arresting the cast of the play *The Beard* almost nightly a few years ago, most newspapers described the act of simulated cunnilingus that triggered the arrests as "an unnatural sex act"—a term as pejorative as it was inaccurate. One editor told me he didn't think the "exact nature of the act was all that important to the story." But that same editor would certainly have questioned—and reprimanded—any police reporter who described a bank robbery as, simply, "a criminal act." And woe unto the sportswriter who would have described the playing of the national anthem before a football game as "an unnatural patriotic act."

I came across an even more grievous case of the editor-sitting-as-moral-arbiter early in 1972 at the *Los Angeles Times*. It was one of those dreadfully foggy winter mornings that seem to descend upon the Los Angeles area about five or six times a year. Invariably, the first rain and fog of the year are accompanied by accidents and impenetrably snarled traffic, as cars ricochet off each other with all the thunderous clanging of the climactic pinball championship scene in the movie *Tommy*.

The morning of February 28, 1972, was just such a fog-shrouded morning—there were twelve separate accidents on one two-mile stretch of freeway. Twelve people were hurt, a total of sixty-nine cars were involved and the freeway was closed for more than three hours at the peak of rush hour.

It made a good newspaper story. However, if you caught the headlines in that afternoon's edition of the *Los Angeles Times*, you would have read about a "70-Car Fog Pileup." That's right: 70, not 69. A news editor at the *Times* (since retired) arbitrarily changed 69 to 70 in both the headline and the story because he thought using 69 might somehow offend readers by subconsciously reminding them of the sex act of the same name—er, number.

The *Los Angeles Times* is, as one American magazine recently and correctly noted in an article "Living With Dirty Words," "more courageous in its use of language than the majority of American newspapers." Nevertheless, the story of the 69-cum-70-car freeway pileup is, in many ways, indicative of the timidity and hypocrisy of the American daily newspaper in dealing with what has become—if it was not always—everyday language for a great many of its readers.

To be sure, editors and publishers are not as timid as they once were. After all, most *did* use the Jimmy Carter "screw" story, and most *did* quote then-President Nixon saying, on one of the Watergate tapes, "I don't give a shit what happens. I want you to stonewall it." But these are exceptions—made grudgingly, prompted by historical necessity. Words like "damn," "hell," "bastard" and "son of a bitch"—once as difficult to find in a newspaper as a nymphomaniac in a nunnery—may appear with some regularity now, but, often, only after prolonged debate. And their more pungent four-letter associates are still routinely eschewed.

You could argue, I guess, that everyone knows "f---" is "fuck" (or is it "fart"?) and that "questioned his ancestry" obviously means "son of a bitch" (or is it "bastard"?), and that there is no need to spell out what is so readily apparent. But we spell out other words—and other situations— don't we? Everyone knows "Former President N----" is "Former President Nixon," but we spell out his name. It's obvious that "hit a h--- r--" in a sports story means "hit a home run," but we spell it out. If the four-letter words are equally obvious, why not follow the same practice? Why play games with blanks and dashes and euphemisms?

I don't for a moment deny that some people are offended by these words. Nor am I ignorant of what cancelled subscriptions and advertising contracts mean to any newspaper. But I don't think either would reach epidemic proportions. This is, after all, the last quarter of the 20th century; readers may finally be somewhat more sophisticated than editors think. (The few publications that did *not* censor Earl Butz' remarks about blacks in 1976 found themselves swamped with calls from readers outside their circulation area who wanted to know just what he'd said; a few papers that *didn't* print Butz' exact words but did invite readers down to read the remarks for themselves were also swamped: The Lubbock (Texas) *Avalanche-Journal* published such an invitation, and was promptly visited by 200 readers—including a farmer and his wife who had come from 70 miles away. The *San Diego Evening Tribune*—a very conservative paper in a very conservative town—offered to mail Butz remarks to anyone writing in for them. More than 3,000 readers wrote in that very week.) Even if some readers would object to "obscene" language, though, I would argue that the nation's press has a higher responsibility than to cater to the unreasonable pruderies and prejudices of a relatively few of their readers—readers who will use a word themselves in anger or in jest but will object when it is used by others in print.

With such genuine obscenities as poverty, corruption, crime, pollution and our prison system all begging for attention and salvation, it seems preposterously self-indulgent for these readers to get upset by words that describe human bodily organs and their functions.

One of the newspaper's functions is to serve as a mirror—reflecting the values and standards of the society it represents. But I think a newspaper —a good newspaper—also ought to help formulate and influence those values and standards, not just reflect them; it ought to anticipate, not just react; to lead, not just follow.

Most newspapers were late in acknowledging, no less deploring, white racism in our society. Had they been in the vanguard, instead of the rear-guard—had they written their voluminous news stories and indignant editorials before Watts, not after—it's just possible there might not have been a Watts. The same may be said of the press' editorial-come-lately approach to the war in Vietnam, the threat to our environment, the conditions in our prisons.

Most papers didn't want to print stories on those subjects until crises or violence made them unavoidable. They were afraid of offending the sensibilities of their affluent, comfortable, middle-class readers, who, presumably, either didn't know about these conditions or, more likely, didn't object to them so long as they were not personally affected.

The same is true of the obscenity issue. Editors know their readers are wrong—foolish—to allow themselves to suffer fits of apoplexy over mere words, arbitrary configurations of letters, directed at no one in particular. The editors know, too, that change is coming—is already under way, in fact.

But newspapers should not just passively await desirable change; they should agitate for it—or, if not agitate, at least encourage it, even implicitly, by refusing to pay obeisance to the blatant sham and hypocrisy inherent in "f---" and "barnyard epithet" and "hurled an obscenity."

Editors may argue that it is self-defeating to risk alienating readers over four-letter words when so many more serious issues must be confronted. Similarly, editors will argue that a newspaper can lead only so far if the readership isn't willing to follow: "You can write about Watts or smog all you want," they say, "but if the readers don't care or aren't ready to worry about it yet, you're wasting your space and their time."

Both arguments have considerable merit—or would have, except that for most papers, it's rationalization, not rational argument.

Most editors—even many of those who personally favor the publication of "profanity"—are no more likely to take those first tentative steps slightly ahead of their readers than to stake out a pioneering position far ahead of their readers. Their dereliction of editorial duty in so relatively trivial a matter as four-letter words, I would argue, is indicative of a widespread and deep-rooted timidity to confront issues of transcendent importance as well . . . in the editorial pages and the news columns. I sincerely believe that attitude is at least partially to blame for the divisiveness and malaise now afflicting our society. By not doing what it should when it should, by refusing to "offend" readers over certain conditions (and words) until it is "safe" to do so, the press has been, however unwittingly, an accessory to the crimes of oppression, pollution, racism and hypocrisy.

Epilogue: The Future

The daily newspaper—an American institution since 1784—is being challenged today as never before by forces as widely disparate as inflation, urban flight, reader disaffection, unemployment and the automobile—not to mention apartment-house living, a diminished sense of community, trends toward later marriage and childbirth, charges of bias, negativism and irrelevance, and competition from television, radio, special-interest publications and a growing profusion of leisure-time activities.

From 1973 to 1975, the number of daily newspapers sold in the United States dropped 4.6 percent—and the number of people who read a daily paper dropped more than 7 percent . . . the first such declines in more than 40 years.

Since 1970, the three New York newspapers combined have lost 550,000 readers, the two largest Philadelphia newspapers have lost more than 150,000 readers, the two Cleveland papers about 90,000, the two San Francisco papers more than 80,000.

The *Los Angeles Times*, after doubling its circulation in the decade of the 1960s, reached a peak in March 1973, then lost more than 40,000 daily sales from November 1973 to November 1975.

Some newspapers have lost *all* their circulation: since 1960, daily newspapers have gone out of business in New York, Chicago, Los Angeles, Boston, San Francisco, Detroit, Houston and Cleveland.

Many in the newspaper business see this decline as merely a "temporary readjustment," occasioned primarily by poor economic conditions in the country. In the Great Depression of the 1930s, they note, newspaper circulation fell 11 percent, but the nation's economic recovery subsequently carried circulation to all-time highs.

A similar recovery from the 1973–75 recession may, in fact, have already been underway in 1976: preliminary indications are that a number of newspapers regained some of their lost circulation. (The *Los Angeles Times*, for example, regained 34,000 of its 40,000 drop.)

Advertising revenue—which provides about 75 percent of most newspapers' income—has also increased substantially (about 17 percent in 1976.)

But most responsible editors and publishers are still concerned (even apprehensive) about the future of the daily newspaper—especially the large, metropolitan daily; in a recent study, more cited "declining readership" as their biggest problem than anything else.

"If we're not careful," says Barry Bingham, editor and publisher of the *Louisville Courier-Journal and Times*, "we could find ourselves in the buggywhip business; we could phase ourselves right out of existence."

To avoid this untimely end, many papers have authorized exhaustive market research studies on newspaper readership—and most have instituted new features and new policies designed to attract new readers and to retain old ones.

Since the newspaper industry has long suffered from what one academic critic calls "marketing myopia," such research and innovation are probably long overdue; in that sense, the circulation decline of the 1970s may be a blessing in disguise: Just as the Chinese characters for the word "crisis" have two very different meanings—"danger" and "opportunity"—so, in this crisis, the most thoughtful editors and publishers may be able to capitalize on the "opportunity," rather than succumbing to the "danger."

Unfortunately, some papers have, instead, resorted to panicky, short-term circulation-builders that will almost assuredly prove counter-productive—gimmicks like games and sweepstakes, front-page gossip columns, daily soap operas, a sensationalistic, yellow-journalism approach to the news.

Even the historically staid *New York Times*—down 112,000 readers from 1970 to 1975—joined the circulation war in 1976, sponsoring and promoting a search for the Loch Ness Monster.

In Detroit, where the *News* has lost more than 65,000 readers in the last two years, editors circulated an internal memo early in 1976 describing a column on rape, robbery and an auto accident as a "fine example" of the kind of stories they wanted "on top" of page one to regain lost readers.

"It was an example of just the horrors that are discussed at suburban cocktail parties," the memo said. "That's the $18,000-plus income group and 28–40 age group . . . we are aiming our product at.

"I want at least one, preferably two or three stories on [page] 1A that will jolt, shock or at least wake up our readers," the memo said: "Go through the last few weeks of the early edition and you'll see what I want: 'Nun charged with killing her baby.' 'Prison horrors revealed' . . . Look for sex, comedy and tragedy."

Most editors realize this is not a very sound approach to the problems of declining readership, though, and their attempts to resolve the problems have generally been somewhat more positive and substantive.

Many of these changes have been essentially economic and/or technological—the institution of such labor-saving processes as computerized typesetting and page-composition, a centralized home-delivery system, the use of slightly smaller pages to reduce the runaway cost of raw newsprint.

Other changes have been largely cosmetic, designed to make the newspaper easier and more pleasurable to read—color photographs, wider columns, a more detailed index, prominently displayed national and international news digests, specific daily features anchored in the same place every day, sections divided by subject matter, even newsmagazine-style subject headings on each page.

But newspapers are losing readers primarily because readers no longer feel they really *need* a daily newspaper, so most changes are being effected to make the paper more relevant, more valuable, more *necessary* to the reader/consumer.

Studies show that many people have traditionally read a daily newspaper not so much because they were actively seeking information as because they simply enjoyed doing so—or felt obliged to do so. But today, with so many other activities (and obligations) competing for their time (and money)—and with the cost of subscribing to a newspaper having increased 26 percent in the last two years—that is no longer sufficient reason for many to read a paper.

Otis Chandler, publisher of the *Los Angeles Times*, says he doubts that the *Times* (or any other metropolitan daily) is "really essential" to even 50 percent of its readers.

"A lot of my colleagues insist we are essential," he says, "but I think they're listening to their own promotion departments. Our readers just aren't a captive audience anymore; they can do without us."

The newspaper, says columnist James Kilpatrick, has "no intrinsic function. . . . You cannot wear it, drive it, eat it, drink it or live in it." Its basic service/product is information—and for newspapers to survive in contemporary society, they must convince their readers that the information they provide is not just enlightening, not just entertaining, but *useful*.

And yet, to know what is useful to their readers, editors must know precisely who their readers are—and what they consider important. Studies have shown editors rarely know either.

This is especially worrisome in the midst of what pop sociologist Tom Wolfe calls "the ME decade"—a time when many people are less concerned with their communities than with themselves; they are absorbed, indeed obsessed, with their own problems, interests, desires and frustrations.

Great numbers of people simply don't *care* any longer about cosmic issues; that's one reason voter turnout has dropped steadily, from 63 percent in 1960 to 53 percent in 1976.

The traditional newspaper function of keeping readers well-informed about their neighborhood and their nation is of considerably diminished importance to people not only preoccupied with the burdens of inflation but compulsively searching for themselves through est, yoga, Transcendental Meditation, Scientology, Transactional Analysis, Hare Krishna, Primal Therapy. . . .

City magazines have catered to this self-absorption—and flourished. Newspapers have largely ignored it—and suffered.

"Most newspapers just pay too little attention to the daily concerns of their readers," says Tom Winship, editor of the *Boston Globe*. "We're out of touch. We have to show them we're aware of their problems. They're low now; we have to give them a little sympathy, a little hope, a little excitement."

In an effort to do just that, newspapers have recently instituted a wide range of personal advice columns and features—not merely the traditional advice-to-the-lovelorn but advice on shopping, health, grooming, fashions, pet care, home repairs, gardening, dining out, cooking, old age, taxes, investments, hobbies. . . .

Scores of papers have instituted "Action Line" columns through which they actually serve as social/consumer ombudsmen for their readers, responding to complaints about such things as lost pets and auto repair fraud.

Other newspapers provide clip-out coupons for their readers to apply for everything from CB radio licenses to swine flu injections.

Newspapers are also expanding their letters-to-the-editor columns and developing op-ed pages to give readers a greater opportunity to become part of the communications process. A few papers have taken this one step further: the Detroit *Free Press*, for example, invites readers to telephone their "Sound Off" column to voice opinions, which are then published in the paper.

Concomitantly, newspaper editors have decided that since they cannot really compete with leisure-time activities for the readers' time, they will try to become an essential adjunct to these activities—an indispensable guide to what to do, where to do it and, above all, how to do it as conveniently and inexpensively as possible.

"Some years ago, as leisure time increased, a favorite prediction of many newspapermen was that Sunday circulation would decline," says Lee Hills, chairman of the board of Knight-Ridder Newspapers. "The opposite has happened."

In fact, during the 1973–75 circulation slide, Sunday circulation dipped only a fraction of 1 percent, and now, many newspapers are trying to transplant to their weekday editions some of the features that have made their Sunday papers so successful.

The *New York Times* is publishing "Weekend," a leisure/entertainment guide, in its Friday editions; the *Los Angeles Times* is publishing "YOU," a consumer/leisure guide, every Tuesday; the *Boston Globe* is publishing "Calendar," a cultural guide for families and youth, on Thursday; the *Louisville Times* is publishing "Scene," a full-color Saturday magazine, complete with dating and astrology advice, tips on how to repair your own car, suggestions on how to spend the weekend, youth-oriented stories on how to shop for blue jeans, even a special children's pullout section called "Jelly Bean Journal."

Many other papers have greatly expanded their weekend weather forecasts and the camping/boating/fishing pages of their sports sections to include information of use to families and outdoorsmen alike.

Such innovations have been loudly trumpeted—ads in the newspapers, signs on the newspaper display racks, commercials on radio and television, promotional shorts in the local moviehouses. . . .

The *New York Times* spent an estimated $150,000 in four weeks to promote its newest addition—a Wednesday food and lifestyle supplement ("The Living Section") that debuted November 10, 1976.

Until quite recently, all this ballyhoo about why you should read your local newspaper had seemed about as necessary as bribing a drunk to attend a beer-bust.

Every year—almost without exception—newspaper circulation went up, advertising went up, profits went up. Then, in the recession/inflation of the 1970s, newspaper production costs soared; the price of raw newsprint alone jumped 58 percent in one 37-month period.

Since newsprint accounts for about 30 percent of most large newspapers' costs (it's 43 percent at the *Los Angeles Times*), newspapers were forced to pass along this—and other—increased costs to their readers (and advertisers).

In 1964, you could subscribe to the *Los Angeles Times* for $2.50 a month—only 25 cents more than in 1951. Now, after four price increases in the last three years, you get a bill every eight weeks for $11.20. (If you live in New York and subscribe to the *New York Times*, the bite is even bigger—as much as $35 for two months' home delivery.)

"The cost of subscribing is something people have to think about now," says Richard Leonard, editor of the *Milwaukee Journal*. "They don't just pay automatically anymore."

Today, for the first time, the cost of a newspaper subscription is not just odd change for the delivery boy at month's end; it's a genuine, budgetable expense—and at a time when the cost of everything else is going up, too.

In most families, expenses must be cut; something must go. In some of those families, that something is the daily newspaper.

Although George Bernard Shaw liked to think of the daily newspaper as "the poor man's university," families low in income and educational and occupational achievement have always been less likely to read newspapers than the better-educated, better-off citizenry; one recent study shows that in today's inflationary economy, there are "many *more* persons [in] the nonreading group with decline in education and income."

This is especially true in the large cities that have become increasingly populated by low-income blacks, Chicanos and whites. The potential market for an English-language newspaper is greatly reduced, for examples, in cities like Los Angeles, New York, Miami and San Antonio, all of which have large and growing Spanish-speaking communities.

The *Miami Herald* now publishes a Spanish-language supplement, but most big-city newspapers have deliberately discontinued delivery in certain low-income areas that were difficult to collect and not especially productive for advertisers anyway.

All this helps explain the drop in circulation nationally from 1973 to 1975. But it is only a partial explanation.

"I just don't think the cost of the paper is that significant a factor for most readers," says John Cowles, chairman of the board of Cowles Newspapers. "I think the demands on the readers' time count for ten or twenty times more cancellations than the cost of the paper."

Cowles is probably right. After all, at 15 cents a copy, a newspaper—a good newspaper, one that fulfills its readers needs—is still quite a bargain, a fraction of the cost of a magazine or a hamburger or a gallon of gas.

Besides, poor people and middle-class people are not the only ones discontinuing their newspaper subscriptions:

"We found, on careful analysis of our readership surveys, that our biggest circulation losses are among those in the upper-income, better-educated and white-collar classes," says Robert Clark, executive editor of the *Louisville Courier-Journal and Times.*

"Those are the people we have always thought of as our mainstays," Clark says, and to lose them is "alarming."

Readers, it seems clear, are not dropping their subscriptions so much because they can't afford them as because they choose not to spend their available money (and time)—both now at a premium—on something they feel they don't really need.

Almost every study of newspaper circulation shows that far more people say they quit subscribing because of poor delivery service than because of cost or any other single factor. That is somewhat misleading, though.

Newspaper delivery—like most other services in contemporary society —*has* deteriorated. But readers used to put up with missed delivery, soggy papers and papers thrown in the street and flowerbeds; they had no alternative.

Now, with all the competition for their time—and for their channels of information input—they can afford to be impatient, demanding.

Still, this is not a sudden change. Although circulation didn't actually begin to decline until 1973, there had long been signs of the impending crisis:

- More and more households were taking only one newspaper, instead of two or three.
- Almost invariably, when a newspaper went out of business, its readers did not subscribe to one of the remaining papers.
- Newspaper growth has lagged far behind both population growth and Gross National Product grown since 1950; the slide has just become more precipitate since 1970.

In fact, argues sociologist Richard Maisel, this is perfectly consistent with "the development of the . . . post-industrial society, [which] does not support the rapid growth of mass communications; rather, it stimulates the growth of specialized media."

In the 1960s and 1970s, it has, indeed, been the specialized publications that have thrived—be their specializations geographic (as in the case of city magazines and suburban newspapers) or subject matter (as in the case of magazines devoted to photography, auto racing, nudity, horticulture). While *Life, Look* and the *Saturday Evening Post* were dying, the special-interest publications were doubling and tripling and quadrupling their circulation and advertising.

But the newspaper remains a mass-appeal publication—a cafeteria, a department store, a sociointellectual service station.

Thus, the problems confronting the daily newspaper today are, essentially, more sociological than economic.

Many people see television as the most pervasive of these sociological forces: "If people can get everything they need from television, why read newspapers?" asks William F. McIlwain, managing editor of the Bergen (N.J.) *Record*.

One study says 65 percent of the people in America now get most of their news from television; another study says the average adult now watches 50 percent more television news than he did a decade ago.

Ours is a visual generation, not a linear generation, says Marshall McLuhan: Americans no longer read; television has produced a nation of illiterates.

Not quite.

There is no question, of course, that in the coverage of such dramatic, fast-breaking events as riots, wars, earthquakes, assassinations and election returns, television is the more engaging medium.

As NBC's John Chancellor says, newspapers just "can't show you Nixon pushing Ziegler. [They] can't show you beads of perspiration."

The gradual expansion of the evening TV news—in an era filled with events that almost seemed designed precisely for television—has clearly affected newspapers: It is no coincidence that evening newspapers have lost readers at about twice the rate of morning papers in recent years—nor that newspapers increasingly move toward the illumination and interpretation, rather than the mere presentation of news.

The largely blue-collar work-force of earlier generations left home for the factory early each morning and returned home in plenty of time to read the afternoon paper before dinner. Now, more people have white-collar jobs and more (78 percent of the work-force) drive to and from work every day; they leave home later and—with traffic getting heavier —they return home later still (often stuck in the same traffic that delays trucks delivering afternoon newspapers).

They've probably heard the late news on the car radio, and they can watch more on television—over dinner—if they wish. They have neither the time nor the inclination to read an evening paper that (1) requires more effort than TV, and (2) is probably several hours behind TV anyway.

Afternoon newspapers in America have traditionally been oriented more toward human-interest features, sensationalism and a light approach to the news than toward the hard news and news-analysis of the better morning papers anyway; their audience is especially vulnerable to television news, with its personal immediacy, conversational format and shorter stories.

But TV news is not always "news." A Syracuse University study of 1972 presidential campaign coverage, for example, shows that nightly network newscasts too often ignored the issues and covered only "hecklers, crowds, motorcades, balloons, rallies and gossip."

The television audience "doesn't want to sit for ten minutes to watch a well-done, well-written story," says Walter Jacobson, coanchorman for CBS News in Chicago. "They want ten seconds of the school crisis and ten seconds of Liz and Dick."

If people prefer that to their newspaper, says one editor, "it says more about the paper than it does about TV *or* the people."

In fact, people who watch television news usually read newspapers, too—and people who don't read newspapers seldom watch all that much television news.

Newspaper subscribers watch television news "significantly more than nonsubscribers," a 1975 Indiana University study shows—and when there's a major news (or sports) event, people who see the event on television then want to read about it in the newspaper.

"If the Redskin game has been on TV Sunday, we will sell 3,000 to 5,000 more copies that we can't explain any other way," says Benjamin C. Bradlee, executive editor of the *Washington Post*. "The same thing happened with the moon shot and the Ervin committee."

People who watch television news usually do so, it seems, for one of two reasons: Either they are news buffs or they are television buffs. If it is the former, television merely whets their appetite for the more detailed coverage available in their newspaper; if it is the latter, they see TV news primarily because the TV set is always on, not because they actively seek out TV news in preference to newspapers.

Thus, television *does* compete with newspapers, but more as a convenient and immediate home entertainment center (and an advertising medium) than as a purveyor of news; television and newspapers compete more for the reader's time than for his mind.

As for the theory that people no longer read newspapers because they no longer read *anything*, that, too, is arguable.

"Reading is a habit that will survive as long as we give people something worth reading," says Tom Boardman, editor of the *Cleveland Press*.

Dr. Daniel J. Boorstin, Pulitzer Prize winning historian and head of the Library of Congress, agrees: "People are probably reading as much and maybe more than ever," he says, and statistics would seem to confirm that judgment.

Magazine sales, for example, have increased at a slightly faster rate than the population since 1960, and weekly newsmagazines sales have increased at more than double the population rate.

Contrary to prevailing opinion, there isn't even a decline in reading among the young: the alternative press and such successful magazines as *Rolling Stone, People* and *Psychology Today* all rely heavily on young readers. Moreover, young people—aged 18 to 24—buy 24.6 percent of all books sold, despite comprising only 17.6 percent of the population.

The young may not read newspapers, but they read—and they don't watch much television news: only 40 percent as much as their share of the adult population. Most of the young just aren't all that interested in news, whether on TV or in newspapers.

Still, many editors are clamoring for young readers. The *Boston Globe* publishes two full pages of high school sports results every week. The *Cleveland Press* publishes a weekly page of letters from young readers. The *St. Petersburg Times* convenes a panel of young readers each week to talk about how the paper can best serve them.

Newspaper readership among the young is declining at an even faster rate than it is among the general population, and all across America, editors are lamenting this disaffection—worrying that if the young don't acquire the newspaper-reading habit early, they never will.

William F. Thomas, editor of the *Los Angeles Times*, thinks that is a false—and dangerous—concern.

"Sure," he says, "you need some things in the paper for the young reader, just as you have to answer the legitimate needs of any other reader. But young people—those under 24 or so—have never read the newspaper much, and any editor who gears a significant effort to get people who don't really care about your basic purpose anyway is crazy.

"That's just an easy way out—to make it look like you're doing something, instead of working to improve the paper. You wind up diverting resources and space and attention from your basic purpose—the presentation and interpretation of the news."

Many criticisms the young make about newspapers are echoed by their elders, though—that newspapers are dull, repetitive, impersonal, that they require too much time and effort. The young want excitement. The young demand relevance. The young are skeptical of institutions and formality. But many older readers increasingly share these attitudes.

Traditionally, the regular newspaper reader has been married, a parent, working, a homeowner—someone with a stake in his community . . . interested, involved, rooted.

But people are marrying later today—if at all; they're having children later—if at all. Many are out of work; many have chosen to rent apartments, rather than own homes.

Since 1960, the birthrate in the United States has declined 37 percent. The number of single women aged 20 to 24 has increased 42 percent. The number of households comprised of nonrelated adults has increased almost 50 percent.

In 1960, only 17 percent of all new housing starts in this country were for buildings of three or more units. By 1973, the figure was 42 percent—and in metropolitan areas, it was 53 percent. (In Los Angeles, people living in single-family homes outnumbered apartment-dwellers in 1960 by slightly more than 3–1; today, the margin is less than 2–1.)

People who live in apartments not only tend to be less involved in their community (and less interested in the daily newspaper) than homeowners, they are also more difficult to sell and deliver a paper to in purely logistical terms—especially if they live in modern, big-city security buildings, guarded by doormen, double-locks and closed-circuit television cameras.

Apartment-dwellers also spend less time at home than homeowners; they go to more movies and plays and concerts and restaurants and parties. Many just don't have time—won't make time—to read the paper every day.

Ironically, it is the very success of newspapers that has contributed to this "time" problem; the advertising boom of the 1950s and 1960s made possible the bulging daily papers that now take so long to read.

(At least one newspaper—the *Los Angeles Herald-Examiner*—has tried to turn this circumstance to its advantage, advertising its own slim editions as "the newspaper for people who don't have all day to read one"—an obvious swipe at the much bulkier *Los Angeles Times.*)

Reader mobility, too, is a problem for the modern daily newspaper.

"At least a fifth of all Americans move one or more times each year," says sociologist Vance Packard, "and the pace of the movement of Americans is still increasing . . . at least 40 million Americans now lead feebly rooted lives."

Moreover, says UC Berkeley sociologist Claude Fischer, the people who move today are increasingly white-collar workers—the natural audience for the daily newspaper—rather than the poor who were most often "pushed" from their homes in earlier generations.

Thus, if newspapers try to capture readers by emphasizing local news—on the theory that television cannot compete successfully with them in that regard—they may lose more than they gain: the mobile, rootless reader is not much interested in local news; he is, says one critic, "a resident of the world at-large."

So how do newspapers attract these readers?

Robert Haiman, executive editor of the *St. Petersburg Times*, thinks newspapers must become more visually appealing.

"Today's generation sees the world in living color," he says, "in television, movies, billboards. Look at our drab, dull, gray product. We need something that can jump off the doorstoop in the morning and say, 'Wow! I'm exciting! Read me!' "

Other editors agree. That's why so many newspapers are experimenting with a flashier appearance—larger photographs, color, cartoons, more white space, different typefaces, shorter stories, subject labels that make stories easier to find (and read).

Certainly, the continued growth of the weekly newsmagazines proves there are people interested in news but not in the way newspapers have traditionally presented the news.

The *St. Louis Post-Dispatch* recently developed prototypes of three "new" newspapers (each called the "*St. Louis Mirror*"), and hired a research firm to mail them out and seek reader comments on them, solely to guide *Post-Dispatch* editors in planning changes at the paper.

Two of the prototypes were essentially jazzed-up feature newspapers —heavy on human interest and sensationalism, light on news; the third was most like the *Post-Dispatch* in that is concentrated on news, but it, too, tried to present the news in a more visually attractive package.

Respondents clearly preferred the latter to the present *Post-Dispatch*, and editors are now in the process of incorporating into the *Post-Dispatch* many of the innovations introduced in that prototype—a page-one news summary, stronger coverage of participant sports, clearly labeled divisions of the news ("International News," "National News," "Consumer News").

But reader rejection of the gaudier, less substantive prototypes would seem to indicate that readers still want NEWSpapers—perhaps newspapers-cum-magazines, but newspapers nonetheless.

"The news has to carry the paper," says the *Los Angeles Times'* Thomas, "or else we're in the wrong business; we might as well put out comic books."

If newspapers make too many changes in an effort to attract new readers, says A. M. Rosenthal, managing editor of the *New York Times*, "they may wind up offending their old readers. There are so many people out there who ought to read the paper that we really have to figure out how to get *them*," not the so-called "new readers" who probably wouldn't read the paper anyway.

But even Rosenthal and Thomas agree newspapers must do something different, both to serve and to awaken their readers. Moreover, the rootless (like the young) are an ever-growing group and (like the young) they reflect many of the concerns and characteristics of society at-large. Many editors think newspapers can rebuild circulation in both groups, as well as in their base readership.

How?

By producing a better newspaper, Rosenthal and Thomas believe.

"I'm astonished that readers put up with so damn little in so many papers" Rosenthal says. "Many newspapers just do a lousy job. Thirty years ago, it didn't matter very much if a paper did a poor job; there was no competition. But now. . . ." He shrugs.

Now, a paper that is poor journalistically may quickly become poor financially as well.

Few newspapers can afford the $32-million annual editorial budget the *New York Times* has, of course, but most can improve their product considerably nonetheless.

"Everyone's looking for the patent medicine, the gimmick, the one little thing in your bag of tricks—two columns of local news or a new consumer column—to solve the problems of metropolitan papers," says Gene Roberts, executive editor of the *Philadelphia Inquirer.*

"The problem is much broader and more fundamental than that; it involves everything from superficial news coverage to generally dull writing. We've gotten so stock and so routinized in our presentation that we're just uninviting for most readers.

"There are probably 50 or 60 or 70 things we ought to reexamine—page by page, section by section, subject by subject."

There have been several national studies in recent years to help newspapers with these reexaminations. Representatives of the American Newspaper Publishers Association and the Newspaper Advertising Bureau are now engaged in just such a project.

But the major shortcoming of all these national studies is precisely that: they're national. Although newspapers clearly have some common problems, their differences may be more significant.

In Los Angeles, for example, year-round warm weather and heavy reliance on the automobile enable people to spend a great deal of time away from home—in a boat, on the beach, with a backpack. All these activities take the reader away from his home—and his newspaper. He can even listen to the news on the car radio en route to any of these pursuits—and on his way to work as well.

In contrast, New Yorkers—often kept indoors by inclement weather, generally commuting to work by train or subway or taxicab, rather than by automobile—have far more time to read their newspapers. But urban flight and a poor economy give New York newspapers their own indigenous problems.

Similar differences exist between other American cities.

Nevertheless, just as New York has been the ultimate crucible of the contemporary urban crisis, so the *New York Times* can be seen as a case study (albeit an exaggerated one) of the problems facing the metropolitan newspaper today.

For many years, the problems of the *New York Times* were camouflaged: as one after another of its competitors went out of business— five New York newspapers folded from 1949 to 1967—the *Times'* position of preeminence seemed to solidify.

But, all the while, its affluent, well-educated readers were moving further and further into the suburbs.

Even if *Times* executives had been more aware of the impending crisis, they would have had to overcome formidable obstacles to effect the necessary changes:

- Restrictive and costly labor union settlements severely hamstrung the paper's technological innovations.
- An old, almost calcified management team was neither individually prescient nor collectively efficient. ("A managerial nightmare," said *Business Week* magazine, with "no organizational structure, merely a group of warring factions and fiefdoms working against each other.")
- The *Times'* own strong sense of tradition inhibited any change.

"We don't like to rush into new things and then have to back out," says Publisher Arthur Ochs (Punch) Sulzberger, who took over the paper in 1963. "If any other newspaper changes its editor, they get one paragraph in *Time*. If the *New York Times* does it, three operas, four ballets, two movies and a half-dozen books are written about it."

Having failed with a West Coast edition and a few haphazard suburban pages in the 1960s, *Times* executives were long wary of any further innovations that could prove similarly embarrassing and fruitless.

Then, in the 1970s, disaster struck: Circulation dropped 12 percent. Advertising dropped 7 percent. The company's stock dropped from $53 a share in 1968 to $7.50 a share in 1975. Pretax earnings plunged 58 percent in 1975.

In New York City itself, the *Times'* penetration dipped from 51 percent to 39 percent of all households—and in the burgeoning suburbs, smaller newspapers like *Newsday* and the Bergen (N.J.) *Record* began to reach two to five times as many households as the *Times*, even outselling the *Times* among the affluent, well-educated readers who are the *Times'* prime target audience.

The dismal figures stunned the *Times* into bold if belated action.

Sulzberger made sweeping managerial changes, consolidated the daily and Sunday staffs, expanded the daily news summary and index, replaced almost half the editorial board, diversified corporate holdings with the purchase of other newspaper and broadcast properties, expanded market research by 80 percent and dictated a tough negotiating stance with the unions.

The *Times* also shifted to a six-column format (from the traditional eight) to reduce newsprint costs by 5 percent, and is in the process of changing from two sections to four on most days to give readers a more attractive and manageable news package.

To get away from what Sulzberger calls "the ridiculous situation of having the city's biggest factory in the middle of Times Square," the *Times* has built a $37-million printing plant in the suburbs.

The *Times* is also experimenting anew with becoming a national newspaper; 25 percent of its daily circulation (30 percent on Sunday) is already outside the three-state New York metropolitan area, and about 4,000 to 5,000 copies a day are now being flown to Atlanta in a market test to determine the paper's allure in selected large cities.

But the *Times'* greatest effort is with its own city and suburban readers. Many suburban readers, for example, bring the paper to work with them on the train in the morning, then throw it away—leaving neither news nor advertising behind for later use. To counter this, the *Times* is aggressively trying to persuade suburban readers to take not one but two copies of the Times—with the second copy at a discount. Thus far, fewer than 15,000 dual subscriptions have been sold.

The *Times* has been considerably more successful with its new "Weekend" section, which has increased Friday circulation by 40,000 and advertising by 20 percent; in November 1976, the *Times* introduced its second new section—"The Living Section"—and plans are underway for a third section (incorporating fashions and columns by several of the *Times'* better writers) and, perhaps, a fourth.

Two new suburban sections were also introduced in 1976, two more were added early in 1977, and *Times* executives—with circulation, advertising, income and profits all up this year—say they are optimistic about the future.

Other big-city changes are trying to effect similar change. The *Chicago*

Tribune, according to one estimate, has spent $1 million in revamping its paper, and the *San Francisco Examiner* has shuffled its staff, changed some typefaces, added new columns and a page-one news summary and become more serious in tone and style.

"There's never been a time when as much experimentation was going on in newspaper format and content," says Leo Bogart, general manager of the Newspaper Advertising Bureau.

Most newspapers are making a special effort to attract suburban readers—and with good reason. From 1960 to 1973, central cities in the nation's 50 largest metropolitan areas grew only 2 percent; the suburbs grew 41 percent. Suburbs now have 56 percent of the people who live in metropolitan areas; by 1980, it is estimated they will have 62 percent.

Suburban newspapers have grown—and will continue to grow—accordingly, both as a news and an advertising medium. And it is suburban advertising—local advertising—that all newspapers must have to survive, now that television has cut drastically into their national advertising. (In 1945, newspapers had 11.9 percent of all national advertising; television had none. In 1975, newspapers had 7.8 percent; television had 25.3 percent.)

Metropolitan daily newspapers cannot, of course, compete with smaller suburban dailies and weeklies in covering community news. But, clearly, they must provide their readers with some community coverage, as well as with broader stories that are as relevant to the suburban reader as to the inner-city reader.

Thus, the *Chicago Tribune* added two new suburban sections and expanded two others in 1976. The *San Francisco Examiner* is now publishing a suburban "Peninsula" edition. The *Cleveland Press* has begun distributing seven separate weekly newspapers with the *Press.* The *Philadelphia Inquirer* has developed a staff of 30 suburban reporters and editors to produce weekly lifestyle sections in its three-state suburban market.

"The suburban zone sections have helped save the *Los Angeles Times'* life," says Seth Baker, president of the company that publishes *Los Angeles* magazine.

"L.A. was always just a bunch of suburbs anyway, so the *Times* had to make that move faster than most other papers, and it was the best thing that ever happened to them."

But the *Los Angeles Times*—which has been publishing suburban sections since 1950—has much the same problems other papers do in trying to be what Publisher Otis Chandler calls "both a class and a mass newspaper."

The paper's major thrust now is toward the "mass" audience on the theory that, as Chandler says, "The class audience really has no place else to go if they want the kind of package of news, interpretation, analysis and cultural criticism we give them."

But the much larger mass audience "can get almost everything they want from us elsewhere," he says. "That's why we have to become less a traditional newspaper and more a regional newsmagazine. . . . We must more and more explain the relationship between facts and what the significance of these facts might be to our readers' lives."

That is the philosophy behind the new "YOU" magazine, as well as more consumer-oriented features in the financial section and lifestyle stories and family activity guides in the View section.

The *Times*, like other metropolitan newspapers, must, however, guard against offending this mass audience by being what Chandler calls "too shrill, too unthinking, too uncaring, too bloodthirsty . . . cynical."

In the aftermath of Vietnam and especially Watergate, newspapers have become increasingly determined to disclose wrongdoing and hypocrisy in high places. That, most would agree, is as commendable as it is valuable. But it can be overdone.

The *Los Angeles Times*, for example, sent conflict-of-interest questionnaires to all elected state officials, asking them to list their income and investments.

Chandler now feels that project was misguided.

"It would have been a good topic for the editorial page," he says, "but we got carried away. We decided to play God, and that's just not our role."

Many readers feel the same way about press coverage of other issues— and they're tired of all the "bad news" that coverage produces.

One *Times* study showed that some readers actually cancel their subscriptions because they don't read such stories—and then feel guilty about not having done so.

One such reader said, "I feel guilty. I should know what's going on. An earthquake in Guatemala, starvation in Pakistan, war in Northern Ireland. . . . Good night, it's just too much. I feel sorry for all these people, but I'm powerless to do anything about it."

Her solution: cancel her subscription.

If many more feel like her, and if newspapers are not able to meet the changing needs and desires of these readers, canceled subscriptions could become epidemic.

The imminent demise of the daily newspaper has been predicted before, though, and as University of Texas journalism professor William Mindak says, "History has proved most of these gloomy prognosticators wrong IF (and this is a big if) the media reacted intelligently and quickly to their changing environment."

Newspapers *are* responding to their changing environment; whether their response will prove to have been quick enough—and intelligent enough—is something that can only be judged by future generations of readers . . . and nonreaders.

Certainly, the audience is still there. The higher-income, well-educated people who comprise the newspaper's basic readership are growing in numbers every year; in 1965, for example, there were 10 million college graduates over the age of 25 in the United States; in 1975, there were 15 million; by 1985, it is estimated there will be 25 million.

Thus, what seems most likely is that the daily newspaper—or, at least, some daily newspapers—will survive; but, like other endangered species, they will do so only by adaptation and accommodation. The strong will become stronger—and the weak will die.

More than 1,000 of the nation's 1,756 newspapers are published by just 174 companies—monopoly operations in small-to-medium-sized cities; largely free of the economic burdens and competitive pressures of their big-city brethren, they should continue to do quite well.

In metropolitan areas, 287 newspapers already account for 63 percent of the total circulation. Only three big cities—New York, Chicago and Philadelphia—still have three daily newspapers. Most other have only two.

In time, say most editors and publishers, every metropolitan area— with perhaps an exception or two—will have only one large daily newspaper.

In each city, that newspaper will be the one that best serves the changing needs of its readers.

77 78 79 80 9 8 7 6 5 4 3 2 1